Computational Design Methods and Technologies:

Applications in CAD, CAM, and CAE Education

Ning Gu
University of Newcastle, Australia

Xiangyu Wang
Curtin University, Australia

Managing Director:	Lindsay Johnston
Senior Editorial Director:	Heather Probst
Book Production Manager:	Sean Woznicki
Development Manager:	Joel Gamon
Development Editor:	Hannah Abelbeck
Acquisitions Editor:	Erika Gallagher
Typesetters:	Lisandro Gonzalez
Cover Design:	Nick Newcomer, Greg Snader

Published in the United States of America by
Information Science Reference (an imprint of IGI Global)
701 E. Chocolate Avenue
Hershey PA 17033
Tel: 717-533-8845
Fax: 717-533-8661
E-mail: cust@igi-global.com
Web site: http://www.igi-global.com

Library of Congress Cataloging-in-Publication Data

Computational design methods and technologies: applications in CAD, CAM, and CAE education / Ning Gu and Xiangyu Wang, editors.
    p. cm.
  Includes bibliographical references and index.
  ISBN 978-1-61350-180-1 (hardcover) -- ISBN 978-1-61350-181-8 (ebook) -- ISBN 978-1-61350-182-5 (print & perpetual access) 1. Computer-aided engineering. 2. Computer-aided design. 3. CAD/CAM systems. 4. Education--Data processing. I. Gu, Ning, 1975- II. Wan, Xiangyu, 1979-
  TA345.C63155 2012
  620'.00420285--dc23
                              2011043974

British Cataloguing in Publication Data
A Cataloguing in Publication record for this book is available from the British Library.

All work contributed to this book is new, previously-unpublished material. The views expressed in this book are those of the authors, but not necessarily of the publisher.

Editorial Advisory Board

Table of Contents

Detailed Table of Contents

This chapter presents a conceptual model of the architectural design process, spanning from ideation
to realization, but not focused on stages in the process. Instead, the model identifies four primary
meta-systems in design (representational, proportional, indexical, and operational) that are connected
through, and supported by, a range of enabling tools and technologies. The purpose of developing this
model is to support a heightened understanding of the parallel evolution of the design process and of
enabling technologies. Thereafter, the chapter introduces seven recent trends in computational design
and technology, each of which serves to enable the design process. The seven developments are: Building
Information Modeling (BIM), parametric design, generative design, collaborative design, digital
fabrication, augmented reality, and intelligent environments. The chapter offers a critical review of
proposed definitions of each of these technologies along with a discussion of their role as a catalyst for
change in the design process.

New media and methodologies are being employed in changing the conceptual understanding of what
digital design is and may become. New experience is beginning to emerge in relation to novel key
design concepts, computational methods, and digital technologies in the use of, and interaction with,
digital media in design. The chapter describes an experimental program, the objective of which was to
identify and map novel design concepts and relevant methodologies of digital design. In making the
survey, analysis, and the categorization of relevant concepts and emerging precedents in this field, the
authors made an attempt to formulize a theoretical basis for the conceptual mapping of this field. The
conceptual mapping of this field is termed DDNET: Digital Design Network. The DDNET is a seman-

tic system divided into the following conceptual levels: Key-concepts, sub-concepts, computational models and techniques, and precedent level. As a first step in this research, the authors made a survey of emerging knowledge from both praxis and theoretical resources, and then formulated and presented proposed set of design models, concepts, relevant methodologies, and precedents. Next, the authors mapped a network representation around leading key-conecpts. The final step was to accommodate and apply this representation as a new basis for a pedagogical experiment in teaching digital design. The research has been conducted in Experimental Digital Design Studio in the Faculty of Architecture and Town Planning at the Technion, Israel.

Chapter 3

This chapter describes the teaching of shape grammars within an architectural design program. Developed over thirty years ago, shape grammars remain today a distinctive computational paradigm – a slow paradigm – for generative design. Shape grammars are visual and perceptual and, at root, non-digital. They are expressive and interpretive, as well as creative and generative. They foster unhurried, reflective design computing. To promote these unique computational features, shape grammars are taught using a manual approach in a collaborative, learning-by-making environment. An overview of the teaching of shape grammars at the Massachusetts Institute of Technology is given here. The potentials and challenges for slow computing versus fast computing by machine, in teaching and in design practice, are considered.

Chapter 4

Parametric designing, its instruments, and techniques move architectural design education towards novel avenues of deep learning. Akin to learning and working environments of engineering and manufacturing, it offers similar advantages for architects. Yet it is not as simple as using another tool; parametric designing fundamentally shifts the engagement with the design problem. Parametric designing allows architects to be substantially deeper involved in the overall design and development process extending it effectively beyond production and lifecycle. Leaning parametric design strategies enhance architects' critical engagement with their designs and their communication. Subsequently, the computational aid of parametric modelling alters substantially how and what students learn and architects practice.

Chapter 5

Architecture, engineering, and construction industries maintain a long standing desire to enhance design communication through various forms of 3D CAD modeling. In spite the introduction of Building Information Modeling (BIM), designers and builders expect varying amounts of communication loss once construction has started due to indirect construction techniques or hand based methods to manufacture buildings. This is especially true for houses and small structures, buildings that makeup the core of villages and suburbs. Unfortunately, paper documentation and reading 3D CAD models on screen continue the trend of indirect production defined in most manufacturing industries as error. The emerging application of CAD/CAM within design and construction industries provides hope for elevated communication between design and building. With CAD/CAM, it is possible to manufacture buildings of all types and sizes directly from CAD files similar to mass produced artifacts, thus reducing complexity in communication between parties. This chapter is presentation of one process of direct manufacturing from CAD and the emerging possibilities for small building production using digital fabrication. The chapter will focus on houses to illustrate the potential of direct manufacturing of buildings from CAD data.

Chapter 6

The practice of architecture is changing rapidly due to an influx of new technical, procedural, and organizational innovations in the building delivery process. Building Information Modeling (BIM) is a key technical component of this evolution in practice, encompassing newly available modeling, fabrication, and communications technologies. BIM represents a key enabler of other innovations, by creating value and incentives for rethinking aspects of conventional practice, from contractual roles and responsibilities to the format and content of project information.

Chapter 7

In the early stages of the adoption of Building Information Modeling (BIM), the AEC (Architecture, Engineering, Construction) professionals were often the leaders, and some university faculty were caught unprepared. More recently, many universities have responded to the adoption of BIM technologies in the profession. No single approach to BIM curricula will suffice; each academic program is different, with unique and often innovative ways in accomplishing its goals of BIM integration. At USC, School of Architecture, rather than concentrating on a single strategy, multi-dimensional approaches are being developed that include at their core the recognition that the building delivery professions and academia must be better integrated, communication and interoperability are key components, and that BIM is one step, albeit with flaws, towards developing fully parametric design solutions. BIM technology should be broadly integrated throughout the curriculum; advanced seminars should stress interoperability and sustainability components; and the schools have a mission to outreach to the profession through conference hosting and executive education while being receptive to professionals' advice. Not everyone is in agreement as to how this can be done or what methods should be implemented, and similar to the integration of CAD software and 3D modeling over the past 20 years, dissenting voices, heated dialogues, and solutions born in the crucible of academic/professional debate will accompany change.

Chapter 8

This chapter presents an educational case study of applying Building Information Modeling (BIM) as an integrated design platform for interdisciplinary building and construction projects. The course is meant to focus on utilizing BIM for commercial construction. Students examine 3D geometry, spatial relationships, geographic information, quantities of materials, and properties of building components in this course. The students also learn the processes that make up BIM so they will be able to apply this information in a company. The purpose of the initial study was to assess the need for and receive feedback on the syllabus of the first commercial construction computer graphics course at Purdue University through a survey that was sent to industry professionals. The class was taught in the Fall 2009 semester and was successful according to the students in what they learned. The course was a 400 level course in which both upper level undergraduates and graduate students participated. The professor took the approach of a real world job and incorporated it into the content of the course. This chapter will discuss the initial case study of industrial professionals, the initial course creation, the development, and ultimately the final curriculum delivered within the course, as well as student feedback received at the end of the semester.

Chapter 9

In the authors' design teaching, they have been employing virtual world technologies, allowing students the capacity to collaborate and design within a constructivist immersive design platform such as Second Life and Active Worlds. These environments support synchronous design communication and real-time 3D modelling. Particularly, 3D immersive design environments have the potential to make a major contribution to design education as constructivist learning environments. Based on authors' teaching experience and the students' learning experience, this chapter discusses 3D virtual world as constructivist learning environments that support team-based design and communication skill-building and presents the challenges faced by design education today. The chapter firstly provides a critical analysis of various design learning and teaching features offered in 3D virtual worlds as constructivist learning environments, secondly, identifies a number of key issues in addressing engagement and interaction in virtual design learning, thirdly, addresses the core skills and cognitive processes of designing in 3D virtual worlds, and finally, provides several strategies for the facilitation of virtual worlds as the constructivist design teaching platform.

Digital Media Design (DMD) sits between ICT and the creative arts. DMD uses computers as a design tool. The ubiquity of the computer means DMD is available to a broad range of people. It is used in everyday design practices – creative, professional, commercial, academic, and casual. In an educational context, the way it is taught needs to meet students' expectations from a broad range of capabilities and requirements. Unlike more traditional forms of design practice, peculiar to DMD is the use of online collaborations. In turn, this demands different cognitive learning structures to traditional design practices. Online collaborations include a socialising element. Hence, current DMD practice is as much about social interaction as it is about design problem solving. Problem solving exercises in design teaching are traditionally explored in a project setting. In DMD this now includes the socialising element of online collaboration. This chapter describes a method for analysing DMD practice and, in particular, online design collaboration using a 3D Collaborative Virtual Environment.

Chapter 11

This chapter presents a study on the impact of design scales on collaborations in 3D virtual environments. Different domains require designers to work on different scales; for instance, urban design and electronic circuit design operate at very different scales. However, the understanding of the effects of scales upon collaboration in virtual environment is limited. In this chapter, the authors propose to use protocol analysis method to examine the differences between two design collaboration projects in virtual environments: one large scale, and another small scale within a similar domain. It shows that the difference in scale impacted more on communication control and social communication.

Chapter 12

The case for utilizing computer game modding in an architectural design curriculum is a strong one. The rich intertwining of real-time spatial, material lighting and physical simulations reinforce spatial visualization, navigation, and mental rotation. In the past two decades many researchers have implemented games engines in architectural curricula, but in every case, the courses have been in upper years of their students' degrees, with small, elective classes rather than core courses. That this is in contrast to the wider computer game modding community, suggesting that the difficulties previous researchers have had may actually be mitigated by implementing the technology, along with aspects of computer game modding culture, in large first year classes. Case studies of student work collapse Stockburger's distinction between the game designer and the game player to further his extension of Lefebvre's and Soja's thinking about space as it relates to computer gaming. The chapter concludes by reconsidering the term 'player' as a 'game designer in testing mode'.

Chapter 13

Mi Jeong Kim, Kyung Hee University, Korea
Xiangyu Wang, Curtin University, Australia & Kyung Hee University, Republic of Korea
Xingquan Zhu, University of Technology Sydney, Australia
Shih-Chung Kang, National Taiwan University, Taiwan

A growing body of research has shown that Augmented Reality (AR) has the potential to contribute to interaction and visualization for architecture and design. While this emerging technology has only been developed for the past decade, numerous journals and conferences in architecture and design have published articles related to AR. This chapter reviews 44 articles on AR especially related to the architecture and design area that were published from 2005 to 2011. Further, this chapter discusses the representative AR research works in terms of four aspects: AR concept, AR implementation, AR evaluation, and AR industry adoption. The chapter draws conclusions about major findings, research issues, and future research directions through the review results. This chapter will be a basis for future research of AR in architecture and design areas.

Chapter 14

John I. Messner, The Pennsylvania State University, USA
Robert M. Leicht, The Pennsylvania State University, USA

To implement computational design applications into design education successfully, it is critical that educators consider the available facilities which allow students to develop, communicate, and experience their designs. A variety of media spaces can be used to facilitate greater interaction with digital content, along with the potential to foster greater collaboration on team focused activities. An interactive workspace can be designed to enhance authoring and interaction with digital content by using the INVOLVE framework, which includes seven elements: Interaction, Network, Virtual Prototypes, Organization, Layout, Visual Real Estate, and Existential Collaboration. This framework focuses on first identifying the fundamental uses and needs of the space, along with identifying the types of tasks to be performed within each physical space or room. For example, if a department has three different rooms available to students in a design studio or course, then the activities to be performed within the different spaces, e.g., design review, digital design authoring/modeling, fully immersive navigation of a model, collaborative brainstorming, et cetera, would suggest different displays and means of interaction. Once the use of each space is identified, then the framework guides the user toward the selection of fundamental space attributes, equipment and resources that should be available to students within each space. Exciting new technologies will allow future students to be more easily engaged in the digital content while gaining easy access to data and information which was previously difficult to generate.

Chapter 15

This chapter provides an overview of interactive architecture relating to the design and implementation of ubiquitous computing technologies. The kernel of interactive architecture is augmenting spaces that can sense, think, and respond to change. A theoretical framework is provided for contextualization of interactive architecture. A model of interaction is proposed to identify a set of processes, functionality and principles that guide the design of interactive architecture. Key capabilities are identified with respect to interactive architecture: sensitivity, smartness, and responsiveness. Examples of some research projects are provided to demonstrate the capabilities. Methods and techniques for developing such capabilities are described according to the model of interaction. Applications for using ubiquitous computing technologies in interactive architecture are reviewed.

In this chapter, the view that Interactive Architecture (IA) practice ought to produce (digital) interactive interventions designed to affect people's actions and behaviours is firstly introduced. After presenting the challenges arising when integrating these two different conceptions of the word: Atoms and bits, reviewing the interpretations of IA and the lessons learnt from design methods theory in architecture, a novel way of approaching the intersection between architectural design, methodology, and emerging interactive technologies is proposed. This chapter attempts to make strong connections between design philosophy and project work, in aid of reinforcing the intellectual side of IA projects. Very often these types of projects are the result of technological pursuits rather than intellectual ones. Furthermore, this study demonstrates some strategies for ensuring the collaboration of design with related scientific and intellectual domains: architecture, computer science, and behavioural and social studies.

Chapter 17

Design for effective information engagement through interactive sonification and visualization can be divided into two parts: (1) interface and interaction - designing the method of manipulating, investigating and interrogating information representations; and (2) information design - designing the representation, interactivity and user-customizability of the data content. The user experience is affected by the responsiveness and intelligence (awareness, contextual knowledge, situated interactivity) of the representation design. The purpose of information visualization and sonification is to transform data into information, that is, to enable users to find meaningfulness in the data.

Chapter 18
Christiane M. Herr, Xi'an Jiaotong-Liverpool University, China

This chapter presents a digitally supported approach to creative thinking through diagrammatic visuals. Diagrammatic visuals can support designing by evoking thoughts and by raising open questions in conversational exchanges with designers. It focuses on the educational context of the architectural design studio, and introduces a software tool, named Algogram, which allows designers to employ diagrams in challenging conventional assumptions and for generating new ideas. Results from testing the tool and the way of approaching conceptual designing encouraged by it within an undergraduate design studio suggest a potential for refocusing of attention in digital design support development towards diagrams. In addition to the conventional emphasis on the variety of tool features and the ability of the tool to assist representational modeling of form, this chapter shows how a diagram-based approach can acknowledge and harness the creative potential of designers' constructive seeing.

Chapter 19
Caroline Lecourtois, School of Architecture of Paris La Villette, France
François Guéna, School of Architecture of Paris La Villette, France

This chapter presents an original teaching method carried out at the School of Architecture of Paris La-Villette (ARIAM-LAREA) whose aim is to prepare future architects for parametric design. Unlike most of the parametric design studio, the authors of this chapter do not want to teach a specific design method. They believe that the students have to find out their own method from the knowledge of architectural usages of parametric design. Theoretical courses linked to a studio will better train them in the usage of parametric tools. During theoretical courses focused on parametric design activity, the authors ask the students to analyze computer activities of architects in order to identify their design methods. The students are trained under a method to analyze design activities based on "Applied Architecturology." During the studio, they ask the students to reuse the identified methods. The students apply the methods in their own project and adapt them in order to build their own parametric design method. The works produced by the students in the courses and in the studio bring up new questions for the ARIAM-LAREA research laboratory and constitute bases for the development of new software tools for parametric architectural design.

Chapter 20
Dean Bruton, Southern Cross University, Australia

This chapter aims to develop awareness of the changing characterization of design and design education in response to the impact of global crisis and the ongoing introduction of innovative computational design methods and technologies. This chapter presents a strategic vision that includes a range of major concerns in relation to design education's learning and teaching needs in higher education. The purpose of the chapter is to reconsider the foundation and consequent assumptions required of a vital relevant design education in the 21st century. It reflects on a general academic reassessment of the nature of design education in the light of the impact of computational methods and technologies and asserts a need for the re-envisioning of design education pedagogies in terms of networked interaction and global issues. Specifically it maintains that computational methods and techniques and the institutional adoption of interaction as a key factor in education has transformed the conception and construction of content as well as the delivery of communications across the broad spectrum of both the arts and sciences. It acknowledges the theory of institutional transformation, explores the evidence for such a theory, and discusses design education's potential pedagogical strategies for reform of higher education.

Chapter 21

A new generation of design computation systems affords opportunities for new design practices. This calls for potentially new teaching requirements in design education, in particular the development of the requisite spatial thinking skills. In this chapter, the authors review the pertinent literature, followed by two case examples that illustrate how spatial thinking was taught in two undergraduate design courses. The authors' experiences suggest that early exposure to spatial thinking concepts, coupled with practice using computational design tools in the context of a project, can significantly help students to improve the skills necessary to design in a digital environment. Through the use of team projects, the authors discovered the potential variances in design representations when students switched between digital and physical modeling. They propose further research to explore the spatial processes required in computational design systems and the implications for design education.

Chapter 22

This chapter describes two case studies concerning the introduction of computational design methods and technologies in new undergraduate architectural curricula, one in Portugal and the other in Brazil. In both cases, the immediate goal was to introduce state-of-the-art technologies in the curriculum to promote creative design thinking. The ultimate goals were to fulfill the criteria of intellectual satisfaction, acquisition of specialized professional skills, and contribution for the economic development of society that should underlie university education. The chapter describes the theoretical framework, the various courses and labs that were devised and implemented, as well as the strategies used to implement them. Then it presents the final results and concludes with a discussion of the pros and cons of each strategy. The main lesson drawn from both efforts was that cultural and organizational aspects are at least as important as technical aspects for the successful integration of computer media in architectural education.

Computational Design Methods and Technologies: Applications in CAD, CAM and CAE Education surveys five major categories of contemporary computational technologies and explores their applications in, and interactions with, design and design education. The five categories of technologies are: Generative and parametric design systems; BIM; collaborative virtual environments; virtual and augmented reality systems; and interactive and intelligent environments. This final chapter reflects on the impact of these computational design methods and technologies, using Ostwald's System-enabler Model as an underlying conceptual structure. The chapter explores changing relations between the representational, proportional, indexical, and operational systems in the design process, as well as emerging opportunities and challenges that arise from these methods and technologies. The impact of these new technologies and approaches is also discussed in the context of design education. The chapter draws together this significant body of work in order to provide a point of reference for the interpretation and critique of the new design knowledge and phenomenon encompassed in the five categories.

Preface

The rapid development of computational design technologies has significantly impacted on design and design education beyond the replacement of drawing boards with computers or pens and papers with Computer-aided Design (CAD), Computer-aided Manufacturing (CAM), and Computer-aided Engineering (CAE) applications. The emergence and adoption of these technologies has greatly challenged and is still changing the ways of design and educating designers. *Computational Design Methods and Technologies: Applications in CAD, CAM and CAE Education* presents the state-of-the-art developments in computational design methods and technologies and explores their applications in and interactions with contemporary design and education.

BOOK OVERVIEW

Computational Design Methods and Technologies: Applications in CAD, CAM and CAE Education is a significant body of work including the following 23 chapters of original contributions from a cohort of international experts in the following areas: (1) research and development of computational design methods and technologies; (2) theory and practice of computational design; and (3) design education. This book reflects on the current trends and inspires future extensions in the advancement of computational design methods and technologies as well as the evolvement of design and education under such influences, by exploring and challenging the interactive relationships between the two. With such foci, the book provides unique references for design research, education and practice, to the following primary reader groups:

- Researchers in the broad domain of computational design.
- Academics who are interested in applying computing design methods and technologies in teaching and learning.
- Pedagogic scholars who study the role and impact of computational design on education.
- Developers of computational design technologies.
- General design communities who follow the latest developments and applications of new media and technologies in the field.

The book presents and demonstrates design education as an important test field for applying new computational design methods and technologies, providing significant research evidence to validate the effectiveness of these methods and technologies in design. It was observed that firstly, design researchers often explore, validate, and refine research through self-reflection. Because most academic researchers are also educators, educational case studies become ideal revenues for such reflective purposes. Secondly, the introduction of leading-edge computational technologies and computational thinking brings tremendous benefits to design students, exposing them to new ideas and practices, and better preparing them for the future. Students with exposure to such knowledge and challenges are most likely to support and sustain the innovation, leading the design and the industry.

The emphases of the following 23 chapters can fall into three categories, with many across multiple categories.

- **Category I:** Introduction and current development of computational design methods and technologies.
- **Category II:** Educational case studies of utilizing these methods and technologies.
- **Category III:** New theories and future trends in the field.

Category I aims to showcase and critically evaluate the state-of-the-art development of computational methods and technologies in design, and discuss their impacts on design and design education. Examples of the work in this category include research into the development and application of fundamental theories and techniques for design, through computation or computational thinking, for example, the concepts of design generation and optimization through grammatical, parametric, diagrammatic, and other knowledge-based approaches. Works also include the research into the development and application of computer-mediated tools for design, collaboration and management, for example, the development and application of digital fabrication tools, BIM systems, collaborative virtual environments, computer game engines, virtual and augmented reality systems, sensory and interactive devices, and so on.

Category II focuses on the presentation and reflection of a variety of successful educational case studies that adopt different computational design methods and technologies, which aim to explore and better understand their roles in design and design education, supported with cognitive evidences or critical reflections of the design experience and/or outcome.

Category III emphasizes the impact and implication of the evidences and results presented in Category II. Based on these understandings, some re-assess educational design theories and formulate new principles or guidelines. Some discuss how these understandings can assist design educators in developing, refining, and implementing curricula that best utilize the technologies and suit the current design culture. Others suggest and highlight future theoretical and technological trends in computational design.

INTRODUCTION TO CHAPTERS

Computational Design Methods and Technologies: Applications in CAD, CAM and CAE Education will take readers on a journey to the domain of computational design. The journey starts with two introductory chapters, which provide two conceptual frameworks in order to develop an overall understanding about the field. These two frameworks are developed from two different perspectives that compliment each other. In *Systems and Enablers: Modeling the Impact of Contemporary Computational Methods and Technologies on the Design Process*, Michael Ostwald introduces the System-Enabler Model. The model provides a formal approach to develop an elevated understanding between the evolution of the design process and the roles of different computational design technologies, while Rivka Oxman's DDNET semantic system, as introduced in *Novel Concepts in Digital Design*, provides a methodological and pedagogical basis for contemporary computational design.

Following this introduction, readers will then experience each of the main topic areas in contemporary computational design, through scholarly writings of a combination of technological developments, pedagogical cases, and up-to-date critiques of theories and practices. These main topic areas are generative and parametric design systems, digital fabrication, BIM, collaborative virtual environments, virtual and augmented reality systems, and interactive and intelligent environments. Many of these areas share common concepts and purposes. Therefore these groupings can be useful for thinking about a complex field, but they are not necessarily definitive.

- **Generative and parametric design systems:**
    - *Slow Computing: Teaching Generative Design with Shape Grammars* by Terry Knight, and
    - *Learning Parametric Designing* by Marc Aurel Schnabel.
- **Digital fabrication:**
    - *Direct Building Manufacturing of Homes with Digital Fabrication* by Lawrence Sass.
- **BIM:**
    - *Building Information Modeling and Professional Practice* by Dennis Shelden,
    - *Advancing BIM in Academia: Explorations in Curricular Integration* by Karen Kensek, and
    - *Applying BIM in Design Curriculum* by Clark Cory and Shanna Schmelter-Morret.
- **Collaborative virtual environments:**
    - *Constructivist Learning Theory in Virtual Design Studios* by Leman Figen Gul, Anthony Williams, and Ning Gu,
    - *Understanding Collaborative Digital Media Design in the 3DCVE: A Vygotskian Approach* by Theodor Wyeld and Ekaterina Prasolova-Førland, and
    - *Will Different Scales Impact on Design Collaboration in 3D Virtual Environments?* by Jerry Jen-Hung Tsai, Jeff Kan, Xiangyu Wang, and Yingsiu Huang.
- **Virtual and augmented reality systems:**
    - *Implementing Computer Gaming Technology in Architectural Design Curricula: Testing Architecture with the Rich Intertwining of Real-Time Spatial, Material, Lighting and Physical Simulations* by Russell Lowe,
    - *Augmented Reality Research for Architecture and Design* by Mi Jeong Kim, Xiangyu Wang, Xingquan Zhu, and Shih-Chung Kang, and
    - *Experiencing Digital Design: Developing Interactive Workspaces for Visualizing, Editing and Interacting with Digital Design Artifacts* by John Messner and Robert M. Leicht.

The journey continues by examining two specific approaches to computational design and education: A diagram-based approach by Christiane Herr (in *Supporting Design Thinking with Evocative Digital Diagrams*), and an Architecturological approach by Caroline Lecourtois and François Guéna (in *Architectural Design Education and Parametric Modeling: An Architecturological Approach*).

Applying the above computational design technologies and methods in design curricula creates both opportunities and challenges to all parties involved. These complex issues are discussed in the final section of the book from the relatively higher level of institutional transformation by Dean Bruton (in *Design Education and Institutional Transformation*), to the development of specific skill set by Halil Erhan, Belgacem Ben Youssef, and Barbara Berry (in *Teaching Spatial Thinking in Design Computation*

Contexts: Challenges and Opportunities), and specific curricular implementation by José Duarte, Gabriela Celani, and Regiane Pupo (in *Inserting Computational Technologies in Architectural Curricula*).

The book concludes with *Computational Methods and Technologies: Reflections on Their Impact on Design and Education*, provided by Ning Gu and Michael Ostwald, aiming to contextualize the knowledge presented in this book, to create a foundation for further work, and to act as a point of reference for the development and critique of new design knowledge.

SUMMARY

In the remaining of the book, readers will find the latest technological and theoretical developments, empirical research findings, educational case studies, pedagogical theories, design reflections, future trends and many more. Each chapter has been double blind reviewed by the Editorial Advisory Board to maintain the highest possible standard. Readers will be critically informed how applying research and pedagogical outcomes and reflections in the field of computational design have influenced and will continue to transform design and education into the future.

Ning Gu
University of Newcastle, Australia

Xiangyu Wang
Curtin University, Australia

Acknowledgment

We would like to express our gratitude to individual authors of the chapters. We could not possibly thank you enough for your great intellectual input and time commitment in making *Computational Design Methods and Technologies: Applications in CAD, CAM and CAE Education* a great success. We must acknowledge the invaluable contributions of the members on our Scientific Peer Review Board. You took on one of the most important roles in shaping this book by providing the authors and us with constructive feedback to ensure the quality of the content. We would also like to thank other researchers, academics and designers who submitted abstracts and/or full chapters during different stages of the project. We regret that it was not possible to accommodate your contributions due to the limited volume of the book. We hope to have the chance to collaborate with you in the future. Finally we must acknowledge and thank the colleagues in IGI-Global, especially Hannah Abelbeck, our very dedicated Development Editor, whose on-going hard work and determination have assisted us greatly in completing this book project.

Ning Gu
University of Newcastle, Australia

Xiangyu Wang
Curtin University, Australia

Chapter 1
Systems and Enablers:
Modeling the Impact of Contemporary Computational Methods and Technologies on the Design Process

Michael J. Ostwald
The University of Newcastle, Australia

ABSTRACT

This chapter presents a conceptual model of the architectural design process, spanning from ideation to realization, but not focused on stages in the process. Instead, the model identifies four primary meta-systems in design (representational, proportional, indexical, and operational) that are connected through, and supported by, a range of enabling tools and technologies. The purpose of developing this model is to support a heightened understanding of the parallel evolution of the design process and of enabling technologies. Thereafter, the chapter introduces seven recent trends in computational design and technology, each of which serves to enable the design process. The seven developments are: Building Information Modeling (BIM), parametric design, generative design, collaborative design, digital fabrication, augmented reality, and intelligent environments. The chapter offers a critical review of proposed definitions of each of these technologies along with a discussion of their role as a catalyst for change in the design process.

INTRODUCTION

Historians generally trace the rise of the architectural profession to Ancient Egypt and specifically to the Third Dynasty (c2600BC). Records from that era suggest that, for the first time, an individual was granted the honorific title "chief builder" by the Pharaoh Djoser (Kostof, 1977). In the years that followed, many Pharaohs appointed a chief architect who, in turn, trained the next generation of designers in the arts and sciences of visualizing and constructing buildings. In this way, successive generations of architects, typically drawn from the same families, continued to serve the state and support the completion of major projects. While the Ancient Greeks and Romans also maintained that the role of the architect included the strengthening of existing structures and the construction of

DOI: 10.4018/978-1-61350-180-1.ch001

fortifications and machines (Vitruvius, 1914), the primary role of the architect has been, and remains to the present day, the visualization of a design and the communication of this intent, in such a way as to support the construction of a building. While this, the architect's overarching role, has not changed substantially since the Renaissance, the mechanics of the design and construction process have evolved in countless ways. In particular, the tools and technologies that once simply supported the design process have, more recently, begun to alter the way in which architects work.

This chapter commences with the presentation of a new model of the architectural design process and traces how it has changed over time. Rather than being a conventional "design as process" model, the new model is focused on the relationship between the meta-conditions of design (representation, proportion, information, operation) and the tools, devices and technologies that enable these conditions to be met. Thus, this is a framework recording the relationship between

conceptual *systems* and practical *enablers* and therefore could be described as a *system-enabler* model of the design process.

Conventional models are concerned with the stages that occur in a design process; typically including conceptualization, sketch design, developed design, documentation and reflection (Figure 1). These stages have been presented, with variations, in many different works (Schön, 1983; Cross, 1997; Lawson 2005) and while they offer a reasonable facsimile of a design process, they say relatively little about the primary conditions placed on a design, or the methods, techniques and technologies that support the process. The new model is loosely founded on the traditional design process, not only identified in architecture but also in engineering, interior and industrial design (Miller 1995; Dorst 1997: Cross 2000), but with several key differences. First, it is a comparative model; its purpose is to chart changes in design practice and process. Second, its focus is on the shifting relationship between the meta-issues in

Figure 1. A traditional design process model

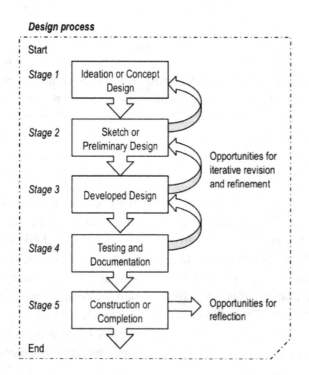

architecture and the tools used to support them. In the traditional design process framework the tools are invisible and the model affectively suggests that the wax tablet, the drawing board and CAD are all essentially the same, what matters is the process the designer takes. Without rejecting this view, the *system-enabler* model takes a different perspective on the design process in order to explain how it has changed in the past, and how the development of new technologies, tools and devices will support change in the future.

In the second part of the chapter seven contemporary enablers – computational design tools and technologies – are described. Three of the seven are concerned with the expanded capacity of the CAD model; they are *Building Information Modeling* (BIM), *parametric design* and *generative design*. Two more of the enablers provide assistance for the conceptual model to be translated into a completed building or object. These two are *collaborative design* support mechanisms and *digital fabrication* (rapid prototyping) systems. Finally, in an age of mobile computing there is a heightened capacity to not only create designs within the computer, but also to interact with the real world through the computer. Two sets of tools, *augmented reality* and *intelligent environments*, round out the overview of contemporary enablers in architecture and design. The chapter describes these seven enablers in turn, positioning them within the overarching conceptual model presented in the first half and discussing the development and application of each. In this way the reader will be able to understand not only several critical recent developments in computational design, but they will be able to visualize the part of the architect's work process that these technological enablers have the most influence over. Finally, while this chapter is largely framed around the architectural design process, the *system-enabler* model is also relevant to the fields of engineering design, industrial design and interior design all of which will be changed, in subtle or dramatic ways, by the introduction of new methods and technologies.

A META-MODEL OF THE DESIGN PROCESS

From ancient times to the present day, the architectural profession has relied on a combination of three major conceptual systems – *representational*, *proportional* and *indexical* – to describe any planned, but as-yet unbuilt, structure. In addition to these three, over time particular *operational* systems were developed to assist the design to be realized or constructed. When viewed together, these four systems could be considered to constitute a conceptual framework of the architects' conventional role; the production of designs that lead to completed structures.

The first of the four systems, the representational, includes the most visible manifestations of the architects' work; models and drawings of buildings. The first true architectural drawings can be traced to Ancient Egypt and the practice of inscribing or carving lines into flat panels of wood, as a permanent, record of a designer's spatial and formal intentions. Conversely, the earliest architectural models are typically traced to the ancient Greek world where, despite a lack of surviving examples, the language of the era included words for a model of a complete building and a wax model of an ornamental detail. While both models and drawings of existing buildings were produced in earlier times (for example, the Minoan Civilization is responsible for the earliest model buildings ever recorded), the use of representational systems to pre-figure architecture and support the construction process, occurred much later (Kostof, 1977; Morrison and Ostwald, 2007).

The second system – the proportional – was required to connect the representational media of drawings and models to the real world. In its earliest form, proportional systems were extrapolated from elements of the human body; the cubit, the foot and the dactyl (digit) are examples. To avoid variations, each civilization developed local standards that operated, to a greater or lesser extent, within their geographic boundaries (Jones, 2007). For example, the Roman civilization not only standardized each of these measures using ebony rods but they transported replicas or impressions of these rods to each colony to be used as a uniform system for translating representational forms, typically drawings, into constructed buildings. By the late 18th century most countries had acknowledged the need to formalize systems of measurement and the metric system was proposed in France and soon thereafter the Imperial system was ratified in Britain. Regardless of the system of measurement adopted by each successive generation, architecture has remained reliant on a strong conceptual link between the representational and the proportional to allow the designs of the architect to be constructed.

The next system that has traditionally supported the transition from unbuilt proposition to constructed reality is concerned with information and is entitled the indexical. The word "indexical" has two related meanings in this context. In conventional use, the word "index" describes a process that isolates particular components of a larger set and gives them a new order. Thus, the index in a book records the location of words in a larger text, and alphabetizes this list for ease of access. In semiotics though, the word indexical has a slightly different meaning, it refers to any way of methodically ordering and connecting one set of information to another. In any profession, a list of common abbreviations is one form of index while a key to a set of recurring symbols is another. Regardless of whether the first or second definition is adopted, the indexical in design could be regarded as relating to a type of rigorously ordered information. In architecture, for example, the form of a proposed design may be described though a combination of scale models and drawings (proportionally consistent representational systems), but this is not enough information to construct a building. The architect must also communicate something about the materials they wish the building to be constructed from or the expected standards to which the building must perform; both of which are forms of ordered information. The

Ancient Romans adopted a simple and pragmatic solution to this problem. Their drawings were supplemented with a list of additional information, including construction materials, which were not only defined by place and performance criteria but samples were frequently presented as part of the process. Thus, the Roman architect Vitruvius defines one construction material for a design as, "white tufa" from "Venetia [...] which can be cut with a toothed saw, like wood" (Vitruvius, 1914: 49). Thus, the representational system is supplemented with an indexical system that defines specific types of construction materials and performance criteria for a building.

Until the early 19th century these three systems remained sufficient for the majority of designs to be constructed. However, following the industrial revolution, the construction industry became increasingly complex, with tighter time-frames, greater expectations regarding financial predictability and a new reliance on material suppliers and sub-contractors. By the 20th century the process of guiding a building from its design stage through to completion had become larger and more complex than the remainder of the process it supports. While ancient Roman architects also required sufficient charisma, negotiating skills, political knowledge and imperial warrants to support the construction process, this was a relatively minor part of their role. However, in the later years of the 20th century the role has become so specialized that a new profession, Construction Managers, has arisen to share responsibility for the operational side of the process. Furthermore, with design frequently being undertaken by large teams, in part to assist the high level of indexical information required for every project, operational systems, as an extension of the design process, have come under increasing pressure.

It should by now be apparent that these four systems, the representational, the proportional, the indexical and the operational cannot function in isolation. In order to support or connect these systems a range of tools, techniques or protocols are required. For example, in Ancient Greece, the architect might present a client with an etched drawing on a soft-timber panel, a wax model, notes on a wax tablet, a set of drawers and a state warrant. The drawing and the model, part of the representational system, have been enabled through the use of primitive right-angled triangular guides, knives, scrapers and a stylus. The tablet contains a simple diagram, also produced by stylus, of the footprint of the building set out in multiples of *podes* or *poes* (a foot, being precisely 296mm long), *orgyia* (6 *podes* or the length between the tips of the fingers of a man with outstretched arms) and *stadia* (100 *orgyia* or 600 *podes*). For the builder to interpret the diagram they would need access to the state's official measures from which they could procure a copy, for construction purposes, of the *Attic* standard *pode* and *orgyia*. Such proportional enablers, typically wooden copies of stone rods, were amongst the most important of the ancient realm. The set of draws

contains chips of stone, their origins engraved into the front of the draw, as reference materials for the builder. The sample drawers are an ideal example of an indexical system that both contains and orders information. Finally, the warrant is an authority to build; an operational enabler (Figure 2). In this example the design process is focused on the representational and the proportional, as the most important systems and leaving the indexical and the operational as relatively minor components of the process. Moreover, the four systems are essentially disconnected, and each have their own specialized enablers.

Since the Renaissance architects have produced and annotated their drawings with both dimensions and graphic scales and with acronyms and abbreviations that signify certain materials or performance criteria. Such drawings were often signed and affixed with wax seals and accompanied by small scrolls of notes. There are several enablers present in this second example. First, the

Figure 2. System-enabler model: The design process in Ancient Greece

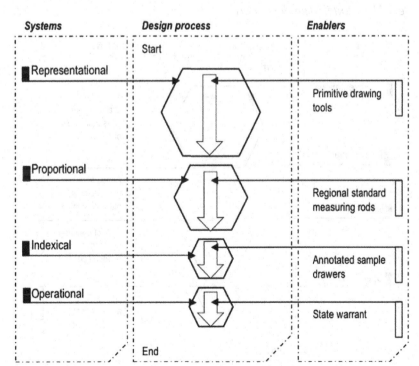

architect has used a set of tools to construct the drawing. These include a drawing board, set squares and a pair of compasses along with various inks, scribes, nibs and quills. These are the primary enablers of the representational media. The second set of enablers serves to connect systems. In this instance they include the graphic scale on the drawings which is a primitive proportional enabler, and the material acronyms and other symbolic notations on the drawings, which are early indexical enablers. The authority to construct, an operational enabler, is now literally stamped on the drawing and authorized or witnessed. The small scrolls contain more extensive advice on materials and minimum performance standards (Figure 3). The emphasis in this example is still on the representational although the proportional, aided by a national distributed standard, is somewhat less important. The proportional has also become partially connected to the representational while the indexical remains largely isolated as too does the operational.

In the aftermath of the industrial revolution, and throughout the early years of the 20th century, legislation diminished the problems of proportional systems, technical standards began to clarify and expand the indexical and management processes associated with tendering and construction grew in complexity and importance. The architectural drawing, now more densely annotated and with a conventional graphic and numeric scale, remained the primary representational and proportional source. However, because technical and scientific standards had increased the quantity of indexical information required for a design, parallel systems of drawings were required (one for each consultant and for each layer of services) to coordinate multiple levels of information. These were soon supplemented with technical specification documents containing further additional information often associated with minimum standards of workmanship. By the middle years of the 20th century the indexical had grown to become the largest system, closely followed by the operational. The representational

Figure 3. System-enabler model: The design process in the Renaissance

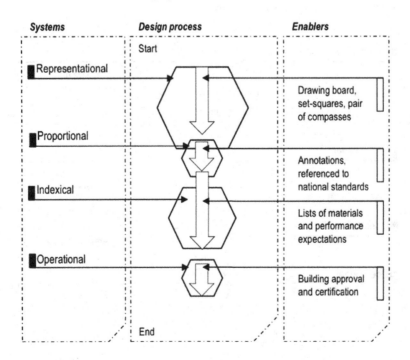

Figure 4. System-enabler model: The design process in the mid to late 20th century

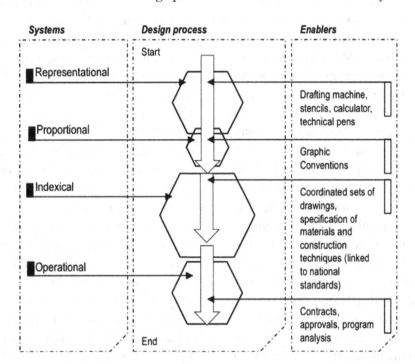

remained slightly less important and the proportional had almost disappeared from the design process as a serious concern. The contemporary architecture or design student would probably no longer be aware that the proportional was once such a significant challenge (Figure 4).

It wasn't until the end of the 20th century that the first of the major changes in the system-enabler model can be detected. With rise of CAD, the largely separate existence of the representational, the proportional and indexical began to break down. The first of these to be challenged was the role of the proportional as a separate entity. The virtual space of the computer is without fixed-scale and therefore the representational drawing could be constructed at full scale. Another way of looking at this change is that the question of scale was now only of importance to the way the drawings were printed. But this was simply the first of several major developments in enabling technology that were to challenge the conventional relationship between the four architectural meta-

systems. In the remainder of the chapter seven enabling tools are described and their impact on the system-enabler model of the architectural design process is considered. The first three, BIM, parametric models and generative design, could all be described as developments in CAD, although they serve a larger purpose and effectively relegate CAD to a minor support role.

ENABLING TOOLS AND TECHNOLOGIES

Building Information Modeling (BIM)

One of the primary conceptual goals of the CAD movement was to create a tool or device to diminish the gap between representational and proportional systems. While a CAD model or drawing may be effectively scale-less in the computer, the proportional relationships between the component parts are fixed and once a scale is set for one part, the entire model is now scalable. While this characteristic of CAD was initially celebrated it wasn't long before it was also acknowledged as a weakness. For example, Sherif (2008) argues that CAD systems "produced representations interpretable only by humans […] and they required endless effort to comprehend the full geometrical detail of those representations […] making them highly open to errors" (86). Sherif argues that, while CAD software effectively solved the problem of proportionality, it had no significant impact on the parallel problem of indexicality. In order to respond to this limitation, CAD software had to be reinvented in such a way so as to not only connect to the indexical system, but to place it at the forefront of the design process. This is, in essence, the intent of Building Information Modeling (BIM); a name which literally places the indexical ("information") centrally between the proportional ("building") and the representational ("model").

Krygiel (2008) defines the functional properties of BIM in two ways. First, BIM is focused on a single virtual model supported by a database where all of relevant information is interconnected and any "changes to an object within the model are instantly reflected throughout the rest of the project in all views" (26). Second, BIM serves to provide "information used for design decision making, production of high-quality construction documents, prediction of building performance, cost estimating, and construction planning" (27). Smith (2009) proposes that the strategic goal of BIM is to

tie all the components of a building together as objects imbedded with information. A simple computer graphic turns into an object pregnant with information that tracks its manufacture, cost, delivery, installation methods and labor costs, and maintenance all the way through to its replacement value. More importantly, BIM makes possible the erection of the building in a computer model form before putting a shovel in the ground. This goes

a long way to identifying and solving the typical errors that occur during their creation. (xi)

Smith's description could be considered typical of the more sanguine visions of BIM as solving the historic disconnection between drawings, material specifications and the construction process. Ambrose (2006) agrees proposing that BIM supplants the primacy of "composition, scale and abstraction" (effectively displacing the representational and the proportional) "with literal re-presentation" (183). Ambrose is critical of architects for relying for too long on the representational and the abstract; "[p]lans […] are merely representations of ideas composed in distorted two-dimensional abstractions of three-dimensional space. […] They are a linguistic system, a visual, graphic language, and as such they are inherently an abstract system of symbolic representation" (2006, 183). For Ambrose, the aim of BIM is to construct a virtual building, accurate and consistent in all of its parts. Krygiel (2008) concurs proposing that a "BIM model contains the building's actual constructions and assemblies rather than a two-dimensional representation of the building that is commonly found in CAD-based drawings" (26).

Despite these claims, most researchers are more circumspect in their descriptions of the potential of BIM, perhaps realizing that a virtual model, however accurate, is still simply a representation of a completed structure and that it has the same conceptual strengths and weaknesses as any set of drawings. Furthermore, while it may, theoretically, be possible to model each and every element of a building in the way Krygiel and Ambrose suggest, the reality is that current fee structures, timescales and risk mechanisms will not allow this to occur. Furthermore, site conditions are never definitively known until excavation has been completed, material qualities and quantities are not entirely predictable and BIM assumes a uniform, perfect and consistent standard of construction. For all of these reasons, the more evangelical proponents of BIM are far less convincing than those who see it simply as an important enabling tool; a critical step beyond CAD and towards some future, as yet unidentified system. In this sense Russell (2008) offers a pragmatic definition of BIM as the act of "adding a semantic layer to the three-dimensional [representation] to create a single building or data model" (532). Laiserin (2003) similarly focuses the innovative potential of BIM in the indexical realm stating that BIM is

designed to capture and re-present [information] in a way that is meaningful to the users of that information. That information should encompass the architect's design intent with respect to the building program, site, budget, building systems, energy performance, aesthetics, building codes, etc. For the contractor it should include construction methodology, quantity takeoffs, costing information, schedules, construction simulation, and so on. (np)

While the more utopian propositions may be difficult to support, BIM has certainly integrated indexical systems into the design process in a holistic, adaptive or responsive way for the first time.

Parametric Design and Generative Design

Mitchell (1995) defines a parametric system as one that may be described "in terms of a small number of independent (usually dimensional) variables" (477). Eastman (2008) argues that in parametric design, "[o]bjects are defined using parameters involving distances, angles and rules like *attached to*, *parallel to* and *distance from*." (29) Thus, the qualities of the object are not only able to be described using dimensional variables, but these are located within a hierarchical system that relates sets of dimensional variables to rules or goals. For example, in a traditional CAD program objects are infinitely flexible whereas in a parametric system, the object will have some rules embedded in it and when it is resized in the

computer the other parameters of the object will adapt to ensure that the rules can be met.

A good definition of a parametric model contains at least the following four elements. First, parametric objects are typically defined by a combination of dimensional, innate and rule-based parameters. That is, the virtual object has shape or form, it has simulated material properties (strength, resilience, color) and it serves a purpose (to transfer loads, to isolate areas, etc.). Second, parametric objects have connotative rules; this means that any change in one parameter will have an impact on any others within the object. Thus, Burry (2003) notes, "[e]ach time a value for any parameter changes, the model simply regenerates to reflect the new values" (212). The third characteristic is that parametric objects will either not allow themselves to break established rules or they will signal to the designer if they are forced to breach the rules or requirements of the system. Burry (2003) describes this as being "over-constraint"; the situation wherein "a value for a parameter cannot be fulfilled due to a constraint of another parameter" (212). Finally, parametric objects are able to "broadcast or export sets of attributes" (Eastman, 2008: 14). This implies that a parametric model can output various forms of data. This could include representational data (scale drawings, renderings and animations), proportional data (tolerance schedules for off-site manufacturing, cutting and wastage schedules) and indexical data (tables of lighting levels, or thermal performance information).

Kolarevic (2003) argues that parametric models "provide for a powerful conception of architectural form by describing a range of possibilities, replacing in the process stable with variable, singularity with multiplicity" (25). He goes on to propose that not only is the parametric process useful for generating multiple alternative design solutions, but that it may provide support for the process of assessing the viability of each alternative. For Kolarevic, *[i]n parametric design, it is the parameters of a particular design that are declared, not its shape. By assigning different values to the parameters, different objects or configurations can be created. Equations can be used to describe the relationships between objects, this defining an associative geometry – the "constituent geometry that is mutually linked." That way, interdependencies between objects can be established, and object behaviour under transformations defined. (2003: 25)*

While the combination of BIM and parametric modeling has the potential to radically alter the design process in most commercial architectural firms, there are, nevertheless, serious challenges inherent in this combination of enablers. For example, Burry argues that, despite the hype, the reality is that most of the complex, rule-based parameters cannot be easily programmed by architects and this leaves the designer susceptible to having their work shaped by rules which they have little or no control over. Furthermore, in practice the majority of the parameters are still geometric and formal; a situation which has not changed in the last decade. Therefore, Burry suggests that,

[i]n this sense, parametric design is more accurately referred to as "associative geometry", for in the cases that I have experience, [that is] at the front-end use of the software, the only parameters that can be revised in acto are those that define the measurements of entities and distances along with their relative angles, and the ability to make formal associations between these elements. (Burry, 2003, 211)

Generative design is closely related to both BIM and parametric design and it shares characteristics with both of these enabling technologies. The title generative design, or more correctly auto-generative design, typically describe a loose series of related processes which architects have separately branded "iterative" (Sharples *et al.,* 2002), "algorithmic" (Terzidis, 2006), "evolutionary"

(Watanabe, 2002), "morpho-ecological" (Hensel and Menges, 2008) and "emergent" (Hensel *et al.,* 2004). All of these design tropes share a common set of three features. First and foremost they celebrate a system's innate capacity for autonomous development. Each of the strategies describes a set of conditions wherein a design is able to grow or change without overt human influence. Second, this process is never random, it occurs within certain preordained limits; often called "reflexive" parameters (Castle, 2002). This feature suggests that their capacity for evolution is constrained by rules or boundaries. Such rules could be derived from spatial limits, social patterns, functional requirements or material properties. The third and final feature of the auto-generative design approach is that it does not produce a singular design solution. Instead, it operates by defining a set of conceivable solutions to a design problem. Thus, the system produces a constrained continuum of possibilities, typically as an animated sequence recording the evolution of a series of forms, all of which are shaped by different combinations of rules (Fear, 2001). Rocker (2006) offers the definition that in the generative design process,

[t]he computer is no longer used as a tool for representation, but as a medium to conduct computations. Architecture emerges as a trace of algorithmic operations. Surprisingly enough, algorithms – deterministic in their form and abstract in their operations – challenge both design conventions and, perhaps even more surprisingly, some of our basic intuitions. (4)

Despite the apparent power of generative and parametric systems, a growing number of scholars have become critical of different parts of this process and of the architecture it has produced (Ostwald, 2004). For example Burry is critical of the way in which the parametric and generative systems produce an "'implied design process' that is the enemy of intuition" (Burry, 2003, 210). Terzidis (2006) is critical of generative design

Figure 5. System-Enabler model: The design process at the start of the 21ˢᵗ Century

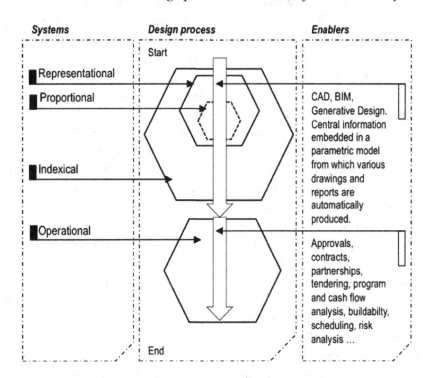

for celebrating the complexity of computational systems; a complexity which few architects truly understand. The present author has previously demonstrated how a range of values are invisibly embedded in parametric and generative design software; a situation which is problematic for the efficacy of the design process (Ostwald, 2006; Ostwald, 2010a). Rocker (2006) has expressed a similar damning view that

[m]ost architects now use computers and interactive software programs as exploratory tools. All their work is informed by, and thus dependent on the software they are using, which inscribes its logic, [...] onto their everyday routines. Such users of software packages have little or no knowledge of the algorithms powering the programs they employ. Most of the interactivity is reduced to a manipulation of displayed forms on the screen, neglecting the underlying mathematical calculations behind them. All of this – even though implemented on computers – has little to do with the logics of computation. (23)

While acknowledging these criticisms, the combination of BIM, parametric design and generative design have potentially had the greatest impact of any enabler on the architectural design process since ancient Roman times (Figure 5). In essence, they have collectively sought to place the representational and proportional systems within an indexical framework. Information, for the first time, has become the central feature of the design process. Moreover, BIM, parametric design and generative design have collectively enabled the production of a consistent set of documents and controls for the construction and manufacturing process.

Collaborative Design and Digital Fabrication

The last century has seen a growth in complexity of the design and construction process that has resulted in a situation where project teams are now, collectively, the primary progenitors of a design.

As a result, project team dynamics have increasingly become the focus of specialized research.

The concept of collaborative design involves a shift in "network practices"; what Burke and Tierney (2007) define as the non-technical issues that govern the human component of the design process. In an abstract sense, Burke and Tierney see collaborative design as taking advantage of the "creative potential of physical, social, and technical networks" (27) to respond to "changing environmental parameters" (27). In practice though, the majority of research into collaborative design has been associated with two aspects of the design process; sharing virtual models and improved communication strategies between consultants through the use of virtual environments. The first of these has, in part, been described as a component of BIM; the capacity for not only sharing a single design model, but also for allowing, within certain approval hierarchies, for any member of the team to modify components of the design which they have been given influence over. To date, much of this work has been focused on software and interface development. This problem could be considered a technical one which will, in time, be solved in such a way as to seamlessly allow an integrated design team to share information and responsibility for decision making (Krygiel 2008). The second part of the collaborative design concept has set out to use virtual environments to enable improved communication and possibly to support the more tangible sharing of design information. For example, Whyte (2002) argues that one of the problems with sharing representational and indexical models is that the level and form of interaction lacks immediacy. Thus, while it is possible to solve the problems of model sharing, without some immersive parallel environment, where that sharing is manifest, the collaborative benefits are limited. This realization has tended to encourage collaborative design researchers to consider the benefits of virtual environments including Second Life and large-scale on-line gaming environments. Additional uses have included virtual design studios (Chen *et al.,* 1998), in un-

dergraduate education, where Dave and Danahy (1998) argue that the "virtual design studios can serve as contexts in which students develop their abilities to function as team members" (102).

Collaborative design enablers do not have a single point of impact (Figure 6) in the system-enabler model. While they assist in bridging between the indexical and the representational systems in the newly merged BIM environment, they are potentially active throughout the entire design process, cutting across other systems, to facilitate progress. A similar impact is felt by a different form of enabling technology; digital fabrication which may have a direct role in connecting design to construction, but is, like collaborative technology, active in multiple stages of the design process. Digital fabrication and rapid prototyping both refer to the automated process wherein a computer file is used to control the construction of an object by a machine. While they are often used semi-interchangeably, the former is more correctly associated with full-scale manufacturing while the latter is more commonly used to produce models or prototypes as part of the design process.

Rapid prototyping is typically employed when the object being constructed is a representation or model of some finished object or component. Burry (2003) notes that rapid prototyping "provides affordable opportunities to investigate a design within an iterative process: both words 'rapid' and 'prototyping' in this conjunction imply a physical testing of concept somewhere along a path of design refinement" (210). Several authors have argued that computer renderings of a design are at best a loose representation of a completed building, whereas models, either handmade or digitally fabricated, provide a more experiential, and thereby useful, form of representation (Ostwald 2010b; Burry 2010). Kenzari (2008) notes that such prototypes "are often displayed in architectural exhibitions in the form of models of buildings" (62). Bonewetsch *et al.* (2006) similarly argue that in architecture this technology is largely limited to "design studies in a model scale" (490).

Figure 6. System-enabler model: The impact of collaborative design and digital fabrication

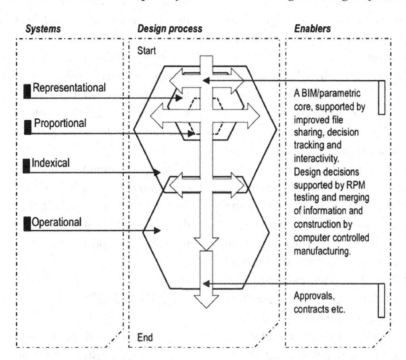

The title digital manufacturing is more commonly used to refer to the automated construction of actual building parts from the data contained in a BIM model. For example, Eastman (2008) notes that

some companies [...] already have CNC machines of different kinds, such as rebar bending and cutting machines, laser cutters for steel profile or plates, or sophisticated conveyor and casting systems for precast concrete. For some fabricators, these technologies may be drivers for adopting BIM; for others, they will be new, and BIM will enable their introduction. In either case, it is important to consider the information requirements and the interfaces that are supported by the BIM software. (268)

Ultimately, despite differences in scale and intent, technological enablers like digital manufacturing and rapid prototyping (which take computer files and automatically construct objects from them) are important for the advancement of effective design. While their most significant financial impact may occur when the design model is used to automate construction (in the overlap between indexical and operational systems), the greatest impact on the quality of the finished design will occur much earlier in the process (Figure 6).

Augmented Reality and Intelligent Environments

Definitions of augmented reality tend to agree on the key elements. For example, Caudell and Barfield (1992) define augmented reality as the application of "advanced human-computer interface technology that attempts to blend or fuse computer-generated information with our sensations of the natural world" (6). Azuma (1997) proposes that augmented reality "allows the user to see the real world, with virtual objects superimposed upon or composited with the real world" (2). White (2002) proposes that in augmented reality "systems overlay virtual and real world imagery allowing the user to interact with both the virtual and real world" (5). Finally, Choi (2006) suggests that augmented reality is "an advanced information technology that links digital information such as computer graphics, sounds [and] haptic systems [...] and real objects in physical environments" (54).

One of the few different insights into augmented reality comes from Schnabel (2008) who identifies that there is a complex continuum that exists between real environments, which may be digitally enhanced (augmented reality) and virtual environments, which may also be digitally enhanced with additional information (augmented virtuality). Both of these variations are useful in the design process; the former for assisting people to visualize the impact of a proposed design and the latter for adding layers of information in a virtual model. Novak (1997) offers a similar distinction but for the purpose of defining a different enabling system, intelligent environments. For Novak, there is a technical continuum between the real world and the virtual world that is not defined by the level of augmentation, but by the level of "intelligence" (meaning computational responsiveness) embedded in the system. Novak argues that at one extreme are "actual environments with ubiquitous computing embedded in every available device" while at the other are "purely immersive virtual spaces accessible only through technological mediation"(Novak, 1997, 418).

More conventionally, an intelligent environment is typically a space, structure or building which has had technology embedded into it for the purpose of assisting, monitoring or optimizing its performance. Bowen-James (1997) argues that the driving force behind attempts to create intelligent environments is the desire to "anthropomorphize technology and mechanize humanity"; suggesting that just as "our artifacts are becoming more like us", so too "we are becoming more like [...] our artifacts" (354). Intelligent environments are useful in a range of circumstances and at different scales. For example, Hookway and Perry (2006) propose that

[t]ypical scales of focus might thus include reflexive and adaptable infrastructures for interior or small-scale environments. At the scale of the interior, this could be office, lobby and gallery landscaping systems, including the secondary scales of furniture, ceiling and partitioning systems, as well as lighting, sound and temperature infrastructures. At the scale of the exterior, it might include building skins, roofing landscapes and sidewalk furniture systems. (77)

Together augmented reality and intelligent environments have a range of potential impacts on the design process with the former focused in the earlier stages of the system-enabler model and the latter after project completion.

CONCLUSION

This chapter has demonstrated that it is possible to construct a history of the architectural design process largely from the point of view of the shifting relationship between conceptual systems and technical enablers. A critical part of such a history is the gradual growth in capacity, or "intelligence", of the design enablers. Enablers were once simple wooden tools, the most basic devices used to translate the architects' ideas into a consistent conceptual system; to describe the extent of a design, set its scale and define the materials that will be used in its construction. Today, the computational enablers have all but solved the historic problems of representational and proportional systems and by placing information, the indexical, at the heart of the design process have encouraged the greatest change in the standard architectural design process in many hundreds of years. But problems also arise when enablers no longer simply support the design process, as the present chapter records. BIM, parametric modeling and generative design can all blur the distinction between support tools and design process; a practice that some architects and scholars may applaud, but a growing number are concerned about. This will be an ongoing challenge for the next generation of architects and the creators of future computational design tools and techniques.

ACKNOWLEDGMENT

An ARC Fellowship (FT0991309) and an ARC Grant (DP1094154) supported this research.

REFERENCES

Ambrose, M. A. (2006). *Plan is dead: To BIM, or not to BIM, that is the question.* Computing in Architecture / Re-Thinking the Discourse (pp. 182–189). Sharjah, United Arab Emirates: ASCAAD.

Azuma, R. (1997). A survey of augmented reality. *Presence (Cambridge, Mass.)*, (August): 335–385.

Bonewetsch, T., Kobel, D., Gramazio, F., & Kohler, M. (2006). *The informed wall: Applying additive digital fabrication techniques on architecture.* Synthetic Landscapes (pp. 489–495). Louisville, KY: ACADIA.

Bowen-James, A. (1997). Paradoxes and parables of intelligent environments. In P. Droege (Ed.), *Intelligent environments: Spatial aspects of the information revolution* (pp. 354–383). Amsterdam, The Netherlands: Elsevier.

Burke, A., & Tierney, T. (2007). *Network practices: New strategies in architecture and design.* New York, NY: Princeton Architectural Press.

Burry, M. (2001). *Cyberspace: The world of digital architecture.* Melbourne, Australia: Images.

Burry, M. (2003). Between intuition and process: Parametric design and rapid prototyping Architecture. In B. Kolarevic (Ed.), *Digital age: Design and manufacturing* (pp. 147–162). New York, NY: Spon Press.

Burry, M. (2010). Models, prototypes and archetypes. In M. Ostwald, P. Downton, & A. Fairley (Eds.), *Homo Faber volume 3: Modelling, identity and the post digital* (pp. 187 – 196). Melbourne, Australia: Melbourne Museum.

Castle, H. (Ed.). (2002). *Reflexive architecture.* London, UK: Wiley-Academy.

Caudell, T., & Barfield, W. (2001). *Fundamentals of wearable computers and augmented reality.* New Jersey: Lawrence Erlbaum Associates.

Chen, Y., Fram, I., & Maver, T. W. (1998). A virtual studio environment for design integration. *Advances in Engineering Software*, *29*(10), 787–800.

Choi, J. W. (2006). A technological review to develop an AR-based design supporting system. In X. Wang & M. A. Schnabel (Eds.), *Mixed reality in architecture, design and construction* (pp. 53–57). Sydney, Australia: Springer.

Cross, N. (1997). Descriptive models of creative design: Application to an example. *Design Studies*, *18*(4), 427–440.

Cross, N. (2000). *Engineering design methods: Strategies for product design.* New York, NY: Wiley.

Dave, B. D., & Danahy, J. (1998). Virtual study abroad and exchange studio. Digital design studios: Do computers make a difference? *ACADIA Conference Proceedings*, (pp. 100-115). Québec, Canada: ACADIA.

Dorst, K. (1997). *Describing design - A comparison of paradigms.* Delft, The Netherlands: Technische Universiteit Delft.

Eastman, C. (2008). *BIM handbook: A guide to building information modeling for owners, managers, designers, engineers, and contractors.* Hoboken, NJ: Wiley.

Fear, B. (Ed.). (2001). *Architecture and animation.* London, UK: Wiley-Academy.

Hensel, M., & Menges, A. (Eds.). (2008). *Versatility and vicissitude: Performance in morphoecological design*. London, UK: Wiley-Academy.

Hensel, M., Menges, A., & Weinstock, M. (Eds.). (2004). *Emergence: Morphogenetic design strategies*. London, UK: Wiley-Academy.

Hookway, B., & Perry, C. (2006). Responsive systems, appliance architectures. *Architectural Design, 76*(5), 74–79.

Jones, M. W. (2006). Ancient architecture and mathematics: Methodology and the Doric temple. In S. Duvernoy & O. Pedemonte (Eds.), *Nexus VI: Architecture and mathematics* (pp. 149–170). Torino, Italy: Kim Williams Books.

Kenzari, B. (2008). Digital design and fabrication. *Proceedings of the 13th International Conference on Computer Aided Architectural Design Research in Asia* (pp. 61-67). Chiang Mai, Thailand: CAADRIA.

Kolarevic, B. (2003). *Architecture in the digital age: Design and manufacturing*. New York, NY: Spon Press.

Kostof, S. (1977). The practice of architecture in the ancient world: Egypt and Greece. In S. Kostof (Ed.), *The architect: Chapters in the history of the profession* (pp. 3–27). New York, NY: Oxford University Press.

Krygiel, E. (2008). *Green BIM: Successful sustainable design with building information modeling*. Hoboken, NJ: John Wiley & Sons.

Laiserin, J., & Barron, C. (2003). Graphisoft on BIM. *The Laiserin Letter, 19*.

Lawson, B. (2005). *How designers think: The design process demystified*. Burlington, MA: Elsevier.

Miller, S. F. (1995). *Design process: A primer for architectural and interior design*. New York, NY: Van Nostrand Reinhold.

Mitchell, W. J., & McCullough, M. (1995). *Digital design media*. New York, NY: Van Nostrand Reinhold.

Morrison, T., & Ostwald, M. J. (2007). Shifting dimensions: The architectural model in history. In P. Downton, M. Ostwald, A. Mina, & A. Fairley (Eds.), *Homo Faber: Modelling architecture* (pp. 142–156). Melbourne, Australia: Melbourne Museum.

Novak, M. (1997). Cognitive cities: Intelligence, environment and space. In P. Droege (Ed.), *Intelligent environments: Spatial aspects of the information revolution* (pp. 386–419). Amsterdam, The Netherlands: Elsevier.

Ostwald, M. J. (2004). Freedom of form: Ethics and Aesthetics in digital architecture. *The Philosophical Forum, 35*(2), 201–220.

Ostwald, M. J. (2006). Ethics and geometry: Computational transformations and the curved surface in architecture. In S. Duvernoy & O. Pedemonte (Eds.), *Nexus VI: Architecture and mathematics* (pp. 77–92). Torino, Italy: Kim Williams Books.

Ostwald, M. J. (2010a). Ethics and the autogenerative design process. *BRI: Building Research and Information, 38*(4), 390–400.

Ostwald, M. J. (2010b). On the value of labour: Rethinking the physical model and questioning the CAD/CAM model. In M. Ostwald, P. Downton, & A. Fairley (Eds.)m *Homo Faber volume 3: Modelling, identity and the post digital* (pp. 175–186). Melbourne, Australia: Melbourne Museum.

Rocker, I. M. (2006). When code matters. *AD Architectural Design, 76*(4), 16–25.

Russell, P., & Elger, D. (2008). The meaning of BIM. *Architecture in Computro, Conference Proceedings* (pp. 531-536) Antwerpen, Belgium: eCAADe.

Schnabel, M. (2008). *Mixed reality in architecture, design and construction*. Dordecht, The Netherlands: Springer.

Schön, D. A. (1983). *The reflective practitioner*. New York, NY: Basic Books.

Sherif, M. (2008). Building information modeling and architectural practice: On the verge of a new culture. *International Conference on Critical Digital Matters*, (pp. 85-90) Cambridge, MA: Harvard University Graduate School of Design.

Smith, D. K., & Tardif, M. (2009). *Building information modeling: A strategic implementation guide for architects, engineers, constructors, and real estate asset managers*. Hoboken, NJ: John Wiley & Sons.

Terzidis, K. (2006). *Algorithmic architecture*. Oxford, UK: Elsevier.

Vitruvius, M. (1914). *The ten books on architecture*. New York, NY: Dover Publications.

Watanabe, M. S. (2002). *Induction design: A method for evolutionary design*. Basel, Switzerland: Birkhäuser.

Whyte, J. (2002). *Virtual reality and the built environment*. Oxford, UK: Architectural Press.

KEY TERMS AND DEFINITIONS

Design Enablers: The set of tools, techniques or protocols required to support the design process. For example, if the process is to produce a representation, then the tools might be pencils, rulers, or CAD software. If the process is to support operation systems, then the enablers might include BIM, project planning software and industry standard protocols (for example, quality assurance operational standards).

Design Process Model: A common trope in the design disciplines is to view design as a linear process (with some potential feed-back loops) that commences with conceptualization and then gradually refines the concept though schematic and developed stages until technical resolution is required. This model typically does not extend to the construction or manufacturing stage, but might include prototyping and testing.

Indexical Systems: The information required to define the practical properties of a form designated in a representation. This information is typically associated with material or structural properties but could also include, lighting, acoustic and thermal properties as well as a wide range of other issues (like maintenance scheduling). In the late 20th century this information was typically provided as a key on drawings in combination with a specification document and schedules of performance criteria.

Meta-Design Systems: The set of systems required, as part of the design process, for a concept to be translated into a building, structure or object. The four systems are *representational, proportional, indexical* and *operational.*

Operational Systems: The managerial and legislative systems required to support the construction process. In the late 20th century these typically included everything from building approvals by consent authorities, to materials delivery schedules, critical path plans and cashflow programming.

Proportional Systems: A benchmark measure and associated scale which allows a representation to be converted into a full-size construction. In the 20th century this typically included the imperial and metric systems in combination with standard representational ratios (that is, 1:200, 1:500 etc.).

Representational Systems: Any medium that is used to communicate the formal and spatial intent of a design. The most common examples include scale drawings and models but renderings and animations may also be used to provide additional, qualitative information.

Chapter 2
Novel Concepts in Digital Design

Rivka Oxman
Technion - Israel Institute of Technology, Israel

ABSTRACT

New media and methodologies are being employed in changing the conceptual understanding of what digital design is and may become. New experience is beginning to emerge in relation to novel key design concepts, computational methods, and digital technologies in the use of, and interaction with, digital media in design. The chapter describes an experimental program, the objective of which was to identify and map novel design concepts and relevant methodologies of digital design. In making the survey, analysis, and the categorization of relevant concepts and emerging precedents in this field, the authors made an attempt to formulize a theoretical basis for the conceptual mapping of this field. The conceptual mapping of this field is termed DDNET: Digital Design Network. The DDNET is a semantic system divided into the following conceptual levels: Key-concepts, sub-concepts, computational models and techniques, and precedent level. As a first step in this research, the authors made a survey of emerging knowledge from both praxis and theoretical resources, and then formulated and presented proposed set of design models, concepts, relevant methodologies, and precedents. Next, the authors mapped a network representation around leading key-concepts. The final step was to accommodate and apply this representation as a new basis for a pedagogical experiment in teaching digital design. The research has been conducted in Experimental Digital Design Studio in the Faculty of Architecture and Town Planning at the Technion, Israel.

INTRODUCTION

The evolution of digital design as a unique field of design knowledge, supported by new technologies, and producing unique understanding of designs is a phenomenon that is rapidly crystallizing in this decade. Our assumption is that the very nature of design is radically changing today. If the new media is indeed the common thread - there is the need first, to pioneer a new understanding of the nature of designing in relation to digital design media. Furthermore, if the very nature of design is radically changing, how then can we accommodate

DOI: 10.4018/978-1-61350-180-1.ch002

and recognize emerging theories of design? And how we accommodate these as a basis for a new didactics and pedagogy?

Among the significance of digital design for the design theoretical community is the way that this form of highly mediated design is beginning to evolve unique conceptual content. A new understanding of digital design as a unique set of design phenomena demands a theoretical and methodological formulation of the symbiosis between the product of design and the way it is now conceived, generated and modeled in digital media. The clarification and meanings of conceptual relationships between models, concepts, systems, and their applications in precedents, appears to provide advantages in the formulization of novel bodies of knowledge concepts and techniques. Having created a body of novel precedents in emerging practices, new methods and processes of mediated design have reached the point of maturity in conception and practice that now demands a broad and general theoretical formulation.

THE EMERGENCE OF NEW DISCOURSE

Early attempts to deal with digital design as an important theoretical threshold in architecture were realized by various theoreticians (Oxman, 2006). *Folding in Architecture*, the special issue of the journal *AD* (Lynn, 1993) created an influential body of early theoretical sources and had an important impact in determining the constituents of an incipient digital design theory. Early contributions by Lynn (1999) provided introductions to potential philosophical sources, to studies of technological innovations, to descriptions of experimental projects, and to identity of their relevance in the formulation of a theory of the digital in design. This combination of diverse theoretical, philosophical, methodological, technical and professional sources has characterized the discourse of digital architectural design in its first decade. In parallel, emerging technologies began to influence central issues in design theory. From the mid 1990's digital architectural design became engaged with the exploration of complex geometries (Rashid and Couture, 2002), with so called, 'free forms' (Pottmann, 2010) as well as with related materialization processes of fabrication and manufacturing technologies (Schodek et al., 2005; Sass and Oxman, 2006). Recently, *Digital Culture in Architecture* - an introduction for the design profession examines the influence of digital culture on architecture (Picon, 2010) and in a recent AD book, the *New Structuralism* is proposed as a new theory of structuring in architecture as part of a new material practice (Oxman and Oxman, 2010).

Furthermore, the formulation and publication of a theoretical discourse, novel precedents have been associated with *practice gained theory*. Among such significant monographs on *digital theoretical practice* are UN-Studio, van Berkel and Bos (1999), Rashid and Couture (2002), Oosterhuis (2002), Zaero-Polo and Moussavi (2003), and Spuybroek (2004) each of which is a significant theoretical work promoting digital design as a unique set of processes. Furthermore, there was a growing impact of innovative experimentation in design and construction. In architecture, the Bilbao Guggenheim by Frank Gehry (1992-1997) was the most prominent catalyst of theorizing new formal directions and postulating new design methods (Lindsey, 2002). Other formative works that helped to generate theoretical discourse include the Greater London Authority Headquarters, (2002) and the Swiss RE building (2004) designed by Foster & Partners and Arup Associates etc. Recently works such as the Cagliari Contemporary Arts Centre in Cagliari designed by Zaha Hadid Architects (2007), the Skipper Library by *Formtexx* (2010) and works completed by Gramazio & Kohler (2008) are proposed as part of the *New Structuralism* (Oxman and Oxman, 2010).

Digital Design Education

Following the evolution of the field in praxis it has influenced the development of novel concepts and significant terms such as "digital design" and "digital design thinking". Understanding the way novel concepts are changing our conceptual and ideation processes has become essential. Furthermore, if digital design ideation constitutes a new conceptualization of design then there is a need for a new education and pedagogical and didactic framework. The conventional educational model in the design studio generally employs a simulation of praxis as a didactic model. That is, the didactic stages are driven by a theoretical interpretation of program, site and conditions carried through stages of conceptualization, schematic design and design development. Most studios still employ well accepted knowledge-bases and traditional typologies as well as traditional media such as paper-based sketches. However, as we attempt to re-evaluate the logic of the Schön model, we find the need to re-define the concept of "material" and to understand the impact of digital design in design thinking. Schön's classic characterization of visual reasoning in the design as a "dialogue with the materials of the problem" and the process of backtalk from visual images (Schön, 1983) may be re-interpreted today and gain new perspective. Within the framework of this orientation to a critical formulation of new educational agenda, the following issues were considered (Oxman, 2008):

- If conventional knowledge base is obsolete, what are we teaching when we teach digital design? How can we, in fact, define, capture, collect and teach new knowledge?
- If we assume that digital design is so different from traditional paper-based design than many of our root concepts must be reformulated. If this is the case, how can we begin to conceptualize and formulate novel ways of designing?

- In this case if conventional teaching approaches are obsolete, what are we teaching when we teach digital design? How can we teach novel concepts, new technologies and techniques associated with emerging new knowledge?

The evolution of digital design as a unique field of design endeavor, motivated by its own body of theoretical sources, and a culture of discourse, is beginning to evolve unique ideology, methodologies and formal content (Liu, 2005, Oxman 2006). Works such as Kolarevic (2003); Kolarevic and Malkawi (2005) Pottmann (2010) and Oxman and Oxman (2010) may provide a conceptual basis of methodological and technological content.

Conceptual Structure of Digital Design

The awareness of change between traditional and digital design are stimulating the need for a conceptualization of digital design foundations. As a result the following points have been identified (Oxman, 2008):

- Digital design thinking is more than simply a set of formal preferences. It is the *abandonment of the modernist design ontology* that is predicated upon formal and typological knowledge (e.g. formal languages, typological classes and generic design, etc.) It is non-typological and non-deterministic in supporting and preferring the differentiated over the discrete and the typological.
- There is an emerging *new symbiosis* between the digital product of design and the way it is conceived, generated and produced in digital media. These stages are fundamentally different from those of modernist design. It is the understanding and formulation of this procedural symbiotic relationship between conception, gen-

eration, production and the product itself that appears to be of high priority today.

- Digital technologies appear to have *freed the image from traditional concepts of image-based representation.* We no longer represent discrete shapes in the conventional paper-based sense. This condition has enhanced the denial of classical notions of representational conventions such as static space, and has introduced new concepts of dynamic and responsive space and form that are producing new classes of designs.

- In many cases approaches to form generation exploit *generative-based transformational processes* in which digital media are the enabling environment. This in many ways is *replacing the experimental visual nature of the paper-based sketching process.*

- Context in the modernist sense may possess iconic, stylistic, or configurative content that can implicate design through visual or formal content. Context in digital design is considered a *per-formative shaping force* acting upon shape structure and material.

The objective of the research presented in this paper has been to address this evolving synergy and its theoretical imperative. The main question raised in this research was related to means by which we can capture and map this knowledge in order to define it and make it useful in design. Our approach to this task has been to access and define a conceptual structure in order to collect and construct a semantic map of the key concepts of this field.

DDNET: CONCEPTUAL MAPPING OF DIGITAL DESIGN

In the following sections we present the DDNET. DDNET (**D**igital **D**esign **NET**work) is a first attempt to formulate a conceptual mapping for the field of digital design. According to Sowa (Sowa, 1991) *a semantic network or net is a graphic notation for representing knowledge in patterns of interconnected nodes and arcs.* Earlier versions have long been used in philosophy, psychology, and linguistics and recently they are implemented in computational systems. What is common to all semantic networks is a declarative graphic representation that can be used either to represent knowledge or to support the reasoning about the semantics of specific network. The conceptual mapping and the notations presented in the next section *represent the semantics* of the DDNET system.

Semantic networks and our proposal of enriching this formalism through describing the meaning of conceptual clustering and multiple levels of clusters have proven relevant as a tool of discourse analysis. They help to clarify important semantic relationships as well as identifying scientifically meaningful, as compared to the purely descriptive, terminology that is associated with ideology. The first experiment underling the knowledge acquisition and network construction process was carried on in an educational situation in which a team of student-researchers collaboratively constructed a generic knowledge base for the conceptual and methodological applications in a specific design library of theoretical material and case studies. The initial stage of the research was based upon the collection of theoretical materials as well as a systematic survey of relevant precedents employing the ICF formalism (Oxman, 1994; 2003).

In the following sections we present the DDNET structure, the conceptual levels and the theoretical constructs of DDNET.

DDNET: Novel Key Concepts, Computational Models and Digital Technologies

DDNET is a structure of a semantic network which attempts to relate the body of theoretical constructs with the key concepts, models, methods and technologies and leading precedents of the field. Once the mapping of the levels of conceptualization is completed, we believe that the theoretical foundations of the field will emerge as a distinct body of theory and related design practices. Such clarified terminological and conceptual distinctions should also serve to ameliorate the effects of an ideologically charged interpretation that has characterized much of the design practice and the research in this field.

The proposed structure of DDNET is composed of key concepts, sub-concepts computational models, digital technologies and precedents. Concepts and sub-concepts are those concepts which have emerged as central to a sub-discourse in digital design. We have also proposed that in design there is a highly conventionalized acceptance of the constituents of models (important models of digital design such as *performance-based models*), and methods (important methodological/technological foundations for system development such as *parametric methods and techniques*) and illustrative precedents. The conceptual structure and of the conceptual levels in DDNET: *Key concept, Sub-concept, Computational Models Digital Technologies and Digital Design Precedents,* are illustrated below (see Figure 1).

These indications of conceptual change are starting to emerge from the formulation of the conceptual content and terminology of digital design.

Figure 1. Conceptual levels in DDNET: Key concept, sub-concept, computational models digital technologies and digital design precedents

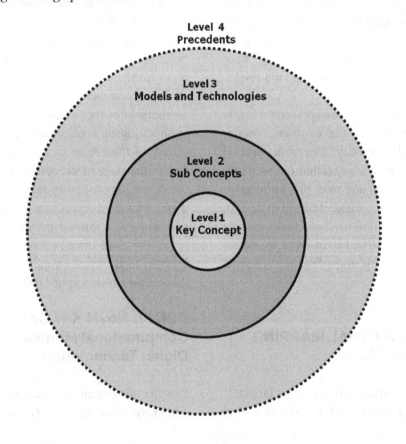

Computational Models

A formulation through the identification of relevant early models of design has been developed by the author (Oxman, 2006). The classification of paradigmatic models include: CAD models, formation models, generative models, performance models and integrated compound models. This classification enables the definition of underlying current digital design models.

- *CAD Models:* Traditional CAD models signify the initial attempt to depart from paper-based media. They had little qualitative effect on design in comparison to conventional paper-based models. In traditional CAD the interaction with formal representations supports the a posteriori automation of design drawings and visual models. First CAD systems were mainly descriptive, employing various geometrical modeling / rendering software.

- *Formation Models:* In digital design the centrality of traditional concepts of paper-based representation are no longer valid conceptions for explicating the thinking and processes associated with digital design. Furthermore, in certain formation processes of digital design the formal implications of the concept of representation are negative and unproductive. Emerging design theory has transformed the concept of form into the concept of formation associated with topology, parametrics and animation. Topological design is based on the exploitation of topology and non-Euclidean geometry. Parametric design is based on principles of parametric design (Bury, 1999). And generative components, animation, morphing (Lynn, 1999) and other range of motion and time-based modeling techniques are based on the propagation of multiple discrete instantiations in a dynamic continuum.

- *Generation Models:* Generative models of digital design are characterized by the provision of computational mechanisms for formalized generation processes. Here, as compared to formation models, shapes and forms are considered to be a result of pre-formulated generative processes. Currently there is a rich theoretical body of research-related applications of generative models. Two main distinct current sub-approaches are shape grammars (Knight and Stiny, 2001) and evolutionary models (Frazer, 2002).

- *Performance Models:* Performance-based models are driven by performance and potentially integrated with formation and generative processes. Forces in a given context are fundamental to form-making in digital design. External forces may be considered as environmental forces including structural loads, acoustics, transportation, site, program etc. Information itself is also considered as an external "force" that can manipulate the design (Oxman, 2009).

Key Concepts

Concepts and sub-concepts are those concepts which are central to a sub-discourse in digital design. Each key concept is linked to one or more sub-concepts that define the meaning of a key-concept and may provide an underlying computational model. Sub-concepts are linked to one or more computational systems which are implemented on the basis of underlying computational technologies and techniques.

The following conceptual structures of selected key concepts are represented and illustrated below:

Free Form

The term, *free-form*, constituted what was in the early 1990's the new promise of architecture freed from the constraints of orthogonal geometry and rational standardized construction.

Inexact as it is from both a geometrical and descriptive point of view, the term symbolized the relationship between architectural theoretical positions regarding form and the formal potential of new productive possibilities in *non-standard architecture* and through *mass-customization* and *fabrication*. Free Form thus illustrates the complexity of constructing a coherent approach to conceptual structuring. On the one hand it relates both to its means of modeling (e.g. *MESH systems* or *NURBS systems*) and production methods as well as to its knowledge sources (e.g. *complex geometry*) (see Figure 2).

The term and the set of relationships have become an ideological position now, replaced by new and more exact terminology. The next related concept is deriving from conceptual associations with terms such as *Topology*.

Performance

Performance, or Performance – based Design is driven by simulations. Performance here is defined as the ability to directly act upon the physical properties of a specific design. In addition to quantitative properties, these classes of properties could eventually be broadened to include qualitative aspects such as spatial factors in addition to technical simulations such as structural and acoustical performance. (See Figure 3)

Today, there exist a wide range of digital tools for *simulation*, analysis and evaluation of performance aspects (Kolarevic and Malkaawi, 2005). Current theories and technologies of digital design suggest a shift from analytical simulation for evaluation to *simulation for synthesis and generation* (Oxman, 2008; 2009).

Figure 2. Free form: Semantic network and conceptual levels

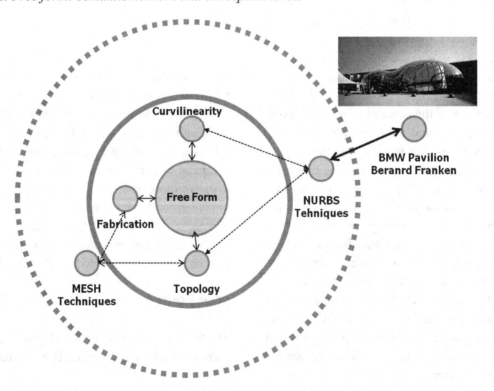

Figure 3. Performance: Semantic network and conceptual levels

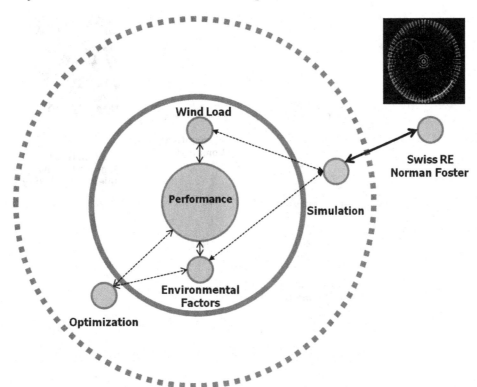

Parametricism

As an example of the dynamics of theoretical discourse, *Parametrics* and *Parametric Design* have now emerged as two key contemporary terms. Various designers and researchers (Burry and Murray, 1999) view parametrics and the related body of theoretical, modeling and methodological concepts as the seminal concept of current digital design and a distinguishing characteristic of digital architecture. Parametrics (Meredith, M., et alia, 2008) is essentially a design enabling technology. Coupled with other concepts such as *associative design*, it enables the exploitation of *topological diversity* and transformations. Furthermore, parametric design supports the existence of design models such as *generative components* that are among the foundation of important contemporary design technologies. (See Figure 4).

On the other hand, parametrics also underlies advanced engineering design practices and methods e.g. flux structures, (Sasaki, 2007). Thus the conceptual constellations of this term are both complex to represent and rich in interpretative potential. Figure 4 illustrates a well-know precedent, the Segrada Familia by Antonio Gaudi. The remodeling of the Segrada Familia is associated with parametric systems (Burry and Murray, 1997). The next related concept is deriving from conceptual associations with terms such as *Morphogenesis*.

Morphogenesis

We have seen that the terms *free form* and *parametrics* are characterized by diverse meanings and connotations that have developed and evolved historically. The presence of theoretical, design models and methodological/technical content

Figure 4. Parametricism: Semantic network and conceptual levels

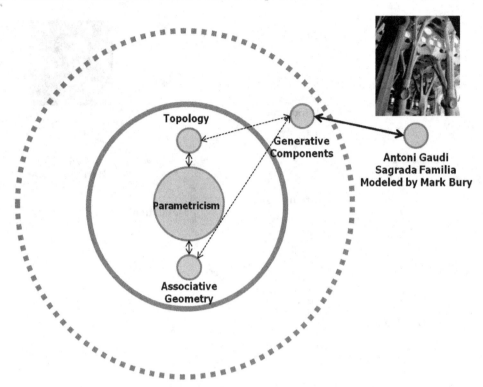

makes the visual characterization of conceptual relationships difficult. Certainly, in additional to scientific and computational content, these concepts also contain ideological content. The fourth term which we present is *morphogenesis*. This term further illustrates the rich body of discourse (or in other words, the complexity of the conceptual network) that canonic terms can generate. Morphogenesis essentially relates to processes of *form evolution* and particularly to modeling of *"natural"* processes of form generation (Hensel, Menges, and Weinstock, 2004). In design, the term is strongly related to the historical tradition of *form-finding* and *self organization* in the work of designers such as Frei Otto. Furthermore, it is associated with the terminology of *performance-based design*, the methods of *per-formative analysis* and the potential of *performance driven generation* (Oxman, 2008; 2009). The discourse of morphogenesis has become associated with studies of the principles of form generation in nature and

their exploitation in design (*biomimicry*) and with the associated contemporary discourse on material in design (Oxman N., 2008; 2010).

This term is proposed as a key term in an emerging body of key concepts that contribute to generative models, methods and techniques related to emergence in design (see Figure 5).

The term thus exemplifies a highly complex level of discourse in which multiple key terms are interrelated in new processes of conceptual development.

Material

The current shift in design and production technologies requires an integrated and seamless design approach that supports the interdependence of form, structure and material from design to fabrication. The *New Structuralism* is a first attempt to define this emerging paradigm (Oxman and Oxman, 2010). The following concepts and

Figure 5. Morphogenesis: Semantic network and conceptual levels

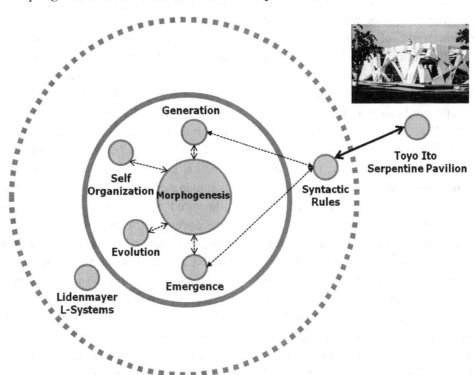

processes contribute to the theory of the *New Structuralism*: Digital Material and Fabrication concepts extend the scale of conventional construction methods and current craft-based methods, performing complex and large scale *customized* tasks. Digital fabrication and computational programming of production data integrates design with the materialization process. This process shapes both the design of structural and material elements in an encoded formal design process. In this case, the construction process is controlled. This defines fabrication as a generative process. Material conditions and assembly logic are now integrated and used as the basis for design generation (Gramazio and Kohler, 2008). *Fabrication of digital materials* with heterogeneous properties across a wide array of scales and applications has significant impact on the future of design. They promote the application of material subsequent to the generation of form. This principle calls for a

shift from a geometric-centric design to a *material-based design fabrication* (Oxman N., 2010).

EXPERIMENTAL PEDAGOGY

The prevailing model of modernist design is a formalist model in the profound sense of what we might term design ontology. Modernist design is formulated about the sequential development of symbolic representations of the design. It traditionally begins with considerations of space, with the major emphasis being upon the manipulation of visualizations of the design object - the design of form - through the stages of conceptual design, schematics, design development and materialization. The formal foundations of modern art and design have been theoretically defined and the evolutionary process of formal-graphical evolution in design representation has been well-formulated by various theoreticians.

We are now moving beyond this formal syndrome. The parametric, topological, geometric and generative characteristics of current digital design are in profound theoretical contradiction to shape production in the formalist models. Irrespective of how unique that shape may be, it is still the process of shape production as the production of a static form. Digital design characterized by generative processes related to movement and time is neither formalistic nor static. Form generation, beyond formalism, produces conditions of pliancy and continuity in both the conception and geometry of form.

Parametric formation, generation and performance are the motivating forces in the new design. They, as concepts and processes, begin to condition new design models that are uniquely conceptual. The characterization of the digital design model is completely contradictory to models of design such as *visual-based design* in which the visual representation of the design is manipulated by visual reasoning through a succession of stages generally in the medium of sketching. This interpretation of sketching as design thinking through iterative stages of visual discovery is the antithesis of the digital model. Digital design brings new design ontology such as generative and per-formative which control generative processes beyond the visual interpretation of form. The term digital design system, according to our definition implies the digital synthesis and integration of properties related to *form structure and material.*

The need for the integration of both the digital model and the physical model is still important. The physical models are still very useful for feel and touch in exploring principles of form, morphology and structure. Since current descriptive geometrical modeling lacks material and structural logic, the physical model provide a complementary medium. Physical studies can then be translated into digital *fabrication models* for transformation and versioning. Fabrication processes (*from file to production*) were found to be extremely meaningful.

Experimental Design

The objectives of our initial experimental research were to take first steps through a process rethinking many of the root assumptions of current computational conventions. We determine the relevance of these findings for conceptualizing new pedagogy in the design studio, and carried out and evaluated these approaches in a series of experimental studios. Our didactic approach in guiding the following paradigmatic project is presented and illustrated below. The project presented below was developed by exploiting digital key and sub concepts, models and techniques presented in the DDNET structures that suited the theoretical and conceptual content of the project. In this case key concepts provided a medium for the development of the formal, structural and material concept through its evolution. Our didactic process consists of the following four basic tasks. The first task is to select a key concept. The second task is to define a unique model and digital technique. The third task is to define a generic model. The fourth task is to select a context that can best demonstrate the behavior and adaptability of the generic model in relation to its contextual specifications.

In the following sections we demonstrate and illustrate these didactic steps.

Experimental Project: Digital Typology

The following project demonstrates a thinking process and didactic stages taken in our experimental design framework. The following DDNET network components were defined:

TITLE: Parametric Typology
KEY CONCEPTS: Parametricism; Performance
MODELS: Per-formative Model (Performance-
    based Generation) and Adaptive Model
MODELLING SYSTEM: Rhino and Grasshopper
    Modeling and Parametric Systems
PRECEDENT: Housing for the 21st Century -
    Evolo Housing Competition Fall 2009

The project termed "Parametric Typology" aims to demonstrate ways in which a generic typology can be developed and respond to various constraints projected by programmatic and environmental conditions.

Anthony Vidler, in his article "The third typology" (Vidler, 1977), presents a number of various typologies which nourished the process of architectural design since the middle of the 18th century. The first typology is based on the rational order of nature. The second typology identifies the emergence of ideal types at the end of an evolutionary process. The third typology points out the relationship between a building and its urban environment. The conceptualization of the project was based on key concepts represented by *parametricism and performance-based design that were based on* principles of material organization of organic organisms (see Figure 6). The project explored ways to apply principles of helical organization of organic material and apply them to typology of a Skyscraper. The idea behind these studies was to apply parametric performance-based transformations.

In order to study how these principles can be applied to building typology, natural growth systems were studied, formulated and implemented by algorithmic scripting and parametric modeling techniques (see Figure 7 and Figure 8). The success of this research is based on the existence of digital modeling technique that follows the behavior of natural systems to examine, analyze and finally design a novel architectural typology.

To conclude, we hope that in the near future the semantic knowledge of DDNET including key concepts, sub concepts, computational models and techniques and precedents; may become accessible by constructing a computational semantic network system that will be employed in any specific project.

Figure 6. Material: Semantic network and conceptual levels

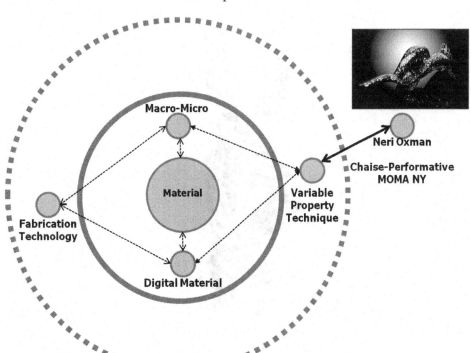

Figure 7. Organic Structures (©[photographed by Limor Goldhaber and Ron Alon] used with permission)

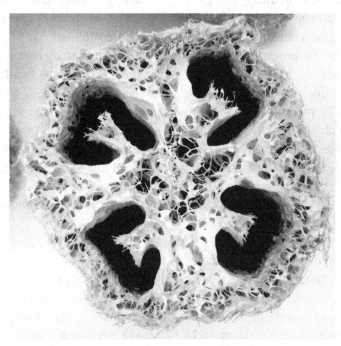

Figure 8. Study of Parametric Helical Typologies (©[Limor Goldhaber and Ron Alon] used with permission)

CONCLUSION

Our research has presented an attempt to construct conceptual structures for the field of digital design that may contradict the prevailingly accepted logic of image-based design. Rather than the employment of digital technologies, it is these emerging conceptual structures that strongly influence the logic of architecture and its design methods. These conceptual changes become the content of new pedagogical methods of design education. Our qualitative observations have demonstrated the following:

- Digital Design is not simply a discovery of new formal vocabularies. It has established new approaches to digital design which have made it a novel discipline.
- Among these, the ability to understand the knowledge of this discipline, to add, select, or use key concepts, sub concepts, computational techniques and models, and understanding leading precedents will constitute a new knowledge and recognized skill in the field of digital design.
- Design thinking precedes intuitive design learning. However, it can do so only by directly articulating and working with conceptual structures as pedagogical material. It is in this endeavor that we have established our studio for experimental didactics.
- The exploitation and experimentation with DDNET has proved to be an articulate environment for design learning in which learning by making is transfigured by its conceptual, rather than computational, content. A rigorous formulation of such emerging concepts does not yet fully exist, however this work is a first step – being yet unformulated body of concepts, it is in itself experimental research oriented.
- The most problematic concept in digital design is the term *Digital Architecture*.

Whether distinct architectural phenomena actually exist and justify such a term is a question of some import. Given that such phenomena do exist and that they are simply stylistic indicators, it seems doubtful that they justify the claim of a "new architecture". Certainly the meaning of the new digital presence in design is that we are able to at last, abandon the dinosaur sanctuary of the visual form.

To conclude – the DDNET formulation is still in progress. Future developments will complement the present formulation. However, the awareness of change and conflicts can stimulate the necessary theorization and conceptualization for better understanding of this field and to new approaches in digital design didactics.

ACKNOWLEDGMENT

The students Limor Goldhaber and Ron Alon participated in my Digital Studio 2009-2010, who contributed to this chapter are deeply acknowledged for their deep involvement and their creative work.

REFERENCES

Burry, M. (1999). Paramorph: Anti-accident methodologies. In Perella, S. (Ed.), *Architectural design: Hypersurface architecture II* (pp. 78–83). Chichester, UK: Wiley.

Frazer, J. H. (1995). *An evolutionary architecture*. London, UK: The Architectural Association Publications.

Gramazio, F., & Kohler, M. (2008). *Digital materiality in architecture*. Lars Müller Publishers.

Hensel, M., Menges, A., & Weinstock, M. (Eds.). (2004). *Architectural design, emergence: Morphogenic design strategies*. London, UK: Wiley.

Knight, T., & Stiny, G. (2001). Classical and non-classical computation. *Architectural Research Quarterly, 5*(4), 355–372.

Kolarevic, B. (Ed.). (2003). *Architecture in the digital age*. New York, NY: Spon Press.

Kolarevic, B., & Malkaawi, A. (Eds.). (2005). *Performative architecture: Beyond instrumentality* (pp. 85–96). New York, NY: Spon Press.

Lindsey, B. (2002). *Digital Gehry*. Bern, Switzerland: Birkhäuser.

Liu, Y. T. (2005). *5th FEIDAD Award: Demonstrating digital architecture*. Bern, Switzerland: Birkhäuser.

Lynn, G. (1993). Architectural curvilinearity: The folded, the pliant and the supple. In Lynn, G. (Ed.), *AD architectural design: Folding in architecture* (pp. 8–15). London, UK: Wiley.

Lynn, G. (1999). *Animate form*. New York, NY: Princeton Architectural Press.

Meredith, M. (2008). *From control to design: Parametric/algorithmic architecture*. Barcelona, Spain: Actar.

Oosterhuis, K. (2002). *Architecture goes wild*. Rotterdam, The Netherlands: 010 Publishers.

Oxman, N. (2007). Get real towards performance-driven computational geometry. *IJAC: International Journal of Architectural Computing, 4*, 663–684. doi:10.1260/147807707783600771

Oxman, N. (2010). *Material-based computation*. PhD Thesis Dissertation, Dept. of Architecture, MIT, Cambridge, 2010

Oxman, R. (1994). Precedents in design: a computational model for the organization of precedent knowledge. *Design Studies, 15*(2), 141–157. doi:10.1016/0142-694X(94)90021-3

Oxman, R. (2003). Think-maps: Teaching design thinking in design education. *Design Studies, 25*(1), 63–91. doi:10.1016/S0142-694X(03)00033-4

Oxman, R. (2006). Theory and design in the first digital age. *Design Studies, 27*(3), 229–265. doi:10.1016/j.destud.2005.11.002

Oxman, R. (2008). Performance based design: Current practices and research issue. *IJAC International Journal of Architectural Computing, 6*(1), 1–17. doi:10.1260/147807708784640090

Oxman, R. (2009). Performative design - A performance-model of digital architectural design. *Environment and Planning B, 36*, 1026–1037. doi:10.1068/b34149

Oxman, R., & Oxman, R. (2010). The new structuralism - Design engineering and architectural technologies. In *Architectural design: New structuralism* (pp. 79–85). London, UK: Wiley. doi:10.1002/ad.1101

Picon, A. (2010). *Digital culture in architecture: An introduction for the design profession*. Bern, Switzerland: Birkhäuser.

Pottmann, H. (2010). Architectural geometry as design knowledge. In Oxman, R., & Oxman, R. (Eds.), *Architectural design: New structuralism: Design engineering and architectural technologies* (pp. 72–76). London, UK: Wiley.

Rashid, H., & Couture, L. A. (2002). *Asymptote: Flux*. New York, NY: Phaidon.

Reiser, J., & Umemoto, N. (2006). *Atlas of novel tectonics*. New York, NY: Princeton Architectural Press.

Sasaki, M. (2007). *Morphogenesis of flux structures*. London, UK: AA Publications.

Sass, L., & Oxman, R. (2006). Materializing design. *International Journal of Design Studies*, *27*(3), 325–355. doi:10.1016/j.destud.2005.11.009

Schodek, D., Bechthold, M., Griggs, K., Kao, K. M., & Steinberg, M. (2005). *Digital design and manufacturing, CAD/CAM applications in architecture and design*. New York, NY: Wiley Academy Press.

Schön, D. A. (1983). *Educating the reflective practitioner*. New York, NY: Basic Books.

Sowa, J. (1991). *Principles of semantic networks*. San Francisco, CA: Morgan Kaufman.

Spuybroek, L. (2004). *NOX: Machining architecture*. New York, NY: Thames and Hudson.

Van Berkel, B., & Bos, C. (1999). *UN Studio: Move*. Amsterdam, The Netherlands: Architectura & Natura.

Vidler, A. (1977). The third typology. In Cuthbert, A. (Ed.), *Designing cities* (pp. 317–339). UK: Blackwell Publishing.

Zaero-Polo, A., & Moussavi, F. (2003). *Morphogenesis: FOA's ark*. Barcelona, Spain: Actar.

KEY TERMS AND DEFINITIONS

Digital Design: A term that reflects how new media and methodologies are changing our conceptual understanding of design and designing.

Digital Material: A computational model that represents a shift from geometric centric design to material-based design.

Free Form: Complex geometrical shapes modeled by novel software tools and modeling techniques such as Rhino; CATIA; NURBS-based modelers, etc.

Morphogenesis: Relates to 'natural' processes of form generation particularly in evolution, self organization and form finding models.

New Structuralism: Seamless design that supports the interdependence of form, structure and material from design to fabrication.

Performance-based Design: A computational model which is driven by performance.

Parametric Design: A seminal concept of current digital design, related to theoretical, concepts such as associative geometry and topology and modeling techniques such as generative components.

Chapter 3
Slow Computing:
Teaching Generative Design with Shape Grammars

Terry Knight
Massachusetts Institute of Technology, USA

ABSTRACT

This chapter describes the teaching of shape grammars within an architectural design program. Developed over thirty years ago, shape grammars remain today a distinctive computational paradigm – a slow paradigm – for generative design. Shape grammars are visual and perceptual and, at root, non-digital. They are expressive and interpretive, as well as creative and generative. They foster unhurried, reflective design computing. To promote these unique computational features, shape grammars are taught using a manual approach in a collaborative, learning-by-making environment. An overview of the teaching of shape grammars at the Massachusetts Institute of Technology is given here. The potentials and challenges for slow computing versus fast computing by machine, in teaching and in design practice, are considered.

INTRODUCTION

This chapter describes the teaching of shape grammars within an architectural design program. Developed over thirty years ago, shape grammars remain today a distinctive computational paradigm – a *slow* paradigm – for generative design.

DOI: 10.4018/978-1-61350-180-1.ch003

Shape grammars are visual and perceptual and, at root, non-digital. They foster unhurried and reflective computation through shape ambiguity and emergence. They foster explanation and understanding of design computations in addition to the generation of designs. Shape grammars are not solely a means to an end (the production of designs) but an end in themselves. To promote these unique computational features, shape grammars are taught using a manual approach in a collaborative, learning-by-making environment. Deliberative, by-hand shape calculations allow students to develop a rich understanding of shape grammars, and computation in general. They build a command over the development and consequences of computations and are better able to generate successful results. Computers do not have a central role in this learning environment. Students are the computers – slow computers.

The teaching approach described here has some parallels with ideas from theories of education and learning, in particular, situated learning (Lave and Wenger, 1991) and constructionism (Harel & Papert, 1991). It shares with situated learning the idea that social interaction and collaboration among learners in an activity-based environment is key to learning. It shares with constructivism that idea that learning is most successful when learners make tangible, public artifacts for reflection and for conversation with others. In general, the pedagogy for teaching shape grammars described here assumes that a good appreciation and understanding of shape grammars cannot be transmitted abstractly from teacher to student, rather it must be created through active doing and making.

The teaching approach described here also has some very loose affinities with ideas from "slow" movements (Honoré, 2004) – for example, slow design (Strauss & Faud-Luke, 2008), slow technology (Hallnäs & Redström, 2001) and slow education such as slow reading and writing (Bauerlein, 2008). The agendas of these various movements range from the personal to the political, and are difficult to encapsulate. However, the approach here shares with slow theories their general advocacy for the benefits of slow, reflective, physical or sensory engagement in activities. While slow theories usually do not argue for or against digital technology or computers, the idea is that when technology is used it must be put to the service of reflection and awareness. Where digital technology is seen to impede understanding, as some argue is the case for reading and writing,

then it should be avoided or supplemented with other media. A premise of the approach here is that computers do not help initial learning about shape grammars, and therefore are not part of introductory teaching.

The remainder of this chapter is organized in three sections. Shape grammars and their distinctive characteristics and mechanics are introduced in the *Background* section. They are discussed relative to other generative design approaches and situated in the early history of computation. A brief review of shape grammar research and teaching over the years is also given.

The next section, *Teaching Slow Computing*, describes a two-semester sequence of shape grammar courses in the Department of Architecture at the Massachusetts Institute of Technology (MIT). The objectives, structure, teaching approach, and outcomes of the courses are discussed. The foremost objective of these courses, especially the first semester course, is for students to begin to see the design potentials of shape grammars and to begin applying shape grammars in their own work with just a minimal introduction to the mechanics of shape grammars. Slow, in-class exercises with pencil and paper and with physical 3D shapes are central to this goal. Teaching follows a spiral approach giving students multiple opportunities to absorb and practice shape grammar fundamentals at varying levels of complexity, and in the context of different design activities and problems – from analysis to synthesis, in 2D and in 3D, and in team and individual work. Student projects are an important aspect of learning, and importantly, they often inspire new avenues of research in the field. In this regard, recent student work combining forms with material properties and physical behaviors in grammars is highlighted.

Challenges for advancing slow computing within and beyond introductory shape grammar courses are discussed in the last section, *Conclusion and Future Directions*. Roles of fast computing using computers and digital technologies in academic and professional settings are discussed.

BACKGROUND

The formative ideas for shape grammars were conceived in the late 1960s by two MIT undergraduates, Jim Gips and George Stiny. The two went on to develop and formalize shape grammars in their doctoral dissertations at Stanford and the University of California, Los Angeles (UCLA), respectively. Gips (1975) focused on applications of shape grammars; Stiny (1975) on their mathematical foundations. Soon after, Stiny (1977) generalized the idea of shape grammars to parametric shape grammars, merging the powerful notion of parametric design with generative, rule-based design. Minor details of shape grammars (both standard and parametric) have changed over the years, but the basics have remained the same.

Shape grammars have foundational features that distinguish them radically from other generative design systems. First, shape grammars are visual systems. Shape grammars compute directly with shapes, rather than with numbers, symbols, words, or other abstract structures that represent visual shapes indirectly – as, for example, in graph grammars, L-systems, scripts or computer programs. The shapes in a shape grammar can be defined in almost any conceivable way. They can be made up of points, lines, planes, or volumes, and can be defined in spaces of any dimension – OD, 1D, 2D, 3D, or more. Shapes can be rectilinear or curved. Importantly, shapes in shape grammars are treated as nonatomic and ambiguous. They do not have definite parts and can be freely decomposed and recomposed by the user of a grammar, as a design is being generated. Shape ambiguity in shape grammars goes hand in hand with another singular property of shape grammars – shape emergence. An emergent shape is a shape that is not predefined in a grammar, but one that arises through rule applications. Further, emergent shapes can not only be generated by rule applications, they can also be recognized and used in subsequent rule applications.

The visual and perceptual properties of shape grammars are tied to a second foundational feature of shape grammars. Shape grammars are, at root, nondigital. They are based on work in the field of formal languages and automata, and were envisioned as an algorithmic approach to design as technically rigorous as computer programs or other formal algorithms. However, they need not be implemented on a computer. As Gips wrote in 1975: "The formalism for shape grammars is designed to be easily usable and understandable by people and at the same time to be adaptable for use in computer programs." (Gips, 1975, p.1). As it turned out, it is not straightforward to adapt shape grammars, particularly their visual, perceptual features, to computer programs. Research on a general computer implementation for shape grammars has been ongoing for thirty years but has had limited success. (However, programs for particular shape grammars are more feasible and many have been developed.) Ambiguity and emergence are very natural for people, but not at all for computers.

A third foundational feature of shape grammars has to do with their purpose. Shape grammars were developed in the tradition of earlier generative grammars to be explanatory or expressive – to give insights into the objects they generate. They are not solely a means to an end (the production of designs) but an end in themselves. What rules say about the designs they generate is often as important as what they do. Thus, shape grammars serve an analytic and interpretive function as well as a creative and generative one.

Although shape grammars have unique features that set them apart from other generative design systems, they are embedded in a rich history of work on computational systems in general. Figure 1 shows a very abbreviated history of the first fifty years of computation. This history begins with the work of various mathematicians and philosophers in the 1930s who formalized the notion of computation: what it means to compute something, and what the limits of computation

Figure 1. The first fifty years of computation

Early History of Computation

	logical	biological
1930s	formal theories of computation (Turing, Gödel, Church, ...)	
	logical	**biological**
1940s	production systems (Post)	neural nets (McCulloch & Pitts)
1950s	generative grammars (Chomsky)	cellular automata, parallel computation (von Neumann)
1960s	pattern grammars (Fu)	evolutionary computation
1970s	shape grammars (Gips & Stiny)	
1980s		artificial life (Langton), self-organizing systems
	.	.
	.	.
	.	.

are. The first theoretical models of computers (automata) and grammars were developed at this time. Computational work then developed more or less along two strands: logical and biological. Work in the logical strand was based on abstract ideas from logic and mathematics. Work in the biological strand was based on ideas from biology and the natural world. Today there is considerable overlap between work in these two strands, and distinctions between biological and logical are difficult to make.

The logical strand begins with the work of the logician Emil Post and others on production systems for characterizing and understanding abstract logical languages. Chomsky then took this work into a new domain with his work on generative grammars for natural languages. A decade later, K. S. Fu, a computer scientist, initiated work on pattern grammars, the first grammars for modeling and generating 2D visual patterns, albeit indirectly with symbols representing 2D patterns. Shape grammars were invented a decade later in the 1970s. Today, there are many descendants and variations of shape grammars.

The biological strand begins with work of McCulloch and Pitts on artificial neural networks, in particular, with their idea to use the human nervous system (neurons) as a model for computation.

Around a decade later, the mathematician von Neumann developed cellular automata, along with the novel concept of parallel processing, as a computational model for artificial self-reproduction. Evolutionary computation, using principles from natural evolution such as mutation, crossover, fitness, and selection, was developed in the following decade. Christopher Langton drew on these and earlier ideas to found the field of artificial life in which computation is used to model artificial life-like systems. Around the same time, interest in computational systems that mimic the natural phenomena of self-organization and emergence began to grow.

These two strands of computation have had somewhat different perspectives or goals. The biological kind of computation tends to emphasize results or output – what you get at the end of a computation, as opposed to how the computation works or what it explains about the output. The speed and power of computers are often indispensable in carrying out this goal. The logical kind of computation, on the other hand, began historically with an emphasis on explanation. The right results are necessary, but the more important emphasis is on understanding. Shape grammars were developed within this tradition.

A shape grammar looks much like other formal grammars in the logical line of computation, at least in terms of its components. A shape grammar consists of a set of shape rules and a starting shape, called the *initial shape*. A shape rule has the form A → B. The rule says that a shape A can be replaced by, or changed into, a shape B. A rule A → B applies to a shape C if the shape A, or any shape geometrically similar to it, can be found in the shape C. In other words, the shape A must match a shape in C. More formally, the rule applies to the shape C if there is a similarity transformation *t* that makes the shape A a part of the shape C. If there is a transformation *t* that does this, then the rule can be applied to the shape C to generate a new shape C'. The rule applies by subtracting the transformation of A from C, and then adding the same transformation of B. Thus, the new shape C' is equal to [C - *t*(A)] + *t*(B).

In a parametric shape grammar (Stiny (1977), one or both of the shapes A and B in a rule are parametric, that is, the shapes have variable geometric or other properties. These variable geometric properties are specified by associating variables – or parameters – with the shapes. In order to apply a parametric shape rule, an assignment of values must first be made to the variables in the shapes. The rule then applies in the way described above. A parametric shape grammar embeds the concept and the affordances of parametric modeling within generative rules. However, in contrast to most current parametric softwares which focus on output (the production of design alternatives) and can involve unwieldy and impenetrable symbolic models to generate that output, parametric shape grammars emphasize understanding the output through clear visual rules and generation processes.

The rules of a standard or parametric shape grammar apply recursively to the initial shape to generate designs. The step-by-step application of rules to generate a design is called a computation. Different sequences of rule applications can gener-ate different designs. The set of designs generated by all possible computations is called a *language*.

Figure 2, shows a simple shape grammar. The one rule of the grammar shifts a square along a diagonal axis of the square. The dotted X in the rule acts as a registration mark, showing the positions of the squares on the left and right sides of the rule relative to each other – in other words, the "before" and "after" locations of the square. The rule applies under different similarity transformations to move the square along a diagonal up or down to the right or the left. The initial shape of the grammar consists of two squares. A computation of a design is shown to the right. Note how emergent squares are generated and used in the computation. The rule can be applied in many other ways to generate different designs. A parametric shape grammar based on this grammar is shown below. The shapes in the rules are now parametric. They can be rectangles of any size or proportion depending on the numerical values assigned to the parameters *w* and *l*. The initial shape consists of two rectangles. A computation of a design is shown to the right. Many other designs can be generated by the rule.

Shape grammar research, applications, and teaching have been ongoing for the last thirty-five years. Theoretical research has focused on understanding and expanding the underlying capacities of shape grammars; for example, through the development of parametric shape grammars, parallel shape grammars, and shape grammars made up of shapes of multiple dimensions. Another line of research has focused on programming and automating shape grammars. Other work has centered on applications of shape grammars. Applications have cut across all areas of design from architecture to landscape design to furniture design to painting to product design to mechanical and engineering design. They have addressed two complementary and overlapping design activities: analysis and creative design (or synthesis). In analysis applications, shape grammars are developed for existing design languages, styles, or

Figure 2. A shape grammar and a parametric shape grammar

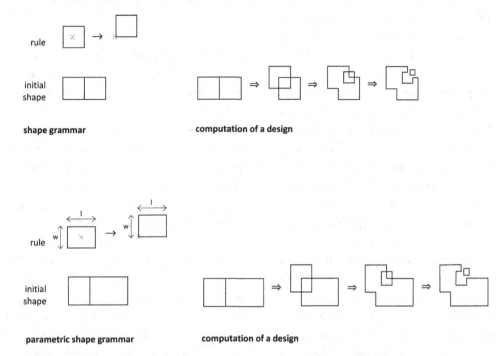

brands, as a way of capturing and representing design knowledge and understanding about these languages. In creative design applications, shape grammars are developed from scratch or from precedents to generate new and original designs. Done mostly in academic settings, these applications have provided important proofs of the validity and varied uses of shape grammars.

The teaching of shape grammars has developed in parallel with research. The first courses dedicated exclusively to shape grammars were taught by Stiny and his colleague William Mitchell at UCLA in the early 1980s. These early classes were structured much differently than the classes described here, but like them, were taught mostly without the involvement of computers. Shape grammar teaching began independently some time later at Carnegie Mellon by Ulrich Flemming (Flemming, 1990) and others. Successive generations of students have taken shape grammar teaching to academic institutions worldwide from the UK to Portugal to Brazil to Turkey to Hong Kong to Australia and numerous other countries.

Courses have ranged from seminars to design studios, and have focused on different aspects of shape grammars from theory to computer applications to design projects.

TEACHING SLOW COMPUTING

Objectives

A two-semester course sequence on shape grammars, taught by the author, is described in this section. The courses build on teaching begun at UCLA in the late 1980s and continued at MIT. Each course is 12 to 13 weeks long, and classes are held once a week for a 3-hour period.

The first semester course is presented to students as an introduction to a rule-based, generative approach to design using shape grammars. More specifically, the aim of the course is to give students the broadest possible understanding of the nature and capacities of shapes grammars with the least amount of formal lecturing and the most hands-on practice. With this aim in mind, the 3-hour time block for each class is organized to allow for some lecture time as well as ample time for students to practice new concepts. There are no prerequisites for the course, and no background in computing or computer programming is assumed. The course is an elective, and students from any degree program and from any department are welcome. Teaching is therefore geared for a mix of students from undergraduate to PhD, mostly from the Department of Architecture, but also from other MIT departments and from Harvard's Graduate School of Design. The course attracts students interested in the idea of design and computation in general, or shape grammars in particular, but not necessarily in programming or the more technical aspects of computation.

The second semester course is also an elective. A formal prerequisite is the first semester course. However, motivated students without this prerequisite are welcomed into the course with the understanding that they will need to do some catch-up work. In the first part of this course, advanced shape grammar topics such as color grammars (Knight, 1989) and parallel grammars (Stiny, 1981) are introduced, and a quick review of fundamentals is given for newcomers. However, the real objective is to give students an extended opportunity to deploy and test their learning from the first semester course and this one, in the development of a research or design project of their own choosing. The second half of the course thus concentrates on the development of student initiated projects. Classes revolve around student presentations and group discussions of work-in-progress in a workshop/studio type of setting.

The following discussion focuses primarily on the first, introductory course. However, student projects from the second course are included in the discussion as this work is an outcome of student learning from the first semester, as well as the second.

Structure and Approach

The introductory course is structured in five parts: (1) overview, (2) shape grammar fundamentals, (3) analysis applications, (4) creative design (or synthesis) applications, and (5) projects. The *visual*, *nondigital*, and *expressive* aspects of shape grammars are woven throughout. Shape grammars are an unfamiliar concept and approach for students. Thus, students are told to "suspend their disbelief" in the early parts of the course, and reminded that the potentials of shape grammars may not be apparent to them until the end of the course or even much later. As the course progresses, lecture time in general becomes shorter and more class-time is devoted to slow, hands-on work with practice problems. Students share and assess their solutions with one another in class. This collaborative work also allows students to pool and benefit from their different ways of understanding grammars. As the course progresses, students gradually assume more responsibility in their practice with grammars: first by applying or *following rules* that are given to them, next by inferring or *finding rules* that will generate designs that are given to them, and last by *making up rules* according to their own design intentions or criteria. (This sequential approach is similar to one used in collaborative design workshop with Duarte (Duarte, 2004, p. 94) and in Duarte's subsequent teaching.)

Beginning assignments follow a conventional MIT problem set format. Later assignments and the final project are more open-ended and are viewed as experiments in which the students' settings of problems and goals, and their processes for reaching them, are as important, if not more so, than the final results. Readings of shape grammar papers supplement some assignments.

Overview

In the first class, shape grammars are introduced in the broader context of computational or generative design. The idea of formal algorithms or rules in design is discussed, and important distinctions made between rules that are prescriptive and imposed from without (such as rules in architectural treatises like those of Alberti or Palladio) and rules that are made up and individualized. The unique foundational features and history of shape grammars are then reviewed. A quick preview of the shape grammar formalism is given. The generality of shape grammars and their applicability to any kind of design produced at any phase of a design process is stressed. The relationship of shape grammars to traditional design is discussed. The process of developing a shape grammar is explained as a conventional design process that involves the same competencies associated with good design: trial-and-error, artistry, intuition, discipline, experience, knowledge, and so on. Instead of designing a single design, however, an algorithm for a set of designs is designed. The initial time and effort in designing rules may be considerable, but the returns in terms of the range and quality of potential solutions to a design problem are usually worth the initial investment. To illustrate all these points, example applications of shape grammars in analysis and synthesis are shown.

In their first assignment, students are asked to read introductory papers on shape grammars (Knight, 1999; Knight 2003), and to formulate questions about what they have read. This exercise allows students to articulate their uncertainties about shape grammars and computational design, in general, and makes for a lively discussion in the following class.

Fundamentals

The mechanics of shape grammars – the meta-rules for defining and using shape grammars – are introduced in two class sessions. Because of their technical and abstract content, these classes are challenging to teach to a range of students often with very different backgrounds, interests, and abilities. Some students find the material intuitive and straightforward; others find it remote, even vexing. A mix of conceptual, perceptual, and physical work is essential to motivate students and to bring them all to roughly the same level of technical competence. Formal definitions are minimized as much as possible. Definitions are conveyed mainly through examples drawn by hand – slowly – at the blackboard, rather than with pre-prepared slides.

All work is based on simple 2D linear shapes in order to clarify mechanics. Students are told that definitions and examples can be extended to more complex shapes in 2D or 3D, and the generality of definitions is demonstrated, wherever possible, by showing how they are instantiated in more detailed analysis or synthesis applications in architecture or other areas of design. Nonetheless, it is a challenge at this point for students to extrapolate beyond what they see and work on in examples to more complex design situations. Students are also reminded that the ability to grasp the intent of shape grammars is more important in the end than quick, technical aptitude. Indeed, by the end of the semester, all students have a good enough understanding of the mechanics of shape grammars to be able to use grammars independently.

The fundamentals classes begin with a discussion of *shapes*, the components of rules. Next, an *arithmetic of shapes* is introduced. The arithmetic consists of formal relations and operations for comparing, combining, and manipulating shapes. All of these relations and operations come into play in the application of shape rules. Analogies with number arithmetic are made to give students familiar grounding for these unfamiliar concepts. At the same time, contrasts are made with number arithmetic to underscore fundamental differences between shapes or visual material and numeric or symbolic material. Students are given shape arithmetic problems to solve in class. These are students' first encounter with slow, by-hand computing.

Shape rules are introduced next. Recursion and recursive systems are discussed as background for

Figure 3. A shape rule and its application to generate designs

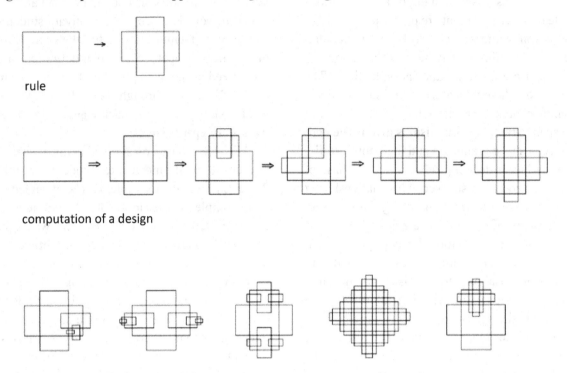

rule

computation of a design

some of the many other designs that can be generated by the rule

understanding the power and appeal of rules in general. The basic format of a shape rule is then shown, and described informally as an *If-Then* statement. The *If* part specifies the condition for doing something to a design, the *Then* part is what happens if the condition is satisfied. A simple example is used to illustrate a shape rule and how it applies in a step-by-step computation to generate a design (Figure 3). The rule is based on a familiar Greek cross pattern. Students' attention is directed to the visual, nondigital, and expressive aspects of the rule and the computation. The shapes in each step of the computation can be read in multiple ways, the rule can apply to new rectangles that emerge from parts of previous ones, the rule is easy to understand and encapsulates clearly the basis for all the designs it generates. Students are then asked to *follow* this rule by applying it to generate new designs beyond the ones shown to them. After students have an informal feel for

rules, they are given formal definitions like those given in the Background section above. However, students rarely appeal to formal definitions to clarify their understanding.

The generality of shape rules is demonstrated to students by showing a range of rules that correspond to familiar design moves – such as rules for adding shapes, subdividing shapes, subtracting shapes, moving shapes, and replacing shapes – and by showing rules that correspond to familiar design processes – such as top-down and bottom-up processes. To develop their understanding further, students are asked to solve simple problems that involve *finding* rules. They are given abstract designs and must infer rules that generate those designs. In order to prove to themselves and to the rest of the class that they have found correct rules, they must *follow* their rules, that is, they must draw step-by-step computations that lead to the given designs. This exercise is often not straightforward as students make incorrect assumptions about how rules work and do not realize that rules must contain all the information necessary for anyone or anything to carry them out correctly. They are encouraged to work and draw slowly, individually and in groups, to understand and debug their rules.

The fundamentals part of the course concludes with a discussion and practice with two mechanisms that allow for finer control over rules and the designs generated by them: *labels* which restrict or *specialize* the ways rules apply, and *parameters* which *generalize* the ways rules apply.

Assignments consist of short problems finding and following rules. There may be multiple correct answers to a problem, and care is taken to try to understand how students arrive at their answers regardless of whether their answers are correct. Emphasis here and throughout the course is on the process through which students arrive at solutions and how they understand and use grammars.

Analysis

Following the introduction to fundamentals, students are engaged rapidly in more complex applications of shape grammars. Analysis applications are introduced first. The central task in analysis applications is inferring or finding rules given a starting point, or corpus of existing or historic designs. The objective of analysis applications is classification and explanation of the given designs and others like them.

The analysis section takes place over two class sessions. It begins with a brief introduction to the concept of *style*. Style is described as an ordering principle for grouping or distinguishing things according to shared characteristics. In architecture and design, style could refer, for example, to the style of an individual, culture, geographic region, or time period. A style classification is often just a first step toward examining the relationship of a style to larger cultural, social, political issues. Shape grammars are presented as an algorithmic,

computational way of representing and understanding style. They offer an approach to style that is often deeper, more rigorous and explicit than traditional art historical approaches. A shape grammar can be defined to generate a language of designs that is the formal equivalent of a style. The aim of an analysis grammar is to generate a language that contains all and only designs in a given style. The language may contain not only extant designs but also new, hypothetical designs like the existing ones. These new designs provide more evidence by which to judge the value of a grammar as a particular theory of a style.

The task of writing an analysis grammar is explained to students as a subjective and often laborious one. Extracting or inferring rules from a corpus of designs requires a slow and careful visual examination of the designs. In general, there can be alternative, competing grammars for any given style depending on what aspects of the designs are considered to be significant or meaningful – that is, on what aspects of designs one chooses to see. External documentation about the designs may or may not be helpful in this regard, and can easily bias how designs are seen. Because the rules that are inferred from designs are visual, they are able to express the salient features of designs more directly and succinctly than other, symbol or text based generative design systems (for example, with computer programs or scripts). All in all, the *visual, nondigital,* and *expressive* aspects of shape grammars are central to analysis applications.

Students are shown two contrasting examples of analysis grammars – a short, 4-rule grammar for Chinese ice-ray lattice designs (Stiny, 1977) and a longer grammar for Palladian villa plans (Stiny and Mitchell, 1987). The ice-ray grammar describes a vernacular style practiced by many people over a long period of time and with many design examples. The Palladian grammar, on the other hand, generates the "high-style" of a single architect practiced over a relatively short period of time and with a limited set of examples. The

Figure 4. Two excerpts from "sketches" for a shape grammar for some of the work of the architecture firm Coop Himmelb(l)au. (a) Rules in section (Murat Mutlu and Steffen Reichert, 2008). (b) Rules in plan (Rizal Muslimin and Sung-O Park, 2008).

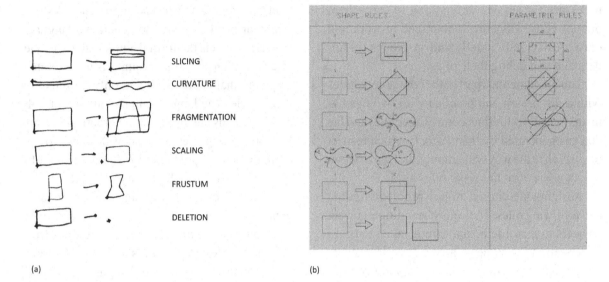

(a)   (b)

rules of both grammars are more complex and detailed than the rules students have seen previously. As each grammar is shown and explained in class, students practice and extend their technical understanding of shape rules by following the rules to generate extent and new designs. Students share their results and this gives them a chance to debate the value of shape grammars as an analytic, interpretative, and pedagogical tool.

Students are then immersed in a one-week, out-of-class, analytic exercise, called "Authoring a Grammar". They are given a contemporary style of architecture – a style with well-documented designs and/or built work – and asked to sketch a shape grammar that generates existing designs in the style, as well as new designs in the same style. The term "sketch" is used in figurative and literal senses. Students need only develop an informal outline for a grammar (they do not have sufficient technical skills or time to write a full-fledged, technically correct shape grammar), and they are asked to draw or sketch as much as possible what they consider to be the important features of designs and then translate these sketches into shape rules. They are required to work in teams of two or three students so that they must confront and negotiate alternative points of views about possible grammars. They quickly come to understand the subjective and personalized nature of defining rules, the hard work and effort involved in formulating rules to express their intuitions and understandings, and the major insights gained from slow, visual thinking. The second class of this section is devoted entirely to presentations and reviews of this assignment. Most students agree that they learn more in one week about an architect's work from this exercise than from any other type of analysis they have undertaken. Figure 4 shows excerpts from two "sketches" for grammars for the work of Coop Himmelb(l)au, reflecting different interpretations of the firm's work. One grammar is comprised of general, loosely defined rules in section, the other of more precise parametric rules in plan. This analytic exercise is a potential first step towards a more formal shape grammar that could be developed in a final project for the course.

Creative Design

The creative design part of the course is the longest. Students learn new material in this section and at the same time they revisit and practice fundamentals in a new context. They are introduced to computing with 3D shapes, and are given sets of small, rectilinear blocks to use for the remainder of the semester.

The focus in this part of the course is on using shape grammars as a creative design tool or medium in the design process. In contrast to analysis applications, which involve inferring or finding rules from a given starting point, creative design applications involve making up rules, often without a clear starting point. However, these two kinds of applications are not always distinct. For example, creative design can begin with the analysis of precedent designs, and then continue with the adaptation or transformation of the inferred rules to create new rules for new designs.

Students are introduced to a hierarchy of types of shape grammars – beginning with very simple grammars and building to more complex ones. The premise of this hierarchy is that very simple grammars are easy to develop, understand, and control and thus are most useful in the initial stages of designing, in exploring and forming design concepts, intentions, and goals. Then, design ideas are developed by detailing and fine-tuning rules to build more complex grammars.

The first grammars that students work with are called *basic grammars*. These are just one or two rule grammars but they can generate a multitude of surprising, interesting, and productive design possibilities. The foundation for these grammars were developed very early by Stiny (1980) and then expanded by the author in teaching (Knight (1994). Students are given an approach for defining basic grammars that requires the introduction of just a few new, technical concepts – the last such concepts to be introduced in the course. The approach begins with the selection of one or two shapes and an arrangement between the shapes

called a *spatial relation*. Depending on whether the shapes in the spatial relation are the same or different, a rule or pair of rules is defined from the spatial relation. Each rule adds a shape in accordance with the spatial relation. Next, the rule (or pair of rules) is labeled in different ways, using a specific labeling scheme, to define a series of *basic rules*. Last, these rules are combined with an initial shape to define a series of basic grammars. Each basic grammar utilizes the same beginning spatial relation in a different, repetitive way to create a different *basic design*. Basic grammars thus identify all of the simplest, most basic design consequences of one, simple spatial relation or compositional idea. The number of basic grammars that can be defined from any spatial relation is easily calculated, giving students a good sense of the range of design alternatives possible with their starting idea. Figure 5 shows the steps in developing basic grammars beginning with a spatial relation.

The fundamentals of basic grammars are illustrated with 2D and 3D examples drawn at the blackboard or on pre-prepared slides. However, students come to understand 3D basic grammars almost entirely through hands-on work with their blocks. For virtually all students, grasping the technical, conceptual, and perceptual underpinnings of computing with 3D shapes is impossible with slides or paper-and-pencil alone. They learn by using their blocks to follow sample rules given to them in class. The construction of physical forms with blocks not only externalizes learning, it also enables productive conversations among students about using shape grammars in design. Students are surprised by how quickly they learn to apply rules and how easy it is to generate complex and attractive designs. However, work at this point is abstract, and it is challenging for students to imagine using shape grammars for real-world design problems.

The first opportunity students have to design with grammars on their own is in a two-week abstract exercise. This exercise involves a major

Figure 5. The steps in developing basic grammars beginning with a spatial relation. In this example, the spatial relation is between two oblongs. One of the many basic grammars that can be defined from the spatial relation is shown.

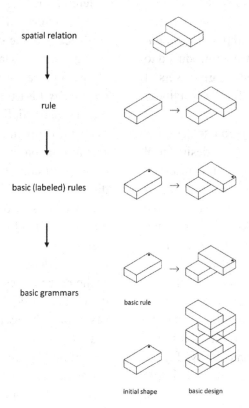

shift in responsibility for students, from following rules that are given to them to making up their own rules. The exercise is straightforward. Students are asked to define their own spatial relation between any 3D shapes of their choosing, and then to develop basic grammars and designs from the spatial relation. Although students are allowed to represent their grammars in 2D if the underlying shapes or spatial relations are too complex to model physically, they are required to make 3D physical models of the designs they generate. Students can choose their starting points randomly, but more often they think carefully about the shapes and spatial relations they begin with in order to generate designs of interest (aesthetic or otherwise) to them. Working through this assignment introduces students in a small but telling way to the problem of how to define

a shape grammar (or other generative system) that generates designs to match design intentions or goals. Slow work with rules enables students to direct their explorations in a disciplined and informed way towards particular goals. A class session is devoted to review of this assignment. In their presentations, students are required to show how their rules communicate and express their design intentions and their results. Figure 6 shows one student's response to this assignment.

Following this assignment, students are shown some computer programs that automate basic grammars in 2D and in 3D. They are able to understand these programs only after their practice with basic grammars by hand. Next, students are introduced to more complex grammars that include different and more complex kinds of rules than basic rules. As before, students do practice work

Figure 6. A student project for basic grammars (Miho Chu, 2009). The starting spatial relation is between two tetrahedra. One of the many sets of basic rules defined from this spatial relation, and some of the many basic designs generated by basic grammars, are shown.

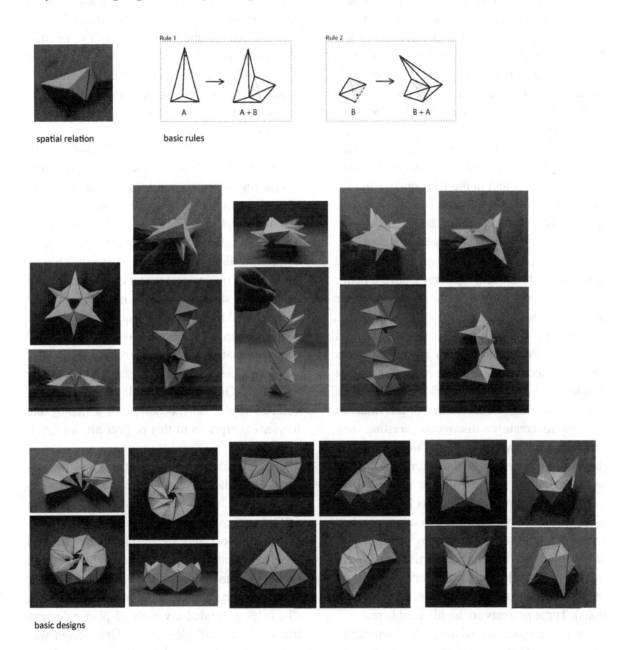

with these grammars with their blocks in class. In the last three to four weeks of the course, students work on a final project.

Projects

The final project in the first semester course, as well as in the second semester course, is open-ended. Students can work individually or in teams on an analysis, creative design, or other project of their choosing. They can develop or use any kind of grammar, from basic to more complex. Most important, students must declare an initial problem, intentions, or goals to guide their work. These invariably change over the course of their work, but students must have a set starting point. Students are encouraged to view their project as an exploration or experiment, that is, as research. The results are judged successful or not with respect to the parameters of the experiment that each student sets up. While students are working on their projects and in the final review, the focus is on students' processes as much as on their final results. The difference between the first semester project and the second semester one is that the second semester project is longer and more in-depth. Students generally have a better grasp of shape grammars in the second semester so expectations are different.

The open-ended, research nature of the final project in both semesters means that some students need considerable guidance in setting up an initial problem and following through on it. However, it also allows more experienced or adventurous students to create or discover interesting new problems and applications for shape grammars (beyond the foresight of the instructor), and to take research in the field in new directions. In this regard, a number of students have recently explored and advanced the potentials of slow computing with physical forms by working with shapes that have material properties or physical behaviors difficult to understand or compute with indirectly (for example, with digital representations). Three projects are highlighted here.

In one project, a student studied tensegrity structures. Tensegrity structures have unique visual and structural properties that are complex to model formally or abstractly. Inspired by the work of Kenneth Snelsen, the student analysed Snelsen's work as aggregations of different tensegrity modules. She then invented her own octahedron module, and used this as the starting

point for generating a wide terrain of original tensegrity structures. Her exploration process was deliberate and thoughtful. She studied different spatial relations and basic grammars to begin with, then defined parametric variations of some rules to expand on design possibilities. Her exploration depended the use of physical models (made from wooden dowels and rubber bands), which she later documented with drawings. Figure 7 shows excerpts from this project.

In two other projects, students explored the potentials of foldable/unfoldable forms, but from contrasting starting points and with different objectives. In both projects, the students' understandings and appreciation of the folding behaviors of the rules and designs were facilitated by computing directly with physical, tangible forms. The goal of one project was the development of deployable structures for houses. The student defined a 3D foldable (to a plane) shape and a 3D rigid shape to begin with, and then used these 3D shapes in spatial relations and rules to generate a variety of designs either partly or wholly foldable to a plane. One of the foldable designs was developed further in the design of a deployable house. Excerpts from this project are shown in Figure 8.

The goal of the other project was the development of foldable/unfoldable materials, for example, fabric for clothing. The student began with a 3D shape, called a *muri,* derived from a *miura*-fold or rigid origami. In contrast to the previous project, this student began with a 3D shape in its folded or planar state, and then used the planar shape to define planar spatial relations and rules. The rules generated a variety of planar designs that could be unfolded to 3D. One design was used in the design and fabrication of a dress. Excerpts from this project are shown in Figure 9.

Figure 7. A student project exploring tensegrity structures (Lisa Hedstrom, 2009). An original tensegrity module, shown at the top, formed the basis for this physical exploration. One of the spatial relations and basic rules defined by the student, and some basic designs generated by the rule, are shown. Parametric variations of a basic design are shown at the bottom.

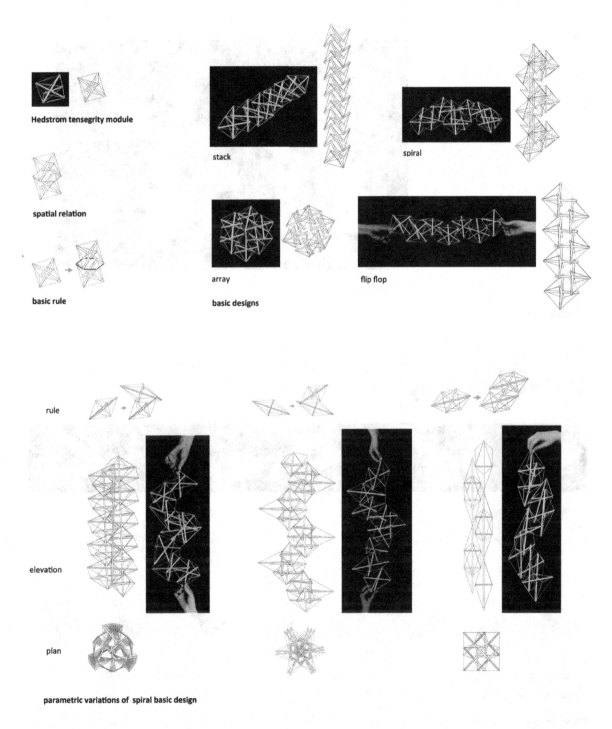

Figure 8. A student project exploring deployable houses (Arash Adel Ahmadian, 2009). Form explorations used foldable and rigid shapes, spatial relations, and rules. One foldable design was developed further for a deployable house structure.

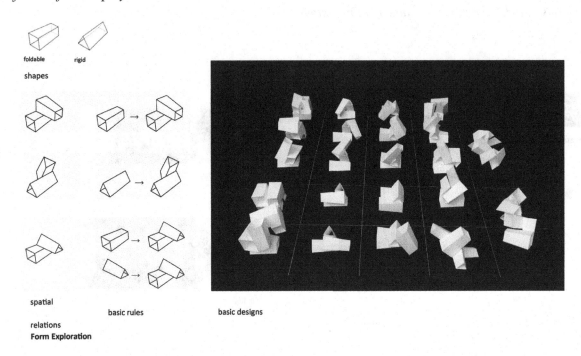

Form Exploration

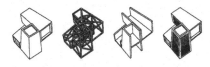

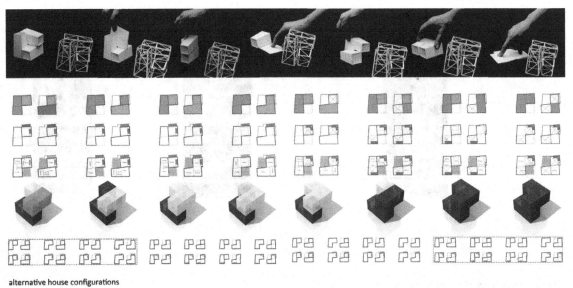

alternative house configurations

Deployable House

Figure 9. A student project for (un)foldable materials (Bianca Costanzo, 2009). A 3D muri shape, folded flat, was the basis for planar spatial relations and rules that generated a variety of planar designs that could unfold to 3D. One design was used for a dress.

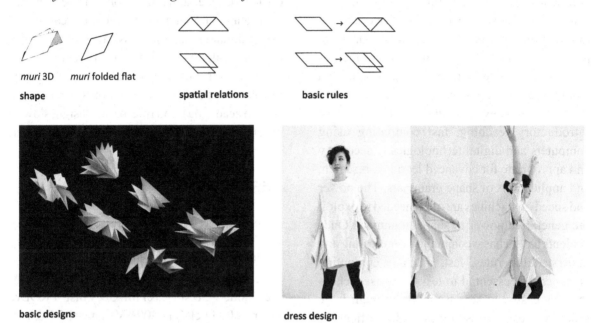

CONCLUSION AND FUTURE DIRECTIONS

This chapter overviewed the use of slow computing for teaching generative design with shape grammars. Slow computing promotes the unique visual/perceptual, nondigital, and expressive features of shape grammars and gives students mastery over rules, computations, and their outcomes. Nonetheless, issues remain to advance the benefits and reach of slow computing.

In the introductory courses described here, two challenges stand out from year to year. One is the continuing need to balance the amount and timing of formal/technical work with practical work. Currently, technical content is introduced at the beginning of the course, but it may make sense to postpone these lectures until later in the semester when students may be more primed to appreciate technical issues. Another challenge is to develop and incorporate new and different approaches to

defining analytic grammars and design grammars. For example, the structured method for defining grammars based on precedents and archetypes, proposed by Duarte (2008), is very promising.

Beyond the introductory courses, an important issue is the transfer of slow computing ideas and learning to other courses. Students from the introductory courses are somewhat successful in doing this informally on their own. In history/theory courses, students use the ideas of spatial relations and rules as analytic devices. In studio courses, students use grammar ideas at different points in a conventional studio design process as a way of analyzing their design concepts and taking them further. In other, computation or digital technology courses, students sometimes sketch their ideas with visual (shape) rules as precursor to scripting or programming. In digital fabrication courses, students use grammars informally to define component-based systems for physical fabrication of designs. However, in all of these scenarios, there is no support structure or culture to encourage or help students implement or experiment with slow computing ideas. An obvious solution and next step is to introduce explicit teaching of slow computing in other courses, in particular, design studio courses where the potentials of shape grammars for teaching design would be great, though controversial.

Although slow computing is the focus of introductory teaching, fast computing using computers and digital technologies is necessary and appropriate for advanced learning, research, and applications of shape grammars. The power and speed of machines are often needed to exploit the generative power of shape grammars. Once students have a basic command over creating and understanding rules, fast, machine computing is sometimes essential to test the consequences of rules easily, to search rapidly through large spaces of design possibilities, and to efficiently select designs that match intentions and goals. However, the successful use of fast computing always depends on slow, reflective thinking of the kind engendered by slow computing. Much research has gone into approaches for automating grammars, for either stand-alone software or plug-ins to existing software. Still, there are significant computational and interface problems that need to be resolved to achieve practicable machine implementations, especially for novice users and designers. Indeed, many of the thorny issues described ten years ago (Gips, 1999) still remain.

A last, important frontier for slow and fast computing with shape grammars is professional practice. The culture and demands of practice call for special ways to introduce and embed shape grammars, and generative design more broadly, within a professional setting. Many designers do not have the time or interest to learn or practice slow computing, and many do not have the technical competence or interest to use automated grammars for faster computing. Technical consultants or the assimilation of a new generation of computation-savvy designers might solve this issue. Nonetheless, the benefits of grammars will likely outweigh, in the end, any temporary difficulties. Certainly, the economic benefits are significant. Grammars expedite the creation, re-use, and adaptation of successful design strategies and design alternatives in many different contexts. Practice has been quick to realize the advantages of parametric design for this purpose (even more so than academia), and rule-based design, slow or fast, takes these advantages one giant step further.

REFERENCES

Bauerlein, M. (2008). Online literacy is a lesser kind. *The Chronicle Review, 55* (4), B10. Retrieved May 13, 2010, from http://proquest.umi.com.libproxy.mit.edu/ pqdlink?index=31&did=1564036981& SrchMode =3&sid=2&Fmt=3&VInst=PROD& VType= PQD&RQT=309&VName=PQD&TS= 1277424696&clientId=5482&aid=1

Duarte, J. P. (2004). MIT-Miyagi 2002: An experiment in using grammars for remote collaboration. In Bento, J., Duarte, J. P., Heitor, M., & Mitchell, W. J. (Eds.), *Collaborative design and learning* (pp. 79–115). Westport, CT: Praeger Publishers.

Duarte, J. P. (2008). *Mass customization of housing: Models and algorithms. Unpublished Habilitation Exam, Course Report and Synthesis Lesson.* School of Architecture, Technical University of Lisbon.

Flemming, U. (1990). Syntactic structures in architecture. In McCullough, M., Mitchell, W. J., & Purcell, P. (Eds.), *The electronic design studio* (pp. 31–47). Cambridge, MA: The MIT Press.

Gips, J. (1975). *Shape grammars and their uses: Artificial perception, shape generation and computer aesthetics.* Basel, Switzerland: Birkhaüser Verlag.

Gips, J. (1999). *Computer implementation of shape grammars*. Paper presented at the NSF/MIT Workshop on Shape Computation, Cambridge, MA.

Hallnäs, L., & Redström, J. (2001). Slow technology – Designing for reflection. *Personal and Ubiquitous Computing, 5*, 201–212. doi:10.1007/PL00000019

Harel, I., & Papert, S. (1991). *Constructionism*. Norwood, NY: Ablex Publishing Corporation.

Knight, T. (1999). Shape grammars in education and practice: History and prospects. *International Journal of Design Computing, 2*. Retrieved from http://wwwfaculty.arch.usyd.edu.au/ kcdc/ijdc/vol02/papers/ knightFrameset.htm

Knight, T. W. (1989). Color grammars: Designing with lines and colors. *Environment and Planning. B, Planning & Design, 16*, 417–449. doi:10.1068/b160417

Knight, T. W. (1994). Shape grammars and color grammars in design. *Environment and Planning. B, Planning & Design, 21*, 705–735. doi:10.1068/b210705

Knight, T. W. (2003). Either/or → and. *Environment and Planning. B, Planning & Design, 30*, 327–333. doi:10.1068/b12927

Lave, J., & Wenger, E. (1991). *Situated learning: Legitimate peripheral participation*. Cambridge, UK: Cambridge University Press.

Stiny, G. (1975). *Pictorial and formal aspects of shapes and shape grammars*. Basel, Switzerland: Birkhaüser Verlag.

Stiny, G. (1977). Ice-ray: A note on Chinese lattice designs. *Environment and Planning. B, Planning & Design, 4*, 89–98. doi:10.1068/b040089

Stiny, G. (1980). Kindergarten grammars: Designing with Froebel's building gifts. *Environment and Planning. B, Planning & Design, 7*, 409–462. doi:10.1068/b070409

Stiny, G., & Mitchell, W. J. (1978). The Palladian grammar. *Environment and Planning B, 5*(1), 5–18. doi:10.1068/b050005

Strauss, C., & Fuad-Luke, A. (2008). The slow design principles: A new interrogative and reflexive tool for design research and practice. In C. Cipolla & P. P. Peruccio (Eds.), *Changing the change* (pp. 1440-1454). Allemande Conference Press.

ADDITIONAL READING

Celani, G. (2004). *Notes on the educational use of shape grammars*. Paper presented at Workshop 6, Cognition And Computation In Digital Design, Design Computing and Cognition 04, Cambridge, MA.

Chase, S. C. (1989). Shapes and shape grammars: from mathematical model to computer implementation. *Environment and Planning. B, Planning & Design, 16*, 215–242. doi:10.1068/b160215

Chase, S. C. (2002). A model for user interaction in grammar-based design systems. *Automation in Construction, 11*, 161–172. doi:10.1016/S0926-5805(00)00101-1

Chau, H. H., Chen, X. J., McKay, A., & de Pennington, A. (2004). Evaluation of a 3D Shape Grammar Implementation. In Gero, J. (Ed.), *Design Computing and Cognition 04* (pp. 357–376). Dordrecht: Kluwer Academic Publishers.

Heisserman, J., & Callahan, J. (1996). *Interactive grammatical design*. Workshop notes on Grammatical Design, AI in Design '96, Stanford, CA.

Jowers, I., Prats, M., Lim, S., McKay, A., Garner, S., & Chase, S. (2008). Supporting Reinterpretation in Computer-Aided Conceptual Design. In C. Alvarado & M-P Cani (Eds.), *EUROGRAPHICS Workshop on Sketch-Based Interfaces and Modeling* (pp. 151-158).

Knight, T. W. (1992). Designing with Grammars. In Schmitt, G. (Ed.), *Computer-Aided Architectural Design* (pp. 33–48). Wiesbaden: Verlag Viewag.

Krishnamurti, R., & Stouffs, R. (1993). Spatial grammars: motivation, comparison, and new results. In U. Flemming & S. Van Wyk (Eds.), *5th International Conference on Computer-Aided Architectural Design Futures* (pp. 57-74). Amsterdam: North-Holland Publishing Co.

Li, A. I. (2001). Teaching style grammatically, with an example from traditional Chinese architecture. In M. Burry, S. Datta, A. Dawson & J. Rollo (Eds.), *The Proceedings of Mathematics & Design 2001: the Third International Conference* (pp, 270–277).

Li, A. I. (2002). A prototype simulated interactive shape grammar. In K. Koszewski and S. Wrona (Eds.), *Design e-ducation: connecting the real and the virtual, Proceedings of the 20th conference on education in computer aided architectural design in Europe*, (pp 314–317). Warsaw: eCAADe.

McGill, M., & Knight, T. (2004). Designing Design-Mediating Software: The Development of Shaper2D. In *22nd eCAADe Conference Proceedings* (pp. 119-127).

Piazzalunga, U., & Fitzhorn, P. (1998). Note on a three-dimensional shape grammar interpreter. *Environment and Planning. B, Planning & Design*, *25*, 11–30. doi:10.1068/b250011

Stiny, G. (1980). Kindergarten grammars: designing with Froebel's building gifts. *Environment and Planning. B, Planning & Design*, *3*, 409–462. doi:10.1068/b070409

Stiny, G. (1981). A note on the description of designs. *Environment and Planning. B, Planning & Design*, *8*, 257–267. doi:10.1068/b080257

Stiny, G. (2006). *Shape: Talking About Seeing and Doing*. Cambridge, MA: MIT Press.

Stiny, G., & Gips, J. (1972). Shape Grammars and the Generative Specification of Painting and Sculpture. In C. V. Freiman (Ed.), *Information Processing 71* (pp. 1460-1465). Amsterdam: North-Holland Press. Republished (1972) in O. R. Petrocelli (Ed.), *The Best Computer Papers of 1971* (pp. 125-135). Philadelphia, PA: Auerbach Publications.

Tapia, M. (1999). A visual implementation of a shape grammar system. *Environment and Planning. B, Planning & Design*, *26*, 59–73. doi:10.1068/b260059

Trescak, T., Esteva, M., & Rodriguez, I. (2009). General Shape Grammar Interpreter for Intelligent Designs Generations. In *Computer Graphics, Imaging and Visualization, CGIV'09, Vol. 6* (pp. 235-240). IEEE Computer Society.

Wang, Y., & Duarte, J. (2002). Automatic generation and fabrication of designs. *Automation in Construction*, *113*, 291–302. doi:10.1016/S0926-5805(00)00112-6

Wong, W. K., & Cho, C. T. (2004). A Computational Environment for Learning Basic Shape Grammars. In *International Conference on Computers in Education 2004* (pp. 287-292).

KEY TERMS AND DEFINITIONS

Basic Design: A design generated by a basic grammar. It is constructed by recursively adding shapes in accordance with a single spatial relation.

Basic Grammar: A shape grammar consisting of one or two simple and limited rules, called basic rules, that apply recursively to generate designs by adding shapes in accordance with a spatial relation.

Label: A symbol associated with a shape in a shape rule that is used to control or restrict the way the rule is applied.

Parametric Shape Grammar: A shape grammar with rules defined in terms of parametric shapes, that is, shapes with variable geometric or other properties.

Parametric Shape Rule: A rule of a parametric shape grammar. It has the form A → B, where one or both of the shapes A and B are parametric shapes. It specifies that a shape defined by assigning values to variables in A can be replaced by, or changed into, a shape defined by assigning values to variables in B.

Shape: A visual-spatial entity defined in terms of any combination of points, lines, planes, or volumes defined in a space of any dimension – 0D, 1D, 2D, 3D, or more.

Shape Grammar: A set of shape (visual) rules that apply recursively to a starting shape to generate a set of designs.

Shape Rule: A rule of a shape grammar. It has the form A → B, where A and B are shapes. It specifies that a shape A can be replaced by, or changed into, a shape B.

Spatial Relation: An arrangement of one or more shapes in space.

Chapter 4
Learning Parametric Designing

Marc Aurel Schnabel
The Chinese University of Hong Kong, Hong Kong

ABSTRACT

Parametric designing, its instruments, and techniques move architectural design education towards novel avenues of deep learning. Akin to learning and working environments of engineering and manufacturing, it offers similar advantages for architects. Yet it is not as simple as using another tool; parametric designing fundamentally shifts the engagement with the design problem. Parametric designing allows architects to be substantially deeper involved in the overall design and development process extending it effectively beyond production and lifecycle. Leaning parametric design strategies enhance architects' critical engagement with their designs and their communication. Subsequently, the computational aid of parametric modelling alters substantially how and what students learn and architects practice.

INTRODUCTION

Parametric design techniques offer obvious advantages for engineering and manufacturing processes, now architects have emerged to apply these methods in their working environment suggesting solutions and novel designs at an earlier stage of the process. Through the coupling of architectural design with parametric modelling methods, the chapter presents techniques that enhance students' learning and knowledge about designing and architectural building processes. This allows a deeper comprehension of the design objectives and aids architectural designers in their decisions to find solutions.

A dilemma of semester-based teaching is that students reach their highest level of skills and experience at the end of a term, after which they leave for their break and are therefore unable to apply their freshly gained knowledge immediately. At the beginning of the next following term, however, the knowledge and skills they had gained earlier are likely to be either inactive or not employed, and learning foci may have shifted to other aims. The architectural design studio presented here addressed these issues by integrating the learning experience from the beginning by focusing on parameters that create or inform about the design. The objective of this 'parametric designing' was to allow students to understand the impact each step and variable has on the design and follow the impact it has onto the project. Students developed

DOI: 10.4018/978-1-61350-180-1.ch004

Figure 1. Right: Pieter Bruegel's 'Tower of Babel. Right: Archigram's Plug-in City

and communicated their design parameters by utilizing their knowledge throughout the design-studio environment. Because of this, students began to think about design problems in different ways. The studio explored design by basing it on parameters and their connecting rules. In order to build up a philosophy around parametric dependencies and relationships, the participants used digital instruments that aided them to create and express their designs. With these instruments, they could develop expertise to engage creatively in designing. The studio cumulated in an architectural art exhibition highlighting the coupling of architectural design with digital modelling and fabrication methods. Students presented architectural solutions that challenged and addressed environmental and programmatic issues, dimension, space and volume, as well as theoretical and conservational topics, resulting in novel designs created with freedom of innovation, interpretation, and definition some of which without any boundaries. The notion of non-conformity added to the core of this collection of works, held together by the idea of spatial concepts and parametric designing in architecture.

BACKGROUND

Pieter Bruegel, a Netherlands' Renaissance painter, depicted a representation of the 'Tower of Babel' as a building that is constantly redefining its needs, as it grows larger and more complex (Figure 1). The painting shows a tower nearly reaching the clouds and illustrates all the problems then associated with cities, buildings and life within and the constant change and reaction to new situations during the process of building.

The exploration of the relationship between human beings and the natural world, and the subsequent implications of interactions between them, has deep roots in our social and cultural understanding of society. Cities, therefore, are direct reflections of their inhabitants, as their architectural expressions directly influence the living conditions of their people. In recent practice, architects have designed and described buildings through the means of (master-) plans, sections, elevations, or descriptions of render-perfect, complete architectures in which change was not part of the picture. A few, however, have tried different approaches to communicate architecture.

In the 1960s and early 1970s, Archigram already presented an idea that reacted against the permanence of houses in what it called the "Plug-in City" (Figure 1, right). They proposed architecture that is ever changing and adaptable to different social and economic conditions (Karakiewicz, 2004). Their proposal did not develop further than a conceptual stage, yet it lays in contrasts to the common practice that also Le Corbusier describes as non-intelligent building machines, whereby these machines would not think, and would therefore be unable to adapt to change.

More recently 'LAB Architecture Studio' translated planning codes of Beijing's 'Soho Shang-Du' into series of parametric design rules whereby the outcome both complies with and confounds the rigid regulations (Davidson, 2006). As a result, the architects did not prescribe a fixed definition of architecture, but a set of rules and instructions that inform about and can generate the outcome. This allows a reaction on a variety of site-specific variables that can be modified according to the need, yet fit into the overall design intents of the architects.

These samples point out the constant demand for architecture to adapt and react to a variety of parameters that are driven by its use and context. The gap between the architectural design conceptions and the translation of these designs into the real built environment can be addressed fundamentally differently by an intersection of process and outcome (Eastman, 2004). Parametric design and digital fabrication techniques suggest controllable and adaptable solutions at an earlier stage of the process that react to the given situations and the outcomes.

PARAMETRIC DESIGN STUDIO

Architectural design studios are an essential learning experience for architectural students. Their traditions and proceedings are well established. Studios go beyond pure skill training and require reflection upon, and the creation of, knowledge. These studios are, additionally, informed and supplemented by courses and seminars that contribute to the overall learning goals. Yet there can be a gap between skill training and application of knowledge. At the end of the studio, students may not be able to identify how they arrived to their solution and solves a given problem, or what were the individual contributors that made their design successful.

In computational architectural studios, the same phenomena can be observed. These studios present the underlying concepts of architectural design using computational instruments, and have at the same time to provide for software skills and other technical knowledge (Kvan, 2004A). The integration of digital media into design studio curricula often fails, because the compound acquisition of skills prevents a deep exploration of design and the theoretical aspects involved at the same time. Participants can employ computational instruments within a studio context only after they have learned subject matters and acquired proficiency in their skills. By then, the studio may consider these skills no longer valid or has ended.

Parametric applications have inherited two crucial elements. These are that all entities start in a multi-dimensional space and allow the study of architectural conditions in a cloud of data and variety of representations, rather than the conventional two-dimensional or layered design environment. The underlying notion of parametric designing is based on the contextual construction of a formal and spatial systemic intelligent simulation; or in other words data, variables, and their relationship to other entities, which can then respond to variations of necessities (Ambrose, 2009). Students learn about cause and effect in both abstract environments as well as at specific situations of their design task. This is where architectural education is in the process of changing fundamentally. Design studios and courses are now increasingly reacting to the quantum leap architectural computing has presented to design education, and introducing computational parametric tools to the design studios that go beyond Computer Aided Design (CAD) (Picon, 2010). Yet one has to be careful that novel technologies and learning methodologies offer current pedagogies to address certain known issues and cannot eliminates all problems connected with learning and education.

PARAMETRIC DESIGNING

Architecture in general can be expressed and specified in a variety of ways. Commonly, drawings describe geometric properties that can explain, depict, and guide the construction of buildings or streets. Alternatively, performance specifications can describe observed behaviours. It is also possible to describe properties as relationships between entities. Spreadsheets, for instance, specify the value of each cell as the result of calculations involving other cell entries. These calculations or descriptions do not have to be explicit. Responsive materials change their properties in reaction to the conditions around them. A thermostat senses air temperature and controls the flow of electric current, and hence the temperature of the air supplied. Using such techniques, artists have created reactive sculptures and architects have made sentient spaces that react to their occupants or other relevant factors. Streetlights turn on if light levels fall below a threshold; traffic flow can be regulated according to need; walls can move as users change location.

Links to a variety of data can be established and subsequently serve as the bases to generate geometric forms using parametric design instruments. When designing spaces, it is usual to collect some data of the type of architectural qualities desired. These are then, for example, translated into master plans, which are themselves specific spatial descriptions. Performance requirements for spaces can then be written, linking the description of the architecture to experiential, financial, environmental, or other factors (Picon, 1997).

Design studios mimic the typical working processes of the architectural profession and are the essential learning experience for architectural students. Research is now looking into how the framing of design problems using parametric methods enhances the overall process (Schnabel et al., 2004). The here presented studio, therefore, couples parametric methodologies within the generation of architectural design, ultimately reframing the problem and proposing new answers to design thinking and learning. Participants in this study solved a typical architectural design problem using computational applications that focused on the parametric dependencies of spatial entities, generative scripts, and form finding. The re-representation of the design intent sharpens the question at its centre (Gao and Kvan, 2004), while taking full advantage of available parametric modelling software to explore it. This approach tested the limitations set by conventional, design-only methods. The cognitive aspects of the design generation and their relationships to parametric design methods operated as an influential factor for the understanding of the projection of design intent, framing, generation of spatial knowledge within architectural design and the reflection about the outcome produced in this process (Ambrose, 2009).

Problem Framing

The studio engaged the participants in design processes by using sets of variables and series of relations to question, create, and define the form and function of the resulting designs. Thus, the students examined interaction techniques between their design intent, their framing of the design problem, their subsequent generation and reflection on their development by testing the rules and parameters. Participants engaged in a collaborative architectural design studio involving the creation and fabrication of architecture. This formed the basis for a transfer of knowledge to the larger context of the issues ahead in their future professional careers (Riese and Simmons, 2004).

The studio took a distinctive neighbourhood within the larger urban context of Sydney, Australia as its base of exploration. The specific site

Figure 2. Four phases and exhibition of the design studio with learning reflections and projections

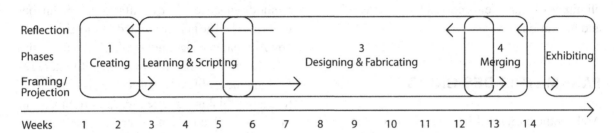

surrounding, a mix of residential, public and commercial buildings, offered a medium dense area with a variety of architectural languages.

Driven by a fast growing population, an architectural strategy that steers further development was sought. The city's scale, its growth through migration and the need for new housing have an impact on its inhabitants' sense of place and sense of community. Earlier urban planning did not anticipate the changes that arose over years of population growth. Hence, a new strategy for development that could address these issues was sought to create a new identity for the place and the city itself (Forrest et al., 2002).

The site of the studio had typical architectural characteristics and requirements. Located at a riverbank, in close proximity of a parkland, cultural-, office- and residential buildings, the site offered a variety of inspiration as well as constrains for an architectural design exercise. Students had to address and responded to the local and overall conditions of open space, city, work, living and environment.

The studio built upon design studios where participants explored design methods and tools beyond their original definitions and perceived limits (Schnabel et al., 2004). To allow the students both to acquire skills and training within their studio and to apply this knowledge to their design, the studio had an integrated digital media component that addressed parametric modelling in architectural design.

Two groups of fifteen students of the postgraduate architectural program each joined this studio, which was guided by two design tutors and one architectural consultant in digital media. The studio was structured in four phases that related to and built upon each other (Figure 2). The aim was to acquire and integrate parametric design knowledge and to use it as the base of the design creation of their architectural proposal. As a result, the final design could be modified and manipulated based on the parameters and their dependencies, allowing the students to gain a deeper understanding of their design processes and outcomes as well as the reaction of their proposals with the various influences of the site.

Creating

The project's first component included the collection and understanding of data that arrived from the site. In order not to overwhelm the students, the tutors asked them during this first stage to limit them to investigating only two points of interests, which became their key-parameters. Hereby the students could focus on the selections of parameters that they believed would influence their building proposal or their site's perception, this parameter could be a real or abstract item (Figure 3).

The parameters they chose informed them about the variables and correlation of their guiding design principles that formed their initial rules. These provided them a description based on de-

Figure 3. Two parameters (floor-heights) used by a student team (R Beson & N Minasian)

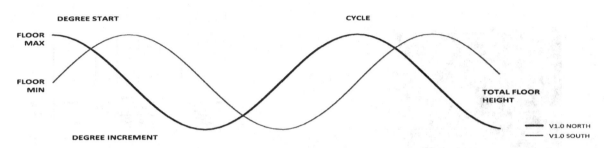

pendencies and interconnected relationships of relevant information. The chosen parameters helped the students to understand what impact certain variables may have on a design strategy and the design itself. This component concluded after two weeks with presentations of data, parameters, and individual interpretations of the site.

Learning

The program's second component focused on the understanding and creation of parametric concepts and the acquisition of design-application skills that allow rule-based three-dimensional design. Participants were trained intensively during studio time in the use of *Digital Project ™* (2004). This software allows users to not only create three-dimensional models, but also to establish rules, create parameters and their dependencies on a variety of entities (Figure 4).

Parametric functions require a different understanding of the conceptual approaches to design. Creating rules and dependencies, which then create the design, involved the students in a higher level of problem framing and definition of the concept of design. It allowed the visualization and modelling of highly complex forms that may result from non-traditional design data, such as noise data or spatial requirements.

The students focused on their own parametric and rule-based design analyses from the first component and subsequently studied mainly only the aspects relevant to these in relation to the use and operation of the software, the creation of rules, and parametric and generative design. During this phase, they used the time allocated to the design studio to establish a basic understanding of the software in its relationship to the design intent developed during the first phase. After three weeks of intensive training in architectural computing, the students reached a sufficient level of skills that enabled them to use the parametric software as an aid for the creation of their own designs.

Scripting

'Script' is derived from the term for written dialogue in the performing arts, where actors are given directions to perform or interpret. Subsequently, 'scripting' is a creative process that describes the artistic intent of the designer. Scripts can define a set of rules that combines parameters in the named way. Software applications can be programmed and adjusted by scripts allowing for example repetitive tasks to be automated or to generate solutions that fit to a range of parameters (Biloria et al., 2005). Instead of using only compositional methods for designing, the students utilized scripts to form their own generative properties and base for their design exploration (Figure 5). Sourcing related or suitable general available scripts students quickly learned how to edit and control their design by amending the parameters or rules to fit their design intent (Celani, 2008). This phase differs greatly from conventional studios because students are engaging in software training and skill

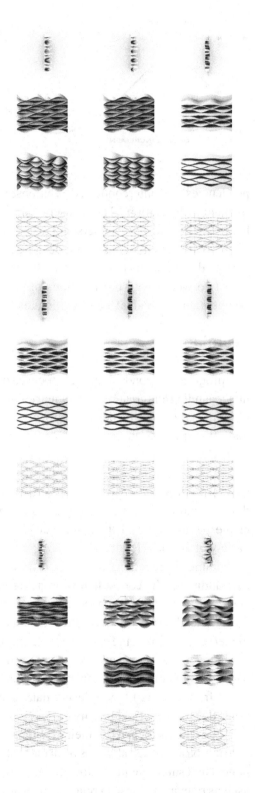

Figure 4. Development of parameters, dependencies and rules within software analogue (left) and digitally (right) (Beson & Minasian)

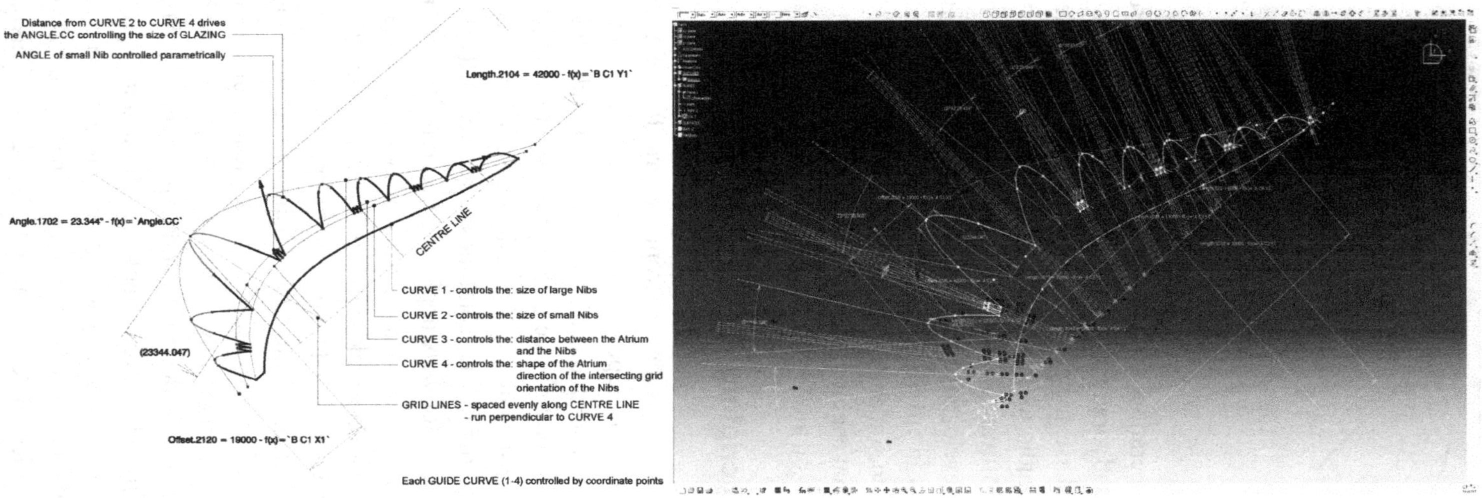

Distance from CURVE 2 to CURVE 4 drives
the ANGLE.CC controlling the size of GLAZING
ANGLE of small Nib controlled parametrically

Length.2104 = 42000 - f(x) = "B C1 Y1'

CENTRE LINE

CURVE 1 - controls the: size of large Nibs
CURVE 2 - controls the: size of small Nibs
CURVE 3 - controls the: distance between the Atrium
                        and the Nibs
CURVE 4 - controls the: shape of the Atrium
                        direction of the intersecting grid
                        orientation of the Nibs
GRID LINES - spaced evenly along CENTRE LINE
             - run perpendicular to CURVE 4

Each GUIDE CURVE (1-4) controlled by coordinate points

Angle.1702 = 23.344° - f(x) = "Angle.CC'

(23344.047)

Offset.2120 = 19000 - f(x) = "B C1 X1'

Figure 5. Variations generated by a script to modify facade-tiles (Beson & Minasian).

acquisitions of how to generate and manipulate instructions for computer programmes that can aid their design process.

Designing

The program's third component, scheduled for seven weeks, concentrated on design creation, reflection, and the communication of architectural design proposals. Using the data of the first component and the skills of the second, the students then started to establish and visualize their designs in three-dimensional forms that created spatial expressions of their findings and explorations.

Due to the emphasis on parameters, the studio was in particular interested in describing a building form by creating dependencies of parameters that defined the relationship of data to architectural expressions. With the use of a parametric modeller, it was easy to create geometric entities, solids and voids, and relate them to the context of the design task. This method made it obvious how one can learn about design and understand the various steps and elements through the logical steps laid out by the chosen parameters, variables, rules or scripts.

Fabricating

Another stage in the creative process is the fabrication of the digitally created designs. Recent computational applications and digital fabrication technologies have allowed architecture to take novel directions. The combination of architectural computation with computer-controlled machinery has nearly made it possible for shapes, however complex or irregular they seem to be, to be rationalized and created as physical entities with the ultimate aim to result in a buildable architecture (Oxman and Oxman, 2010). The studio subsequently made extensive use at all stages to explore the transformation of virtual design conceptions to physical objects via the use of computer-aided manufacturing (Figure 6).

Merging

The program's next following component brought together the various aspects and results of the earlier modules. Within two weeks, the students merged their individual designs into larger cluster files. This synthesis created compound descriptions and dependencies that were highly complex and interrelated, yet both the content as well as the tool allowed seamless communication to a larger

Figure 6. Facade details from the digital model fabricated by rapid-prototyping (Beson & Minasian)

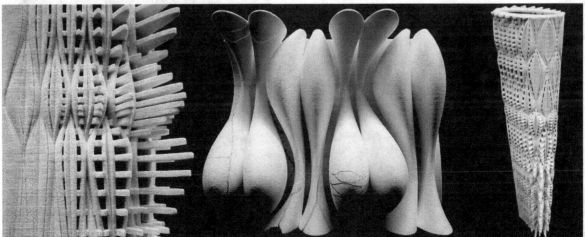

Figure 7. A joint model that combined facade, interior spaces and atrium details

audience by describing the rules and parameters (Figure 7). This phase created a design with shared authorship of all participants and allowed the students to study and understand the complexity and the interrelationships of architectural designing that they normally would have been unable to perceive immediately. Through their collaboration and exchange the students built up a collective intelligence that was driven by the individual contributions. The change of a single variable modified the whole design. Participants understood therefore the complex dependencies that one variable has in a large building and the impact it can have on the design.

Exhibiting

The design explorations culminated in an exhibition displaying the designers' engagement with parametric designing and fabrication (Figure 8). To mark the distinctive final stage in a celebrative conclusion of design development, the event

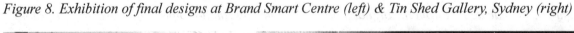

Figure 8. Exhibition of final designs at Brand Smart Centre (left) & Tin Shed Gallery, Sydney (right)

exemplified how digital architectural design can conceptually and artistically engage with a particular site, where a variety of solutions to problems in architectural design were developed from a diversity of multi-faceted and eccentric approaches (Schnabel and Bowller, 2007). The participating designers pushed creativity to new boundaries in definition of their artwork and cultural contexts, setting the direction for poetic viewpoints on innovation in architecture and spatial design. The exhibition forms a crucial learning experience whereby both processes and outcomes are presented in a formal way that is self-explanatory to a wider audience.

The compiling of all projects into a single exhibition removed the designers from the context of individual ownership, providing them with the invaluable opportunity to reflect on both, their own and their colleagues' proposals as a coherent collection of contributions towards one common engagement of design.

OUTCOMES

Participants of the parametric design studio were able to employ digital media skills from very early on throughout the studio and expand on these with their understanding and communication of design issues from there.

The students had already acquired a very high level of skills in using a specific parametric instrument within the first half of the studio. This enabled them to employ the instrument as an amplifier to learn about their designs. Subsequently, they were not limited by their knowledge or level of skills in order to be able to express themselves. The students produced a variety of individual design proposals as well as one large design-cluster. They created rules, scripts and parameters that allowed complex and interrelating designs to emerge. These representations could not be generated or communicated using traditional architectural design methods or instruments.

For example, one proposal related street lighting, neon-signs and display-windows with human activity around the building site. These parameters provided the engaging surface for the building mass. Subsequently they controlled the use, orientation and appearance of the building. The author took references to Japanese inner cities, where innovative ways of spaces are created by the means of lights, advertising and projections. Void, volume and density is controlled and created by the rhythm and intensity of lights. The student transferred this concept into parameters, which redefined the spatial understanding of the site and used these variables to create an architectural proposal.

Other results used parameters that related to the relationships between people and attraction to spaces with responsive structures. Students created self-opening canopies that reacted to people, activities, ferry schedules, weather conditions and the possibilities to collect rainwater to provide a comfortable environment in all conditions. One team reacted with different floor-heights to various needs of public and private programme of their building and related their spaces to vista and light penetration of their building (Figures 3-6). These explorations then were merged with parameters controlling the interior space, atrium and program to form an overall design of a mix use building (Figure 7).

In the studio's last component, all students presented in-depth clusters of multifaceted architectural design proposals for the site. They demonstrated a high level of thinking processes resulting in the generation of compound rules and dependencies that finally create the architectural design schemes. Each student contributed simultaneously to create a variety of design proposals. The participants gained a high level of expertise with digital parametric tools as part of their development at the studio, and used this knowledge to design parametrically. The outcome clearly showed that thinking, learning and creating within parametric designing requires a novel and deeper understanding of the overall design goal and its anticipated outcome. The studio also showed that a social engagement with team members created a common knowledge to which everyone not only contributed but also benefitted. Students subsequently build up a social intelligence that allowed them to address both skills and design problems.

Students reported of the step learning curve of understanding how parametric software is structured differently to conventional software. They reported that they could not just design intuitively as they would do in conventional studios and had to stick to the rigour process of the parametric design methodology. The skill training in the software and the translation of the design intent proved not always to be straight forward. Some students only gained the full understanding of the potential parametric modelling offers at the end of the studio where all solutions were presented. While others had difficulties in developing a logic string of design steps that relate to the parametric approach, they preferred or felt back to intuitive or conventional designing.

Parametric modelling subsequently does not solve all issues connected with design-learning. It allows however, an alignment of cause and effect and a reflection of the design intent, the process and outcome. This differs from conventional design studios where these dependencies only seldom can be established. The studio allowed participants to learn about designing and problem framing. They were able to theorize and reflect on design creation for this and other design tasks. Consequently students engaged in a deeper learning that allows them to transfer and adapt their knowledge to new situations. Results can be explored at: www.parramatta.tk and www.disparallelspaces.tk.

DISCUSSION

In the early stages of computational architecture, designing in layers was a popular enrichment to conventional designing because it allowed architects to deal with problems that are more complex, with each different layer playing a specific role. It singled out issues and allowed dealing with them one at a time. Items that are more complex were divided into separate issues and dealt with one by one. Parametric design opens up a novel set of opportunities. It enables architects to study causes of problems and their relationships to, and dependencies on, other elements directly within a three-dimensional environment.

This shift of design thinking and creation needs to be addressed in the teaching and learning of design. Additionally, parametric designing provide for unpredictable events in connection with an overall architectural framework. Architects and architecture itself can respond to unplanned changes and their resulting consequences. The outcomes of this design studio showed that parametric dependencies allowed for such a level of ambiguity that is desired and required in creative and learning environments.

One objective of the studio was to frame an intellectual question that created design descriptions based on rules, scripts and parameters. The more interesting outcomes resulted from the ability to redefine and reframe the problems themselves by stepping out of preconceptions based on experience and exploring sets of unpredictable answers and then reflecting back on the starting point. Hence, in certain ways, parametric designing act at a higher level of the problem framing. The establishment of meta-rules has instituted a form of problem framing that demands the reference of one problem or parameter with other ones.

The learning outcomes of the parametric design studio demonstrate how non-linear design processes led to architectural design understandings that differ from conventional approaches to design learning due to their different nature of design thinking, framing, creation, and intuition. Despite three-dimensional representations of an architectural space being only a medium aiding the understanding and communication of spatial arrangements, the designers' comprehension of complex spatial qualities was enhanced by the parametric design environment, partly due to the logic structure and dependencies of one step to the next. The steep learning curve and the time needed to adjust to the parametric and sometimes stringent or seemingly limiting methodology of parametric designing shows that conventional designing is the pre-dominant approach to design and deeply routed in the design-thinking of students. Yet despite these difficulties students unanimously reported that the here presented studio helped to understand how to design and they highly valued the approach to thinking about and executing designing.

The use of parametric instruments allowed all students to design within an environment based on rules and generative descriptions, amplifying their understandings of creative processes and their learning outcomes. Each designer bridged the rift between their knowledge and ambition, creating architectural designs and learning about the act of architectural designing.

NEXT STEPS

The increasing marginalization of architects in the building industries (Bennetts, 2008) suggests that professional and educational ideals and professional work are poorly aligned. Unlike other professions, architects are trained in a variety of fields of knowledge and skills that are not directly related to the daily routine of the architectural praxis. Subsequently architecture students have an increasing amount to learn following graduation. Architects have discovered how digital instruments alter any aspects of their routines of working. However, academic and educational environments are not able to follow in the same speed. Learning designing has shifted from the single learner to a collective engagement with a variety of learners, novices, experts and instruments that aid, analyze, generate, design and

review. Less than a decade ago many schools of architecture did not allow students to deliver CAD drawings for design projects assuming that would limit the exploration and understanding of design. In fact, the early experiments in using the computer in the design process quite often failed only because of the restrictions of the available infrastructure, facilities and skills. Today, students are familiar with architectural computing even before they enter the university (Dokonal and Hirschberg, 2003).

Still many questions remain unanswered and new questions arise in the relationship between architectural design and architectural computing. Architectural design is both an imagination and the ability to convey this idea. The learning of architectural design has to make use of the advantages that complex architectural computing offers without loosing the qualities of the established conventional methods. The current 'Net-Generation' (Oblinger and Oblinger, 2005) of learners, who are more conversant in using computational instruments than their teachers, are changing the dynamics of architectural education. This is a challenge to established curricula and institutions.

The herein presented studio is a successful attempt to integrate architectural computing into the learning environment by aligning skills and knowledge of the students with the objective to generate knowledge about designing, computation, architecture and realization.

Akin to Maver's (1995) comments, parametric designing and for that matter, architectural computing is certainly far from being resolved and offering the perfect solution. As the needs, goals and problems are rapidly developing architectural design and its learning needs to facilitate the evolution and progress. Synergies between the different realms, media and technologies are constantly evolving and adjusted to foster the evolution of architectural praxis and the building industry (Eastman et al, 2008).

CONCLUSION

The parametric design studio method presented in this chapter addressed computational concepts of architectural designing that influence the recent learning environment of architectural education. It coupled the setting of studio-learning with an in-depth digital media training in order to close the gap between acquisition of skills and the reflection of knowledge, as well as to explore new avenues of framing and integrating compound design issues. The use of digital parametric instruments allowed the participants to design within an environment based on rules and generative descriptions, amplifying their design understanding and their own learning. The students connected their knowledge with their ambition to create their own design proposals.

The synthesis of all individual projects removed the students from individual ownership of their designs, but allowed them to reflect on both their own and their colleagues' designs as a complete cluster of contributions (Kvan, 2004B). This related to earlier research into design studios based on the same principle, in which media were applied outside their normal pre-described purposes, and innovative design methods were deployed by interplaying digital media and design explorations (Schnabel et al., 2004).

With the employment of parametric design methods that allowed students to experience the dependencies and rules of the various individual contributions spatially, as well as the overall common proposals, the design was communicated using digitally controlled manufacturing processes and digital representations.

The studio was phased in such a way that each section built upon the next and became an essential part of the overall design learning and creation. They addressed and expressed certain aspects of the process. A holistic discussion about design, form, function, and development is consequently established - a significant venture not only within the architectural realm, but also in all other dialogues involving spatial representation.

REFERENCES

Ambrose, M. A. (2009). BIM and comprehensive design studio education. In *Proceedings of the 14th International Conference on Computer Aided Architectural Design Research in Asia* (pp. 757-760). Yunlin, Taiwan: CAADRIA.

Bennetts, R. (2008). Reasserting the architect's position in pursuit of sustainability. In S. Roaf & A. Bairstow (Eds.), *The Oxford Conference: A re-evaluation of education in architecture* (pp. 11-16). Southampton, UK: WIT Press.

Biloria, N., Oosterhuis, K., & Aalbers, C. (2005). Design informatics. In *Smart Architecture: Integration of Digital and Building Technologies* (pp. 226–235). Savannah, GA: ACADIA.

Celani, M. G. C. (2008). Teaching programming to architecture students. *Revista Gestão & Tecnologia de Projetos, 3*(2), 1–23.

Davidson, P. (2006). *The regular complex.* Paper presented at the NSK Wolfram Science Conference, Washington, DC. Retrieved May 10, 2010, from http://www.wolframscience.com/conference/ 2006/presentations/davidson.html

(2004). *Digital Project* ™. Los Angeles, California: Gehry Technologies.

Dokonal, W., & Hirschberg, U. (Eds.). (2003). *Digital design.* Graz, Austria: eCAADe and Graz University of Technology.

Eastman, C. (2004). New methods of architecture and building. In *Fabrication: Examining the Digital Practice of Architecture* (pp. 20–27). Cambridge, Canada: ACADIA & AIA Technology in Architectural Practice Knowledge Community.

Eastman, C., Teicholz, P., Sacks, R., & Liston, K. (2008). *BIM handbook: A guide to building information modeling for owners, managers, designers, engineers and contractors*. New Jersey: John Wiley & Sons.

Forrest, R., La Grange, A., & Yip, N.-m. (2002). Neighborhood in a high rise, high density city: Some observations on contemporary Hong Kong. *The Sociological Review, 50*(2), 215–240. doi:10.1111/1467-954X.00364

Gao, S., & Kvan, T. (2004). An analysis of problem framing in multiple settings. In Gero, J. (Ed.), *Design computing and cognition* (pp. 117–134). Dordrecht, The Netherlands: Kluwer Academic Publishers.

Karakiewicz, J. (2004). City as a megastructure. In Jenks, M., & Dempsey, N. (Eds.), *Future forms for sustainable cities* (pp. 137–151). Oxford, UK: Architectural Press.

Kvan, T. (2004A). Collaborative design: What is it? *Automation in Construction, 9*(4), 409–415. doi:10.1016/S0926-5805(99)00025-4

Kvan, T. (2004B). Reasons to stop teaching CAAD. In Chiu, M.-L. (Ed.), *Digital design education* (pp. 66–81). Taipei, Taiwan: Garden City Publishing.

Maver, T. W. (1995). CAAD's seven deadly sins. In M. Tan & R. The (Eds.), *The Global Design Studio, Proceedings CAAD Futures* (pp. 21-22). Singapore: Centre for Advanced Studies in Architecture, National University of Singapore.

Monedero, J. (2000). Parametric design: A review and some experiences. *Automation in Construction, 9*(4), 369–377. doi:10.1016/S0926-5805(99)00020-5

Oblinger, D. G., & Oblinger, J. L. (Eds.). (2005). *Educating the Net generation*. Washington, DC: Educause.

Oxman, R., & Oxman, R. (Eds.). (2010). Special issue: The new structuralism: Design, engineering and architectural technologies/ *Architectural Design, 80*(4).

Picon, A. (1997). Les annales de la recherche urbaine. *Le Temps du Cyborg dans la Ville Territoire, 77*, 72-77.

Picon, A. (2010). *Digital culture in architecture: An introduction for the design professions*. Basel, Switzerland: Birkhäuser.

Riese, M., & Simmons, M. (2004). The glass office - SCL office and showroom in Brisbane, Australia. In *Fabrication: Examining the digital practice of architecture* (pp. 28–33). Cambridge, Canada: ACADIA & AIA Technology in Architectural Practice Knowledge Community.

Schnabel, M. A., & Bowller, N. (Eds.). (2007). *Disparallel spaces*. Sydney, Australia: The University of Sydney.

Schnabel, M. A., Kvan, T., Kuan, S. K. S. & Li, W. (2004). 3D crossover: Exploring - Objets digitalise. *International Journal of Architectural Computing – IJAC, 2*(4), 475-490.

ADDITIONAL READING

Derix, C. (2009). In-Between Architecture Computation. *International Journal of Architectural Computing – IJAC, 7*(4), 565-586.

Iwamoto, I. (2009). *Digital Fabrications: Architectural and Material Techniques*. New York: Princeton Architectural Press.

Jones, C., Ramanau, R., Cross, S., & Healing, G. (2010). Net generation or Digital Natives: Is there a distinct new generation entering university? *Computers & Education, 54*(3), 722–732. doi:10.1016/j.compedu.2009.09.022

Karakiewicz, J., Shelton, B., & Kvan, T. (2010). *From Vertical to Volumetric: prototypical Hong Kong*. Routledge.

Rahim, A., & Jamelle, H. (Eds.). (2007). *Elegance-Architectural Design AD. 77(1)*. London: John Wiley & Sons Ltd.

Schumacher, P. (2010). *The Autopoiesis of Architecture*. London: John Wiley & Sons Ltd.

Sterk, T., & Loveridge, R. (Eds.). (2009). *reForm() Proceedings of the 29th annual conference of the Association for Computer Aided Design in Architecture*. Chicago, Illinois: ACADIA

Tidafi, T., & Dorta, T. (Eds.). (2009). *Joining Languages, Cultures and Visions/Joindre Langages, Cultures et Visions - CAADFutures 2009*. Montréal, Canada: Les Presses de l'Université de Montréal.

Wang, X., & Schnabel, M. A. (Eds.). (2009). *Mixed Reality Applications in Architecture, Design, and Construction*. Amsterdam, Netherlands: Springer-Verlag. doi:10.1007/978-1-4020-9088-2

KEY TERMS AND DEFINITIONS

Architectural Computing: Architecture that is aided or generated by computational means.

Computational Architecture: Architecture and its design that arrived from or in collaboration with computational means, instruments or aids.

Design Education: The pedagogical approach to teach and learn to design.

Design Learning: Learning of how to design with the aim to become a good designer.

Design Process: The elements that contribute to the making of a design.

Parametric Designing: Designing using a parametric methodology that employs parameters, rules, and systems.

Parametric Design Studio: Design Studio that employs parametric designing as core method of enquiry.

Chapter 5
Direct Building Manufacturing of Homes with Digital Fabrication

Lawrence Sass
Massachusetts Institute of Technology, USA

ABSTRACT

Architecture, engineering, and construction industries maintain a long standing desire to enhance design communication through various forms of 3D CAD modeling. In spite the introduction of Building Information Modeling (BIM), designers and builders expect varying amounts of communication loss once construction has started due to indirect construction techniques or hand based methods to manufacture buildings. This is especially true for houses and small structures, buildings that makeup the core of villages and suburbs. Unfortunately, paper documentation and reading 3D CAD models on screen continue the trend of indirect production defined in most manufacturing industries as error. The emerging application of CAD/CAM within design and construction industries provides hope for elevated communication between design and building. With CAD/CAM, it is possible to manufacture buildings of all types and sizes directly from CAD files similar to mass produced artifacts, thus reducing complexity in communication between parties. This chapter is presentation of one process of direct manufacturing from CAD and the emerging possibilities for small building production using digital fabrication. The chapter will focus on houses to illustrate the potential of direct manufacturing of buildings from CAD data.

1. INTRODUCTION

For centuries, architects and builders have pursued systematic ways to design and deliver homes at low cost in production and high quality in output. New arguments around home production are directed at machine based manufacturing of buildings opposing common handcraft construction techniques (Kiernan & Timberlake 2005). This process, typically described as prefabrication, is a century old, westernized system of home production in factories by assembly of large units with cranes on site. It has survived many decades of reinvention while also struggling for

DOI: 10.4018/978-1-61350-180-1.ch005

broad acceptance as a worldwide industrialized system of building production (Davies 2005). In particular prefabrication has not caught on in developing countries or as a means to produce low cost housing in westernized environments.

This chapter argues prefab is complex in production maintenance, it suffers from the limitations of space and skilled labor, both impede the number of modules produced daily when demand for prefabricated homes is high. These factors also jeopardize the financial security of each manufacturer when unit sales are low. Also noted is the high cost of factory startup and operations curtailing new ventures within impoverished countries and states.

Digital fabrication or CAD/CAM is emerging as the next method of building delivery with built examples as experimental and exotic structures (Sass 2006) (Iwamoto 2008). It is a low cost, high precision manufacturing from CAD data commonly used today for furniture manufacturing. Specific to home construction one benefit of digital fabrication is that it can expand the range of production beyond the local contractor. With digital production manufacturers of metal, stone, plastic and wood based trades can fabricate components anywhere and at anytime. Manufactured components can be delivered to the project site or factory supporting assembly only production systems with low skilled labor. Digital fabrication of components assures component assembles with few discrepancies between the digital representation in CAD and the physical artifact. As a production system it allows for replication and recombination of digital models potentially supporting mass customized home manufacturing (Duarte 2005). Best is that digital fabrication can increase the efficiency of Building Information Modeling (BIM) by empowering *direct building manufacturing* from CAD based product models (Eastman 2008).

The grand challenge for *direct building manufacturing* will be discovery of new process pathways that bridge the physical divide between 3D building information models and machine data. This limitation stems from industry maintenance in hand tooling and assembly with handheld machinery as the core production method. For wood framed housing the standard material is dimensional lumber processed with standard tools such as power saws, screwdrivers and nail guns. Power tools and dimensional lumber do not take advantage of the efficiency of CAD modeling or CAD/CAM machinery. Precise machine cutting of is often difficult without special machine setups and rigging, the industry of wood framed housing maintains a need for highly skilled crafts people.

The aim of this chapter is to provide a context for digital fabrication as a mode of building production from a design by presentation of a process with two built examples. The chapter starts by presentation of industrialized manufacturing as the background for our home product manufacturing goals (Section 2). Next, past methods of controlled home manufacturing is presented illustrating the limitations and error in construction leads to higher cost and lower quality construction (Sections 3-5). Digital fabrication is presented as a method of production along with and explanation of its limitations (Sections 6-7). Materializing Design is systematic way to compute a design model for digital fabrication along with illustrations of the transformation process (Sections 8-9). The chapter ends by discussion on next steps as they related to the integration of other building systems such as plumbing, electrical, solar, etc.

2. INDUSTRIALIZED MANUFACTURING

As we stand at the threshold of new demands for energy-efficient green homes, we are also faced with the need for advanced systems that control design and home delivery. More than ever before, consumers expect new homes to perform in ways similar to mechanical products like automobiles, computers, and airplanes. Demands for increased building performance, reduction in cost, and speed in delivery all drive the desire for homes to be built in controlled environments.

The American housing industry supports three common home-delivery systems. The first—wood framing on site with dimensional lumber—is considered to be the least controlled by the designer. Here methods of production are governed by the local contractor and vary between contractors. The second form is factory-built homes as an assembly of framed boxes or prefabricated housing. Units are designed and manufactured in a factory setting as a way to control labor and materials processing. Last is a panelized system. The process starts with metal or timber framing infill with wood or metal panels. Both panelized and box fabrication require delivery by truck and on-site assembly with the assistance of cranes. All of the three methods are used by many home manufactures and designers.

The production of a prefabricated house starts with the customer's selection of predetermined designs from a catalog of glossy photos and renderings. Design styles are limited to rectangular shapes for easy transportation; cylindrical and nonplanar building shapes are uncommon. Once the order is placed, designers can then tailor each home to meet the environmental and regulatory needs of the town and site.

The efficiency of prefabricated production is its ability to standardize the mode of production. For example, the structural framing of most homes is assembled from dimensional lumber and plywood. In spite of the standards, though, every factory-made home requires some number of design changes due to variations in building site, codes, utility hookups, and the foundation. Therefore, paper drawings are generated for each new home project to guide the workers through production on the factory floor. After factory fabrication, local contractors are responsible for attaching the prefabricated boxes or panels to the foundation, as well as adding exterior siding, electrical and plumbing hookups, roofing, and finishes.

Unlike in the building industry, the design and production of goods in other major industries (e.g., automobile, computer, cell phone, aeronautical) is made up of *Original Equipment Manufacturers* (OEMs) whose responsibility is based on the assembly of products in factories (wheels, body panels, etc.), the result of which are branded products (Herbig & O'Hara 1994). The definition of OEM is not clear; each industry has its own terms and definition. In this chapter "OEM" refers to the producer of the home. Unlike home manufacturers, the assembler physically produces a minority of the assembled components; rather, they design, integrate parts, and assemble purchased products.

Digital fabrication makes this type of production possible by including the same or similar CAD data used in design as part of the machine manufacturing and assembly process. In the automobile industry, for example, integrated CAD systems are a critical part of manufacturing plastics and thin metal auto-body parts (Stauber & Bollrath 2007). Efficient production of plastic auto-body parts from a variety of vendors is possible because the design models from the assembler are shared by the designer and plastics fabricators (Figure 1).

Prefabricated-housing factories aspire to operate and to manufacture homes in ways similar to the OEM model. They fall short of this goal, however, due to wasteful processing and low precision. Although it is not a typical constraint in building construction, precision in manufacturing allows for the perfect fit between parts. Once high precision is available, manufacturers can have subcontractors compete to provide the factory with precisely fitting components at the lowest possible cost.

3. CONTROLLING DESIGN WITH DRAWINGS

A common theme in design control over quality, cost and time is controlled through documentation such as instructional books, CAD models,

Figure 1. Exploded diagram of a CAD model for a car produced by an automobile assembler. The chassis is built by one manufacturer, whereas panels, dashboard, and mechanical components are built by other manufacturers and then factory-assembled.

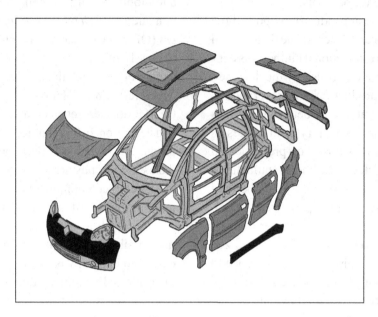

and design automation. One standing tradition is the control of style and process with rules illustrated on paper a method that dates back to the architectural treatise: Vitruvius (Vitruvius 1960) Palladio (Palladio 1965), Alberti (1986), and Serlio (1996). The seventeenth-century architect Durand pursued a similar interest through his *Précis des Leçons d'Architecture*, published in 1819—a text illustrating ways to build public buildings and statues (1802). A current form of design control can be found in architectural pattern books, which guide the production of styles and functions at the scale of a town or community (Gindroz & Robinson 2004). It is important to note that pattern books do not propose individual designs as an assembly of elements, such as columns, stairs, or window and door details, the way a treatise might. Instead, pattern books detail ways of organizing the physical elements of a community (streets, statues, street signs, etc.).

Contemporary design control as an automated process has been explored through shape-grammar methods and generative systems (Stiny 1980). A shape grammar produces designs in a certain architectural language via the application of shape transformation rules. These transformational rules allow for shape evolution from an initial shape. One example of shape-grammar production is the Queen Anne Grammar developed by Ulrich Flemming. The drawings that resulted from the grammar were used to produce designs for a pattern book as part of Pittsburgh's redevelopment initiative in the 1980s (Flemming 1987) (Flemming et. al 1986). More recently, a modern shape grammar called Malagueira Grammar was used to generate house designs in the style of Alvaro Siza (Duarte 2005). Both housing styles—Queen Anne and Malagueira—were generated by a grammar that resulted in 3D representation as drawings or CAD models. One valuable reason to consider shape grammars as a method of design generation is that the process can be automated. Unlike generating designs one at a time through keyboard entry of commands into a CAD program, an automated shape grammar program can, in minutes, generate hundreds of alternative design schemas based on a particular style. The customer can then select the best fit.

Unfortunately, all three examples (treatises, pattern books, and shape grammars) only demonstrate a way to produce design concepts and details as drawings for interpretation by builders. They do not control physical production, cost, or final product quality. Once the design is complete, all of these methods still require many laborious physical steps to build a home.

4. CONTROLLED DELIVERY WITH MACHINES

Alternatively, there are those who venture control over production by combining design and delivery. Architects and builders such as Karl Strandlund, Walter Gropius, Frank Lloyd Wright, and Konrad Wachsmann built delivery systems they hoped would make well-designed houses affordable. They collapsed the extensive relationship between the designer and contractor into companies that provided both.

Sears and Roebuck started the process through the sales of traditional and arts-and-crafts home styles from their catalog in 1895. They brought craft to the masses with a factory-based delivery system that employed artisans who had once built fine products from furniture to houses. A delivery system for housing was invented that gave access to customer-driven home design and delivery; no two houses were alike (Sears 1990) (Cooke & Friedman 2001). Variation was a major factor in sales and marketing. In time, over 400 designs, in many traditional styles, were offered to customers. Sears and Roebuck employed many artisans to manufacture components with handheld tools and machines in a well-lit factory. For efficient delivery, lumber pieces were precut and labeled before shipping by U.S. rail. The resulting assembly on-site was a balloon-framed structure clad with a variety of materials from shingles to brick. Sears and Roebuck survived as a home producer until the late 1930s, when it began offering financing as part of home sales, which unfortunately led to the company's destruction. Sears and Roebuck had positive sales combined with a negative cash flow.

By contrast, Walter Gropius, founder of the Bauhaus, an influential school of art in the twentieth century, was interested in a standardized, rational approach to design and home delivery (Gropius 1956). It was his way of countering crate-based variation in cost and quality due to variations at the hand of the artisan. His interest in moving past craft-based delivery systems to machine-based production was shared in the United States by his business partner, Konrad Wachsmann; together they started the General Panel Company in 1942 (Wachsmann 1961). Their product—The Packaged House—was a modest modern-style building expected to be factory built, delivered by truck, and assembled on-site with no postfactory production. It is clear in Wachsmann's writing that he thought machines and mass production were a means of controlling quality and cost. The machines enabled some automation in production. Wachsmann focused on the concept of element modularity as a way of controlling assemblies between machine-produced metal components. The Gropius–Wachsmann standardized building system considered ways of repeating the manufacture of one type of joinery with variations in panel production. They worked with standard metal machines of the 1940s set up in large spaces ready for building the components of many houses at one time. Unfortunately, the company was reduced to building only doors, and after five years of startup and preparation, it was unable to secure any housing contracts.

Finally, a notable contribution to the industry of home delivery was the Lustron House developed by Carl Strandlund in 1945. His houses were also factory-based products that took advantage of industrial machining and new materials processing. His company produced 2,500 homes from a handful of designed models available in four different color finishes. Exterior and interior walls were manufactured steel panels with a porcelain finish, assembled on-site with nuts and bolts (Knerr 2004). Each house was assembled from over 30,000 small components, which required many manhours in labor. In fact, the manhours needed to screw bolts and gaskets drove the house price out of the affordable range. The company lasted only nine years. It was not the concept of precise machinery in a comfortable controlled environment (i.e., the factory) that made the Lustron a short success. Its demise was due to a laborious assembly system and inflexible panel making that limited variations between designs.

Today's best prefabricated systems resemble the processes employed by Strundland and Wachsmann/Gropius—hand based, hand tooled with inflexible machinery—with the exception of a few factory-based methods in Japan (Noguchi 2003) and Europe and the use of digital design. Prefabricated housing companies continue the legacy of low-precision, high-cost production at the hand of the artisan. A notable step forward in production-based research can be found in a system that integrates a structural system into the design computing system (Benros & Duarte 2009).

5. ERROR AND THE ARTISAN

As mentioned earlier, this is not the case in the manufacturing of common industrialized products—such as cell phones, computers, and automobiles—that use the OEM model. In any product design process, prediction and elimination of error is a key activity in the design process (Goh et al. 2005). In contrast to product design, error in home construction originates from overlapping operations between construction workers and the process of visual interpretation of the drawings. This conflict is due to measuring and cutting components with manual tools, then re-measuring previously assembled building elements and new cutting. In construction, design and shop drawings merely illustrate "design intent." Workers can and do deviate from notations on the drawing due to unforeseen obstacles in the field. For example, the process steps in Figure 2 show a designer who produces data output as drawings. These are interpreted by construction workers (a). The information from the drawing is manually transferred to a material substrate (b), hand cut (c), and assembled with handheld tools (d). This low-precision process requires time for measuring and cutting each new element. Steps c, d and e in Figure 2 are then repeated for each new element (as when fabricating a stud wall), so time is needed in order to measure previously assembled studs and to deal with any inaccurate cutting of new studs. As the complete artifact is assembled, the elements may well have little or no relationship with the designer's drawings and models. In craft-based construction, every component is hand measured, hand cut, and assembled with little dimensional relationship with the original drawing.

Figure 2. Traditional craft-based home production starting with CAD drawings

  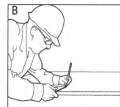  

6. CREATIVE USE OF DIGITAL FABRICATION

For higher precision in cutting and assembly, CAD drawings can be sent to a digital fabrication device for precise measuring and cutting. Digital fabrication is a flexible three-part process from digital modeling to a fabrication device and hand or machine assembly that brings together a relationship between materials, machining and CAD modeling. In contrast to the artisanal work discussed in the previous section, digital fabrication is computer-based measuring, computer-controlled cutting, and hand assembly of precise components. An extensive explanation of digital fabrication machinery, machining methods with examples is found in Schodek (2007). There are two flavors of digital production for the field of architecture.

The first being project based digital design and digital manufacturing. Digital fabrication in the field of architecture is defined by architects who create one-of-a-kind buildings as sculptural artifacts. Design commissions completed by architects such as Frank Gehry who fabricates buildings of metal and wood, theorist Greg Lynn and Bernhard Cache postulates ideas about fabrication through prototyping. Lisa Iwamoto, Nader Tehrani and Mark Goulthorpe are proof of the creative potential behind these new technologies by fabrication free form exhibitions of fabrication. These architects represent their designs with advanced curved surfaces as well as solid and parametric modeling software, and then physically produce complex designs by CAD/CAM manufacturing. They employ a combination of sophisticated technologies such as curved surface CAD modeling tools to simplify areas of design complexity. For most design and construction professional direct manufacturing is reserved for a few areas of construction such as building exterior only, interior surfaces, and the structural members only. A summary of one-of-a-kind projects and methods of production including both traditional and CAD/CAM fabrication can be found in Bernstein (2010). One built example of a creative design can be found in the Amsterdam Pavilion in lower Manhattan built of digitally fabricated plywood components. This project was modeled in CAD traditionally with key board entry of modeling commands. Components and assembly are with metal fasteners and a hand finished surfacing (www.unstudio.com). An example to follow is a project built by the Institute for Advanced Architecture Catalonia of a solar paneled house. This project is also a digitally fabricated plywood structure with assemblies sustained by metal fasteners (www.iaac.net/projects/fab-lab-solar-house-3).

The second type of digital fabricated architecture is as a production system where multiple iterations of a design are generated and manufactured. The first example Contour Crafting is one example of rapid digital fabrication of houses by using layered concrete dispensed from a computer-controlled machine. The greatest potential of Contour Crafting relates to housing in developing countries in need of original and replacement concrete structures (Koshnevis 2004). A second example of a production system is defined as materialization. It is a systematic method of subdividing geometry into constructible components ready for digital fabrication. A pilot project built summer of 2005 demonstrated the potential of digital fabrication as a system of building production. The project was a small cabin built completely of interlocking plywood components manufactured from CAD/CAM machines. The structure measured of 8' x 10' x 15', was elevated 24" off the ground. A detailed description of the process and computation can be found in Sass (2005) (2007). A second example of a materialized design was also constructed using from interlocking plywood components three year later. This version was constructed as part of a museum exhibition was assembled with few tools and assemblies that were sustained by friction from part interlocking (Bergdoll 2008). From these two examples of digitally fabricated structures it is possible to mass produce many of these buildings from the same data. It also means manufacturing is possible anywhere using similar machines controlled by computers. A series of construction rules were developed from the two examples.

Digitally Fabricated Structures

1. Computer generated designs are manufactured from computer controlled machines
2. A variety of complex components can be manufactured by the machine
3. The structure is built of layers of materials that compose a lattice & surface
4. Each element includes interlocking geometry for direct association with other components
5. Elements are fabricated as 2D parts
6. Parts are assembled with few tools possible to sustain by friction

7. PROBLEMS WITH DIGITAL FABRICATION

A core problem in digital design and fabrication is the many design steps associated with modeling physical objects in CAD as described by Sass and Oxman (2006). The paper outlines three limitations in design production: complexity in component design, generating assembly descriptions in CAD and scaling models from physical prototypes to full scale construction. Design automation can address these problems with computer programs built for rapid model generation. Researchers in electronic design automation use CAD tools and libraries to design and generate information for printed circuit boards (Jansen 2006). For digital fabrication automated CAD systems will aid in conversion of 3D design models to 2D data for digital fabrication CAD/CAM. An integrated process of design generation will elevate the impact that computational analysis and optimization tools have on designs and fabrication.

8. MATERIALIZING A DESIGN

A systematic process of object production is discussed here as a pathway towards building physically based automated design tools. This process, defined as *materializing* is intended for production of many 3D artifacts, the process assumes each artifact to differ in shape or composition of shapes with the same physical language of production. This system of production is alternative to methods used by design architects to build a kind of sculptural artifacts. *Materializing* is a computational production system that allows designers to rapidly realize visual and physical goals from three-dimensional CAD models. In summary, *materialization* is a three-stage process of shape transformation from (*a*) an initial shape model to (*b*) CAD/CAM manufacturing and (*c*) assembly by hand or with robots (Figure 3). The contribution of this system defines the mathematical relationship between the designer's CAD model and the physical building production—the critical step in the relationship between computer-aided design to computer-aided manufacturing. As for buildings a close relationship between flexible CAD modeling and flexible digital fabrication will lower process and material waste by removing process steps commonly found in craft based construction. The work in this chapter is not automated with CAD tools as mentioned above, however the format and steps provide a format for building product automation.

Alternative to the three part physical shape production illustrated above, building production requires many steps in translation. With computation quality and time is controlled by converting steps that would otherwise be handcrafted steps to computable steps. Figure 4 is an illustrated process summary that shows three of many computational steps in converting a design model generated in CAD to sets of machine tool paths. Each pathway assists full scale assembly of components with computable features between components. The first step captures geometric char-

Figure 3. Three step materializing process from a shape model (a) in CAD to laser cutting (b) and hand assembly (c)

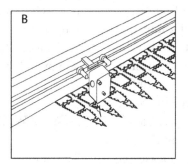
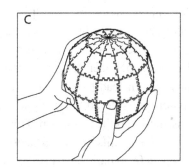

acteristic of the starting Shape for structural analysis and data storage (Figure 4). If the shape is structurally sound the next steps are focused on structural contours along the three axes (x, y & z) or a new shape is generated and edited for structural compliance. The new shape is composed of structural contours as interlocking geometries of varying depths depending on loading and location. The second step is the addition of attachment features to each contour, these features join the surface geometry with the contour geometry. Here the assembly alignment and final attachment between each element is an integral part of the elements geometry. Integral attachments of this type were popularized by research in plastics as a way to measure and manufacture plastic fasteners. The fourth step in the process is subdivision of exterior surface and contours into smaller parts related to the machine and material constraints. The resulting geometric model in a finished collection of elements defines a construction model (*Construction model*)). The last function is translation or development of three-dimensional elements to two dimensions (Manufacturing)a function is common in the field of descriptive geometry. Developed elements and their attachment features are packed and sorted in two-dimensions before final CAD/CAM fabrication. Construction modeling of the type in Figure 4 is complex, labor intensive CAD modeling through keyboard entry of commands.

Figure 4. Broad steps in materializing a model of a building from a shape model to a series of interlocking components

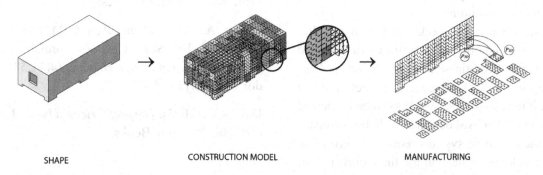

SHAPE   CONSTRUCTION MODEL   MANUFACTURING

9. CONCLUSION

This chapter starts by descriptions of houses as manufactured products designed digitally yet manufactured by hand. The claim is that a physical disconnect between tools in design and physical construction lead to errors in production unfortunately considered the rule and precision based construction is the exception. This imprecision in production results in many process steps in manufacturing from hand measuring and re-measuring by hand of previously built components.

Digital fabrication for home construction introduces precision in manufacturing, assembly and component integration. Precision manufacturing throughout the design and construction process elevates the impact and purpose of computation analysis tools and design optimization. The resulting components can be assembled on site with low skilled labor due to semantic nature of each piece.

Beyond this chapter, a search for holistic approaches to building design, computation and production requires further development in methods to generate component descriptions. In this text computational systems decompose an initial shape into sets of components for digital fabrication in ways similar to carpenters on site. This system also illustrates how the shape of a building can be analyzed and optimized for assembly and fabrication controlling cost and the quality of design delivery. Illustrated are abstract steps in construction modeling for the internal structure, external surfacing and final production data. It is considered first steps leading to design automation for digital fabrication only for the structure of a building.

Future work will seek integration of other building systems beyond structure into interrelated systems such as rain-screens, insulation, air-handling, electrical, plumbing, etc. It is believed that most if not all of these systems can be fabricated through CAD/CAM design as well. It also means that each of these systems requires re-invention and development beyond the three dimensional methods of common construction towards 2D productions that assemble into 3D buildings. New research in digitally based construction systems will lead to similar breakthroughs in construction where all systems can be designed rapidly in CAD and manufactured with machines.

ACKNOWLEDGMENT

The author thanks Dennis Michaud and Daniel Smithwick for their dedicated service in building the exhibit structure, the Department of Architecture at MIT, and the Rockefeller Foundation, which was the primary sponsor of the MoMA exhibit. Additional thanks go to the American Institute of Architects and Boise Cascade, as well as to Shopbot Tools for fabrication.

REFERENCES

Alberti, L. (1986). *The ten books of architecture*. New York, NY: Dover Publications.

Benros, D., & Duarte, J. (2009). An integrated system for providing mass customized housing. *Automation in Construction, 18*, 310–320. doi:10.1016/j.autcon.2008.09.006

Bergdoll, B., & Christensen, P. (2008). *Home delivery: Fabricating the modern dwelling*. New York, NY: Museum of Modern Art.

Bernstein, P., & Deamer, P. (2010). *Building (in) the future: Recasting labor in architecture*. Princeton Architectural Press.

Cooke, A., & Friedman, A. (2001). Ahead of their time: The Sears Catalogue prefabricated houses. *Journal of Design History, 14*(1), 53–70. doi:10.1093/jdh/14.1.53

Davies, C. (2005). *The prefabricated home*. London, UK: Reaktion Books.

Duarte, J. (2005). Towards the mass customization of housing: The grammar of Siza's houses at Malagueira. *Environment and Planning B, 32*(3), 347–380. doi:10.1068/b31124

Durand, J. (1802–1805). *Leçons d'Architecture Partie Graphique des Cours d'Architecture*. Paris, France: Chez l'Auteur.

Eastman, C., Teicholz, P., Sachs, R., & Liston, K. (2008). *BIM handbook: A guide to building information modeling for owners, managers, designers, engineers, and contractors*. New York, NY: John Wiley & Sons.

Flemming, U. (1987). More than the sum of parts: The grammar of Queen Anne houses. *Environment and Planning B, 14*(3), 323–350. doi:10.1068/b140323

Flemming, U., Coyne, S., Pithavadian, R., & Gindroz, R. (1986). *A pattern book for Shadyside: Technical report*. Department of Architecture, Carnegie-Mellon University, Pittsburgh, PA.

Gindroz, R., & Robinson, R. (2004). *Urban design associates: The architectural pattern book*. New York, NY: W.W. Norton & Company.

Goh, Y., McMahon, C., & Booker, J. (2005). Development and characterization of error functions in design. *Research in Engineering Design, 18*, 129–148. doi:10.1007/s00163-007-0034-x

Gropius, W. (1956). *The new architecture and the Bauhaus*. Boston, MA: Charles T. Branford Company.

Herbig, P., & O'Hara, B. (1994). The future of original equipment manufacturing: A matter of partnership. *Journal of Business and Industrial Marketing, 9*(3), 38–43. doi:10.1108/08858629410066854

Iwamoto, L. (2008). *Digitally fabrications, architectural and material techniques*. New York, NY: Princeton Architectural Press.

Jansen, D. (2006). *The electronic design automation handbook*. Kluwer Academic Publishers.

Kiernan, S., & Timberlake, J. (2005). *Refabricating architecture: How manufacturing methodologies are poised to transform building construction*. New York, NY: McGraw-Hill.

Knerr, D. (2004). *Suburban steel: The magnificent failure of the Lustron Corporation, 1945–1951*. Columbus, OH: The Ohio State University Press.

Koshnevis, B. (2004). Automated construction by contour crafting-related robotics and information technologies. *Construction and Automation, 13*(1), 1–19.

Noguchi, M. (2003). The effect of the quality-oriented production approach on the delivery of prefabricated homes in Japan. *Journal of Housing and the Built Environment, 18*(4), 353–364. doi:10.1023/B:JOHO.0000005759.07212.00

Palladio, A. (1965). *The four books of architecture*. New York, NY: Dover Publications.

Sass, L. (2005). A wood frame grammar: A generative system for digital fabrication. *International Journal of Architectural Computing, 1*(4), 51–67.

Sass, L. (2006). Synthesis of design production with integrated digital fabrication. *Automation in Construction, 16*(3), 298–310. doi:10.1016/j.autcon.2006.06.002

Sass, L. (2007). Synthesis of design production with integrated digital fabrication. *Automation in Construction, 16*(3), 298–310. doi:10.1016/j.autcon.2006.06.002

Sass, L., & Oxman, R. (2006). Materializing design, the implications of rapid prototyping in digital design. *Design Studies, 26*, 325–355. doi:10.1016/j.destud.2005.11.009

Schodek, D., & Bechthold, M. Griggs, K., Kao, K., & Steinberg, M. (2007). *Digital design and manufacturing: CAD/CAM applications in architecture and design*. New York, NY: John Wiley & Sons.

Sears & Roebuck. (1990). *Home builders catalogue, The complete illustrated 1910 edition.* New York, NY: Dover Publications.

Serlio, S. (1996). *Sebastiano Serlio on architecture: Books I–V of Tutte l'Opere d'Architettura et Prospetiva.* New Haven, CT: Yale University Press.

Stauber, R., & Bollrath, L. (2007). *Plastics in automotive engineering: Exterior applications.* Munich, Germany: Hanser.

Stiny, G. (1980). Introduction to shape grammars. *Environment and Planning B, 7*(3), 343–35. doi:10.1068/b070343

Vitruvius, M. (1960). *The ten books on architecture* (Morgan, M. H., Trans.). New York, NY: Courier Dover Publications.

Wachsmann, K. (1961). *The turning point of building.* Wurzburg, Germany: Reinhold Publishing Corporation.

KEY TERMS AND DEFINITIONS

BIM: Generation and management of building data, typically a 3D model, throughout its life cycle representing spaces, products and some means and methods of production. The model can be updated for changes made between design, finished construction and renovation.

Construction Modeling: 3D component based description of a design in CAD. This description challenges component at the scale of assemblies. Each digitally fabricated component is represented in 3D.

Design Modeling: 3D description of a design in CAD. This description is a formal representation used for visual evaluation of a design.

Development: Development follows the term developable, as in geometry that can be flattened to 2D from a 3D shape.

Digital Fabrication: Direct manufacturing of physical artifacts from CAD files.

Layered Manufacturing: Similar to additive manufacturing where artifacts are produced from layers of material. Each wafer thin layer is manufactured from a CAD model and automatically assembled to the previous layer.

Materialization: Translation of a 3D design model into 2D elements for CAD/CAM manufacturing.

OEM: Original equipment manufacturer is the company that originally manufactured a specific product.

Rapid Prototyping: Automated production of a physical 3D object from a CAD description.

Chapter 6
Building Information Modeling and Professional Practice

Dennis R. Shelden
Massachusetts Institute of Technology, USA

ABSTRACT

The practice of architecture is changing rapidly due to an influx of new technical, procedural, and organizational innovations in the building delivery process. Building Information Modeling (BIM) is a key technical component of this evolution in practice, encompassing newly available modeling, fabrication, and communications technologies. BIM represents a key enabler of other innovations, by creating value and incentives for rethinking aspects of conventional practice, from contractual roles and responsibilities to the format and content of project information.

INTRODUCTION

In this chapter we consider the general trends of computational applications to design from the specific vantage of practice – the methods, activities, and conventions beyond the designer or engineer's office and outward to the collaborative enterprise of realizing built projects. These are the core considerations of Building Information Modeling (BIM) – a set of advances, founded on technological developments but broadly pointing to new ways of working. BIM is specifically concerned with the activities of documenting and communicating aspects of the design throughout the processes of project execution. These include the development of building permit and contract documents, engineering solutions, instructions for fabrication and placement of components in the field, and a host of other activities.

BIM is about tools, but more significantly about how building projects are developed and the role of information in these activities. Rather than consider the topic from the emergence of specific tools sets, it is perhaps more appropriate to consider the topic from the vantage of activities – how new tools enable new ways of working, what tools must be developed to allow alternative means of production, and how production and technology are likely to evolve given advances in both.

The term Building Information Modeling itself covers a broad territory of inter related advances and as such is somewhat is ambiguous, referring to both the tools themselves as well as the overall processes, and new techniques in conjunction with

DOI: 10.4018/978-1-61350-180-1.ch006

existing methods. Over the many overlapping attempts to define BIM, the most succinct may be the best. The AIA contract documents state:

" A Building Information Model … is a digital representation of the physical and functional characteristics of the Project … which term may be used … to describe a Model element, a single Model or multiple Models used in the aggregate. "Building Information Modeling" means the process and technology used to create the Model" (AIA, 2008).

Building information Modeling is, roughly, the tools through which project documents are developed and the collaborative processes by which this documentation is developed and used. It is specifically applied when we consider project descriptions and delivery processes centered on three dimensional, information rich models of project geometry and systems. But by nature of the data driven approach to developing such information, the term potentially encompasses not only the three dimensional artifacts directly developed through BIM processes, but also by implication all other data that can be derived from or linked to 3D.

BIM's impact on the profession of architecture assumes the level of significance that it does, in part because of the fundamental layer at which its impacts occur. Because BIM impacts the substrate of architectural communications – the graphical and geometric structures of instruments of service - its implications are broadly felt across architectural work and the overall building enterprise. These impacts are profound due to the subtle and myriad ways in which the conventions of practice are interwoven with those of two dimensional project descriptions, and the ways in which practice must retool to support fundamentally new descriptive techniques.

In "pre-bim" practice, many aspects of 3D and even information intelligent models and drawings exist. 3D software has been used for rendering and animation for over twenty years, while three dimensional models have been used

for analyzing the performance of structural systems for a similar time period. Two dimensional CAD systems have, for over two decades, supported the ability to develop drawing symbols with attributes that can appear on a plan and also be extracted to tabular schedules (for example doors and windows, room names and sizes, etc). By in large, however, design information is communicated through disaggregated two dimensional drawings, and it has been up to the diligence and intelligence of designers to maintain the coordinated view between different drawings and other documents. This process of red lining and quality control – a process of immense intellectual labor on even the simplest projects – is one of the areas of practice that BIM most substantially impacts. The state of BIM in practice is still a long way away from what is believed to be promised – a unified view of the project and all its descriptions and uses. But simple and profoundly beneficial utility is available through current BIM capabilities for automating the coordination of information across different subsets of the project description. Drawings – still a foundation of much of inter-and intra firm communication – can largely be generated from the 3D model. Automated annotation is largely available and used, as is the ability to selectively render objects on a given drawing and affect the linework associated with different building systems. Additional effort is required to create the initial project model versus developing a two dimensional drawing set, but the efficiency benefits over time – in updating drawings and quality controlling – already outweigh the costs.

The second fundamental characteristic of BIM of great impact on project delivery is that BIM takes formerly *static* drawing information and makes it *operative*. Traditionally, project documents are developed to convey specific information content within a specific context and with stated or implied limitations of use. As project descriptions become increasingly operative –where design descriptions have the capacity to impact project decisions far beyond the specific intent under which they were created – the conventions by which projects are controlled and, indeed, by which they are delivered, become increasingly called into question. The use of a BIM model developed by the architect has potential or repurposing for activities throughout the project supply chain – often well beyond the level of resolution or determination developed during the design phase.

These combined impacts – replacing the structure of design communication from a predominately two dimensional and often symbolic medium to one that is directly spatial in nature, and drawing on a means of documentation that is operative beyond the specific context of its authors' intentions – together combine to create a context for practice that is profoundly different than that of the past century. New conventions must be defined, and are being defined in real time on contemporary projects. These fundamental changes can be more or less contained in the mechanisms of existing practice, but often at the loss of the potential for broader opportunities that are suggested by more sweeping changes.

A "SIMPLE" BIM PROCESS

In order to illustrate the potential, variabilities and complexities of BIM based collaboration, it make sense to offer a snapshot of how a project might be conducted through the exchange of BIM data. This example illustrates the potential applications as well as some of the shortcuts – or reversions back to conventional practice – that take place in today's evolving landscape of practice.

The process begins in the architect's studio, in communication with the client, during schematic design. The building design at this stage is fluid and absent of much of the construction and even programmatic detail. Building masses are developed using three dimensional solids, and general program areas are identified within these masses. Basic structural notions are incorporated but the precise layout of columns, beams and secondary structural elements are likely not incorporated.

The goal at this phase is to lay out a concept that compellingly solves the building program requirements, given a very preliminary understanding of the building's final systems and performance.

The models may interchange with other media – physical models can be developed from the project geometry by direct or indirect means – cutting building elements with laser cutters or from elevation studies, or 3D printing of massing models. The generative formal techniques discussed in other sections of this book are increasingly drawn in developing the project's formal qualities and may become part of the overall BIM project record that is evolved over the development of the project. The BIM geometry may be incorporated into computer renderings, with the addition of entourage or detailed geometry that suggests but does not define the final resolution of the design.

Figure 1. 3D printed massing model- Architect: Gehry Partners

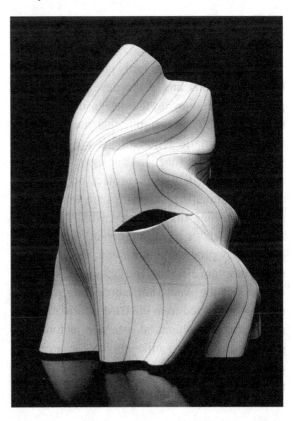

Figure 2. Two dimensional plan produced from the BIM model-MIT Stata Center, Architect: Gehry Partners

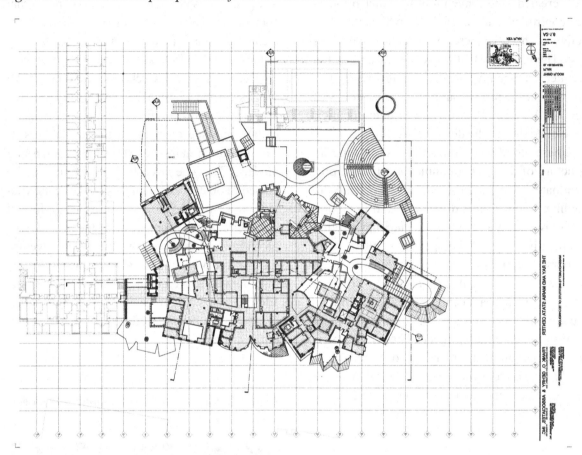

A critical output from this phase will be sections, elevations and plans developed for the purposes of conveying the design intentions to the client, and demonstrating that at a high level the programmatic requirements are satisfied: required program functions and associated areas are incorporated, overall project organization and programmatic relationships are worked out, and the building fits on the site while observing zoning offsets or other site conditions. Critical preliminary program information - heights from grade, program elements and associated areas are indicated on the plans. Simple budgeting activities may be conducted from the BIM information, as rough area or volume takeoffs are factored by precedent costs for similar projects to arrive at rough project cost given the level of knowledge available.

There will likely be several or many iterations through these activities; some will be shared with the client while others represent simply transitional states in the architect's internal design process. These activities can be satisfied using many available tools, both those labeled as BIM tools as well as many other software applications that are perceived to be "just CAD". These tools all present greater or lesser difficulties in achieving each of these activities and the interchanges between them, and sometimes the simpler tools are the easiest and most effective. The critical aspect of this phase in terms of collaboration is that the interaction is between the designer and client, the information is preliminary, and the level of detail required for construction is not needed at this point in time.

Figure 3. Integrated system BIM model - One Island East Tower

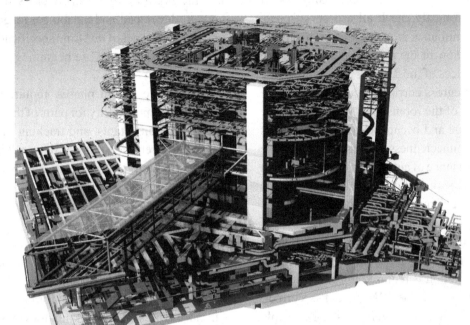

During successive design stages, the design team expands to include structural, mechanical and other specialist consultants. Questions of division of responsibility, partitioning of authorship, and establishing relationships and processes between parties' work become more critical during this phase. An expanded set of performance analysis models and tools becomes part of the collaborative information development, including structural analysis solvers, wind loading and energy modeling tools, mechanical equipment sizing algorithms, etc. While some of these analyses can be conducted within BIM authoring tools, many of these studies are carried out in external engineering solvers with information exchange between these tools and the project model(s).

The BIM model may be organized as an aggregation of separate models associated with each of the engaged firms, with means to overlay the models into some common viewing environment. Or, models may be passed back and forth between parties, checked out by one party to edit and then returned to a repository with distributed access.

Clash detection techniques allow automated means of quality controlling the integrated model, by detecting locations where the work of one party conflicts spatially with that of another. The "collaborative red-lining process" begins to include a process of detecting these conflicts and assigning responsibility for remodeling one or more systems' designs to remove these coordination errors. Automated drawing production is again used to produce drawings from the individual or aggregated models, and various additional reports are extracted from the aggregated model, including schedules and tables of information that become part of the working tools of designing the project and the end products of approval and contract documents.

Automated checking of additional project requirements, including the potential for checking project systems for code compliance – are beginning to become available. Such tools have the capability of analyzing dimensional information in the models against those required by code. The sophistication or complexity of code requirements still exceeds the capabilities of software to robustly check all aspects of code, and code compliance requires a level of fidelity and information in the models that exceed the current practices of most firms. For example, the sizing of an egress corridor requires knowledge in the model of the rooms this egress serves, the square footage and occupancy of each room, as well as the connectedness of the spaces along the corridor. Existence of automated fire suppression systems and the fire rating of enclosure materials also impact the sizing or egress. There are complex relationships between many different aspects of the overall design that require consideration of many special cases. And robust quality control of this information is required to ensure that the input provided into the BIM model is correct; minor changes to a few parameters (for example mis-labelling the occupancy of a space) can have major impacts on the correctness of the resulting code calculations. However, we can anticipate that as BIM practices become more central to firms' practices the utility of such automated techniques will become pervasive.

The intelligence of the information collaboratively developed during this phase becomes a more significant issue of consideration. The structural definition and architectural intentions are intertwined; the structural grid, and elements of the superstructure have both architectural and engineering implications and require authorship by both architect and engineer. Various means for undertaking this collaboration in a shared information process have been devised, but all expose the problematic aspect of assigning responsibility in an iterative, collaborative process. The architect may control certain aspects of the design – say the exterior envelope, while the engineer maintains the structural grid and locations of columns. Or the architect may define the overall grid and structure, while the engineer is allowed access to size the elements.

During the final phases of design document development, additional sets of data are integrated into the overall project definition. Specification texts are developed, and capabilities for generating or linking passages of text from specifications with elements of the model are beginning to become available.

During the design phases, requirements for allocating responsibility for parts of the BIM data set among consultants, and tracking of changes among different iterations of the model, are low relative to the requirements in later phases. The engagement between designers and engineers can be fairly free flowing and collaborative, and indeed must be necessarily so given the degree of change that can occur over design iterations. At the end of contract document phases and beginning of tendering questions of control, permissioning, and permitted usage of BIM information become far more critical. The working drawings become part of the contract between owner and builder, and the correctness, completeness, intent and use of information provided to the builder are critical components of this relationship. The role of the BIM data as part of the contract documents is a critical question in the collaborative development of the project during tendering and construction phases. At the point of writing, many projects using BIM provide only the output two dimensional documents as part of the of the formal contract documents, not the 3D models themselves. When these models are provided, they are often provided with restrictions on usage and instructions that the builder has no right to rely on the models, or that in cases of conflict the two dimensional drawings supercede the information in the BIM model. This aspect of the project collaboration – whether BIM data is provided by the design team at all, and if so what authority the contractor is permitted to assume in the data provided, creates a significant point of departure in how the project unfolds during bidding and construction phases.

If provided as part of bid documents, BIM models provide a wealth of information that can help clarify or delineate the scope of the project. For example, quantities of materials and piece counts of components can be derived from the model and used as part of pricing exercises by bidders. When not provided by the design team, contractors are increasing developing BIM models for the purposes of understanding the project and developing their own, more operative, views of the project documents from the two dimensional documents.

During construction, models are of potential utility for many aspects of the further development of project details, construction, and communication between design and construction teams. Further detailed design and engineering of building components is conducted by the contractor and subcontractors, that expands the intent expressed in the contract documents to the point where actual fabrication and installation can occur. This work may be conducted by repurposing the geometry provided by the design team, and the enhanced fabrication descriptions are typically communicated back to the design team through submittals. For example, a steel column may be represented in the design BIM as a correctly sized extrusion of the appropriate steel section. But additional engineering and associated geometry is developed as part of the scope of the steel subcontractor – splice locations and construction details are developed, bolt and plate geometry and engineering design occurs. Some of this additional intent may be directed by the design team in detail drawings or performance requirements, but other aspects are the purview of the fabricator in determining the means and methods of construction. Once the proposed detailing is approved, additional information may be developed to provide the specific shop tickets by which elements are fabricated in the shop, including potentially tool paths of CNC (Computer Numerical Controlled) fabrication equipment. Concrete walls and slabs may be broken into individual pours by concrete contractors, and formwork, scaffolding and other temporary work may be developed by the contractors in 3D. Additional clash detection and quality control in the aggregate will typically be conducted by

the contracting team, to ensure that the further detailed elements are of the correct size and do not conflict in space, prior to actual fabrication and construction.

The evolution of project information conducted by the contracting team is substantial, to the effect that a second, *construction BIM*, derived from but distinct from the *design BIM*, is developed by the construction team. This model will include additional detailing, additional geometry of construction systems, different ways of breaking the project up into scopes of work, and additional attributes on project geometry. The construction BIM may be developed by extending the provided design models, and certainly can be overlaid with the design models for comparison and error detection.

Sequencing and assembly models may be developed, that tie project schedules together with component geometries to plan and assess the process of installation – both temporary works as well as the final project components. The BIM geometry may be used for fabrication, placement of components, and quality control of location. Increasingly BIM is integrated with digital surveying techniques: placement points may be pulled from the model, and provided to digital surveying equipment to allow semi-automated positioning of building elements.

More recently, point cloud surveying capabilities are used to broadly sample site conditions, either to verify that components are correctly developed, or to adjust the locations or attachment points of components placed later in construction based on the exact location of primary building systems.

At the end of construction, the aggregate BIM data set – including the original designs, perhaps revised to accumulate decisions and changes made during construction, combined or resolved with the construction BIM, maybe be provided to the owner as an electronic record of the project. This information may be linked to documents such as warranties and operating manuals and provided as an electronic record set or "as built" model.

Figure 4. Construction BIM with temporary works in 4D model - Marina Hotel, YAS Island, Architect: Asymptote

Figure 5. BIM Model with overlaid cloud of points surveying - Lincoln Center – Alice Tully Hall. Architect: Diller Scofidio + Renfro

Figure 6. BIM model used in facilities operations

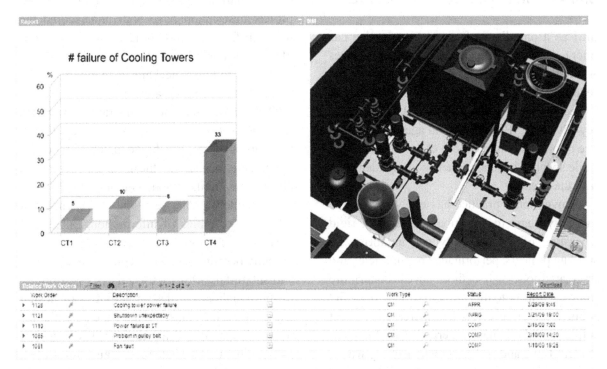

These models may be integrated with facilities management systems or environmental control systems and become part of the ongoing operation of the project. If so used, an ongoing process of continual BIM development must be assumed by the building owner / operator, as changes to the building begin to occur through ongoing use of the facility.

The above view of the use of BIM in the evolution of building projects demonstrates the transitional state of building development. Many aspects of BIM processes are used to develop enhance or support traditional project information development and consumption. The use of BIM is integrated with traditional practices, and not infrequently the ambitions of collaborative information development and use are tempered by current limitations of specific parties' abilities, the persisting efficiencies of some less information rich processes, or the lack of precedent and agreed upon practices for specific information interchanges in the contractually established communications between design team, owner, approval agencies and contractors. The application of BIM practices is expanding at a very rapid rate, and we can expect that many of these issues will become resolved over time and become part of established practice, some potentially by the time this manuscript is published and read. In the mean time, BIM has established significant value in many aspects of project delivery, even as it occurs in conjunction with conventional ways of working.

This section has outlined some of the many ways that BIM is being used in practice – to serve specific functions and activities as well as to form the underlying basis of overall project information development and collaboration. The sections that follow describe in additional detail some of the technical, procedural and contractual challenges of applying BIM as a medium for project development.

BIM AND INTEGRATED PRACTICE

BIM as a paradigm of change in practice has emerged in synergy with other recent advances in practice. Certainly a related evolution is the general topic of integrated practice or Integrated Project Delivery (IPD)[1]. As with BIM and other key advances, IPD is a general agenda in the nature of practice that is as of yet unresolved, even while specific instances are becoming identified with the agenda.

Conventional practice has evolved over the past fifty years to encompass aspects of rigid separation of responsibility and authority. As building projects, performance requirements and associated codes and methods have become more complex, the potential for errors and potential liability for these errors has increased. Project delivery methods have emerged with the intent of identifying and isolating responsibility within the overall scope of what is a complex and inter-related collaborative enterprise. This evolution of identifying scope and responsibility has occurred relative to specific features of traditional project

documentation development. BIM's impacts on project description have both underscored the necessity for revisiting the underlying assumptions of how responsibility is allocated and tracked, as well as providing a mechanism enabling alternative models of collaboration.

There are many types of documentation used on projects, and it is worth considering a few of them in specific. The broad palette of project documentation includes the usual plans, sections, elevations, details, but also includes study models or rendering data sets, text documents, and schedules or tables of information. Subsets of these are used in formal, contractual services – specifically permit documents, contract documents, and submittals. Other data is used less formally in the collaborative design activities of design and engineering firms. All have the potential for integration by BIM. While the complete treatment of BIM in a unified data set remains unfulfilled, project models are increasingly at the heart not just of practices within firms, but also beyond.

Conventional design – bid – build practice is organized as a hierarchy with simple document

Figure 7. Industry contracting organization

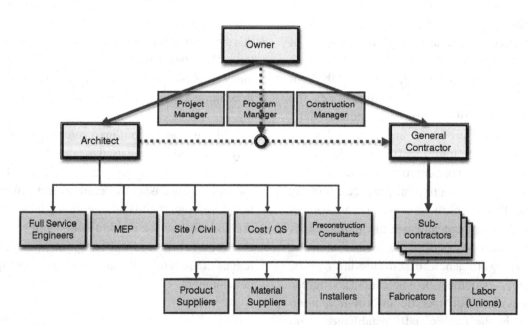

controls in place that map to this organizational structure. Documents and communications flow between parties along these communication channels, and even informal discussions between parties across the hierarchy are controlled and often restricted.

Mapping against this is the flow of 2D documents and their contents across project boundaries. In conventional practice, authority, responsibility, risk, and compensation structures are marked against the development and distribution of drawings. The drawing represents a defined container of information that defines a specific set of project information, often in a format that is partly geometric but also partly symbolic in nature. This restricted view of the overall project in specific documents serves to define boundaries of scope, responsibility, liability and ultimately intent of the authoring designer. Responsibility for the information content of any specific drawing in the collaborative aggregation of project information is assigned to a specific party of the project. This responsibility is both contractual – representing the delivery of information purchased from the particular entity – and legal –certifying that the document has been developed with the professional standard of care by the signing professional. The responsibility for extracting this intent into further project information – perhaps by a fabricator for shop drawings – typically falls on the receiving party, who revises the received document with further intent and perhaps modifications.

Two dimensional CAD represented the first potential erosion of this specific taking of authority in the preparation of documents. With the availability of technologies by which information could persist across the specific project representations provided by individual organizations without specific acts of transcription, the distinction of responsibility has become less clear. An architectural background that "appeared" in the structural documents affected an automated transfer of content between different collaborators. Errors could propagate unnoticed between disciplines in

a manner that has become increasingly difficult to trace and assign responsibility.

BIM has significantly increased the ambiguity of responsibility between the collaborators. A building element may require authorship by multiple parties, but this authorship potentially occurs on a common component within the BIM and the ability to contain individuals' authorities in a potentially integrated database of evolving components in an integrated context is far less clear. Instead, BIM offers greatly improved means for visualizing the performance and potential conflicts across disciplines, through a common spatial repository of design decisions across parties. Specific sets of building objects – potentially associated with specific parties of the design process, can be combined into a common spatial and visualization environment. The potential for detecting and correcting errors is substantially higher than that formerly possible by visually comparing individual drawings, and the aggregate coordination model is potentially available to the overall team and the members of all organizations on the project. Automated software for detecting spatial interferences between parties is commonly available in these environments.

In contemporary BIM practices, the overall project database is often still disaggregated into specific data sets authored by the individual parties of the project, and the overlay of these different data sets does not require the individual objects to be subsumed into a common project database. In other words, the aggregate building models are still overlays of individual building information databases developed and identified with specific parties to the project.

BIM AND PROJECT TIMELINE

BIM methodologies impact the level of required completeness of the design intent expressed in the design team's documents in important ways. The term *design intent* is one that implies specific expectations and also limits. In practice, the scope of information contained in contract documents is necessarily limited and incomplete. Traditional contract documents do not completely delineate all geometry of all systems, but are developed in order to express only the *necessary* intent for the purposes of procuring the project and demonstrating compliance with regulations. The requirement for filling out the project geometry to a level necessary to build falls on others within the construction team. Conventional documents are in aggregate developed to widely varying degrees. Overall building plans and sections have relatively simplified geometry of building systems and do not convey all of the details of subsystems. Specific detailed drawings are called out in the documents that illustrate detailed assembly conditions, including the layering of subsystems. Building systems must be expressed somewhere in the documents, but the entire variability of the geometry of these systems at each location are not expressed. The result is an aggregate set of information that has specific and varying localized levels of detail and geometric resolution.

BIM has the potential to required significant additional resolution in the description of project geometry, if models are to become part of the provided project documentation. When BIM models are used solely for the purposes of providing traditional sets, this requirement is less clear. But when BIM models are provided as a basis for 3D project delivery methods one can not provide models with varying levels of geometric detail across the project and expect the models to be used in any consistent fashion. The level of detail of resolution is still not "complete" in BIM based processes, nor is the required level of detail provided by any participant resolved in the conventions of practice. But in order for contractors to rely on the information it must be correct and complete to an understood level of detail, if the data in the model is to be used for extraction of quantities or for the basis of developing submittals. "The reality is that drawings and specifications have an inherent level of ambiguity and questions which architects and contractors do not know the answers to until the work is underway in the field. Design intent itself may not be fully understood until all parties contribute their knowledge" (Lum, n.d.).

In conventional documentation, the construction team is not permitted to directly rely on the geometry in the drawings as the basis for construction, but only those dimensions which are explicitly called out in the documents. These explicitly expressed dimensions are required to be observed in construction, in order to satisfy code compliance and perhaps minimum standards for the building's performance. These might include the required offset of a door jamb from a wall corner, or minimum dimensions of building materials in an assembly developed in a system detail. The dimensions which are not explicitly called out in the documents are the responsibility of the construction team to define and coordinate in response to a number of conditions including construction tolerances, circumstances discovered in the field, etc. The design team, in turn, is required only to develop a set of design intentions that offer the potential of being satisfied by the builders. This illustrates the deliberate ambiguity or lack of specificity in the design process, and the realm of design development that is left to parties beyond the design team.

Unlike drawings, BIM models do provide explicit geometric definition, even in cases where the precise geometric conditions are not fully known given the detailed construction the contracting team is responsible for. This creates a paradox where the geometry provided potentially contains more information than the design team can actually commit to. A roof may be somewhat thicker than the architect could anticipate given a particular construction system. Or the nominal dimension may be correct but some ambiguity is required given construction tolerances.

One can imagine a similar approach being applied to conditions where BIM models are provided as part of the contract documents. The models would be provided as an overall geometric framework, but the construction team would only be allowed to rely on specific dimensions that are

Figure 8. Level of detail table - AIA document E202

§ 4.3 Model Element Table *Identify (1) the LOD required for each Model Element at the end of each phase, and (2) the Model Element Author (MEA) responsible for developing the Model Element to the LOD identified.* *Insert abbreviations for each MEA identified in the table below, such as "A – Architect," or "C – Contractor."* *NOTE: LODs must be adapted for the unique characteristics of each Project.*															Note Number (See 4.4)
Model Elements Utilizing CSI UniFormat™			LOD	MEA	LOD	MEA	LOD	MEA	LOD	MEA	LOD	MEA	LOD	MEA	
A SUBSTRUCTURE	A10 Foundations	A1010 Standard Foundations													
		A1020 Special Foundations													
		A1030 Slab on Grade													
	A20 Basement Construction	A2010 Basement Excavation													
		A2020 Basement Walls													
B SHELL	B10 Superstructure	B1010 Floor Construction													
		B1020 Roof Construction													
	B20 Exterior Enclosure	B2010 Exterior Walls													
		B2020 Exterior Windows													
		B2030 Exterior Doors													
	B30 Roofing	B3010 Roof Coverings													
		B3020 Roof Openings													
C INTERIORS	C10 Interior Construction	C1010 Partitions													
		C1020 Interior Doors													
		C1030 Fittings													
	C20 Stairs	C2010 Stair Construction													
		C2020 Stair Finishes													
	C30 Interior Finishes	C3010 Wall Finishes													
		C3020 Floor Finishes													
		C3030 Ceiling Finishes													
D SERVICES	D10 Conveying	D1010 Elevators & Lifts													
		D1020 Escalators & Moving Walks													
		D1030 Other Conveying Systems													
	D20 Plumbing	D2010 Plumbing Fixtures													
		D2020 Domestic Water Distribution													
		D2030 Sanitary Waste													
		D2040 Rain Water Drainage													
		D2090 Other Plumbing Systems													
	D30 HVAC	D3010 Energy Supply													
		D3020 Heat Generating Systems													
		D3030 Cooling Generating Systems													
		D3040 Distribution Systems													
		D3050 Terminal & Package Units													
		D3060 Controls & Instrumentation													
		D3070 Systems Testing & Balancing													
		D3090 Other HVAC Systems & Equipment													
	D40 Fire Protection	D4010 Sprinklers													
		D4020 Standpipes													
		D4030 Fire Protection Specialties													
		D4090 Other Fire Protection Systems													

7

indicated by the design team. However, such an approach would invalidate much of the potential efficiency of providing the project geometry in the first place.

The preferred alternative is to provide the geometry of the project to some explicitly defined level of detail, with defined provisions on the intent, use, and ability or restrictions on parties' right to rely on this geometry. This notion of level of detail as being developed in synergy with intended use is captured in some of the emerging standards for BIM usage and contractual definition. The American Institute of Architects has recently developed a contract document (AIA, 2008) concerned with the provisioning and maintenance of BIM data for the project. The document is intended to be incorporated by reference into the Owner Architect agreement and similarly incorporated into other follow on contracts, including the owner contractor agreement. The document describes several levels of detail (LOD) with corresponding authorized and intended use of the information, from LOD 100 which corresponds roughly to overall building massing analogous to schematic design documents, through LOD 300 which corresponds to the level of detail of "traditional construction documents and shop drawings", while LOD 500 corresponds to as-built documentation of the final project. Project teams develop this agreement by specifying the level of development provided for the varying project systems, phases and the Model Element Author (MEA) that is responsible for the authoring of the information, and is responsible for the quality of the information provided. This structure allows models to be developed and used with some standard agreements in terms of useage and required level of detail.

ENCODING THE LOGIC OF PRACTICE

The practice of project delivery is conducted according to rules. These rules are developed and described across manifold media. Some rules – such as codes or methods of structural solution – are explicitly developed. Other rules are not explicitly defined at all, but rather may be considered part of the "standard of care".

Many rules of practice can be seen to directly impact the products of practice and – the rules of practice impact the structure of the ensuing documentation. This notion - of the geometry of designs being rule driven and being traceable back to the logics of design – has been a subject of research in computation and design for some time. However, this agenda has been complicated historically by a number of factors.

First, the rules of practice on the one hand, and those of the geometric logics on the other, have evolved over centuries. Many of the rules of practice have not been explicitly defined, are those that have been defined are often incomplete, and may be occasionally self conflicting. The most explicit such rule sets are found in the building codes. Some of these rules are prescriptive, in that they provide specific instructions for the organization of building elements. These rules include egress rules, for example the layout of stair treads, rises, and maximum distance of travel between landings. Others are more performance based, in that they mandate not the specific organization of building elements, but rather the outcomes of system performance when applied within the context of the overall building organization. Such rules might include the maximum deflection of a floor given prescribed occupancy and loading conditions.

These rules make reference to the ultimate products of design, not their descriptions encoded in design documents. The rules of documentation exist in the heritage and culture of practice, but are not explicitly proscribed. Texts exist to guide the education of the practitioner in the techniques and conventions of drawing, but there is wide variability in the specific conventions of plan, section, elevation and detail development.

Much research has been done to deduce the rules of shape organization and project description of various building typologies, including automating aspects of code compliance. Generally in these techniques, some representation of the overall three dimensional organization of the design is required. Some of the most successful such developments are concerned with analysis and solution of building structures. For more than three decades, finite element structural analysis techniques have been used to automate the design of aspects of building structural systems. These techniques initially automated the analysis of structural performance, but have rapidly incorporated the ability to determine the optimal sizing of structural frame elements given required loading conditions. The introduction of these techniques has radically altered the work of structural engineers. Before the advent of finite element analysis, a majority of the engineers' efforts were directed toward manually performing the required calculations of stress, strain and deflection. The requisite calculates were performed member by member throughout the frame.

The automation of this work has radically impacted the day to day work of structural engineers. Where analysis and calculation previously formed the predominant work before, the design of the structural system has taken on an increased percentage of the engineering work. This design work includes the selection of structural systems and materials, and defining the macro and micro spatial organization of the overall building massing and the individual member locations. The documentation of the project itself has changed, from individual sheets demonstrating the load and response calculations of individual members to generating overall reports and tables of member performance from the analysis software. Building structural systems are increasingly optimized by considering the overall system's performance as a totality, resulting in lighter and more efficient building frames. And, of course, these techniques have enabled more complex project geometries to be solved for, freeing designers to incorporate the

contemporary generation of building geometries as part of the potential set of design alternatives.

These developments have significantly impacted the practice of structural engineering discipline, and came about by the emergence of digitally founded technique. However, as this advance occurred in the context of a single profession, its total potential impact was constrained by the necessity of expressing the results of this advanced technique through traditional project communications. The process of documenting the structural systems in the project working drawings required manual drafters to interpret and apply the description of the digitally derived results back into less operative information sources.

This example illustrates a one central point: without a global, cross disciplinary project approach to building information, point solutions can have significant impacts on specific problems in the building delivery process but are constrained in terms of the overall project impact. Second, three dimensional representations are a critical component of advancing the process of building delivery, simply because the process of developing building intelligence from two dimensional representations requires techniques for re-integrating building knowledge between disparate representations. While this reconciliation work has been done for centuries by building practitioners, it is fraught with potential error, conflict, ambiguity and inefficiency.

AUTOMATION OF DESIGN INTENT

One of the more promising aspects of BIM based project delivery is the ability to apply automated or generative procedures to the detailed design and documentation of building systems. As previously discussed, in conventional project development, detailed studies of component assemblies are usually undertaken by the design team only for typical or isolated special locations in the building.

The effort required to manually design document every condition in its full geometric instantiation prior to construction would vastly increase the cost of developing these documents beyond what clients are prepared to pay for design services. This cost is further exacerbated by the burden of maintaining this level of detail over frequent design iterations. For these reasons, the burden of determining exact conditions into their actual geometric resolution is left to the construction phase and performed by the contractors and subcontractors. This, however, creates significant problems since the design is purchased on the basis of incomplete information, which may in fact contain infeasible instructions that are detected only after tendering. The application of these detailed instructions – when applied throughout the project – are a source of many of the RFIs (Requests For Information) communicated by the construction team, and a source for errors and changes in cases when the specified detailed construction instructions turn out not to be exactly applicable to the site conditions.

Automation techniques change the dynamics and economics of this relationship when applied as part of detailed design development. Computer generated detailing can vastly increase the knowledge of the localized expression of system strategies, and can be refined or modified over multiple iterations with far less cost than traditional manual production methods. Parametric techniques can allow detailed project geometry to automatically adjust to dimensional changes in the project geometry. These techniques are allowing far greater insight into the system configurations before tendering, allowing greater confidence of designers, owners and bidders that the proposed systems will work, and reducing the prices of bids by reducing the factors of safety that bidders apply to accommodate for unknowns in the designers' instructions.

This ability to incorporate additional and more detailed knowledge before contracting greatly changes the dynamic between designer and builder, implicitly shifting the line of responsibility and authority toward the design team. This creates the opportunity for the architect to have greater control over the detailed qualities of the design, and to have greater confidence in the feasibility of the design, and implicitly to affect the demarcation of design intent versus means and methods of construction, and potentially the standard of care of practice.

CONCLUSION

This chapter has described aspects of Building Information Modeling from the perspective of its impacts on practice. These impacts are expansive and expanding. BIM impacts not only the operations of design, engineering, procuring and building, but the roles, responsibilities, authority and dynamics of project control.

This manuscript is written at a time of ongoing change in practice, fueled by both changes in project description and parallel changes in project delivery. We can expect that these changes will continue for the next decade and in doing so radically affect the traditions of practice and the nature of what it means to be a design professional within the collaborative context of building.

REFERENCES

AIA. (2007). *Integrated project delivery: A guide, version 1*. AIA National / AIA California Counsel.

AIA. (2008). Contract document [Building information modeling protocol exhibit.]. *E (Norwalk, Conn.)*, 202.

Lum, E. (n.d.). *On design intent*. Retrieved from http://www.aia.org/practicing/ groups/kc/ AIAB081947

ADDITIONAL READING

Eastman, C. (2009) What is BIM? Retrieved April 18, 2011 from http://bim.arch.gatech.edu/?id=402.

Eastman, Teicholz, Sacks, and Liston (2011) *BIM Handbook: A Guide to Building Information Modeling for Owners, Managers, Designers, Engineers and Contractors.* Wiley

General Services Administration's National 3D-4D-BIM Program (2007-2009). Retrieved April 18, 2011 from http://www.gsa.gov/ portal/content/105075.

Jones, S. (2008) *McGraw-Hill Construction SmartMarket Report on BIM.* Retrieved April 18, 2011 from http://construction.ecnext.com/coms2/summary_0249-296182_ITM_analytics

Kymmel, W. (2008). *Building Information Modeling: Planning and Managing Construction Projects with 4D CAD and Simulations.* New York: McGraw Hill.

Messner., et al. (2009) BIM Project Execution Planning Guide. Retrieved April 18, 2011 from http://www.engr.psu.edu/ ae/cic/bimex/index.aspx.

National Institute of Building Sciences. (2007), National Building Information Modeling Standard (NBIMS) Version 1.0. Retrieved April 18, 2011 from http://www.wbdg.org/ bim/nbims.php

Smith, D. (Ed.). (2007-2011) Journal of Building Information Modeling, a publication of the National Institute of Building Sciences (NIBS). Retrieved April 18, 2011 from http://www.wbdg.org/ references/jbim.php.

Smith and Tardif. (2009). *Building Information Modeling: A Strategic Implementation Guide for Architects, Engineers, Constructors, and Real Estate Asset Managers.* Wiley.

KEY TERMS AND DEFINITIONS

4D Modeling: Modeling that incorporates BIM with construction scheduling to simulate and analyze construction logistics.

AIA Contract Documents: A set of standard contract templates that delineate the transactions, roles and responsibilities of owners, architects, contractors and other parties in building design and project execution. The AIA documents are frequently used as the basis for contracts in the US. Other contract standards such as the ConsensusDOCs and regional standards define organizational models that are generally similar but may differ significantly in the specifics of parties' responsibilities.

Building Information Modeling (BIM): A set of modeling technologies and techniques that draw on 3D and metadata rich models of building objects and collections to automate tasks including modeling, drawing and information extraction, and communication.

Computer Numerical Controlled (CNC): Fabrication machinery that can be controlled by digital descriptions of tool paths and other machine operations. CNC fabrication can be driven from BIM model geometry to automate aspects of physical modeling or component manufacturing.

Integrated Project Delivery (IPD): A collection of project delivery innovations including contractual, technical and other changes to conventional practice to improve communication and collaboration, information sharing, and overall project efficiency. IPD is often used with BIM modeling and data sharing technologies and in often pursued specifically to support enhanced building information sharing among project participants. IPD is often used specifically in reference to the teaming or alliance relationships among parties as expressed in the AIA Contract Document C191-2009 "Standard Form Multi-Party Agreement for Integrated Project Delivery" and related documents.

Parametric Modeling: 3D modeling that generates geometric configurations through formulaic relationships among shape descriptions and other object parameters. Parametric modeling is used in BIM applications to embed design, engineering and fabrication intent into building models, by encoding these intentions as geometric rules and relations on object geometries.

Project Delivery: The collective activities, transactions, and deliverables involved in the realization of a building or other construction project. Project Delivery includes design, engineering, planning, bidding, fabrication, and construction.

Chapter 7
Advancing BIM in Academia:
Explorations in Curricular Integration

Karen M. Kensek
University of Southern California, USA

ABSTRACT

In the early stages of the adoption of Building Information Modeling (BIM), the AEC (Architecture, Engineering, Construction) professionals were often the leaders, and some university faculty were caught unprepared. More recently, many universities have responded to the adoption of BIM technologies in the profession. No single approach to BIM curricula will suffice; each academic program is different, with unique and often innovative ways in accomplishing its goals of BIM integration. At USC, School of Architecture, rather than concentrating on a single strategy, multi-dimensional approaches are being developed that include at their core the recognition that the building delivery professions and academia must be better integrated, communication and interoperability are key components, and that BIM is one step, albeit with flaws, towards developing fully parametric design solutions. BIM technology should be broadly integrated throughout the curriculum; advanced seminars should stress interoperability and sustainability components; and the schools have a mission to outreach to the profession through conference hosting and executive education while being receptive to professionals' advice. Not everyone is in agreement as to how this can be done or what methods should be implemented, and similar to the integration of CAD software and 3D modeling over the past 20 years, dissenting voices, heated dialogues, and solutions born in the crucible of academic/professional debate will accompany change.

BACKGROUND

"A computer-aided design system is most useful when the structured design inside the computer can be used for something besides merely producing a picture. As soon as the process of computer-aided design is considered as building a description of the object being designed rather than as a process of simply drawing the object, horizons become tremendously expanded." Ivan E. Sutherland (1973) – quoted from Mark Smith (about 1986)

DOI: 10.4018/978-1-61350-180-1.ch007

Ivan Sutherland was one of the earliest developers of computer graphics through his invention of Sketchpad and other systems. Still over 35 years ago, he was looking beyond the merely pictorial aspects of his creations to what would eventually become object based modeling, user-defined parametrics, and the current concept of the virtual building or Building Information Modeling (BIM, although an inaccurate term, will be used to refer to a 3D modeling program where objects are parametrically driven with data attached). Key players that assisted in the development of 3D solid modeling were often from engineering fields such as aerospace and electrical design, "where early concepts of product modeling and integrated analysis and simulation were developed" (Eastman et. al. 2008, pg. 27). Ironically, in many schools it was 2D CAD and not 3D modeling, let alone parametric design, where architecture students experienced their first interaction with mouse and monitor in developing their designs. As late as 2007, when 2D and 3D modeling, rendering, and animation software were in use by a majority of architecture students, and BIM software was available, it was lamented that although CAD was everywhere, and students saw it as an essential tool towards getting a job in the profession, BIM was harder to find in the curriculum (Ibrahim 2007, p. 653).

As more firms use BIM software, increasing numbers of students and faculty are realizing that this enabling technology should be explored at the university level, not only as just another software package, but as a way to investigate the changing nature of the architecture and construction professions with regards to Integrated Project Delivery (IPD), collaboration, sustainable design, and even facilities management and "smart" occupancy of buildings. (Becerik-Gerber and Kensek 2010, p. 146). This chapter outlines some goals within a university environment and specifically three strategies to incorporate BIM into the curriculum of a school of architecture. By no means are these presented as the only methods; there are additional

exciting and innovative approaches occurring at other universities. These examples are partly based on the successes and failures that have been achieved in the past twenty years for the integration of other digital technologies.

The three strategies being pursued are:

- *BIM Technology:* Broad integration throughout the curriculum. This section has examples from an introductory seminar, a required professional practice course, and reflections about integration in the design studios.
- *Advanced Seminars:* Interoperability and professional connections. This section traces the evolution of an advanced course on BIM over several years.
- *Engaging the Profession:* Executive education and conference hosting. This section summarizes two methods of continuing education for professionals and how professional education is reflected back into academic courses. One special topic seminar is summarized that demonstrates this feedback loop.

STRATEGY 1: BIM TECHNOLOGY:BROAD INTEGRATION IN THE CURRICULUM

To be enthusiastically accepted by students, BIM education must be presented as an integrated part of the full curriculum of the architecture program. It is important to integrate BIM into the course work from the earliest stages, especially in non-computing courses, but also not neglecting advanced elective courses where teaching can go into more depth without the overload associated with the design studio. Although this goal has not yet been fully realized, this section briefly summarizes an introductory computer course, a required professional practice course, and different approaches to integrating BIM in the design studio.

Introductory Architectural Computing

The first implementation of BIM at USC was its incorporation into an elective introductory computer course. Initially, assignments were given in both ArchiCAD and Revit as examples of BIM software, a "new" type of software conceptually different from the modeling, rendering, and animation programs more frequently in use by architects. As the importance of BIM became more apparent, the course started focusing more on the issues involved with this emerging technology. This course is currently based on the assertion that the architecture and construction professions are facing at least three important transformations: The integrated practice and transformation of its delivery systems, the re-emergence of sustainable design, and BIM – BIM as a digital paradigm shift that is likely to have wider implications than CAD did on the structure of the architecture office and the relationship of architecture to construction, engineering, and facilities management. In the class, BIM is explored as a method for achieving 2D/3D coordination and designing parametric objects, but more importantly, as a method for interoperability between performance based software. There has been increasing sophistication, accuracy, and user friendliness of software available for performance-based simulation including daylight harvesting, energy calculations, and carbon footprint calculations. Included with this has been an increased desire and ability to provide better integration between geometric and analytical models, a "complete" virtual building model that contains the necessary information to predict the behavior of a building while it is still digital. Performance simulation is becoming increasingly common, and although used heavily by engineers, "the full integration of simulation within the design process is far from complete" (Kolarevic and Malkawi 2005, pg. 93).

Interoperability and the transfer of information becomes a significant issue in the course as the students examine the intersection of BIM and sustainable design – ideas of solar access, weather tools, basic energy concerns, and carbon footprint calculations (Figure 1). The students' readings support these themes and reinforce the premise that "BIM and sustainable design do not yet have the perfect marriage of integrated parts to make the solutions obvious and accessible. Yet we recognize the need within the design community to inspire better design through communication and knowledge management. This will greatly assist us to trying to get our carbon footprint to zero so that we can create a healthier planet" (Krygiel and Nies 2008, pg. 209).

One significant problem with the class was that it was trying to accomplish too much in eight weeks. The course was expanded with more units and class time. This enabled it to have the resources to more strongly integrate two other key topics: (1) investigations of the opportunities of parametric conceptual modeling used with energy simulation software (Figure 2), and (2) a stronger emphasis on the role of BIM in the construction industry including project team integration and collaboration, clash detection, project phasing, and code checking.

Required Professional Practice Course

Since spring 2009, the School of Architecture has experimented with extending the scope of an NAAB required undergraduate professional practice course on project documentation and the virtual office to include BIM and other changes in the profession. Under the leadership of Professors Enright and Dombrowa (later with Kensek, Gerber, and Lampert), it has been offered in this modified version three times so far and will continue evolving as BIM technology changes. This work built upon the cross-curriculum teaching that Enright successfully explored while at Sci-Arc in a class that brought together design and

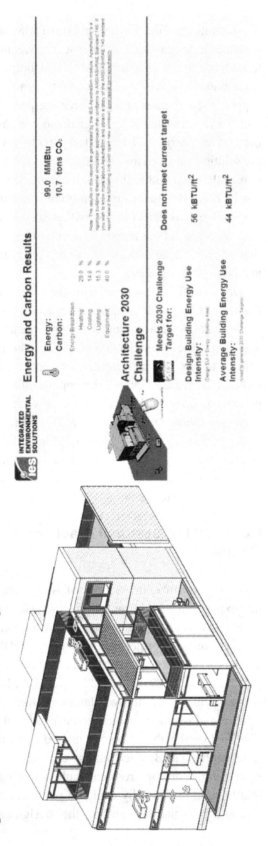

Figure 1. Revit and IES, student example, Daniel Camin. (2008, USC. Used with permission)

technology, integration of building systems, and construction set documentation (Enright 2009).

"The course concentrates on the comprehensive manner in which architects communicate built form with technical drawings and documentation to create construction documents. This includes a review of the laws and regulations that affect the practice of architecture as they relate to the creation of construction documents including permitting, review and regulatory agencies, planning and building codes. A parallel lab portion of the course uses BIM as a tool to develop the skills to create comprehensive, fully coordinated, and dynamic construction documents." (from the course description, spring 2010) (Figure 3)

In 2010, Digital Project was introduced into the class to compliment Autodesk Revit Architecture that was primarily used the previous year. Section times were set up to specifically teach software. The lecture portion of the content remained largely unchanged except for a few enhancements. Implementing a grant by NCARB, Enright was able to augment the course with presentations from leading firms that demonstrated real-life BIM scenarios and provided the opportunity for professionals to directly interact with students in individual desk critiques on their projects. In addition, the class size grew due to the increasing enrollment of graduate students. The 136 students were split into two groups for the lab section: Revit Architecture and Digital Project. The two software programs' strengths and weaknesses asserted themselves in the assignments. An end-of-the-term internal assessment was conducted. There were two major criticisms of the integration of BIM in the course, one focused on student perceptions and the other with philosophical differences in the profession. It was apparent that several students were unhappy with the split between those that were taught Revit Architecture versus Digital Project. As many assignments in the course targeted construction

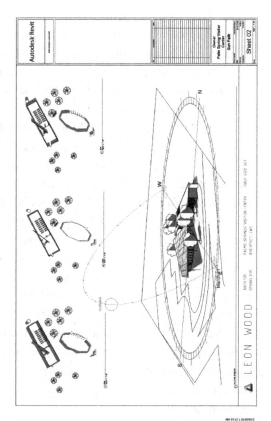

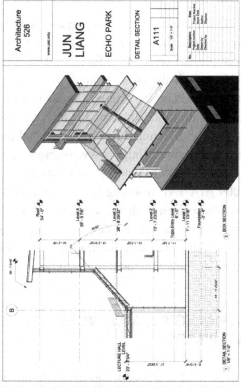

Figure 3. Revit detail student example, Jun Liang and sun path diagrams, Leon Wood. (2010/2011, USC. Used with permission)

documentation, Revit users had a clear advantage as many of its tools are designed precisely for that. Yet, Digital Project was seen as "more advanced," and some enterprising students were able to create parametric models by the end of the semester that were more complex than those developed by the Revit users. The second issue was whether or not the course should focus on more traditional 2D construction documentation supplemented with 3D views or have the students explore methods of using only 3D documentation as a method of communication between architect and contractor.

In 2011, it was decided that all the students would learn both software programs with a split emphasis on construction documentation and the implications of parametrics in design development. Additional evening help sessions were set up, and the class project changed from being mainly one of documentation to a small design project. It was a tremendous amount of work for the students. Continuing discussions (with the additional assistance of the Vice-Dean Murphy, Undergraduate Chair Kimm, Director of M.Arch. Programs Borden, Prof. Coleman) about the future development of the course are focusing on how to balance workload, more strongly integrate the required lecture material with the homework assignments, and strengthen the forward thinking aspects of the course. It is expect that the 2012 version of the course will continue to evolve. More emphasis will be given to the role of collaboration and teamwork in a project-based environment, exchange of information through multiple software programs, and increased participation of visiting professionals. The students need to not only learn software and understand the current implications of BIM, but be enthusiastic and visionary about the sweeping changes that BIM is causing in the profession and what directions it may be heading. These include the opportunities afforded by technologies such as CNC fabrication, smart phones and tablets, cloud servers, and others. The fundamental changes in this required professional class will ripple through other required courses in both the undergraduate and graduate curriculum.

Design Studio

BIM technologies are being applied by students in their design studios both in the undergraduate and graduate programs. In a bottom-up approach, some students have independently decided that BIM is an imperative part of their design process – or at least a useful method for coordinating their 2D drawings with their 3D models. Hand drawings, physical models, and other methods of representation remain supported and are integrated with the BIM model. As with the introduction of CAD into the curriculum over two decades ago, there has been contention over the appropriateness of one brand/type of software over another. In addition, the range of responses from faculty has included some trying to ban the use of BIM software in their studio to others embracing its use. Appropriateness to the task, learning objectives of the studio, and individual student skill set are three of many considerations. It is expected that these kinds of dialectics will continue for many more years. Slightly discouraging is that some of the arguments used against BIM were first heard as arguments used against the use of CAD over 20 years ago. More encouraging have been professor evangelists in the studio who employ BIM in creative ways, whether it is for advanced parametric design in graduate studios or an undergraduate studio in design development. The following course description discusses the use of BIM to develop construction documents; linking it to performance based software for energy and natural ventilation studies and structural analysis; and collaboration between students at another university.

"Integrative Reconstruction: The first phase of the studio will develop and fully document five separate building designs for reconstruction in Haiti. We will design two single family residential types and three community / commercial types. These will all be built in Haiti, probably within the next year, using Structural Insulated Panels (SIP) developed by Pacific Green Innovations and currently being manufactured on site. We will evaluate design alternatives and evaluate environ- mental performance using BIM software models in conjunction with the Arch 519 class and the Arch692a class. We will also meet with and exchange ideas and feedback with a similar topic studio at Cal Poly Pomona [author note: the instructor at Cal Poly is Juintow Lin] working on the same building types. The final product for each building type will be a full set of documents detailing each and every building component as well as a set of installation instructions for assembly by semi-skilled Haitian labor. Because these projects are "real" - they will be built prototypes, which, depending on results, may be replicated throughout the country - the emphasis will be on design as the optimization of resources for maximum performance in structural and environmental terms." (partial course description, Eric Mar, fall 2010)

Other universities are doing an excellent job with fully utilizing BIM in the design studio. For example, the IP/BIM studio at the University of Wisconsin-Milwaukee School of Architecture and Urban Planning offered a studio that brought together multiple stakeholders to "create a collaborative communal enterprise around professional objectives" (http://www.aia.org/practicing/groups/kc/AIAB079440). This was one of the 2009 AIA TAP Building Information Modeling awards recipients in the category of academic program or curriculum development and is just one of many excellent examples that strategically integrate BIM into the design studio.

STRATEGY 2: ADVANCED SEMINARS

The new BIM tools open avenues for the design and delivery of a substantially improved building product. To begin to achieve these goals, the participants must do more than simply adopt the technology as BIM is as much about process as about product. The students not only have the opportunity to research the current state-of-the-art in practice, but also to explore new ways of working. It is intended that they learn how BIM will change the profession that they will be entering and how they can help implement that transformation.

Advanced Computing Course: Performance, Parametric, Interdisciplinary, Explorative

BIM as a tool readily allows itself to be paired with other pertinent architectural concerns. This graduate level course, in many respects, mirrors issues faced in the undergraduate elective: 2D/3D coordination, parametric families, sustainable design, and constructability. The author is still trying to find a balance in her course that teaches specific skills in BIM and incorporates these items. The course has been offered three times so far, evolving, but in all cases trying to respond to the idea of performance based architecture including sustainable design, parametric development, interdisciplinary concerns, and explorative design issues.

Performance Based and Sustainable

A goal in the class is to explore BIM's potential to be used for communicating and transferring building geometries to performance-based tools that can test assumptions and design ideas. Students explored intra/inter operability with energy simulation software, 3D modeling and rendering programs, structural design, tools within the BIM program itself (shadow casting, green material databases), and others (Figure 4). These explorations were not always successful. One drawback is the lack of true interoperability between software programs. Interoperability is not only a moving target, but also a goal that changes intent and complexity, and it is unlikely

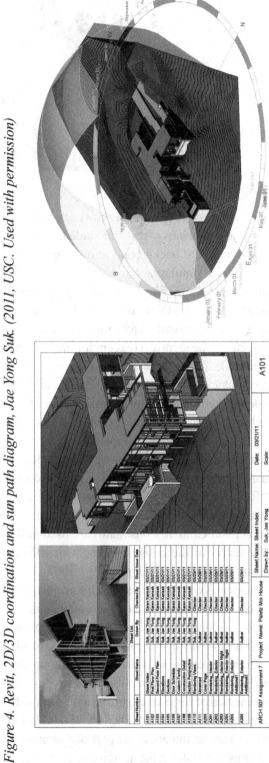

Figure 4. Revit, 2D/3D coordination and sun path diagram, Jae Yong Suk. (2011, USC. Used with permission)

Figure 5. Revit, exterior and interior renderings, Jae Yong Suk. (2011, USC. Used with permission)

to be fully resolved. Another drawback with the course assignments is that the students did not always have the background knowledge to run sophisticated simulations. So although the images can be compelling (Figure 5), the actual numeric values produced in the software (daylight factors, energy usage, and carbon footprint) were strongly suspected to be incorrect (except for the sun path diagrams). This course is not primarily about energy calculations or lighting design; and the students' simulations are approximate and are used to help roughly shape design decisions. The course is not intended as a replacement for more advanced energy, lighting, or sustainable design classes. In an interesting reversal, Lin describes a "Tools for Sustainability" professional elective where software described earlier (for example, Ecotect and Climate Consultant) are used in the early stages of the design process with BIM as the sub-theme (Lin 2010, pp. 189 – 196).

Student Kenneth Griffin used his project from this class in a different course on energy simulation to explore seven different energy programs and examine why heating and cooling load results varied based on the software used for the simulation, its underlying assumptions, and strengths or weaknesses of his own expertise with each software program (Figure 6). The role of simulation should also be integrated as part of the process that is used to inform the design (for example, in

the design studio) so that it can change as the graphic and numeric results provide feedback; in one example, this was done for sustainability analysis including sun shade design and lighting simulations (Techel and Nassar 2007). This provides a high degree of cross-pollination between building science courses and the design process.

Parametric

A second incarnation of this course maintained the essential principles of BIM and sustainable design, but focused more directly on the opportunities afforded by the development of architectural parametric families. Combining two technologies, parametric modeling and performance calculations, BIM has the opportunity to enable architects and engineers to explore performance based concepts early in the design process. For example, by adding data to the parametric objects, it is possible to produce digital models that allow for studies on areas such as solar energy collection, water harvesting, energy savings, CO2 reductions, and daylight usage. BIM is a convenient nexus for this type of integration. Assignments were given to encourage the students to develop their own "green" families.

Typical of student homework assignments, the results ranged from somewhat simplistic to highly interesting, from "the family doesn't work" to

Figure 6. Revit model and comparison of heating and cooling loads in seven different energy programs, student, Kenneth Griffin – instructor Professor Murray Milne. Note that the bars on the charts are not the same height indicating that different results were coming from the different software programs. (2009, USC. Used with permission.)

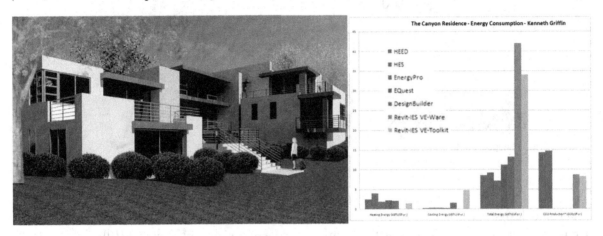

"this is an excellent idea." A list of their submitted proposals includes solar panels and mechanical air handling units (Figure 7), rainwater collection tanks, operable louvers and sun screens for window shading, bike racks for LEED points, low-E and dual glazing window specification, recycling bins, solar hot water heaters, wind turbines, light shelves and skylights, roof ponds, green roofs, Trombe walls and straw bale construction, solar powered radiant floor, low flow toilets, and "five easy LEED Revit family points" (Kensek 2009, pp. 31 – 35).

Other parametric studies were also tried using adaptive components where the students were given a limited scope design project in this case, a parametric bridge (Figure 8). This assignment will be expanded in future semesters to include structural calculations determining member size as the parameters change.

Interdisciplinary

The third incarnation of the course still focused on 2D/3D coordination, interoperability with

Figure 7. Revit air handling unit and PV families, Victor Aspurez and Xing Wu (2009/2010, USC. Used with permission)

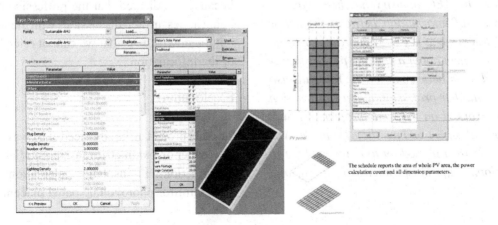

Figure 8. Revit, adaptive components, student Jae Yong Suk (2011, USC. Used with permission)

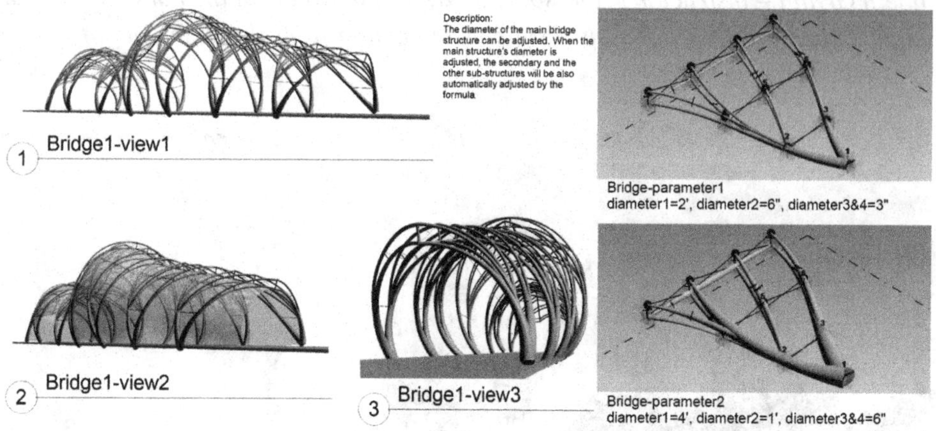

sustainable design tools, and parametric design. Due partly to the presence of construction management and civil engineering students in a class dominated by architecture graduate students, additional emphasis had been added on the role of BIM in the construction industry. This also fit well with the assertion that "in the absence of owner and designer-driven BIM efforts, it is vital that contractors establish leadership in the BIM process if they are to gain the advantages for their own organization and better position themselves to benefit from industry-wide BIM adaption" (Eastman et. al. 2008, pg. 208).

For the final project, teams of two students each developed case studies of BIM process based on this assertion:

"One stumbling block in seamless integration of BIM in the AEC industry has been gaps in the transfer of information between the major players. Interview a key BIM coordinator at an architecture firm about a specific project that is completed or is near completion. You will also interview another professional at a construction firm that worked on the same project. You will discover and report on how the BIM model was created and then passed on to the next stage of its development, what problems occurred, and

how to improve this process." (description from course assignment, spring 2010)

The students, through readings and other research, were also suppose to supply insights on how to improve the use of the BIM and its transfer between the architecture and construction firms.

The author was surprised to discover how difficult it was to find architect/contractor teams who were willing to share experiences and information about the process – usually either one or the other volunteered, while the other demurred. It was also intended that the students' case studies would be edited, verified, and then made public. Major stumbling blocks to this have occurred, especially legal concerns presented by both the architects and contractors that their private comments be made public. This was a positive point because it indicated that the professionals were being honest in their discussions with the students, but the downside is that we cannot release much of the information.

Explorative

Another project in the advanced class was inspired by a paper on parametric massing studies used in combination with insolation calculations, which are useful for photovoltaic panel placement and natural daylighting decisions. It described a high-rise project where conceptual, parametric tools allow architects to explore alternatives based on both qualitative and quantitative feedback during the initial design process (CASE Design 2010). The intent was to bridge the divide between design and predictive analysis and provide examples where analysis informs design, and the design evolves based on the performance goals and results. The students developed simple conceptual massing studies that were informed by solar radiation studies and programmatic requirements. The main objective was not to produce any single design, but to instill in the students the importance of iterative design development using BIM and performance based tools (Figure 9). The results from this assignment were mixed; further thought will be needed to develop it into a more informative project. A less complex version of this assignment was also included in the undergraduate elective course.

STRATEGY 3: ENGAGING THE PROFESSION

A University's educational mission must reach beyond their main constituents, the full-time student population, to the profession. It is critical that this is a two-way relationship. In the two examples described below, the School of Architecture has brought together professionals in sessions moderated by faculty to explore BIM. The information produced in these continuing education sessions and symposia inform both the profession and academia to critical issues in building information technology.

Executive Education 2010

In summer 2010, USC launched an executive education series to appeal to top level practitioners. BIM was chosen as one of the topic areas of prime importance and was developed in conjunction with Professor Gerber. When the event was originally planned, the faculty set up a framework and a series of presentations by industry leaders that would focus the participants' thoughts and inquiry into the subject of the future of BIM and its impact on the profession including building the business and profitable BIM; information transfer; risk mitigation; the architects', contractors', and owners' perspectives; computational and exploratory design; BIM + the Academy; and BIM disasters or is BIM missing the point. At times, it even appeared that BIM shared its headline status at the executive education session with a related topic, IPD (Integrated Project Delivery) – incentives, contracts, variations, and the importance, but also legal consequences, of collaboration. In retrospect, the coming together of industry leaders was informative, but the outreach to those who really needed the knowledge could have been better orchestrated. The second summer Executive Education was offered, the intent shifted towards a strong emphasis on fewer projects being discussed with much greater detail and interaction between the participants and speakers. Although both of these versions were excellent for the people present, only one or two students were involved, and the knowledge gained did not affect the general student curriculum.

Conference Hosting

Central to the goal of cross information exchange between the university and the profession, we have developed a set of annual conferences that provide platforms for engaging emerging issues. Although not directly related to the undergraduate or graduate curricula, these symposia are important for the role they play in continuing education for our graduates and others. They provide a timely source of case studies, new techniques, and differing philosophy on the current issues facing the profession in BIM. They also provide opportunities to invite these speakers later to have dialogues with students both as guest lecturers and as professionals to be interviewed, host field trips

Figure 9. Vasari student example: Conceptual massing study, checking for floor plate sizes, solar radia-tion and preliminary energy studies, and parametric design of curtain wall panel. Finished poster, Ruby Chong. (2010, USC. Used with permission.)

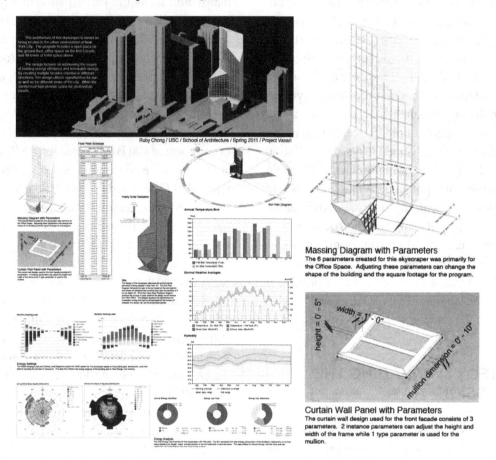

(both at the architecture firms and construction sites), and in some cases, lead to a graduate level seminar being offered.

Five BIM symposia have been hosted at USC so far. Generally the audience is from southern California, about a dozen people from out of state, approximately 200 -300 people (it varies each year), and distinguished speakers. These events are free, and the speakers volunteer their time and efforts. A summary of each year is given below.

BIM SYM 2007 AND BIM BOP 2008

To assist architects, a range of digital tools is available to predict energy consumption, carbon footprint, daylight availability, natural ventilation opportunity, and other important performance criteria in buildings. These analytical models take us beyond hand waving and the "well-behaved arrows" of our diagrams and drawings to a scientific method of evidence/simulation based architecture. In conjunction with an increased understanding of the potential application of BIM and the knowledge that has been accumulated through education and experience, architects can produce more sustainable designs. The BIM SYM

2007 and the BIM BOP 2008 conferences brought together architects, educators, and some students to explore the current status of the intersection of BIM and sustainable design.

Even before 2008, sophisticated uses of BIM + sustainable design tools were being achieved at all scales of architecture design from houses to company headquarters. In a sense, what was surprising at these two conferences was the lack of surprises. Architecture firms were already implementing analytical modeling tools with BIM to predict the performance of their designs; most schools of architecture are doing the same, both in studio and elective classes.

BIM CON!FAB 2009

The third conference explored BIM in construction and fabrication and encouraged presentations that included both the architect and construction professional. In the opening sessions, software representatives gave an overview of their products followed by AEC professionals presenting individual case studies to demonstrate how they utilize BIM during the design, construction, and fabrication process. This conference captured the state of the art of BIM in construction while also showing some tantalizing uses in fabrication. Academia is following this lead and in some cases leading research in the area of fabrication. These uses range from the relatively mundane, but pervasive, use of laser cutters by students to CNC milling machines to advanced bricklaying robots as superbly demonstrated by Fabio Gramazio and Matthias Kohler of ETH Zurich (http://www.dfab. arch.ethz.ch/).

BIM Analytics 2010: Performance Based Design

BIM isn't BIM without Information. For decades, faculty, researchers, and software companies have been developing software tools that are intended to support the work of designers. These tools have typically been stand-alone tools that provide a specific analytical capability. The range and depth of these tools has been astonishing, and yet lamentably many of these tools have not been significantly integrated into the design processes of professionals. BIM is a promising technology to encourage improved integration of design analysis into the building model. For the Fourth Annual BIM + Symposium, the nature of analytical modeling throughout the design and construction of the building was explored. It demonstrated opportunities for a more responsive integration of the evidence/simulation based design decision-making both in academia and the profession. This is exactly one of the goals in the advanced BIM seminar course described earlier.

Extreme BIM 2011: Parametrics and Customization

In Extreme BIM 2011, the speakers were asked to describe cutting edge BIM. The presentations tended to cluster around three different themes of customization (the stated subtitle of the symposium), rethinking the nature of documentation, and the role of collaboration. Several lecturers (both architects and engineers) demonstrated different tools that they have created in-house, for optimization of panels and bracket designs, parametric solar shades, and links between software programs (Figure 10). These presentations lead to the realization that schools must more fully keep up not only with BIM, but its connection to graphic algorithmic design that is strongly making its presence felt in both the profession and academia. The debate about the nature of construction documents continued; this relates directly to lectures given in professional practice undergraduate classes. Elaboration on collaboration techniques between architects, engineers, and contractors and the role of IPD was both hinted at and addressed directly. These issues are those that also effect faculty directly when used as

Figure 10. Parametric panel design for a stadium. (2011, NBBJ, supplied by Nathan Miller. Used with permission.) Parametric shading device components. (2011, Perkins+Will, supplied by Mario Guttman, Tim Meador, author. Used with permission.)

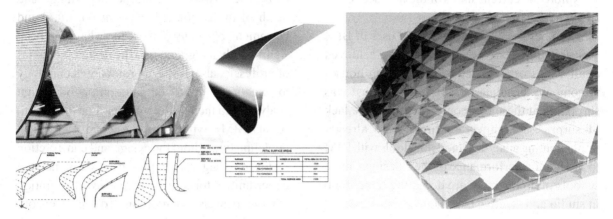

models for structuring new methods of teaching that create truly integrated studios.

Conclusions about Conference Hosting: Special Topics Classes

In many respects, the conferences validated the direction taken for the BIM instruction in the course work including sustainable design, construction and fabrication, and parametrics. The use of BIM as a front-end to simulation software is in practice both in the early design stages by the architect and for more detailed studies by the engineer. Although there are many potholes in the process and results may be misunderstood, it is a relatively easy addition to existing courses.

In the most recent symposia, Extreme BIM, three other themes emerged: customization, 2D/3D documentation, and collaboration. These provide indications for changes both in the design studio and other classes and allow for opportunities where integration and overlap of material can occur. For example, writing code is an essential skill for use in an office setting, and students must at least be aware of how customization occurs. Scripting can be also used for exploring the process of creating architecture and providing a platform for learning how to critically evaluate

results. Advanced courses should be taught that teach these skills; in fact, one of the speakers at the symposium, Nathan Miller, gave a graduate seminar similar to that for our students. This is an excellent example of positive feedback from the professional symposia to a classroom setting.

The profession maintains a strong leadership role in BIM that should be mined. This educational strategy to tap directly into the wealth of professional expertise is necessary to maintain relevance and exchange of ideas between the profession and academia. Invited local and regional practitioners have given lectures, case studies, and interactive learning sessions focused on their experiences and unique approaches to BIM technology. Although not always the case, some of these were directly related to contacts made at the BIM symposia. In one advanced seminar class, BIM evangelist Kimon Onuma taught his revolutionary non-traditional way of re-envisioning BIM: Web-based, interdisciplinary, quick paced, platform independent, concentrating on early planning stages of design -- a BIMStorm™. The course description by Onuma emphasizes the process, opportunities, and importance of collaboration and interoperability (Figure 11):

Figure 11. BIMStorm seminar class at USC (2010, Onuma Inc., used with permission)

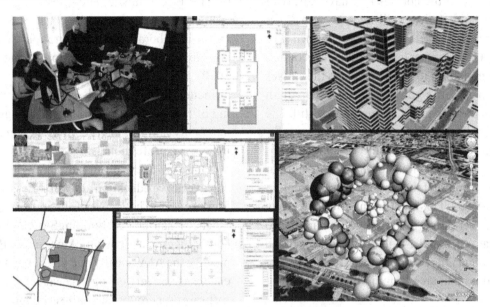

"The seminar will culminate in a real-time BIM-Storm charrette project where we will collaborate with other teams around the world. Being green is not just about using green materials. Studies have shown that the design and construction process contributes to upwards of 30% waste. Green processes for the building industry are possible. Car/air plane trips, documenting methods, and courier shipments are not environmental. There are smarter and greener ways to collaborate and quickly forecast negative decisions. Low Carbon Collaboration techniques use open standards to manage project information with the same data throughout the project life-cycle. BIM-Storms™ minimize the need for traditional carbon heavy communications like face-to-face meetings and travel. The building industry is poised to promote a 'green practice' with sustainable project management processes." (partial course description, Kimon Onuma)

CRITIQUE

Three strategies were discussed as methods of achieving wide spread use of BIM: integration into the curriculum in undergraduate elective and required courses; advanced seminars with discussions of interoperability including sustainable design tools and parametric modeling; and an active professional outreach through executive education and conference hosting. These strategies were partially based on years of experience with trying to achieve integration of earlier digital tools into the curriculum.

Integration into the curriculum at the undergraduate level is possible. At first, courses might focus more heavily teaching the software and implications of its use, but the syllabi can be transformed so that the classes are not seen as "training" but have their own content distinct from the BIM tools being employed. This is very similar to the incorporation of CAD software, modeling, rendering, 3D printing, CNC machining, etc. The intent may be to teach design or construction or color theory or furniture design. Content is this case can be separable from method, and in all likelihood the courses that have a heavier emphasis on technical skill become something else over time as their mission is redefined. For example, CAD courses became modeling courses that may transform to BIM courses as the classes try to keep up with significant software paradigm shifts. This is happening; nothing stands still. The greatest challenge is actually to find strategies for incorporating new content into existing courses in meaningful ways; it is not always possible or desirable to completely re-write ones curriculum every few years. This is not unique to architecture; civil engineering curricula are also changing to incorporate BIM and as with CAD courses in the past, the intent is not to teach software, but explore critical ideas that are changing the profession.

"In the ▢rst semester that the course was offered, approximately 40% of the lecture hours and 60% of the frontal tutoring hours were devoted to teaching use of the BIM tool. This proved to be unnecessary, as the students proved adept at learning to use the tool. In subsequent semesters, all of the lecture hours previously given to BIM tool instruction were devoted to more general issues of BIM, including concepts, review of the different engineering analyses that can be run on building models, case study projects and the use of BIM in architectural, mechanical/electrical/plumbing, curtain-wall, and other building design areas. Tutorial and homework hours devoted to learning the BIM tool remained unchanged" (Sacks and Barak 2010).

Advanced seminars have their own challenges and often the greatest potential as they draw directly on the expertise and interests of the faculty teaching the course. The author has an interest in both BIM and sustainable design, so her courses find ways to incorporate both. This is not to say that the courses previously described are unique. In the case of BIM, there is ample opportunity to focus on other related issues. For example, professors may emphasize IPD, the parametric nature

of BIM (see Schlueter and Thesseling 2008, pp. 218-219), connection to the construction industry, or collaboration and integration (see Jordan and Henderson 2010 and Armpriest and Gulling 2010). It is apparent that these courses can serve as incubators for research or conversely for testing of research ideas. This is one strength of the university and can also serve as a connection to innovative professionals.

Outreach to the profession through symposia and executive education allow for cross-fertilization of ideas. The National Institute of Building Sciences has hosted buildingSMART Alliance conferences with EcoBuild America (NIBS 2009, pg. 27); the AIA, locally and at its annual conference, has actively engaged speakers about BIM; software user groups focused towards practitioners abound. Although faculty often participate in these events, hosting conferences at universities provides a different, mainly neutral, venue where a mix of ideas and discussions of projects can be presented. It is advantageous in some respects that these are not academic conferences, but presentations by professionals to their peers. One challenge has been to keep up the quality of the presentations, not be subject to software representatives' desire to promote their products, and showcase BIM in a variety of insightful and innovative ways that speak to a variety of participants: high-level users of BIM, students, owners, architects, contractors, and facility managers.

Although others have done so (see Taiebat and Ku 2010), one form of outreach that we have not seriously attempted is to poll the profession on its expectations of what they expect as part of the skill set of recent graduates from our program.

The role of BIM research has not been adequately addressed in this chapter. Yet its role is critical not only in preparing the next round of forward thinkers and teachers, but also as one method in producing innovative ideas and papers that will help the profession progress more quickly. How this is done differs across the university spectrum (Becerik-Gerber and Kensek 2010); my work tends to focus on what I call "Building Analytical Modeling" – BIM plus simulation tools for sustainable design or other forms of performance-based design. This, however, is beyond the scope of this chapter and has been described in others.

CONCLUSION

"Building Information Modeling (BIM) is a new approach to design, construction, and facility management in which a digital representation of the building process is used to facilitate the exchange and interoperability of information in digital format. BIM is beginning to change the way buildings look, the way they function, and the ways in which they are designed and built" *(Eastman et. al. 2008, back cover).*

BIM is changing the nature of the AEC profession. It is also impacting directly the curriculum for AEC students. This chapter discussed a range of approaches that the author tried towards integrating BIM in the curriculum and gave examples of how professional expertise can complement traditional coursework. BIM technology can be integrated broadly throughout the curriculum; advanced seminars can focus on interoperability and interdisciplinary work; and professionals can be engaged through executive education and symposia.

Integration: Students are learning that BIM should not be a separate technology from design studio and other courses in environmental systems and structures, but can be completely integrated design-support activity. Although easy to declare, this is harder to actually put in practice. For many schools, it took decades between the release of relatively inexpensive hardware and CAD software before it was incorporated into the curriculum. Optimistic hopes were pinned on CAD as the framework for the integration of technology in design studios, but having learned from that experience, more success may be possible with

BIM. In every case, the instructors changing the course should consider the advantages for further integration, appropriate use of new software and hardware and paradigms that they engender, and what will have to be given up in the course to make room for new material.

Interoperability: The capability of BIM to work with analytic and representational tools offers a great opportunity for students and architects to reinforce their design capabilities. This works only if tasks of interoperability do not present major hurdles. The migration of data between systems should be nearly seamless with two-way communication between the software programs. Sustainable design is one critical area that can benefit from this. Other areas include structural analysis, construction management, water resource optimization, geographic information, facilities management and operation, and even interoperability with programs specifically for the early stages of design. Yet, schools should not wait until software communicates better between each other. Seamless communication is a goal that may never be reached. Ad hoc, "sloppy," kludgy solutions are often opportunities for students to be innovative and learn how to progress despite obstacles. It can also be frustrating and time-consuming, but instructors should be able to help students with connections between software programs that is rewarding.

Interdisciplinarity: BIM tools significantly widen the opportunities for interdisciplinary cooperation, allowing for a truly integrated design process. Faculty, students, architects, engineers, and construction professionals are recognizing that building information modeling requires a much tighter working relationship and that each of the participants has much to offer to the others. BIM allows, and sometimes even demands, collaboration as the digital models are edited, re-worked, and passed through the design and construction process. In the studio, not only could building designs integrate architecture, structure, and construction, but the students could also learn to develop project management skills within group dynamics (Dong 2008). No single profession or school or department is going to be able to advance the capabilities of BIM without enthusiasm and cooperation from all of the participants.

A final note: BIM is *not* as advertised (tongue-in-cheek) "a fully featured virtual building model with complete, seamless interoperability that can do everything and anything, reduce expenses, and save the profession in an collaborative, integrated manner. Nor is it a cure-all for the education of future architects. Dedicated teachers concerned about the future of architecture and students actively engaged in their own education are critical, with or without BIM.

ACKNOWLEDGMENT

Thanks to Douglas Noble for his help, my students for the use of their images, and the professionals who volunteer their time to speak at the annual symposia.

The opinions presented in this chapter are purely those of the author.

REFERENCES

Armpriest, D., & Gulling, D. (2010). Teaching architecture technology: Shifts in subject matter and pedagogical practices from 2006 to 2009. In B. Goodwin & J. Kinnard (Eds.), *RE.building, 98th ACSA Annual Meeting* (pp. 762 - 768). Washington, DC: ACSA Press.

Becerik-Gerber, B., & Kensek, K. (2010). Building information modeling in architecture, engineering and construction: emerging research directions and trends. *Journal of Professional Issues in Engineering Education and Practice*, 136(3), 139 – 147. American Society of Civil Engineers, 2010-7.

Design, C. A. S. E. Inc. (2010). *Conceptual design modeling in Autodesk Revit Architecture*, 2010. White Paper, Autodesk.

Dong, K. (2008). *BIM in education: Collaborative design studios integrating architecture, engineering, & construction*. 2008 buildingSMART alliance™ National Conference, December 8-13, 2008, presentation.

Eastman, C., Teicholz, P., Sacks, R., & Liston, K. (2008). *BIM handbook: A guide to building information modeling for owners, managers, designers, engineers, and contractors* (pp. 27, 208). Hoboken, NJ: Wiley Publishing.

Enright, J. (2009). Applications in cross-curriculum teaching the synthesis of the design studio and building technology seminar. *ARCC Journal 09. Affecting Change in Architectural Education*, 6(1), 14–22.

Ibrahim, M. M. (2007). Teaching BIM, what is missing? The challenge of integrating BIM based CAD in today's architectural curricula. *Embodying Virtual Architecture: The Third International Conference of the Arab Society for Computer Aided Architectural Design*, ASCAAD 2007, (pp. 651 – 660), 28-30 November 2007, Alexandria, Egypt.

Jordan, N., & Henderson, L. (2010). *Teaching for collaboration: Bringing our practice to our teaching. JBIM, Journal of Building Information Modeling, Spring 2010* (pp. 31–33). Houston, TX: Matrix Group Publishing, Inc.

Kensek, K. (2009). Sustainable parametric objects. In *AUGI | AEC Edge, Fall 2009* (pp. 31 – 35). Extension Media LLC. Retrieved July 27, 2010, from http://digitaleditiononline.com/publication/?i=25028

Kolarevic, B., & Malkawi, A. (Eds.). (2005). *Performative architecture: Beyond instrumentality* (p. 93). New York, NY: Spon Press.

Krygiel, E., & Nies, B. (2008). *Green BIM: Successful sustainable design with building information modeling* (p. 209). Indianapolis, IN: Wiley Publishing.

Lin, J. (2010). Design for quantitative and qualitative performance: a pedagogical approach for integrating environmental analysis into the early stages of the design process. In B. Goodwin & J. Kinnard (Eds.), *RE-Building, 98th ACSA Annual Meeting* (pp. 189 - 196). Washington, DC: ACSA Press.

NIBS- National Institute of Building Sciences. (2009). *Annual Report to the President of the United States.* Retrieved from www.nibs.org

Sacks, R., & Barak, R. (2010). Teaching building information modeling as an integral part of freshman year civil engineering education. *Journal of Professional Issues in Engineering Education and Practice, 36*(1), 30–37. doi:10.1061/(ASCE) EI.1943-5541.0000003

Schlueter, A., & Thesseling, F. (2008). Balancing design and performance in building retrofitting, a case study based on parametric modeling. In A. Kudless, N Oxman, M. Swackhamer (Eds.), *Silicon + Skin > Biological Processes and Computation, ACADIA 08 Conference Proceedings* (pp. 214- 221). Association of Computer Aided Design in Architecture.

Taiebat, M., & Ku, H. (2010). Industry's expectations of construction school graduates' BIM skills. *46th Annual Associated Schools of Construction International Conference Proceedings, in conjunction with the Annual Meeting of the International Council for Research and Innovation in Building and Construction (CIB) Working Group 89,* Wentworth Institute of Technology, (p. 35). Retrieved from ascpro.ascweb.org/chair/paper/CEUE217002010.pdf

Techel, F., & Nassar, K. (2007). Teaching building information modeling (BIM) from a sustainability design perspective. *Em'body'ing Virtual Architecture: The Third International Conference of the Arab Society for Computer Aided Architectural Design* (ASCAAD 2007), November 28-30, 2007, Alexandria, Egypt, (pp. 635-650).

ADDITIONAL READING

100Annual Meeting, A. C. S. A. 19: Digital Simulation. *Theoretical Implications of BIM: Performance and Interpretation* (Folan and Poerschke, session leaders) AIA document E202 2008 - http://www.aia.org/contractdocs/ training/bim/AIAS078742

Annual Meeting, A. C. S. A. *Digital Aptitudes.* Conference proceedings. https://www.acsa-arch.org/conferences. March 1-4, 2012. Co-chairs: Mark Goulthorpe, Massachusetts Institute of Technology; Amy Murphy, University of Southern California. Host School: Massachusetts Institute of Technology. These thematic sections are especially relevant to this topic area

100ACSA Annual Meeting8: The Effect of Computation on Design Process. *Becoming Computational: Restructuring/ Reconsidering Pedagogy Towards a (More) Computational Discipline* (Beorkrem and Senske, session leaders).

100ACSA Annual Meeting10: Parametric Performance. *Design Computation: Parametrics, Performance, Pedagogy and Praxis* (Kensek, session leader).

100ACSA Annual Meeting14: Digital Networks: Collaborative Praxis. *Integration, Not Segregation: Interdisciplinary Design Pedagogy for the Second 100 Years* (Doerfler and Dong, session leaders).

Eastman, C., Teicholz, P., & Sacks, R. (2008). *Rafael; Liston, Kathleen. BIM Handbook: A guide to Building Information Modeling for owners, managers, designers, engineers, and contractors.* Hoboken, NJ: Wiley Publishing.

Hardin, B. (2009). *BIM and Construction Management: Proven tools, methods, and workflows.* Indianapolis, IN: Wiley Publishing.

Jernigan, Finith. *BIM BIM, little BIM.* Salisbury, MD. 4Site Press, 2008.

Krygiel, E., & Nies, B. (2008). *Green BIM: successful sustainable design with Building Information Modeling.* Indianapolis, IN: Wiley Publishing.

Kwok, A., & Grondzik, W. *The Green Studio Handbook, second edition, environmental strategies for schematic design*, Oxford, Burlington, MA: Architectural, Elsevier, 2011.

McCullough. (1990). *Malcolm; Mitchell, William; Purcell, Patrick. The Electronic Design Studio: architectural education in the computer era.* Cambridge, MA: MIT Press.

Mitchell, W. (1990). *The Logic of Architecture: design, computation, and cognition.* Cambridge, MA: MIT Press.

Smith, D. K., & Tardif, M. (2009). *Building Information Modeling: A strategic implementation guide for architects, engineers, constructors, and real estate asset managers.* Hoboken, NJ: Wiley Publishing.

KEY TERMS AND DEFINITIONS

AECO: Architecture, Engineering, Construction, Operations. Often just listed as AEC, but recently operations have been added to demonstrate the importance of facilities management.

BIM: Building Information Model is an integrated, structured, virtual graphic database, informed by the AECO industry that consists of three dimensional parametric objects and allows for interoperability.

CAD: Computer Aided Drafting is a vector based software program that has been optimized for producing 2D contract documents for the description of objects such as a buildings, airplanes, mechanical parts, electrical layouts, etc. The term Computer Aided Design (also CAD) has been expanded to include 3D programs, usually surface or solid model based.

IPD: Integrated Product Delivery is a method of professional practice, often bound by legal agreements, where there is strong collaboration between the owner, architect, and contractor and the sharing of financial risks and rewards. Integrated teams, often including the engineers and subcontractors, meet throughout the design of the building so that stakeholders' concerns can be discussed and resolved in a sharing of ideas and expertise.

Interoperability: The ability of software programs to share data without loss of information.

Parametric: The general word parametric refers to having a value that can be changed. For example, a BIM might contain a parametric door where the width and height dimensions are variable.

Parametric Design: The process of parametric design involves selecting appropriate sets of parameters for a problem and establishing a series of functions, expressed in terms of variables and geometrical relationships. It allows the exploration of many solutions; however, the product variation depends on how the designer approached and defined the problem and its constraints.

VDC: Virtual Design and Construction is often used interchangeably with BIM, but whereas BIM usually refers to the product and software, VDC often refers to the management process.

APPENDIX: OTHER RESOURCES

These organizations usually hold annual conferences that produce excellent proceedings on topics related to computer-aided design, building science, or education.

ACADIA: Association for Computer Aided Design in Architecture. http://www.acadia.org/

ACM SIGGRAPH: the Association for Computing Machinery's Special Interest Group on Computer Graphics and Interactive Techniques. http://www.siggraph.org/

ACSA: Association of Collegiate Schools of Architecture. https://www.acsa-arch.org/

ASCAAD: Arab Society for Computer Aided Architectural Design. http://www.ascaad.org/

BTES: Building Technology Educator's Society. http://www.btesonline.org/

BuildingSMART: international home of openBIM. http://www.buildingsmart.com/

CAADFutures:http://www.caadfutures.org/

CAADRIA: The Association for Computer-Aided Architectural Design Research in Asia. http://www.caadria.org/

eCAADe: Education and research in Computer Aided Architectural Design in Europe. http://www.ecaade.org/

SBSE: Society of Building Science Educators. http://www.sbse.org/

SiGraDi: Sociedad Ibero Americana de Grafica Digital. http://sigradiorg.uchilefau.cl/

Chapter 8
Applying BIM in Design Curriculum

Clark Cory
Purdue University, USA

Shanna Schmelter-Morrett
Holder Construction Company, USA

ABSTRACT

This chapter presents an educational case study of applying Building Information Modeling (BIM) as an integrated design platform for interdisciplinary building and construction projects. The course is meant to focus on utilizing BIM for commercial construction. Students examine 3D geometry, spatial relationships, geographic information, quantities of materials, and properties of building components in this course. The students also learn the processes that make up BIM so they will be able to apply this information in a company. The purpose of the initial study was to assess the need for and receive feedback on the syllabus of the first commercial construction computer graphics course at Purdue University through a survey that was sent to industry professionals. The class was taught in the Fall 2009 semester and was successful according to the students in what they learned. The course was a 400 level course in which both upper level undergraduates and graduate students participated. The professor took the approach of a real world job and incorporated it into the content of the course. This chapter will discuss the initial case study of industrial professionals, the initial course creation, the development, and ultimately the final curriculum delivered within the course, as well as student feedback received at the end of the semester.

INTRODUCTION

Construction has been an ever evolving industry with changes in technology as well as materials and method used to construct buildings. It is this change that has prompted Purdue University's Computer Graphics Technology (CGT) department to take a look at the current curriculum for the focus of Construction Graphics Technology to update it to those changes in industry. The curriculum in the past was focused on residential construction with a hint of commercial construction graphics. With the Architectural, Engineering, and Construction (AEC) economy in the current situation it is in, students were having an impossible time finding

DOI: 10.4018/978-1-61350-180-1.ch008

employment in the residential construction area after graduation. There were a selected few though that were interviewing for commercial construction positions, and obtaining them. The reason for their employment was those students took control of their education and went to the Building Construction Management (BCM) department within the College of Technology and took additional construction courses. This additional education was the deciding factor for obtaining employment. Ultimately the problem of the study was to determine a need from construction professionals if there is a lack of education in the College of Technology's construction graphics area that delivers Building Information Modeling (BIM) to Purdue University CGT students for their future profession. The study evaluated the CGT 460: Building Information Modeling for Commercial Construction course content to provide feedback from the industry who will potentially be hiring Purdue University CGT graduates. This study collected and analyzed demographic feedback, course curriculum feedback, and general course comments to improve and align it with industry standards.

The chapter will give a background as to current AEC technological trends; followed by a process & survey created for the AEC industry in order to create a curriculum dictated by industrial standards; identify a sixteen week curriculum outline defined by the AEC professional's survey; talk about implementation of that curriculum into a new course proposed in the Fall 2009 semester at Purdue University, and lastly give results in the form of feedback from students who took the course. From the above information, the author has analyzed the feedback and has drawn some conclusions for the future of the course to make it substantially better.

Objectives of Survey:

- Review of current AEC technological trends for construction education

- Identify Building Information Modeling in higher education curriculums
- Review 16 week outline for proposed course
- Identify focal BIM standards within curriculum
- Review of course setup and implementation
- Identify key components that made course successful
- Identify key components of course that need improvement

BACKGROUND

The popularity of BIM in the commercial construction industry is increasing everyday (Sullivan, 2007). A recent survey of construction projects and program owners stated that more than one third of them used BIM on one or more of their projects. This further illustrated that educational settings are in need of creating new courses and challenging existing ones to facilitate the need of industry (Building Design and Construction, 2007). The educational and industrial programs that focus on construction graphics are at the front of this need. Companies are recruiting students with computer graphics skills to BIM positions because of the modeling knowledge. Most construction companies are slowly redefining their efforts to incorporate BIM technology and methods. The contractors are "using 3D technology to identify interferences, link data to schedules, and produce 4D (four dimensional) animations, which help discover dynamic interferences of construction activities" (Constructech, 2007, p.25). These companies are looking for individuals straight out of college that are knowledgeable about computer graphics and have a good sense of visualization in construction. Merriam-Webster (2007) described visualization as the "formation of mental visual images or the process of interpreting in visual terms or of putting into visible form". It is suggested that visualization tools may help enhance the students' understanding of certain construction aspects (Messner & Horman, 2003).

While AEC companies are redefining their efforts and processes to incorporate BIM, higher education in BIM are few and far between. A quick Bing or Google search identified less that a dozen universities that incorporated or currently have a BIM curriculum or course. And while most universities include some sort of 3D modeling, that is just the start of the process for BIM and could technically be defined as not BIM at all. Inclusive BIM curriculums are extremely rare to find online. Most links selected were individual courses introducing BIM and the others selected were professional organizations like American General Contractors (AGC) or Autodesk extended educational courses on BIM.

Computer Graphic Technology (CGT) students at Purdue University who would like to specialize in Construction Graphic Communication (CGC) are taught residential construction processes with 2D drawings and 3D tools; however, there are many more opportunities in commercial construction that are not explored by the CGT department that could be explored in similar manners. The New Jersey Institute of Technology (NJIT) offers a BIM class and design studio where they use Revit Architecture as the main BIM tool to further teach BIM concepts. They are also researching how to incorporate other BIM tools such as Revit MEP and Revit Structure into their curriculums (Autodesk, 2007).

Associate Professor of Construction Management, Willem Kymmell at Chico State University in Chico, CA has created a BIM curriculum that has been incorporated into their school to enable students to understand BIM concepts and become familiar with BIM tools. BIM assists in information transfer and collaboration settings. Through this curriculum students are given the opportunity to connect how visualization, communication, and collaboration all apply to the scope of BIM. Furthermore, the curriculum is unique because it was designed to suit the attending audience

and has basic modules developed to break BIM into manageable concepts. The students are able to interact with industry projects where they are learning how to document construction processes and techniques by working with industry professionals. Then the students can compare physical observations with their BIM observations. The BIM models are still able to be manipulated after this interaction (Kymmell, 2006).

Currently, there are no commercial construction classes taught at Purdue University through the CGT department which if taught or introduced could be useful to these students in their future careers. The course could potentially do several of the following: Increase their visualization of 2D into 3D information, increase their understanding of the coordination of commercial construction documentation and technology, increase familiarities with the current technologies in BIM, increase understanding of cooperation with architects and clients, etc. Furthermore, the lack of these visualization tools and this course may be a contributing factor to the lack of knowledge in commercial construction processes. This course was proposed to greatly enhance the student's commercial construction knowledge through the use of BIM techniques to enhance future success in industry.

INITIAL STUDY

The purpose of the initial study was to demonstrate BIM techniques to educate students on commercial construction to assist them in learning "geometry, spatial relationships, geographic information, quantities and properties of building components" (Purdue University, 2007, p.1). Students will be able to receive education on professional practices and "explain how BIM is used in the industry and the processes that make up BIM as they apply to information in a company that uses BIM techniques" (Purdue University, 2007, p.1). There are no commercial construction courses in CGT which ultimately can hinder a student's visualization, understanding of commercial construction concepts, and future opportunities. This proposed course may increase students' knowledge, visualization skills, and perhaps enhance their learning environment. The course objectives are (Purdue University, 2007):

- Increase spatial visualization.
- Increase individual as well as group production productivity.
- Coordinate construction documentation and technology.
- Become familiar with the current technologies in BIM and what is utilized for MEP (Mechanical, Electrical, and Plumbing) systems.
- Understand principles of BIM and incorporate them into current projects in the AEC industry.
- Develop independent and teamwork skills of BIM, and know how to cooperate with architects, clients, and everyone dealing with the need for information visualization in construction graphics.
- Develop the ability to evaluate and incorporate multiple file formats into one that will evaluate collision of MEP and structural systems within a structure.
- Embed and link vital information such as vendors for specific materials, location of details, and quantities required for estimation and tendering.
- Explain how BIM is used in the industry and the processes that make up BIM as they apply to information in a company that uses BIM techniques.
- Assess a BIM project and develop a BIM project assessment.
- Become aware of the career opportunities in BIM.

An evaluation tool was utilized to assess the course and laboratory material by professionals in the industry. This study hypothesized that evaluations from the industry would prove that the course could be effective in teaching commercial construction and BIM. Also, feedback from the professional sources assisted in adjusting the course curriculum to be most effective for the CGT students.

Initial Study Results

The methodology consisted of designing course content and implementing an assessment criterion to provide feedback on the content. This content and feedback were then integrated into the lecture and laboratory section of CGT 460: Building Information Modeling for Commercial Construction course curriculum at Purdue University. This feedback from the assessment was used to further aid students in applications of visualization and documentation in commercial construction by the use of BIM theories and software. The study was developmental due to the course syllabus that was created for assessment and then later assessed upon critiques.

Selecting Participants for Assessment/Sample Size

The researcher completed the necessary documentation and received permission to proceed with the study from Purdue University's Internal Review Board (IRB) committee by an expedited review protocol. The individuals that assisted in assessing the course syllabus were industry professionals in design/build firms that had specific involvement in the design or BIM discipline. The industry professionals were employed by firms across the country and of varying age groups. The first sample was derived from research of design/build firms from educational professionals at Purdue University. The final sample that was contacted was taken from research of the design/build firms that have resources and departments to complete the assessment. After permission was granted from IRB, the industry design professionals were notified and asked to participate. The sample size was approximately 70 design professionals with a return rate of 27.1% which was 19 assessments.

Pre-Experimental Task - Course Content Formation

The course syllabus was written by Clark Cory and further edited by the researcher to meet Purdue University guidelines and policies. This course was developed according to the Purdue University's standard guidelines for developing new courses. The course outline included:

- Specific learning objectives.
- A 16 week lecture and laboratory schedule.
- Textbooks to be used in the course.
- Grading evaluation outlined.
- Student conduct and polices.
- Course resources for students' needs throughout the course.

Study Implementation - The Assessment

The researcher created a survey to obtain feedback on the CGT 460 course syllabus to further aid students in commercial construction and BIM knowledge. The survey was chosen to obtain statistical feedback. The assessment given to the industry professionals included the course content outline and survey questions about improvement of the course from an industry viewpoint. The reliability of the assessment survey was found by the expert assessment of the survey prior to distribution. Also, the questions were developed with help from educational professionals and statistical consultants to receive feedback on the correct material. This assessment and course outline was delivered by an e-mail asking for participation with a link to an assessment survey and the course outline attached. The e-mails were sent out from a Purdue e-mail account to the selected design/build firms. The questions for the survey are as follows:

- What percentage would you say your firm uses BIM?
- Describe how your department uses BIM?
- What is your previous knowledge of BIM?
- Do the course outcomes meet the industry standard?
- What software package are you using in your firm for BIM operations?
- When looking at the 16 week outline, are there any topics that you would add?
- Are there any resources that would be helpful to the students?
- Would you suggest a course like this be offered at Purdue University?
- Would you hire a student that had BIM commercial knowledge?
- What are your suggestions for improving this course outline?

Instrumentation

The survey was designed in Purdue's CGT department and placed on a local server with a maximum of fourteen questions. The questions asked the industry professional to assess the course syllabus from their viewpoint and had areas to expand on any further comments or suggestions they may have to improve the course. The first group of survey questions asked was demographic questions about the professionals and their firm. The second group of survey questions asked them about their previous knowledge of BIM and how they used BIM in their firm. The final group of questions assessed the course content and asked if they would hire CGT graduates with this knowledge. The survey questions will be a combination of a six-point Likert-type scale questions with zero being the highest level (strongly agree) and five being the lowest (strongly disagree) and fill in the blank questions. The survey results were completed anonymously due to the survey returning information unattached to the responder. The industry professionals were not required to participate; however, if they chose there was no risk associated with participation. The industry professionals were given approximately five weeks to complete the syllabus review and online survey. The course content was then adopted as the assessments that were analyzed by the instructor to further meet the industry expectations.

Measures

The participant's responses were measured to compare the results and validate if the curriculum we are teaching is valid and/or needs revision. The responses were measured from the 19 participants that provided a response to the survey. The measure of variables was direct because everything was exposed to the industry professionals that chose to participate.

Data Collection

The data was collected on a server at Purdue University. The participants were assigned a random number when they completed the survey for analysis purposes. All data was collected anonymously according to the requirements of IRB. This data was then sorted in a spreadsheet and coded to be placed into SAS, a statistical analysis software, for data analysis.

Analyzing the Data

This study has independent, dependent, and intervening variables. The independent variable was the assessment survey that the industry professionals responded to. The dependent variables were the responses and comments of the industry professionals about BIM and its assistance in learning. The intervening variables were any malfunctions of the survey or e-mail while in use. The data for the first variables was nominal because the assessment associated numbers with the responses to categorize them. The order of the categories was arbitrary. For nominal data, statistical concepts such as mean and standard deviation would not be

helpful for this data so the statistical consultants at Purdue University chose the Fisher's exact test to analyze the data. The Fisher's exact test is used to find statistical significance in categorical data. It is used with small sample sizes to find an association between two variables. The p-value is computed as if the margins are fixed. Since we had a relatively small sample size and some values in the table cells were below 10, the chi-square test was not appropriate to use. The exact test was perfect to use for this study's data analyses because the data was non-parametric and unbalanced (Fisher, 1922). Also, the probabilities of the questions were analyzed separately to assess the likelihood of the potential case will happen.

The rest of the data was of qualitative content because of the suggestions and comments given. The industry professionals that suggested or recommended similar changes were taken into serious consideration. All recommendations were compared closely with information in the literature review. The greater amount of responses on a particular topic validated that those recommendations would further assist in education and should be incorporated into the BCM 460 curriculum. After the above analysis, the results were further analyzed by the instructor and the researcher to further make appropriate improvements to the course curriculum. Furthermore, the descriptive analyses that will be used are percentiles, comparison by the Fisher's exact test, and qualitative recommendations.

Summary of Analysis Results

The educational implications of these findings are that the integration of commercial construction and BIM principles in the CGT curriculum may be helpful for students that would like to participate in the commercial construction industry. The results explain the positive impacts this course may have on Purdue University students by industry standards. These findings are speculative due to the relatively young age of this specific discipline. However, most importantly the industry professionals that participated in the survey confirmed that:

- 100% of the firms that responded agree or strongly agree that the syllabus outcomes that they reviewed do meet the industry standards.
- 89.5% agree in some way that the resources in the syllabus meet the student's needs.
- 73.7% agree in some way that the 16 week outline in the syllabus would be expected for a student to learn about BIM in their current and future careers.
- 100% of the firms that responded agree or strongly agree that the course that they reviewed should be offered at Purdue University.
- And 89.5% of the firms that responded agree in some way that the future graduates that they hire will need BIM knowledge.

Furthermore, any research in the commercial industry is stating that there is a need for educated BIM professionals. Due to the industry trends, it further could be assumed that educational institutions are the best place to start teaching the students basic fundamentals of commercial BIM knowledge. The BIM engineer or manager is not just a luxury on construction sites today but a fundamental and integral part of the model based construction process. The BIM Manager's multi-faceted skills have a direct effect on the quality of projects and the reduction of overall project execution time. Due to the limitations and recommendations of the study, these findings have raised enough aspects to further research the course and its material to further aid and enhance Purdue University's CGT students. Repeating this study and gathering even more participants will likely strengthen the current claims and find many more associations between survey questions to understand trends of the data to allow even further improvement of the course.

CURRICULUM OUTLINE

A preliminary outline was created from the survey above and submitted to the AEC members one more time for additional feedback. Once that feedback was received from the AEC professionals and a careful analysis of the research data was done; a combined and revised 16-week outline was created. The course would be an upper level undergraduate course and it was also determined that portions of the course would take on components of a graduate course such as a submitted journal article or conference presentation. Table 1 identifies the 16-week outline with weekly lecture topics as well as lab problems.

Implementation into Classroom

The normal classroom setup for a Construction Graphic Class at Purdue is two one-hour lectures in which one is based on theory and one is a demonstration of technology. The students also have a two-hour lab toward the end of the week. This being a 400 level course, the trick was to create the course that paralleled what is done in industry per professional recommendations.

First, Facility Management at Purdue University was called first to obtain a set of construction documents for one building on campus. After several weeks of negotiation on use of documents and then scanning of original documents to obtain PDF prints, the student received a complete set of construction documents for two buildings; KNOY Hall and Electrical Engineering buildings were selected. The construction documents did not include the MEP or Structural set of prints. Those two items were to come at a later date which Facility Management did not identify as to a specific date. Fig. 1 partially shows the quality of the original documents.

The beginning of the semester had started and the students were paired up with another student in order to start the model with the architectural PDF prints. The pairs were placed with two

Table 1. 16-week outline of the course

Week	Theory Lecture	Demonstration Lecture	Lab
1	Intro to Course	Introduction, Interface, and Sketching	Sketching Assignment
2	2D CAD vs BIM	Levels, Grids, Walls, Floors, Dimensioning, and Ceilings	Sketching Assignment Due Small Office Assignment Paper 1 Assigned Project 1 Assigned
3	Going Parametric and Using BIM	Doors, Windows, Stairs, and Roofs	Small Office Assignment Due Small Office Assignment 2 Project 1 Continued
4	Who needs BIM?	Databases, Views, Visibility, Elevations, Curtain Walls, Options, Sections, and Sheets	Small Office Assignment 2 Due Small Office Assignment 3 Project 1 Continued
5	What projects need BIM? How is BIM used in the industry?	Components, Tags, Schedules, Rendering, and Family Creation	Small Office Assignment 3 Due Small Office Assignment/Family Creation Assignment Project 1 Continued
6	MEP Using BIM	Site Plans	Small Office Assignment/Family Creation Assignment Due Site Plan Assignment Project 1 Continued
7	Structural Construction	Revit and Sustainable Design	Site Plan Assignment Due Sustainable Assignment Project 1 Continued Final Project Assigned- Group project
8	Midterm Review Navisworks Intro	File Importing - bring the entire model together in Navisworks!	Sustainable Assignment Due Project 1 Continued Final Project Continued Paper 1 Due
9	Design Constraints, Design Information Organization	Estimation	Paper 2 Assigned Final Project Forum Research Project 1 Due Final Project Continued
10	Spring Break	Spring Break	Final Project Continued Paper 2 Continued
11	Domain-Specific Knowledge	Final Project Forum/BIM/CAD - Project management, work-flow, scheduling, system management and standards implementation.	Final Project Continued Paper 2 Continued
12	Interdependencies	Integration: Using Revit with 3DS Max and Auto CAD	Final Project Continued Paper 2 Continued
13	Component Design	Contractual/Legal Aspects of BIM and Participants/Coordination with Others	Final Project Continued Paper 2 Due
14	Delaying Specificity- Massing	Clean Up of Interference	Final Project Continued
15	Is Architecture Engineering?	Development Trend of BIM and Future Insights or Thoughts (Further Resources)	Final Project Continued
16	Developing Trends in BIM- Future of Construction Graphic Documentation	Presentations	Final Project Due
Finals Week	Final Exam- Date to be announced!		

Figure 1. (Quality of original documents) © 2009 Purdue Research Foundation

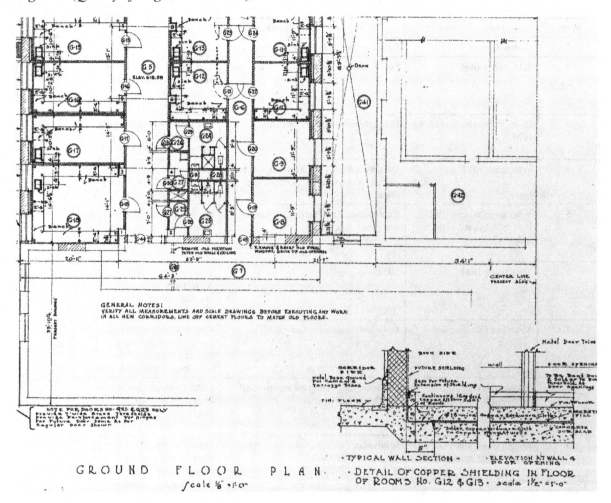

GROUND FLOOR PLAN.
Scale ⅛" = 1'-0"

· DETAIL OF COPPER SHIELDING IN FLOOR
OF ROOMS No. G12 & G13 · scale 1½" = 1'-0"

other pairs to make a group of six. The idea was for one pair to work on the architectural prints using Revit Architecture- the second pair was to work on the MEP utilizing Revit MEP and the third pair was to work on the structural models utilizing Revit Structural software. Three weeks into each group's assignment, they were to switch technologies and models. So if they started working on the architectural model, they would get the model from MEP or structural and continue to work on it. This caused some very interesting dilemmas for each group. They had to develop a system of file naming conventions along with create a standard of software standards in order to pick up where the other group left off. Software standards and file naming conventions were most important items that the industrial professionals identified as being extremely important during a project. The industrial professionals get files from multiple subcontractors and inevitably have to utilize their models or redraw the entire structure from scratch. Either way, file naming and graphic standards were to become a critical factor for each group. The instructor of the course made it extremely clear to each group that the suggestions of the industrial professionals were to be taken very seriously and adhered too. The instructor also pointed out that each company that he consulted with had spent as few as two months and as much as two years identifying, defining, and documenting the file organization, file naming, internal drawing and graphic standards they were to use in the company for each project. The idea being that if one employee were to get called away to a project another could open up and be productive with what he/she was working on without delay. Some students started working on the project without regard to this warning and ended up spending an entire week rethinking the way they set up the initial file. An entire week wasted because they did not initially sit down to talk. Most AEC professionals will identify that BIM is forcing everyone involved with the building to plan everything out initially before construction begins. So a week of wasted production time to redefine file formatting and drawing standards was a great learning example they will not soon forget.

Each building modeled was three-story high with multiple basement levels. Each level per building was approximately 25,000 square feet, so it was imperative that the student work together to get each floor completed by the end of the 16-week semester. While one pair was working on the architectural model, another pair was working on the structural components of the building. Facility Management finally sent the Structural and MEP for each building five weeks into the semester. So two of the pairs could break off the architectural model and start on each component they had to complete. Each student in the 6 student group had a chance to work on the architectural component for the first five weeks. It was now time to start rotating pairs so they got introduced to MEP and Structural components within the building. It was determined that six weeks was all that could be afforded until they had to start getting familiar with Navisorks and prepare for the final formal presentation. It was understood that a majority of the MEP and Structural would not be completed by presentation time but one entire floor of MEP of the building and the entire structural model was expected to be finished by each group. Figure 2,Figure 3, and Figure 4 show each model of one group.

Figure 2. Building architectural model-

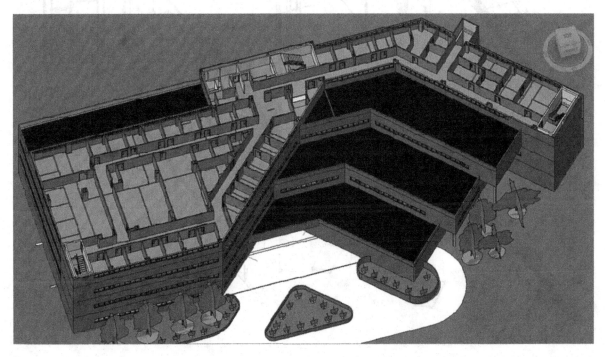

Figure 3. Building structural model-

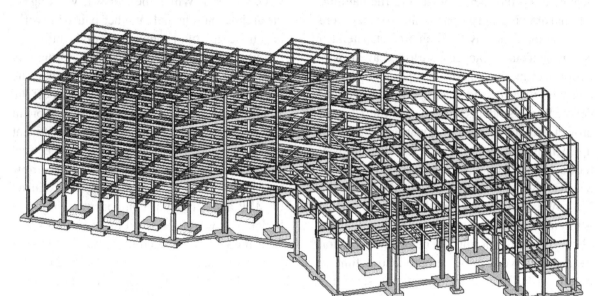

Figure 4. Building MEP model-

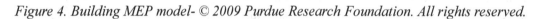

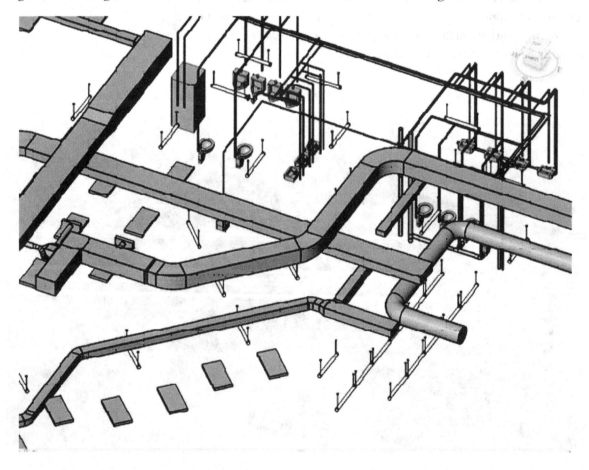

After each model for the architectural, structural, and one floor of MEP was completed to the satisfaction of the instructor, the groups were to take them into Navisworks to run collision detection. Most industrial professionals are currently utilizing Navisworks or Solibri in current practices; therefore it was crucial for students to get introduced to Navisworks since that was the technology accessible to the students. The students soon realized that the file naming and graphical standards they should have spent time identifying and utilizing came back to haunt them one more time. If the group did not identify a unified origin for each model, when they imported each into Navisworks the groups quickly found out that each model did not coincide with the other models and in some instances was off by 25 feet in an East/West direction for one model and 50 feet in the North/South direction for the other model compared to the architectural model. Several groups then had to go back into each technology and physically move each model to a predeter-

mined origin allowing the combined Navisworks model to align properly. After another week of Navisworks importing stress, it was a group effort to run through tutorials and run collision reports for each component within the building. This is where most groups found out how important communication between the technologies was during the process. There was not enough time to go back to change any component within the collision report. They were able however to see how the structural, architectural, and MEP components interact in the complete BIM building. Figure 5 shows one of the Navisworks collision images where the HVAC goes thru the structural component.

The 16th week was the formal presentation of each group project. There were four groups in total and the evaluation was done as a competition. All groups submitted their presentational documents in a plain manila envelope simulating a sealed bid. Groups were told that late presentational documents would not be accepted. Best

Figure 5. (Collision Detection Report) © Autodesk Navisworks®. Autodesk screen shots reprinted with the permission of Autodesk, Inc.

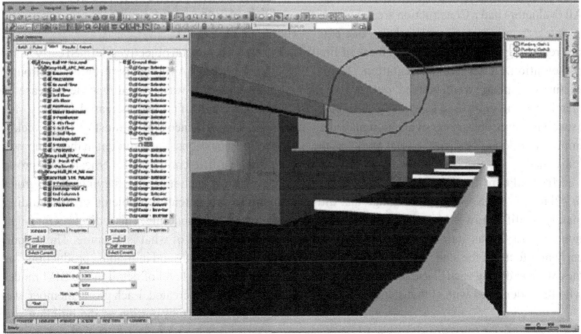

overall document and presentation won the bid and contract with the client to build the structure, and received the only A grade in the class. Presentation day found students dressed in semi matching formal attire for their groups. There were also groups that had the presence of mind to create business cards to pass out just before their presentation. The order of the presentation was decided randomly. Evaluations were done by the professor of the course, two invited professors and two graduate teaching assistants within CGT. All evaluators had a Construction area of interest or research expertise. Figure 6 shows one exterior rendering produced by a group for their final presentation. After the presentation, formal evaluation sheets were handed out and each member in the group had to evaluate each other as well as themselves. Peer evaluation played an important role in deciding the final marks of the individuals.

Mike LaFevre (2008) of Holder Construction in Atlanta, GA USA created an image that ultimately identifies how BIM is utilized in Construction. Figure 7 was introduced to the students early and focused the students to identify where they were at during each phase of the project and who they identified with at that stage.

Once they understood the relationship each member had in the overall construction process, a clearer picture, (Figure 8) of the middle team portion was introduced on what BIM could do for the design group, the company, and ultimately the client. It was initially the hope that they would take the image to heart and follow its team interest message with a unified team effort while creating the models.

Evaluation: Achieving Course Objectives

There were several objectives defined early in the course creation. As the course progressed through the semester, it was evident that the increase of spatial visualization had increased in every student. The evidence was in most of their weekly group discussions. Each student in the group was assigned a different area and overhearing the group discussions, each student was trying inform group members of potential problems of the building they would be modeling. This indicates a foresight of visualization of what is to come. The second objective of group and individual production was obtained by the level of detail in the BIM model each group had created. Each group member was assigned a different portion of the building and

Figure 7. BIM common ground- © 2009 Mike LaFevre. Used with permission .

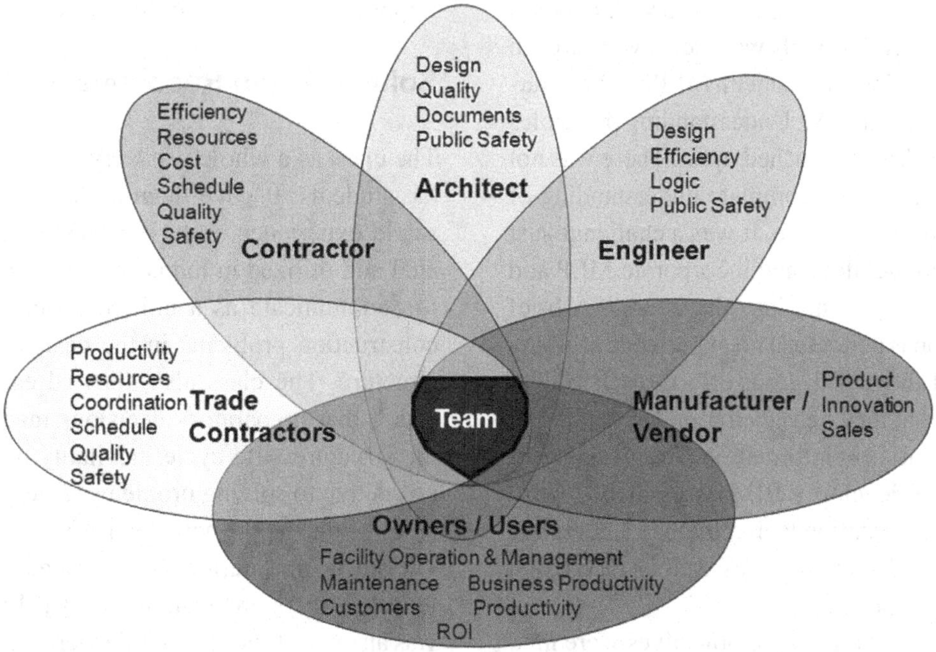

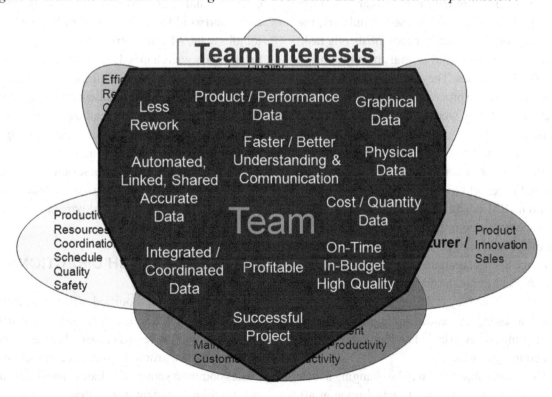

Figure 8. Team interest- BIM common ground- © 2009 Mike LaFevre. Used with permission .

then they had to pull each model together for the entire building. Coordination of documentation and technology definitely was met as well as each student becoming familiar with MEP and Structural components of BIM. Understanding principles of BIM was briefly touched upon. There was not enough time to get a complete understanding of 4D or 5D into the course. It was a challenge just to get the model done and incorporate MEP and structural components into the course. A brief introduction is better than no experience at all. As mentioned above with group efforts- each student identified that they had a better understanding of the collaboration of information. The groups were also able to develop a BIM assessment report. The final presentation had to include a complete construction document set as well as a collision assessment report.

Although several of the objectives were met, there were a few that was not. With the amount of details included in the model, it was time that prohibited getting vendor information or location of detail in their end of year report. As for explaining how BIM is used in industry, the students could not really accomplish this task. They could only identify what their group did with BIM processes. They might have had a few components of the processes, but could not verify whether what they were doing was accurate for industry or not.

As for the last course objective and becoming aware of career opportunities, the students were required to report twice through the semester on potential BIM positions. This meant they either had to contact a company personally or look online to get information. The reports turned out to be a huge discussion rather than a report by each student. Each came in and started talking to each other about what they had found. The discussions were interesting and ended up taking the entire lecture time and even ended up running over time on a couple occasions.

The course objectives will be changing a little because a couple were not touched upon at all.

So each will be reviewed and critiqued as to its importance or utilization in the course.

Solutions and Recommendations

The class as a whole was very well received by the students. It gave them a chance to get real world experience on how a BIM model is created and utilized in industry and how they need to communicate as a unified group to resolve construction problems in the design stage of a structure. The class also allowed each student to see that preparatory decisions made early in the structures life cycle inevitably makes them pro-active to solving problems rather than being reactive during the actual construction process.

The course defined and created from AEC industrial recommendations for a BIM curriculum was an overall success. While there were glitches in the beginning due to lack of information, the overall course went very smoothly. According to end of year evaluations, each student thought the class was challenging but very helpful in their education and would benefit them later while applying for jobs in the AEC industry. The overall schedule for the class was changed multiple times through the semester due to lack of information obtained or lack of knowledge on students understanding of MEP or Structural print reading but in the end each came away with a greater understanding of their future roles in the AEC industry.

And even though a few course objectives were not accomplished, the ones that were achieved will help the students in future employment scenarios.

FUTURE RESEARCH DIRECTIONS

The course will be modified slightly in future semesters to include a complete set of construction documents presented at the end of the course. Since it is a construction graphics curriculum, it makes common sense to include a set of working construction documents to be submitted since each student will be producing those every day in industry. Also, there will be smaller projects assigned. The two buildings selected in the initial course were extremely large to accomplish everything in one semester. Future building projects will be ½ the size of the building selected for this course. The group sizes will also be cut in half. This will force each student to take on more responsibilities as well as get introduced to more technologies.

Each modification was a direct result of information obtained by industry, the instructor's observation and experience in AEC industry, or student comments from semester evaluations. Surprisingly, most students were very vocal when it came to course input for future course content. While most are wrapped up with finishing finals or interviewing for jobs, these students were trying to help create a course that would benefit future students. The instructor was pleased to read so many comments about course improvements. The students that took the class for the first time all mentioned that they see the benefits of industrial input and the comments they included were a way to give back to Purdue for all it has done for them.

CONCLUSION

The course presented above was created from data collected from AEC professionals with years of construction and BIM experience. The curriculum is an ongoing and evolving entity at Purdue University in the Construction Graphics area of focus within Computer Graphics Technology. Real world experiences with hands on focus are how most technology students learn. While the AEC industry is going through the greatest changes it has seen in the last 25 years, the curriculum at Purdue will remain in constant state of change and update due to technological advancements and how the BIM is utilized in the AEC industry. With the help of the AEC industrial professionals that consult with Purdue University faculty, the students are receiving the best education possible

which inevitably will jump start their professional careers with internships and ultimately obtain them permanent positions in the AEC industry.

REFERENCES

Autodesk. (2007). *Revit building information modeling: BIM goes to school.* Retrieved November 16, 2007, from http://students2.autodesk.com/ ama/ orig/BIM_Goes_To_School.pdf

Autodesk. (2007b). *Frequently asked questions.* Retrieved October 16, 2007, from http://usa.autodesk. com/adsk/ servlet/index?siteID=123112&id= 8497694#section2

Building Design and Construction Magazine Website. (2007). *BIM adoption accelerating, owners study finds.* Retrieved November 20, 2007, from http://www.bdcnetwork.com/ bim-adoption-accelerating- owners-study-finds

Constructech. (2007). BIM builds its case. *Constructech Magazine, 10*(9), 25-28.

Dowhal, D. (1997). A seven – dimensional approach to graphics. *ACM Asterisk Journal of Computer Documentation, 21*(4), 26–37. doi:10.1145/270871.270875

Fisher, R. A. (1922). On the interpretation of χ^2 from contingency tables, and the calculation of P. *Journal of the Royal Statistical Society, 85*(1), 87–94. doi:10.2307/2340521

Kymmell, W. (2006). *Outline for a BIM curriculum.* Retrieved September 25, 2007, from http:// www7.nationalacademies.org/ FFC/willem_kymmell_csu.pdf

Merriam-Webster Online Dictionary. (2007). *Visualization.* Retrieved from http://www.merriam-webster.com/ dictionary/visualization

Messner, J. I., & Horman, M. J. (2003). Using advanced visualization tools to improve construction education. *Proceedings of CONVR 2003, Conference on Construction Applications of Virtual Reality*, Blacksburg, VA, (pp. 145-155).

Purdue University. (2007). *CGT 460: Building information modeling for commercial construction. Course syllabus*. Retrieved October 16, 2007 from http://www2.tech.purdue.edu/ cgt/courses/cg460

Sullivan, C. (2007). Integrated BIM and design review for safer, better buildings: How project teams using collaborative design reduce risk, creating better health and safety in projects. *McGraw Hill Construction Continuing Education*. Retrieved November 16, 2007, from http://construction. com/CE/ articles/0706navis-3.asp

KEY TERMS AND DEFINITIONS

2D CAD: Current method of construction documentation based on limiting drawings in two dimensions. 2D CAD communicates the design intent with the following characteristics: Replicating manual drafting process (low-tech); Often having missing, inconsistent, or erroneous information; Hard to support collaboration; Conflicts detected at construction site; Expensive to fix and maintain; Containing only lines and shapes.

3D Images: Images that simulate 3D perception of an object in a 2D computer screen display that provides more information such as depth. This information enhances the observers' detection of image edges which allows an observer to extract specific information.

4D Construction: A computer-generated model that is three-dimensional and adds a time component such as a schedule. When the aspect of time is added to three-dimensional project components to generate construction schedules automatically integrated in the 3D model, we achieve a 4D representation, which dynamically manages the resources over time.

BIM: "Building Information Modeling (BIM) is the creation and use of coordinated, internally consistent, computable information about a building project in design and construction. The ability to keep this information up-to-date and accessible in an integrated digital environment gives architects, engineers, builders, and owners a clear overall vision of their projects and contributes to the ability to make better decisions faster—helping raise the quality and increase the profitability of projects" (Autodesk, 2007b).

Collision Detection/Avoidance: Digital plans can be merged to illustrate areas where installed materials interfere spatially.

Construction Sequencing Planning/Phasing Plans/Logistics: The element of "time" can be added to the model to create a visual construction sequence plans and aid in the development of Site Logistics plans.

Design Visualization: Visualization often with 3D view that helps clarify the design intent.

Scope Clarification: Design can be dissected for each subcontractor to reveal his or her portion of the work.

Visualization: The formation of mental visual images or the process of interpreting in visual terms or of putting into visible forms.

Chapter 9
Constructivist Learning Theory in Virtual Design Studios

Leman Figen Gül
TOBB University of Economics and Technology, Turkey

Anthony Williams
University of Newcastle, Australia

Ning Gu
University of Newcastle, Australia

ABSTRACT

In the authors' design teaching, they have been employing virtual world technologies, allowing students the capacity to collaborate and design within a constructivist immersive design platform such as Second Life (www.secondlife.com) and Active Worlds (www.activeworlds.com). These environments support synchronous design communication and real-time 3D modelling. Particularly, 3D immersive design environments have the potential to make a major contribution to design education as constructivist learning environments. Based on authors' teaching experience and the students' learning experience, this chapter discusses 3D virtual world as constructivist learning environments that support team-based design and communication skill-building and presents the challenges faced by design education today. The chapter firstly provides a critical analysis of various design learning and teaching features offered in 3D virtual worlds as constructivist learning environments, secondly, identifies a number of key issues in addressing engagement and interaction in virtual design learning, thirdly, addresses the core skills and cognitive processes of designing in 3D virtual worlds, and finally, provides several strategies for the facilitation of virtual worlds as the constructivist design teaching platform.

1. INTRODUCTION

Recently the developments in and extensive use of internet technologies have brought about fundamental changes in the way designers practice and collaborate. This has led to the transformation

DOI: 10.4018/978-1-61350-180-1.ch009

of their organizations through implementation of higher levels of IT-based strategies. In response to these changing trends in design practice, design schools have been using these advanced information and communication technologies in design curricula. Design education is concerned with teaching theory and applications in the design of artefacts that could occupy human activities. Historically, schools of architecture taught "descriptive geometry" (Lee and Reekie 1949), based on an Euclidean understanding of form and space. The revolution of the paper making technology in the fifteenth century can be considered as the "application" that enabled "the intellectualization of buildings", leading the notion of architecture as we know it today (Kvan et al. 2004). Innovative approaches to design education should consider the impact of computer technologies on creating "new ways of designing" (Kvan et al. 2004) and integrating digital skills (craft) and design thinking (art) (Kvan et al. 2004; Gül et al. 2007).

In relation to this view, 3D virtual worlds offer many opportunities for design teaching and learning, the most known of which is the support for constructivist learning. There are approaches which integrate the emerging fields of digital design into design education, such as employing parametric design, interaction design, experiential design, graphic design, product design, etc. Although these studies use new technologies in design education, there is still a general lack of research and practice which explores the potential of design teaching in 3D virtual worlds as constructivist learning environments. Perkins (1991) classified constructivist paraphernalia including information banks, symbol pads, construction kits and task managers. According to Perkins, computational tools facilitate human memory and intelligence to interpret experience and to refine mental models. Thus computer-supported constructivist learning environments focus on how representations and applications can mediate interactions among learners and natural or social phenomena (Dede 1995).

2. A CONSTRUCTIVIST VIEW OF DESIGN LEARNING

2.1 Introduction to Constructivist Learning

A constructivist view of learning focuses on the process of knowledge construction with concept development achieving a comprehensive understanding of the goals (Resnick 1986; Fosnot 1996). Constructivism is characterized by an approach where individuals construct their own understanding and knowledge of the world, through confronting new experiences and reflecting on those experiences (Huitt 2003; Mahoney 2004). According to the constructivist view, the learning process involves the following two concepts:

1. Knowledge is obtained and understanding is expanded through active (re)constructions of mental frameworks (Piaget through Bransford et al. 2000; Abbott and Ryan 1999), and the learner's previous knowledge constructions, beliefs and attitudes are considered in the knowledge construction process (Murphy 1997); and

2. Learning is an active process involving deliberate progressive construction and deepening of meaning (Spady 2001). Learning situations, environments, skills, content and tasks are relevant, realistic, authentic and represent the natural complexities of the 'real world' (Murphy 1997).

In contrast to behaviourism which centres on students' efforts to accumulate knowledge of the world and on teacher's effort to transmit it, in the constructivist view of learning, teachers play the roles of coordinators or facilitators. A subtle difference between behaviourism and constructivism is that behaviourism emphasizes observable and external behaviours, constructivism takes a more cognitive approach, has profound implications for all aspects of a theory of learning (Murphy 1997).

Table 1. Characteristics of a behaviourist compared to a constructivist approach

	Behaviorist	**Constructivist**
Focus of teaching	Learning for doing	Learning for being
Knowledge produced	Practical	Experimental
Curriculum structure	Processes	Issues
Teaching style	Demonstrations	Facilitation
Role of teacher	Master	Collaborator
Teaching strategies	Practical demonstrations	Participation

Researchers articulate differently the constructivist view of learning by emphasizing different components, such as the types of knowledge, skills and attitudes, the role of teacher and learner, and how goals are established, etc.

The constructivist theories provide the basis for much of the considerations of learning at the tertiary level at this time. Rather than delve into the psychological learning theories, however, let us look at what learning means to us as tertiary teachers. Table 1 documents the characteristics of the models of learning.

According to Phye (1997) constructivism is a movement that combines cognition from a developmental perspective with other important issues, such as motivation, self-directed learning and focus on the social context of learning (as cited in Chen et al. 2003). Cognitive constructivism – focusing on the cognitive processes people use to understand the world and social constructivism (see Durkheim 1973) – focusing on learning as a social process wherein students acquire knowledge through discussion with others, both primarily impact the "competent, creative, mindful, collaborative and constructive dimensions" of learning (Spady 2001). The social version of constructivism emphasizes how students can gain new strategies through peer collaboration by interpersonal discourse (Forman and Cazden 1985). The influential psychologist Bruner (1966) makes the case for education as a knowledge-getting process:

"To instruct someone... is not a matter of getting him to commit results to mind. Rather, it is to teach him to participate in the process that makes possible the establishment of knowledge. We teach a subject not to produce little living libraries on that subject, but rather to get a student to think mathematically for her/himself, to consider matters as an historian does, to take part in the process of knowledge-getting. Knowing is a process not a product" (1966: 72) (as cited in Smith 2002).

According to Bruner (1973), learning is a social process, whereby students construct new concepts based on current knowledge. They select information, construct hypothesis and make decisions by integrating new experiences. Based on Bruner's theory (1973), a constructivist curriculum should provide the followings:

1. Instruction must be commensurate with the experiences that make the students willing and able to learn (readiness);
2. Instruction must be structured so that it can be easily understood by the students (spiral organization); and
3. Instruction should be designed to facilitate extrapolation (going beyond the given information).

Based on the above views, learning is a process of constructing meaningful representation, and of making sense of one's experiential world. Thus learning emphasizes the process and not the final product. Von Glasersfeld (1995) pointed out that "from the constructivist perspective, learning is not a stimulus-response phenomenon. It requires self-regulation and building of the conceptual structures through reflection and abstraction" (Von Glasersfeld 1995). We have adapted the above approaches into our design teaching curriculum which includes problem-solving situations and design collaboration in a virtual design studio context.

2.2 A Constructivist View of Design Learning

Broadly, the educational approaches for various design disciplines fall into three groups: Those evolving from a fine-arts background and generally conforming to a studio-based Beaux Artes educational model; those evolving from a technology background and generally conforming to an applied science educational model; and those who have sought alternative approaches, generally being combinations of Beaux Artes and scientific models.

Interest in alternative educational approaches to design education has been gradually increasing since the Bauhaus experiments of the 1930s in Germany and their "migration" to America in the post-war years and then to design education institutions throughout the developed world. The "Reflective Practitioner" philosophy of Donald Schön (1983) of the University of Wisconsin Milwaukee, USA, focused particularly on architectural and engineering education, was developed from Bauhaus principles and led initially to the introduction of "Problem-Based Learning" by Donald Woods (1985) of McMaster University, Ontario, Canada for undergraduate engineering design education. Woods' approach was a form of experiential learning focusing on integration of diverse knowledge and skills, and problem-solving praxis to meet "real world" relevance expected by employers, all brought together through reflection.

A variation on a combination of Schön's and Woods' themes was a "cognitive apprentice"

model (also called "Problem-Based Learning") developed by Howard Barrows (1986) for medical education. This, in turn, was further adapted to architectural and other design education domains, including particularly a "Block" model in architecture and related design programs at TUDelft (Westrik et al. 1994) Netherlands and an "Integrated Learning" model and a "Research-Based Learning" model in architecture (Maitland 1985) at the University of Newcastle, Australia. The outstanding success and acceptance of Woods', Schön's, Barrows', Delft's and Newcastle's models led to further adaptations across a wide range of design education disciplines.

Many design educators reacted against these innovations and entrenched themselves in "scientific" design education approaches based on rigorous analytical design routines. A majority, however, adopted various combinations of scientific and studio-based approaches, with studio-based tutorials and master classes for some parts of their programs, and analytical, procedural approaches for the other parts, often using parts of Schön's and Woods' theories to justify existing conventional studio-based tutorial and master-class design teaching practices.

As an ongoing process, constructivism can be employed as a design teaching approach which includes the facilitation of the emerging information and communication technologies. The term constructivism refers to the idea that learners construct knowledge for themselves, each individual construct meaning as s/he learns (Hein 1991). Von Glasersfeld (1987) talked of constructivism as a theory of knowledge which involves two basic principles:

1. Knowledge is actively constructed by the learner, not passively received from the environment; and

2. Coming to know is a process of adaptation based on and constantly modified by learner's experience of the world (Jaworski 1993).

Powers (2001) stated that the design "studio is an excellent place for the outgrowth of constructivism. The nature of design with its uncertainty and irregularities are congruent with the epistemology and ontology of constructivist pedagogy. Inclusion of constructivist ideology within the current curriculum and studio courses will help add theoretical credibility to existing studio teaching practices and most importantly increase learning and advance construction of knowledge".

3. APPLYING CONSTRUCTIVIST LEARNING THEORY IN VIRTUAL DESIGN STUDIOS

Research of educational use of Virtual Reality (VR) provides compelling evidence of the potential of the emerging 3D virtual worlds to facilitate constructivist learning activities (Winn 1993; Dede 1995; Dede et al. 1996). One of the main advantages of VR identified is that students are able to view an object or setting from multiple perspectives (Dede 1995). Dede (1995) points out that virtual environments offer many benefits including opportunities for experimentation without real-world repercussions, opportunities to "learn by doing", or "experiential learning" and ability to personalize an environment.

From the mid 1990s, virtual design studios (Kahneman and Tversky 1996; Maher 1999; Kvan et al. 2000; Kolarevic et al. 2000; Schnabel et al. 2001) have been established in architecture and design schools internationally. These virtual design studios aim to provide a shared "place" where distant design collaboration can take place especially synchronous communications and design activities. The forms of virtual design studios vary from the early approach of digital design data sharing to the more recent 3D virtual world approach where the designs as well as the designers and the learners, are simulated and represented in the virtual worlds allowing "design and learning within the design". This new phenomenon has caught the attention of many design academics.

The underlying principles of learning and cognition are the same for all media and learning environments (Wilson and Lowry 2000), including virtual environments. Winn (1993) identified four different approaches in educational computing. The first one is based on behavioural theory that gave rise to traditional approaches to instructional design (Dick and Carey 1985; Gagne et al. 1988) that includes:

1. Predicting students' behaviour (Reigeluth 1983);
2. Reducing necessary knowledge and skills by using appropriate analytical techniques (Landa 1983); and
3. Following a set of procedures to ensure that instruction developed by their systematic application will work effectively without further intervention from designers or teachers (Winn 1993).

The second approach is based on how information is presented to students (Fleming and Levie 1993). The emphasis in this approach is on how students process information and has a greater impact on what they have learned rather than on the accuracy of task reduction and prescription of instructional strategies on the basis of content (Winn 1993). Psychologists realize that cognitive theories of learning and instruction provide resources for instructional designers to draw upon for guidance rather than behavioural theory (Winn 1993).

The third approach which is based on cognitive theories arose from the belief that the nature of the interaction between the students and instruction is a determinant of learning equal to, if not of greater importance than content or how information is presented (Winn 1993). For example, Anderson's ACT cognitive theory (Anderson 1976; Anderson 1983) formed the basis of 'intelligent' computer-based tutors which included the following principals:

1. Identifying the goal structure of the problem space;
2. Providing instruction in the context of problem-solving;
3. Providing immediate feedback on errors;
4. Minimizing working memory load;
5. Adjusting the "grain size" of instruction with learning to account for the knowledge compilation process; and
6. Enabling the student to approach the target skill by successive approximation.

The fourth approach relies on an understanding of how students interact with courseware; the assumption is that, knowledge is constructed by the students themselves, not through the delivery by the courseware (Winn 1993). In this constructivist view, the knowledge is constructed, not transmitted and the students actively learn (Jonassen 1999). To enhance learning, students should be given opportunity for exploration and manipulation within the environment as well as opportunities for discourse between students (Dickey 2007). Within this content, students have opportunity to apply new knowledge and skills in a collaborative shared environment (Gül et al. 2007). In learning as constructivist activities, the role of teachers is "to help and guide the student in the conceptual organization of certain areas of experience" (Glasersfeld 1983).

In our development of designing and applying 3D virtual worlds in design education, we maintain the last two approaches of Winn's to emphasize the use of 3D virtual worlds as design and learning environments, providing structured tutorials, immediate feedbacks and the opportunities to interact within the environments. Integration of communication and information technologies into design curricula offers significant potentials for design schools, through their capacity to facilitate designing in new learning environments, advancing research and development in learning theories. Our research distinguishes itself from these studies by exploring the potential of 3D virtual worlds

as constructivist learning environments in design education. Further, we teach subjects that regard 3D virtual worlds as a design discipline in its own right. This is because 3D virtual worlds distinguish themselves from other networked technologies by having place characteristics (the use of the place metaphor in designing and constructing 3D virtual worlds). 3D virtual worlds are not just another medium of communication but rather the ultimate "world" where we shop, are entertained and get educated (Kalay and Marx 2001). Therefore virtual worlds can be perceived as an important extension of built environment for exploring and "inhabiting" spatial design in addition to supporting design simulation and remote team collaboration. Thus the aspect of 3D virtual worlds for design and collaboration is equally essential in these course developments. We characterize the application of constructivist learning in virtual design studios in the following sections:

3.1 Facilitating the Engagement in Virtual Design Studios

Virtual design studios provide the constructivist environments in which knowledge is created and determined viable through functional and social interaction. Based on the social constructivism approach, the world is accessible to us only through our shared interpretations, and the idea of an independent reality is at best an irrelevant abstraction and at worst incoherent (Gasper 1999). "'Truth' or 'reality' will be accorded only to those constructions on which people of a social group agree" (Heylighen 1993).

Our design teaching experience shows that in order to achieve the best outcome, constructing a shared goal and an understanding of the given problems are essential for the students in the virtual design studios. In most cases visual and verbal language provide the shared structure necessary for communicating meaningful ideas and concepts in the design situations. "Since the meaning is derived from language and language is interdependent between two or more persons, it follows that socio-cultural processes of negotiation, cooperation, conflict, rhetoric, ritual, roles, social scenarios, and the like are crucial factors in the development of meaning and reality" (Powers 2001).

Once the quality of an academic's teaching was the primary consideration, quality often measured in the quantity of content imparted. Now the shift in focus is to what the students are learning. We as academics should be shifting our thinking from what we do when we present sessions to students, to focus on the learning experience the student will have as a result of our teaching. This would include the knowledge skills and perhaps even values or attitudes that our students will have as a result of their learning.

Below is a summary of some of the principles:

3.1.1 Learning Must be Active

The virtual environment provides a student with a significant opportunity to engage in all aspects of the design process from problem analysis through to design and "construct" in the virtual domain. Students have the ability to develop not only the design but the design context and to bring into play themes which would not normally be available in a real world context. The opportunity to continually test their designs against the design parameters they created provides for the continual engagement of the student in the design. This raises the student engagement in designing and evaluating within self generated parameters.

The virtual domain also provides for a diversity of communication and design management scenarios and activities, again these engage the student in continual activities in the design process.

3.1.2 Focusing on the Learner through the Relevance of the Content

This is one of the most difficult and often overlooked aspects of university teaching. Knowledge is often irrelevant without the terms of reference by which students are able to evaluate it. As such it is important for us as teachers to provide a relationship between what we are asking the student to confront and the professional context for which the student will use the skill. An example of this situation evidences itself when engineering students are asked early in their university studies "what does an engineer do?" Often students in the lower years of their studies do not know, because at that time they have probably studied more science subjects than engineering subjects. Although the science subjects may provide "scaffolding" or foundation knowledge, to the students this is not readily apparent as they have no relevance to the profession of engineering.

As educators when introducing new content, especially if it is leading edge and not being fully utilized in the profession, we have to ensure the students understand how it is relevant to the profession and in the case of this chapter that may mean forecasting the relevant activities a learning experience may relate to, specifically remote collaboration and Building Information Modelling (BIM) systems as often occurred in a virtual design studio but not necessarily in a traditional face-to-face design studio.

3.1.3 Developing Clear Objectives to Provide Direction to Student Learning

Students' initial engagement with the virtual domain sees their levels of apprehension rise because of the lack of "structures" associated with the domain. Students in this situation of uncertainty invariably look to well developed learning objectives as their "safety net". Therefore it is important for the teachers of this type of activity to have clearly articulated learning outcomes expressed in terms of both project and personal developments.

3.1.4 Articulating Knowledge and Learning Experiences

Effective education in the context of higher education is composed of three complex and closely interrelated operative components, with the implementation of virtual reality into the curriculum it is important that these components align:

1. Course curricula must be considered as setting the content of a the virtual learning experience but also to be seen as setting the detailed outcome-objectives of the virtual learning experience;

2. Teaching protocols which are generally considered as methods of delivery of a course must be aligned with the strategies and tactics for achieving the virtual learning experience outcomes, this will involve teachers approaching the teaching of the students in a different way, most notably using the virtual domain as the teaching "location"; and

3. Assessment protocols which are generally considered as tests of individual students' achievement in terms of the content, but can also be seen as strategies and tactics for monitoring the student achievement of the learning outcome.

In practical terms, what we teach and how we teach it should be derived from criteria for assessment. The assessment being the focus of the student engagement with learning, the assessment becomes the initiator of learning in which it focuses the students' attention on synthesizing the information into design. The assessment criteria need to be explicit in their description of the expected outcomes. The learning resources must then support the needs of the learner as they confront the assessment item. The methodological approach to the delivery of the information needs to also be appropriate to the learning experience, for example providing information in lectures may not support a very heuristic design problem being confronted by students. The assessment and the criteria which detail the learning outcomes drive the learner, and the teaching and resources which support the learner must be appropriate for the situation.

3.1.5 Ensuring the Application of Effective Feedback Mechanisms

Feedback is critical to students' new learning experiences, therefore it is imperative to develop appropriate "formative" feedback strategies. These strategies will not only give a student clear indications of their performance against the learning outcomes for the experience but will also provide encouragement and support students in their confrontation of the new learning experiences. This is especially important when students are facing new learning environments such as the virtual design studios as this will challenge them by taking them out of their normal learning environment, the real world. Students in such situations invariably look to feedback for support. Such support will not only give them confidence in the new environment but it will also encourage creativity, the opportunity for creative thinking is significant in the virtual domain. It will be through the effective feedback strategies that confidence to confront new learning experience will be fostered. This is especially the case early in the project where it will facilitate them engaging and exploring new design boundaries with confidence.

3.1.6 Employing Effective "Scaffolding" in the Organization of the Learning Experiences

Students have a great deal of difficulty transferring knowledge and skills across context boundaries when a virtual learning experience is introduced. This provides opportunity for the teacher to develop strategies and projects that will encourage and support the development of this capacity.

Students will not necessarily enjoy their virtual learning experience unless a range of preparatory knowledge and skills are imparted to support their introduction experience. These skills which the problem solving processes require must be supported.

3.1.7 Encouraging Collaborative Learning

There is a wealth of evidence indicating that peer learning and teaching is extremely effective for wide range of goals, content, and students of different levels and personalities (Johnson et al. 1981). Collaborative learning appears to play an important part in design education. Students often learn more when interacting with other students than listening to instructors alone. In a virtual learning context, students experience problems in building trust and social communication as well as receiving and giving timely feedback. The use of variety of methods and tools for monitoring tasks, communication and design should be encouraged.

3.2 Exploring Design Opportunities within Virtual Design Studios

Today the communication and information technologies bring new challenges and opportunities to design education which require the consideration of new pedagogical approaches when employing emerging design fields. An innovative approach to design education should include a demonstration of the impact of computer technologies on "new ways of designing" (Kvan et al. 2004) integrating the teaching of digital skills (craft) and the concept of design thinking (art). In relation to this view, the emerging field of 3D virtual worlds offers many opportunities for design teaching that requires understanding the principles of virtual worlds design, in addition to the well-known design simulation aspects with metaphorical references to built environment design.

3.2.1 Virtual Worlds Design and Interaction Design

Designing in virtual worlds can go beyond imitating the built environment yet still focuses on accommodating human activities, in particular, interactions that are not readily available in the physical environments. A unique property of virtual worlds is the capacity for the architecture, objects or avatars (animated virtual characters) to be dynamic and interactive, adapting and responding to the actions of their inhabitants (Maher and Merrick 2005). Unlike the built environment, where behaviour is usually attributed to characters (inhabitant or user of the design), or sometimes objects or appliances, in virtual worlds behaviour can be attributed to any element of the environment. For examples, rooms may be able to change size or shape for different activities or furniture may be able to rearrange or reconfigure itself as needed. The examples of virtual world design as interaction design include the largely popular interactive online games and the recently emerging agent-based intelligent worlds. Situated in such an environment, a software agent is capable of reasoning about the world and acting upon its beliefs and desires (Wooldridge 2000). Mediated with software agents, 3D virtual worlds become intelligent networked environments. Smith et al. (2003) develop 3D virtual worlds that respond to their inhabitants in reflective, reactive and even proactive modes. This is achieved by applying a multi-agent model which enables each component in the virtual world to be an agent. Using a design agent model, Gu and Maher (2005) develop dynamic 3D virtual worlds that are designed and modified as needed during use. These examples provide valuable exploration and validation contributing to the understanding and scenario development of interactive architecture.

3.2.2 Designing within the Design

Maher and Simoff (2000) first characterize the design activities in 3D virtual worlds as "Designing within the Design". Unlike in the general CAD systems designers in virtual worlds are represented as avatars that are immersed within the design. This characteristic enables the designer to actively engage as a part of the design rather than only observing the design as an "outsider". This concept has also been studied to enhance remote team collaboration in design practice (Rosenman et al. 2005). 3D virtual worlds provide an integral platform that utilizes team collaboration, design representation, modelling and in the case of designing virtual worlds, even design realization.

3.3 A Virtual Studio that Facilitates Constructivist Learning

To demonstrate the principles discussed above for employing virtual worlds as constructivist learning environments, we introduce the following collaborative virtual design studio. Together with other teaching cases, it also serves as a means for our teaching evaluation and reflection. "Designing Virtual Worlds" was offered as a 10-credit unit. The weekly schedule includes one hour lecture and a two hour design studio.

In "Designing Virtual Worlds" we not only structured a virtual design studio that support collaborative design and learning, we also encouraged students to explore design potentials in 3D virtual worlds and to consider designing 3D virtual worlds an unique design discipline in its own right. Following is the details of the course.

3.3.1 Course Introduction

The aim of the course was for students to understand and develop the essential skills of collaborative design and modelling using 3D virtual worlds; to develop the understanding and hands-on experience of 3D virtual worlds as the simulation and extension of traditional built environment. The course content has two major components:

1. Understanding collaborative design and developing the essential skills for collaborative design in 3D virtual worlds; and
2. Understanding and applying the principles and practical techniques for designing and implementing 3D virtual worlds.

In order for students to develop the understanding of collaborative design in 3D virtual worlds, firstly, relevant theories such as the development of core skills for teamwork, as well as design and collaborative cases in 3D virtual worlds were introduced and discussed, the concepts associated with collaborating across cultures were also raised. Secondly, students were guided to inhabit and critically assess a wide variety of design examples in 3D virtual worlds, as well as various design (3D modelling and rendering) and communication features (synchronous and asynchronous communication) supported in the constructivist design platform. In order for the students to develop and practice the design and collaborative skills for 3D virtual worlds, a remote collaborative design project was used as the major assessment item.

Our first collaboration in 2008 attracted 36 University of Newcastle (Australia) students from the second year undergraduate architecture program. They were divided into groups consisting of three to four individuals. Each group was then paired with one to two remote collaborators from Rangsit University, Thailand, who were enrolled in their third year undergraduate architecture program. Students from both universities remotely collaborated over the period of five weeks on a design project titled "Virtual Home" in Second Life. Students were expected to collaborate also outside of the scheduled studio times. With scheduled supervision in design development supplemented by technical tutorials supporting students' technical skill development, the collaborative design project provided opportunities for students to:

1. Experience and practice collaborative design in 3D virtual worlds; and
2. Develop and apply principles and technical skills for virtual world design.

The design brief required each group to design and implement a place in Second Life which will demonstrate their concept of a virtual home and this will challenge the boundaries of the concept of home as a traditional built environment (developed by students in an earlier traditional architectural studio).

3.3.2 The Design and Collaboration Process

As we are employing the constructivist learning approach in the virtual design studio it is important to establish a prior knowledge of the students. Thus we acquired background information of the students; based on the information the groups are formed to ensure each group had students from both universities and that they can complement each other's design skills and interest. The students functioned as a remote collaborative design team. They are required to explore the potentials of virtual worlds, and design and model a virtual home in Second Life. Each of the groups went through a process of formal introduction and had the opportunity to hold more informal discussions prior to the collaboration; this was to minimize the expected cultural issues.

The virtual home project was to challenge the traditional design concept of home as a built environment, and reflect the unique characteristic and experience possible in virtual worlds. In relation to the constructivist theory, the aim of the task is to provide a condition for ambiguity and uncertainty, and because "the embedding of learning within relevant context is important" (Powers, 2001). Therefore the virtual design studio provided a constructivist learning platform for learning situations, skills, content and tasks that are realistic and authentic. Each team was assigned a plot of "virtual land" in Second Life for project design and implementation which requires problem-solving and higher-order thinking skills as well as a deep understanding of design concepts.

Within each design of the virtual home, each team member is required to design and "own" a personal item such as an individual area, a piece of virtual furniture, a virtual object, an ornament, and so on. This personal item would share a consistent style of the virtual home and contribute to the overall place making of the virtual home.

Each team was required to design its team dynamics and to establish team management protocols. This involved them defining the roles of team members, and to discuss their plans and protocols with their tutor during the early weeks of the project. Providing an environment that encourages social negotiation is an integral part of constructivist learning. In the virtual design studio students were required to plan and set their own goals, reflect and assess their progress as well as determine how to proceed. The tutor's role in this instance was to offer advice and assist in the facilitation. The tutor's role in these activities would diminish over the project allowing the student design groups to take ownership of their decision making.

The quality of the communication between the individuals in the groups was critical to the outcomes of the project on both the design level and the team management level. To facilitate the communication each design team are required to use Second Life or to be supplement with other electronic communication tools such as Skype, MSN Messenger, email, etc. (if needed) to conduct at least one project meeting per week during the collaboration. The expectation was that at least one third of these meetings were to be conducted synchronously in Second Life with full attendance and participation of team members in the design activity. Each team was also required to keep weekly project meeting logs or comprehensive communication records such as blog entries or compiled email messages.

3.3.3 Project Outcomes

The project outcomes were demonstrated by the following:

1. A virtual home collaboratively designed and modelled in Second Life;
2. A PowerPoint presentation; and
3. Weekly meeting logs or communication records that demonstrate effective remote team collaboration.

The outcomes achieved by the students were diverse and they provided much for both the students and us as educators to reflect on, in terms of the design potential of virtual worlds. Selected designs of virtual homes are illustrated in Figure 1, each of which represents a different approach to virtual world design. We briefly summarize each of the selected design as follows:

1. "Zero Gravity": Virtual worlds have no physical constraints such as gravity but still support various activities. This design uses (non) gravity as the design trigger to challenge the constraint of gravity and to have different spaces hanging upside down within a sphere, as shown in 1;
2. "Interactive Home": The design interprets virtual home as series of isolated places for supporting series of activities (interactions). The combination of these places can change

and is purely determined by the needs of the activities, as shown in 2.

3. "Archi-Bio": The design is inspired by bio-mechanisms and the students compose and transform those dynamic and growing modules of "home components" into their virtual home in Second Life, as shown in 3.

4. ANALYSIS OF 3D VIRTUAL WORLDS AS DESIGN LEARNING ENVIRONMENTS

Most 3D virtual worlds offer constructivist learning environments and can enhance learning by:

1. Providing opportunities for exploration and manipulation in the virtual environments;
2. Providing opportunities for discourse between students and other users' of the environments; and
3. Providing opportunities to actively build skills and knowledge in relation to their interest.

Reflecting on our experience, we maintain the last two approaches of Winn's to emphasize the use of 3D virtual worlds as design and learning environments, providing structured tutorials, immediate feedbacks and the opportunities to interact within the environments. The following section discusses 3D virtual worlds as constructivist learning environments in terms of:

Figure 1. Three selected virtual home designs

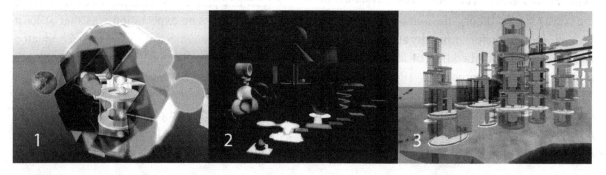

Figure 2. The unique appearance of selected student designs, an interior of a space (left) and a landscape design (right)

1. Design features in 3D virtual worlds which are essential for supporting constructivist learning; and
2. Two aspects of human behaviour (core skills and cognitive behaviour) which should be considered when teaching in constructivist learning environments.

4.1 Evaluations of Design Features in 3D Virtual Worlds

3D modelling features: 3D virtual worlds offer many possibilities for understanding and testing different design objects and their spatial arrangement to develop student's spatial abilities. Second Life supports different viewpoints including both the first-person view and third-person view. Changing the camera view and flying over the places are also possible for design exploration in the virtual world.

Second Life supports the parametric design method which comprises a set of objects whose forms are determined inside the world by selecting geometric types and manipulating their parameters. They can also be freely adjusted within the world at any stage. Design platforms that support

the parametric design method are therefore modelling tools as well. The affordance of Second Life encourages students to generate design models that look unique (Gül et al. 2008). Figure 2 shows some of the student's designs which have their own unique style.

As a constructivist design teaching platform, Second Life represents the natural complexities of the "real world" providing personal relevance. Providing personal relevance can be achieved by simulating authentic problems without lowering the cognitive complexity. "Since these problems are similar to the challenges students will face in their real world, tasks requiring problem-solving become more engaging" (Powers, 2001). Second Life provides a platform where students can start designing from the early stage using basic geometric forms. However, this can be a challenge for some students who were novice designers. Some students commented that they had to sketch their design ideas on paper in order to understand the overall design layout, prior to modelling the design in Second Life.

Collaborative Design and Workspace Awareness: Second Life supports the presence of designers/learners and their collaborators (awareness of self and others), use of place metaphor (awareness of the place); navigation and orientation (way finding aids). Most virtual worlds support synchronous communication which often has a text-based and/or voice-based communication features. Users can communicate by typing in the chat dialogue box in Second Life; the texts appear above the avatars' heads. Users can talk to each other using their microphones and speakers. Figure 3 shows one of the chat sessions where the speeches of the users' appear above their avatars. In addition the sequence of the discussion can be followed from the left corner of the screen. In virtual design studios, it is important to moderate the discussion in a large class as multiple trends often emerge during online discussion which can easily lose the topic focus if there is not adequate moderation.

Second Life provides more workspace awareness through "consequential communication" and "feed-through". In consequential communication,

the characteristic movements of an action (for example typing including hand movements or walking including leg and body movement) communicate its character and content to others (Segal 1995). In feed-through, the feedback produced when objects are manipulated provides others with clues about the manipulations (Dix et al. 1993). For example, in Second Life, when a student is modelling/manipulating an object, a light blob that shows a link between the avatar and the object will appear, and when the student communicates using the keyboard, the avatar also appears to be typing in the virtual world. This feature supports workspace awareness through "consequential communication". In addition, in Second Life, when a student is transferring or moving an object, these manipulations are visible to others. This is an example of "feed-through" behaviours that support workspace awareness. Due to these features of Second Life, the students

Figure 3. Text balloons displayed above the heads of the avatars and the list of messages displayed on the bottom left of the window during the discussions.

are aware of each other's actions and can focus more on the development of the design model in a collaborative design task.

The ability to model collaboratively and to share models is essential for collaborative design in virtual worlds. In Second Life, the ownership of the objects can be flexibly arranged and shared, but one user only can manipulate an object's properties/location at a time. This means that students need to determine the overall concept of the design and separate the parts to construct the model. Thus these features of the 3D modelling environments might encourage the designers to work individually on separate parts of the design model in a collaborative task.

Scripting/programming for interactivity: Second Life enables in-world scripting to support interactions in the virtual environment. Second Life scripting is robust, as it supports a scripting language called LSL (Linden Script Language)[1], a programming language similar to Java.

The robust scripting environments do support advanced interactions well. However it can be quite difficult for designers without a computing background to master.

4.2. Evaluations of Human Behaviour in 3D Virtual Worlds

Teaching virtual design studios in a constructivist learning environment requires an understanding of students' design and learning behaviour, in particular an understanding of the key aspects of human communication and cognitive processes.

Core skills for teamwork in 3D virtual worlds: The core skills are essential for design collaboration in 3D virtual worlds; therefore they are important for students to master and should be embedded in virtual design studios taught in 3D virtual worlds. Bellamy et al. (2005) identified the following core skills for designers to effectively participate in collaborative design:

- Leadership is important because it decides the balance of relevant skills and contribu-

tions required from team members. Team leader(s) need to be able to create teams that identify the important "social links" between team members (Baird et al. 2000);

- Co-ordination and structuring skills are required for team members to work collaboratively in a virtual environment (Lahti et al. 2004);
- Feedback abilities are also important skills for team members. This is crucial because large amounts of information often need to be validated in virtual worlds (Baird et al, 2000);
- Interpersonal relationships between virtual team members can impact on the team's ability to provide a satisfactory product. In addition, social collaboration appears to play an important part especially when researching and determining limitations; and
- Trust is not easily created in a computer-mediated environment including 3D virtual worlds, especially when team members have no prior experience. The commitment of others fosters trust, but this trust may not reach its highest level until the end of a task (Jarvenpaa and Liedner 1998).

We have emphasized the above issues during the delivery of the virtual design studio. One of the objectives of the studio was for students to exercise group collaboration skills. Based on students' previous design experience and programming/scripting skills, the groups were formed. Since the main consideration of forming the groups was the students' background, trust and shared understanding of the design context took some time to establish between group members. In our experience, we require the groups to submit weekly collaborative design journals and weekly online meeting records as minor assessment items to reinforce the collaboration, and to encourage the students to exercise the core skills.

Communication in 3D virtual worlds: In general, communication presents a challenge in virtual worlds. A number of factors constrain these interactions, for example:

- A lack of visual cues and auditory input might affect the quality of shared understanding. Even when visual cues are used (e.g. augmented with video conferences or web cameras) team members' abilities to communicate using non-verbal interactions (such as body language) can be inhibited (Hoyt 2000);

- The technology does present some advantages when communicating over distance as they often allow more focused and concise information exchange between team members (Gabriel and Maher 1999; Maher et al. 2000), and assist team members keeping to their task (Cleland and Ireland 2002);

- Baird et al (2000) find that the virtual environment may not foster skills such as feedback. Furthermore, Williams and Cowdroy (2002) note that communication is easier if team members have previously worked together;

- Synchronicity is also an issue as virtual teams can operate in both synchronous and asynchronous virtual environments (Maher et al. 2000); and

- Research has shown that simply mimicking co-located settings such as teleconferences may result in fewer social interactions between team members as well as difficulties in sharing visual information (Gabriel and Maher 1999).

Our students collaborated both synchronously and asynchronously. Synchronous collaboration usually occurs during allocated meetings in remote locations. The students also reported that they used in-worlds communication tools which based on text as well as other synchronous platforms such as MSN Messenger, and asynchronous communication tools such as email and blog.

Collaborative design process in 3D virtual worlds: Understanding the processes of collaborative design is crucial for the development of learning materials and tools in virtual environments. Collaborative design activity requires the participation of individuals for sharing information and organizing design task and resources (Chiu 2002). Kvan et al. (1997) point out that as collaborators come together in design, the nature of their activity does not change, since collaboration still requires a designer to attend to design as an individual task, as well as collaborating. With the recent developments in virtual environments, there is a change in the way that design-related professionals collaborate and design. Researchers (Gül and Maher 2006; Maher et al. 2006) point out that the design process and the realization process are different between the co-located sketching and the designing in 3D virtual worlds. Therefore it is necessary to consider those differences during course development. These studies indicate that:

- Designing in 3D virtual worlds encourages immediate and detailed design decisions: The designers had the situation of immediacy to construct the design representation in the 3D virtual world, rather than exploring alternative design solutions. They concretized their design solution without much iteration in the design process, because designing in remote locations require extra attention that resulted longer attention spans and less iterations (Gül and Maher 2009). They often quickly decided on a particular design idea and constructed it;

- Designing in 3D virtual worlds encourages individual designing on the model: The designers stayed in the distributed design situation in the 3D virtual world, where they often worked on individual tasks and then came together for negotiation and evaluation, staying in lower-level design ideas; and

- Spatial adjacency of the objects become the main design activity: The designers created the 3D model through the "continue" action in longer spans, thus allowing them to focus on the spatial relationships of the 3D objects (see Gül 2007 for more details).

Being consistent with the findings from the above collaborative design studies, we observe that a large number of groups maintained the same design concept which was developed in the early stages and spent most of their time on developing and refining the model and the implementation. Structured collaborative activities including task allocations, determining the roles and monitoring the process are also occurred during the project. To effectively support conceptual design in a computer-mediated environment is an open research question.

5. STRATEGIES FOR FACILITATING CONSTRUCTIVIST DESIGN LEARNING IN VIRTUAL DESIGN STUDIOS

Constructivist learning has emerged as a major approach to teaching during the past decade (Gagnon and Collay 1996). This shift represents a paradigm shift from an education based on behaviourism to an education based on cognitive theory. A constructivist approach to course planning focuses on student centred activities, which include selecting information, constructing hypotheses and making decisions. The cognitive paradigm of constructivism shifts the responsibility of learning from the teacher to the learner who is active in constructing new knowledge and understanding.

Over the years, design educators have explored different applications of 3D virtual worlds in design learning and reflected on their experiences. For example, it is argued that virtual design studios allow students to learn more about the design process, while the traditional design education has

focused on the product (Kvan 2001) 3D virtual worlds provide "experiential" and "situated" learning (Dickey 2005). The use of 3D virtual worlds can support social awareness when students from different cultural backgrounds design and learn collaboratively (Wyeld et al. 2006); and the role of place in virtual learning environments can encourage "collaboration and constructivism" (Clark and Maher 2005). Our teaching experience shows that to design and implement successful learning environments for virtual design studios require careful integration and adaptation of the following issues.

5.1 Embedding Learning in Experience and Knowledge Construction in a Problem-Solving Environment

From our experience the virtual design studio shows that the curriculum should be organized in a spiral manner so that students build upon what they have already learned. According to Bruner (1973), students construct new concepts based on existing knowledge aiming for combining the latest experiences with his/her existing mental construct. Students cannot learn by means of rote learning; they can only learn by "directed living" in which concrete activities are combined with theory (Dewey 1966). "Learning always proceeds from the known to the new" (Wilhem et al. 2001), and therefore the metaphor of scaffolding is also used. Scaffolding is a process of guiding the learners from what is presently known to what is to be known (Murphy 1997) by constructing an edifice that represents the student's cognitive abilities. The construction of knowledge starts from the level zero, on the foundation of what is already know and the new is built on top of the known. Teaching in virtual design studios should facilitate the basic components of this design activity through using a new medium or environment in which their existing design skills can be applied. It also engages the students to collaborate in a new context.

In general the design task involves the creation of an object which may have some functions with some practical and/or aesthetic values. The process of designing is considered a problem-solving activity that requires defining and analyzing the problem, proposing solutions, synthesizing and evaluating the design solutions. Note that there are synergies with the constructivist approach described above.

The efficient use of design representation, along with employing this generic design cycle, is essential in design teaching. Representations have many functions in design and their role is significant in virtual worlds through:

Firstly, they act as memory aids by offering external tokens for the design concepts/objects that must otherwise be kept in mind and freeing working memory to perform mental calculations on the objects. Another memory function of the design representation is to promote creativity by reminding the user about the conceptual knowledge which is necessary for problem-solving (Goldschmidt 1994; Suwa and Tversky 2002).

Secondly, design representations carry information that can be directly perceived and utilized without being interpreted and explicitly formulated, such as visuo-spatial and metaphoric calculation, inference and insight (Cox and Brna 1995). Inferences that are based on size, form, distance and directions are clearly made from design representations. Insights, particularly those based on spatial arrangement of the objects such as proximity and grouping may be facilitated by inspection of representations.

Finally, design representations serve as visual aids for design thinking in several ways, particularly, facilitating the formulation of a mental representation of a design concept as well as communication of design ideas.

The design problem-solving activity requires extra attention in virtual worlds: The detailing of many aspects of the objects such as working on position and location of the object in the world $(x, y, z$ coordinates) and elaborating sizes, shapes, colour and materials (Gül 2007). In addition,

studies show that when designers manipulate and modify the design artefact in virtual worlds, they produce more perceptual activities (attending the grouping, proximity, alignment etc.), produce more low-level design solutions (detailing objects) and inference about the structural aspects of the design artefact (Gül 2007). The virtual reality platform provides an enhanced design development and simulation space where designers/students develop prototypes of the end product, test and evaluate the design solution. Thus in constructivist virtual design studios, design tasks should be organized in a manner which includes above aspects of designing.

5.2 Encouraging Collaborative Learning

Many constructivist theories identify the importance of the role of social and cultural aspects to the construction of meaning (Resnick et al. 1991 as cited in Wilson et al. 2000). According to the social learning approach, knowledge is constructed whilst individuals are engaged in activities, receiving feedback, and participating in other forms of human interaction in public and social context (Henning 2004). Since cognition is not considered an individual process, learning and knowing are developed by the kinds of interactions a student has with others and the context within these interactions occur (Hill et al. 2009). Collaborative activities with others, promoted by the learning environment, allow them to develop multiple perspectives where some type of "shared reality" is produced (Cunningham 1991). The virtual world constructivist learning environment has great potential to provide a platform for social learning through remote interactions.

Our experience confirms that the virtual design studio provides an outstanding environment for collaborative learning and co-design situations in which students share the same goal, and achieve this goal through working and learning together on the 3D model. This 3D model becomes the ground on which conflicts, collaboration, critique and negotiation take place. Working on a shared 3D model also requires design and modelling coordination such as editing and modifying controls, monitoring the process and monitoring the other's activities etc. In addition, virtual worlds also provide features which support this facet of collaboration through such facilities as providing information about the presence of others and an awareness of other's activities.

Virtual design studios offer an excellent environment for students to learn from the experiences of their peers and co-participants through observing the actions of others, participating in open forums and discussions, which are more readily observable in the virtual world.

5.3 New Role for Teachers and Students

The constructivist approach to teaching design is based on the engagement with problems and tasks, this being the core to effective design education. Driver et al. (1994) defined two important components of a teacher's role in a constructivist classroom: The first is to introduce new ideas or cultural tools where necessary and to provide the support and guidance for students to make sense of these for themselves. Secondly to listen and diagnose the ways in which the instructional activities are initially being interpreted by students then used by them to inform further action. In this approach, the teacher steps out of the more traditional "didactic role" (Hanson and Sinclair 2008) and takes the role of facilitator, mentor, organizer, or leader, the teacher coaches students in a cognitive apprenticeship (Collins 1991). According to Von Glasersfeld's (1995) view, teachers play the role of a "midwife in the birth of understanding" instead of being "mechanics of knowledge transfer". The role of teachers is not to provide knowledge but to provide opportunities and incentives to build it up (Von Glasersfeld 1995).

In constructivist design studio, student's role is considered as active learners allowing them to construct their own knowledge by looking for meaning and associations. In this approach students interpret what they hear, read and see based on their previous experiences and knowledge. "From the constructivist perspective, learning is not a stimulus-response phenomenon. It requires self-regulation and the building of conceptual structures through reflection and abstraction" (Von Glasersfeld 1995). Student's learning is enhanced in the first-hand experience of engaging with realistic problems, projects, cases, simulations and experiments (Hanson et al. 2008). The virtual design studio enhances the opportunity to provide this experience through enhanced opportunities for synchronous and asynchronous co-design activities.

The constructivist virtual design studio provides a learning platform where the students have ownership of their learning and their "learning space", they also take responsibility for what to learn and how to learn. Taking the responsibility of their learning encourages students to become active in the knowledge construction and skill development process. In a virtual design studio, teachers on the other hand facilitate, coordinate, guide, or assist students in understanding and making sense of the concepts, skills and experience learnt.

REFERENCES

Abbott, J., & Ryan, T. (1999). *Constructing knowledge, reconstruction schooling.*

Anderson, J. (1976). *Language, memory and thought.* Hillsdale, NJ: Erlbaum Associates.

Anderson, J. (1983). *The architecture of cognition.* Cambridge, MA: Harvard University Press.

Baird, F., Moore, C. J., & Jagodzinski, A. P. (2000). An ethnographic study of engineering design teams at Rolls-Royce Aerospace. *Design Studies,* *21*(4), 333. doi:10.1016/S0142-694X(00)00006-5

Barrows, H. S. (1986). A taxonomy of problem-based learning methods. *Medical Education, 20*, 481–486. doi:10.1111/j.1365-2923.1986. tb01386.x

Bellamy, T. R., Williams, A. P., Sher, W. D., Sherratt, S. M., & Gameson, R. (2005). Design communication: Issues confronting both co-located and virtual teams. *Proceedings of the Association of Researchers in Construction Management 21st Annual Conference*, London.

Bransford, J., Brown, A., & Cocking, R. (Eds.). (2000). *How people learn: Brain, mind, experience and school*. Washington, DC: National Research Council.

Bruner, J. (1966). *The process of education: Towards a theory of instruction*. Cambridge, MA: Harvard University Press.

Bruner, J. (1973). *Going beyond the information given*. New York, NY: Norton.

Chen, Q., Grundy, J., & Hosking, J. (2003). *An E-whiteboard application to support early design-stage sketching of UML diagrams. Prodeecings of HCC*. IEEE.

Chiu, M.-L. (2002). An organizational view of design communication in design collaboration. *Design Studies, 23*(2), 187–210. doi:10.1016/ S0142-694X(01)00019-9

Clark, S., & Maher, M. L. (2005). *Learning and designing in a virtual place: Investigating the role of place in a virtual design studio. Proceedings of eCAADe, 2005*. Technical University of Lisbon.

Cleland, D., & Ireland, L. (2002). *Project management: Strategic design and implementation* (4th ed.). New York, NY: McGraw-Hill.

Collins, A. (1991). Cognitive apprenticeship and instructional technology. In Idol, L., & Jones, B. F. (Eds.), *Educational values and cognitive instruction: Implications for reform* (pp. 121–138). Hillsdale, NJ: Lawrence Erlbaum.

Cowdroy, R. M., & Williams, A. P. (2002). Assessing design activity: Issues and actions. *Proceedings of the 7th International Design Conference, DESIGN 2002*, Croatia.

Cox, R., & Brna, P. (1995). Supporting the use of external representations in expert problem-solving: the need for flexible learning environments. *Journal of Artificial Intelligence in Education, 6*(2).

Cunningham, D. (1991). Assessing construction and constructing assessments: A dialogue. *Educational Technology, 31*(5), 13–17.

Dede, C. (1995). The evolution of community support for constructionist learning: Immersion in distributed virtual worlds. *Educational Technology, 35*(5), 46–52.

Dede, C., Salzman, M., & Loftin, R. B. (1996). The development of virtual world for learning Newtonian mechnics. In P. Brusilovsky, P. Kommers & N. Streitz (Eds.), *Multimedia, hypermedia and virtual reality* (87-106). Berlin, Germany: Springer.

Dewey, J. (1966). *Democracy and education*. New York, NY: Free Press.

Dick, W., & Carey, L. (1985). *The systematic design if instruction*. Glenview, IL: Scott Foresman.

Dickey, M. D. (2005). Three-dimensional virtual worlds and distance learning: Two case studies of active worlds as a medium for distance education. *British Journal of Educational Technology, 36*(3), 439–451. doi:10.1111/j.1467-8535.2005.00477.x

Dickey, M. D. (2007). Teaching in 3D: Pedagogical affordances and constraints of 3D virtual worlds for synchronous distance education. *Distance Education, 24*(1), 105–121. doi:10.1080/01587910303047

Dix, A., Finlay, J., Abowd, G., & Beale, R. (1993). *Human-computer interaction Europa*. Printice Hall.

Driver, R., Aasoko, H., Leach, J., Mortimer, E., & Scott, P. (1994). Constructing scientific knowledge in the classroom. *Educational Researcher*, *23*(7), 5–12.

Durkheim, E. (1973). *Emile Durkheim on morality and society*. Chicago, IL: University of Chicago Press.

(1985). Exploring Vygotskian perspectives in education. InForman, E. A., & Cazden, C. B. (Eds.), *Culture, communication, and cognition: Vygotskian perspectives*. Cambridge, UK: Cambridge University Press.

Fleming, M. L., & Levie, W. H. (1993). *Instructional message design: Principles from the cognitive and behavioral science*. Hillsdale, NJ: Educational Technology Publications.

Fosnot, C. (1996). Constructivism: A psychological theory of learning. In Fosnot, C. (Ed.), *Constructivism: Theory, perspectives, and practice* (pp. 8–33). New York, NY: Teachers College Press.

Gabriel, G., & Maher, M. L. (1999). *Coding and modelling communication in architectural collaborative design*. ACADIA' 99.

Gagne, R. M., Briggs, L. J., & Wager, W. W. (1988). *Principles of instructional design*. New York, NY: Holt Rinehart and Winston.

Gagnon, G., & Collay, M. (1996). *Teacher's perspectives on a constructivist learning design*. Retrieved from http://www.prainbow.com/ cld/cldp.html.

Gasper, P. (1999). Definitions of constructivism. In Audi, R. (Ed.), *Cambridge dictionary of philosophy* (2nd ed., p. 855). Cambridge, UK: Cambridge University Press.

Glasersfeld, E. v. (1983). Learning as constructive activity. *Proceedings of the 5th Annual Meeting of the North American Group of PME*. Montréal, Canada: PME-NA.

Glasersfeld, E. v. (Ed.). (1987). *Learning as a constructive activity: Problems of representation in the teaching and learning of mathematics*. Hillslade, NJ: Lawrence Erlbaum.

Glasersfeld, E. v. (1995). A constructivist approach to teaching. In Steffe, L., & Gale, J. (Eds.), *Constructivism in education* (pp. 3–16). Lawrence Erlbaum Associates, Inc.

Goldschmidt, G. (1994). On visual design thinking: The vis kids of architecture. *Design Studies*, *15*(2), 158–174. doi:10.1016/0142-694X(94)90022-1

Gu, N., & Maher, M. L. (2005). Dynamic designs of 3D virtual worlds using generative design agents. *Proceedings of CAAD Futures* 2005, Dordrecht, The Netherlands: Springer.

Gül, L. F. (2007). *Understanding collaborative design in different environments: Comparing face-to-face sketching to remote sketching and 3D virtual worlds*. Key Centre for Design Cognition and Computing. Sydney, University of Sydney. PhD.

Gül, L. F., Gu, N., & Maher, M. L. (2007). *Designing virtual worlds: A case study of design education in and of 3D virtual worlds*. CONNECTED 07, International Conference on Design Education, Sydney.

Gül, L. F., Gu, N., & Williams, A. (2008). Virtual worlds as a constructivist learning platform: Evaluations of 3D virtual worlds on design teaching and learning. *ITCon. Special Issue Virtual and Augmented Reality in Design and Construction*, *13*, 578–593.

Gül, L. F., & Maher, M. L. (2006). The impact of virtual environments on design collaboration. *24th eCAADe Conference Proceedings*, Volos, Greece. ISBN 0-9541183-5-9

Gül, L. F., & Maher, M. L. (2009). Co-creating external design representations: Comparing face-to-face sketching to designing in virtual environments. *CoDesign*, *5*(2), 117–138. doi:10.1080/15710880902921422

Hanson, J., & Sinclair, K. (2008). Social constructivist teaching methods in Australian universities - Reported uptake and perceived learning effects: A survey of lecturers. *Higher Education Research & Development*, *27*(3), 168–186. doi:10.1080/07294360802183754

Hein, G. E. (1991). *Constructivist learning theory*. Retrieved from http://www.exploratorium.edu/IFI/ resources/constructivistlearning.html

Henning, W. (2004). Everday cognition and situated learning. In Jonassen, D. (Ed.), *Handbook of research on educational communications and technology* (pp. 143–168). Mahwah, NJ: Erlbaum.

Heylighen, F. (1993). Epistemology, introduction. *Principia Cybernetica*. Retrieved from http://pespmlcl.vub.ac.be/EPISTMI.html

Hill, J., Song, L., & West, R. (2009). Social learning theory and web-based learning environments: A review of research and discussion on implications. *American Journal of Distance Education*, *23*, 88–103. doi:10.1080/08923640902857713

Hoyt, B. (2000). Techniques to manage participation and contribution of team members in virtual teams. *WebNet Journal*, *2*(4), 16–20.

Huitt, W. (2003). *Constructivism: Educational psychology interactive*. Valdosta, GA: Valdosta State University.

Jarvenpaa, S., & Liedner, D. (1998). Communication and trust in global virtual teams. *Journal of Computer-Mediated Communication*, *3*(4), 1–32.

Jaworski, B. (1993). *Constructivism and teaching - The socio-cultural context*, v. 1.0. Retrieved from http://www.grout.demon.co.uk/ Barbara/chreods.htm

Jonassen, D. H. (1999). Designing constructivist learning environments. In Reigeluth, C. M. (Ed.), *Instructional design theories and models* (pp. 215–239). Mahwah, NJ: Erlbaum Associates.

Kahneman, D., & Tversky, A. (1996). On the reality of cognitive illusions. *Psychological Review*, *103*(3), 582. doi:10.1037/0033-295X.103.3.582

Kalay, Y. E., & Marx, J. (2001). Architecture and the Internet: Designing places in cyberspace, reinventing the discourse. *Proceedings of the 21 Annual Conference of the ACAADA, How Digital Tools Help Bridge and Transform Research, Education and Practice in Architecture* (pp. 230-241). Buffalo, New York.

Kolarevic, B., Schmitt, G. N., Hirschberg, U., Kurmann, D., & Johnson, B. (2000). An experiment in design collaboration. *Automation in Construction*, *9*(1), 73–81. doi:10.1016/S0926-5805(99)00050-3

Kvan, T. (2001). The problem in studio teaching - Revisiting the pedagogy of studio teaching. *Proceedings of the 1st ACAE Conference on Architecture Education*, National University of Singapore.

Kvan, T., Mark, E., Oxman, R., & Martens, B. (2004). Ditching the dinosaur: Redefining the role of digital media in education. *International Journal of Design Computing, 7*.

Kvan, T., Schmitt, G. N., Maher, M. L., & Cheng, N. Y.-W. (2000). Teaching architectural design in virtual studios. In Fruchter, R., Pena-Mona, F., & Roddis, W. M. K. (Eds.), *Computing in civil and building engineering* (pp. 162–169). Stanford. doi:10.1061/40513(279)21

Kvan, T., West, R., & Vera, A. (1997). *Tools and channels of communication: Dealing with the effects of computer mediation on design communication*. 1st International Conference on Creative Collaboration in Virtual Communities, University of Sydney.

Lahti, H., Seitamaa-Hakkarainen, P., & Hakkarainen, K. (2004). Collaboration patterns in computer supported collaborative designing. *Design Studies*, *25*(4), 351. doi:10.1016/j.destud.2003.12.001

Landa, L. (1983). The algo-heuristic theory of instruction. In Reigeluth, C. M. (Ed.), *Instructional design theories and models*. Hillsdale, NJ: Lawrence Erlbaum Associates.

Lee, L. A., & Reekie, R. F. (1949). *Descriptive geometry for architecs and builders*. London, UK: Arnold.

Maher, M. L. (1999). *Variations on a virtual design studio*. The 4th international Workshop on CSCW in Design, Universite de Technologie de Compiegne.

Maher, M. L., Bilda, Z., & Gül, L. F. (2006). *Impact of collaborative virtual environments on design behaviour. Design Computing and Cognition '06*. the Netherlands: Springer.

Maher, M. L., & Merrick, K. (2005). Agent models for dynamic 3D virtual worlds. *Proceedings of 2005 International Conference on Cyberworlds*, Singapore, (pp. 27-34).

Maher, M. L., & Simoff, S. (2000). Collaboratively designing within the design. *Proceedings of Co-Designing 2000*.

Mahoney, J. (2004). What is constructivism and why is it growing? *Contemporary Psychology, 49*, 360–363.

Maitland, B. S. (1985). A problem-based course in architecture. In Boud, D. (Ed.), *Problem-based learning in education for the professions*. Sydney: HERDSA.

Murphy, E. (1997). *Constructivism: From theory to practice*. Retrieved from http://www.stemnet. nf.ca/~elmurphy/emurphy/cle.html

Perkins, D. (1991). Technology meets constructivism: Do they make a marriage? *Educational Technology, 31*(5), 18–23.

Phye, G. (1997). Learning and remembering: the basis for personal knowledge construction. In Phye, G. (Ed.), *Handbook of academic learning: Construction of knowledge* (pp. 47–64). San Diego, CA: Academic Press. doi:10.1016/B978-012554255-5/50003-X

Powers, M. (2001). *Applying a constructivist pedagogy to design studio education*. ARCC Spring Research Conference, Virginia Technique.

Reigeluth, C. M. (1983). *Instructional design: What is it and why is it?* Hillsdale, NJ: Lawrence Erlbaum Associates.

Resnick, L., Levine, J. M., & Teasley, S. D. (1991). *Perspectives on socially shared cognition*. Washington, DC: American Psychological Association. doi:10.1037/10096-000

Resnick, L. B. (1986). Introduction. In Resnick, L. B. (Ed.), *Knowing, learning and instruction: Essays in honor of Robert Glaser* (pp. 1–24). Hillsdale, NJ: Lawrence Erlbaum Associates.

Rosenman, M. A., Smith, G., Ding, L., Marchant, D., & Maher, M. L. (2005). Multidisciplinary design in virtual worlds. *Proceedings of CAAD Futures 2005*. Dordrecht, The Netherlands: Springer.

Schnabel, M. A., Kvan, T., Kruijff, E., & Donath, D. (2001). The first virtual environment design studio, architectural information management. *19th eCAADe Conference Proceedings*, Helsinki, Finland.

Schön, D. A. (1983). *The reflective practitioner: How professionals think in action*. New York, NY: Basic Books.

Segal, L. (1995). Designing team workstations: the choreography of teamwork. In Hancock, P., Flach, J., Caird, J., & Vicente, K. (Eds.), *Local applications of the ecological approach to human-machine systems* (pp. 392–415). Hillsdale, NJ: Lawrence Erlbaum.

Smith, G., Maher, M. L., & Gero, J. S. (2003). Designing 3D virtual worlds as a society of agents. *Proceedings of CAAD Futures 2003*, the Netherlands, Kluwer Academic Publishers.

Smith, M. K. (2002). Jerome S. Bruner and the process of education. In *The encyclopedia of informal education*.

Spady, W. G. (2001). *Beyond counterfeit reforms: Forging an authentic future for all our learners*. Lanham, MD: The Scarecrow Press.

Suwa, M., & Tversky, B. (2002). How do designers shift their focus of attention in their own sketches? In Anderson, M., Meyer, B., & Olivier, P. (Eds.), *Diagrammatic representation and reasoning*. Springer. doi:10.1007/978-1-4471-0109-3_14

Westrik, J., De Graaff, E., Chen, S. E., Cowdroy, R. M., Kingsland, A., & Ostwald, M. J. (1994). Development and management of the new PBL-based curriculum in architecture. In *Reflections on problem based learning* (pp. 189–200). Sydney, Australia: Australian Problem Based Learning Network.

Wilhem, J., Baker, T., & Dube, J. (2001). *Strategic reading: Guiding students to lifelong literacy*. New Hampshire, USA, Heinemann, Reed Elsevier Inc.

Wilson, B., & Lowry, M. (2000). Constructivist learning on the Web learning technologies. In Burge, L. (Ed.), *Reflective and strategic thinking*. San Francisco, CA: Jossey-Bass, New Directions for Adult and Continuing Education.

Winn, W. (1993). *A conceptual basis for educational applications of virtual reality. Human interface technology laboratory*. Washington Technology Center, University of Washington.

Woods, D. (1985). Problem-based learning and problem-solving. In Boud, D. (Ed.), *Problem-based learning in education for the professions* (pp. 19–42). Sydney, Australia: Higher Education Research and Development Society of Australasia.

Wooldridge, M. (2000). *Reasoning about rational agents*. Cambridge, MA: MIT Press.

Wyeld, T. G., Prasolova-Forland, E., & Teng-Wen, C. (2006). *Virtually collaborating across cultures: A case study of an online theatrical performance in a 3DCVE spanning three continents*. Sixth International Conference on Advanced Learning Technologies.

KEY TERMS AND DEFINITIONS

3D Virtual Worlds: 3D virtual worlds are interactive simulated 3D environments accessed by multiple users through an online interface.

Collaborative Learning: This is an approach where students attempt to learn something together.

Constructivist Learning: This approach argues that learning is an active process of creating meaning from different experiences in particular, allowing students to learn themselves by trying to make sense of something. In this approach the teacher plays the role of a guide to help them along the way.

Evaluation of Design Feature: This includes the evaluation of the 3D modelling features (creating complex geometric objects, editing tools etc.), collaborative design features (text channel, video channel), awareness of each other's actions, and scripting and programming for interactivity.

Evaluation of Human Behaviour: The evaluation of human behaviour includes understanding the impact of the 3D virtual worlds on the development of the core communication skills and design process.

ENDNOTE

[1]   See http://wiki.secondlife.com/wiki/LSL_ Portal for more details on LSL.

Chapter 10
Understanding Collaborative Digital Media Design in the 3D CVE:
A Vygotskian Approach

Theodor Wyeld
Flinders University, Australia

Ekaterina Prasolova-Førland
Norwegian University of Science and Technology, Norway

ABSTRACT

Digital Media Design (DMD) sits between ICT and the creative arts. DMD uses computers as a design tool. The ubiquity of the computer means DMD is available to a broad range of people. It is used in everyday design practices – creative, professional, commercial, academic, and casual. In an educational context, the way it is taught needs to meet students' expectations from a broad range of capabilities and requirements. Unlike more traditional forms of design practice, peculiar to DMD is the use of online collaborations. In turn, this demands different cognitive learning structures to traditional design practices. Online collaborations include a socialising element. Hence, current DMD practice is as much about social interaction as it is about design problem solving. Problem solving exercises in design teaching are traditionally explored in a project setting. In DMD this now includes the socialising element of online collaboration. This chapter describes a method for analysing DMD practice and, in particular, online design collaboration using a 3D Collaborative Virtual Environment. It provides a framework for analysis using Vygotsky's (1978) Zone of Proximal Development (ZPD) and Wenger's (1999) approach to learning communities and communities of practice, providing a case study for discussion. The results of this study are that a radical shift in teaching approach is needed to foster the sorts of deep learning outcomes graduates of DMD require to meet the demands of contemporary design work practices.

DOI: 10.4018/978-1-61350-180-1.ch010

INTRODUCTION

In general terms, to design is to 'make a sign' or 'mark-out'. Moreover, design is about problem solving. But, design is not an easily understood process, and there are many methods for studying the design process. The work of Cross, Christians and Dorst (1996) in Protocol Analysis (PA) at Delft in the 90s is perhaps the most common method for studying the design process. However, PA relies on the analysis of participant reflections on recorded conversations and actions. These reflections, divorced from the original context, may not be a reliable method for analysing the design activities. Furthermore, PA does not directly address pedagogical settings nor is it a practical method for large groups of students. On the other hand, Activity Theory, while originally conceived in the context of industrial work practices and their social settings, is more suited to studying large groups of participants socially engaged in a problem solving task. In particular, Vygotsky's (1978) Zone of Proximal Development (ZPD).

Vygotsky's ZPD is focussed on shared learning practices in pedagogical settings. It recognises the social dimension of learning as a key factor in individual and group outcomes. It suggests that traditional top-down teaching methods are flawed and that instead deeper learning outcomes are achieved by student-led investigation of the learning material. In short, ZPD can be defined as the distance between the actual developmental level of a learner as determined by independent problem solving and the level of potential development as determined through problem solving under the guidance of a teacher or in collaboration with more capable peers.

According to Vygotsky (1978, 1981), all activity is social by nature. Hence, social interaction is central to any study of learning practices. Vygotsky's method emphasises the study of patterns of change in behaviour where work activity is the basic unit of study.

Vygotsky's ZPD was used to analyse the case study outlined in this chapter. It is an investigative research project in the form of an online design project with students collaborating across three continents, cultures and timezones. The participants come from diverse backgrounds and bring a range of skills to the project. A 3D Collaborative Virtual Environment (3D CVE), supported with other design and social software, was used as the vehicle for the study as it simulated the sort of workplace environment the students might encounter on graduation. In this sense it has real-world applicability. The fabled *Tower of Babel* was used as the project narrative. It was chosen because it is an historically distant concept yet easily understood and lends itself to a design exercise. Although much of the software encountered in the project was new to the students the online socialisation component was already well known to them. The familiarity with the online socialisation component made it easier for them to engage with the project. With the 3D CVE and its support software students could share resources, skills and ideas. The goals of the project were explicit but negotiable from the outset. Hence, the goals were also led by the groups and individuals within groups and across groups.

The sorts of activities performed in the 3D CVE were typical of workplace environments – a common graduate attribute goal of the institutions involved. By contrast, the project, and the way it was organised, was a radical departure from the normal teaching mode. The risk of allowing students to direct their own learning trajectories was not inconsiderable. Vygotsky's ZPD was instrumental in guiding this process. His ZPD was used to identify changes in patterns of behaviour throughout the project and provided a framework for the role of teachers and students. The results show that, overall, the students were more active in their own learning and problem solving. The tools they used and the cultural artefacts created were unique to the project yet transferable to other design work practices. And, their identity as individuals and groups, an important part of the social interaction, was preserved by the 'signs' they created in the project: National flags, terms and phrases used in their chats, and so on. This project is the latest in a series of similar sequentially organised projects conducted by the authors since 2004. This method is now adopted as the defacto Digital Media Design (DMD) teaching and learning method in the institutions involved.

DESIGN AND COMPUTERS

Digital media design sits between ICT and the creative arts – the digital media designer needs some knowledge of how computers work and some creative flair to produce an aesthetic outcome. The ubiquity of the personal computer means it is increasingly an essential part of the designer's toolkit (artists, architects, engineers, commercial/industrial designers and so on). It is also used in many other contexts which require some creativity but not necessarily proficient computing or artistic ability as such. Once separate, ICT and the creative arts are now merged in the practice of designing on the computer.

In a pedagogical context, design computing, multimedia and digital media design are (only a few of) the sorts of names given to the process by which 'digital design' is done using computers. Digital design tools open new possibilities in design – for 3D, print and web among other media. Digital design courses concern themselves with the middle ground between ICT and the creative arts. Their students come from both domains and may or may not be proficient in either. As such, digital design is increasingly seen as a domain in itself. Where it fits within the traditional design domain is less clear. What is clear, however, is that digital design follows many of the same processes as for other types of design practice.

Digital design provides opportunities for individuals and groups to be creative from a broad spectrum of society. Once taught in a decontextualised environment – divorced from its everyday personal use – today, increasingly, digital design is more about outcomes than the systems that underlay them. This is especially so in the digital design domains of Multimedia, Interaction Design, Computer Graphics, 3D Games and 3D Animation. Such pursuits are increasingly attracting students from a range of degree studies, not just traditional design. This is especially so where there are little or no programming skills involved. Hence, it follows that, in more general terms, the non-programming use of digital media is a mainstream integral, creative and essential part of the design student's development.

Peculiar to digital design is the emphasis on collaboration and online promotion and resources. Increasingly, students both source much of their inspiration and raw materials online and promote and share their creativity via the same medium. Added to this is the increased socialisation and sharing of resources online collaboration affords. This online design collaboration is distinctly different from more traditional forms of design practice. It is both a product of the Internet and all that it represents and at the same time it is also sustained by the Internet.

Computers and the design software they support (3D CAD programmes, Photoshop, video editing programmes and so on) provide a context for activity which promotes the development of different cognitive structures than more traditional activities, such as pen and paper, paint, sculpture, modelling and so on. Nonetheless, computers, software, pen and paper all have their own peculiar socio-cultural ontogeny and significance for individuals and groups depending on how they are culturally defined, within a social context and use. They arise also from the same socio-cultural ontogeny. Collectively, they can be thought of as cultural artefacts. The study of university students' use of digital design media provides an example of the social ontogeny of knowledge and quality of learning possible with this media in a pedagogical setting.

As an integral part of the student's development, in its use and study, digital media design can be seen as linked to other forms of cultural activity and social interaction. Hence, a systematic method for studying the effects of this on student learning is critical to understanding contemporary learning in general. More particularly, online collaborative design provides a vehicle for the study of the cultural contexts and artefacts 'thrown up' (in Heidegger's (1977) terms) by increasingly popular everyday digital design activities.

STUDYING DESIGN PRACTICE

The word 'design' originates from the Latin *designare* (1540) – *de* 'out' + *signare* 'to mark' from *signum* 'a mark or sign' – which means to 'mark out' or make a 'sign'. Traditionally, this is achieved with pencil, ink, brush, stone, steel, clay or other media in an artistic gesture or purely functional way. By contrast, to digitally mark out or make a sign produces highly resolved gestures – from a palette of 2D strokes, patterns and colours (such as in Adobe Photoshop) to fully formed 3D objects ready to assemble (such as in SecondLife). Whether the product of the digital designer's creative labour can be called a 'good design' remains open to debate. However, the *act* of designing with digital tools is indisputable. Understanding what designers know and do is less easily defined.

In Lawson's (2004)*What Designers Know* he explores the knowledge structures that designers rely on to communicate with each other. He claims, unlike other disciplines, there is no taxonomy of design problem-solution relationship – there is no easy way to map the problem solving process onto the solutions arrived at. Attempts to impose a structure to the problem-solution relationship have generally failed. Indeed, design problems are often solved without having been completely stated. Different design teams given the same brief will invariably arrive at different solutions

suggesting the solution comes from what the team and its individuals bring to bear on the problem rather than any clearly definable logical path to a solution. This suggests designing comprises a number of different mental activities. A common method for making sense of this process is using Protocol Analysis (Cross et al, 1996).

Protocol Analysis relies on verbal descriptions from videotaped conversations and conversations about drawings and sketches as aids to the conversations and reflections on the videotapes by the participants in design exercises. In protocol analysis activities are broken down into temporal (or time slices – useful in large-scale analysis of activities) and relational (separating out of events – useful in the small-scale analysis of activities). To make sense of the two, one needs to project a framework onto the data (Gero et al., 1998). The framework includes identifying events such as: Drawing, physical actions, modelling, gesturing, acting and reflecting. These events are often referred to as design 'moves' (Schon, 1983). According to Lawson (2005), the characteristic role in design conversations can be defined as comprising the: Learner, informer, critic, collaborator and initiator.

Following Cross et al's (1996) Protocol Analysis method, the design process follows the cycle: Identification of the problem, clarification, framing of the solution space, followed by design moves towards a solution. A lexicon of words is created in the collaboration which is part of an overall design language. From the final solutions come schemas which are drawn upon in future problem solving exercises. Collectively, Cross (1982) refers to this as a 'designerly way of knowing'. Drawings and the words that accompany them create bridges in the design process or language of design. However, Protocol Analysis relies on recorded verbal accounts of the design process and this may not be a good indicator of the thinking process itself (Lloyd et al., 1996). Hence, Protocol Analysis may not be the most reliable method for analysing design. Instead, the artefacts that the design process throws up lend themselves to analysis in more general terms as simply a part of human activity. More specifically, part of a community of practice. In a pedagogical context, this is about student development and their roles in learning communities. Instead, Vygotsky (1978), Leont'ev (1981) and Engestrom's (1987) Activity Theory (AT) can be used to analyse the activities of these communities.

Activity theory is based on the work by Vygotski (1978), Leont'ev (1981) and later Engestrom (1987). The fundamental unit of analysis is human activity, which is directed towards an object, mediated by cultural artefacts and is social within a culture (Bardram, 1997).

Activity theory is based on the idea that culturally defined tools, or *artefacts*, mediate all activity. This is illustrated by Figure 1 where S is a subject (a person), A is a mediating artifact and O is the object or result of the activity (Bardram, 1998). An artifact can therefore be thought of as a tool for mediating activities. Engestrom summarizes the main components of the theory in the activity structure illustrated in Figure 2 (Engestrøm, 1987):

The main components of the triangle are artefacts, object, division of labour, community, rules, and subject. The components in Figure 1 represent the top of this pyramid. Individuals and groups can be seen as 'subjects' situated in *com-*

Figure 1. The basic structure of mediated human activity (adapted from Bardram, 1998)

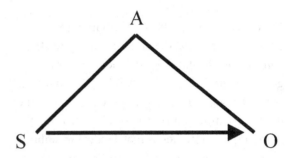

munities mediated by rules of participation and division of labour. The artefacts are placed centrally since all human work is characterized by the collaborative production of artefacts; each of them is made with the purpose of mediating a certain activity. The mediating characteristics of an activity is crystallized or objectified into these artefacts (Bardram, 1997). The artefacts are continuously modified and shaped to meet the evolving needs. Once focused on a single artefact, we can now consider a whole set of connected artefacts (Engestrøm, 1987). This results in a system that includes not only multiple cognitive artefacts but also primary ones used in daily practice.

Figure 2. Activity structure (adapted from Engestrøm, 1987)

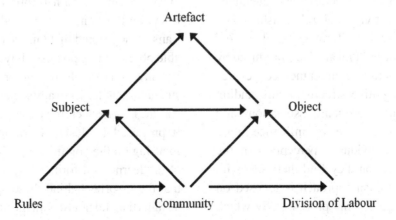

VYGOTSKY'S ZONE OF PROXIMAL DEVELOPMENT

Vygotsky's (1978, 1986) contribution to the psychology of human development in educational contexts is substantial. His socio-cultural ontogenetic approach provides a vehicle for a unified view of student development. He brings together human cognition and situated action in a way that mere empirical studies cannot. Under the umbrella of AT, his notion of the Zone of Proximal Development (ZPD) provides a framework from which shared learning experiences can be investigated. It challenges the social organisation of the teaching institution in a way that demonstrates learning both on the part of the student and the teacher through the experience of their co-interaction.

Most teaching and learning situations are not value free, objective or divorced from everyday personal concerns. No more so than when students use social software in their university learning experiences. Social software provides for sometimes intense social engagement. As such, it challenges many of the pre-existing epistemological beliefs and assumptions underlying traditional educational practice.

All activity, according to Vygotsky, is social by nature, whether it be personal or group. Hence, an individual's subjective view, their context and knowledge derived from past experience, by there very nature, shape that individual's interpretation of the goals of their activities. This directs their needs and purposes, the actions and meanings they attach to an activity, their relationships with others and the socio-cultural arena they find themselves in. The cultural artefacts produced by these associations further direct their conscience and evolving cognitive structures surrounding the activity. In turn, these same associations, and the cognitive structures created, influence future actions and the individual's perception of the reality of the situation they find themselves in. Hence, the Vygotskian approach is focused on patterns of change and the processes by which

people are changed. It is the shared consciousness of change that matters. And it is in the shared cultural artefacts, language and tools that a shared consciousness is articulated.

Learning institutions such as universities are part of larger socio-cultural settings and student-teacher interactions are situated within this. More particularly, student-student and student-teacher interactions have a socio-cultural ontogeny. Vygotsky's cultural historical approach, which pays attention to the history of the individual and group activity and the socio-cultural context in which it occurs, is thus particularly suited to exploring design activities. Vygotsky's non-absolute forms of consciousness is readily adapted to the study of the ephemera of the design professions. This is reflected in the fields of Computer Supported Cooperative Work (CSCW) and Computer Supported Cooperative Learning (CSCL) where the use of AT as a methodological framework for studying collaborative activities is well understood (Kuutti, 1994; Bardram, 1998; Gifford & Enyedy, 1999).

Kuutti (1994) uses work activity as a basic unit for analysing cooperative work situations, and Bardram (1998) argues that AT helps us understand the way in which work activities are cooperatively realized in order to design efficient cooperative technologies. Learning activities are the unit of analysis in the fields of CSCW and CSCL. Prior to this a number of different methods had been used for facilitating learning in communities and groups in the CSCL field. For example, the Domain Centred Design (DCD), based on the transmission model of knowledge transfer, suggested that knowledge is an identifiable object that is possessed by a person and can be conveyed from the instructor to the mind of the student, detached from any social context. Another was the Learner Centred Design (LCD) approach. It proposed to design learning technology by focusing on the cognitive capabilities and needs of the learner. Gifford & Enyedy (1999) argued that the theories behind these approaches led to designs that did not fit with the basic participation structures in a classroom. For example, the DCD model rewards imitation and memorization while limiting sense-making and meaningful dialogue. By contrast, LCD sees the learning as a highly individual activity and does not provide enough support for peer interaction. Gifford & Enyedy concluded, that both these approaches ignore the social context of learning and the role of conversation and collaboration. Instead, AT was seen as a more appropriate theoretical framework because it emphasizes the social nature of learning and considers learning as a participation in cultural practice. Hence, unlike the DCD and LCD which do not consider the importance of the social dimension in learning, an activity centred learning design places the activities performed by learners in the centre of the model (Figure 3). At the same time, all the activities are placed on a learning trajectory, followed by the learners during their development. A trajectory in this context can be defined as a continuous motion through successive forms of participation, connecting the past, the present and the future (Wenger, 1999). Other elements in the model are the cultural tools (artefacts), teachers and collaborative user groups.

The structure of an activity centred learning model can serve as a checklist for the design of learning environments in general. Hence, the implications for the design of learning environments includes:

- Social interaction and conversation play a fundamental place in learning, and
- The way activity is organized can only be understood from its historical context.

This means that teachers should pay attention to the interaction between multiple trajectories of individuals. Trajectories include the development of cultural practice, the development of people within a practice and development of ways of participating within the cultural practice. An example can be a student's movement through different forms of participation in a project group: From a novice to an expert and a leader.

In practice, this means that the teacher-as-researcher is also an integral part of the learning process. The teacher-as-researcher is embedded in the study and the outcomes are shared by participant and teacher alike. The teacher-as-researcher is looking for those cultural artefacts that signal, in Vygotsky's (1978) terms, a shift in teaching and learning episteme.

Figure 3 Activity centred learning (adapted from Gifford & Enyedy, 1999)

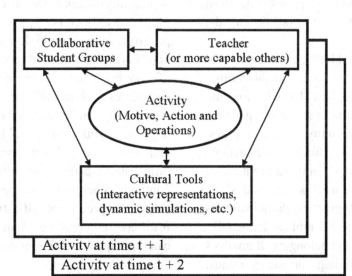

This shift occurs across and within the socio-cultural environments teachers and learners find themselves in. They occur within a local cultural framework and across the community of learners. It is through the social interaction of the teachers and learners and their communities that new learning occurs.

The study described here follows Vygotsky's community of learners interacting individually and as a part of a group which includes members from different cultures, timezones and continents connected by the Internet. They are engaged in an online design collaboration project. They support each other by bringing to the project different cultural capital in the form of skills and prior socio-cultural understandings. Over the course of the project many expressed a new understanding about each other and the role of the technology and design collaboration. For the duration of the project, collectively, they formed a community of practice unique to themselves and the project.

Community is a central component of Activity Theory. Particularly relevant to the discussion and analysis in this chapter is the seminal work on learning communities and communities of practice presented by Wenger (1999, p86). For Wenger, "communities of practice can be thought of as shared histories of learning." Each activity is situated on a learning trajectory, so that learners move through activities, progressing from partial to full participants (Gifford & Enyedy, 1999; Wenger, 1999).

According to Wenger (1999), continuous negotiation of meaning is at the core of social learning and involves two processes: Participation and reification, together forming a shared repertoire. The repertoire of a community includes routines, tools, words, ways of doing things, stories, actions and concepts that the community has produced or adopted in the course of its existence, and which have become part of its practice. Participation is the "complex process that combines doing, talking, thinking, feeling, and belonging. It involves our whole person including our bodies, minds,

emotions, and social relations." Reification is the "process of giving form to our experience by producing objects that congeal this experience into thingness" (Wenger, 1999, pp56, 58). Hence, learning communities can also be thought of as shared histories of participation and learning. Members have different roles as master and apprentice and there is a progression through these roles along the learning trajectories. Therefore, there is a need for artefacts that can comprise the outcome of the activities and thus serve as the shared repertoire of the community and as the indicators of a learner's movement along trajectories (Tolsby et al., 2001). The collection of such artefacts can be used by the subjects of the community in further activities and to support their movement along the learning trajectory as well as self-reflection and construction of meaning.

Another important concept is identity. Identity is defined by Wenger (1999) as negotiated experience, community membership, learning trajectory and nexus of multi-memberships. A learning community can strengthen the identity of participation by incorporating its members' past into its history and opening new trajectories. As identity is connected to the activities on the learning trajectory, it can be expressed by the artefacts that comprise the outcome of the activities. In this way, the past experiences and history of community members are reified within the shared repertoire as documents, plans, etc. Another aspect of identity is multiple memberships, which involves reconciliation of boundaries and creation of bridges across the landscape of practice. In some cases, the boundaries are reified with explicit markers of membership, for example, titles and degrees, or with boundary objects. They connect and coordinate different practices and communities. Participation and reification can create continuities across boundaries. For example, an artefact, or product of reification, can be present in different communities. At the same time, people can participate in different communities at once.

Wenger argues that learning should be primarily addressed in terms of identities and modes of belonging and only secondary in terms of skills and information. In this perspective, experiences involving new forms of membership, multi-membership and ownership of meaning are at least as important as the curriculum coverage. Social relations and interests thus clearly play an important role in the development of a learning community.

ONLINE COLLABORATIVE DESIGN

Communities of practice involve cooperative human activity towards shared goals. With increased efficiencies in telecommunications and file sharing, distributed work practices in the design industries (among other industries) has become a common community of practice. Remote design collaboration is now a routine part of many design practices (architecture, engineering, digital design and so on). Initially comprising file transfer, email, fax, telephony, video-conferencing, and so on, other forms of online collaboration are being trialled. One such media is the 3D collaborative virtual environment (3D CVE). It is being investigated as a means for collaborative design interaction.

Online collaborative design is essentially a socialising process (Mitchell et al, 1998). As such, the 3D CVE provides a 'place' for both design and socialisation to occur. Hence, the research emphasis in 3D CVEs tends to be on the efficacy of the instrument to provide a visually captivating experience and engendering social interaction. Collaboration can be between individuals or groups. In its infancy, most 3D CVE research still occurs between teaching institutions, which include student participants and incorporates a pedagogical component.

For the 3DCVE, as in more traditional forms, the 'place' collaboration occurs is established through social interaction. Connected to and forming part of this place is the legibility of the environment surrounding it and the paths that lead up to it. This 'place' is not a space but an experience, and, in time, it forms part of a collective memory and discourse of a community – the social interaction, reflection, paths and experience form the collective discourse of the community in the 3D CVE. Unlike more traditional forms of collaboration, the 3D CVE provides a level of intimacy and interaction between collaborators that is unique.

Remote collaboration projects emphasise the need for social cohesion (Wojtowicz, 1995; Maher, 1995). They try to emulate the actions and interactions found in the traditional design studio. Indeed, the intellectual power of the community resides in the interactions between its participants. An important feature of these systems is the incorporation of face-to-face communication (which can be achieved with video conferencing). This increases the social familiarity over time between the various participants facilitated by the personalised content.

The prevailing practices and rituals in a 3D CVE are often loaded with the same symbolic meanings that express the value-laden culture of the traditional design studio. Focussed and unfocussed, active and passive information exchanges are just as important in traditional face-to-face interaction (Cuff, 1991; Heath & Luff, 1996; Mitchell et al, 1998) collaboration as they are in a 3D CVE. Its importance is in the way it unintentionally conveys important content and context information contributing to group cohesiveness and effectiveness. It is the passive transactions that much of current design education ignores yet is critical to the socialisation process. Hence, in an era which is increasingly reliant on distributed work practices the 3D CVE has a clear role.

The Project

In an attempt to study the social interaction of students engaged in online design collaboration, a 3D CVE project was coordinated between three cooperating institutions: *The University of Queensland* (Australia); the *National Yunlin University of Science and Technology* (Taiwan); and, the *Norwegian University of Science and Technology Trondheim* (Norway). It built on a series of similar projects conducted by the authors (see Wyeld and Prasolova-Førland, 2008; Prasolova-Førland and Wyeld, 2006 and 2008; Wyeld, Prasolova-Førland and Viller, 2007; Wyeld, Prasolova-Førland and Chang, 2006 and 2007). The project discussed in this chapter centres on a virtual design and construction of the fabled *Tower of Babel*.

The remote design collaboration of a *Tower of Babel* in a 3D virtual environment was formed as an exercise to address the need for digital media students to work in an internationalised cross-cultural environment. The *Tower of Babel* story was chosen as a historically and culturally distant text to bring into sharp focus differences with contemporary culture and within its own story – the confusion arising from the diversity of languages interfering with communicating a common goal. Using a suite of tools, central to which was the 3DCVE *ActiveWorlds* (AWs), students worked in teams collaborating across time zones on a single project complimenting each other's skills and learning about new ways to work and learn in a global community. This fostered deep understandings of alternative meanings to everyday occurrences and work practices.

The introduction of design interaction to the curriculum in the form of a remote collaboration exercise was made adaptable and flexible so it reflected and respected the various local conventions of the learners involved. This was conducted in a playful atmosphere where students were actively encouraged to experiment with the tools given and cultures encountered within and across teams. This is a known approach to effective learning (Hubbard, 1980; Bourdieu & Wacquant, 1992; Dewey, 1957). It followed a process of acculturation to a new knowledge community (Leidner & Jarven-

paa, 1995), resulting in participants reinforcing and expanding their ability to comprehend new challenges, risks and opportunities. Trust was a crucial mitigating factor in cooperation between remote team partners and hence overall feelings of control and satisfaction of the students within the exercise (Clear and Kassabova, 2005; Jarvenpaa & Leidner, 1998; Seifert, 2004; Marks et al, 2001). A key factor in groupwork motivation for the students was addressing the need for explicit and implicit 'meaning' in the project – how it related to the wider world of the students' experiences.

There were nine groups of 11 students each (six Australian, four Norwegian and one Taiwanese) ranging in age from 18 to 25 and individual ICT ability from little prior knowledge to good programming skills. Students had divergent prior experiences with social software and the 3D CVEs used. They were all familiar with using a computer for social communication. Most students relished the opportunity to explore a new form of social networking, this was despite many of them having trouble conceptualising the three dimensional spaces encountered. Nonetheless, all agreed that the perceived 'presence' the 3D CVE afforded required only a brief transition period before the new knowledge needed to be productive in such spaces was mastered.

Groups were formed with members from each institution. Each group included a team leader who organised various forms of contact, including email, chat, videoconferencing and meetings in AWs. Explicit tasks were allocated to Australian, Norwegian and Taiwanese team leaders by the teachers. Norwegian team members were allocated the task of designing 20 different building blocks to use in the final tower design. Taiwanese team members were required to assist in designing specific functions for the building blocks such as hyperlinks, teleports, textures, animations, and so on. Australian team members were required to design the overall towers using the allocated blocks and their functions.

All other design decisions were the domain of the individual groups to negotiate amongst themselves. Teachers only intervened if irreconcilable difficulties arose – these were rare. Design and construction of the tower involved the manipulation of the blocks, managed through the simple 3D AWs interface. It allowed students to move, copy, and change the type of blocks and add simple scripts. These blocks were then arranged following the individual groups' design guidelines to create a tower. Restrictions to the tower construction included the use of only twenty different types of blocks and a maximum height that represented the limit of the AWs application (see Figure 4).

Another important restriction imposed by the AWs concerns existing possibilities for collaborative building. Building in AWs is inherently an individual process where only the owner has the right to modify his/her objects. It is possible to share building rights by the use of the so-called 'privilege password' but this option was not always functioning properly. Another possibility was introducing a fictitious user account and letting students use that account while building. This option was, however, not feasible when the number of builders is significant and when most of the construction effort was happening simultaneously.

A different solution was adopted in this project in order to overcome these limitations. To allow flexible simultaneous building by a large number of users, the students were asked to log in and build as 'tourists', hence everyone had access to objects built by others. This solution, though

Figure 4. Typical construction space in Active Worlds browser showing the chat field below

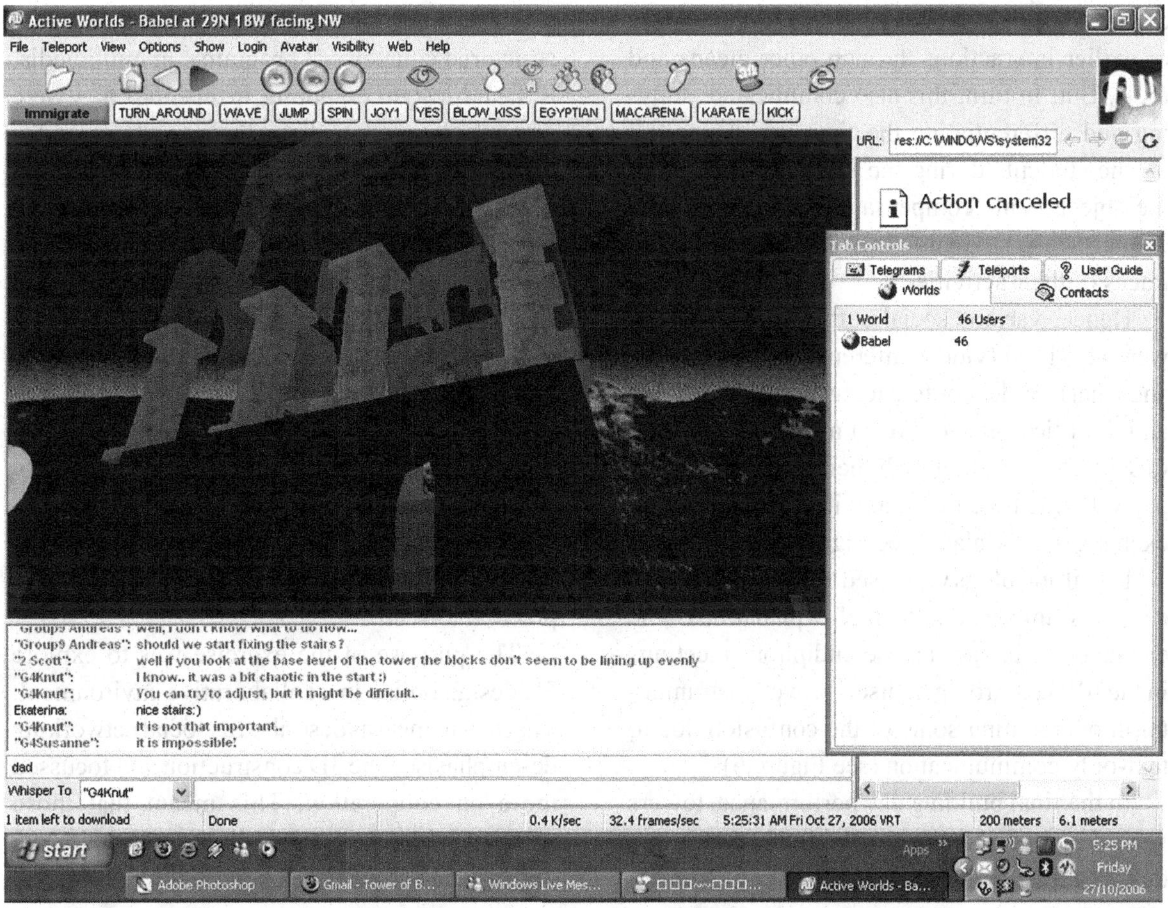

allowing collaborative construction and brainstorming, had some drawbacks. The unlimited access to altering objects built by others imposed a certain responsibility and was highly dependent on good communication to succeed. It resulted in some conflicts on the final build day when misunderstandings led to deleting each other's work causing frustrations and friction between and within groups. There were also cases of malicious interventions and 'virtual terror' when an unidentified participant deleted pre-prepared buildings stones the day before the main building effort.

This choice also influenced the case in terms of the students' movement along Wenger's participation trajectories as logging in as tourist only allowed the choice of only two avatars and thus reduced the means for students to express their identity and cultural belonging. This was however compensated by other means, such as choice of names, verbal communication, identity expression through construction and the history of earlier interactions through other means and tools. But, in turn, this also complicated studying and differentiating the 'implicit' traces left by the students during the building (user id on the objects) only compensated for by being able to analyse the students' notes and other 'explicit' traces of their activities.

Hence, various social software applications were also used (videoconferencing, email, blogs and chat). Videoconferencing was essential as an initial 'ice-breaker' to get members of a team to start collaborating with their, remote counterparts. It was here that many interesting cultural exchanges took place (see Figure 5).

Email and blogs were used to exchange design concepts, images and textual explanations. The exchange of images and serendipitous meetings in the AWs environment itself proved instrumental in overcoming some of the confusion due to text-only communication (see Figure 6).

In the final building day performance, towers were designed and constructed from scratch in a one hour time limit per group (three groups build-ing at the same time, hence total time for all nine groups was three hours). A number of practice designs preceded the final design. Towers constructed during the practice sessions were critiqued by group members and designs were continuously being modified until considered appropriate within the constraints given. On completion of the project, students were required to prepare reflective essays on their experiences in the teamwork exercise. Their reflective essays were used in combination with the researchers' notes and collected chat logs for analysis and application of Vygotsky's ZPD.

ANALYSING DESIGN WORK PRACTICES

The students that participated in this study came from diverse backgrounds – culturally, skill-wise and artistically. From, ordinarily part of highly structured coursework programs, in multimedia, ICT, and design computing, in this study they were given the freedom to direct their own learning according to their own needs (assessment, interest and motivation), perceptions (roles, where they fit within the ICT to creative art spectrum, and fairness) and socialisation (within and external to their groups and the larger community).

For many this was a radical shift in learning emphasis. It presented many challenges, for students and teachers alike. But it also rewarded those who engaged in the process. The Activity Theory methodological framework we used assisted in guiding and making sense of the complex interrelationships generated by the community of practice formed.

The purpose of the exercise was to explore 3D design online in a collaborative environment. That the theme was described as social networking de-emphasised the 3D construction and focussed more on cooperation. This meant that those students who would normally be reticent to get involved in cooperative exercises were forced to

Figure 5. Active Worlds browser use in conjunction with MSN videoconferencing

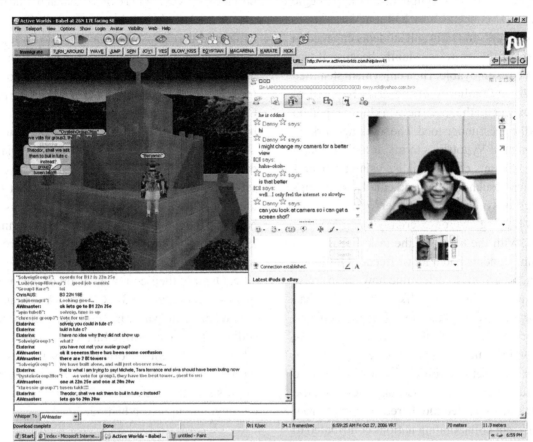

Figure 6. Blogs were set up by the students for sharing their ideas as images

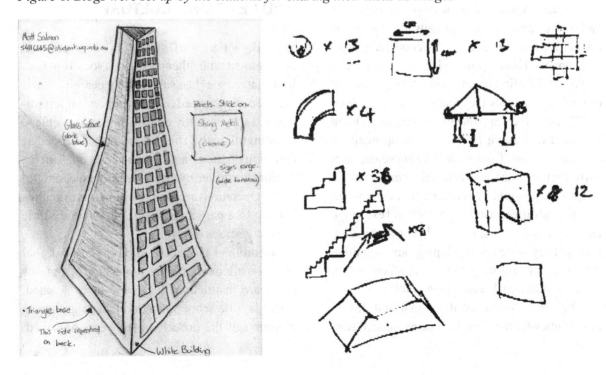

and those students who might ordinarily struggle with the 3D concepts now had a new reason to get 'involved'. In reality, all students engaged in all parts of the exercise. Mainly because it was perceived as enjoyable. Their enjoyment stemmed from the unfamiliarity of the tasks required of them, except for the social networking component which they best understood. The social networking was a sign in Vygotsky's terms. It took different forms. Students could socialise using asynchronous means such as email and email attachments or blogs, or synchronously either logged onto the 3D CVE using chat or externally using MSN or Skype. With the theme of the task discussed as a group, students had a lot of freedom individually and as groups to determine how the exercise would proceed in a studio-like setting. They had to negotiate roles with their overseas counterparts.

Working in groups, there was much sharing of new information and knowledge between groups. This set up a different social context to the traditional closed classroom. New cultural artefacts were created and shared as students from the different collaborating nations contributed to the group tasks. Language, images, symbols and methods were shared. Students were empowered by their ability to share knowledge that only they had. For example, some students acted as interpreters for the 'English as a Second Language' participants. This empowered those students who could use their first language in a foreign country (whereas previously they had felt isolated). Such as a Chinese overseas student studying on a visa in Australia interpreting for her local group members communications from their Taiwanese counterparts. Participants had to adjust their expectations of how they would be received by others when the cultural differences in approach and exchange became apparent. Some were better at this than others. They were all developing new cognitive structures for exploring the media (although they were not necessarily conscious of this).

Their conceptions of the social and design possibilities for the 3D CVE and associated support tools was extended over time. Each time they moved back and forth between email, Skype or MSN and the 3D CVE their activities were re-contextualised. For example, students often had to overcome their frustration with the lack of information provided by their overseas counterpart. Or, in other instances, some students reported being offended by the nature or behaviour of their overseas counterpart. This was invariably due to cultural misunderstandings. It was their self-resolution of many of these issues that saw them grow in their understanding of the task at hand and the role of the technology underpinning it. In instances where misunderstandings were not self-resolved appropriate counselling was available. Overall, their comprehension of the task at hand – designing in a 3D CVE – was enhanced beyond that achievable in a traditional classroom setting. This was confirmed at the end of the study, when many students reported ongoing friendships with their overseas counterpart and an interest in pursuing the use of 3D CVEs in their future employment upon graduating.

THE SHIFT IN TEACHING AND LEARNING CULTURE

Vygotsky's notion of *Activity* is about personal engagement with other people in a social context, how that person then subjectively perceives their and the common needs of the group and opportunities and subsequently chooses actions to achieve meaningful goals. This can be further defined as conscious *actions* and unconscious *operations*. Actions are driven by *needs* to achieve meaningful *goals*. Operations are the transformation of actions leading to a particular result. They require little or no conscious effort.

Traditional classroom exploration of digital design is often focussed on procedural operations (software instruction) that need to be learned. There is little scope for individual or group exploration of the underlying concepts broached.

On the other hand, as an exercise embedded in a socialised forum, the use of the 3D CVE described in this study allowed students to investigate its design possibilities as part of their everyday socio-cultural experiences.

The typical curriculum requires that students be ready to face the sorts of workplace environments they will encounter upon graduation. However, most traditional digital media design training focuses on operational skills acquisition and tends to ignore the social aspects of cooperative work. Yet, it is this cooperative work practice that makes up a large part of the everyday socio-cultural experience that the digital media design student faces upon graduation. Hence, to address this, a transformation in the cultural definition of teacher and student was needed. The exercise described in this chapter was a radical departure from the typical teaching and learning methods used previously. To achieve the goal of work-ready graduating students – as stipulated in the various institutions' graduate attribute statements – we found it necessary to facilitate the free exploration of the media used rather than operational understandings alone. It resulted in a deeper understanding of the potentials for that media. This recognises that, where once the operationalised method for teaching design served a purpose – mostly in the ICT domain – nowadays, with the proliferation of computing devices and the software they support being used by a wide spectrum of society, a more socio-culturally acceptable method needed to be used in learning digital design.

The introduction of a 3D CVE into the curriculum was a major departure from the normal top-down teaching methods in a digital media design program. With the 3D CVE students were mostly in charge of their own learning. The teachers' role was merely as facilitator. The new forms of activity which this promoted provided a new socio-cultural context for the students, teachers and the school more generally.

Normal student-student and student-teacher relationships were challenged by this study.

For example, peer-to-peer interaction outside of teamwork was encouraged instead of being seen as a form of cheating. Teachers needed to be receptive to the learning of their students as a student-led pedagogy, unlike the teacher-knows-all model that normally prevails. There were no precise instructions on what was required of each student and assessment was self-regulated by the students. The outcomes of this process were analysed using AT as a methodological framework. More specifically, Vygotsky's Zone of Proximal Development (ZPD).

VYGOTSKY'S ZONE OF PROXIMAL DEVELOPMENT AND LEARNING COMMUNITIES APPROACH

Vygotsky's zone of proximal development (ZPD) can be interpreted as the characteristic, common, patterns of communication and interaction experienced by individuals and between groups constituted within the context of particular activities. In a traditional classroom the ZPD would be constituted by the formal instruction communicated from teacher to student. The teacher assumes that their needs, goals and intentions are shared by the students. However, this ignores the personal experience of the students, which is invariably subjectively interpreted differently by different students within their own greater socio-cultural context – none of which is ordinarily the concern of the traditional teaching practice. Traditionally, students understand their role as discovering what the teacher requires of them and accurately reproducing the culturally appropriate information and procedures as determined by the teacher. This is only interrupted when openly questioned by the students.

In light of the traditional approach, the 3D CVE activities would seem marginal to the core curriculum needs. However, it was found that by extending the classroom activities outside the traditional school socio-cultural environment and students were more active in their own learning, that they were forced to overcome problems by sharing solutions. Instead of deferring to the teacher for solutions to problems, they were now participating in problem solving of their own accord. The process of problem solving could be seen through the process of reification, which together with the dual process of participation allowed negotiation of meaning, forming a shared repertoire (Wenger, 1999).

As a learning community, the students participating in the study shared a history of participation and learning where members had different roles as master and apprentice and there was a progression through these roles, along learning trajectories. The students' designs comprised the outcome of the activities and thus served as the shared repertoire of the community and as the indicators of a learner's movement along a trajectory (Tolsby & Sørensen, 2000).

Their designs (and their intermediate artefacts: Sketches and blogs) were important for expressing their identity. Wenger (1999) defines identity in terms of negotiated experience, community membership, learning trajectory and nexus of multimemberships. Identity is connected to the activities on the learning trajectory and is expressed by the artefacts that comprise the outcome of the activities. The past experiences and history of community members were reified within the shared repertoire as documents, plans (sketches, email and chat communications) and the 3D constructions. Membership involved reconciliation of boundaries and creating bridges across the landscape of practice. The boundaries were reified with explicit markers of membership, such as national identity (e.g. national flags in the constructions), or with boundary objects, connecting and coordinating different practices and communities (such as teleportation links connecting constructions sites of subgroups within a bigger group).

During the project, the students used various tools to mediate their activities. Some of them used blogs, paper sketches and pre-built building blocks in Active Worlds for further customization and copying. They put information about their design activities and ideas in the blogs and on the building sites as notes and design fragments. In this way, the students put 'experiences into thingness' (Wenger, 1999, p58). They formed the landscape and the artefacts according to their personality and negotiated design ideas. They left traces of their activities, participation and identity in the design spaces. For example, they made culturally explicit identifying signs such as "G'day mate" and national flags. By leaving these traces in the places where students worked, and collaboratively creating a Babel tower across national borders, the

Figure 7. The students' forms of communication can be seen as the artefacts of their socialising. Their need to be socially organised mediated the social actions that followed.

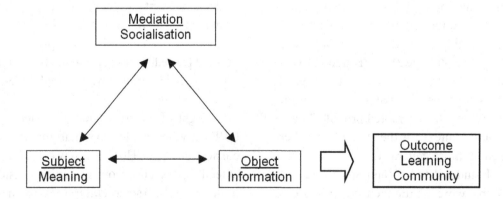

students expressed their trajectory of membership and social roles. Through the design of the towers (complexity) and the artefacts constituting their interiors (furniture and text) they provided an indication of their expertise. By mastering the new technology, helping peer students and learning to overcome language differences by means of the 3D CVE, IRC and videoconferencing, the students progressed along learning trajectories from apprentice to master. From representing different nations, the students moved towards creating a common community of practice.

We observed that not only students but also artefacts progressed along trajectories as the project unfolded. From simple sketches to final constructions, one could see that the virtual places that the students created (i.e. the Babel towers) could be considered as artefacts as well as the mediating of their identities and cross-cultural activities. The belonging of the artefacts developed as they moved from individually owned ideas to a group's property and then finally ending as a part of the whole community's shared repertoire.

Along the way students met many difficulties. Many had not previously encountered the software being used. Many had not worked with 3D design software before. At first, they sought guidance on what was required – 'would this be sufficient in this way or that?' Increasingly however, they developed a method for taking control of their own endeavours – once they understood the freedom they had to do so. The students' confidence grew as the project progressed. This was recorded in their weekly journal entries – on reflection, they could see their own progress.

In terms of their shared ZPD, the social characteristics of the setting, revolved around problem definition, argument, decision making, role play, task allocation, online communication, experimentation and collaboration. They had made the project their own. While some students struggle with traditional teaching practices, most of the students in this study found the online collabora-

tion both straightforward and rewarding. Whereas traditional digital media design instruction is typically focussed on skills acquisition, requiring students to memorise procedures and how to apply them, they often do not retain the personal consciousness necessary for actual problem solving. By contrast, we found that by providing a creative learning environment, this allowed the students to own the project, self-solve problems and take responsibility for the outcomes. The online activities as part of the 3D CVE provided this setting. It required a radical shift in power relationships and social organisation between students and students, and students and teacher, and administrators.

The traditional activity of producing a lesson using pre-prepared notes and tutorial guides involves little conscious intellectual activity on the part of the teacher. It simply involves operations within an assumed conceptual framework. Representing the information in a new form, directed by the students, required personal involvement – a radical power shift. Students progressed from a place of discomfort to an empowering state. Through this we observed them progressively improve their own cooperation skills and knowledge about the technology itself as well as their own social interactions mediated by the technology. Students saw themselves as a part of a system of collective learning activity in which their individual knowledge and prior experiences mattered. This was in stark contrast to previous, more traditional, learning practices.

CONCLUSION

Most students graduate from university with a view of digital media design as a legacy of code and procedures that need to be rote learned and reproducible when and wherever needed. The traditional transmission model of learning in digital media design is still prevalent in many universities. This is reinforced by the perceived needs of academic staff to be able to quantifiably justify the results of their students – usually by exam. This is despite the realities of the workplace – teams of digital media design professionals working collaboratively on a single solution. That design is now no longer simply the purview of the creative artist, but rather most design experiences are now mainstream everyday communications using digital media, suggests that, more generally, the way it is taught needs to change also. This chapter outlined a framework for the analysis of Digital Media Design (DMD) practice and a 3D CVE using Vygotsky's (1978) Zone of Proximal Development (ZPD) and Wenger's (1999) approach to learning communities. The results of this study were that a radical shift in teaching approach was needed to foster the sorts of deep learning outcomes graduates of DMD require to meet the demands of contemporary digital media design work practices. The implications/lessons learned from the study can be summarized as follows:

- The collaborative design process progressed along the learning and participation trajectories as predicted by Wenger. This involved both learners and the artefacts created by them
- Participants' cross-cultural design experiences moved along participation trajectories between different memberships, from being parts of different nations towards a shared "virtual" cultural membership and community of practice as predicted by Vygotsky's ZPD.
- And, the final design results, the intermediate design artefacts as well as the understandings achieved, procedures adopted and so on, comprise the shared repertoire of the learning community. Therefore, the collaborative design process is most appropriately described by the duality of participation and reification as espoused by Wenger.
- More specifically, the 3D CVE lent itself to this investigation and subsequent conclu-

sions as its features and properties helped to illustrate and visualize the processes involved a ZPD study. For example,

- The means for constructing identity in 3D CVE, though still imperfect in terms of graphical quality and richness of body language, provided a heightened sense of freedom of expression and flexibility, thus facilitating progression along the participation trajectories. Boundary objects could be easily constructed and visualized (such as the Babel towers) and explicit markers of membership (such as user names, avatar appearance, and flags in the buildings).
- The mediating artefacts produced by the participants comprise the outcome of the learners' activities and therefore served as indicators of the learners' movements along their learning trajectories. In this sense, artefacts in the 3D CVE provided for flexible transformations and modifications, as well as linking and displaying metadata. In this, we saw a more direct and immediate reflection and visualization of the learners' progression along their trajectories. The same flexibility also provided additional support for mediation of the learners' activities.
- 'Places' in the 3D CVE, considered as artefacts, were used to mediate the learners' activities and comprised the outcome of the activities by containing traces of learners and events, meetings, construction activities, and so on. The virtual places could be 'stored' for future use as a part of the shared repertoire of the learning community.

As a methodological framework for investigating this type of design activity, AT has demonstrated its applicability to the digital design domain. This suggests it may also be suitable in different educational contexts in 3D CVEs, as well as different technological platforms.

REFERENCES

Amonashvili, S. A. (1984). Development of the cognitive initiative of students in the first grades of elementary education. [in Russian]. *Voprosy Psihologii, 5,* 36–41.

Argyris, C., & Schon, D. A. (1978). *Organisational learning: A theory of action perspective.* Reading, MA: Addison-Wesley.

Bardram, J. E. (1997). Plans as situated action: An activity theory approach to workflow systems. In *Proceedings of ECSCW 1997,* September 7-11, Lancaster, UK, (pp. 17-24). Kluwer Academic Publishers.

Bardram, J. E. (1998). *Collaboration, coordination, and computer support: An activity theoretical approach to the design of computer supported cooperative work.* Doctoral Dissertation (PB-533), DAIMI, University of Aarhus.

Bedny, G., & Meister, D. (1997). *The Russian theory of activity current applications to design.* London, UK: Lawrence Erlbaum Assoc.

Bourdieu, P., & Wacquant, L. J. D. (1992). *An invitation to reflexive sociology.* Chicago, IL: University of Chicago Press.

Bruner, J. (1986). *Actual minds, possible worlds.* Cambridge, MA: Harvard University Press.

Cartwright, D., & Zander, A. (1968). *Group dynamics: Research and theory.* New York, NY: Harper Collins College Div.

Clear, T., & Kassabova, D. (2005). Motivational patterns in virtual team collaboration. In A. Young, & D. Tolhurst (Eds.), *Proceedings of Australasian Computing Education Conference 2005, Conferences in Research and Practice in Information Technology,* Newcastle, Australia, vol. 42.

Cole, M. (1990). Cultural psychology: A once and future discipline? In J. J. Berman (Ed.), *Cross-cultural Perspectives, Nebraska Symposium on Motivation* (vol. 37, pp279-335). Lincoln, NE: University f Nebraska Press.

Cross, N. (1982). Designerly ways of knowing. *Design Studies, 3*(4), 221–227. doi:10.1016/0142-694X(82)90040-0

Cross, N., Christians, H., & Dorst, K. (Eds.). (1996). *Analysing design activity.* Chichester, UK: Wiley.

Cuff, D. (1991). *Architecture: The story of practice.* Cambridge, MA: MIT Press.

Davydov, V. V. (1988). Problems of developmental teaching: The experience of theoretical and empirical psychological research. In *Soviet Education,* Part I: *30*(8), 15-97; *Part II: 30,* 3-38; *Part III: 30*(10), 3-77.

Davydov, V. V. (1990). *Types of generalisation in instruction: Logical and psychological problems in the structuring of school curricula.* Reston, VA: National Council of Teachers of Mathematics.

Dewey, J. (1957). *Experience and education.* New York, NY: MacMillan.

Engstrom, Y. (1987). *Learning by expanding: An activity-theoretical approach to developmental research.* Helsinki, Finland: Orienta-Konsultit.

Engstrom, Y., Miettinen, R., & Punamaki, R.-L. (1999). *Perspectives on activity theory.* Cambridge, UK: Cambridge University Press.

Gero, J. S., & McNeill, T. (1998). An approach to the analysis of design protocols. *Design Studies, 19,* 21–61. doi:10.1016/S0142-694X(97)00015-X

Gifford, B. R., & Enyedy, N. D. (1999). Activity centered design: Towards a theoretical framework for CSCL. In *Proceedings of Computer Supported Collaborative Learning 1999,* December 12-15, Palo Alto, CA, USA, (pp. 189-196). Lawrence Erlbaum Associates.

Guba, E. (1981). Criteria for assessing the trustworthiness of naturalistic inquiries. *Education Communication and Technology Journal, 29*(2).

Guba, E., & Lincoln, Y. (1998). Competing paradigms in qualitative research. In Denzin, N., & Lincoln, Y. (Eds.), *The landscape of qualitative research*. California: Sage Publications.

Heath, C., & Luff, P. (1996). Convergent activities: Line control and passenger information on the London underground. In Engestrom, Y., & Middleton, D. (Eds.), *Cognition and communication at work* (pp. 96–129). Cambridge University Press.

Hedegaard, M. (1986). Instruction of evolution as a school project and the development of pupils' theoretical thinking. In M. Hildebrand-Nilshon & G. Ruckreim (Eds.), *Workshop contributions to selected aspects of applied research. Proceedings of the 1st International Congress on Activity Theory* (Vol. 3), Berlin, Germany: System Druck.

Hedegaard, M. (1987). Methodology in evaluative research on teaching and learning. In van Zuuren, F. J., Wertz, F. J., & Mook, B. (Eds.), *Advances in qualitative psychology: Themes and variations* (pp. 53–78). Lisse: Swets & Zeitlinger.

Hedegaard, M. (1990). The zone of proximal development as basis for instruction. In Moll, L. (Ed.), *Vygotsky and education: Instructional implications and applications of sociohistorical psychology* (pp. 349–371). Cambridge, UK: Cambridge University Press.

Jarvenpaa, S., & Leidner, D. (1998). Communication and trust in global virtual teams. *Journal of Computer-Mediated Communication, 3*.

Johnson, B. (2001). Unfocused interaction in distributed workgroups: Establishing group presence in a Web-based environment. In B. de Vries, J. van Leeuwen, & H. Achten (Eds.), *Proceedings of the International CAAD Futures Conference*, 8-11 July 2001, Eindhoven, The Netherlands, (pp. 401-414).

Kuhn, T. S. (1996). *The structure of scientific revolutions*. Chicago, IL: University of Chicago Press.

Kuutti, K. (1994). *Information Systems, cooperative work and active subjects: The activity-theoretical perspective*. Ph.D. Thesis, Research Papers Series A 23, Department of Information Processing Science, University of Oulu, Finland.

Latour, B. (1987). *Science in action: How to follow scientists and engineers through society*. Cambridge, MA: Harvard University Press.

Latour, B. (1994). *We have never been modern*. Hertfordshire, UK: Harvest Wheatsheaf.

Lawson, B. (2004). *What designers know*. Elsevier Architectural Press.

Lawson, B. (2005). *How designers think*. London, UK: Architectural Press.

Leidner, D., & Jarvenpaa, S. (1995). The use of Information Technology to enhance management school education: A theoretical view. *MIS Quarterly*, September.

Lektorsky, V. A. (1984). *Subject, object, cognition*. Moscow, Russia: Progress.

Leont'ev, A. N. (1978). *Activity, consciousness, and personality*. Englewood Cliffs, NJ: Prentice-Progress.

Leont'ev, A. N. (1981). *Problems of the development of the mind*. Moscow, Russia: Progress.

Lloyd, P., Lawson, B., & Scott, P. (1996). Can concurrent verbalisation reveal design cognition? In Cross, N., Christians, H., & Dorst, K. (Eds.), *Analysing design activity* (pp. 437–463).

Maher, M.-L. (1995). Using the Internet to teach in a virtual design studio. In *Proceedings of DECA 95: Information Technology and its Influence on Design Education*, RMIT, Melbourne, 1995.

Marks, M., Mathieu, J., & Zaccaro, S. (2001). A temporally based framework and taxonomy of team processes. *Academy of Management Review, 26*, 356–376.

Marx, K., & Engels, F. (1968). *The German ideology*. Moscow, Russia: Progress.

Mead, G. H. (1938). *The philosophy of act*. Chicago, IL: University of Chicago Press.

Mitchell, W. J., Yee, S., Naka, R., Morozumi, M., & Yamaguchi, S. (1998). The Kumamoto-Kyoto-MIT Collaborative Project: A case study of the design studio of the future. In N. A. Streitz, S. Konomi, & H.-J. Burkhardt (Eds.), *Cooperative Buildings, Integrating Information, Organisation, and Architecture. Proceedings of the First International Workshop, CoBuild'98*, Darmstadt, Germany, February 1998, (pp. 80-93).

Oxman, R., & Streich, B. (2001). Digital media and design didactics in visual cognition. In Hannu, P. (Ed.), *Architectural Information Management, Proceedings of eCAADe19* (p. 357). Helsinki, Finland.

Prasolova-Førland, E., & Wyeld, T. (2008). The place metaphor in 3D CVEs: A pedagogical case study of the virtual stage. *International Journal of Emerging Technologies in Learning, 3*(1), 54–60.

Prasolova-Førland, E., & Wyeld, T. G. (2006). Online 3D cave performance of T. S. Elliot's Cocktail Party: An example of virtual stage. In *Proceedings of Web-Based Education 2006*, Puerto Vallarta, Mexico, January 23-25.

Schon, D. A. (1983). *The reflective practitioner*. London, UK: Temple, Smith.

Schutz, W. (1958). *Firo: A three-dimensional theory of interpersonal behaviour*. New York, NY: Holt, Rinehart, and Winston.

Seifert, T. (2004). Understanding student motivation. *Educational Research, 46*, 137–149. doi:10.1080/0013188042000222421

Suchman, L. A. (1987). *Plans and situated actions: The problem of human-machine communication*. Cambridge, UK: Cambridge University Press.

Tolsby, H., Sorensen, E. K., & Dirckinck-Holm-feld, L. (2000). *Designing virtual portfolios for communities of practice*. In the Seventh World Conference on Computers in Education, WCCE 2001, Copenhagen, Denmark, 2000.

Vygosky, L. S. (1978). *Mind in society*. Cambridge, MA: Harvard University Press.

Vygosky, L. S. (1981). The genesis of higher mental functions. In Wertsch, J. V. (Ed.), *The concept of activity in Soviet psychology* (pp. 144–188). Armonk: M.E. Sharpe.

Wenger, E. (1999). *Communities of practice: Learning, meaning and identity*. Cambridge: MA Cambridge University Press.

Wertsch, J. V. (1990). *Voices of the mind*. Cambridge, MA: Harvard University Press.

Wittgenstein, L. (1953). *Philosophical investigations*. London, UK: Basil Blackwell.

Wojtowicz, J. (1994). *Virtual design studio*. Hong Kong: HKU Press.

Wyeld, T., & Prasolova-Førland, E. (2008). Using activity theory to assess the effectiveness of a learning community: A case study in remote collaboration using a 3D virtual environment. In Akoumianakis, D. (Ed.), *Virtual communities of practice and social interactive technologies: Lifecycle and workflow analysis*. Hershey, PA: IGI Global.

Wyeld, T. G., Prasolova-Førland, E., & Chang, T.-W. (2006). The 3D CVE as a cross-cultural classroom. In *Proceedings of Game/Set/Match 2006*, Delft, Berlageweg, Holland, March 29-April 01.

Wyeld, T. G., Prasolova-Førland, E., & Chang, T.-W. (2007). 3D remote design collaboration: A pedagogical case study of the cross-cultural issues raised. In *Proceedings of the 11th International Conference on CSCW in Design* April 26-28, 2007, Melbourne, Australia.

Wyeld, T. G., Prasolova-Førland, E., & Viller, S. (2007). Theatrical place in a 3D CVE: An online performance of Plato's allegory of the cave in a distributed 3D CVE. In [Guadeloupe, French Caribbean.]. *Proceedings of The Second International Multi-Conference on Computing in the Global Information Technology, ICCGI, 2007*(March), 4–9.

KEY TERMS AND DEFINITIONS

3D Collaborative Virtual Environment: A 3D modelling environment, are typically available online, which includes at least text messaging, such as ActiveWorlds, SecondLife and online games.

Activity Theory: Vygotski (1978), Leont'ev (1981) and Engestrom's (1987) Activity Theory focuses on human activity directed towards an object, mediated by cultural artefacts and is social within a culture (Bardram, 1997). Culturally defined tools, or *artefacts*, mediate all activity.

Avatar: One's representative icon or three dimensional embodiment when immersed in a 3D modelling environment that supports collaboration or cooperation.

Cultural Artefact: Within the context of any collaborative activity and its social context, cultural artefacts are produced, such as shared learning, reflective questioning and technological processes.

Cultural Capital: In Bourdieu's (1996) terms, one's cultural capital, knowledge or power can be exchanged in socialised situations.

Digital Media Design: Digital Media Design combines computing and the creative arts. Due to the ubiquity of the computer it is available to a broad range of design-related practitioners.

Learning Trajectory: Learners move through successive forms of participation, connecting the past, the present and the future, progressing from partial to full participants (Gifford & Enyedy, 1999; Wenger, 1999).

Protocol Analysis: Analysis of participant reflections on recorded conversations and actions. The analyst looks for common terms, phrases or actions that indicate a process is being followed.

Zone of Proximal Development: Vygotsky's (1978, 1986) socio-cultural ontogenetic ZPD provides a framework from which shared learning experiences can be investigated through studying the experience of co-interactions.

Chapter 11
Will Different Scales Impact on Design Collaboration in 3D Virtual Environments?

Jerry Jen-Hung Tsai
University of Sydney, Australia

Jeff WT Kan
Taylor's University, Malaysia

Xiangyu Wang
Curtin University, Australia

Yingsiu Huang
Tunghai University, Taiwan

ABSTRACT

This chapter presents a study on the impact of design scales on collaborations in 3D virtual environments. Different domains require designers to work on different scales; for instance, urban design and electronic circuit design operate at very different scales. However, the understanding of the effects of scales upon collaboration in virtual environment is limited. In this chapter, the authors propose to use protocol analysis method to examine the differences between two design collaboration projects in virtual environments: one large scale, and another small scale within a similar domain. It shows that the difference in scale impacted more on communication control and social communication.

INTRODUCTION

Collaborative design is a process of dynamically communicating and working together in order to collectively establish design goals, search through design problem spaces, determine de-

DOI: 10.4018/978-1-61350-180-1.ch011

sign constraints, and construct a design solution (Hennessy and Murphy, 1999; Lahti et al., 2004). Traditionally, face-to-face (FTF) manner is the most common way of designers' communication in collaborations. However, it requires significant amount of time and financial investments on coordinating and relocating resources, which can often lead to additional costs and unexpected project delay. 3D virtual worlds combined with high-bandwidth network provide a way of design communication and collaboration by participants immersing into the same environment. It has shown great potentials for supporting synchronous and asynchronous multiple-time-zone and multiple-location design collaborations without the need of designers physical presenting for design collaboration. Currently, the majority of studies on design collaboration in virtual environments mainly focus on analysing collaborative design behaviours in virtual worlds (Gabriel and Maher, 2002; Maher et al., 2006a; Gul et al., 2008), seldom if any on the studies of collaborative design behaviours affected by different scales of design projects. Scale refers to the size or extent of something, especially when compared with something else (Hornby and Wehmeier, 2007). In a 3D environment, should the tools that support urban design collaborations be the same to that support interior design collaborations? A study of design collaboration behaviours in virtual environments related to design projects with different scales will help developers of 3D virtual worlds to further enhance tools for design collaborations in different scales.

In this chapter we assume human use different cognitive resources to handle different scale objects and this will affect the way they communicate and collaborate. We conjectured that the ability for human to observe the environment and to examine smaller objects is decoded by using different cognitive resources. It is further conjectured that the use of different cognitive resources to read the environment (large-scale) and to handle objects (small-scale) carries on in the 3D virtual environment. To give an example, when apple came out with QuickTime VR (also known as QuickTime Virtual Reality), it had two modes, a Panoramic mode and an Object mode. In the panoramic mode viewers look out to get a sense of place; while in the object mode, viewers look in toward the central object. Thus our notion of scale refers to the way human interacts

with it rather than in a relative term. For example we can examine or appreciate a car as an object (small scale) by walking around the car to look in toward it in different angles, but we can also sit in the drivers' seat and look out to appreciate the interior.

We propose to us protocol analysis as a tool to investigate the effects of scales upon 3D virtual collaborations. It is a rigorous methodology for eliciting verbal reports of thought sequences as a valid source of data on thinking. By analyzing the information expressed as verbalized thoughts, it is possible to assess the validity of the verbalized information (Ericsson and Simon, 1993). Protocol analysis had been used to study design collaboration (Gabriel and Maher, 2002).

Following our previous preliminary comparative study (Tsai et al., 2008), we focus on and present how the scale of design project (large and small) in 3D virtual environments affects the designers' behaviours during the collaboration in this book chapter. The large-scale design project defined in this chapter is a design of a building which people can move within it. In contrast, the small-scale design project is defined as a design of furniture which people can manipulate it but cannot move within it. A studio and a workstation are designed in the large-scale design project and the small-scale design project respectively. Both of them are performed in the virtual environments in Second Life (http://secondlife.com/). A coding scheme derived from Gabriel and Maher (2002) and Suwa, Prucell and Gero (1998) as well as inspired by Gero (1990) is developed for protocol analysis to understand how designers collaborate in 3D virtual environments on their design projects.

This chapter commences from brief reviews of design collaborations in 3D virtual environments and protocol analysis. It is followed by the descriptions of the large-scale design project and the small-scale design project, i.e. Design Project I: a studio, and Design Project II: a workstation, including design project settings and design outcomes. A coding scheme developed is then followed. Protocol analysis results and discussions for both design projects are presented at the end of this chapter.

BACKGROUND

Design Collaboration in 3D Virtual Environments

3D virtual worlds, virtual architecture or cyberspace can be understood as networked virtual environments designed using the place metaphor. One of the main characteristics that distinguish 3D virtual environments from conventional virtual reality is that 3D virtual environments allow multiple users to be immersed in the same environment supporting a shared sense of place and presence (Singhal and Zyda, 1999). 3D virtual environments provide a consistent context for people to browse digital information, interact with the environment, and communicate with each other.

Collaborative design is a common occurrence with designers communicating their ideas with their peers in the form of verbal representations (voiced or typed) and graphical representations (Gabriel and Maher, 2002). In general, especially in the past, FTF manner is the most common way of designers' communication in collaborative design. The emergence of virtual environments combining with computer technology and the Internet is gradually changing the way of design representations and communications for collaborative design. The employment of computers can support design documentation, design computing and design development. The application of the Internet provides a new way for virtually remote design communications. Computer-supported collaborative design via the Internet creates a new platform for designers to communicate and develop designs in virtual environments. With the support of collaborative 3D virtual environments, designers can remotely collaborate on projects without concerning the barriers of locations and time differences. Designers can also have access to synchronous and asynchronous digital communications and real-time building simulation data. Current development of such systems, for example, DesignWorld (Maher et al., 2006b) supports video chat, message board chat, collaborative modelling and multidisciplinary building information viewing for architects and structure engineers.

Design Study and Protocol Analysis

Design is one of the most important intentional acts of human being. It has been viewed as one of the most complex endeavors. However, the understanding of this ability is still limited. Depending on the domain and position, the meaning of "design" varies. Designers with different cognitive abilities and style will approach design differently. Product designers focus on the creating of objects, while landscape designers concern the environment change. Cognitive abilities can be seen as how good certain aptitude a designer possess, and cognitive style is seen as the preferred way how a designer designs.

Protocol analysis has become the de facto method for studying the cognitive processes of designers in the past two decades. Cross et al. (1996) stated that "... protocol analysis ... has been regarded as the most likely method (perhaps the only method) to bring out into the open the somewhat mysterious cognitive abilities of designers." Ericsson and Simon (1993) laid the foundation of using verbal protocols, concurrent reporting, as quantitative data for studying thought process. Eastman (1970) conducted the first formal protocol analysis that studies designing. His study contributed to the current understanding of what architects do when they design in the form of an information process model. Eastman viewed designing as a process of identifying the problems and testing alternative solutions. This view was challenged by viewing designing as a reflective conversation with materials (Schn and Wiggins,

1992) in which the basic structure is an interaction between designing and discovering. Protocol analysis has also been used to study design teams (Goldschmidt, 1995; Gabriel and Maher, 2002; Maher, et al., 2006a). In studying the team collaboration, their communications were usually taken as the raw data of protocol.

Protocol studies have shown it affects the behaviour of the collaborators for design collaboration in 3D virtual environments. For example, Maher et al. (2006a) showed that two designers collaborating in a 3D virtual environment spent more time on management of tasks and less in design compared with the same pair designing face-to-face. Kan (2008) also showed that when collaborating in 3D virtual environments the design processes contain very little reformulation of behaviour and function. We are unaware of studies that examine the impact of design scales upon the collaboration in the virtual world.

The review of design collaboration in 3D virtual environments and design study and protocol analysis shows the lack of studying effects of design scales to design behaviours and collaborations during design developments in 3D virtual environments. It also provides a foundation that we can apply protocol analysis by using designers' communications as the raw data of protocol to study design collaborations in the progress of design development.

COLLABORATIVE DESIGN IN 3D VIRTUAL ENVIRONMENTS

Collaborative Design Projects

The collaborative design projects are performed by design teams in 3D virtual environments in Second Life (http://secondlife.com/). A design team includes two students from Design Computing discipline in the Faculty of Architecture, Design and Planning at the University of Sydney and two students from Digital Design Department at MingDao University. They are design novices,

undergraduate Year three students with about two to three years of design-experience. Two collaborative design projects are:

- *Design Project I*: A large-scale design project (LS), a studio design
- *Design Project II*: A small-scale design project (SS), a workstation design

Each design project is completed in forty minutes. Design project participants consider the requirements of the projects to develop the style and layout of both design projects.

The design requirements of Design Project I (LS) are: This studio should consist of public spaces and private spaces. There are different rooms for individual design group members (as private spaces) and a multi-function room for group meeting and entertainment (as a public space). Design group members can decide the shape, size and colour of their own private spaces. The public space is designed by all group members. The style of private spaces and public spaces should be consistent.

The design requirements of Design Project II (SS) are: This workstation should satisfy the specific needs for each individual member and a universal function for all design group members. This workstation will be placed in the studio developed. Design group members work together for the shape, size and colour of the workstation.

Collaborative Design Outcomes

Design Project I: Studio Design in the Virtual Environment

Figure 1 shows the collaborative design outcome of a studio for the large-scale design project (LS) in the virtual environment (VE) in Second Life, Design Project I. This studio is assumed to be located beside a beach. It is a three-level building with a multi-functional area on the ground level, a meeting room and a balcony on the first level, and a kitchen and four private rooms for

Figure 1. Collaborative design outcome of a design studio with three levels in the virtual environment (VE), Design Project I

four design group members respectively on the second level. Design group members can work and entertain within this virtual building. The ground level is open to the public. The main function is for group presentations. The first and second levels are restricted to design group members' use only. On the first level, there are a projector, a big screen and some furniture, such as several comfortable chairs. Avatar of each design group member can move to here for design brainstorming and discussions. Some outdoors furniture is placed at the balcony. Avatars can sit and relax in this area. The second level is the main private working area where workstations and chairs will be placed. In addition, there is a kitchen where avatars can prepare food.

Design Project II: Workstation Design in the Virtual Environment

Figure 2 shows the collaborative design outcome of a workstation for the small-scale design project (SS) in the virtual environment (VE) in Second Life, Design Project II. This workstation with specific features is required to suit the needs of every individual design member. It will be placed in the private rooms of the studio designed in Design Project I. Using 3D objects provided by Second Life, design group members can create and modify the workstation as well as place it into private rooms very easily. This workstation, in Figure 2, is made of timber. It consists of a foldable rectangle desktop and two shelves for storing avatars' stationaries and personal belong-

Figure 2. Collaborative design outcome of a workstation in the virtual environment (VE), Design Project II

ings. The desktop and the shelves are supported by two pieces of oval-shape timbers. The height of the workstation is adjustable according to the needs of each avatar of design group members.

CODING SCHEME

The coding scheme for studying the impact of large and small design scales for design collaborations in 3D virtual environments is divided into three main categories, including communication control, design communication and social communication, shown in Table 1. Details of each coding scheme are as follows. In regard to protocol analysis segmentation setting for both design projects, i.e. Design Projects I and II, each segment is thirty seconds. In total, there are eighty segments for each design project performed in forty minutes.

Table 1. The coding scheme for collaborative designs in both real and virtual environments (after Gabriel and Maher 2002)

Communication Control	Code	Description
Interruption	**INT**	When a design member interrupts another member.
Hand-over	**HAN**	Handing over the conversation from a design member to another member. May be through questions or by specifically naming the next speaker.
Pause	**PAU**	Pauses during the communication.
Design Communication	**Code**	**Description**
Design Concept		*What is communicated*
Introduction of Idea	**IDE**	When a design member directly or indirectly introduces an idea.
Acceptance of Idea	**ACC**	When a design member accepts an idea of other members.
Rejection of Idea	**REJ**	When a design member does not accept a particular idea of other members.
Clarification of Idea	**CLA**	When a design member explains why the idea is appropriate.
Development of Idea	**DEV**	When a design member further develops an idea.
Design Detail		*What the characteristic is concerned*
Discussion of Size	**VSZ**	When design members discuss about the size of a 3D object.
Discussion of Shape	**VSP**	When design members discuss about the shape of a 3D object.
Discussion of Colour/ Texture	**VCL/VTXT**	When design members discuss about the colour & texture of a 3D object.
Design task		*How the design is implemented*
Task Questioning	**TKQ**	When design members question about their design task.
Instructing	**INS**	When a design member gives instructions to another member. e.g. 'draw the door here.'
Working Status	**VWS**	When design members state what they are currently doing or what they have done. e.g. 'I just finished the walls.'
Social Communication	**Code**	**Description**
Non-task-related social communication	**NTR**	When design members talk about non-task-related things.
Joking	**JOK**	When a design member laughs or gives a joke.
Gesture	**VGT**	When a design member gives a gesture in Second Life.

Communication Control

The coding scheme of communication control includes interruption (INT), hand-over (HAN) and pause (PAU). Interruption (INT) is to describe a design member interrupts another member and it is associated with simultaneous speech [10]. Hand-over (HAN) is to describe a speaker hands over the conversation to another member. A speaker can hand the conversation over to another by asking questions, using stereotyped questions, such as "isn't it?" or statements as "you know", or by specifically naming the next speaker [10]. Pause (PAU) is used when there is a temporary cessation of conversation between the design group members. In the protocol analysis, pauses occur often during the design collaboration in the virtual environment, in Second Life.

Design Communication

The coding scheme of design communication are categorised into design concept, design detail and design task.

* *Design Concept:* How design ideas are manipulated during the design process, e.g. introducing, accepting, rejecting, clarifying and developing design ideas.
* *Design Detail:* How the design project is created and modified in virtual environments by using 3D objects, e.g. considering object size, shape, colour and texture.
* *Design Task:* What actions are taken to get the design task done, e.g. task questing, instructing and working status.

Design Concept: The coding scheme of design concept is similar to [8] and includes introduction of idea (IDE), acceptance of idea (ACC), rejection of idea (REJ), clarification of idea (CLA) and development of idea (DEV). The difference is to introduce development of idea (DEV) here to replace refinement (REF) in [8]. DEV is used

when a design member further develops an idea. In both Design Projects I and II, when design group members were not satisfied with the design idea, they normally developed new ideas rather than refined it.

Design Detail: The coding scheme of design detail includes discussion of size (VSZ), discussion of shape (VSP), and discussion of colour/texture (VCL/VTXT) of 3D objects. In virtual environments, in Second Life, designers use objects provided to develop their design projects. When design group members develop a design project, they mainly focus on the discussions of object characteristics, including their size, shape, colour and texture. Design group members can easily create and modify their design projects by using basic 3D objects (e.g. box, prism, cylinder and sphere) and edit functions provided (e.g. rotate, stretch and select texture). They can also upload images they have for the 3D objects.

Design Task: The coding scheme of design tasks includes questioning (TKQ), instructing (INS) and working status (VWS). Task questioning (TKQ) is used when a design member questions about their design tasks. It may be referred to a previously agreed plan or schedule, or making design decisions in advance. Instructing (INS) is occurred when a design member gives instructions on how or what to create in virtual environments. Working status (VWS) applied to virtual environment collaborations is used when design group members state what they are currently doing or what they have done. The other design group members might follow these WVS to keep working on the project design. In collaborative design in Second Life, design group members create or modify 3D objects in real time. VWS is used to prevent confusions and conflicts of the working design activities.

Social Communication

The coding scheme of social communication includes non-task-related social communication

(NTR), joking (JOK) and gesture (VGT). In collaborative design, design members might talk about some things which are not related to the design project. Non-task-related social communication (NTR) is used when there is a non-task-related talk happened in collaborative designing. Joking (JOK) is used when design members laugh or give jokes in collaborative designing. Gesture (VGT) is applied to virtual environment collaborations, in Second Life, when a design member gives a gesture for fun. Joking (JOK) and gesture (VGT) are used and represent verbal and non-verbal social communication in collaborative design.

RESULT AND DISCUSSION

The following presents protocol analyses of the two design projects, i.e. the large-scale design project and the small-scale design project, with some discussions.

Communication Control

In Design Project I, the large-scale design project, the "pause" (PAU) percentage occupies two third of the total communication control, Figure 3. There are only a few "interruptions" (8%) and a low percentage of "hand-over" (HAN) (25%). Comparatively, the distribution of types of com-

munication control in Design Project II, the small-scale design project, is more even. "Pause" still represents the highest percentage (46%) but it is much lesser than it is in Design Project I. The "hand-over" and "interruption" (INT) percentages are higher than that of the Design Project I. In a nut shell, the hand-over and interruptions are interactions. This result suggested that there are more interactions in the small-scale design project. Reviewing the protocol, we observed that in Design Project I, the division of labour was very clear at the beginning and the collaboration was loosely coupled; whereas in Design Project II, the collaboration was closely coupled – design group members were tied to the same design process and object. In the large-scale design project, i.e. a studio design, design group members spent time exploring the environment and space according to their own preferences while in a small-scale design project, i.e. a workstation design, they were forced to focus on the object.

Design Communication

The coding scheme of design communication includes design concept, design detail and design task. Figure 4 shows the overall coded result of the design communication. There is a slightly higher percentage of design concepts in Design Project I (35% vs. 28%). The percentage of De-

Figure 3. Analysis of communication control

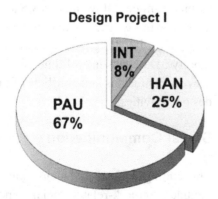
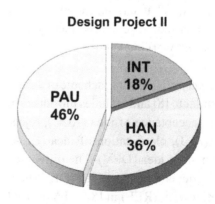

Figure 4. Analysis of design communication

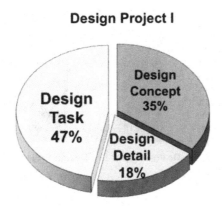

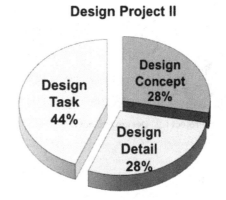

sign Details is much higher in Design Project II (28% vs. 18%). The percentages of Design Tasks are roughly the same. In the Design Concept category, the large-scale design project has more room for communication with design ideas and design concept. In contrast, the small-scale design project has higher percentage of detailed design; the protocol shows design group members often discuss colours and textures of the workstation.

Design Concept

Figure 5 compared the percentage break down of the Design Concept. There is no "development of idea" (DEV) in Design Project I, the large-scale design project, which is surprising. Design Project II, the small-scale design project, also has very little amount of idea development. The design

Figure 5. Analysis of design concept

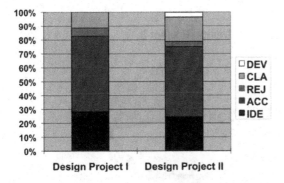

group members are novice designers. In studying single designers, Kavakli and Gero (2003) showed that the novice designer used a lot of cognitive resources to generate ideas but did not have the experience to take important ideas and further develop it. On the other hand the expert designer was very efficient in anchoring and developing important ideas. In these two design projects, once the design group members had accepted an idea, they will develop it further and go ahead to implement the idea.

In both design projects the "rejection of idea" (REJ) percentages are low. Design group members in both design projects tried to maintain harmonious process of collaborating.

The clarification of ideas (CLA) in Design Project II, the small-scale design project, occurred more frequently compared with the percentage of CLA in the large-scale design project. Design group members were more engaged in the discussion in the small-scale design project.

In both design projects, the percentage of "acceptance of idea" (ACC) far exceeds the percentage of "introduction of idea" (IDE). When someone raised an idea, other design group members expressed their acceptance.

Overall, there is no significant difference in terms of design concept communication in both design projects. The major difference is in the "development of idea".

Figure 6. Analysis of design detail

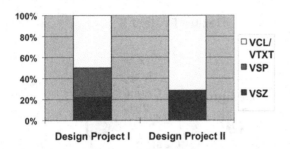

Figure 7. Analysis of design task

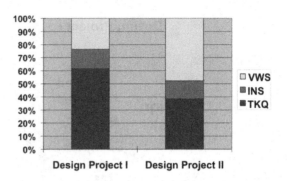

Design Detail

Figure 6 shows the percentage break down of the design details. In both design projects, the colour and texture (VCL/VTXT) show the highest percentages. In Second Life, designers can easily change colour and texture of objects and see the results. In the small-scale design project (Project II), there is no discussion on shapes of objects (VSP). Design group members used 3D objects provided in Second Life directly to work on the small-scale project design (Project II). They did not challenge nor discuss shapes of objects.

Design Task

Figure 7 shows the distributions of design tasks related to communications. Both design projects had similar percentages of "instructing" (INS). In the large-scale design project, over 60% was about task questioning (TKQ) whereas in the small-scale design project, a workstation design, TKQ was below 40%. In the large-scale design

project, the studio, design group members might spread to different areas in the studio while they were working on design tasks. Design group members in the workstation project, the small-scale design project, had higher percentage of "working status" (VWS) communications. They had more interactions because they informed each other about the tasks.

Social Communication

Figure 8 shows the analysis of the social communications in both the large-scale and small-scale design projects. There was no communication with gestures (VGT) in Design Project I. The percentage distributions of non-task related (NTR) and jokes (JOK) of the two design projects are opposite. Design Project I had very little jokes (10%). 90% social communication is non-task related communication. Design Project II con-

Figure 8. Analysis of social communication

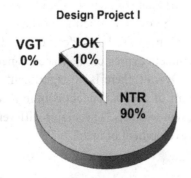

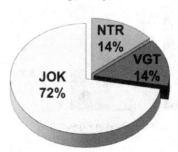

tained 72% of jokes and 14% of non-task related social communication.

In Design Project I, the large-scale design project, design group members were scattered at different levels so they were not able to see the avatars of each other. Therefore, there is no gesture. In Design Project II, the small-scale design project, design group members saw each others' avatars most of the time. They used gestures in Second Life as a mean to communicate with each other.

Discussion

Comparing design collaborations of the large-scale and the small-scale design projects in 3D virtual environments, the main impacts were found at communication control and social communication.

In both large-scale and small scale design projects:

- "Pause" (PAU) in communication control represents a higher percentage comparing with "interruption" (INT) and "hand-over" (HAN). One of the main reasons is that design group members spent a lot of time on using objects to develop their design projects in Second Life.
- In design communication, design task represents the highest percentage compared with design concept and design detail. In general, design group members are concerned about how the design is implemented.

However, in the large-scale design project, a studio design, Design Project I:

- Design group members spend time to explore the environment and space according to their own preferences. There are fewer interactions between design group members.
- Design concept is concerned more than design detail.

- Task questioning (TKQ) is highly concerned in design tasks. The reason is that the large-scale design area is much broader than the small-scale design area. Design group members are dispersed. They need more efforts to coordinate and manage design tasks with each other. No gesture was used, since design group members were not able to see the avatars of each other.

In the small-scale design project, a workstation design, Design Project II:

- Design group members were forced to focus on the object. There were more interactions between design group members.
- Design group members have a higher percentage of "working status" (VWS) communications for design tasks. This indicates design group members were more interactive in their collaboration because they informed each other who concerned the tasks.
- Design project members could see each others' avatars most of the time. Therefore, they could use the gesture function in Second Life as a mean for social communications.

In summary, in the virtual environments, design group members working on the small-scale design project had more interactions and spent more time on details of the design project, since they gathered around the design subject, the workstation in Design Project II. The avatars that represent the design group members can see each other. Therefore, gestures were also applied for communications. However, in the large-scale design project, design group members moved around different areas or rooms in the design subject, a studio in Design Project I. It was not easy for them to have a whole picture of the studio. Therefore, they spent more time on the development of ideas than details of the design subject. In addition, they might not able to see other design group members. Gestures were not used for communications.

CONCLUSION

This chapter presents a case study of how different design scales impact on design collaboration in 3D virtual environments in Second Life including a large-scale design project and a small-scale design project, i.e. a studio design (Design Project I) and a workstation design (Design Project II). In order to isolate "scale" as the primary variable, the participants and the design projects were controlled. Design group members were all students from the same domain of study. They were novice designers with basic design knowledge and computer skills being capable to work collaboratively for design projects in both real and virtual environments.

In this study, protocol analysis was used as the method of investigation. A coding scheme was developed to categorise protocols of the two projects into communication control, design communication and social communication. Kan (2008) argued that coding scheme unique to data hinders the advance of our understanding of designing because results cannot be compared from different studies. Also, with the limited cases it is impossible to generalize the results. Nevertheless, the software aided time based segmentation applied in this case shows the advantage of quickly obtain initial understanding of different scales impact on design collaboration in 3D virtual environment.

This case shows that different scales impact more on communication control and social communication than design communication on design collaboration in a 3D virtual environment. It suggested that when designing in a larger scale, if in the virtual environment the developer provides a function to scale down the artifacts into hand hold-able objects (an object mode), it will encourage the participants to interact more. In a way, the suggestion sounds trivial and is common in any computer-aided design/drafting softwares.

However, the case presented in this chapter provides a scientific way of observing users' design behaviour in a 3D virtual environment.

This case also indicates that if the education agenda it to let student to learn to communicate and collaborate in a virtual environment, it is better to start with a smaller scale project so that they can learn the art of communication control in the environment. The further research will work on:

- protocol analysis of both large-scale and small-scale design projects to study how communication control, design communication and social communication are conducted in design collaboration in 3D virtual environments progressing in different time sessions
- comparisons of different scales impact on design novices and experts on design collaboration in 3D virtual environment
- collect more data so as to be able to obtain statically generalizable results

These works provide a foundation to further investigate the different scales impact on design collaboration in 3D virtual environments so as to suggest improvement in virtual environment to better support design collaboration.

ACKNOWLEDGMENT

The authors would like to thank the students at the Faculty of Architecture, Design & Planning of the University of Sydney, Australia, and at the Digital Design Department of the MingDao University, Taiwan, who attended the course DECO2010 in 2008. Especially, they would like to acknowledge the design teams that collaboratively worked on and produced the projects shown in Figures 1 and 2 in this chapter. They also extend their thanks to IT supports from both Universities.

REFERENCES

Cross, N., Christiaans, H., & Dorst, K. (1996). Introduction: The Delft Protocols Workshop. In N. Cross, H. Christiaans, & K. Dorst (Eds.), *Analysing design activity* (pp. 1-14). John Wiley & Sons.

Eastman, C. M. (1970). On the analysis of intuitive design processes. In Moore, G. T. (Ed.), *Emerging methods in environmental design and planning* (pp. 21–37). Cambridge, MA: The MIT Press.

Ericsson, K. A., & Simon, H. A. (1993). *Protocol analysis: Verbal reports as data.* Cambridge, MA: The MIT Press.

Gabriel, G. C., & Maher, M. L. (2002). Coding and modelling communication in architectural collaborative design. *Automation in Construction, 11*(2), 199–211. doi:10.1016/S0926-5805(00)00098-4

Gero, J. S. (1990). Design prototypes: A knowledge representation schema for design. *AI Magazine, 11*(4), 26–36.

Goldschmidt, G. (1995). The designer as a team of one. *Design Studies, 16*(2), 189–209. doi:10.1016/0142-694X(94)00009-3

Gul, L., Wang, X., Tanyel, B., Bülbül, T., Çağdaş, G., & Tong, H. (2008). Global Teamwork: 2008, a study of design learning in collaborative virtual environments. In *CD Proceedings of 2008 Design Research Society Biennial Conference.*

Hennessy, S., & Murphy, P. (1999). The potential for collaborative problem solving in design and technology. *International Journal of Technology and Design Education, 9*(1), 1–36. doi:10.1023/A:1008855526312

Hornby, A. S., & Wehmeier, S. (Eds.). (2007). *Oxford advanced learner's dictionary.* New York, NY: Oxford University Press.

Kan, W. T. (2008). *Quantitative methods for studying design protocols.* Sydney: The University of Sydney.

Kavakli, M., & Gero, J. S. (2003). Difference between expert and novice designers: An experimental study. In Lindemann, U. (Ed.), *Human behaviour in design: Individual, teams, tools* (pp. 42–51). Berlin, Germany: Springer.

Lahti, H., Seitamaa-Hakkarainen, P., & Hakkarainen, K. (2004). Collaboration patterns in computer supported collaborative designing. *Design Studies, 25*(4), 351–371. doi:10.1016/j.destud.2003.12.001

Maher, M. L., Bilda, Z., & Gul, L. F. (2006a). Impact of collaborative virtual environments on design behaviour. In Gero, J. (Ed.), *Design Computing and Cognition '06* (pp. 305–321). Dordrecht, The Netherlands: Springer. doi:10.1007/978-1-4020-5131-9_16

Maher, M. L., Rosenman, M., Merrick, K., & Macindoe, O. (2006b). DesignWorld: An augmented 3D virtual world for multidisciplinary, collaborative design. *CAADRIA, 2006*, 133–142.

Schn, D. A., & Wiggins, G. (1992). Kinds of seeing and their functions in designing. *Design Studies, 13*(2), 135–156. doi:10.1016/0142-694X(92)90268-F

Singhal, S., & Zyda, M. (1999). *Networked virtual environments: Design and implementation.* New York, NY: ACM Press.

Suwa, M., Purcell, T., & Gero, J. S. (1998). Macroscopic analysis of design processes based on a scheme for coding designers' cognitive actions. *Design Studies, 19*(4), 455–483. doi:10.1016/S0142-694X(98)00016-7

Tsai, J. J.-H., Wang, X., & Huang, Y. (2008). Studying different scales of collaborative designs in real and virtual environments. *ANZAScA, 08*, 277–284.

KEY TERMS AND DEFINITIONS

3D Virtual Environments: A networked virtual environment provides a consistent context for multiple users to browse digital information, interact with the environment, and communicate with each other.

Communication Control: Communication control covers interruption, hand-over and pause in design commuincations.

Design Collaboration: A process of dynamically communicating and working together in order to collectively establish design goals, search through design problem spaces, determine design constraints, and construct a design solution.

Design Communication: Design communication includes communications of design concept, design detail and design task in design.

Design Scale: Design scale refers to the relative size or extent of something in design.

Protocol Analysis: A rigorous methodology for eliciting verbal reports of thought sequences as a valid source of data on thinking. It has become the de facto method for studying the cognitive processes of designers.

Scale: Scale refers to the size or extent of something, especially when compared with something else.

Social Communication: Social communication includes non-task-related communications and gestures in design.

Chapter 12
Implementing Computer Gaming Technology in Architectural Design Curricula:
Testing Architecture with the Rich Intertwining of Real-Time Spatial, Material, Lighting and Physical Simulations

Russell Lowe
University of New South Wales, Australia

ABSTRACT

The case for utilizing computer game modding in an architectural design curriculum is a strong one. The rich intertwining of real-time spatial, material lighting and physical simulations reinforce spatial visualization, navigation, and mental rotation. In the past two decades many researchers have implemented games engines in architectural curricula, but in every case, the courses have been in upper years of their students' degrees, with small, elective classes rather than core courses. That this is in contrast to the wider computer game modding community, suggesting that the difficulties previous researchers have had may actually be mitigated by implementing the technology, along with aspects of computer game modding culture, in large first year classes. Case studies of student work collapse Stockburger's distinction between the game designer and the game player to further his extension of Lefebvre's and Soja's thinking about space as it relates to computer gaming. The chapter concludes by reconsidering the term 'player' as a 'game designer in testing mode'.

INTRODUCTION

Section one will contextualize the chapter by making a case for utilizing computer game modding in architectural design curricula and briefly surveying serious games from a wide variety of fields (including military and surgical training through to economics and other social interactions). The section will then compare and contrast computer game modding with conventional architectural animation to build an argument that computer game environments are more than 'skin deep'. The section will conclude with the proposition

DOI: 10.4018/978-1-61350-180-1.ch012

that computer game environments can be considered as both a computational technology and methodology.

Section two considers the implementation and interface of computer gaming technologies within architectural design curriculums. Questions arise such as; should the use of computer game engines be limited to small classes in the upper years of their degrees? What experience in computing do students need to be able to engage the technology effectively? Are there examples of collateral learning going on? What are the weaknesses? This section is bound together by a consideration of the culture surrounding computer game modding and the lessons that might be learnt or methodologies that may be transferred. For this reason section two will focus on four commercial (as opposed to independent developers) game engines with large modding communities. Case studies here will focus on curriculum design and development rather than student work directly.

Section three considers the 'World Builders' of computer game engines as a medium, as one might consider traditional sketching or painting with watercolours. By referring to case studies of student work this section examines the effect that designing utilising computer game engines has on architectural outcomes. Do the plans or sections of a student's project resemble those designed using conventional digital modelling for example? Is the media promoting a new architecture? Section three will also outline representation and conceptual issues raised by computer gaming technologies and the implications of these for students. Finally this section will argue that looking beyond the distraction of weapons and vehicles present in many modifiable computer games is critical so that they may become instruments that are able to contribute to architectural design and interaction.

Section 04 presents two case studies on work outside the architectural design studio and notes on the use of computer gaming technology in practice.

Note: to fully appreciate the architectural tests and resulting innovations described in Sections

03 and 04 the author would like to share the full computer game environments. There are however, some practical impediments in doing so (as noted in Section 02). To facilitate the richest engagement with the case studies described in Sections 03 and 04, in an easily digestible fashion, links to video captures are provided via author's website: www.russelllowe.com/publications/cdmt/cdmt. htm. Alternatively readers can email the author directly to request specific computer game files; a current email address will be provided within the webpage noted above.

SECTION 01: A CASE FOR USING COMPUTER GAME MODDING WITHIN AN ARCHITECTURAL DESIGN CURRICULUM

To understand why academics or students should consider using computer gaming technology within the context of an architectural design curriculum a brief overview of the computer games historical and cultural development alongside its key elements is useful.

Recently a new category of games has emerged; called serious video games they take advantage of a technology that has been pushing the envelope for the past 30 years (Microsoft, 2004). For followers of contemporary media it's not surprising to find that computer games are capable of being "serious". Looking back to the late 50's and early 60's one finds that the origin of the technology had very serious purposes indeed; military air defence systems such as projects "Whirlwind" and "SAGE" (Rheingold, 1991). So even though one should understand serious games as a technological imperative coming full circle rather than emerging innocently from our entertainment media there is one obvious and major difference this time around; many, many more people are involved.

One set of statistics describing American computer gamers in 2010 (Online Schools, 2010) show that 65% of US households play computer games with almost half of them in the 18 - 49 year old bracket. Combining those statistics and the fact that two out of five gamers are female you are more likely to find that a gamer is a woman in the 18 - 49 bracket than the more typically understood boy of less than 18 years of age (19.6% vs. 15%). So, in terms of serious games, what might our 35 year old female gamer be playing?

She might be studying physics at the University of Worcester where under Colin Price (Price, 2006) she would be learning "Physics by Inquiry where students are encouraged to actively investigate, probe, search and explore the physical world through observing, questioning and finding answers to their questions". Price argues "this approach is equally valid for virtual worlds, provided they contain a valid physics engine". In Price's class our gamer might be experimenting with "Potential Hills", or eight other physical concepts, in Unreal Tournament 2004. (As an aside, in the paper noted above, Price also provides us with a range of projects that use game engine technology from 1995 through to 2005 and finds that "the development of dedicated educational materials may not always lead to environments rich enough for most learners. It also does not engage with the familiar game culture.")

Our gamer might be a surgical resident or attending physician undergoing advanced medical training with James Rosser at the Rosser Top Gun Laparoscopic Skills and Suturing Program. Describing an experiment on "The Impact of Video Games on Training Surgeons in the 21st Century" conducted within the program Rosser (Rosser, et al., 2007) references many of the "disturbing negative correlations" concerning video game play but notes some of the positive benefits including "increased performance on eye-hand coordination tasks; spatial visualization, and mental rotation".

At yet another moment our gamer might be playing Second Life; as an entrepreneur she might be developing a business model to buy and sell digital real-estate; for real-world currencies. In his article subtitled "Economics and Ownership in Second Life" Cory Ondrejka (Ondrejka, 2004) notes that "strong and efficient markets also lead to rapid evolution of user-created content, as observed within Second Life". His unselfconscious referencing of real-world theories to illuminate issues within Second Life implicates parity between real and virtual economic systems.

These three examples show the wide range of uses that computer gaming technology can be put to beyond the spectrum of entertainment. While many would understand physics, spatial visualization and the evolution of user created content to have diverging concerns, Architects and Engineers recognize three themes that are intrinsically entwined within their professions.

The introduction so far has been concerned with a 'typical' serious computer game player. In a survey published by the author at CAADRIA2008 (Lowe, 2008b) first year architecture students were asked to indicate how many of the games they had played from a list that represented examples of games with both official modification tools and those with third party modification tools. That 74% of the students had played at least one of the games on the list was not entirely surprising, given their popularity, but it is a little higher than average (when compared to the American statistics noted above). What was more surprising was that from the 86 students who had played one or more of the games, 50 of them had modified them in some way. Put another way, just under half of the entire number of students coming to study architecture at the author's university were game modders. These numbers point to a level of experience, familiarity and expertise with both playing and modifying computer games that could be taken advantage of within an architectural design curriculum.

To reveal some of the key advantages that using computer gaming technology can bring to an architectural design curriculum the following will compare and contrast computer game modding with conventional architectural animation (its closest 'relative' within architectural representation).

In many instances traditional key frame animation in architectural representation takes the form of the 'fly-through'. In the fly-through a disembodied camera follows a predetermined path through a virtual film set. The pathways, often defined by Bezier curves, are smooth and flowing; not only separated from the subtle undulations of vision that are the results of walking but also unrestricted by gravity or materiality

(see the ArchiForm3d gallery for indicative examples (ArchiForm3d, 2010)). While many critics are able to "visualize [a students] design intentions more clearly with VR than with traditional means of representation" Campbell and Wells (Campbell & Wells, 1994) note that a common negative criticism stems from a lack of interactivity with the environment; for example "several design critics and jury members commented that they would have gotten more out of the experience had they been able to walk or fly through the design themselves rather that depend on views from a particular path flown for the presentation."

The ability for designers and critics to freely navigate a virtual environment has emerged with the development of computer games. In 'The Language of New Media' Lev Manovich (Manovich, 2000) claims that "navigable space ... is now a common way to visualise and work with any data". A year later Shiratuddin and Thabet (Thabet, Shiratuddin, & Bowman, 2002) recognized that off the shelf 3D game engines, such as Unreal Tournament, not only give users the ability to "navigate a virtual environment as if in the real world" but were also "low cost, [had] networking support, collision detection, support for high frame rates per second and entry level hardware requirement" (this chapter also usefully tabulates the "major VE projects utilising 3D Games Engines" immediately prior to 2001).

Up until recently however this level of immersion and interactivity has come with a cost;

real-time graphics have been less realistic than is achievable with 'off-line' rendering. With more contemporary computer games however the 'gap' in realism between real-time computer game graphics and off-line rendering has closed ... and for many students has even flipped (the computer game Crysis is a leading example). After the 'Imagina 2007' computer graphics industry conference 3dWorlds editors (3dWorld Editors, 2007) noted that video game based "simulations of light, fluids and behavior [sic] have reached such a high level of realism and effectiveness that they are on the verge of supplanting all other traditional approaches". While the editors of 3dWorld saw this development emerging within the computer graphics industry this author has seen an architecture undergraduate student's ability to create a realistic visualization skyrocket because of computer gaming technology.

But within architectural design visual realism is only scratching the surface. Of much more significant interest is the ability for students to use the graphics, physics and artificial intelligence engines of contemporary computer games to experiment with real-time atmospheric, material, structural and interactive simulations. Working in this way students not only experience the end result of their design process but are able to experiment within the design itself. In this way, by facilitating high level real-time simulation, computer game environments are not only a computational technology but can also be considered a computational methodology. The case studies of specific student work in Section 03 will develop these ideas in more detail. But to fully appreciate how students are able to make the leap from simply using computer game environments as a computational technology to using a computational technology as well as a computational methodology it's necessary to understand how these environments have been implemented; first in elective courses and then in core architecture design studio courses.

SECTION 02: IMPLEMENTATION AND THE CULTURE OF GAME MODDING

While the author's recent implementations of computer game engines in architectural design curricula are significant in a few important dimensions a number of key researchers have laid valuable groundwork. In 2002 Saku Lehtinen (Lehtinen, 2002) claimed that "games engines have been tested [for creating and navigating virtual environments] for at least a decade". He went on to say that "ease of use" was a major limiting factor, resulting in a "select few" students working with the technology. Lehtinen's classes were so select that there were only seven students over a three year period. While seven students seems like incredibly low number, at that time it was actually quite typical. In 1998 Achten and Turksma (Achten & Turksma, 1999) ran a studio using only six computers and while Moloney's (Moloney, 2002) 2002 design studio had 26 students it still couldn't be considered large. In addition to small class sizes the notion that computer game modding was especially challenging in terms of skill acquisition resulted in classes being targeted towards senior students. However it might be that ease of use as a major limiting factor may be more connected with perception rather than fact; in any case it's an understanding that is persisting. In 2003 Hoon and Kehoe (Hoon & Kehoe, 2003) found that to successfully negotiate their course "necessitated a many-layered infusion of new skill sets for both students and instructor. They noted "only a cursory relationship between game engine tools and 'industry-standard' architectural visualization tools" and found that as a result of this many experienced digital designers were easily frustrated". More and Burrow (More & Burrow, 2007) present an illuminating contradiction in their paper "Observing the Learning Curve of Videogames in Architectural Design"; they find "inexperienced designers have difficulties in progressing through typical design milestones" ... reinforcing the notion that imposing computer gaming technology on an otherwise unaltered (or typical) design curriculum will create difficulties. As recently as 2007 Shiratuddin and Fletcher (Shiratuddin & Fletcher, 2007) surveyed a mix of 27 undergraduate and graduate students to find that 56% of them found "learning to operate the software" was "difficult"; 74% found the software was unreliable and 60% found the software speed was too slow. They do note however that even though the majority of ratings by the class was low "a number of students produced high quality work".

In 2003 the initial implementation of the Unreal Tournament 2003 world builder, UnrealEd3, by the author reflected the conditions and reinforced the findings outlined above. The class was small and consisted of senior students; all successfully created interactive virtual environments but only a few produced really innovative and conceptually challenging work.

Following this experience a hypothesis was developed that small class sizes filled with experienced digital designers might be reinforcing the perception that computer games are difficult to modify rather than mitigating it. To put it another way, one only has to look at the internet to see evidence of thousands (if not tens of thousands) of young and inexperienced game modders who are producing technically advanced, if not for the most part conceptually challenging, environments without formal instruction.

While the exact number of people modifying computer games is difficult to ascertain there are indications that it is a relatively large community (Sean Pickersgill (Pickersgill, 2007) notes that the community supporting the game Unreal Tournament 2004 is not only large but also extremely well organised). One indicator of the size of the game modding community is the amount of game modding tutorials, and the numbers of people viewing them, that are available on dedicated computer game modding websites. One popular modding website, called www.moddb.com, has 399 tutorials for a range of game engines and world builders including the Hammer editor for the HL2 series, the Unity engine, Unreal Tournament 3 (UT3) and the Cryengine3. There had been 2,120 views of those tutorials on the day the author visited the site with 1,902,863 views in total (as of 29/03/2010). Another popular community site is www.3dbuzz. com which has 1,161 tutorials focusing on game development (primarily UT3). The amount of tutorials created by the modding community is far in excess of those produced by the creators of the development tools themselves. In addition to the numbers of people modding computer games these numbers also indicate a culture of sharing and mutual support.

With these parameters in mind the author undertook to develop courses where the use of computer gaming technology, and the culture surrounding modifying it, supported studio design in large classes with students in the early stages of their formal architectural education. One should note that the case studies described below do not utilise the broad range of game engines that are available to modify; and are being modified in architectural design studios around the world; a long, but still incomplete, list is published on the Wikipedia (Wikipedia, 2010a) ... the Quest3D and Unity engines are notable absences. Instead, reflecting on broader game modding cultures, the case studies below focus on one particular subset; incredibly popular games noted for (and perhaps successful because of) their advanced graphics and physical interactivity.

The first large course developed by the author to encompass these ideas was called DESN104: Introduction to computer for designers. Over three years, beginning in 2004, this course enrolled approximately 90-120 first year design students per semester who were intending to complete degrees in Architecture, Interior Architecture, Landscape Architecture, Industrial Design and Digital Media Design. Most of the students had no prior knowledge of 3D modelling software, and as such were not familiar with the industry standards for software operation and interface.

The inclusion of real-time interactive environments using the UnrealEd3 world builder further strengthened and broadened their introduction to digital modelling; which at the time also included surface (3D Studio Max) and solid (Solidworks) modelling (previously the course only included SolidWorks for digital modelling). In addition to this the inclusion of the UnrealEd3 world builder added a distinctive and important aspect to their design work; the ability to test architectural designs through an immersive experience of the space. In this way the design of spaces and environments became truly experimental; recalling the jury member's comments from Section 01, this is in contrast to traditional key frame animations where the experiential outcome is predefined by the animator.

In addition to the anti-intuitive notion that larger classes with less experienced students would make implementing computer game engines in an architectural design curriculum easier, there were two other factors that enabled the author to overcome obstacles that had faced previous curriculum designers.

In 2002 Lehtinen (Lehtinen, 2002) noted "all game creation tools currently lack any easy way to import from any common CAD-software". The following year Epic games released Unreal Tournament 2003 which provided the first world builder from a major developer that facilitated content creation in third party software. While alienating many within the game modding community this move suited those with access to high end modelling software; which includes most architectural faculties around the world. From this point on Epic Games (Epic Games Inc, 2010) described the UnrealEd world builder as a "content creation tool filling the void between 3D Studio Max and Maya, and shippable game content".

The second factor depended on the multi-disciplinary nature of the course. For reasons of efficiency computer game rendering engines render only one side of each polygon. With surface modellers the designer must pay special attention to the direction the polygons are facing and avoid both open meshes and overlapping co-planer surfaces. The PhD research assistants to O'Coill and Doughty (O'Coill & Doughty, 2004) found that even very small models (with only 400 polygons) might have over 100 errors upon compilation (a process where a digital model is translated into a game engine readable format). DESN104 introduced students to Solidworks, a solid modeller intended for use by Industrial Designers. Solid models have the advantage that resulting meshes are 'watertight' and without overlapping polygons (solving two of the major issues that resulted in O'Coill and Doughty's PhD students giving up on computer game engines altogether).

In 2007, and in a new faculty and country, the author was asked to design a first year studio course that enrolled students who were studying towards Architecture, Architectural Computing and Engineering with Architecture degrees. The class size was around 200 and no computer lab facilities would be formally scheduled. To implement the course students were encouraged to purchase high end graphics quality laptop computers. The university policy only requires students to have access to computing facilities without specifying graphics capability (access to faculty computer labs outside of class time was available to students to mitigate equity issues). While the absence of computer lab facilities made implementation more complicated (especially for the students who now had to install the software and ensure their hardware would perform adequately) it offered an opportunity to more closely replicate the wider computer game modding culture. To both mitigate further costs, promote the concept of a portable office and further parallel computer game modding culture the course employed open source, free or very inexpensive software.

The resulting course, called ARCH1102: Architecture Workshop 1 (Lowe, 2007a), developed "inquiry, literacy, and compositional skills in architectural design placing a focus on manual as well as digital techniques of architec-

tural representation. In doing so it consider[ed] the similarities and distinctions between manual and digital techniques as well as developing potential overlaps." The course consisted of three experiments which developed sequentially to build the conceptual and representational skills required to form an immersive engagement with Architecture. During the course the students made drawings of two dimensional textures, sections, axonometrics, and perspectives. They created models in Google SketchUp, environments for UT2004 (using the UnrealEd3 world builder). Finally, they imported models from SketchUp into UT2004 and developed interactive attributes.

To achieve the workflow from Google Sketch-Up to the UnrealEd3 world builder the author (Lowe, 2009c) modified a plug-in for SketchUp to create an exporter that would create ASCII files that were properly configured for UT2004. Following video tutorials created by the author students were able to apply hand drawn textures to models inspired by sections, axonometric or perspective drawings and insert them into real-time interactive environments. In addition to stills and video captures of the finished environments the student's work was assessed by tutors who loaded the 'levels' into UT2004 and navigated them in real-time. Some especially interesting examples of these will be discussed in Section 03.

When asked (in an anonymous online feedback mechanism the university manages as a part of its teaching and learning strategy) what was strong in the course was one student commented; "Challenging our way of thinking and designing by using computer software like Unreal 2004. It forced me to think beyond what was 'reality' and to create 'unreal' environments." In 2005 Burrow and More (Burrow & More, 2005) asked "are non-real world scenarios of benefit to the spatial designer?" and answered that while they thought they were they observed "Participants tended to preserve the continuity of space, allowing literal movement through the designs. In particular utilising walking through space as the main form of navigation, a direct effect of the game engine mechanics". The student continues "Also, the program was fun to use (although it took some time learning it). There was much freedom in design and so results varied greatly across the students." Another student noted: "Strong sense of peer helping peer in studio classes. Good collaboration."

The second experiment, that focused on creating an environment solely using the UnrealEd world builder, student learning was supported by a series of video tutorials produced by Jason Buzzby (Epic Games Inc, 2004) (Buzzby owns the website www.3dBuzz.com, mentioned above). Perhaps inspired by the tutorials and forums on that site one student made the following suggestion on how to improve the course: there should be "An online forum, so students can discuss problems related to unreal editor. Distribute unreal editor on disk rather than making us buy it."

In response to this feedback and in an effort to capture the knowledge that occurs across a large studio group the author implemented a discussion forum in the following year using Google groups. The forum, with 1574 messages, is now archived but can be viewed online (Lowe, 2009a). In the anonymous online survey noted above 85% of students agreed or strongly agreed that the course was effective for developing their thinking skills (e.g. critical analysis, problem solving). The studio forum shows many examples of these skills in action. In 2010 (with the introduction of Crysis Wars) the anonymous online survey showed that 97% of students agreed that the course was challenging and interesting, 92% agreed that the course was effective for developing their thinking skills and 97% agreed that the course encouraged them to be self directed in their learning.

The second part of the students comment was a relatively common one amongst the cohort; and points to concerns beyond the simple purchase price (which was less than $15). The computer game UT2004 (and UnrealEd3) was three years old by this point and only available to purchase new via an online mechanism called Steam. Steam is commonly understood (Wikipedia, 2010b) as "a digital distribution, digital rights management, multiplayer and communications platform developed by Valve Corporation. Steam is set apart from similar services primarily by its community features [and] completely automated game update process." While there are some convenient aspects to the services described above the digital rights management and automated game update process can be a major source of anxiety when modifying games or frequently changing ones online/offline status. Often students found themselves denied access to Steam managed products if they hadn't followed the correct steps before going offline to attend class. In another course, a final year Architecture graduation project where the students were modifying the game Half-Life 2, an automatic update occurred one week before final submission. The update made changes to the directory system of the game, breaking reference pathways critical to compiling and running the game environments. A fix was discovered and implemented within a few hours, but the added stress at that particular time of the year was unwelcome to say the least.

In 2008 the author designed a first year course for 60 students studying towards a degree in Architectural Computing called BENV2423: Real-Time Interactive Environments (Lowe, 2008a). In this first iteration the course used a workflow from Solidworks, through 3D Studio Max to the new world builder for Unreal Tournament 3 (UT3). In this case the studio ran in a computer lab environment. While the UT3 engine is undoubtedly powerful in terms of rendering, physics and general interactivity (the appearance of 'Kismet', a visual scripting interface within UnrealEd multiplied interactive opportunities exponentially compared with UT2004) there was also a corresponding reduction in ease of use. For example, the lighting and cast shadows depend on a second set of texture mapping coordinates alongside the primary set that align diffuse, specular and normal maps to an objects surface. In many cases lighting and cast shadows will not only be unrealistic but quite distracting unless the object has had its texture mapping 'unwrapped'. In contrast UT2004's lighting is usually acceptable without requiring advanced texturing skills. In short, with a high level of expertise UT3 environments can be stunning but with low to medium expertise students had achieved more immersive results with the older, less sophisticated, game engine for UT2004. The following year saw the adoption of the 'Crysis Wars' game engine (Lowe, 2009b). This class experimented with two possible workflows; from Google SketchUp or 3D Studio Max to the Sandbox2 world builder. The Crysis Wars game engine doesn't require a second texture mapping channel for very realistic, real-time, lighting and shadow casting. Models are simply textured and exported directly to the game engine. When given the option to use either modelling option almost all of the students utilized Google SketchUp. This reflected the types of models the students were making; that is, static Architecture rather than vehicles, weapons, or character models. As Google SketchUp doesn't support 'rigging' or 'skinning' geometries if the students attempted to design Architecture that was conceptually more challenging (i.e. more like a vehicle, weapon or character model) they would have to use 3D Studio Max. In either case however for all students the process and results were many times superior to what the best students were able to achieve the previous year with the UT3 engine.

In anonymous feedback via the online feedback mechanism noted above a student commented: One of the courses best features "would be the diversity in programs used. I very much enjoyed using gaming programs not simply because they were "games" but because it revealed a more educational side to them."

The editors of 3dWorld may well have been talking about early demonstrations of the Crysis game engine when they saw "simulations of light, fluids and behaviour" that were "on the verge of supplanting all other traditional approaches (3dWorld Editors, 2007). With Crysis Wars the author has seen the first example in computer game modding of an increase in sophistication alongside an increase in ease of production. In other words undergraduate students find the workflow for modding Crysis Wars is less complicated than modding UT2004 with results that can match an industry expert's modding of HL2 or UT3. Reinforcing this, the author notes that his tutorial (Lowe, 2007c) for creating a custom object for the HL2 engine was approximately 50 steps long and that his current tutorial (Lowe, 2010c) to model a similar object in Google SketchUp for Crysis Wars (using a plug-in for Google SketchUp called "PlayUP" (PlayUpTools, 2010)) is approximately three steps long.

On the basis of this the author has implemented the Crysis Wars game engine within a first year architecture design studio course; which in 2010 has almost 260 students. While the three experiment structure, commitment to hand sketching and the freely available Google SketchUp remains consistent with previous years curricula some changes have been made to experiments two and three to capitalize on real-time lighting effects and sophisticated terrain modelling that are facilitated by the Sandbox2 world builder. Case studies from the third experiment will be discussed in Section 03.

While the emphasis above has been on the growing ease in implementing computer gaming technology within an architectural design curriculum some continuing shortcomings should be noted.

Graphics Demands on Hardware

The graphics demands of computer games engines surpass those required for general architectural modelling (this has been the case for the last 10 years and the trend shows no signs of reversing; indeed, as noted in Section 03, industry standard architectural modellers are only beginning to approach the graphics demands of computer games by utilising the mechanisms of computer games).

The downside to this is that to participate in a mobile studio environment effectively students must have access to a laptop computer currently costing $2500 or more; the upside is that students will be well equipped to handle any other computing task required of them during their undergraduate studies. The fact that Crysis Wars, UT3 and HL2 all require a Windows operating system is less of a shortcoming than in previous years with more recent Apple computers being able to boot into Windows natively; there is an additional cost consideration however. The ongoing commitment to student owned laptops (as opposed to booked computer labs) within these implementations does highlight the current plethora of operating systems … students in the authors first year architecture studio class currently run Windows XP, Vista, and Windows 7 in both 32 and 64 bit versions on both PC's and Macintosh's via Boot Camp. Each of these systems offers peculiarities with installations, some of which can be seen on the class forum (Lowe, 2010b). It should be noted that while the class forum is an invaluable medium for supporting a student's installation responding to technical questions (which is shared by the course coordinator, tutors and students) and generally managing a forum that seeks to replicate those found in wider computer game culture averages 2-3 per week over the duration of a 12 week course.

Sharing Real-Time Environments

While file sizes of computer game environments can be much less than a typical video animation to experience a game environment (in contrast to simply playing a video) often requires significant setup. Typically computer game environments require the installation of the game the modification is based upon. UT2004 requires 5.5 gigabytes of free hard drive space; Crysis Wars requires 12 gigabytes of free space. Most of these games have the ability to set up some kind of mod structure that facilitates exchange between players (which is of course a priority also for the developers). A few,

the Unity or Quest3d game engines for example, have web based players or can produce stand alone executables. While web players and stand alone executables are undoubtedly useful within a professional context, the advantages are less within an architectural design curriculum where all participants have the game software installed.

Software Compatibility

Mention was made above of the automated game update process employed by Steam that negatively affected modifications to HL2. In addition to this game developers have in some cases operated on different development schedules than the software developers that they rely on to deliver game content. The most recent example of this see's the developers of Crysis Wars choosing not to release an update for their 3D Studio Max plug-in to make the 3D Studio Max 2010 compatible with their resource compiler (it seems Crytek's logic is that a new SDK will be released with the new CryENGINE3). The current solution is to use 3D Studio Max 2009, which presents some licensing complications to both the authors university and for the students using student licenses. An alternative is to use the PlayUp tools for Google SketchUp, but one should keep in mind that these are free and developed by a third party; so no warranty or continuity is expressed or implied.

Lack of Wider Peer Assistance and Relevant Tutorial Content

As noted in previous research (Lowe, 2009c) students modding computer games to create environments that focus on architectural content can find themselves somewhat alienated. In small senior level classes where there is not a critical mass to establish a supportive culture students depend on online tutorials to gain knowledge and develop skills (with many instructors facing the same pressure (Hoon & Kehoe, 2003)). Unfortunately the emphasis of many of these tutorials is on creating objects rather than architecture. Once again larger class sizes can mitigate this if support media commonly found within the computer game modding community are employed; studio blogs and forums for example (Lowe, 2010a).

Licensing (within Academia)

In the case of the games UT2004, HL2, UT3 and Crysis Wars the End User License Agreement's (EULA's) are very clear when they state that modifications of the games cannot be used for commercial gain. Many academics are reluctant to incorporate these game engines within their curricula for fear of litigation. The developers of these games, Epic Games, Valve Software and Crytek have responded to these concerns by making educational licenses available for modest fees or for free. Unfortunately some of the educational licensing agreements still have room for improvement. For example, the current educational agreement for Crytek's CryENGINE3 has clauses relating to the territory of the licensee and non-competition which seem aimed at protecting the engines source code ... which most (if not all) architecture schools would have little use for. These clauses would make running classes in a university computer lab problematic. With a commitment to student owned laptops the obvious alternative, and the one employed to date, is that each student purchases an authentic copy of the game (or downloads a free version as supplied by the developers). The result of this is that each student is bound by the EULA of the particular game they are modifying; to reinforce the non-commercial nature of the student work the author requires that all students submissions of game environments are submitted via publically accessible file sharing websites (such as filefront) and links to them are provided from their publically accessible blogs.

Lack of Quantitative Evidence of the Benefits to Design

There is a great deal of qualitative evidence of the benefits of using this technology in the design studio. Many authors made observations of increased enthusiasm (Lehtinen, 2002; Shiratuddin & Fletcher, 2007), increased immersion of students (Achten & Turksma, 1999; Johns & Lowe, 2005; Johns & Shaw, 2006; Lehtinen, 2002) and critics (Moloney, 2001) and a rich (including sometimes alternative/challenging) understanding of the spatial experience of the design (Achten & Turksma, 1999; Johns & Shaw, 2006; More & Burrow, 2007; Pickersgill, 2007; Shiratuddin & Fletcher, 2007). Observations of obstacles are less well covered but primarily relate to compatibility between traditional CAD and computer gaming software (including norms of use) (Hoon & Kehoe, 2003; Pelosi, 2010b) steep learning curves (More & Burrow, 2007), professionalism of the interface ... including violence and other problematic computer game stereotypes ... (Burrow & More, 2005; Hoon & Kehoe, 2003) and software stability (Lowe, 2009c; Shiratuddin & Fletcher, 2007). But as Shiratuddin and Fletcher note (Shiratuddin & Fletcher, 2007), we need more "comprehensive and quantifiable data to measure the performance of our students when using 3D games development tools in comparison to using conventional 3D modelling and animation tools". In an engineering course Coller and Scott (Coller & Scott, 2009) have quantitatively supported their hunch that "something unusually good was happening educationally". Their study compared student performance in a numerical methods course, which used the design of a video game to structure the course, with traditional numerical methods courses. In their study success was directly related to the number of concepts recalled and the amount of logical connections that map between them. While a numerical approach will not capture many of the qualities in architecture that demonstrate high performance there is research to support that the variety and number of iterations of an architectural scheme is related to creativity (Schoon, 1992). Obtaining quantifiable data regarding increased performance afforded by using computer gaming technology may well be necessary to convince more reluctant colleagues that there is a place for computer gaming technology within the core architectural design curriculum. There is a great deal of opportunity for further research in this area.

SECTION 03: THE MEDIA AFFECTING THE WORK, REPRESENTATION AND CONCEPTUAL ISSUES

In 'Playing the third place: Spatial modalities in contemporary game environments' Axel Stockburger (Stockburger, 2007) considers Henri Lefebvre's spatial theories to present an understanding of spatiality as it relates to contemporary computer gaming environments. He argues that "what makes Lefebvre's theory so significant for the development of a novel perspective on game space is his precise analysis of different types of space and the notion of the dynamic interplay between them, resulting in the notion of 'spatial practice'." According to Stockburger the post-modern theorist Edward Soja effectively captures the relativities of the different types of spaces when he "identifies perceived space (Firstspace) with the real, and conceived space (Secondspace) with the imaginary, leading to lived space (Thirdspace) as a field of both, imagined and real. The hybrid mix between real and imagined spaces that is provided by digital game universes reverberates strongly with this conception of 'Thirdspace'. This insight is crucial because it defies the idea of computer games as merely 'virtual' and purely imaginary spaces. It is precisely the interaction between real and imagined spatiality that makes this medium so compelling and unique."

When Stockburger is talking about the real spaces of computer gaming, in 'Playing the third

place: Spatial modalities in contemporary game environments', his examples are quite literal; they are spaces at home, or at internet cafés and Local Area Network parties where the bodies of computer gamers actually exist. To these we might add the physics computer lab at the University of Worcester or a lounge at the Rosser Top Gun Laparoscopic Skills and Suturing Program (to reflect our serious gamer from Section 01). But Stockburger's, and now the author's, examples of real spaces reflect his continuation of difference between the "game designer" and "player". To extend Stockburger's work this author would argue that a space that should find itself within his hybrid mix is the spatial practice of architectural design; specifically, where the designer is creating digital models for computer game environments. In this case the distinction, and consequentially space, between designing and playing has been collapsing over the past few years. As much as one has seen the interfaces of computer game world builders become closer to 'industry standard' modellers we have also seen industry standard modellers utilizing the same physics engines as computer games (the Havok physics engine is an example of this (Havok, 2010)) and even incorporate real-time rendering engines; Blender (Blender, 2010) and more recently the BIM tool ArchiCAD 12 (Graphisoft, 2010) for example. See Section 04 for further notes on the use of game engines in architectural practice. Where the computer games UT2004 and HL2 require a sometimes lengthy compiling process before one can 'playtest'. In UT3 and Crysis Wars one can be playtesting as quickly as making a simple keystroke. In games such as GarrysMod (GarrysMod, 2010a) one is able to design, using predefined objects, construction and representational tools, in game. Taking it an important step further Crytek, the creators of the new CryEngine3, claim that their engine "is the only 100% real-time game development engine in the market. But what does this mean? It means that from content creation to actual game-play, there are no delays caused by the engine crunching the numbers. Changes made anywhere by any developer are immediately playable (MyCryEngine, 2010)." With their new engine Crytek, in much the same way as Architect Lars Spuybroek (Spuybroek, 1998) challenges oppositional concepts of the "real and the virtual, the material and immaterial", would see designing and playing "not in opposition, or in some metaphysical disagreement, but more in an electroliquid aggregation, enforcing each other, as in a two part adhesive."

Spuybroek's electroliquid aggregation manifests itself most directly in the case studies presented below through the cycle of *testing* that developed and develops within each project. In fact it's worthwhile to understand the term 'player' below as a 'game designer in testing mode'.

The case studies below begin by describing the work of senior students in small classes (both core and elective) and conclude by describing the work of first year students in large core architectural design classes; following the developmental trajectory outlined in Section 02.

Case Study 01

Simultaneously reinforcing and challenging the physicality of making within the computer game environment: Engaging with the premise that (in 2007) "recent advances in digital gaming technology allow us to create/theorize significant portions of our design in real time" (Lowe, 2007b) Shawn Li created a 'workshop' that would test a player's understanding of making. Li used video captures from the GarrysMod environment to construct a film (Li, 2007) that demonstrated the experience of one protagonist. The film begins with a text from Li that says: "He woke up in a strange place, hewn from wood and steel and stone. Searching for a way out he found none, but he found tools contained in his mind. Tools filled with objects from his memories and those that alter the reality he is in. Bit by bit he would piece together a contraption. A contraption that will grant him passage out of the void." Li's protagonist then systematically tests the capabilities of the interactive Tools menu in an 'online tutorial' style that is familiar

to many computer game modders. Li's protagonist creates his contraptions using 'constraints' (axis, slider, pulley, rope, and weld for example) and 'construction' tools (thrusters and balloons) but departs from the documentary style of online tutorials by exploring real-time post processing such as the motion blur and morph tools. The end result is a space that simultaneously reinforces and challenges the physicality of making within the computer game environment. In one example thrusters cause an object to spiral out of control due to asymmetric placement ... but only after the protagonist releases an impossible constraint 'connecting' the object to thin air. In another example ropes connected between balloons and objects lift those objects with them skywards but as the objects get jammed in the built fabric the ropes pass straight through walls, floors and ceilings ... that is, the ropes have no body of their own and maintain some reasonable physical relationships (length) while contradicting others (collision). In each of these cases a user implicitly understands what will happen ... one doesn't need a degree in physics to understand a rope will tighten when something pulls on one end of it ... what is strange is, by the overwhelming novelty of virtual physics in action, one's suspension of disbelief is maintained even though the ropes continuity isn't.

Case Study 02

Testing spaces with human participation: In this project final year student Julian Cromarty created a series of spaces that he used to test participants spatial recognition and memory (Cromarty, 2008b). To do so he utilized the ability of the Unreal Tournament 3 game engine to have players trigger animated geometry in real-time. Cromarty's experimental hypothesis was that "architecture that is hard, angular and brutal imposes itself on the memory in different ways to architecture that is smooth, delicate or voluptuous (Cromarty, 2008a)." He goes on to describe his experiment ... "In this experiment the subject is presented with a variety of internal spaces each with varying geometric, lighting, and textural complexities. After each space is experienced the subject moves to the same room that warps and distorts. The subject can stop the space warping at any time when they are satisfied that it is the same as the previous static room they were in. By varying light, geometry and material textures this experiment is able to determine what factors are of greatest use in recognizing spaces and what combinations are to be encouraged or avoided for the benefit of those already struggling with memory." In this experiment Soja's notion of perceived space and conceived space collapses via the interrogation of spatial memory; where the player is required to overlay present and past experiences of space to determine best fit. When one is successful their spatial memory becomes real and imaginary at the same time.

In another experiment Cromarty uses a sequence of spaces linked by teleporters to test spatial recall that relies on group interaction. Because the teleporters give players no indication of destination, that is, they may teleport the player into an immediately adjacent space or one separated by a great distance, players need to take advantage of "multiple viewpoints to complete the picture" (other players at a distance are able to note teleport entry and exit points within the environment where the similarity of the teleported players immediate vicinity obscures this for them). In this case perceived and conceived spaces are communicated (verbally and visually) and held in a common social space; to navigate with a path or strategy in mind players need to compare their own perceptions and conceptions against those of the group. Another option would be subjugate to another's strategy and follow their directions without reflecting one's own perceptions or conceptions. In this experiment the social space of the environment is the permutation of all players perceived and conceived spaces.

Case Study 03

Testing promotes an architecture that defies plans and sections: Rather than considering the following projects individually this case study will consider a common theme that has been developed in different ways within all of them; that cyclically testing architecture between perceived, conceived and lived spaces promotes an architecture that defies conventional plans and sections. It should be noted here that 'conventional' refers to the convention of plans and sections rather than some connection to a particular or traditional style.

Using the UnrealEd3 world builder first year students Oren Oaariki and Hye Bin Sung created environments that considered a person's navigation through space. In Oaariki's case the resulting three dimensional sculptural architecture (based on the two dimensional shapes of graffiti tags) required multiple iterations and testing to ensure his architecture could accommodate the ergonomics involved in navigating continuingly sloping surfaces that occurred beneath, beside and over the user (Oaariki, 2006). A two dimensional, planar, section plane would describe an architecture that is disjointed and fragmented when in navigating the architecture the opposite is true. In Hye Bin Sung's environment individual rectilinear spaces are offset from one another inspired by a set of drawers by Droog design (Sung, 2006). Each space tests one's navigation by locally altering a usually global physical property. For example, one of Hye Bin Sung's spaces has its gravity set to pull the player upwards. In the same way as one expects the north point to orientate the plan on the page one expects gravity to orientate a section. One also reasonably expects the orientation provided to the section by gravity is consistent across its entirety; the presentation to viewers of a section on an ordinary sheet of paper absolutely depends upon this (the materiality of the paper unable to support reorientation of local elements without ripping them … literally as well as substantively … from the rest of the sheet). In this way Hye Bin

Sung's architecture defies the consistent global orientation of a section.

In experiment three of the core course ARCH1101: Architecture Design Studio (2008) first year student Vincent Hao Hsiu Hsu also used UT2004 to create two offices and a meeting space between them (Hao, 2008). While Hao Hsiu Hsu's uses moving elements innovatively in many parts of his environment of particular interest is the meeting space. In this space a series of concentric rings creates a diaphragm that, when triggered by the player's presence, seems to 'flex' between three levels. At different times through its flexing cycle the diaphragm either connects, conceals or reveals pathways between his client's offices. In this space Hao Hsiu Hsu has created a dynamic three dimensional ramp that not only fuses plan with section but simultaneously binds both together in a constant flux of negotiation and renegotiation.

In contrast to the examples immediately above senior student Harry Legaspi developed a project that took advantage of a modification of GarrysMod called WireMod (GarrysMod, 2010b). WireMod allows one to construct virtual electronics and artificial intelligence systems in real time. Legaspi's construction consisted of a series of found elements, virtual sensors, thrusters and anti-gravity 'hoverballs'(Legaspi, 2009). His construction looked for the player in the environment and attempted to follow them. The architecture of Legaspi's project existed not only in his construction but also in the space between it and the player. This space between is being constructed in negotiation between the player and the artificial intelligence controlling the construction. In this case not only is the plan and section contingent on a collapse between player and designer but is the result of shared authorship; between the player/designer and his architectural Frankenstein.

Case Study 04

The Physical Effect of an Explosion on Porosity: In the first experiment of the core course BENV2423 Real-Time Interactive Environments approximately 60 first year students utilized the Sandbox2 game editor for Crysis Wars to create, "capture and critically reflect on complex inter-relationships between objects, catalysts and space" (Lowe, 2009b). Students created three dimensional fields of objects and carefully placed explosive devices to promote complex physical interactions. The arrangement of their three dimensional fields of objects responded to artist Richard Goodwin's notion of "Porosity" (Goodwin, et al., 2006). The experiment was called The Physical Effect of an Explosion on Porosity. To document their experiments they constructed a complimentary architecture of ramps and platforms from which many different views could be captured.

Billy Tran's experiments were typical of many students' approaches and can be characterized by a systematic engagement with the motion of elements when subjected to a variety of explosive forces (Tran, 2009). Tran sensibly textures the approximately 500 cubes he stacks in various configurations so that they clearly reflect direction, speed and axis of local rotation as well as their global values. In Tran's experiments one sees a developing understanding of the interrelationship between gravitational and explosive forces ... he notes: "the high impact collision causes many higher level cubes to scatter away at high speed". The possibility of this kind of physics-based understanding has only become available with the current generation of computer games engines; and Crysis Wars is exemplarily in terms of the quantity of elements that can physically interact on screen at any one time.

Haley Ng's experiments stood out in that she literally and conceptually challenged the relationship between weapon, projectile and the human body (Ng, 2009). In one experiment, rather than firing a shell from a tank into her three dimensional field, she drops a tank itself into the field while her avatar assumes the point of view of the projectile that more conventionally follows this trajectory. This recalls the many examples of missile-eye-view footage seen during coverage of the recent wars in Iraq. Stockwell and Muir (Stockwell & Muir, 2003) note this war is "different to previous wars in one major way: This war [is] waged as entertainment". Stockwell and Muir go on to say that "by toying with the point of view (POV), experience of the simulation can create new empathies". Ng takes advantage of the missile-eye point of view to bind firing of a weapon with death of her avatar.

Many of Mathew Hunter's experiments blur the relationship between real-time simulation and using machinima (using computer game engines to create films) to document it (Hunter, 2009). They show the collapse of a stack of "ordinary" objects. The simulation is then seemingly played in reverse, but when the result is an alternative form it becomes unclear whether Hunter is compositing video from two collapsing structures or some new physical rules have been brought into the simulation. Either option is plausible when one understands that real world physical constants become real-time variables in a computer game environment. Another of Hunters experiments makes this point by directly engaging the disparity of real-world and in game physics. This experiment overlaid approximately 100 rectangular prisms so that they occupied exactly the same space; appearing as if only one rectangular prism was present. Shooting the assembly seemed to 'wake' the physics engine which, only after this point, sought to respect the volumetric integrity of each element. By experimenting in this space Hunter reminds us that even though we are not physicists we have a, possibly socially constructed, understanding of what to expect.

Case Study 05

Two hundred and sixty students in Crysis: The final case study in this section discusses the work of four students from a cohort of almost 260. The students in the core course ARCH1101 Architectural Design Studio (2010) were studying towards degrees in Architecture, Architectural Computing and Engineering with Architecture. This year saw the implementation of the Sandbox2 editor for the computer game Crysis Wars. All students created hand drawn sections, axonometrics, perspectives and textures, applied them to SketchUp models and exported those to custom environments they created in Sandbox2. Interactive and environmental attributes were also created in the Sandbox2 editor using the Flowgraph visual scripting editor and a particle editor. The brief for experiment three of this course (conducted over the final five weeks of semester one) called for the students to create a bridge over a valley that was inspired by a real valley from one of the chosen clients countries of origin. The clients were Angela Merkel, Miranda Kerr and Helen Keller (three powerful women; with the students choosing two from the three). The bridge was to contain offices for the clients with access to elevators that would take the clients to a 'third space' on the valley floor; where they would find a table around which they would meet.

Matt O'Brien's original motivation for choosing Helen Keller as a client arose from a desire to model a valley inspired by one at Yellowstone National Park in North America which he had recently visited. Using images and topography from Google Earth he was able to construct an accurate facsimile of the valley in the Sandbox2 editor. He commented to the author that he was able to reconstruct many of the same trails he walked when he was there, and the almost photorealistic consistence between images of his landscape and photos of the park itself certainly reinforced his assertion (for a presentation of his work, and the other case studies within this section please refer again to www.russelllowe.com/

publications/cdmt/cdmt.htm). Two other aspects within O'Brien's work directly address the notion of an expanded Third Space. Responding to Helen Keller's blindness and deafness O'Brien created an office and elevator which maximised the effects of wind, inertia and gravity on Keller's senses. The elevator utilised physics enabled ropes and relied on moving elements and a pulley system to reposition the elevator both horizontally and vertically (O'Brien, 2010). It's important to stress that O'Brien's elevator was not an animation, but a real-time simulation of physical properties and processes. Finally, O'Brien's video captures, or Machinima, of these spaces and interactions display a sophisticated understanding of film production. The carefully shot, sequenced and edited video captures remind the viewer that in the contemporary world the ways in which we understand our environments are often mediated by popular forms of representation such as film and computer games. From 'real' experiences of trail walking through 'real' nausea as one swings on a rope elevator to reflections on our mediated perspectives within the world O'Brien's scheme inadvertently designs Soja's Third Space.

Christine Pan's valley was inspired by the urban environment of Chicago; the multistorey office buildings forming the valley walls with a series of low bridges across the river creating the valley floor. Pan links the buildings with a vast web of cables, which in her words mirror "the vast network of cables running along the city, connecting both sides like threads or power lines. It suggests communication, co-corporatisation (Pan, 2010)." Seemingly reacting against the corporate dominance of the contemporary city Pan meticulously hand draws her own versions of building facades and applies them to the models within the computer game. The result reminds us of the presence of our bodies within the city and captures those qualities within Chicago in a profoundly visceral way.

Millie Lakos chose Mount Whitney as inspiration for her valley. This area, known as the Ala-

bama Hills, reflects her client's, Helen Keller's, place of birth. In contrast to both O'Brien and Pan, Lakos recreated a mountainous environment with multiple interconnected valleys. As a consequence her bridge cannot simply span from one side to the other. Lakos says: "The bridge's main structure is to be two intertwining ribbons that are anchored to the sides of a small valley. A third ribbon is to connect the bridge visually and act as a path for the elevators to the valley floor. The ribbon has played an important historical role as a declaration of support, it is a symbol of connectedness, belonging and guidance. An internal ribbon will act as a guiding path for Keller to move throughout the space comfortably from one side of the bridge to the other (Lakos, 2010a)." Lakos' ribbon swirls between interior and exterior spaces. Her Machinima shows the landscape and architecture at night with snow falling and fires blazing (Lakos, 2010b) adding dynamic atmospheric effects to support the physical role of the ribbon in navigation. By employing these qualities within the natural environment Lakos extends former students Oren Oaariki and Hye Bin Sung's project on navigation (case study 03) further testing the ability of plans and sections to capture the extent of architecture in ways they could possibly imagine but not bring into effect only a few years prior.

Jarrod Hinwood describes a notion of power as it relates to one of his clients ... "Merkel's offices consist of exposed steel frames filled in by a collection of prefabricated roof, wall and floor elements. The organisation of these prefabricated elements [and] frames is representative of the power that Merkel posses which is channelled through rigid government framework an[d] policy (Hinwood, 2010a)." Apart from the qualities of light and shadow which are modulated dynamically by shifting elements of the built fabric (and triggered by the presence or otherwise of the elevators) it is Hinwood's attention to structure and construction that makes this project worthy of noting here (Hinwood, 2010b). That Hinwood writes unselfconsciously about prefabrication is not so surprising when one remembers that each architectural element within the computer game environment was prefabricated in Google SketchUp before being exported to (or delivered to) the site of the Sandbox2 editor (as in prefabrication as it is conventionally understood in the construction industry the SketchUp to Sandbox2 workflow also privileges standardisation and repetition of parts). By splitting the virtuality of these two softwares Hinwood's workflow creates a parallel Virtual and Third Space to Soja's described above.

The consideration of construction in the final case study in this section forms a good introduction to Section 04.

SECTION 04: BEYOND DESIGN

While this chapter has focused on the application of computer gaming technology within the architectural design curriculum there are also significant opportunities for application in other parts of the curriculum. Curriculum areas such as construction, structures, project management and ergonomics can benefit from the enhanced interactivity provided by computer gaming technology. As mentioned in Section 02 Coller and Scott (Coller & Scott, 2009) present a game based numerical methods course in their paper "Effectiveness of using a video game to teach a course in mechanical engineering" whilst also providing a useful summary of the learning principles embedded in computer games drawing on authors such as Gee and Kelly (Gee, 2003; Kelly, 2005). In collaboration with Newton and Zou the author has noted that virtual simulations have the potential to replace direct student exposure to construction sites (in an upcoming paper, "Learning and Teaching Domestic Construction Competence Using Serious Video Game Technology", to be presented at the 10th International Conference on Construction Applications of Virtual Reality,

2010). It also forms the basis of a pilot project and an Australian Learning and Teaching Council grant application with a view to enabling first-year construction management students to learn and demonstrate their technical competence in domestic construction.

Case Study 06

The distraction of subject matter: This case study involves a research project conducted in collaboration with Associate Professor John Mitchell and employed recent architectural graduates, Julian Cromarty and Vinh Nguyen. A significant part of the project involved the translation of a Building Information Modeling (BIM) model from ArchiCAD to Crysis Wars to test various ergonomic scenarios. The BIM model included selected units of a 1.3 billion dollar hospital in Australia. A critical component of that project and a critical concept for computer game modding more generally, until now not discussed, is the reimagining of standard computer game assets. The aesthetics and subject matter for First Person Shooters such as Unreal Tournament, Half Life 2 and Crysis Wars can be described as aggressively militaristic (as is probably obvious from their titles). Indeed, Burrow and More (Burrow & More, 2005) specifically chose the UnrealEngine2 Runtime version of UT2004 to use in their elective class because it provided "an environment for design experiences that avoids the problematic videogame stereotypes concerning violence and destruction that are associated with traditional game-engines." Unfortunately, as can be seen in the case of Burrow and More, the overtly violent subject matter often distracts from opportunities hidden just below the surface. In the project above a civilian vehicle from Crysis Wars (resembling a Toyota light truck) was reconfigured as both a wheelchair and a hospital bed. The civilian vehicle was chosen as the base of these configurations due to its physical similarity to them; it has four wheels. Another version of the hospital bed was constructed in Unreal Tournament 3, but this time it used a military tank as the underlying structure. As the tank was a tracked vehicle that could turn on the spot (rather than requiring some forward motion to turn, as in the case of the civilian vehicle) it more closely represented the capability of the four wheel steering hospital bed in practice. The resulting wheelchair and hospital bed bear no visual resemblance to the vehicle they build upon. The important point to take from this is that many computer games prioritize subject matter and narratives that distract from their underlying capabilities; looking beyond subject matter and narratives is vital for higher levels of engagement. In the same way that civilian vehicles and armoured tanks can become wheelchairs and hospital beds, weapons become portable devices that interact with other participants at a distance and avatars become user centred animated geometries. Reimagining the scale, materiality, function and intention of standard game assets in this way may lead the reader to surprisingly challenging architectures.

Case Study 07

Real-Time Porosity: This final case study presents an ongoing research project that is a collaboration between the author, Professor Richard Goodwin (University of New South Wales, College of Fine Arts) and the New South Wales, Emergency Information Coordination Unit and supported by the Australian Research Council. This project uses embedded environmental sensors to track pedestrian movement which is then translated in real-time to computer game environments. By using a series of visualisation methods we call 'Porosity Lenses' observers are able to understand pedestrian movements in new ways. Initial stages of the research are presented in "Computer Gaming and Porosity" (Lowe & Goodwin, 2009) but of particular interest in this context is the opportunity to extend Mallasi's work on activity workspaces (Mallasi, 2004) with a view to both understanding the spatial dynamics of people involved in

the construction process and avoiding workplace conflicts. Recent field trials in urban Sydney, using wireless sensors developed by Dr Mark Hedley at the CSIRO (CSIRO, 2008), have confirmed the systems viability in challenging real world environments. Opportunities exist to integrate this work with the "Learning and Teaching Domestic Construction Competence Using Serious Video Game Technology" project outlined above to enable students to train alongside workers in real-time.

Notes on the use of Computer Game Engines in Practice

While prohibitively expensive licenses have prevented widespread uptake of computer gaming technology in architectural practice there are indications this may be about to change. Two notable exceptions to this are the firms HKS who licensed the Unreal3 game engine (HKS, 2007) and Enodo, formerly IMAGTP, who in a high profile example used the CryENGINE 2 game engine to support Foster+Partner's proposal for the New York Public Library (Crysuki, 2008). In a positive move Crytek is offering the opportunity to register for four different types of CryENGINE3 license; Game Development, Simulation, Education and Visualisation (Crytek, 2010). At this stage pricing and availability are still unconfirmed.

In his comparison of CAD and BIM software with three dimensional computer games engines Pelosi (Pelosi, 2010b) identified three primary areas of concern; view navigation, spatial quality of the representation and geometrical interoperability. Pelosi notes BIM models and models used in most computer games are currently optimised to satisfy disparate needs. Drawing on six years of teaching undergraduate students CAD, BIM and computer gaming software he found that there was "an emerging generation of AEC workforce that have grown up immersed in complex and sophisticated 3D computer games."

Traditional architectural software developers are responding to demand for this type of technology in architectural practice. Since version 12 Graphisoft's ArchiCAD software has been supported with a "Virtual Building Explorer" which they describe as enabling "Real-time 3D navigation in an architectural design – enhanced with gravity, layer control, fly-mode, egress recognition and pre-saved walkthroughs for the ultimate design exploration (Graphisoft, 2010)." The website AECBytes supplements GraphiSoft's description by adding "using familiar video game controls (Bobrow, 2009)". One of Graphisoft's main BIM competitors, Autodesk, is also developing a "game engine for architects" for its Revit software (Sheppard, 2008).

The question for software developers and designers is whether it will be more expedient to incorporate notions of topology and tolerance (for example) within computer game engines or to incorporate high levels of atmospheric representation and interactivity (for example) within BIM software. Or whether translation between softwares to capture the best of both worlds will remain the best (if somewhat uncomfortable (Lowe, 2009c)) option?

CONCLUSION

The case for utilizing computer game modding in an architectural design curriculum is a strong one. The underlying technology behind many computer games is not only serious, but has been at the forefront of the technology envelope for the past 30 years. The rich intertwining of real-time spatial, material, lighting and physical simulations reinforce spatial visualization, navigation and mental rotation. The consideration of serious gaming implementations in fields as diverse as physics, medicine and economics reveals themes that are central to the practice of engineering and architecture. Prospective students of engineering and architecture degrees may already know this;

certainly many of them play computer games … and almost half of the students that had enrolled at the author's university to study architecture were already modifying computer games. To put it another way; if there are themes present in this technology that are already scheduled to be developed within an architectural design curriculum, and students are already building experience, familiarity and expertise to develop them using computer games then there is an opportunity to extend on this experience that is too good to miss. Up until recently the advantages of using computer gaming technology, as noted above, came at a cost of realism as compared to traditional architectural animation. This cost has not only closed in recent times but has actually reversed for almost all students.

In the past two decades many researchers have implemented games engines in architectural design curricula but in every case the courses have been in upper years of their student's degrees, with small classes and elective rather than core courses (Pelsoi (Pelosi, 2010a) is an exception to this, using Google SketchUp and the Esperient Creator game engine in a first year course with 100 students, however this course is an elective). That this is in contrast to the wider computer game modding community suggested that the difficulties they were having may actually be mitigated by implementing the technology, along with aspects of computer game modding culture, in large first year classes. At around 2004 a change in focus, to third party content creation, by many computer game developers further aided subsequent implementations. There are some continuing shortcomings however, these include; graphics demand on hardware, sharing environments, printing stills, software compatibility as a result of 'update' cycles, lack of wider peer assistance, licensing complexities and lack of quantifiable data regarding increased learning performance. One can already see the impending resolution of many of these technical shortcomings, but they will require mitigation in any implementations in the near future. Obtaining quantifiable data regarding increased learning (and therefore design) performance afforded by using computer gaming technology would support any argument that this technology deserves its place within the core architectural design curriculum rather than remaining on the fringes in elective courses.

In Section 03 the author collapsed Stockburger's distinction between the game designer and the game player to further his extension of Lefebvre's and Soja's thinking about space as it relates to computer gaming. In this section it was important to understand the term 'player' as a 'game designer in testing mode'. Case studies of student work showed that game environments could be engaged with critically; simultaneously reinforcing and challenging the physicality of making within the computer game environment, defying traditional conventions of architectural representation or implicating the military entertainment complex. They also showed that architecture could be tested with human participation, physics based interaction, artificial intelligence, a consideration of its construction processes or a hybrid of the above.

Section 04 presented examples of significant, and developing, opportunities for application of computer gaming technology in other parts of the architectural curriculum. Ironically, sensors within real world environments that link them to computer game environments may bring competence training and evaluation much closer to reality. Finally we find that the distraction of violence that is ever present in many modifiable computer games may still be a factor in arguments to avoid using this technology within architectural design curricula. But in reimagining military vehicles as wheelchairs and hospital beds the final case study not only shows the humanitarian advantage when such distractions are overcome ... but also reflects once more on the power of computer game engines to synthetically integrate and more broadly implicate the physical, the mental and the social; qualities vital in the creation of great architecture.

REFERENCES

ArchiForm3d. (2010). *3D rendering gallery*. Retrieved 28 March, 2010, from http://www. archiform3d.com/ 3d-gallery/index.php

Blender. (2010). *Blender: Features*. Retrieved 1 May, 2010, from http://www.blender.org/ features-gallery/features/

Bobrow, E. (2009, April 23). ArchiCAD's new virtual building explorer. *AECbytes Tips and Tricks Issue, 41*. Retrieved 7 August, 2010, from http://www.aecbytes.com/tipsandtricks/ 2009/ issue41-archicad.html

Burrow, A., & More, G. (2005). *Architectural designers and the interactive audience*. Paper presented at the Second Australasian Conference on Interactive Entertainment.

Campbell, D., & Wells, M. (1994). *A critique of virtual reality in the architectural design process*. Technical Report: R-94-3. Retrieved 28 March, 2010, from http://www.hitl.washington.edu/ publications/r-94-3/

Coller, B. D., & Scott, M. J. (2009). Effectiveness of using a video game to teach a course in mechanical engineering. *Computers & Education, 53*(3), 900–912. doi:10.1016/j.compedu.2009.05.012

Cromarty, J. (2008a). *Draft2 text*. Retrieved 1 May, 2010, from http://julescromarty.blogspot.com/ 2008/10/draft2-text.html?zx=c8500b3429f482e7

Cromarty, J. (Producer). (2008b). *Draft2_Cromarty.mov: Machinima*. Retrieved from www.russell-lowe.com/publications/ cdmt/Draft2_Cromarty. rar

Crysuki. (2008). *Enodo new info* (formerly IMAGTP). Retrieved August 8, 2010, from http://www.incrysis.com/forums/ viewtopic. php?pid=467288

Crytek. (2010). *Crytek, MyCryENGINE*. Retrieved 8 August, 2010, from http://mycryengine.com/

CSIRO. (2008). *Wireless tracking for challenging applications*. Retrieved May 31, 2010, from http://www.csiro.au/science/ Position-Location-System.html

Epic Games Inc. (2004). *Unreal Tournament 2004, Bonus Disc: Atari*.

Epic Games Inc. (2010). *Unreal Technology: Editor*. Retrieved 29 April, 2010, from http://www.unrealtechnology.com/ features.php?ref=editor

GarrysMod. (2010a). *GarrysMod: About*. Retrieved 1 May, 2010, from http://www.garrysmod.com/about/

GarrysMod. (2010b). *Wiremod*. Retrieved 1 May, 2010, from http://wiki.garrysmod.com/?title=Wire_Addon

Gee, J. (2003). *What video games have to teach us about learning and literacy*. New York, NY: Palgrave MacMillan.

Goodwin, R., McGillick, P., Helsel, S., Tawa, M., Benjamin, A., & Wilson, G. (2006). *Richard Goodwin: Performance to porosity*. Victoria, Australia: Craftsman House, an imprint of Thames and Hudson.

Graphisoft. (2010). *Graphisoft virtual building explorer for ArchiCAD*. Retrieved 1 May, 2010, from http://www.graphisoft.com/ products/virtual-building-explorer/

Hao Hsiu Hsu, V. (Producer). (2008). *ARCH1101 experiment 3: Animation*. Retrieved from www.russelllowe.com/publications/ cdmt/VincentHaoHsiuHsu.rar

Havok. (2010). *Havok physics*. Retrieved 1 May, 2010, from http://www.havok.com/ index.php?page=havok-physics

Hinwood, J. (2010a, 11 August). *Crysis image capture and concept*. http://jarrodhinwood.blogspot.com

Hinwood, J. (Producer). (2010b). *Keller and Merkel_s elevators.flv*. Retrieved from www.russelllowe.com/publications/ cdmt/Hinwood.rar

HKS. (2007). *HKS licenses Unreal Engine 3 for groundbreaking architectural applications*. Retrieved November, 2009, from http://www.hksinc.com/news/ 2007_10_HKS_Licenses_Unreal.htm

Hoon, M., & Kehoe, M. (2003, 24-27 October). *Enhancing architectural communication with gaming engines*. Paper presented at the ACADIA22, Connecting Crossroads of Digital Discourse, Indianapolis (Indiana).

Hunter, M. (Producer). (2009). *BENV2423: Experiment 1*. Retrieved from www.russelllowe.com/publications/ cdmt/MathewHunterEXP1.rar

Hye Bin, S. (2006). *Hye Bin Sung: DESN104 experiment 3 website*. Retrieved 1 May, 2010, from http://www.russelllowe.com/desn104_2006t2/ website_misc/student_work/ hye_bin_sung_exp3_website/index.html

Johns, R., & Lowe, R. (2005). *Unreal Editor as a virtual design instrument in landscape architecture studio*. Paper presented at the Trends in Real-Time Landscape Visualization and Participation, Anhalt University of Applied Sciences.

Johns, R., & Shaw, J. (2006). Real-time immersive design collaboration: Conceptualising, prototyping and experiencing design ideas. *Journal of Desert Research, 5*(2), 15.

Kelly, H. (2005). *Pre-summit paper harnessing the power of games for learning*. Paper presented at the Summit on Educational Games. Retrieved from www.FAS.org

Lakos, M. (2010a, 11 August). *Bridge development*. Retrieved from http://www.millielakos.blogspot.com

Lakos, M. (Producer). (2010b). *Running through bridge.mp4, Elevator1.mp4*. Retrieved from www.russelllowe.com/publications/ cdmt/Lakos.rar

Legaspi, H. (Producer). (2009). *Arch7201_Legaspi.flv*. Retrieved from www.russelllowe.com/ publications/ cdmt/Arch7201_Legaspi.rar

Lehtinen, S. (2002, 18-20 September). *Visualization and teaching with state-of-the-art 3D game technologies*. Paper presented at the Connecting the Real and the Virtual - Design E-ducation, 20th eCAADe Conference, Warsaw (Poland).

Li, S. (Producer). (2007). *shawn_li_workshop. wmv*. Retrieved from http://www.russelllowe. com/cdmt/ shawn_li_workshop.rar

Lowe, R. (2007a). *ARCH1102: Course outline*. Retrieved 29 April, 2010, from http://www.russell-lowe.com/arch1102/ course_info/course_outline. html

Lowe, R. (2007b). *ARCH1501: Course outline*. Retrieved 1 may, 2010, from http://www.russell-lowe.com/ arch1501/course_outline.html

Lowe, R. (2007c). *HL2 tutorial: Model with complex collision*. Retrieved 1 May, 2010, from http:// www.russelllowe.com/desn285_2006t2/ tutorials/ model_with_complex_collision.html

Lowe, R. (2008a). *BENV2423: Course outline*. Retrieved 1 May, 2010, from http://www.russell-lowe.com/ benv2423/index.htm

Lowe, R. (2008b, 9-12 April). *Beyond the boundary object: Sketches, computer games and blogs facilitating design development*. Paper presented at the CAADRIA, Chiang Mai (Thailand).

Lowe, R. (2009a, 21 June 2009). *ARCH1101: Architecture design studio 1, discussion forum*. Retrieved 29 April, 2010, from http://groups. google.com/group/arch1101

Lowe, R. (2009b). *BENV2423: Course outline*. Retrieved 1 May, 2010, from http://www.russell-lowe.com/ benv2423_2009/index.htm

Lowe, R. (2009c). *Computer game modding for architecture*. Paper presented at the 14th International Conference on Computer Aided Architectural Design Research in Asia. Retrieved from http://cumincad.scix.net/cgi-bin/ works/ Show?caadria2009_176

Lowe, R. (2010a). *ARCH1101-2010 blog*. Retrieved 1 May, 2010, from http://www.arch1101-2010.blogspot.com/

Lowe, R. (2010b). *ARCH1101: Architecture design studio 1, discussion forum*. Retrieved 1 May, 2010, from http://groups.google.com/group/ arch1101-2010/topics

Lowe, R. (2010c). *SketchUpToCrysis_mpeg4.avi*. Sydney, Australia: Lowe, R.

Lowe, R., & Goodwin, R. (2009, 5-6 November). *Computer gaming technology and porosity*. Paper presented at the 9th International Conference on Construction Applications of Virtual Reality, Sydney, Australia.

Mallasi, Z. (2004, 7-9 December). *Identification and visualisation of construction activities' workspace conflicts utilising 4D CAD/VR tools*. Paper presented at the eDesign in Architecture: ASCAAD's First International Conference on Computer Aided Architectural Design, KFUPM, Saudi Arabia.

Manovich, L. (2000). *The language of new media*. Cambridge, MA: MIT Press.

Microsoft. (2004). *Computer gaming to enhance CS curriculum* (p. 11). Retrieved from http:// research.microsoft.com/ en-us/collaboration/pa-pers/ computergamingtoenhancecscurriculum.doc

Moloney, J. (2001, 9-12 December). *3D game software and architectural education*. Paper presented at the Meeting at the Crossroads. Short Paper Proceedings of the 18th Annual Conference of the Australian Society for Computers in Learning in Tertiary Education., Melbourne, Australia.

Moloney, J. (2002, 18-20 September). *String CVE collaborative virtual environment software developed from a game engine.* Paper presented at the 20th eCAADe Conference Proceedings, Warsaw (Poland).

More, G., & Burrow, A. (2007). *Observing the learning curve of videogames in architectural design.* Paper presented at the The Fourth Australasian Conference on Interactive Entertainment: IE2007, RMIT University, Melbourne Australia.

MyCryEngine. (2010). *Five reasons to license CryENGINE3.* Retrieved 1 May, 2010, from http://mycryengine.com/?conid=43

Ng, H. (Producer). (2009). *HayleyNGEXP1.flv.* Retrieved from www.russelllowe.com/publications/ cdmt/HaleyNGEXP1.rar

O'Brien, M. (Producer). (2010). *Exp3Part1. mp4, Exp3Part2.mp4, Exp3Part3.mp4.* Retrieved from www.russelllowe.com/ publications/cdmt/ OBrien.rar

O'Coill, C., & Doughty, M. (2004, 15-18 December). *Computer game technology as a tool for participatory design.* Paper presented at the Architecture in the Network Society, 22nd eCAADe Conference, Copenhagen (Denmark).

Oaariki, O. (2006). *Oren Oaariki: DESN104, experiment 3 website.* Retrieved 1 May, 2010, from http://www.russelllowe.com/desn104_2006t2/ website_misc/student_work/ oren_oaariki_exp3_ website/index.html

Ondrejka, C. R. (2004). *Aviators, moguls, fashionistas and barons: Economics and ownership in Second Life.* SSRN eLibrary.

Online Schools. (2010). *Video game statistics.* Retrieved 21 March, 2010, from http://www. onlineschools.org/blog/ video-game-statistics/

Pan, C. (2010, 11 August). *Client spaces.* Retrieved from http://www.arch1101-2010kb.blogspot.com/

Pelosi, A. (2010a). List of game engines used. In R. Lowe (Ed.) (email to author ed., pp. 1).

Pelosi, A. (2010b, 7-10 April). *Obstacles of utilising real-time 3D visualisation in architectural representations and documentation.* Paper presented at the CAADRIA 2010, New Frontiers, Hong Kong.

Pickersgill, S. (2007, 11–13 July). *Unreal Studio: Game engine software in the architectural design studio.* Paper presented at the Computer Aided Architectural Design Futures, Sydney (Australia).

PlayUpTools. (2010). *PlayUp homepage.* Retrieved 1 May, 2010, from http://www.playuptools.com/

Price, C. (2006). A crisis in physics education: Games to the rescue! *ITALICS, Innovation in Teaching And Learning in Information and Computer Sciences, 5*(3).

Rheingold, H. (1991). *Virtual reality.* New York, NY: Summit Books.

Rosser, J., Lynch, P., Cuddihy, L., Gentile, D., Klonsky, D., & Merrell, R. (2007). The impact of video games on training surgeons in the 21st century. *Archives of Surgery, 142*(2), 5. Retrieved from http://archsurg.highwire.org/ cgi/content/ full/142/2/181doi:10.1001/archsurg.142.2.181

Schoon, I. (1992). *Creative achievement in architecture: A psychological study.* Leiden, The Netherlands: DSWO Press - Leiden University.

Sheppard, S. (2008). *We're on to something with Project Newport.* Retrieved 7 August, 2010, from http://labs.blogs.com/its_alive_in_the_lab/ 2008/12/were-on-to-something-with-project-newport.html

Shiratuddin, M. F., & Fletcher, D. (2007, 22-23 October). *Utilizing 3D games development tool for architectural design in a virtual environment.* Paper presented at the Conference on Construction Applications of Virtual Reality 2007, Penn State University.

Spuybroek, L. (1998). Motor geometry. *Architectural Design, 68*(5/6), 7.

Stockburger, A. (2007). Playing the third place: Spatial modalities in contemporary game environments. *International Journal of Performance Arts and digital Media, 3*(2 & 3), 13.

Stockwell, S., & Muir, A. (2003). The military-entertainment complex: A new facet of information warfare. *FibreCulture, 1*, 1. Retrieved from http://journal.fibreculture.org/issue1/issue1_stockwell-muir.html

Thabet, W., Shiratuddin, M. F., & Bowman, D. (2002). Virtual reality in construction: A review. In *Engineering computational technology* (pp. 25–52). Civil-Comp Press. doi:10.4203/csets.8.2

Tran, B. (Producer). (2009). *BillyTranEXP1.flv.* Retrieved from www.russelllowe.com/publications/ cdmt/BillyTranEXP1.rar

Wikipedia. (2010a). *List of level editors.* Retrieved 14 August, 2010, from http://en.wikipedia.org/wiki/List_of_level_editors

Wikipedia. (2010b). *Steam (content delivery).* Retrieved 1 May, 2010, from http://en.wikipedia.org/ wiki/Steam_(content_delivery)

3DWorld Editors. (2007). Imagina20. *3dWorld, 1*. Achten, H., & Turksma, A. (1999, 8-10 April). *Virtual reality in early design: The design studio experiences.* Paper presented at the AVOCAAD Second International Conference, Brussels (Belgium).

KEY TERMS AND DEFINITIONS

Architectural Design Curriculum: The sequence of courses or subjects focused on the learning/instruction of design within undergraduate and postgraduate programs of university study leading to a professionally accredited degree in Architecture. Typically these courses occur in design studios that facilitate physical drawing and modelling; but more recently the introduction of computers has seen the nature of work in the studios transform.

Crysis Wars: Released in 2008. A free to download version of the Crysis game series by German game developers Crytek. It is a multiplayer game where each player engages with the virtual world in first person. The Crysis game series is particularly significant due to its incredibly sophisticated and realistic graphics, setting many benchmarks in this area.

Game Modding: Refers to modifying an existing game. A significant number of contemporary computer games facilitate modification by releasing Software Development Kit's alongside the parent game itself. These kits usually include level, map or world builders that enable non-programmers to design landscapes, atmospherics, interactions, vehicles and avatars and import two dimensional, three dimensional and aural content from other design software. Ultimately, a full modification replaces all of the content of the parent game and only uses the underlying rendering, physics, artificial intelligence engines, etc. making the original theme of the game unrecognisable.

Sandbox2: The level builder for Crysis Wars. The Sandbox2 level builder is a comprehensive set of instruments to amalgamate content created in external design software with content created within the level builder itself. Amongst other features it includes a visual scripting interface, called the Flowgraph, which facilitates non-programmers to build complex computational sequences that underpin rich levels of interaction. A welcome addition to game modding, this level builder provides equivalent, or superior, levels of sophistication to the Unreal Tournament 3 level builder (see below) but with a much lower skill level required.

Simulation: As opposed to visualisation, especially via animation, a simulation does not presuppose an outcome but provides a virtual context to enable experimentation.

Unreal Tournament 2004: Released in 2004. A first person shooter game by American game developers Epic Games. This game was released with the level builder Unreal Editor and was one of the first, if not the first, games to 'outsource' three dimensional content development.

Unreal Tournament 3: Released in 2007. This game followed Unreal Tournament 2004 in the Unreal series and was released with a second generation version of the Unreal Editor. This level builder greatly increased the level of sophistication in terms of possible design outcomes but also significantly raised the skill level required to achieve even basic outcomes.

Chapter 13
Augmented Reality Research for Architecture and Design

Mi Jeong Kim
Kyung Hee University, Republic of Korea

Xiangyu Wang
Curtin University, Australia & Kyung Hee University, Republic of Korea

Xingquan Zhu
University of Technology Sydney, Australia

Shih-Chung Kang
National Taiwan University, Taiwan

ABSTRACT

A growing body of research has shown that Augmented Reality (AR) has the potential to contribute to interaction and visualization for architecture and design. While this emerging technology has only been developed for the past decade, numerous journals and conferences in architecture and design have published articles related to AR. This chapter reviews 44 articles on AR especially related to the architecture and design area that were published from 2005 to 2011. Further, this chapter discusses the representative AR research works in terms of four aspects: AR concept, AR implementation, AR evaluation, and AR industry adoption. The chapter draws conclusions about major findings, research issues, and future research directions through the review results. This chapter will be a basis for future research of AR in architecture and design areas.

INTRODUCTION

During the last two decades, the Architecture/Engineering/Construction (AEC) domain, which heavily relies on visualization, has significant benefited from Virtual Reality (VR) technology. VR

is a technology to simulate a computer-generated world and the potential of virtual visualization has captured the AEC industry's attention. Recently, by enriching interaction techniques and by overcoming the lack of the integration with a real environment, a new emerging technology Augmented Reality (AR) has entered our daily life and world. In the line of the Reality-Virtuality

DOI: 10.4018/978-1-61350-180-1.ch013

continuum (Milgram and Kishino 1994), AR is characterized by the combination of the real and virtual, real time interaction, and registration in 3D (Azuma 1997). The technological advancements of AR have clearly shown the significant sophistication of technological capabilities.

Although the concept of AR is as simple as the idea of mixing the real and virtual worlds, the AR research agenda in architecture and design ranges from its concept generation to industrial adoption. AR involves the human perception with both real and virtual information sources, and accordingly, AR research in architecture and design is an inter-disciplinary research between the AR technology, human factors, and design. The enabling technologies of AR consist of media representations, interaction devices, feedback displays, trackers and computing units. More varied media representations are utilized in AR than VR, where input and output mechanism is considered for object manipulation in the augmented digital information onto a real background. Further, human factor studies are necessary not only in the rigorous methodology, but also in the application of the technology to a targeted domain in which researchers are conducting critical evaluation and validation.

A growing body of research has shown that AR has the potential to contribute to interaction and visualization for architecture and design. The hybrid visualization afforded by AR can potentially impact on the architecture and design practice by changing the way people experience and interact. While this emerging technology has been mainly advanced during the past decade, numerous journals and conferences in architecture and design have published articles related to AR. The current research identified a total of 44 main articles on AR that are especially related to the architecture and design area. They were published from 2005 to 2011. Furthermore, this chapter discusses the representative AR research works in terms of four aspects: AR concept, AR implementation, AR evaluation and AR industry adoption. This

chapter also draws conclusions regarding major findings, research issues, and future research directions through the review results.

The research work in AR has ranged from the conceptual framework to lab-based prototype proof, evaluation, and case illustration. It is necessary to have a comprehensive review of recent significant AR applications in architecture and design, in order to provide a comprehensive understanding of the state-of-the-art work in the field and its impact on architecture and design. Each paper was reviewed by the authors to determine its eligibility and level of relevance. Only current articles published from 2005 to 2011 were considered, with the aim of focusing on the most recent advances. The selected paper had to be AR works in the areas of architecture and design. Considering AR for design is an emerging area, thus both the leading international journals and conferences were searched. The identification of articles involved keyword searches as well as careful examination of the titles of articles. The search was initialized using the keyword combination with one expression chosen from "augmented", "augmented reality, "mixed" and "mixed reality", and one chosen from "architecture", "design", and "digital architecture". Articles that appeared to fit into the category were verified by first reading the abstract and then the entire article to extract the main findings. Many articles that were initially identified via the title or keywords were discarded in the screening process. In the end, only 44 key articles were determined for the content analysis as being associated with architecture and design.

AUGMENTED REALITY RESEARCH IN ARCHITECTURE AND DESIGN

The general characteristics of AR research in architecture and design were identified first. Then the more specific results were reported, along with research issues that emerged through the review of the AR works.

Figure 1. Number of articles from 2005 to 2011

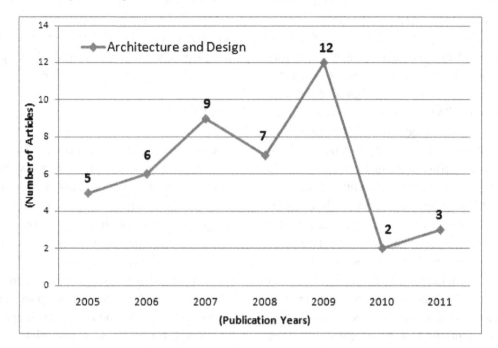

General Characteristics of AR Research

The number of articles by publication year shows a longitudinal perspective of AR researcher as depicted in Figure 1. AR research articles grew considerably in 2009, and the number of articles before 2009 is similar in quantity, but surprisingly, there was a significant drop in numbers in 2010. However, the number of articles climbed again in 2011. It should be noted that the number cited for 2011 is only from the period between January and June because the search of papers ended at the end of June 2011. It is therefore predicted that additional papers will be forthcoming and should be counted towards 2011. It is very clear that AR research in architecture and design is increasing and this trend will certainly continue.

Figure 2 shows the number of articles at each category from 2005 to 2011. Considering the fact

Figure 2. Number of articles in each category from 2005 to 2011

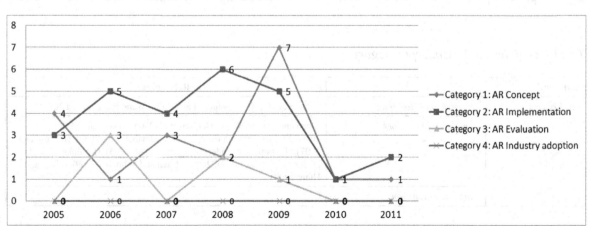

that certain papers might fall into several categories, the sum of the "number of articles" is over 44. As for the category 1, 43.2% (19 articles) of reviewed articles have significant AR concepts and theories involved in their studies. The category 2 implementation has the highest percentage of AR articles (26 articles, 59.1%). This implies that the AR technology has mature enough to enable implementation. 13.6% (6 articles) of the papers have significant evaluations (category 3) of the effectiveness and/or usability studies. Unfortunately, no article has significantly engaged industry adoption in practice. These results depicted a picture of what happened in AR research for architecture and design. It becomes a mature practice to implement AR for design. Formal evaluation to demonstrate their benefits and usefulness have not been much conducted yet, further, industrial adoption of the AR research outcomes have not been realized yet.

Results of AR Research Review

Identifying the current research concentration and paucity is critical to the establishment of the future direction for AR research. It is expected that the identification of whether or not some specific areas have been investigated sufficiently would be a prerequisite for proposing new research issues to be pursued in future AR research. For the convenience of discussing and comparing similar works, we categorize AR research in architecture and design into four aspects: AR Concept, AR Implementation, AR Evaluation and AR Industry Adoption. The following subsections discuss the representative and significant works identified for each aspect and each subsection is highlighted by an identified list of research issues.

AR Concept

The work in AR concept concerns AR algorithms and modeling, conceptual frameworks, and evaluation frameworks. This aspect involves new concepts of how AR can be adopted in the design area and new theories of how AR can be applied to design. Algorithms are an essential part of the development of the AR systems. Conceptual frameworks provide a general idea of what the systems are made up of, and what type of implementation can be built upon them. Evaluation frameworks are essential to form the basis of heuristic guidelines of usability evaluation for the technologies. 29.6% (13 articles) of the papers focused on the conceptual framework of proposed AR systems with sophistication. Only 6.8% (3 articles) of papers have significant works on the development of a new algorithm or modelling. Interestingly, none of articles concerned the development of an AR evaluation framework.

Chung et al.(Chung et al. 2009) proposed an AR system modeling that allows users to visualize the virtual buildings, streets and historic sites with the current actual scene, and interact with the virtual scene in real-time while the user is navigating. They especially developed two-step

Table 1. Articles on AR Concept category

Category		References
AR Concept	*Algorithm and Modelling*	(Chung et al. 2009), (Santos et al. 2007), (Wang and Dunston 2005)
	Conceptual Framework	(Phan and Choo1 2010), (Germen et al. 2006), (Dave and Moloney 2009), (Anders 2007), (Wang 2007), (Schnabel et al. 2007), (Petzold et al. 2007), (Lonsing and Anders 2011), (Lin et al. 2005), (Lertlakkhanakul et al. 2005), (Schnabel et al. 2008), (Chen and Schnabel 2009), (Chen and Hung 2009)
	Evaluation Framework	

solutions for outdoor mobile AR tracking: using GPS and gyro devices, and the built-in camera of the mobile device for vision-based tracking. Santos et al. (Santos et al. 2007) also presented a system architecture of mobile AR applications for collaborative design review, combining a variety of visualization technologies such as multi-tile displays (called powerwall), TabletPCs and HMD (head-mounted displays). The system includes a variety of tracking systems providing the best possible pose estimation for AR modes and a number of multi-modal interaction techniques ranging from speech recognition to two-handed interaction for navigation and selection, and so forth. For the real-time transfer of data between CAD and the AR viewer, Wang and Dunston (Wang and Dunston 2005) proposed the algorithm and implemented an integration of CAD and AR in a prototype system to demonstrate the feasibility of the proposed algorithm. The proposed algorithm requires downloading the 3D solid model description at the client side via networking socket codes and supports only the AR rendering of piping system models.

Anders (Anders 2007) presented the principles for the design of AR compositions and illustrated them through experiments involving architecture and robotics. The author tried to figure out what would characterize the cybrid designs, and how they differed from other forms of design. A novel concept, Mutual Augmentation (MA) where AR and AV co-exist to form a seamlessly integrated space was proposed by Wang (Wang 2007) and a systematic framework of exploring MA was presented for supporting collaboration, communication, and coordination in architecture and design. Lin et al. (Lin et al. 2005) introduced a concept of information portal (IP) as a smart environment composed of a variety of AR architecture components and developed a research prototype of IP that provides interactive experiences in outdoor and indoor settings. To augment information capabilities to places and support interactive media linked to location, they suggested a set of design principles of constructing the IP: Technological,

functional, cognitive, social requirements and experience design. Chen and Schnabel (Chen and Schnabel 2009) emphasized tangible AR as an innovative way to understand the spatial conception and used tangible AR in order to evoke new instructional technology into design learning. They argued that tangible AR allows designers to evaluate the design context and its solution more holistically in an urban context. Through an AR interactive navigation system, Chen and Hung (Chen and Hung 2009) also found that the intuitive user experience is more beneficial when real tangible objects replace the keyboard and mouse. Unperceivable (lost) space can be retrieved and then the design communication can be enhanced by using a variety of visualization methods.

Research Issues

- The use of AR in outdoor settings has been a rather theoretical undertaking due to the poor performance of AR displays, especially in daylight. Virtual models need to be placed into the current scene in a manner that exhibits proper perspective by adopting advanced display techniques (Chung et al. 2009).

- The limited integration between CAD and AR applications has hindered users from maximizing exploitation of their combined strength and complementary advantages. A seamless integration between CAD and AR applications needs to be pursued for architecture and design (Wang and Dunston 2005).

- Mobile devices become a powerful platform as complementary to desktop devices as the computing becomes more and more ubiquitous and ambient. The development of AR visualization using mobile devices need to be more focused to support designers' collaborative works in architecture and design (Santos et al. 2007; Chung et al. 2009).

• AR evaluation frameworks can form the basis of heuristic guidelines on usability evaluation in architecture and design. The development of evaluation frameworks needs to be made based on the theory of human factors in AR research.

AR Implementation

AR Implementation can be further divided into two sub-levels: Software and hardware. The software level concerns agent-based approach, knowledge-based approach, content design, and interaction design.

By proposing and integrating agent models from artificial intelligence into AR systems, AR systems can be developed into intelligent systems. A knowledge-base is a collection of data representing related experiences and knowledge, which can support human decision-making in the problem-solving process. The sub-level 'content design' includes general AR research dealing with the AR-related content that does not belong to the other sub-levels. In AR systems, virtual informa-tion is presented to the real world scene, thus the interaction design for object manipulation is one of important issues in AR research. The hardware level includes the analyses of types of displays, interaction/ input devices, computing units and registration methods and trackers. In the category 2 implementation, there are much more articles dealing with software side (25 articles, 56.8%) of AR as compared to the hardware side (13 articles, 29.6%). Many articles are related to the contents design of AR systems (15 articles, 34.1%) and 10 articles (22.7%) address significantly interaction design. There is no paper that incorporates agent and knowledge-based into AR systems.

Lin et al. (Lin et al. 2005) presented the Digital Yuanmingyuan project to provide the visualization of virtual reconstructions upon the current appearance of the ruins using an AR system. They analysed the technical difficulties of the system regarding real-time accurate registration, display units and modelling scenery and then discussed the design of the proposed system hardware and the tracking algorithm. Moloney and Dave (Moloney and Dave 2011) proposed two approaches

Table 2. Articles on the implementation category

Category			References
AR Implementation	Software	Agent-based AR	
		Knowledge-based AR	
		Contents design	(Tonn et al. 2009), (Lin et al. 2005), (Moloney and Dave 2011), (Choo et al. 2009), (Fukuda et al. 2006), (Liang and Huang 2009), (Anders and Lonsing 2005), (Seichter 2007), (Kinayoglu 2009), (Chung et al. 2009), (Gruber et al. 2010), (Viet et al. 2009), (Moloney 2007), (Dias et al. 2005), (Wang and Wang 2009)
		Interaction design	(Wang and Dunston 2006), (Wang and Dunston 2008), (Kim and Maher 2008), (White et al. 2007), (Papagiannakis and Magnenat-Thalmann 2007), (Tonn et al. 2008), (Tonn et al. 2007), (Chen and Chang 2006) (Belcher and Johnson 2008), (Huang and Ho 2008)
	Hardware		(Wang and Dunston 2006), (Wang and Dunston 2008), (Wang and Dunston 2006), (Kim and Maher 2008), (Wang and Chen 2009) (Papagiannakis and Magnenat-Thalmann 2007), (Liu et al. 2006), (Moloney and Dave 2011), (Choo et al. 2009), (Papagiannakis and Magnenat-Thalmann 2007), (Tonn et al. 2008), (Tonn et al. 2007), (Seichter 2007), (Belcher and Johnson 2008), (Petzold et al. 2007), (Chung et al. 2009), (Gruber et al. 2010), (Viet et al. 2009), (Moloney 2007), (Huang and Ho 2008), (Dias et al. 2005),

for multiple design representations, namely, studio MixR and sit MixR reflecting the distinction between the typical studio based design process and the requirements of a formal design review by the design team and stakeholders. They argued that the representation of 'context' can be extended by two interrelated approaches: The incorporation of the temporal, as well as through the concurrent evaluation of qualitative representations and quantitative information on functional performance. Prototype applications were implemented to illustrate the potential of AR to enhance decision making at the early stages of design. An application with a tangible AR interface on a regular PC system for interior design was proposed by Choo et al. (Choo et al. 2009), where the colour, style or covering of the virtual furniture in a real environment can be modified in real-time on the screen through the tracking markers. Anders and Lonsing (Anders and Lonsing 2005) proposed an AR system called AmbiViewer by which architects could generate 3D compositions – full scale objects – on actual sites, and to view the results as navigable AR. They especially proposed four performance specifications of AR systems as the perceived needs of designers at the initial stages of a project: portability, ubiquity, visualization and indeterminacy. Mobile technology can enable spatial awareness in AR space by turning our living space into geosemiotics via visual, iconic and metaphorical methods, thus this aspect has been recently emphasized in AR research (Liang and Huang 2009). In order to demonstrate the effects of soundscapes on characteristics of place experience, Kinayoglu (Kinayoglu 2009) conducted an experimental study using audio AR. He found that there is a correlation between soundscape and the sense of place that depends on audio-visual congruence, which, in turn, is based on cultural, aesthetic and semantic factors.

The limiting factors of current interaction can be augmented by AR because direct manipulation of objects in AR setup is more natural than the mouse/keyboard setup. While users interact with the real world using objects, the movement of human hands and arms is more natural, thus conveying more expression, gesture and feeling (Wang and Dunston 2006). Towards the effectiveness of the AR tool for design review, they (Wang and Dunston 2008) developed an AR-based face-to-face design review prototype for supporting collaboration and assessed users' experiences with virtual models. They suggested that the AR tool may facilitate problem-solving and the quantity of work in a given amount of time and that virtual design displayed in the mixed scene was a useful aid in the design error detection task. Similarly, Kim and Maher (Kim and Maher 2008) conducted a comparative study using an AR tabletop system with tangible user interface (TUI) and a desktop with a typical keyboard/mouse/display in order to identify how the designers' interaction with the design model are changed in an AR system. They found that the use of AR and TUIs has an impact on designers' spatial cognition, and that these changes affected the design process by increasing their 'problem-finding' behaviours leading to creative design. Tonn et al. (Tonn et al. 2007) proposed an AR planning software SAE-CA with a focus on the potential of AR for the support of colour and material design in the existing built context. Using a mobile hardware setup, they (Tonn et al. 2008) investigated the conceptual and technological foundations for the visualization of interactive 3D data on arbitrary surfaces in real indoor environments and emphasized AR- based user interaction on site using laser pointer tracking.

Research Issues

- A human–computer interface of future AR system versions should be produced by integrating AR with more intuitive and natural interaction techniques. Tangible AR interfaces are one of the multi-modal user interfaces that afford natural human-AR

Table 3. Articles at the evaluation category

Category		References
AR Evaluation	Effectiveness	(Wang and Dunston 2006), (Kim and Maher 2008), (Tonn et al. 2007)
	Usability	(Wang and Dunston 2008), (Wang and Wang 2009)
	Effectiveness+Usability	(Wang and Dunston 2006)

interaction (Kim and Maher 2008; Wang and Dunston 2008).

- The potential of incorporating agent-based into AR systems should be considered for developing AR intelligent systems. For example, agent-based AR simulation systems can examine people's circulation and behaviours within a building design before the real one is built physically (Belcher and Johnson 2008).

- The mobility of the device gives designers flexibility to design and contextual information. AR systems need to be portable, thus they can enable designers to explore design from multiple viewpoints on the fly and to acquire information on the context of a device (Anders and Lonsing 2005).

- For the implementation, the critical features of the AR systems for architecture and design need to be discussed and identified along with their hardware and software, where the interactive potential should be increased (Choo et al. 2009).

AR Evaluation

The AR evaluation aspect is divided into two sub-levels: Effectiveness and usability. Effectiveness evaluation concerns the productivity improvement and other quantitative indicators of how effectively AR systems can facilitate a certain design task. Usability category involves investigating user needs by conducting user interviews or questionnaires, field evaluations with users, and expert evaluations of AR systems. Emerging AR devices introduces a new level of complexity in usability evaluation

because AR augmented a human's cognitive process and provides a hybrid representation. Only 6 articles (13.6%) has rigorous evaluation work, among which 3 articles (6.8%) is related to effectiveness evaluation of performance of using AR for design tasks and 2 articles (4.6%) of the evaluation work focused on usability evaluation, and only 1 article (2.3%) has conducted both effectiveness and usability evaluations. There should be more usability evaluation as additional to the effectiveness evaluation.

Wang and Dunston (Wang and Dunston 2006) argued that AR research has not adequately considered human factors beyond acknowledging ergonomics issues, such as fatigue and discomfort related to wearing an HMD. They analyzed the feasibility of augmenting human abilities via AR applications from the cognitive perspective and then generated partial guidelines to solve ergonomics issues in AR systems. Through an experiment comparing an HMD versus a desktop monitor, they validated that the perceptual incompatibility regarding performance time, accuracy and workload in performing an orientation task. Further, they (Wang and Wang 2009) conducted an experiment to examine some of the co-presence factors with a focus on the image size and viewing distance. Based on the results, they argued that a higher level of co-presence and better effects could be achieved in the AR-mediated collaborative design system. From a cognitive perspective, Kim and Maher (Kim and Maher 2008) performed an evaluation on the effectiveness of TUIs through an empirical study with two interior renovation tasks. They did not evaluate the final design outputs, rather identified specific features of the creative design process using protocol analysis. They conjectured that the epistemic 3D modeling actions afforded by TUIs offload designers' cognition, and the naturalness of the direct hands-on style of interaction promote designers' immersion in designing, thus allowing them to perform spatial reasoning more effectively. Tonn et al. (Tonn et al. 2007) assessed the proposed AR software prototype through a user study, which projects the color and material qualities of a design directly onto any surface within an existing building. Based on the evaluation of the effectiveness in performance, they argued that the support of color and material design using AR has major potential for architectural planning practice.

Research Issues

- Cognitive issues need to be considered as major factors for the development of AR systems because human factors are associated with the use of AR systems. For example, solutions to depth ambiguity in a planar projection view of an AR 3D environment can be found by reference to perceptual psychology and cognitive science (Wang and Dunston 2008).
- AR constitutes an intuitively powerful computer interface for augmented users' interactions and experiences, thus it comes with new human factor challenges. The human factors associated with the AR interfaces need to be identified to successfully operate AR systems in architecture and design (Wang and Dunston 2006).
- The essential factors for evaluating the usability and effectiveness of AR systems for design need to be investigated and identify through empirical studies. For example, more research on performance measuring methods reflecting the characteristics (portability, nomadicity, cognitive load etc.) of AR systems should be conducted.

AR Industrial Adoption

AR Industry Adoption involves the question as to whether the prototype has been tested in industry. The industrial adoption practice is critical in assessing the effectiveness of the tool. Unfortunately, no article has significantly engaged industrial practitioners and tested their systems by means of practical project. The benefits gained from using AR tools in practical projects can convince the industrial complex to adopt the tool into their practice. For example, the dissemination of AR applications directly within the architecture area can help to obtain feedback, thus defining future AR research agenda in design. Furthermore, we investigated whether or not the AR work include domain knowledge and found that only 11.4% (5 articles) of papers have serious domain knowledge studies and applied when implementing their AR systems for design. This percentage is indeed low.

Research Issues

- AR systems need to be tested by means of practical industrial projects in order to assess their effectiveness in real circumstances. Otherwise, the efforts for AR systems will simply be proof-of-concept.
- As one of the effective adoption strategies in industries, the benefits and challenges of AR systems associated with specific practices need to be considered. AR systems for architecture and design should be developed based on their domain knowledge.

CONCLUSION

This chapter reviewed a total of 44 key articles on AR in architecture and design, published between 2005 and 2011 in terms of four aspects: AR concept, AR implementation, AR evaluation, and AR industry adoption. This review chapter details the wide variety of architecture and design applications for which AR systems are now being developed and tested. The published studies, for the most part, still consist of lab-based controlled studies with a lack of industrial practitioner-based control groups, meaning that the studies are mainly geared toward the feasibility or proof of concept testing. However, this type of work is apparently appropriate and necessary for testing a new technology in the early stages of its application. Meanwhile, this summary also confirms that most of the papers reviewed have system implementation components, a fact that implies that AR technology has matured enough to enable implementation. It was also found that very few papers have conducted a significant evaluation of the effectiveness and/or usability studies through a scientific and formal approach. None of the work has significant industrial adoption or piloting. There is no work integrating artificial intelligence methodology (agent and knowledge-based system) into AR to make it intelligent. Most of the work did not considerably involve human factors models theories and did not involve serious domain knowledge from architecture and design.

The results of the review on articles raise two research issues to be considered for the development of future AR systems: 'Human factor' and 'domain knowledge'. AR research has focused more on the technical aspects of prototype development, limited to "proof-of-concept" applications. However, AR can enhance users' perception of the real environment, providing access to information the users cannot directly perceive when unaided (Wang and Dunston 2006). Human factors in AR should be a crucial issue to be considered, which have not been much researched, for more successful technology development and integration. It is expected that the evaluation framework for AR systems can be developed based on the human factor theory. Further, many AR research have focused on prototype systems using AR technologies, however, there have not much understanding of how such AR systems could be employed in design practice. Advanced AR techniques are being introduced without significant insight on

their benefits in practice (Verlinden and Horvth 2009). To utilize AR systems effectively in a specific domain, the domain knowledge should be incorporated into a variety of technologies. The knowledge derived from this research can be sources of inspiration for the future AR studies in architecture and design by forming the basis for the guidelines on AR research and systems.

REFERENCES

Anders, P. (2007). *Designing mixed reality: Perception, projects and practice* (pp. 276–283). Association for Computer Aided Design in Architecture.

Anders, P., & Lonsing, W. (2005). *AmbiViewer: A tool for creating architectural mixed reality* (pp. 104–113). Association for Computer Aided Design in Architecture.

Azuma, R. T. (1997). A survey of augmented reality. *Presence (Cambridge, Mass.)*, *6*(4), 355–385.

Belcher, D., & Johnson, B. (2008). *MxR: A physical model-based mixed reality interface for design collaboration, simulation, visualization and form generation* (pp. 464–471). Association for Computer Aided Design in Architecture.

Chen, C.-T., & Chang, T.-W. (2006). *1:1 spatially augmented reality design environment* (pp. 487–499). The International Conferences on Design & Decision Support Systems in Architecture and Urban Planning.

Chen, I. R., & Schnabel, M. A. (2009). Retrieving lost space with tangible augmented reality. International Conference on the Association for Computer-Aided Architectural Design Research in Asia (pp. 135-142).

Chen, Y. L., & Hung, P. C. (2009). Intuitive augmented reality navigation system design-implementation by Next-Gene20 Project, *International Conference on the Association for Computer-Aided Architectural Design Research in Asia* (pp. 351-360).

Choo, S. Y., Heo, K. S., Seo, J. H., & Kang, M. S. (2009). Augmented reality- effective assistance for interior design: Focus on tangible AR study. *The 27th Conference on Education in Computer Aided Architectural Design in Europe: Communicating Space(s)* (pp. 649-656). Istanbul.

Chung, D. H. J., Zhiying, S. Z., Karlekar, J., Schneider, M., & Lu, W. (2009). *Outdoor mobile augmented reality for past and future on-site architectural visualizations* (pp. 557–571). Computer Aided Architectural Design Futures.

Dave, B., & Moloney, J. (2009). Augmenting time and space in design inquiries. *International Conference on the Association for Computer-Aided Architectural Design Research in Asia* (pp. 523-532).

Dias, J. M. S., Lopes, A. C., & Marcos, J. S. (2005). *Seamless indoor and outdoor location, guidance and visualization in mobile computing.* International Conference on Construction Applications of Virtual Reality.

Fukuda, T., Kawaguchi, M., Yeo, W., & Kaga, A. (2006). Development of the environmental design tool "Tablet MR" on-site by mobile mixed reality technology. The *24th Conference on Education in Computer Aided Architectural Design in Europe: Communicating Space(s)* (pp. 84-87). Volos, Greece.

Germen, M., Artut, S., Ayiter, E., Balcısoy, S., & Sharir, Y. (2006). The representation and navigation of complex data. The *24th Conference on Education in Computer Aided Architectural Design in Europe: Communicating Space(s)* (pp. 406-410). Volos, Greece.

Gruber, L., Gauglitz, S., Ventura, J., Zollmann, S., Huber, M., Schlegel, M., et al. (2010). The city of sights: Design, construction, and measurement of an augmented reality stage set. *International Symposium in Mixed and Augmented Reality* (pp. 157-163). Seoul, Korea.

Huang, Y., & Ho, K.-S. (2008). *An integrated environment of representing digital antiques.* International Conference on Construction Applications of Virtual Reality.

Kim, M. J., & Maher, M. L. (2008). The impact of tangible user interfaces on spatial cognition during collaborative design. *Design Studies, 29*(3), 222–253. doi:10.1016/j.destud.2007.12.006

Kinayoglu, G. (2009). Using audio-augmented reality to assess the role of Soundscape in environmental perception: An experimental case study at UC Berkeley campus. The *27th Conference on Education in Computer Aided Architectural Design in Europe: Communicating Space(s)* (pp. 639-648).

Lertlakkhanakul, J., Lee, I., & Kim, M. (2005). Using the mobile augmented reality techniques for construction management. *International Conference on the Association for Computer-Aided Architectural Design Research in Asia* (pp. 396-403).

Liang, R.-H., & Huang, Y.-M. (2009). Visualizing bits as urban semiotics. *International Conference on the Association for Computer-Aided Architectural Design Research in Asia* (pp. 33-42).

Lin, H. C., Shen, Y. T., & Jeng, T. (2005). IP++: Computer- augmented information portal in place. *International Conference on the Association for Computer-Aided Architectural Design Research in Asia* (pp. 185-192).

Liu, Y., Wang, Y., Li, Y., Lei, J., & Lin, L. (2006). Key issues for AR-based digital reconstruction of Yuanmingyuan garden. *Presence: Teleoperator and Virtual Environments, 15*(3), 336–340. doi:10.1162/pres.15.3.336

Lonsing, W., & Anders, P. (2011). Three-dimensional computational structures and the real world. *International Conference on the Association for Computer-Aided Architectural Design Research in Asia* (pp. 209-218). Hong Kong.

Milgram, P., & Kishino, F. (1994). A taxonomy of mixed reality visual displays. *IEICE Transactions on Information Systems. E (Norwalk, Conn.)*, 77-D(12).

Moloney, J. (2007). Screen based augmented reality for architecture. *International Conference on the Association for Computer-Aided Architectural Design Research in Asia* (pp.577-584).

Moloney, J., & Dave, B. (2011). From abstraction to being there: Mixed reality at the early stages of design. *International Journal of Architectural Computing*, 9(1), 1–16. doi:10.1260/1478-0771.9.1.1

Papagiannakis, G., & Magnenat-Thalmann, N. (2007). Mobile augmented heritage: Enabling human life in Ancient Pompeii. *International Journal of Architectural Computing*, 5(2), 396–415. doi:10.1260/1478-0771.5.2.396

Petzold, F., Bimber, O., & Tonn, O. (2007). CAVE without CAVE: On-site visualization and design support in and within existing building. *The 25th Conference on Education in Computer Aided Architectural Design in Europe: Communicating Space(s)* (pp. 161-168).

Phan, V. T., & Choo1, S. Y. (2010). Augmented reality-based education and fire protection for traditional Korean buildings. *International Journal of Architectural Computing*, 8(1), 75–91. doi:10.1260/1478-0771.8.1.75

Santos, P., Gierlinger, T., Stork, A., & McIntyre, D. (2007). Display and rendering technologies for virtual and mixed reality design review, *International Conference on Construction Applications of Virtual Reality* (pp. 165-175).

Schnabel, A. M., Wang, X., Seichter, H., & Kvan, T. (2007). From virtuality to reality and back. *Conference on International Association of Societies of Design Research* (IASDR) (pp. 1-15).

Schnabel, M., Wang, X., & Seichter, H. (2008). Touching the untouchables: Virtual-, augmented-, and reality. *International Conference on the Association for Computer-Aided Architectural Design Research in Asia* (pp. 293-299).

Seichter, H. (2007). *Augmented reality and tangible interfaces in collaborative urban design* (pp. 3–16). Computer Aided Architectural Design Futures.

Tonn, C., Donath, D., & Petzold, F. (2007). Simulating the atmosphere of spaces– The AR-based support of 1:1 colour sampling in and within existing buildings. *The 25th Conference on Education in Computer Aided Architectural Design in Europe: Communicating Space(s)* (pp. 169-176).

Tonn, C., Petzold, F., Bimber, O., Grundhöfer, A., & Donath, D. (2009). Spatial augmented reality for architecture – Designing and planning with and within existing buildings. *International Journal of Architectural Computing*, 6(1), 41–58. doi:10.1260/147807708784640126

Tonn, C., Petzold, F., & Donath, D. (2008). Put on your glasses and press right mouse button: AR-based user interaction using laser pointer tracking. *The 26th Conference on Education in Computer Aided Architectural Design in Europe: Communicating Space(s)* (pp. 201-208).

Verlinden, J., & Horvth, I. (2009). Analyzing opportunities for using interactive augmented prototyping in design practice. *Artificial Intelligence for Engineering Design, Analysis and Manufacturing*, 23(3), 289–303. doi:10.1017/S0890060409000250

Viet, T. P., Yeon, C. S., Hak, W. S., & Ahrina, C. (2009). AR: An application for interior design. *International Conference on the Association for Computer-Aided Architectural Design Research in Asia* (pp.115-124).

Wang, R., & Wang, X. (2009). Experimental investigation of co-presence factors in a mixed reality-mediated collaborative design system. The 6th International Conference on Cooperative Design, Visualization, and Engineering (pp. 333-340). Luxembourg: Springer-Verlag.

Wang, X. (2007). *Mutually augmented virtual environments for architectural design and collaboration* (pp. 17–29). Computer Aided Architectural Design Futures.

Wang, X., & Chen, R. (2009). An experimental study on collaborative effectiveness of augmented reality potentials in urban design. *CoDesign*, *5*(4), 229–244. doi:10.1080/15710880903320020

Wang, X., & Dunston, P. S. (2005). Real time polygonal data integration of CAD/augmented reality. In *Architectural Design Visualization, Computing in Civil Engineering* (pp. 1–8). American Society of Civil Engineers, ASCE. doi:10.1061/40794(179)10

Wang, X., & Dunston, P. S. (2006). Compatibility issues in augmented reality systems for AEC: An experimental prototype study. *Automation in Construction*, *15*(3), 314–326. doi:10.1016/j.autcon.2005.06.002

Wang, X., & Dunston, P. S. (2006). Potential of augmented reality as an assistant viewer for computer-aided drawing. *Journal of Computing in Civil Engineering*, *20*(6), 437–441. doi:10.1061/(ASCE)0887-3801(2006)20:6(437)

Wang, X., & Dunston, P. S. (2008). User perspectives on mixed reality tabletop visualization for face-to-face collaborative design review. *Automation in Construction*, *17*(4), 399–412. doi:10.1016/j.autcon.2007.07.002

White, M., Petridis, P., Liarokapis, F., & Plecinckx, D. (2007). Multimodal mixed reality interfaces for visualizing digital heritage. *International Journal of Architectural Computing*, *5*(2), 322–337. doi:10.1260/1478-0771.5.2.322

KEY TERMS AND DEFINITIONS

Augmented Reality: A technology to augment a physical world with digital information.

Mixed Reality: A technology to mix the real and virtual worlds.

Virtual Reality: A technology to simulate a computer-generated world.

Virtual Environment: A virtual and digital place created using virtual reality.

Digital Architecture: An architectural design representation made by digital technologies.

Design Computing: An area of design studies done through techniques in computing.

State-of-the-Art Review of Technologies: A review on current technologies involved in a specific area or domain.

238

Chapter 14
Experiencing Digital Design:
Developing Interactive Workspaces for Visualizing, Editing and Interacting with Digital Design Artifacts

John I. Messner
The Pennsylvania State University, USA

Robert M. Leicht
The Pennsylvania State University, USA

ABSTRACT

To implement computational design applications into design education successfully, it is critical that educators consider the available facilities which allow students to develop, communicate, and experience their designs. A variety of media spaces can be used to facilitate greater interaction with digital content, along with the potential to foster greater collaboration on team focused activities. An interactive workspace can be designed to enhance authoring and interaction with digital content by using the INVOLVE framework, which includes seven elements: Interaction, Network, Virtual Prototypes, Organization, Layout, Visual Real Estate, and Existential Collaboration. This framework focuses on first identifying the fundamental uses and needs of the space, along with identifying the types of tasks to be performed within each physical space or room. For example, if a department has three different rooms available to students in a design studio or course, then the activities to be performed within the different spaces, e.g., design review, digital design authoring/modeling, fully immersive navigation of a model, collaborative brainstorming, et cetera, would suggest different displays and means of interaction. Once the use of each space is identified, then the framework guides the user toward the selection of fundamental space attributes, equipment and resources that should be available to students within each space. Exciting new technologies will allow future students to be more easily engaged in the digital content while gaining easy access to data and information which was previously difficult to generate.

DOI: 10.4018/978-1-61350-180-1.ch014

INTRODUCTION

Designers are increasingly using digital content to author and review their creations. For design disciplines within the Architectural, Engineering, and Construction (AEC) Industry, this use of digital content is particularly valuable due to the scope and scale of the artifacts that are being developed. A popular method for authoring this content is through individual interaction with a computer with traditional input devices such as a keyboard and mouse. While this method of interaction with a modeling application may seem natural to some, the interaction limitations can inhibit the ability for developing and reviewing digital models. This limitation is amplified when students work in teams to develop digital design content.

Computational design is becoming widespread with many students devoting significant effort into the development of a digital model of their design. With the increased use of Building Information Modeling (BIM) and digital design, there is a need for educators to focus on the design of interactive workspaces that support greater degrees of interaction with the digital content being developed by students. Unfortunately, the digital media environment is not always planned to enhance the tasks that will be performed within the environment. By developing well designed interactive workspaces that fosters interaction, students and faculty can be more productive and creative as they develop, review, present and engage with digital content.

This chapter presents a framework for designing interactive workspaces with a specific focus on creating learning environments, although there are many similarities to industry workspaces as well. There are many reasons for the development of interactive workspaces within an academic setting which include:

- Collaborative work environments for students and faculty;

- Visualization environments to allow students to be immersed within their designs, possibly through 3D stereoscopic visualization;
- Presentation spaces for conveying design concepts through multimedia presentations; and
- Recruitment environments to attract new students into the profession or university program.

To design an interactive workspace, the following steps are outlined:

- Inventory digital spaces;
- Identify tasks to be performed by students and faculty, e.g., group activities, individual visualization, class presentations;
- Match physical spaces with the task focus; and
- Design the workspace to support the task performance.

Throughout this chapter, we will:

- Describe the value of using interactive workspaces in an educational setting to facilitate student interaction with digital media;
- Present a framework for designing a series of the media environments that can be used to foster interaction with digital media;
- Provide illustrative examples of highly interactive workspaces implemented in various educational settings.

BACKGROUND

Using Media for Communication

Media possess fundamental capability, each of which may be more or less important for a particular task (Brennan and Lockridge 2006). Dennis and Valacich (1999) have defined fundamental media capability categories as:

- *Immediacy of Feedback:* The extent to which a medium supports rapid bi-directional communication;
- *Symbol Variety:* The number of ways in which information can be communicated;
- *Parallelism:* The number of simultaneous conversations that can exist effectively;
- *Rehearsability:* The extent to which a medium enables the sender to rehearse a message before sending; and
- *Reprocessability:* The extent to which a message can be re-examined or processed again.

Choosing one single medium for any task may prove less effective than choosing a variety of media which a team can use at different times to perform different tasks (Chidambaram and Jones 1993; Rubens 2003). This supports the need to develop interactive environments that allow for communication to be supported by many different methods.

Effective communication is essential for effective learning. Therefore, the development of interactive workspaces that promote communication, between faculty, students, and student teams, is critical.

Media capabilities can be matched to the characteristics of different tasks. In Media Synchronicity Theory (MST), tasks can be defined as either conveyance or convergence. Conveyance is the exchange of information, followed by the deliberation of its meaning. Convergence is the development of shared meaning for information. Participants working on convergence strive to agree on the meaning of information and verify that they have agreed. This means that participants understand each other's view (DeLuca and Valacich 2006). By matching media capabilities to task requirements, it has been suggested that certain media, such as email and electronic bulletin boards, are more appropriate for conveyance of information, while media such as face-to-face and telephone are more suitable for convergence tasks. By recognizing these fundamental communication attributes, one can design a media environment to suit the needs of a task.

MST is notable in that it does not propose that any specific medium is inherently better than another. Instead, it recognizes that communication media are flexible. MST indicates that work activities involve a series of communication tasks that need different communication media capabilities. It is also recognized that it is frequently beneficial to use more than one communication media simultaneously, such as face-to-face communication which is supported by written documents or visual presentation content. MST provided a core foundation to the INVOLVE framework discussed later in the chapter.

Modes of Collaboration

Another core concept that is important when designing communication media for a task is to consider the group interaction requirements when performing the task. At a very abstract level, group tasks can be summarized as maximizing or optimizing (Steiner 1972). An optimized outcome is referring to how efficiently and effectively the team spends their time and energy in solving a problem. The term is intended to mean that the team combines their efforts efficiently to meet a preset standard, rather than coming up with the optimal answer. In comparison, a maximizing outcome is used when a team explores the full extent or potential output of their efforts rather than trying to meet a set goal. To use an example in building energy analysis, the team would be optimizing if they were seeking to the least effort to reach a predefined energy use value. They would be maximizing if they were seeking the lowest energy solution possible for the facility.

In addition, Steiner (1972) also identified two options for combining a team's efforts to perform a task: *Divisible* and *unitary. Divisible* tasks can be broken into smaller tasks and then the team members can make individual contributions which can be integrated into the overall team's contribution, or more simply, the divide and conquer method. In contrast, *unitary* tasks are efforts that cannot be divided. An example of a unitary task within the building sector would be the development of an optimal design for incorporating daylighting and energy analysis from an optimum perspective. The two analysis activities are highly related and therefore cannot be divided into individual optimization processes.

The method of group interaction is important to consider when designing an interactive workspace. *Unitary - Maximizing* tasks require more exploration of potential design solutions, and therefore tend to require more flexible, adaptive work environments to support the interactions of the team. At the other extreme, *Divisible – Optimizing* tasks tend to have a clear answer, or solution set of answers, that will meet the defined standard, and the task can be subdivided to be solved by multiple team members. These tasks do not tend to require the same degree of interaction in the media environment during the design or solution generation process. And through some of the activities performed we have found that the set up of the space and media used can actually change the method & process of the teams performing the task.

DESIGN CONSIDERATIONS FOR INTERACTIVE WORKSPACES IN EDCUATION

There are several important design considerations that can be defined through the analysis of interactive workspaces. A framework, titled 'INVOLVE', has been developed by performing a detailed analysis of digitally mediated facilities to define the various parameters of an interactive workspace that should be considered. The components of the framework include:

I   *Interaction:* The modes of interaction of the users with the system. These modes can include writing or sketching; audio / video capture; physical manipulation, e.g., haptics; and 3D navigation and selection.

N   *Network:* The ability to remotely connect to project files, devices, and team members. Networking functionality can make a significant impact of the ability for team members to effectively perform team tasks.

V   *Virtual Prototypes:* The digital information, products, and ability to interact with them. The prototype is the digital model. The level of detail for the model content, along with the interactivity built into the content, impacts the results within the workspace.

O   *Organization:* The collaborative team and their competencies. The team integration into the system includes the collaborative process, team structure, and the location of team members (virtual collaboration or collocated team). It is also important to consider the specific traits and competencies that can impact the team's affinity toward the use and exploitation of the digital media environment. These can include items such as training for the digital environment, comfort with the use of new technologies, and the affinity toward digital media.

L   *Layout:* The physical position and comfort within the workspace to support the tasks. The work environment should be a physically comfortable space with proper indoor environmental factors. This may seem like an obvious feature, yet many computationally intensive work environments are not very comfortable spaces which make them less attractive for use, particularly when a team must spend a significant amount of time in the environment. Proximity to the primary work environment is also an important consideration.

V   *Visualization and Display:* The traits and configuration of the display system(s). This can include the size of the screen(s), resolution, stereoscopic capability, and physical layout. The display also includes audio and haptic feedback.

E *Existential Collaboration:* Teamwork through shared goals and transparent processes is very important for group projects. Teamwork can be facilitated by the interactive workspace traits, e.g., when you provide multiple methods for interaction with a model, then there are opportunities for students with different primary interaction methods to provide valuable contributions to the team's efforts.

Virtual Environments and Display Integration

There are many different types of interactive workspaces. In this section, we will review several example facilities to illustrate some varied capabilities and design intents. The first facility is the Immersive Environments Lab (IEL) at Penn State University (Otto et al. 2005). This facility has three large rear-projected screens. Each screen is six feet tall and eight feet wide. They are arranged with an angled view to provide a wider field of view than a single wall, but they do not completely surround a user (see Figure 1). The display uses stereoscopic vision and large display visualization to aid students and faculty to better experience their design models by enabling one to one scale interaction with the model. The human eye uses stereopsis to register two different images using both eyes to measure depth (Julesz 1971). Stereoscopic visualization, then, is the use of display systems to portray the dual images needed to provide the sense of depth in the visualized model. This display system provides a reasonably high level of visual immersion into a virtual model. The IEL does not include a position tracking system to allow for view modification based on the position of the user so it is only optimized for one focused location in the room, but the facility does allow for all users to see a reasonably scaled version of the model. The key features of this particular display design are the immersive stereo features, the three screen wide field of view with the angled layout, the rear projected images, and the large scale of the visualized content. It also allows for a large group (approximately 30 people) to be in proximity to the display at one time.

Figure 1. User viewing a model within the Immersive Environments Lab at Penn State

Another display system which is also at Penn State is the SSVR contained within the SEA Lab (Whisker et al. 2003). The SSVR display, as shown in Figure 2, has four walls and a floor display which allow for the user to be completely surrounded by the displayed images. The user's head is tracked to allow the computer to adjust the displayed images to the viewer's relative eye location. The unique features of this display system extend beyond the IEL's immersive display capabilities and wide field of view to physically surrounding the user with the four walls and floor of the display, the screens are again rear projected (except the floor), and the view of the digital model are modified in real time to match the user's movements using head tracking. This provides a very visually immersive experience with a model which can provide a user with very accurate, one to one scale (or other scale) interaction with a model. There are some challenges involved in the use of this type of display facility for design education. First, they tend to be quite expensive at this time, although the cost of implementation continues to fall. They are also limited to group sizes of three to four people based on the display footprint. And they can be challenging

to transition model content into the environment since the display uses a virtual reality suite of software that requires content conversion from traditional AEC modeling applications to allow for use in the display.

Another type of advanced visualization display is the Powerwall which is composed of a high resolution tiled display system with 24 tiles, each tile able to display two images for stereoscopic visualization at a resolution of 6144 x 3072 pixels. To support the tiled display, 48 computers are clustered with each connected to one of the 48 projectors, with an additional computer to organize and coordinate the clustered computers. This display system, which can be seen in Figure 3, allows for improved visualization through higher quality, faster rendering and a higher resolution display using the smaller images which make up the overall system. The IMPROVE system customizes the images seen from each of the tiles so the perspective of the outside edges of the screens is manipulated to give added perspective to the immersive views (Santos et al. 2007). A unique feature of this tiled display is the improved speed and quality of the rendered images to enable more realistic views of the content, but at a support cost

Figure 2. User inside the SSVR facility at the SEA Lab at Penn State

Figure 3. The Powerwall display system for the IMPROVE project from Santos et al. (2007).

of the clustered computing needed to render and display the images. The use of multiple screens also allows for multiple images to be displayed concurrently, and with the single wall and capability for multi-user tracking, the display can be viewed from several locations and still provide high quality images.

The previous section has specifically focused on high-end display environments that can be considered for implementation in specialized interactive workspaces. The display system is typically the central consideration in planning an interactive workspace and digital design experience, but needs to be considered within the context and needs of the program. The SSVR system completely surrounds the users, to provide a much greater level of presence and more visual cues. The Powerwall presents the single wall perspective, which is less immersive due to the layout of the display, but provides a much higher quality and resolution image which creates a more realistic feel to the images. The different layouts also influence the use of the space with the SSVR

facility creating a small space for a small group of users and only one receiving the customized view of the virtual prototype. The IEL layout allows for a larger viewing area with a centralized space for optimal viewing of the digital content, and the Powerwall is a straight line layout along a wall, with multi-user tracking abilities to allow for several viewers to receive customized views.

Another very interesting facility used in education is the FISHBOWL facility at Stanford. This facility was developed for ICT augmented project based learning where Fruchter (2006) focused on creating an environment that facilitated:

1. Project based learning by students in cross-disciplinary teams;
2. Mentoring of apprenticing with experienced professionals; and
3. Global virtual teaming.

The FISHBOWL facility is used in conjunction with an AEC Global Teamwork course. It is modeled after the medical school environment where operation procedures are often witnessed by students through glass walls. The facility is used to conduct main sessions facilitated by industry members using an interactive whiteboard, live video and audio feeds, and both physical and remote observers to watch and ask questions. The focus of this facility is not the display system, but the use of the display and tools to facilitate new means of interaction in a global teaming environment, and a different type of experience for the students by witnessing and participating in the activities. The overall findings from the use of the facility suggest that the interaction of the team members and the process are often more valuable in the long term than the short term outcomes of the information created in the session.

Several additional very interesting systems have been developed which focus on interaction with information through multiple display systems. The iRoom at Stanford utilizes three large interactive whiteboards with touch sensitive displays for users to directly interact and write on the projected digital image, with the capability of carrying information across the three displays (Fischer et al. 2002). The interactive elements are focused on allowing the users to more fluidly use the software through the infrastructure and hardware in the space. Another facility is the Interactive Collaboration Lab (ICL) at the University of New Brunswick. The facility includes the use of a wireless infrastructure which allows access to the systems for users on portable laptop computers and other devices to facilitate sharing of information and access to the internet for resources (Rankin et al. 2006).

These spaces demonstrate how the characteristics of the space impact the user interactions within the space. When the display system is the focal point of the space, the display quality and tools to improve the user's visualization experience are highlighted such as the SSVR facility which was purposely built for fully immersive experiences. When interaction is more essential, the tools shift to allow different types of interaction – such as the iRoom tools or the virtual infrastructure of the FISHBOWL.

AN INTERACTIVE WORKSPACE DESIGN PROCESS

The INVOLVE framework provides a means for defining the needs and determining the most valuable aspects for the effective use of an Interactive Workspace. The use of the framework is based around the iterative tasks, *create*, *integrate*, *examine*, and *focus*, defined within the context of AEC design and construction planning. These tasks serve to outline the purpose of collaborative team functions or group settings using digital models for the design and construction planning process. The goal in developing this taxonomy was the ability to align the collaborative objectives of the team with the virtual prototype uses which are best facilitated in an Interactive Workspace.

1. Inventory Digital Spaces

The pre-cursor step in developing a comprehensive strategy toward the development of productive interactive workspaces is to take an inventory of the existing spaces available to students and faculty for authoring, presenting and interacting with digital media. This can include instructional computing labs, digital media rooms, and other digitally enhanced work environments for students. Depending on the variety of available spaces and infrastructure, it is necessary to make sure the array of educational objectives and student needs for using these spaces is covered throughout the inventory of available resources. An inventory of the spaces should include the equipment available to students, the primary uses for the spaces, and the limitations of the space. An example of a Digital Spaces Inventory is shown in Table 1.

Table 1. Inventory of digital spaces for Penn State Architectural Engineering Program (partial)

Location	Description	Primary Use	Equipment	Capacity
107 Engr Unit B	Presentation Meeting Room	Presentations	1 Computer; 3 screen projection system; web camera	30 people
306 Engr Unit C	Immersive Construction (ICon) Lab	Interactive design space; 3 screen presentation space; Group interaction space	3 backlit screens; Console computer; 20 tablet PCs; Interactive Whiteboard; 4 modeling computers; video cameras	30 people
307 Engr Unit B	Intelligent Systems Lab	Interactive meeting space, Small presentation space	3 computers; 1 Interactive Whiteboard; 1 Projector	15 people
308 Sackett	Computer Training Lab	Computing instruction; Individual workspace	30 computers; 1 instructor computer with 2 projectors	30 people

2. Identify Tasks to be Performed by Students and Faculty

The task inventory should include all tasks that students perform throughout a course which rely upon or encourage the use of digital media and modeling. Consider how you would like students to: 1) author models (create), 2) compile large computationally intensive tasks such as rendering, lighting analysis, or energy modeling (integrate); 3) review and navigate their digital models (examine); and 4) present the models to their peers (examine/focus). An example of a task inventory for a collaborative design studio with teams of 6 students working on integrated design projects is shown in Table 2.

There are two important task dimensions to consider when developing the task list. The first dimension is focused on the type of interaction that the students have with the digital model. Tasks can be separated into two primary interaction types: Content creation and content review. Content creation typically requires focused interaction with modeling software. This interaction, primarily single user in nature, requires a space with precise control over the computational tools. An example of productive content creation spaces includes computing labs with multiple monitors for larger screen landscape. Spaces that are focused on content review may not allow for quite as easy modification of the design, but instead focus on the ability for the users to navigate and review the content.

A second dimension which is very important to consider when designing a digitally enhanced interactive workspace is the level of group versus individual design and design review tasks which will occur within each space, as well as the balance of additional spaces which support each task. Group tasks require different types of interaction with the digital content. It can be difficult to design a space, and encourage work processes which are supported by the space, for developing group designs. Frequently, when working in digital tools, one user is controlling the authoring of content while others are more passively involved with the design tasks. This single user interaction mode can limit the impact of the team participants. For this reason, it is particularly important to consider various modes of interaction from all team members when designing interactive workspaces for teams. This can include the development of personal computing clusters where multiple students can work together while

Table 2. Sample task inventory for BIM design studio (AE 597A)

Task Description	Type	Group / Individual	Primary Location	Configuration	Digital Tools	Requirement notes
Design concept generation	Create	Group	306 Engr Unit C (ICon Lab)	Small group	Tablet PCs; VNC Screen Sharing	Flexible space and tools; multiple forms of interaction, e.g., sketching
Design development	Create	Group	306 Engr Unit C (ICon Lab)	Small group	Tablet PCs; VNC Screen Sharing	Flexible space and tools; multiple forms of interaction, e.g., modeling or sketching
Engineering analysis / detailing	Integrate	Individual	307 Sackett	N/A (only one config)	Modeling Computers	Efficient computers to perform modeling and analysis tasks
Design Integration	Integrate	Group	306 Engr Unit C (ICon Lab)	N/A (only one config)	Modeling Computers	Efficient computers to compile modeling content (1 computer per group)
Design Review	Examine	Group	306 Engr Unit C (ICon Lab)	Immersive display	3 screen display	Large field of view, immersion for improved review
Presentation Development	Create	Group / Individual	306 Engr Unit C (ICon Lab)	Small group	Tablet PC	Flexible space and tools; multiple forms of interaction
Presentation	Examine / Focus	Group	306 Engr Unit C (ICon Lab)	Presentation	3 screen display	Efficient presentation environment

each has their own computer, using touch screens to allow for multiple students to interact with the device, or using multiple input devices to allow for easily passing control to team members to express their design concepts. An extension of the group interaction requirements could be the need to support remote collaboration.

Further decomposition of the team dimension is whether teams are collocated or virtual. Virtual collaboration requires another level of requirements to support verbal and video interactions in addition to any digital media manipulation which may be required. Note that the task inventory contained within Table 2 does not include provisions for virtual teaming since the design tasks occur within a collocated design studio.

The development of the collaborative iterative tasks, *create*, *integrate*, *examine*, and *focus*, represents a new taxonomy of team tasks defined within the context of AEC design and construction planning. The taxonomy was developed

from the iterative objectives and processes defined for integrated project delivery from the Integrated Building Process Model (reference Leicht (2009) for additional details regarding the taxonomy development). The goal in developing this taxonomy was to provide a means to align the collaborative objectives of the team with the digital content uses which are best facilitated in an Interactive Workspace. These tasks types serve as a taxonomy for collaborative team functions using virtual prototypes for the design and construction planning process.

3. Match Physical Spaces with the Task Focus

Once the tasks and spaces are identified, a matrix which illustrates the various tasks to be performed in each workspace can be used to identify appropriate component features within the INVOLVE framework.

Table 3. Comparing media synchronicity theory factors to level of synchronicity

	Media Synchronicity Theory Fundamental Factors				
	Rehearsability	**Immediacy of Feedback**	**Parallelism**	**Symbol Variety**	**Reprocessibility**
High Synchronicity	High levels	High	Low	Custom	Lower levels
Low Synchronicity	High levels	Low	High	Custom	Higher levels

To achieve this task, it can be beneficial to identify the level of synchronicity for each space. The level of synchronicity considers the five factors defined within the MST (see Table 3).

In general, tasks that involve creation and integration require higher levels of synchronicity and task that involve examining and focus. Therefore, by analyzing the types of tasks that will occur within a space, the level of synchronicity can be defined. This level of synchronicity can be added to the content in Table 1 for each work space (note that the content is shown as separate columns in Table 4 for ease of display).

For the remainder of the chapter, we will specifically focus on the more challenging spaces to design which are team focused interactive workspaces, supporting the collaborative content authoring and review scenarios. In particular, we will review the use of interactive workspaces for use in design courses which leverage BIM software applications to create and review modeling content for building designs.

The layout, furniture, types of system displays and comfort level can influence the function and value of the facility. The space of the ICL at the University of New Brunswick, for example, is designed to facilitate the breakout of sub-group interaction to allow for parallel discussions and interaction in more intimate settings while still providing the same technological resources. The facility is also believed to create a more informal and consensus oriented team environment to allow for more consistent collaborative decision making (Rankin et al., 2006). In contrast, the layout of the CAVE at Virginia Polytechnic Institute (Kim, 2005), the SSVR facility at Penn State (Whisker et al. 2003), and the virtual room at Helsinki University of Technology (Hiipaaka et al., 2001) are all focused on single user and small group applications due to the single user tracking and limited space within which one can benefit from the display. The layout of the VAE facility is designed for the training of a single user for defined task training and would not be suitable for large groups (Zhang et al., 2005). The spatial considerations and layout directly relate to the ability to support different tasks.

Table 4. Level of synchronicity and space attributes

Location	Description	Level of Synchronicity	Desired Space Attributes
107 Engr Unit B	Presentation Meeting Room	Low	Multiple screen display; video conferencing
306 Engr Unit C	Immersive Construction (ICon) Lab	Medium	Interactive whiteboard; immersive display; multiple input devices; tablet PCs
307 Engr Unit B	Intelligent Systems Lab	High	Interactive whiteboard; multiple input devices; tablet PCs
308 Sackett	Computer Training Lab	Low	Computers with dual monitors
307 Sackett	Computer Training Lab	Low	Computers with dual monitors

Table 5. Concepts for INVOLVE by level of synchronicity of the environment

Workspace Component	Low Synchronicity	Balanced/Flexible	High Synchronicity
Interaction	Single user focused use of display and software interaction	Potential to allow users to connect and interact from individual laptops	Multiple user interaction, range of software to use
Network	Slower connections are ok, need to have local copies of models	Moderate speed/bandwidth, can connect to remote servers, remote video/sharing possible	High speed and designated lines for conferencing, or designated teleconferencing lines, model servers for multiple uses
Virtual Prototyping	Single focused use of model, one or a few views to support that use	Ability to change from single focused use to multiple uses/views	Multiple models/software uses and or views occurring and displayed to team, range of tools on different displays
Organization	Single focused discussion	Dependent on task	Single task, but sub-groups and breakout discussions are necessary and infrastructure will need to support those discussions
Layout / Architecture	Around a table/central display	Can switch between focused display and breakout	Flexible for breakout, shifting focus or display, furniture and floor plan are easily adjustable
Visual Display	Central display system, wider field of view	Several screens, but one central display	Multiple displays, spread out in room
Existential Collaboration	Optimizing tasks (mainly Disjunctive or Discretionary)	Flexible use – both Maximizing and Optimizing tasks	Maximizing tasks (mainly Additive or Conjunctive)

In addition to the spatial considerations, the computers, projectors, and other tools in the space create heat and light which need to be planned to ensure the space's HVAC and lighting account for these loads and the use of the space. The layout and comfort considerations need to be planned so they complement the facility's purpose rather than distracting the users or negatively impacting the value of the facility. While this may seem trivial and obvious, we have encountered multiple spaces that were not used to their potential due to physical comfort considerations.

4. Design the Workspace to Support the Task Performance

Once the communication environments and task considerations are planned, the INVOLVE framework can be used to identify the Interactive Workspace design considerations. The strategy identified in the previous steps help to indicate the approach to the planning of the space for a

particular task as a substantial investment or a secondary use of the space. The breakdown of components in Table 5 shows by each component the general strategy. Considering that strategy within the context of each task, the means of meeting each component goal can be considered and the aggregate plans for the component for all of the tasks can be used to identify the focus and range of infrastructure.

Low Synchronicity Interactive Workspace Design

If the method identifies the need for lower synchronicity in the environment then the tasks identified will be mainly examination and focus tasks, for example the virtual prototype use may be automated clash detection of the system geometries. The interaction needed with the model may include navigation of model element clashes, and focused discussion by the team on one issue at a time. To achieve these tasks most effectively, a single application should be used to perform the task, with input from multiple team members. There is likely also benefit from the ability to sketch on the images to show design changes to solve the problems. The network considerations are simply to have the means to get the files necessary for the review to the local system so they can be viewed in the space. The organization of the team for this task requires technical problem solving capabilities associated with both the design and assembly of the systems. The interpersonal skills will require a balance of creative problem solving with interpersonal skills and team management to allow the reaching of compromised solutions. The layout would benefit from a central display which is easy to see and with reasonably comfortable seating, along with a meeting table or tables to allow team members to take notes or directly model some of the necessary modifications. The visual display will need to have a screen large enough for the full group to be able to see, and at a resolution which will not strain their eyes over an extended period. There may be some benefit from a second screen to show additional information about the clash or to be able to display a secondary view of the issue. Bringing these traits together should help to focus this type of review task and optimizing outcomes.

Flexible or Balanced Interactive Workspace Design

If the planned use of the Interactive Workspace is along the lines of the design-build project, teams may be co-located for the duration of the project then the team may use the facility for a more balanced list of tasks. Early in the design process the team may need to perform more maximizing tasks to explore the design concepts while later on they may perform focused reviews like the use of automated clash detection. To develop a space with a flexible and balanced approach, they might develop an infrastructure more in line with the systems in the ICon Lab which is discussed

in detail later in this chapter. They could have several screens aligned in a display which could be used as a single display, or split into separate images. The interaction could then be aligned as one for the single display, or split to different users for the use of multiple images. When brainstorming ideas in early design they could use the separate displays to show different options, then later when performing design reviews they could use the central display or show several different views as needed. The organization of the team will need to be planned based on the task being performed. The layout of the space should allow for individual or small group work to be performed, but also provide for the space to be used for a central discussion or audience seating for a review. The use of the virtual prototype and the necessary interaction will need to be planned with the task being performed.

High Synchronicity Interactive Workspace Design

If the planned use of the Interactive Workspace develops to focus more on maximizing tasks, such as conceptual design charrettes and team brainstorming activities, the design will need to center more on high synchronicity needs. The interaction should focus on the ability to shift between different users and different means of input as ideas are quickly shared and explained. Methods to allow team members to easily connect their computers to the system for displaying their desktops may be valuable to take advantage of different software and show different visual representations or other forms of information.

With the charrette concept, there will likely be parallel conversations and the need to move furniture and shift focus between different displays around the space. The displays will need to be spread to different areas, but less likely to need a large central display. It may also be acceptable to be lower resolution or smaller sizes. The teams will need to have workspaces or table tops, but the use of interactive whiteboards and tablet PC's would be valuable to allow for different users and different locations to be able to sketch or write on the same content.

A CASE STUDY IN INTERACTIVE WORKSPACES: THE ICON LAB

A more detailed review of the ICon Lab facility illustrates the design of an interactive workspace for students focused on multiple design tasks. The ICon Lab was initially built in 2001 (termed the Immersive Environments Lab at the time) through a partnership of the Information Technology Services, School of Architecture and Landscape Architecture, and Department of Architectural Engineering at Penn State. This collaborative development initiative was originally focused on allowing students to immerse themselves in a digital model at full scale, but was later expanded to service many different needs of the students. The facility currently focuses on servicing multiple functions. These can be summarized as design conceptualization; design review; and presentation. Whenever a space is used for multiple purposes, there will be some level of compromise.

When considering the categories of the IN-VOLVE Framework, the following system attributes can be defined:

I   *Interaction:* There are several primary digital devices which allow for increased levels of interaction. These include use of 20 Tablet PC's, the interactive whiteboard, and the ability to use a wireless mouse and keyboard with the main computing console. In addition, a wireless game controller and joystick are available for navigating models.

N   *Network:* All computers in the ICon Lab are connected to a center network. This allows for the easy transfer of content between the multiple machines. In addition, there are several network devices to specifically address

virtual collaboration activities that occur within the space. These include three cameras for video conferencing, a microphone system for web conferencing, a telephone for conference calls, and a dedicated wireless network to ensure a fast network connection for the tablet pcs.

V   *Virtual Prototypes:* The virtual prototypes and digital content developed for use in the ICon Lab need to be planned for the specific task to be performed. For schematic design, models can be less detailed, while for more detailed examination tasks such as 3D design coordination, the models need to be accurate and detailed. There are also many different types of digital content displayed including sketches, photos, 3D models, 4D models, and other content.

O   *Organization:* The organization of the teams varies with the project or task. The space has been used for multi-disciplinary design charettes, construction team 4D schedule reviews with a general contractor and subcontractors, site logistics activity amongst a team of colleagues to name a few. The key is to make sure the stakeholders in the task are involved and able to participate based on the needs of the task.

L   *Layout:* The layout of the space needs to reflect the size of the group using the space, and the needs of the team to be able to use different media in conjunction with the tasks performed. With the display layout of the ICon Lab small tables are used to create flexibility in the use and layout of the space. The space can be arranged in rows to match a presentation, formed into a central table for a group meeting with views of the different screens, or broken into small group arrangements.

V   *Visualization and Display:* There are multiple display capabilities in the ICon Lab. The primary group displays include a large format, three screen, rear projected display.

Each screen has two projectors which allow for passive stereoscopic visualization. The screens are each six feet tall and eight feet wide. In addition to the three large screens, there is also an interactive whiteboard display. Any computer in the ICon Lab can project to any of the four displays (three large screens or the interactive whiteboard) through the use of VNC for interactive screen sharing. This is controlled by a video switch. This provides a very flexible media environment which can support the display of a large amount of information and quickly switch between various display sources.

E   *Existential Collaboration:* Focuses on teamwork skills for projects performed within the ICon Lab environment.

These elements are demonstrated in a modified version of the model of the ICon Lab shown in Figure 4.

LESSONS LEARNED

Throughout the implementation of several interactive workspace designs, we have learned a number of lessons regarding the design of the spaces. Several important lessons follow:

1. It is important to develop flexibility in the available spaces, and allow them to evolve with the various uses that are identified by the users. For example, in the very early use of the Immersive Construction (ICon) Lab at Penn State, we initially had two screens and we thought (naively) that students would always show their models on both screens to maximize the size and scale of the display. But some students started to actually place alternative physical content on the one screen (literally by taping drawings and sketches to the screen) while using the other screen to show model content. This was a good indicator of an emergent use of the space that we then started to support through the

Figure 4. Identification of the INVOLVE components of the Immersive Construction Lab at Penn State.

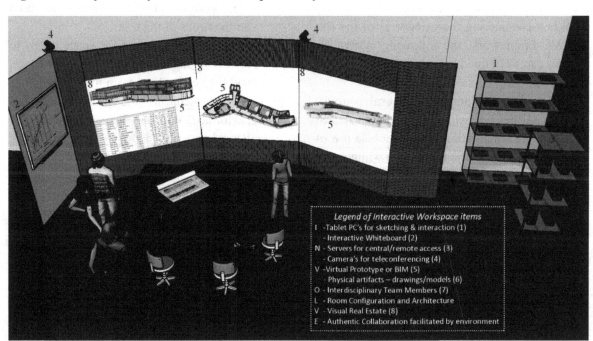

creation of multimedia templates that made it easy for students to create integrative presentations that leverage the multiple screens (reference Balakrishnan 2004). We soon realized that this focused task was only one of many tasks that students need to perform in a design or analysis course, therefore we augmented the workspace design with the capability for each student to use tablet PCs or an interactive whiteboard for collaboration and presentations. And it then became apparent that the need for additional spaces was rising as the demand for the students to use the ICon Lab for an array of activities led to scheduling challenges.

2. People react to the available methods for sharing their ideas, and some people are more disposed to visually expressing these ideas. When group activities are created, it is important that students can share their thoughts. One of the outcomes we discovered in a study of teams performing site logistics brainstorming was that giving all team members a means to display their ideas led to more diverse conversations. In a comparative study, teams were split with half of the teams using an interactive whiteboard for brainstorming site plans while the other half used individual tablet PCs, with the tablets displayed on the different screens of the large display. It was discovered that when the teams used the interactive whiteboard, the students who led the discussions also did most of the sketching. Conversely, when each team member had a tablet PC, the students who were quieter were more likely to be drawn into the discussion based on some element they sketched using the display.

3. Consider the physical attributes of the spaces. First, if you expect people to spend time within the spaces, they must be comfortable. There are sometimes compromises that may need to occur in this area. For example, people enjoy spending time in spaces with natural daylight, yet daylighting is not always practical in projection based environments which may need low lighting levels or with computer screens which may have glare issues if the space is not well designed. Proximity to the workspace is also important. Frequently, students will select a sub-par work environment which is physically close to them instead of traveling a distance to a more appropriate workspace. Also, the thermal comfort of spaces with intensive computing hardware also needs to be considered. If students are not comfortable working in the space they will find another space that allows them to be both comfortable and productive.

4. There are obvious limitations to workspace scheduling within an academic environment which can limit the opportunity to optimize space utilization based on student tasks. For example, some academic settings schedule a class in one space even though it may be best to rotate workspaces based on the types of tasks being performed. It can be benefial when possible to identify different spaces for the design creation tasks and the design presentation tasks, or have an interactive workspace that can be adequately reconfigured to support the needs of the different tasks. Finding a public means of sharing the calendar and allowing students to schedule the use of the space is an important management technique that should be explicitly planned and controlled.

5. Users must sometimes be taught how to work in a new environment and it may take some time for them to feel comfortable with the available tools. Many people will not leverage the advantages from a digitally mediated environment unless they have instruction, and sometime practice (forced or unforced) to get through the initial challenges that they may feel in a new environment or working with new tools. A very simple example is the

use of digital whiteboards. These boards can be very productive for brainstorming and content generation, yet we have seen people who do not get past the slightly awkward feeling that people frequently have when initially using the whiteboard. Once you get accustomed to the new media, it can then become very familiar and comfortable, but not without some familiarity and instruction, e.g., how to align the projector, etc. Creating activities which bring students into these spaces and make them comfortable with the infrastructure will help grow the use of the space. After we introducing an ICon Lab centered activity into a third year class for students at Penn State many of those students more commonly used the lab for meetings and as a workspace in the following two years of their degree. As workspaces become more complex, and aim to support divergent tasks, the level of training and education will need to increase.

FUTURE RESEARCH DIRECTIONS

There are many potential areas for future investigation into the effective design of environments for performing design, design review, and planning tasks, both in industry and educational settings. The continued development of more innovative display and input devices will inspire new systems which can more naturally integrate with the work tasks. For example, the recent release of affordable, large format touch screens; the development of tracking input devices such as the Nintendo Wii controllers and the new Kinectics by Microsoft; the development of mobile computing devices such as tablet PCs, iPads and iPhones; and the development of affordable 3D monitor and TV technologies. While the design of many of these systems is not entirely unique relative to previous high-end virtual reality or computer systems, the large scale commercialization of these devices make it easier and more affordable to develop innovative interactive workspace designs. It will become important to identify the technologies which can add value to the design and design review processes, without distracting the users.

Augmented Reality (AR) is one additional area that will provide potential future educational benefits. AR can be used to develop innovative methods for interacting with models through the use of additional input devices. Eventually, AR may also allow for the extension of the workspace into other environments.

CONCLUSION

Students will learn better with increased engagement in the media that they are using. Therefore, as we move to more digital media, we need to continue to focus on methods to engage students with the media.

As we continue to move toward the greater integration of digital modeling throughout our educational experience, it is critical that we place more emphasis on the design of interactive workspaces which support the authoring and interaction with the digital content. This chapter has outlined a procedure to design interactive workspaces which will support the educational tasks that will be performed within the space. Frequently, you can encounter tradeoffs between sole purpose spaces and more flexible workspaces.

This chapter has presented a structure process for identifying valuable features to include in interactive workspaces in education environments. The INVOLVE framework also provides a list of attributes to consider when designing a workspace. By considering these factors, and maintaining flexibility to allow the workspace to adapt, a more productive work environment for students and faculty can be achieved.

ACKNOWLEDGMENT

The authors thank the many contributors to this research initiative including the ITS Visualization Group, colleagues in the Department of Architecture, and collaborators in the Computer Integrated Construction Research Program at Penn State. We owe special thanks to George Otto, Loukas Kalisperis, Katsu Muramoto, and Jamie Heilman for their efforts with the design process for the IEL and ICon Lab.

REFERENCES

Balakrishnan, B. (2004). *Digital media & virtual reality: A multi-modal approach for architectural design representation*. MA Thesis, The Pennsylvania State University, University Park, PA, May.

Brennan, S. E., & Lockridge, C. B. (2006). Computer-mediated communication: A cognitive science approach. In Brown, K. (Ed.), *ELL2, Encyclopedia of language and linguistics* (2nd ed., pp. 775–780). Oxford, UK: Elsevier Ltd.

Chidambaram, L., & Jones, B. (1993). Impact of communication medium and computer support on group perceptions and performance: a comparison of face-to-face and dispersed meetings. *Management Information Systems Quarterly, 17*(4), 465–491. doi:10.2307/249588

DeLuca, D., & Valacich, J. S. (2006). Virtual teams in and out of synchronicity. *Information Technology & People, 19*(4), 323–344. doi:10.1108/09593840610718027

Dennis, A. R., & Valacich, J. S. (1999). Rethinking media richness: towards a theory of media synchronicity. *Proceedings of the 32nd Hawaii International Conference of System Sciences*.

Fischer, M., Stone, M., Liston, K., Kunz, J., & Singhal, V. (2002). Multi-stakeholder collaboration: The CIFE iRoom. *Proceedings of the CIB W78 Conference 2002: Distributing Knowledge in Building, 6*(13).

Fruchter, R. (2006). The FISHBOWL: Degrees of engagement in global teamwork. *Proceedings of EG-ICE, 2006*, 241–257.

Hiipakka, J., Ilmonen, T., Lokki, T., Grohn, M., & Savioja, L. (2001). Implementation issues of 3D audio in a virtual room. *Proceedings of SPIE*, vol. 4297.

Julesz, B. (1971). *Foundations of Cyclopean perception*. Chicago, IL: The University of Chicago Press.

Kim, J. S. (2005). *Tangible user interface for CAVE based on augmented reality technique*. MS Thesis, Virginia Polytechnic Institute, Blacksburg, VA.

Leicht, R. M. (2009). *A framework for planning effective collaboration using interactive workspaces*. Ph.D. Thesis, Department of Architectural Engineering, The Pennsylvania State University, University Park, PA, USA.

Otto, G., Messner, J., & Kalisperis, L. (2005). Expanding the boundaries of virtual reality for building design and construction. *Proceedings of the ASCE Computing in Civil Engineering Conference*, Cancun, Mexico.

Rankin, J., Issa, M., & Christian, A. J. (2006). Exploring the principles of interactive collaborative workspaces. *1st International Construction Specialty Conference*, Calgary, Alberta, Canada, May 23-26.

Rubens, P. (2003, December 15). Fax - The technology that refuses to die. *BBC News World Edition*. Retrieved from http://news.bbc.co.uk/1/hi/magazine/3320515.stm

Santos, P., Stork, A., Gierlinger, T., Pagani, A., Araujo, B., & Jota, R. … McIntyre, D. (2007). IMPROVE: Collaborative design review in mobile mixed reality. *Proceedings of Human Computer Interaction International,* (pp. 543–53).

Steiner, I. D. (1972). *Group process and productivity.* New York, NY: Academic Press, Inc.

Whisker, V. E., Baratta, A. J., Yerrapathruni, S., Messner, J. I., Shaw, T. S., & Warren, M. E. … Johnson, F. T. (2003). *Using immersive virtual environments to develop and visualize construction schedules for advanced nuclear power plants.* 2003 International Congress on Advances in Nuclear Power Plants (ICAPP), Córdoba, Spain.

Zhang, Y., Sotudeh, R., & Fernando, T. (2005). The use of visual and auditory feedback for assembly task performance in a virtual environment. *Proceedings of the Twenty-First Spring Conference on Computer Graphics (SCCG'05),* (pp. 59–66).

KEY TERMS AND DEFINITIONS

Building Information Model (BIM): A product or intelligent digital representation of data about a capital facility.

Convergence: The underlying communication process which relates to the development of a shared understanding between the people involved in the communication.

Conveyance: The underlying communication process focused on providing information for deliberation among the people involved in the communication.

Interactive Workspace: A team workspace that is augmented with computational devices to support interaction, sometimes defined as a subdomain of ubiquitous computing.

Media Synchronicity Theory: A theory of communication which focuses on the capability for media to support synchronicity (working together at the same time with a common focus).

Virtual Environment: An input environment that is partially or completely computer based.

Chapter 15
Interactive Architecture:
Spaces that Sense, Think, and Respond to Change

Taysheng Jeng
National Cheng Kung University, Taiwan

ABSTRACT

This chapter provides an overview of interactive architecture relating to the design and implementation of ubiquitous computing technologies. The kernel of interactive architecture is augmenting spaces that can sense, think, and respond to change. A theoretical framework is provided for contextualization of interactive architecture. A model of interaction is proposed to identify a set of processes, functionality and principles that guide the design of interactive architecture. Key capabilities are identified with respect to interactive architecture: sensitivity, smartness, and responsiveness. Examples of some research projects are provided to demonstrate the capabilities. Methods and techniques for developing such capabilities are described according to the model of interaction. Applications for using ubiquitous computing technologies in interactive architecture are reviewed.

INTRODUCTION

Ubiquitous computing is a paradigm shift whereby computers can be pervasively embedded into the artifacts, spaces, and environments of everyday life. This paradigm shift occurred with the introduction of a new way of off-desktop human-computer interaction. Computing today is moving beyond the assistance of design environments to the augmentation of our living environment.

DOI: 10.4018/978-1-61350-180-1.ch015

Advances in ubiquitous computing technologies have opened up new opportunities for changing our living environment in a number of ways. These technological methods include:

- Integrating digital world and physical world
- Embedding computers in a huge range of materials and artifacts
- Making objects and spaces more responsive, sensitive, and smarter

- Proactively monitoring human activity and our environment
- Pervasively providing information and services when and where desired
- Multimodal interaction with computers in an intuitive manner (such as gesture and speech)

Each of these changes has its own technical difficulties and specialized areas of research in Human-Computer Interaction (HCI). HCI is a term used to refer to the designing of interactions between people and computers. In the late 1970s, the main concern of HCI was *usability*, involving design and evaluation methods to ensure that technologies are easy to use. During the 1990s, the concerns of HCI started to shift towards communication between people enabled by computers. More recently, HCI has begun to develop techniques for inventing products, spaces, and services that are beyond *usability* to *usefulness*. Designers became heavily involved in HCI. The notion of *interaction design* came to the design practice. During the 1990s, Mark Weiser introduced the area of *ubiquitous computing* and put forth a vision of augmented environments where information and services are provided when and where desired (Weiser, 1991). The notion of ubiquitous computing was elaborated with respect to HCI (Abowd and Mynatt 2000). The philosophical base of human-computer interaction was addressed by examining the concept of embodied interaction- an approach to interacting with software systems that emphasizes engaged practice rather than disembodied rationality (Dourish, 2004). It has been argued that the ubiquitous computing technology does not obviate the human need for place (McCullough, 2005). A theory of place for interaction design called "digital ground" offers an account of the intersections of architecture and interaction design.

Taking a broader view, we need to re-think some fundamental assumptions about the relationship among humans, computers, and architecture.

Digital technologies will continue to proliferate, enabling ever more powerful and networked interactive devices to change the way we interact with our built environment. While computers can be pervasively embedded in built environments, these technologies are likely to change the way in which how we live and how buildings perform. Today's conventional building systems have served us well until now, but they will have to evolve toward a different thinking of architecture.

What may appear to be shifts in emphasis actually represent the convergence on an emerging computer-aided architectural design research area, which is *interactive architecture*- spaces that can sense, think, and respond to change. This chapter introduces three types of interactive architecture with emphasis on the design of interaction space, network space, and kinetic space. A theoretical framework is described for the development of a modular interactive system that can be widely used in smart spaces of the future. Examples of some research projects are provided to illustrate the concept. The chapter closes with a discussion of research issues, challenges, and future research directions.

Interactive Architecture

The term *interactive architecture* is concerned with interactive interfaces between humans and computers. A building is an enclosure that defines the boundaries of a space to support varied activities. Enclosures such as walls, floor, and ceilings can be considered as interactive interfaces. Other terms sometimes used for aspects of intelligent and interactive environments include 'responsive architecture', 'intelligent buildings', and 'smart home'. These aspects define architecture as a dynamic shape-shifting building system that is susceptible to alter its shape and physical properties in response to environmental conditions and user activities (Sterk, 2005) (Fox, 2009). All mean more or less the same objective: *developing an interactive system by extending human capabili-*

ties, enhancing user activities, and augmenting building performance for smart and sustainable living.

Why do we need interactive architecture? The driving force behind interactive architecture is new computing technologies and changing patterns of human interaction with the built environment. Traditionally, architecture is considered as a shelter for living. Buildings are designed by need. There is a constant demand for flexible and adaptable architecture in response to urban and social change. Sustainability has amplified the demand for novel architectural solutions. So far, most buildings are static and single-function designs. There is no way to augment buildings that are capable of response to change, reconfiguration, transformation, and being aware of what is going on around.

How do we develop interactive architectural systems? Like living organisms, buildings have artificial skins. The outer skin of a building is an exterior shell that is designed for weather-proof and security. Aesthetics and building performance are other implications for design of the outer skin (e.g. façade). The inner skin of a building is an enclosure that defines the boundary of a space for supporting varied activities, such as walls, floor, and ceilings. The needed mechanism is not just new features in interactive architecture but require a shift in the way we think about new capabilities of buildings: *sensitive, smart,* and *responsive.*

1. Interactive architecture is *sensitive.* A building envelope might be sensitive to environmental change. For example, a sensing-augmented window can alternately open or close depending on the conditions of outside temperature and sunlight. The sun-shading devices transform themselves to get maximum sunshades. In addition, a wall partition might be sensitive to user activities to create adaptable spatial configurations. The wall surface might be augmented by sensors and motors to enhance human-computer interaction. A common example

is to augment physical space with *sensing* capability, moving from explicit input (e.g. mouse and keyboards) to implicit input (e.g. speech and gesture).

2. Interactive architecture is *smart.* Interactivity is more than the use of an interface. Given the inevitable growth in the range of use of sensors and actuators in spaces, information on users' activities and a building's long-term energy, and environmental performance might be monitored and stored in databases in social and physical context. Context databases coupled with occupancy data acquisition provide a means for making home automation decisions. For example, a window is smart in such a way that it "knows" when and where to open for fresh air unobtrusively. Furthermore, by means of smart operational optimization, all windows communicate and coordinate each other to improve natural ventilation in buildings. The space can learn how to predict human behavior in social and physical context.

3. Interactive architecture is *responsive.* Spaces might transform themselves to adapt to changing conditions. What actions could responsive environments proactively respond? First, responsive environments are climate-responsive in such a way that the internal and external forms are transformable in response to change. Secondly, responsive environments are human-responsive by changing its shape and spatial properties in order to mediate human needs. A fundamental property of such responsive environments is kinetic design. Building envelopes, for example, might change their shape to cut heating costs and reconfigure themselves to improve ventilation.

Sensitivity, smartness, and *responsiveness* are the three major capabilities for interactive architecture to support smart and sustainable living. These three capabilities introduce new challenges for research into exploring design methods and techniques for interactive architecture. One challenge is to explore the dynamics of architectural space by re-thinking architecture beyond conventional static and single-function spatial design. Adaptive response to change should be considered in the preliminary design process prior to the stage of construction and use. The other challenge is to accommodate a new way of manifesting human-computer interaction in architectural design systems. Given the inevitable growth of the range of use of sensors and actuators used in buildings, architecture can be considered as an interaction interface between humans and computers. When integrating computational devices, software, and information into the design of physical space, it demands a new way of thinking about how spaces sense, move, and reconfigure themselves in response to changing needs.

Scenario

Our research group in the Interactive Architecture Laboratory at National Cheng Kung University (NCKU) has built full-scale prototypes of a smart home, an interactive workspace, and kinetic robots integrated with physical space (Jeng, et.al., 2008). The smart home project developed at NCKU creates a sensor-networked space and a variety of computer-embedded everyday products for future living. It has successfully integrated ubiquitous computing technologies, interactive systems, and robots together. Besides, the NCKU smart home has also established a highly interactive lifestyle design platform to collect intelligence by means of Web 2.0 technology. After feasibility tests, the NCKU smart home is now open weekly to attract visitors, and all of the demonstrations are constantly modified based on visitors' feedbacks. The details of the examples are presented in the next section.

As a motivating example, we consider a scenario in a smart space. There will be a variety of interactions and building performance. For the purposes of illustration, we will focus on a responsive interaction relating to dynamic spatial configuration and transformation.

1. In the early morning, a magic mirror in the dressing room shows a daily schedule and weather conditions in real-time.
2. After detecting weather conditions, a window automatically opens for ventilation efficiency.
3. A set of kinetic walls moves together to set up a customized spatial configuration for a teleconference.
4. As soon as the meeting starts, the partition walls' material effect changes from transparent to opaque for privacy.
5. At the meeting, Hannah uses speech and gestures to remotely control her presentation.
6. An augmented-reality greenhouse, after sensing a person's presence, creates an artificial artistic ambience where virtual butterflies fly through physical trees to offer mediation.

This scenario is clearly feasible today for smart and sustainable living. We can expect the required interactive spatial systems and functionality to include climate-responsive windows, human-responsive doors, kinetic walls, robotic moving lights, and an augmented-reality media space with a sensor network. Since it takes time for technologies to reach maturity, there have not yet been sufficient resources to develop the corresponding mechanisms for new kinds of interactive architecture. In this paper, we attempt to explore the underlying theoretical framework required to achieve the desired results. Methods and techniques for developing such capabilities are described, and prototype implementation in support of interactive architecture is reviewed.

Theoretical Framework

There are three lines of approaches to interactive architecture: *human-computer interaction, artificial intelligence,* and *robotics and automation.* Human-computer interaction is primarily concerned with designing more easy-to-use computer interfaces. Interface design is the major focus of this approach. In the past few years, human-computer interaction technologies have changed the way in which people interact with computers from graphical user interfaces to tangible user interfaces using multi-touch, speech, or gesturing. Computers are likely to be embedded in furniture, doors, rooms, cars, and clothing. Sensor networks enable an "Internet of Things" (e.g. products, spaces, and services). Everyday things are embedded with computation, and are able to sense and react to the ways they are manipulated in space. The boundary between computers and the everyday world is shifting. The criterion is shifting from usability, efficiency, and effectiveness to human, cultural, and social values. The design and evaluation of interactive systems that enable human values to be achieved has become important.

Another line of approach is *artificial intelligence.* To develop an intelligent environment, a semantic network of commonsense knowledge is useful in capturing human experience (Minsky, 2000). It has been argued that the complexity of human experience can be resolved by modeling interaction in a formalized logical framework through the representation (e.g. predicate logics) of commonsense knowledge about everyday life (Lieberman et.al, 2004). A smart home, for example, enables an intelligent system to manage and control heat, window coverings, lighting, security cameras, as well as tract electricity, gas and water consumption in real-time. Most intelligent systems rely on a commonsense database to control and monitor a wide variety of home appliances. The control of home entertainment systems (e.g. home theatre) is another example.

The criteria of intelligent spaces or smart homes are to support automatic environmental control, make life more entertaining, and more recently, reduce energy consumption for sustainable living.

The third line of approach is *robotics and automation.* So far, there are only a few model of robotics being applied to household chores. Examples are domestic robots for indoor cleaning and lawn mowing. More research work on social robots has been developed for home entertainment, children education, and elder people's health management. Our interest is in the development of kinetic systems in building applications. An attempt is to integrate embedded sensors and actuators with building components as a means to enhance building performance for sustainability. The criterion is to create a building that can physically re-configure itself to adapt to changing needs. Interactive architecture must respond to change that can be environmental conditions, climate change, and varied user activities within physical spaces.

A theoretical framework of interactive architecture is depicted in Figure 1. The design space of interactive architecture can be categorized in three dimensions: *spaces that sense, spaces that think,* and *spaces that respond to change.* In the first dimension, it takes a human-computer interaction approach to designing user interfaces and sensor networks. The sensing technology is moving computational devices into everyday objects, augmenting user interfaces with sensing and computational capabilities. A sensor network is overlaid onto physical spaces, augmenting them with communication, networking, and remote control capabilities. In the second dimension, it takes an artificial intelligence approach to designing smart systems for home automation. A semantic network is developed to capture human experience and predict user activities. In the third dimension, it takes a robotics and automation approach to kinetic design. The design of kinetic space is moving small robots and devices into building envelopes and structures, augmenting

Figure 1. A theoretical framework of interactive architecture

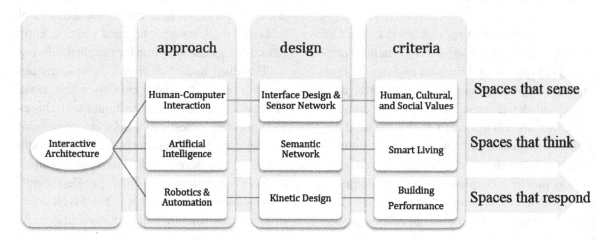

them with interactive capabilities that respond to changes and activities within the spaces.

Based on the theoretical framework of interactive architecture, a question quickly arises: can we integrate these approaches in the implementation of interactive architecture? One answer might be simply integrating human-computer interaction, artificial intelligence, robotics and automation approaches to designing a home of the future. Of course, there is a deeper problem. The needed mechanisms are not just new features but require a shift in the way we think about interaction between humans, computers, and space: a shift to a new model of interaction.

A MODEL OF INTERACTION

What is it hard to design an interactive architecture? Below, some salient characteristics of most interaction design processes are reviewed in a manner of supporting process modeling. Firstly, the computer must vanish into the background and diffuse into everyday objects and settings. For example, a smart home may contain hundreds of sensors, actuators, and computational devices, enabling homeowners to control heat, window coverings, and lighting in real-time. Sensing-based

technologies must be unobtrusive. Sensors must be embedded in everyday objects and settings of home environments in such a way that homeowners are not aware of their presence. Secondly, interactive systems must become perceptually aware, and provide services that are proactively based on a comprehensive understanding of human needs. For example, gesture-based interaction, for example, requires the system to capture the meaning of human gestures in a physical and social context. The computer needs to recognize, understand, adapt to and learn from human interests, activities, goals and intentions. Thirdly, interactive systems must take on physical forms to support embodied interaction. Users perceive the affordance of everyday objects and engage in the interactive system to get work done. By means of embodied interaction, the coupling of action and perception is essential for creating a new user experience. If the motion of interactive systems is far behind the movement of the user's gesture or is mismatched with what the user expects, the effectiveness of the user experience is greatly decreased. Finally, interactive systems must fit into the human environment, rather than forcing humans to enter the computational loop. It is argued that interactive architecture should put computers in the human interaction loop, as

Figure 2. Model of interaction

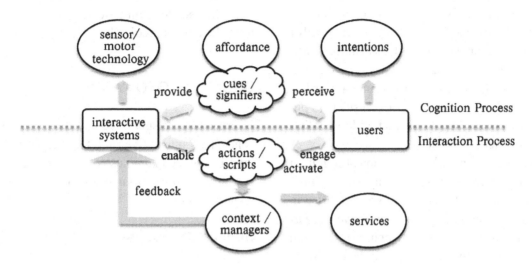

opposed to humans in the computational tool. In another words, we should create environments, which make us smart, not the other way around (Intille, 2006).

In order to build an interactive architecture, a designer needs to know about the users, the process of interaction, and the details of the interactive technologies. Two obvious elements are needed for interaction design: *users* and *interactive systems*. A user is a person who takes an action to reach an intended goal. A set of actions can be programed by a script. In some home automation examples, a user can be augmented by a software agent who follows the script to automate a process. An interactive system refers to an user interface or a place in which interaction between users and the machines occurs. An interactive system can be tangible (e.g. products, spaces) or intangible (e.g. internet services). An interactive system can be simply a computer-augmented interface that accepts input from human users and responds to change. A complex interactive system can be intelligent buildings that can adapt to environmental changes and proactively respond to human needs. A model of interaction is developed for understand-

ing the relations between users and interactive systems, as depicted in Figure 2.

Interaction design can be considered as an exploration process both in the *interaction* space and in the *cognition* space. The interaction space is composed of three elements: actions/scripts, context/managers, and services. When a user engages an interactive system, the system may enable a script for a course of action. An explicit layer is a context manager, observing and translating low-level sensor data to high-level contexts that are relevant to the interaction process (e.g. coordinated activities, integrated environmental and climate conditions). This manager activates information services, while sending signals as feedback to other interactive systems, some on separate rooms, some in different places. Then the interaction process iterates.

The interaction process is not an automated process. Rather, it requires human users to participate in the iteration process. Although a favorite subject of computer technology researchers, however, the goal of interactive architecture seems always to lie well off in the future. Researchers have yet to solve a fundamental problem of *the feedback loop* when interacting with our built environment. The feedback loop for users is important in interaction design. An interactive system must communicate with itself while checking with either an internal or external environment. We can think of the feedback that informs the system constantly performing a task and adjusting the performance towards a meaningful goal. A growing consensus is to put computers in the human interaction loop, rather than the other way around.

This suggests a further dimension of cognition process apart from the interaction process. Three distinct conceptual elements can be identified in the *cognitive* process: *affordances, cues (signifiers),* and *intentions.* It is recognized in design psychology that the perceived affordance defines the possibilities for action in a specific environment. Everyday objects offer *affordances* for possible actions. The perception of the environment inevitably leads to some course of action. Examples are buttons for pushing and handles for pulling. An interactive system makes use of affordances that provide cues, allowing users to act on them, and these cues are spatial signifiers. An architectural example of signifiers is the trails made by people's footsteps across the fields on campus. Here we are interested in designing signifiers to interpret situations for fluid interaction in everyday life. When perceived, signifiers allow users to interpret the situation meaningfully and these are called physical and social signifiers (Norman, 2010).

Let us take the above-mentioned scenario as an example. How can the interactive system guess the user's intention (e.g. meeting)? Designers must install environmental sensors (e.g. cameras, microphones, floor pressure sensors, etc.) in the physical space. Then the computer-augmented space provides physically perceivable cues (e.g. LED floor mat), indicating the possibility of action (e.g. step onto the floor mat). When the user enters the room, the system senses her/his presence. Signifiers are physically perceivable evidence that enable a person to track previous behavior in the room (e.g. previous meeting notes

on a virtual white board). In response to the signifiers, the user determines to have a meeting with her colleague immediately.

DESIGN PROTOTYPES

In order to give substance and demonstrate the concept of interactive architecture, we briefly introduce three examples with respect to *spaces that sense, spaces that think,* and *spaces that respond to change.*

Spaces that Sense

In order to implement spaces that sense, smart floor is chosen to be the first component of interactive architecture for physical prototyping. The aim of smart floor is to identify a user's presence and provide location-aware information when a person walks into a room or a place. Before creating a smart floor, we must analyze a variety of user activities with respect to smart floor in physical and social context, including walking, standing, sitting, watching, and discussion. Based on the analysis of user activities, location sensors can be embedded in a room or a place to detect human presence. Examples of location sensors are capacitance, optical, or magnetic sensors coupled with radio frequency devices. Other commonly used sensing technologies are computer vision and recognition that analyze behavior patterns and interpret the signals of human activities. In our experiments, a matrix of capacitance sensors was installed underlying the floor in a home of the future. When people stepped on the smart floor, a matrix of capacitance sensors underlying the smart floor could trigger the wall-sized display of audio-video projectors in the interaction space.

A problem arises in designing the smart floor. How does the user know the effect of interaction before engaging in the interaction process? According to the above-mentioned model of interaction, the relation between the users and

Figure 3. A matrix of signifiers and user interface design in the built environments

Signifier / Interface	Physical Cue	Physical Signifier	Digital Signifier
Analysis of user activities in space	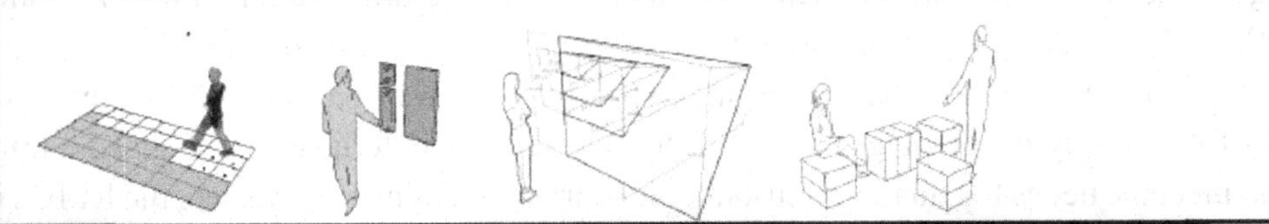		
Smart floor	 floor pads with art installation	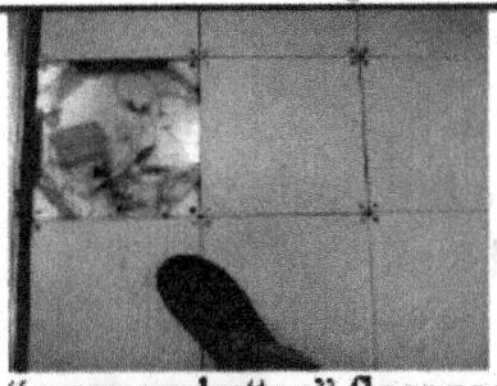 "press-on-button" floor pads	 displays as digital signifiers
Smart walls	 an augmented-reality transparent window	 art installation senses the presence of people	 walls change material effect from transparent to opaque
Ambient displays	 garden of the future	 home of the future	 workspace of the future

the interactive systems is established by means of signifiers/cues and actions/scripts. Consider the design of the smart floor example. The smart floor must provide a signifier in such a way that the user can receive a cue for a course of action in physical context.

Three types of *signifiers* have been designed and tested in our field experiments in developing the smart floor. The first example was an art installation in a garden of the future. In the garden, a matrix of capacitance sensors was installed underneath the floor pads. Underlying the transparent floor pads were natural materials such as pebbles and tree leaves. The natural materials served as a *cue* to attract people standing on the smart floor pads and triggered ambient displays. The second

example used the "press-on-button" metaphor to design a smart floor pad in a home of the future. Like a button, the floor pad went down a little bit when people stepped on it. The movement of the floor pad gave *a physical signifier* to the user awareness. The third example used *a digital signifier* to notify the user about the afforded interaction of the smart floor. A set of computer screens were installed underneath the floor pads, each of which showed a video related to the ambient displays. A matrix of signifiers and user interface design in our built environments (e.g. garden, home, and workspace) is depicted in Figure 3.

The spaces that sense have been developed in conjunction with our projects to develop smart spaces of the future. In the past few years, the

Interactive Architecture Laboratory at NCKU has taken a human-centric approach to integrating sensors, actuators, microcontrollers, and intelligent agents into building elements such as walls, floor, and furniture. At first, we built a workspace of the future. Then, the interactive garden project is followed by developing a home of the future to meet the needs for smart and sustainable living (Jeng, 2009).

Aspire Home is a long-term research project focusing on the achievement of a full-scale smart home of the future. The Aspire Home consists of six major sectors: an interactive 3D multimedia room, an interactive garden, a smart study room, a smart kitchen, a smart bedroom, and a smart living room (Jeng, et. al., 2008). The project includes interactive designs and ubiquitous computing technologies, such as wireless sensor networks, tangible user interfaces, speech recognition, interactive multimedia, and smart product designs. For the purpose of illustration, we will focus on an interaction within the garden.

The interactive garden is a full-scale sensing-based ubiquitous art installation designed for fluid interaction at home. It also affords an augmented reality for sentient interaction within the family. Firstly, the interaction space was designed by installing sensors into floor, chairs, and art installations. We borrowed the notion of a Japanese Karesansui rock garden. LED lights and capacitive sensors were installed inside a set of small rock-like chairs. These chairs lit up the garden when one sat on it. The smart rock calculated the time of sitting and left the LED light on when the user walked away. The more time one sat on the rock, the longer the light stayed on. Colorful butterflies in motion were simultaneously projected on the sandy ground. The "leave a light on" metaphor supports asynchronous social interaction with the family. For example, when the father came home late, he saw the chair's lighting and implicitly realized that someone had been sitting on the rock chair a moment ago. Such an interactive garden

is a context-aware system that senses, connects, and mediates people's emotions.

Secondly, all of the partitions in the Aspire Home were modularized, and each of them was embedded with RFID. The glass mounted on the wall partitions could dynamically changed their material effect (e.g. from transparent to opaque). When connected, the RFIDs in the partition walls detected a state of closure space (i.e. wall connectedness) and triggered the glass wall to turn opaque. The coupling of action and perception is essential to the design of kinetic wall systems (e.g. the motion of kinetic walls combined with the perceived material effects). Based on our surveys and observations, people used the kinetic wall system effectively when they needed a private space for relaxation and meditation. It could be widely applied to housing design in metropolitan areas where dynamic spatial configuration is important since space is a limited resource. Figure 4 shows some perspectives of the interactive garden at the Aspire Home.

The interaction design of smart home of the future concerns with *user engagement* and *coupling action and perception*. Consider, for example, the design of smart homes for supporting sustainable living. Anyone who has experienced in developing a home entertainment system in a smart home is likely to mount a multi-touch screen on a wall. The wall-sized display can also offer visualization of energy consumption in real-time. When the user engaged in the system (e.g. makes a "selection and move" gesture on the screen), the home interactive system must combine action and perception (e.g. the movement of the hand, the motion of images) for effectiveness.

Spaces that Think

After implementing the spaces that sense, we found that the interactive system is not intelligent enough to change its behavior according to physical and social context. We began to think about the possibility of extending the capability from

Figure 4. Some perspectives of the interactive garden at the Aspire Home (left and middle); Visualization of energy consumption using an interactive device (right)

spaces that sense to *spaces that think*. The aim of spaces that think is not to predict human behavior. Rather, the aim is to extend human memory by establishing ambient intelligence in space. The ambient intelligence creates a commonsense of daily routine to provide subtle assistance with daily activities of living (e.g. elderly assistance).

According to the above-mentioned model of interaction, spaces that think must take into account of the mapping between the user's *intention* and the system's *context manager*. The context manager is a software agent who can understand users' intentions in physical and social context. The capabilities required for spaces that think include:

- *A context manger* who translates low-level sensor data to high-level context information,
- *A semantic network* overlaying on a sensor network in a room, and
- *A commonsense database* that is open for capturing knowledge about everyday lives.

The following example will demonstrate the use of context manager to provide service according to the above-mentioned model of interaction.

In order to build up ambient intelligence in space, we used Internet to collect commonsense knowledge about everyday lives, which became a huge open-mind commonsense database for use in smart space. The open-mind commonsense database was based on the user descriptions of everyday lives, which could be formalized into a semantic network (Lieberman, 2004). By connecting sensors and interactive devices in space, each sensing *event* is a node of the semantic network. The link represents event dependencies. Using spreading activation theory, we have implemented a system called *Context Manager* to draw inferences from the semantic network. The *Context Manager* is a software agent who traverses the semantic network to "guess" the user's situation and intention. A script of daily routine is created to check and remind daily activities. An experimental study was conducted in our laboratory. The semantic network and the user interface of the Context Manager is shown in Figure 5.

Figure 5. A semantic network represents events and their dependencies in our everyday lives. (top); The user interface of the Context Manager shows how to "guess" user intention and situated action. (bottom).

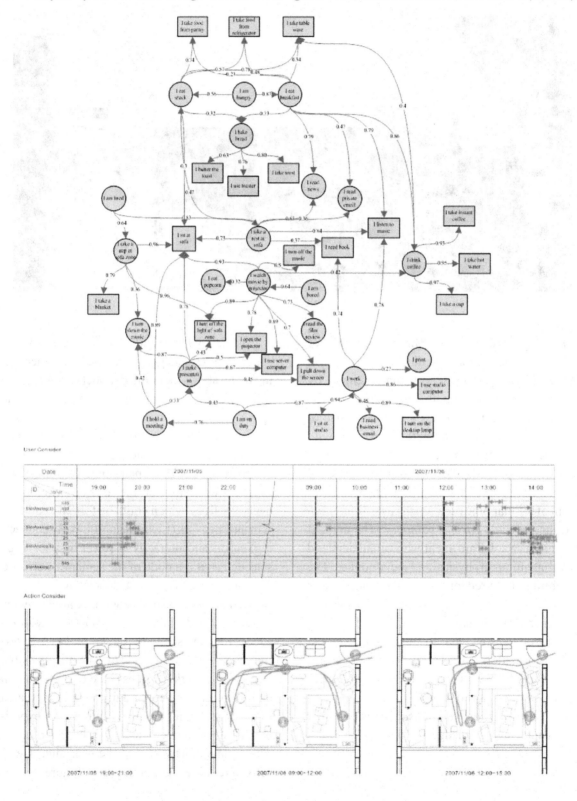

Figure 6. An interactive architecture changes its spatial configuration dynamically. The roof changes its shape to cut heating costs and open skylights to improve ventilation.

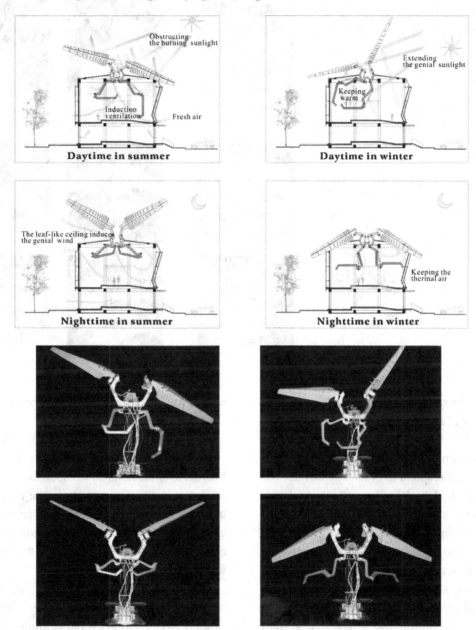

Spaces that Respond to Change

Spaces that respond to change are the most challenging, yet interesting, issue in developing interactive architecture. In the previous session, we described the context manager who attempted to

capture commonsense knowledge to assist elderly in everyday routine. In addition to responding to user needs, interactive architecture may change its physical properties in response to environmental change e.g. weather conditions. A physical change

Figure 7. The development process of physical prototyping of robotic interactive architecture

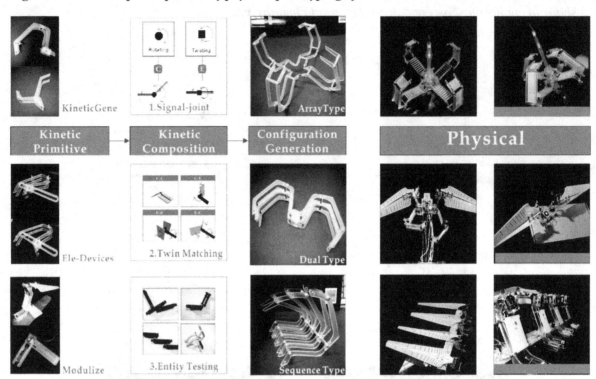

involves a change in physical properties such as shape, material effects, and spatial configuration.

Rather than the human-centric approach, we take an environment-oriented approach to designing spaces that respond to change. Consider the above-mentioned model of interaction. An entire building is the interactive system. When weather condition changes, for example, the building senses the change and enables the execution of a course of action e.g. environmental control. Examples are all skylights that open up to provide natural ventilation in rooms. In addition to environmental control, the interactive system should take into account of user intentions. It is important to put users into the automation loop for flexible control and provide cues for user awareness. Figure 6 shows an example of spaces that respond to change. It shows a building section sketch where the roof changes its shape and open skylights to improve ventilation in response to daily or seasoning weather conditions. The

indoor partitions can change its configuration to support varied activities.

The example depicted in Figure 6 outlines some kinetic features of interactive architecture. In order to understand how responsive architecture works, it is necessary to study the basic unit of building responsive primitives. Due to the high cost of a full-scale building prototype, we decided to use a small-scale building model to study feasibility of kinetic primitives.

A kinetic primitive is a unit of interactive architecture, composed of three kinds of kinetic pair (joints): twisting joints, rotating joints, and sliding joints. The kinetic pairs have three basic actions: sliding, rotating and twisting. The kinetic design is based on a set of kinetic pairs that correspond to different composition of motion joints. A set of composition rules defined in terms of those tectonic relations, together with a set of kinetic pairs, comprise a kinetic design method.

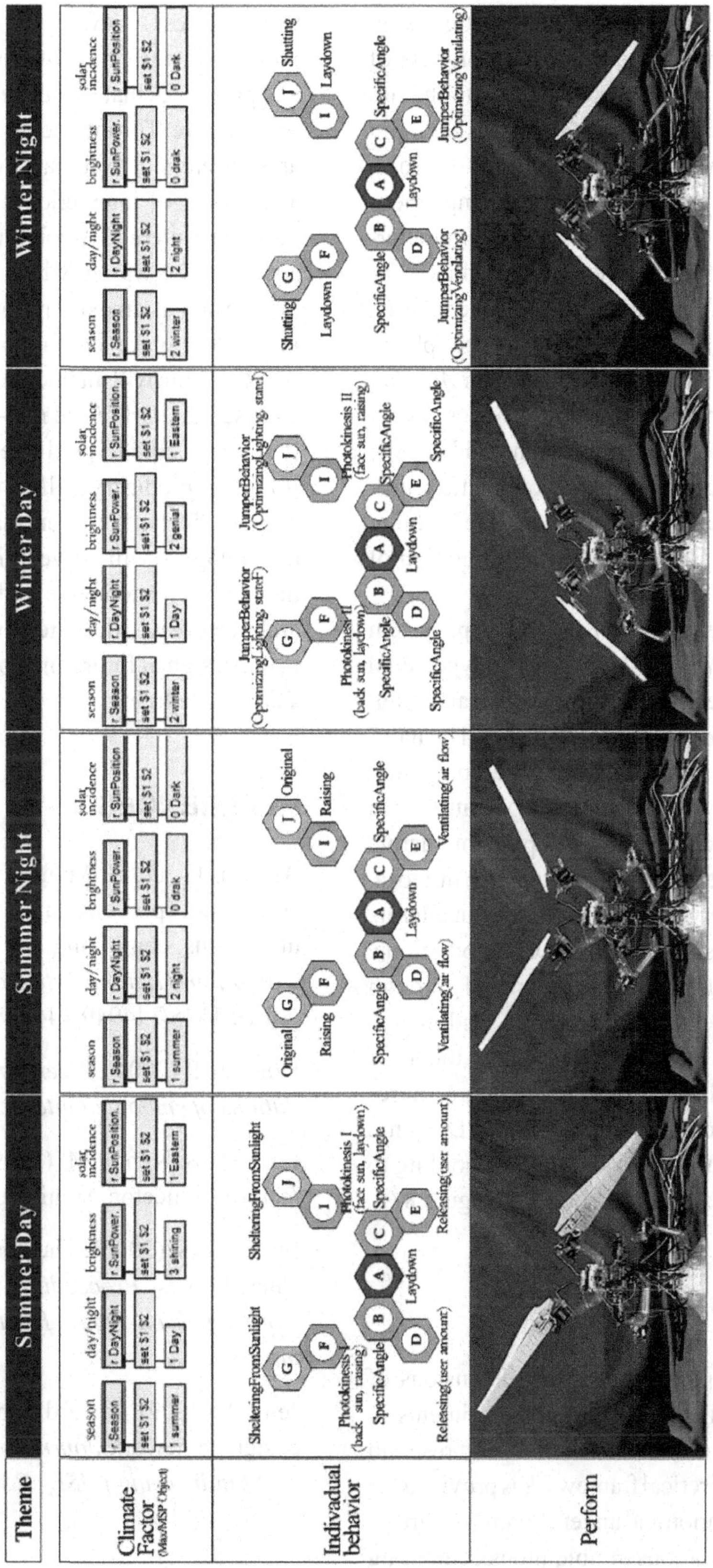

Figure 8. The Mimosa project: The sensing-based intelligent robot simulates dynamic building performance

Based on the above-mentioned kinetic design method, we started the development process of kinetic building model corresponding to the design example. First, we used CNC tools for rapid prototyping of the building components e.g. roof, external skin, internal skeleton. In the implementation of physical computing, a set of computer-augmented roof primitives was produced by embedding light and wind sensors, servo motors, and microcontrollers into a CNC-produced physical entity. Each physical entity used an *Arduino* chip as the microcontroller that receives sensor signals and dispatches action commands to the actuators. After composing a set of kinetic primitives to a robotic building structure, the building model could simulate dynamic configuration of interactive architecture.

The experimental responsive prototype system is called *Mimosa*. The *Mimosa* prototype acted like a large-scale intelligent robot (Pan and Jeng, 2008). The *Mimosa* project was inspired by natural plants (e.g. mimosa) where the compound leaves fold inward when touched. We attempted to transfer bionic ideas to developing interactive architecture. The system prototype, like mimosa, is a responsive organic interface that can alter its shape in response to light and wind conditions. The transformation can be optimized through manipulating the sensors, actuators, and microcontrollers. In the implementation, the roof primitives could rotate to a certain degree in response to varied lighting conditions. Dynamic spatial configuration was simulated according to different seasonal time, as shown in Figure 8.

CONCLUSION

This chapter explores the varied dimensions of interactive architecture with our experiments in developing spaces that sense, think, and respond to change. A theoretical framework is provided for the contextualization and understanding of current trends and applications of ubiquitous computing technologies. A new model of interaction is proposed to identify a set of processes, functionality and principles that guide the design of interactive architecture. The interaction model is expected to apply to any single interactive architecture project. The model of interaction not only provides the necessary interaction constructs, but also requires a shift in the way in which we think of interaction design as an exploration process both in the interaction space and in the cognitive space.

How soon will interactive architecture become an essential part of the real-world environment? It is impossible to predict exactly when or even if building industry will achieve critical mass. It is quite likely, however, that new methods and technologies will drive this paradigm shift to the study of interactive architecture. Interactive architecture will definitely play an important role in the design of future environments for smart and sustainable living.

REFERENCES

Abowd, G. D., & Mynatt, E. D. (2000). Charring past, present, and future research in ubiquitous computing. *ACM Transactions on Computer-Human Interaction*, 7(1), 29–58. doi:10.1145/344949.344988

Dourish, P. (2004). *Where the action is: The foundations of embodied interaction*. The MIT Press.

Fox, M., & Kepm, M. (2009). *Interactive architecture*. Princeton Architectural Press.

Intille, S. S. (2006). The goal: Smart people, not smart homes. *Proceedings of the International Conference on Smart Homes and Health Telematics*.

Jeng, T. (2009). Toward a ubiquitous smart space design framework, *Journal of Information Science and Engineering (JISE)*, 25(3).

Jeng, T. C., Chen, J., Wang, C., Wu, P., Chung, S., & Cheng, J. ... Yang, J. (2008). House of the future relies on multimedia and wireless sensors. *SPIE Newsroom*. Retrieved from http://spie.org/x19165.xml?ArticleID=x19165

Kronenburq, R. (2007). *Flexible: Architecture that responds to change*. Laurence King Publishers.

Lieberman, H., Liu, H., Singh, P., & Barry, B. (2004). Beating common sense into interactive applications. *AI Magazine*, *25*(4), 63–76.

McCullough, M. (2005). *Digital ground: Architecture, pervasive computing, and environmental knowing*. The MIT Press. Norman, D. A. (2010). *Living with complexity*. The MIT Press.

Minsky, M. (2000). Commonsense-based interfaces. *Communications of the ACM*, *43*(8). doi:10.1145/345124.345145

Pan, C., & Jeng, T. (2008). *Exploring sensing-based kinetic design for responsive architecture*. *Proceedings of CAADRIA2008*. Thailand: Chiang Mai.

Sterk, T. (2005). Building upon Negroponte: A hybridized model of control suitable for responsible architecture. *Automation in Construction*, *14*(2), 225–232. doi:10.1016/j.autcon.2004.07.003

Weiser, M. (1991). The computer for the 21st century. *Scientific American*, *265*(3). doi:10.1038/scientificamerican0991-94

ADDITIONAL READING

Communication of the ACM: Special Issue on Organic User Interfaces, 51(6), 70-78.

Jeng, T. (2011). *Interactive Architecture: Space is Medium, Interface, and Robot*. Taiwan: Garden City Publishers.

KEY TERMS AND DEFINITIONS

Human-Computer Interaction: A discipline concerned with the design, evaluation, and implementation of the interaction between users and computers.

Interactive Architecture: An interactive spatial system that is sensible to change its shape, properties or configuration in response to user activities or environmental conditions.

Smart Environments: A technology-empowered living space that is invisibly interwoven with computational devices such as sensors, actuators, and displays.

Chapter 16
A Methodology for Interactive Architecture

Carlos Calderón
Newcastle University, UK

ABSTRACT

In this chapter, the view that Interactive Architecture[1] (IA) practice ought to produce (digital) interactive interventions designed to affect people's actions and behaviours is firstly introduced. After presenting the challenges arising when integrating these two different conceptions of the word: Atoms and bits, reviewing the interpretations of IA and the lessons learnt from design methods theory in architecture, a novel way of approaching the intersection between architectural design, methodology, and emerging interactive technologies is proposed. This chapter attempts to make strong connections between design philosophy and project work, in aid of reinforcing the intellectual side of IA projects. Very often these types of projects are the result of technological pursuits rather than intellectual ones. Furthermore, this study demonstrates some strategies for ensuring the collaboration of design with related scientific and intellectual domains: architecture, computer science, and behavioural and social studies.

INTRODUCTION

"One of the great computational and design challenges of the twenty-first century is to unite the digital with the physical that is to integrate new forms of telecommunications and computing into everyday life" (Greenfield and Shepard 2007).

In the context of this publication, Interactive Architecture explores emerging practices within architecture that aim to merge digital technolo-gies & virtual spaces with tangible and physical spatial experiences. Interactive Architecture research investigates the creation of unique ways of navigating and occupying space by adopting the time based nature of digital technologies. That is, physical spaces in which some aspect of the space changes based on the actions of one individual or a group of people - such as graphical displays, visual projections, sound and lighting.

DOI: 10.4018/978-1-61350-180-1.ch016

CONTEXT

Advances in physics have led to a new understanding of physical phenomena. Advances in biology and neurology have led to new discoveries regarding the human sensory system. Advances in mechanical and electrical engineering have led to development of physical computing systems. Advances in Human Computer Interaction have led to new understanding of embedding physical computing systems. All in all, these advances have contributed an explosion in technology and engineering development in general and digital technology and infrastructure in particular.

Interactive Architecture as noted by Sparacino (Sparacino 2002) is a field truly driven and informed by technology which in turn shapes the architectural thinking and project development. Furthermore, computing technology is the main driver behind Interactive Space Design research and the evolution of the man-machine interface has been a prime force behind the development of new computing paradigms. Grudin (Grudin 1990) was the first to realise that computing evolution could be seen as the story of "computer reaching out", in which the man-machine emphasis moves from being directly focused on the physical machine to incorporate more and more of the user's world and the social setting in which the user is embedded. Grudin's principles can still be seen in current trends in Human Computer Interaction design.

In 1991 Mark Weiser published what is considered to be the seminal paper in Ubiquitous Computing: "The computer for the 21st Century" (Weiser 1991). Weiser argued that "the most profound technologies are those who disappear. They weave themselves into the fabric of everyday life until they are indistinguishable from it". He then set out his vision of a world in which "silicon based information technologies", not the absence of the word computer, have disappeared (this is also known as Weiser's invisibility principle). Furthermore, Weiser perceived that such machines i.e. laptops were nothing more than a "transi-

tional step toward achieving the real potential of information technology". By postulating his vision, Weiser conceived a new way of thinking about computers in the world, "one that takes into account the human environment". In short, Weiser moved computing from two-dimensional to three-dimensional interactions. He placed information technologies in a three dimensional space in which computers will "disappear" and "weave themselves into the fabric of everyday life until they are indistinguishable from it" (Weiser 1991). Today advancements in computer power, the availability of easy to customise software tools which can be coupled with accessible digital interactive hardware (e.g Arduino) are making possible the realisation of Weiser's vision.

IA exploits the relationship between technology and the new possibilities of design that allow for more interactivity in everyday life contexts (e.g. shopping, children's hospitals). The key differential characteristic of IA (a time based design discipline) is information feedback or information reflection. Because "interactive architecture" is changing over time (with interaction) it has a much more directed ability to adapt to temporal conditions. The information feedback and the analogy of "Human Computer Interaction loop" is an exclusive digital issue which underpins and enables the relation between design and human behaviour. This text provides some strategies to ensure design is integrated into, otherwise, purely technologically driven endeavours.

INTERACTIVE INTERVENTIONS

Early perception amongst Architectural Scholars (Kronenburg 2007) was that Interactive Architecture is about automation or intelligent automation in buildings in which "an action that is carried out towards a predetermined result though the process may be changed along the way". This is seen as a built-in reactive quality. From this perspective, the ambition of an intelligent building is to integrate sensor systems that assess the internal and external environment and the condition of a building's systems, and then act on this to achieve maximum operational performance and control level. The areas in which intelligent building systems operate are environmental comfort, safety, security, privacy, sanitation, communications, entertainment, ambience, energy-use and efficiency. The pressure for increased intelligence in buildings comes from perceived improvements that will lead to performance increases and greater safety. From this standpoint a digital layer is the result of developing technologies that are making possible new and better constructional and operational strategies. The aim of these improvements is to make architecture more efficient and sustainable, and also to make the user's relationship with their built environment more comfortable and responsive. Whilst these are perfectly valid applications of interactive technology, the reality is that a true adaptive and predictive building is a very hard problem which relies on the convergence of several areas of knowledge: Ubiquitous or pervasive computing (network capabilities that exploit low-cost computing devices), intelligent systems research (learning algorithms and pattern matchers), context awareness (track and position objects) and user applications and interfaces. Thus far, progress remains slow. More recent studies, however, are focusing less in the predictive and inference capabilities of the technology and more on the interplay between technology and classical architectural and urban design problems. For example, enhancing social awareness in communities has been one of the classical problems in architecture and urban design. In many cases, communities find ways to socialise and interact around common scarce resources such as the village well, or the office coffee machine, but it is important to provide certain deliberate measures to facilitate that process. In particular, transparency in buildings and urban spaces adds to the social fabric of the place. Transparency in this case refers to the quality of a place or building that

enables people to know enough about activities in the common areas that are attracted to them. In her thesis, Kaur (Kaur 2007) proposes a novel sensor network based approach to enhancing the social awareness of people while maintaining low levels of privacy invasiveness in the system development and use. Similarly, Aipperspach et al (Aipperspach, Hooker et al. 2009), have noted the increasing homogeneity of ubiquitously fitted environment and how this can be detrimental for the restorative qualities of the space. In particular, one of the problems they examined was the declining relationship between the home and the community, especially the immediate physical community. This is a traditional architectural problem which tends to be solved with the spatial interplay of private and public spaces. A key element in Aipperspach's design proposals was the ability of people to control exposure to the community by introducing a digital interactive element in the building. They suggested that "the semi-public spaces in buildings provide an interesting place for intervention, allowing for the display of information that might build connections within the local physical community or for the creation of a parallel set of connections to 'virtual neighbours' who have some sort of affiliation with the local community"

This view of Interactive Architecture as digital interactive interventions which affect people's actions and behaviours can be explained from a cybernetics perspective when seen as linear systems. That is, when a zero order cybernetic system (i.e. a reactive digital system which conforms to archetypical structure of the feedback loop) is coupled with a human the resulting system can be seen as a first-order cybernetics because the person (a learning system herself) adjust her goal based on the information yielded by the linear system (e.g. the sensor network proposed in Kaur's work (Kaur 2007). In this case, "information flows from a system (perhaps a computer or a car) through a person and back through the system again. The person has a goal, she acts to achieve it in an environment (provides input to the system), she measures the effect of her action on the environment (interprets output from the system's feedback) and then compares result with goal. The comparison (yielding difference or congruence) directs her next action, beginning the cycle again" (Dubberly, Pangaro et al. 2009)

CHALLENGES

From a spatial perspective, the application of traditional *scales* and divisions such as city, building, and object which are usually associated with built environment professions: Urban designer, architect and interior designer is restrictive and boundaries can be blurred (Calderon 2009). For instance, the Communicative Lighting Facade for the Espacio de Creación Artística Contemporánea in Cordoba, Spain designed by Realities United is physically rooted in the building but it is clear that the most relevant scale here is the 'urban' as this project transcends the physical boundaries of the building and attempts to connect the building to its urban surroundings using a media skin. Similarly, the BIX Communicative Display Skin for the Kunsthaus Graz in Graz, Austria. In this case, the facade as a display extends the communication range of the Kunsthaus, complementing its programmatically formulated communicative purpose. In an abstract and mediated form the media facade transmits the internal processes of the Kunsthaus out into the public. In essence, this intervention provides the Kunsthaus with chance to develop methods for a dynamic communication between building and surroundings, between content and outside perception.

It can also be argued that the interactive nature of these interventions questions traditional architectural notions of *boundaries*. Material boundaries are losing their meaning, and interface and information space are catch words that architects must master. Much of architecture is about boundaries: Defining space and movement

activity space by the thoughtful design of walls, enclosures and openings. Because of the interactive nature of these interventions, boundaries are now active zones of mediation rather than of delineation (Addington and Schodek 2005). We cannot see them, nor can we draw them as known objects fixed to a location. The boundary is no longer delimited by the static planar material surface, instead it may be reconfigured as the zone in which change occurs.

Hence, by investigating the transient behaviour of the material, we challenge the privileging of the static planar surface: Is a line a good *representation* of an interactive flat surface? The boundary is no longer delimited by the material surface, instead it may be reconfigured as the zone in which change occurs. The image of the building boundary as the demarcation between two different environments defined as single states –a homogeneous interior and an ambient exterior- could possibly be replaced by the idea of multiple energy environments fluidly interacting with the moving body. This new type of materials with their transient behaviour and ability to respond to energy stimuli are known as digital materials (Brownell 2006) and may eventually enable the selective creation and design of an individual's sensory experience.

The challenges we face in terms of scale, boundaries and representation are a consequence of attempting to integrate two different conceptions of the word: Atoms and bits (Negroponte 1995). Two things should be kept in mind, when trying to integrate these two interpretations of the word: 1) digital and physical worlds have different properties and are guided by different design principles; 2) a tangible, embodied and embedded interaction is what links atoms and bits (Kirsh 2001).

Architecture is started to enter a new phase: A time when buildings actively co-operate with their inhabitants; when objects know what they are, where they are, what is near them; when social and physical space lose their tight coupling; when walls and partitions change with mood and task. As pointed by leading cognitive psychologist David Kirsh: "Engineers and scientists explore how to digitize the world around us, the classical constraints of design, ruled so long by the physics of space, time, and material, are starting to crumble. (..). Buildings still need to support and enclose. Yet if I am right, the requirements of support and enclosure no longer need dominate or experience of buildings. The digital can take us beyond the tyranny of materials". (Kirsh 2001).

This chapter proposes a novel way of approaching the (pedagogical) intersection between design, methodology and emerging interactive technologies. The chapter is organised as follows: The background section reviews the interpretations of IA and design methodologies in architecture. This section establishes that IA architecture in this text is the design practice of embedding of an online interactive system. Furthermore, it sees interaction as tangible, embodied and embedded in the physical space. The methodology section follows Broadbent (Broadbent 1969) and Lawson's (Lawson 1980) philosophies and presents a model around three concepts: Space, place, and interaction and proposes techniques and attributes for each of these three design generators. Finally, the chapter concludes with a conclusion and further work sections.

BACKGROUND

Interpretations of Interactive Architecture

In the 1960s, a cybernetician whose name was Gordon Pask worked with the architect Cedric Price on his Fun Palace project. Pask's work introduced the concept of underspecified goals to architecture systems. Pask was particular interested in creating systems in which the participant has a creative productive role. This vision profoundly questioned the way interactive computing systems and humans shared an environment. It

moved away from closed-loop feedback technologies towards conversational systems. While simple reactive devices such as those employed in advanced building management systems (i.e. room temperature control; sunlight distribution) are useful, they are based on a close-loop feedback. Current developments in the deployment of interactive digital interventions are following a Paskinian's approach. That is, we are moving from reactive to interactive systems.

Interactive systems are characterised by the ability of the system to engage with the user's input. There are two basics ways in which this can be accomplished: Online and off-line. In short, online systems are those in which users are able to engage with the system in real-time by, for instance, exchanging text messages with each other via a large screen. In off-line systems, on the other hand, this engangement occurs at different points in time. For instance, some interventions are designed so that users can submit art work to be displayed on a screen. This work, in turn, is showed at some point in the future as the installation curator sees fit.

The basic loop of an interactive system is always the same: Input (listening), processing (thinking) and output (speaking). Input and output technologies can be conceptually very different. For instance, physical sensors and cameras are two separate fields of research conducted by two separate types of communities: Electrical engineers and computer scientists. Both, however, can be used as input technology in an interactive intervention. Similarly, output technology can be classified into two categories: Display based and kinetics or moving parts based (e.g. Robots). The use of moving parts as output devices is present in the work of various architects: Dynamic architecture (Fisher 2008), ORAMBA (Sterk 2003) and Living New York (Benjamin and Yang 2006). This interpretation of IA is known as kinetic architecture.

In this text IA is seen as the design practice of embedding of an online interactive system in a designated space.

Table 1. A brief summary of design methodologists in architecture

Design methodologists	Description
First Generation Design Methodologists (c.1960-70)	This generation was seduced by their belief in the validity of applying scientific deductive methods to design process. Search on for set rules for design, usually grounded in mathematical and/or typological theories (e.g. operation research, graph theory)
Second Generation of Design Methodologists (c.1970 - c.1990)	This generation was characterised by search for more effective application in architecture - about 35 'new methods' identified to aid planners and designers in understanding of, and providing for user needs. This translated into a deeper grasp of conventional requirements and nature of scientific process and more ambitious predictive tools (e.g. Space Syntax (Hillier and Hanson 1984))
Third Generation of Design Methodologists (c.1990- ?)	Sophisticated digital media brings new techniques and methodologies integrated into all stages of design: From concept –e.g. parametric design- to fabrication –e.g. digital manufacturing. However, it is still unclear how (or whether) these individualistic trends link up with the scientific methodology that lies at the root of the original movement

(Brief) History of Design Methods in Architecture

The idea of design methods in architecture started gaining acceptance in the early-19th century (Durand 1809). In a man-made world where design problems were increasing in complexity and scale, Durand called into question the prevailing cult of individual creative genius: the "Renaissance Man" with mystical powers.

Over the 20th Century, there has been a quest for the demystification of the design process. This was a quest for a systematised design methodology, based on scientific principles, to replace individualised traditional methods grounded in the Renaissance. It was a quest to demystify the design process by turning it into a process more accessible, accountable and transferable.

Le Corbusier was amongst the leading 20th C pioneers proposing rational design and building procedures: systems building, typology and design methodology (e.g. Domino System (1915); Five Points of a New Architecture (1927); Modular (1948) etc.). Early in the 1960s a series of thinkers began international campaign to give design (of all kinds) a rational scientific basis. Especially influential in UK & USA were Christopher Jones/ Geoffrey Broadbent/ Christopher Alexander. Table 1 describes this movement and subsequent efforts during 1970-1990, and from 1990 till today.

From this review of design methodologists (see Table 1), it can be concluded that, in architecture, designers have not been able to make explicit and record their knowledge in a textbook manner. Hence, designers have been left with imperfect methods of investigating design but no one of these approaches offers the complete answer.

Alongside this debate, today, architecture has been shaped by the observation that traditional habitable patterns are being redefined by cyberspace, physical computation and everything in between these terms (e.g. mixed realities) (c.2000-?). It was William J. Mitchell who initially postulated that these new challenges will "redefine the intellectual and professional agenda of architects, urban designers, and others who care about spaces and places in which we spend our daily lives"(Mitchell 2000). This is now becoming a reality and tangible, embedded and embodied digital interventions are populating the built environment. This paper aims at contributing towards the application and applicability of these digital interactive interventions in public places. To this extent, a methodology for structured design exploration is proposed. The model proposed here follows Broadbent (Broadbent 1969) and Lawson's (Lawson 1980) philosophies. Both methods rely on the notion of concepts as generators to guide design explorations. Broadbent's method relies upon four distinct ways of generating design from which he called, 'pragmatic', 'iconic', 'analogical' and 'canonic' methods. Lawson, on the other hand, proposes a three dimensional model of generators of design problems. Lawson goes further and states that: "There is no evidence that designers actually work like this, but these models are worthy of study and form a useful addition to the designer's toolkit for controlling design thought."

The model proposed here places interaction at the centre of the process. It sees interaction as tangible, embodied and embedded in the physical space. That is, interaction occurs in a physical space where people's cultural experiences are disrupted and transformed (i.e. sense of place). Hence, the model is articulated around three concepts: Space, place, and interaction and it is accompanied by a discussion on which techniques and attributes are deemed as appropriate to encapsulate each of the generators.

A METHODOLOGY

This section proposes a methodology for interactive architecture design which draws ideas, techniques and methodologies from Interaction/Experience Design, Architecture, and Computer science. Furthermore, behavioural and social studies are seen as the underlying sciences (see Figure 1).

This methodology should not be seen as a fixed track to a fixed destination (Jones 1992) but as guidance to the designer's creative process. This methodology follows the basic loop underlined by Simon Herbert in his work "The Sciences of the Artificial" where he discusses the role of analysis (observation) and synthesis (making) as a process of creating man-made responses to the world he/she interacted with. Table 2 illustrates this and includes the stage of implementation as to reflect the outcome of the analysis and synthe-

Figure 1. Interactive architecture is seen at an intersection of: Interaction design, architecture, computer science and behavioural and social studies

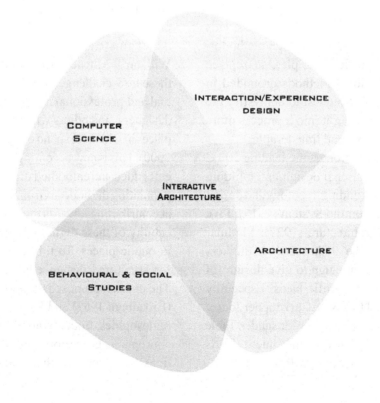

Table 2. Basic stages of design method

Stage
Analysis
Synthesis
Implementation

Table 3. Linking analysis and synthesis to place, space and interaction

Stage		Concept
Analysis	BLACK BOX	Place
		Space
Synthesis		Interaction

sis stages: The implementation of a physical artefact. In this case, this means the deployment of a computing system, which is interactive and tangible, in a public space.

In simple terms, the main objective behind the method outlined here is to facilitate the connection between the two well known stages of a design process: Analysis and synthesis and the three key concepts behind interactive architecture: Place, space and interaction (see Table 3)

Each stage has subsequently divided into attributes which act as further field of specificity for the analysis and synthesis of an interactive architecture intervention. Table 4 illustrates this. The stages and attributes are presented in a sequential order for illustration and analysis purposes, any of them can act as entry point to the "translucent box".

For each attribute a specific technique(s) is proposed as to enable its study. Table 5 illustrates this.

In the next sections, the meaning of the attributes and techniques depicted in Table 3 are explained. Examples, which demonstrate the applicability of this structured methodology, are

selected from two design exercises (briefs) conducted by the author and his group of students over the past two years.

ARCHITECTURAL DESIGN EXERCISES

The first exercise explores the role of information in the city. More specifically, the design exercise investigated how contemporary information technology and interactive programming will lead to a project proposal with the capacity to become a live and dynamic presence within the public realm in Newcastle City Centre. The interventions were required to provide a platform for information and interactive information exchange; provide a platform for a variety of programmed place-based activities; and enhance the appearance, perception, and experience of public space in the city centre. The second exercise's main aim was to propose an interactive and physically-embedded digital system which may induce energy-use reducing behaviours in a public building. The work was commissioned by Newcastle University's Estates

Table 4. Attributes per stage

Stage	Attribute	Concept
Analysis	Cultural Practice	Place
	Morphological	Space
	Conceptual	Interaction
Synthesis	(low fidelity) Prototyping	Place Space Interaction

Table 5. Attributes and techniques per stage

Stage	Attribute	Techniques	Concept
Analysis	Cultural Practice	Focus groups Observational techniques	Place
	Morphological	Site analysis: Movement and usage Physical affordances	Space
	Conceptual	Theoretical intent Precedents Model	Interaction
Synthesis	(low fidelity) Prototyping	Sketching interaction Storyboarding Description of user scenarios Mapping physical computing Information flow diagrams Computing systems diagrams Sections and construction details	Place Space Interaction

department who was inviting design proposals for an interactive digital intervention situated in the Architecture Building to raise energy awareness and promote behavioural change amongst the communities of users. It was assumed that a real-time energy monitoring system was already in place and that this system could measure the electricity consumption of the building. This system (Smart Edd:e ™) will be soon installed in the building.

The design exercises were undertaken by final year architectural students working in groups of three as part of their Bachelor of Architecture degree. The first exercise was undertaken by five groups whereas four groups took part in the second exploration. All of them have access to interaction designers and computer scientists based at Newcastle University.

Analysis: Cultural Practice

Cultural practice refers to the context in which the interventions are situated: Historical, political, social and cultural layers imbued in space as well as its practical organisation. In short, this dimension relates to understanding of "habitation" patterns, activities within the space, and the collective practice of those who occupy it (Calderon 2009).

On the one hand, the practical organisation of space is a mutually constitutive relationship between collective understandings of spaces and the practices and activities that people carry out in them (Dourish and Bell 2007). On the other, cultural organization space refers to the historical, social, and cultural meaning which is, critically, mapped onto habitation patterns. Everyday space is not experienced neutrally; it is experienced as inhabited, with all that that entails (Dourish and Bell 2007).

In order to unlock practices, activities and cultural meaning of spaces in our design exploration we utilize qualitative research methods from social sciences (focus groups and ethnographic studies) as data collection methods.

Observational techniques (Kirwan and Ainsworth 1992) are seen as a general class of techniques whose objective is to obtain data by directly observing the activity(s) or behaviour(s) under study. A wide range of observational techniques are in common use (e.g. direct visual observation, remote of observation via closed-circuit television, video recording, time-lapse photography, etc) and most can be combined or tailored to suit the particular the particular requirements of a study. In our case, the two observational techniques most used were: Direct visual observation (see (Drury. 1992) for detailed description and time-lapsed photography (see (Clancey 2001; Clancey 2001)) for detailed description). Figure 2.illustrates the summary of time-lapsed photographic exercise. The image shows activities linked to time in an outdoor civic space (Newcastle's Monument) where multiple interactions occur throughout the day and night all year around. This exploration and representation was crucial in the design conceptualisation and realisation. In fact, it could be seen as generator of design as, in this specific case, catalysed the group of students in a very specific direction: Enhancing social experience through relaxation, interaction and information. This eventually yielded an interactive and reconfigurable seating area capable of relaying information to the public using a one to one and a one to many strategies.

Focus groups are used as a tool of investigation to enable designers to explore underlying group dynamics and (social/cultural) norms around potential interactive digital interventions. In a focus group participants are more explicitly en-

couraged to talk to one another, as opposed to answering questions of each person turn. A typical session involve between 8-12 people who, guided by the moderator, discuss the topic under consideration for anything between an hour and half and two and a half hours. It is advisable to record the session and/or take written notes. An observer could fill in this role (see (May 2001)) for a more detailed description). The idea of group produces an important side-effect. That is, groups by their own nature imply an assemblage of persons as to form a collective unity. In our case, we have interpreted groups as communities of users of the building. Hence, the first task for students who selected this technique was to identify the representative communities of users. For example, students working on the design of an intervention situated in the Architecture Building to raise energy awareness and promote behavioural change identified the following communities: i) permanent staff (tutors and support staff), ii) students (resident and hot desking), iii) support staff (cleaners and maintenance), and iv) visitors. For each community, time based activities and consumption

Figure 2. Summary of time-lapsed photographic exercise. Bottom left corner is a photomontage image of final intervention.

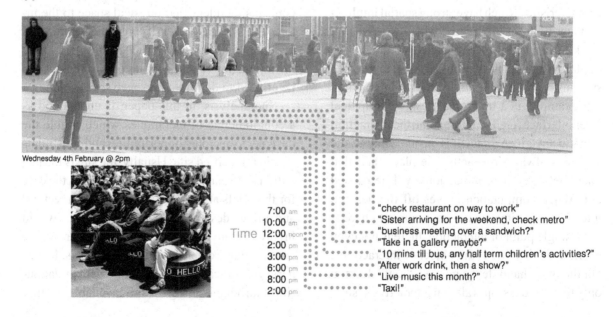

patterns were initially identified (see Figure 3). As a result of this prelimary analysis which used a direct visual observation technique, it was decided to target a particular community (students) and a focus group was held. The focus group revealed that there was key activity common to all resident students independently of the year they are in: gaming. As a result, gaming was used as design generator and shaped their design process. This group eventually developed a wall base intervention in which gaming was the key driver for interaction.

Analysis: Morphological

This section focuses on the morphological dimension or spatial arrangements; that is, the relationship between the deployed interactive system and the space in which it is situated. The type of analysis presented here aims at encouraging the designer to use of the morphological characteristics to simplify interaction and its computational requirements.

Interactive systems have a wide range of applications from entertainment to educational, from environmental to social, as well interactive systems can be presented in various forms or types. However, they share a series of common characteristics which have strong spatial implications or, to put it differently, where good spatial thinking can simplify the design of an interactive digital system. The first problem is that interactive systems do not have a single point of interaction. For example, in a traditional desktop Graphical User Interface (GUI) environment, the interaction focus at any given moment is on one window, the cursor is always in exactly one place, and that place defines where the actions will be carried out. When computation moves off the desktop into the three dimensional environment, there is not a single point of interaction, there is not even a single device that is the object of interactions. On the other hand, let us image a "real" desktop only that this desktop is also an interactive system

designed to detect human interactions. Imagine the act of writing, it comes about through the coordinated use of pen, paper, and ink, not to mention the desk itself and the chair you sit in. Moreover, you might write on the page with your dominant hand while your non dominant hand is used to orient the paper. All these actions are brought together to achieve a task. Thus you act at multiple points at once (Dourish 2001). Another related issue is that interaction in the physical world is "parallel". That is, going back to the desktop example, interactions inside the "virtual" desktop tend to be sequential: One after another. For instance, during the installation of a software package the dialog box will guide you step by step and you will hopefully achieve a successful installation. During this process, the interactions were sequential: One after the other. In the physical world, however, there is no way to tell what I might do next.

With these two problems in mind, in this section I propose two techniques: Site analysis and identification of physical affordances. In a crude and simplified way, the two techniques correspond to two different scales. One, site analysis, deals with the large scale and attempts to situate the intervention in the context in which it is situated (e.g. the building). The other, physical affordances, connects the identified physical space to the interactive system by identifying which features of the built environment aid in the simplification of the interaction (e.g. the width of a pavement can be utilised to delimit a presence sensor range).

Site analysis, in this paper, is understood as a conglomerate of techniques which enable the designer to decipher opportunities and constraints within a specified site. Usually, the site is located within an urban area or a building as it is the case for the briefs at hand. In traditional architectural and urban design sense a site analysis would involve an inventory of: Regulations, resource consent requirements, orientation, views, levels, heritage implications, legal requirements, relationship with neighbouring sites and available utilities,

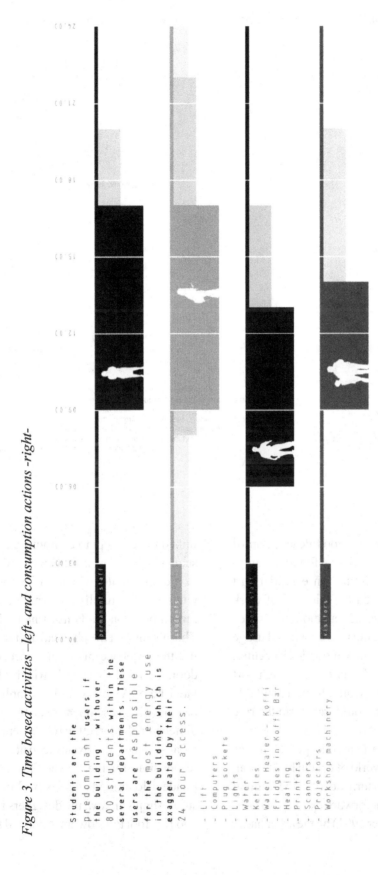

Figure 3. Time based activities –left- and consumption actions -right-

Figure 4. Movement and space use analysis of an urban area in Newcastle city centre

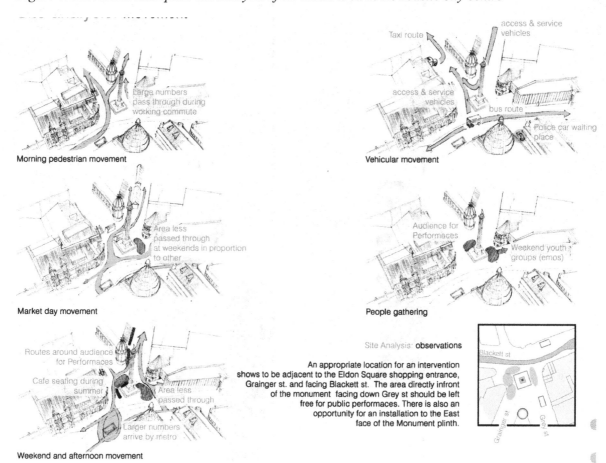

Morning pedestrian movement

Market day movement

Weekend and afternoon movement

Vehicular movement

People gathering

Site Analysis: **observations**

An appropriate location for an intervention shows to be adjacent to the Eldon Square shopping entrance, Grainger st. and facing Blackett st. The area directly infront of the monument facing down Grey st should be left free for public performaces. There is also an opportunity for an installation to the East face of the Monument plinth.

service route and so on. A good description of what site analysis entails can be found in James LaGro's book (LaGro 2008). An essential part of a site analysis required for this type of work is analysis of movement/circulation and space use. Figure 4 illustrates the movement and usage analysis of an urban area in Newcastle city centre. This was employed whilst assessing which part of Newcastle city centre would be more suitable for an intervention that would transform the role of information in the city.

Physical affordance is a concept which was first introduced in the world of design by Norman (Norman 1988) who, in turn, adopted the original concept: affordance put forward by Gibson (Gibson 1977). Gaver (Gaver 1991) on the other hand,

linked the concept to computing technology and sequence. For instance, Gaver gives an example of a door handle, which, in its normal position, lends itself naturally to turning and then, in its turned position lends itself naturally to pulling. This means that the physical design helps in guiding the sequence of actions needed to open the door. This is the principle which I have extrapolated here. A very common application of this principle is to use linearity as to constraint a two dimensional interaction (e.g. a person walking on a flat surface). For example, Antenna design was responsible for the Power Flower intervention. Inside Bloomingdale's (New York department store) shop window, the designers installed thirty two five foot tall flowers. As stated by the design-

Figure 5. Physical affordances simplify the interaction by cleverly using the pavement as boundary and match that distance to the range of the sensors

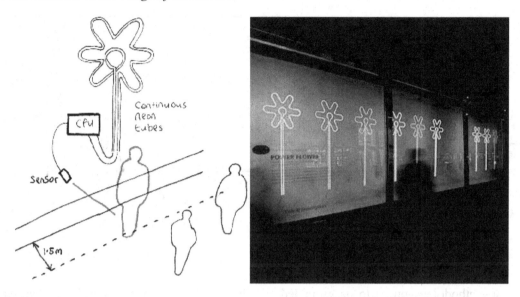

ers: "Each flower was connected to a motion sensor aimed at the sidewalk. The flower remains unlit until a person passes closely in front of it, triggering a sound and causing the flower to light up. As the person continues to move past the windows, the first flowers passed fade out while new ones illuminate, producing a trail of light. To simplify the interaction –which is 2D as a person walks in a 2D plane-, they cleverly used the pavement as boundary and match that distance to the range of the sensors. This is a good example of how the existing physical environment can help in simplifying interaction and system design (see Figure 5). In our own work when exploring interventions to promote energy awareness and actions, after a site within the building was selected –the Kofi Bar-, the students proposed a multi-layer interactive system. The first layer would react to physical presence and used the longitude of the space to facilitate the capture of movement and the display of energy consumption patterns. (see Figure 6).

Analysis: Conceptual

The conceptual stage is where alternative concepts are explored, evaluated and compared. This should not require a substantial time investment and should be developed before proceeding with sections and construction details. In this section theoretical intent, precedents and interactions modes/methods/paradigms are proposed as techniques to help shaping the different design concepts.

Theoretical Intent

Intent is different from function. In previous sections, I have advocated that an interactive computing system ought to be designed to change peoples' attitudes and behaviours. The area of study on how to make (interactive) computing systems more likeable and persuasive is called "captology". An acronym coined by B.J.Fogg (B.J.Fogg 2003) which is based on the phrase: Computers as persuasive technologies. Theoretical intent refers to the theoretical methodology which supports the design intent proposed by the designer. This

Figure 6. Physical affordances simplify the interaction by using the length of the space to facilitate the capture of movement and the display of energy consumption patterns

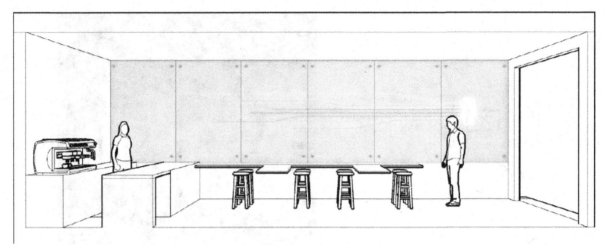

theoretical methodology ought to be grounded on theories and studies from the behavioural and social sciences (e.g. environmental psychology, social anthropology).

The incipient field of Interactive Architecture has engendering behavioural change as its core. Unlike in traditional architecture, interactivity is the enabler property which transforms the physical environment from a passive recipient to an active actuator. Interactivity acts as a connector between theories in architecture, which enhance our understanding of space, and behavioural sciences, which enhance our understanding of human motives and actions in the physical environment.

In our own explorations, for example, play has been used as a behavioural driver for the design of a digital interactive intervention which would enhance energy awareness and engender behavioural change in a public building. Play, in this case, is understood as activities and experiences unbound by time, which are chosen by players and enhance their knowledge of the world and themselves through interaction with others (Baptiste 1995). This translated into an intervention where the user –who belongs to an identified community of users in the building: permanent students- can opt to play a simple game of pong, tennis or air

hockey with a sphere. This sphere graphically represents the real-time energy consumption for this community of users. Similarly other behavioural drivers identified for the same brief were competition and comfort. Competition between different communities of users was seen as a catalyst to encourage energy conservation. As a result, an interactive LED display was embedded in one of the most social areas of the building: A wall in the coffee bar. This interactive LED display had two layers of interaction. Its first layer acts as an ambient display which is triggered by a motion sensor and it displays the overall consumption of energy of the building. The second layer reinforces the dialogue already established with the user by prompting the user towards an RFID reader which will display the community's performance as a LED trace on the wall. Comfort is usually defined in physiological way as "the physical relationship between a person and his or her environment, comfortable 'neutrality' being that state in which the heat generated by the human body is equal to the heat transferred away" (Shove 2003) In this case, however, comfort was used in a wider body-centered definition which is entwined with social practices and expectations. In particular comfort

Precedents

A comprehensive knowledge of good design can be acquired by analysing relevant precedents. Examples of good and bad design yield important lessons that strengthen the designer's tool box and capacity to arrive at creative and appropriate solutions. In our case, precedents, are also sought based on their technological typology. This typology seeks, firstly, to provide a disentangled view of a computer system. It views computer systems as juxtaposition of layers which fulfil the basic requirement of capturing interactions. Secondly, this typology aims at providing a more unified perspective around the idea of interaction. In that sense, at the top of the tree, I distinguish between off-line and on-line. Off-line systems are those that whilst interactive the user's input is not reflected back in real-time. On-line systems, on the other hand, the user's input is processed in real-time or without the user experiencing a feeling of "delay". Table 6 shows the typology.

Model: Interactions Modes and Paradigms

As part of the conceptual stage, the idea of a conceptual model is introduced. Conceptual models have been widely used in designing computer interfaces. They help to answer what, why and how based on the user's needs and other requirements identified. "A description of the proposed system in terms of a set of integrated ideas and concepts about what it should do, behave and look like, that will be understandable by the users" (Sharp, Rogers et al. 2007). More importantly in this context, conceptual models provide ways of linking concept design to interactions.

A first way of conceptualising a system is to think of interaction modes and tasks. A mode refers to distinct method of operation with a computer system for a specific task. For instance, for manipulating and navigating folders in hard drive in a windows computer, we are all familiar with double-click as a way of expanding a folder. Thus students are asked to think of tasks and interaction modes which would best support these tasks. Students are encouraged to use as little interaction modes as possible as to avoid modal behaviour or the situation where the user needs to remember in which mode (state) is he/she in. For example, VCRs were notoriously difficult to operate as they have many modes of operation.

A second approach for conceptual modelling is to think of interaction paradigms. By this it is meant a particular philosophy or way of thinking about interaction design. It is intended to orient designers to the kinds of questions they need to ask. For many years the prevailing paradigm in interaction design was to develop applications for the desktop —intended to be used by single users sitting in front of a CPU, monitor, keyboard and mouse. A dominant part of this approach was to design software applications that would run using a GUI (Graphical User Interface) or WIMP (Windows Icons Menu Pointing) interface. With the advent of wireless, mobile and handheld technologies, developers started designing applications that could be used in a diversity of ways

Table 6. A technological typology

On-Line			Off-line
At the interface with physical contact with interactive elements	Behind the scenes		
	Aware-people	Aware-environment	

Table 7. Interaction paradigms

Paradigm	Description
Pervasive computing	This concept implies the computer has the capability to obtain the information from the environment in which it is embedded and utilise it to dynamically build models of computing
Mobile computing	Mobile computing is fundamentally about increasing our capability to physically move computing services with us
Wearable computing	A variation of mobile computing in which computers are worn on the body
Tangible bits	To give physical form to digital information by making bits tangible

besides only on an individual's desktop machine. This has promoted paradigms that move beyond the desktop. For this purpose and to guide future interaction design and system development, the paradigms I put forward are: Pervasive computing, Mobile computing, Wearable computing and Tangible bits (see Table 7).

SYNTHESIS: PROTOTYPING

There are two main strategies for prototyping: Low-fidelity and high fidelity. A low fidelity strategy (Jim, Ken et al. 1996) is paper-based whereas a high-fidelity relies on the development of a functional prototype and empirical studies for its evaluation. In this section prototyping refers to a low fidelity approach, a paper based approach, which relies on, for example, sketching interactions techniques (Moggridge 2007) such as storyboarding and description of user scenarios for its evaluation. The philosophy behind a low-prototyping strategy is to allow rapid exploration with minimal investment. In other words, it enables designers to externalise their designs quickly, evaluate them and iterate based on the lessons learned. This means that a great level of refinement can be achieved without having to build a prototype. Moreover, the techniques proposed in here have their focus around interaction from two perspectives: The user and the (digital interactive) system (see Table 8).

Table 8. Low-fidelity prototyping. User and system interaction techniques.

User interaction	Sketching interaction: Storyboarding Description of user scenarios
System interaction	Mapping physical computing Information flow diagrams Computing systems diagrams Sections and construction details

User's Interactions

From the user's interaction perspective, the task of sketching interactions can be thought of as analogous to traditional sketching. Using Bill Buxton's words: "Since sketches for interaction need to be able to capture the essence of designs concepts around transitions, dynamics, feel, phrasing, and all the other unique attributes of interactive systems, sketches of interaction must necessarily be distinct from the types of sketches that we have looked thus far" (Buxton 2007). Hence, storyboards and description of user scenarios are proposed as a way of capturing the essence of the user's interaction with the system.

Storyboards and User Scenarios

Description of user scenarios and storyboards can be used for the same purpose sketching user's interactions. The former relies mainly on words

Figure 7. User experience diagram

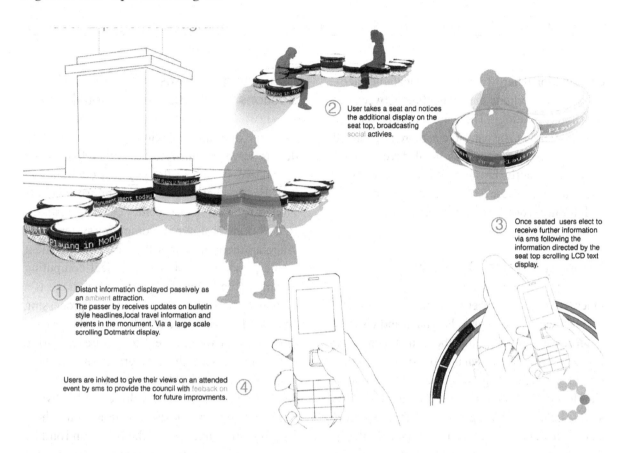

to describe what the user does whereas the latter is a visualisation of that description.

A description of a user's scenario focuses on *what* happens, not *how* it happens. In other words, describing the specific technologies involved in the interaction should be avoided. Instead, the whole environment of the project from the point of view of the person experiencing what you are making should be described. It should be described what that person sees, hears, and feels and what she can do to change the environment. The experience should be described as it unfolds. Changes as the person takes various actions and how her attention and actions are focused by the changes should be explained. Finally, designers should describe why this is engaging to the person and how the sequence of events should work to keep her engaged.

A storyboard is a visual representation of a user's scenario description. Storyboarding is a technique which has been used widely in the preproduction of films and video games as well as for interface design. Storyboarding has the advantage over other representations that it is fairly intuitive and does not require a great deal of explanation or training for architecture students. There is, however, a characteristic which has to be emphasized: Granularity. That is, the story board should clearly illustrate the user's scenario step-by-step. Figure 7 shows an example.

System's Interactions

The techniques describe in this section attempt to bridge the gap between the design and its technological implementation (i.e. software,

Table 9. Mapping physical computing. Adapted from (O'Sullivan and Igoe 2004)

Digital Input	Analog Input	Processing	Digital Output	Analog Output

computational hardware, and physical interface). They try to facilitate the connection between design and technology. These are tools given to the designer so that she can have a degree of control and input over the technological development. More importantly, however, it is the view that, if used correctly, these techniques should make the technology work for the interaction and not the other way around.

Mapping Physical Computing

Once the project has been through a few iterations of being described in plain language and visually explored without thinking about the technology, it should be broken down into the stages of input, output and processing. Next, the input and output should be identified as digital or analog. This should help with starting the search for the perfect transducers: sensor and actuators (see Table 9). Additionally, the sequence of events should be described. Do they happen one after the other? Or do they happen all at the same time? In the former case, they would be serial events, and in the latter would be parallel. This has great implications in terms of system design as parallel event are far more difficult to process.

Information Flow Diagrams

The deployment of an interactive system brings with it the exchange and, sometimes, exposure of data. Adopting a diagrammatic form, usually using "blobs", this diagram explains how the information flows from the systems and systems to the user's interaction(s) (see Figure 8). For the conceptualisation of this process, if applicable, the students are also asked to consider the informational attributes described in Table 10.

Computing Systems Diagrams: Sections and Construction Details

Systems diagrams, sections and construction details serve to illustrate the embedding of the interactive system in the physical environment and, together, act as a feasibility study prior to the implementation stage (i.e. they can help costing a first working prototype). Computing systems diagrams are therefore seen in this case as a refinement to the previously obtained physical computing mapping (see Figure 8). At this stage, there is a mapping between inputs, outputs and processing and specific hardware and software technologies. For instance, if the intervention requires capturing human movement, these diagrams should show which specific technology is used (i.e. cameras) and software which would drive the hardware. Similarly, sections and construction details show the physical components of the system and outline how it would be constructed. Issues of glare, energy efficiency, modularity, durability, and so on are considered here. To consider this an appropriate drawings are presented: Sections, internal and external perspectives, and construction details.

CONCLUSION

The history of design methods warns us against the perils of overly explicit and prescriptive methodologies (i.e. those based on graph theory or operational research techniques). The spirit of the methodology proposed in this study can be encapsulated in Broadbent's words: "A methodology should not be a fixed track to a fixed destination, but a conversation about everything that could be made to happen". Thus, the methodology presented in this chapter should be seen as part of the

Figure 8. Information and process flow diagram.

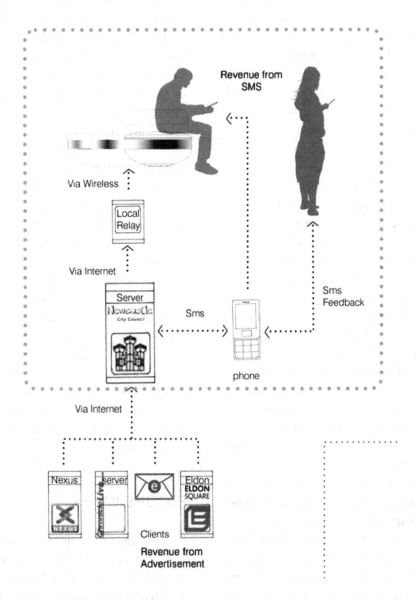

Table 10. Informational attributes

Attribute	Description
Privacy	Information privacy refers to "an individual's claim to control how personal data is collected, distributed, and processed" (Cuff, Hansen et al. 2008). Different country specific regulatory frameworks determine the relationship between what private property is and what is accessible to the public.
Property	Copyright law only protects creative expressions; it does not protect the underlying data. Accordingly, one might be anxious that data will be underproduced because there will be no easy way to incentivise its collection and distribution" (Cuff, Hansen et al. 2008). Current thinking amongst scholars is that instead of financial gain, the incentive would be attribution –recognition-
Information pollution	This deals with an undesirable side effect brought by information technologies: The supply of irrelevant, redundant, unsolicited and low-value information (Nielsen 2003).

designer's toolkit for organising design thoughts. Moreover, this chapter has outlined specific techniques and attributes to link the analysis and synthesis stages of an IA project to the concepts of: Space, place and interaction.

Based on the experience gained during this study, I do believe that outlining specific techniques and attributes is particularly valuable in an education context where students are faced with a novel subject that requires an adaptation of their design thinking process and lack the required experience as very rarely they have designed a digital interactive system before. For example, when I first introduced IA as a design exercise in the School of Architecture at Newcastle University, common feedback comments were: "Interactive space needs to explored a little further", "we did not really pick up on what it was until the last week", "More theoretical justification should be added to inform and refine the concepts beyond gimmickry". These comments have now disappeared. Thus, this seems to suggest that a structured design exploration facilitates the teaching and learning activity as it externalises both the teaching process and expected learning and material outcomes.

Another successful aspect of the framework is the ability to make transparent the link between the three key concepts: Space, place and interaction. This have been noted in the feedback given by the students: (the methodology) "encourages a different perspective on design, developing design ideas rooted in how people behave rather than the more general understandings of physical space". This is particularly critical as IA can be seen focused on the (interactive) object rather than on the (interactive) architectural space.

With regards to the specific attributes and techniques proposed in the methodology, unsurprisingly, the techniques related to the morphological attribute work well as students were familiar with spatial design methods. On the other hand, cultural practice and conceptual techniques were less successful as they require a new set of skills (e.g. ability to conduct successful focus groups).

Low-fidelity prototyping was well received and understood. Storyboards were particularly successful whereas the implementation of techniques to map the interactive system's requirement varied and depended on the level of interest and technical ability of the designer. High fidelity prototyping has been intentionally left out of this discussion as it requires a functional prototype and specific empirical evaluation methods. My view is that high fidelity prototyping should be seen as the first part of the implementation stage. In fact, some practitioners advocate a design method around high fidelity prototyping: Flash Research Physicality (Benjamin and Yang 2006). I do believe this a valid approach which is particularly strong in a practice by experience designers. However, as stated earlier, the approach presented in this text is particularly valuable in an education context where students are faced with a novel subject that requires an adaptation of their design thinking process and lack the required experience as very rarely they have designed a digital interactive system before.

FUTURE WORK

In my view, for the design community to be relevant in technologically driven areas such as IA, the link between technological implementation and intellectual pursue ought to be strengthened. In other words, design needs to inform the technical deployment of these technological interventions. To achieve this, it is my belief that structured design explorations will facilitate this correlation. However, key aspects of future work are to improve: The robustness of the techniques employed to capture data, ability to represent interaction for design and presentation purposes, and the theoretical link between behavioural and social sciences and the design of an interactive intervention.

Capturing Data

The Observational techniques proposed here drew on tasks analysis research (Kirwan and Ainsworth 1992). There are two points for this discussion. The first is a practical and procedural one, observational techniques can be laborious for obtaining and analysis data. It is my experience that clear guidance should be given as to what needs to be obtained and how. For instance, in the case of direct observation is worth discussing what resources are needed, what considerations ought to be taken into account, the procedure, how to create and analyse an event observational form. The same is applicable to video and audio recording and time-lapsed photography. The second point is philosophical. Task analysis has developed from human factor research with focus on the man-machine interface in which the man is seen as an operator who carries out specific and uniquely identified tasks. Whilst this has advantages in terms of very well defined methods and techniques, I believe a future line of research is to develop this further by incorporating philosophical thinking and methodologies from observational techniques developed in ethnographic studies. Ethnographic studies are founded on the idea that humans are best understood in the fullest context possible context (i.e. the place humans work, the improvement they have made to that place, how they provide and use energy, how they communicate, ect). In particular, participant observation research strategies (e.g. life-stories, self-analysis) can be proved to be particularly valuable as they might enable the designer to gain a close understanding of a given group of individuals and their practices their "natural" environment. However, a major caveat is that this type of study tends to be carried out over an extended period of time (e.g. months and years). This is not feasible. Hence, these methods will have to be adapted.

As well as adapting observational techniques, another approach worth considering for capturing data is user centre design. This approach incor-porates the notion of participatory design as the involvement of the user in the design process is formalised. User-centred design methods are imbued with elements of community-art workshop practice and target the development of an intervention based on the requirements and preferences of a user type. In a typical workshop case studies and elemental topics will be addressed, including: Social and environmental factors in the space, feedback loops and potential for points of information, privacy and anonymity, DIY culture and citizenship, technology selection and perceived and actual impacts.

Representation

The challenge for representation is to visualise the dynamics and flow of interaction. Other ways of representing interaction could have been explored. For instance, Bill Buxton has proposed the use of state transition diagrams. Essentially in a state diagram there is a small navigation map attached to each sketch. This enables the sketches to be seen as "states" connected with these navigational paths –"transitions" so that transform the sketch from a static to a dynamic representation. This, in my view, could work well for traditional interaction design based on GUI rather than Interactive Architecture. Similarly, more computational representation could have been used such as Finite State Machine representation. These are abstract graphs used in software design to encapsulate the systems behaviour. Whilst this is an appropriate tool for the conceptualisation of algorithms and software, it is my experience that it is seen as too abstract conceptualisation of the interaction to be used as a representation.

My own thoughts on this are that story board are an appropriate means of initial representation by interactions are too fluid to be captured by a 2D drawing. At times, we have produced 3D time-based animations of the user scenario. Whilst these are clearer, the do come with a drawback: they are time consuming. An idea which I would like to implement is acting the interactions out for an audience. This would easy in terms of production but complex in terms of thought needed.

Behavioural and Social Sciences

As stated by Evans (Evans 1996): "Although architecture as a practice has not embraced the behavioural sciences to the extent hoped for, the education of architects typically includes some exposure to human behaviour. The idea that design affects users and can make a difference in their lives is central to every major design profession".

The initial enthusiasm of collaboration between architects and psychologists (Lang 1975; Moore 1979) has decreased considerably. However recent trends in other design fields suggest increasing interest in behavioural science research. Interior designers, for example, have altered their major scholarly journal, the Journal of Interior Design, to reflect greater involvement in social science research. Similarly, the intersection between criminal behaviour and design is currently seen as a hot topic for research and discussion (Davey 2008). Researchers and designers are exploring the role of the physical environment in affecting crime directly as well as its influence on fear of crime. The interplay of these two processes is well illustrated by the incivilities theory, use of landscape aesthetic principles, and research on the criminal's perspective on crime.

During our explorations behavioural drivers (e.g. play, competition, comfort) were explored but not fully understood. For instance, competition was put forward as key behavioural driver but one of our interventions but it was not fully understood. The reward mechanisms suggested by the designers were naïve in their interpretations (i.e. a beer for every member of the winning community). They failed to notice that using monetary methods to influence behaviour removes the consumer from understanding the greater value of energy and carbon emission reduction. These naïve interpretations were an expected outcome as these

were trained architects who have not had prior exposure to behavioural sciences. I believe that if Interactive Architecture is to progress the link with behavioural sciences needs to be developed.

REFERENCES

Addington, M., & Schodek, D. (2005). *Smart materials and technologies for the architecture and design professions*. Architectural Press.

Aipperspach, R., & Hooker, B. (2009). The heterogeneous home. *Interaction*, *16*(1). doi:10.1145/1456202.1456211

Baptiste, N. (1995). Adults need to play, too. *Early Childhood Education Journal*, *23*(1), 2. doi:10.1007/BF02353377

Benjamin, D., & Yang, S.-I. (2006). *Life size*. New York, NY: Graduate School of Architecture, Planning and Preservation of Columbia University.

Broadbent, G. (1969). *Design methods in architecture*. London, UK: Lund Humpries for the Architectural Association.

Brownell, B. (2006). *Transmaterial: A catalog of materials that redefine our physical environment*. New York, NY: Princeton Architectural Press.

Buxton, B. (2007). *Sketching user experiences*. Morgan Kaufmann.

Calderon, C. (2009). *Interactive architecture design*. Harvard Graduate School of Design, Design and Technology series 2009-2.

Clancey, W. J. (2001). Field science ethnography: Methods for systematic observation on an expedition. *Field Methods*, *13*(3), 223–243. doi:10.1177/1525822X0101300301

Davey, C. (2008). *Design against crime*. Retrieved April 2010 from http://www.designagainstcrime.org/

Dourish, P. (2001). *Where the actions is: The foundations of embodied interaction*. The MIT Press.

Dourish, P., & Bell, G. (2007). The infrastructure of experience and the experience of infrastructure: meaning and structure in everyday encounters with space. *Environment and Planning. B, Planning & Design, 34*, 16. doi:10.1068/b32035t

Drury, C. G. (1992). Methods for direct observation of performance. In Wilson, J. R., & Corlett, E. N. (Eds.), *Evaluation of human work*. London, UK: Taylor and Francis.

Dubberly, H., Pangaro, P., et al. (2009). What is interaction? Are there different types? *ACM Interactions*, January.

Durand, J. N. L. (1809). *Précis des leçons d'architecture données à l'École royale polytechnique*. Chez l'auteur.

Evans, G. (1996). Environmental psychology as a field within psychology. *IAAP Newsletter*, Fall.

Fisher, D. (2008). *Dynamic architecture*. Retrieved 14 July, 2008, from http://www.dynamicarchitecture.net/ home.html

Fogg, B. J. (2003). *Persuasive technology: Using computer to change what we think and do*. Morgan Kaufmann.

Gaver, W. (1991). *Technology affordances*. Conference on Human Factors in Computer Systems CHI'91, New Orleans, ACM.

Gibson, J. J. (1977). *The theory of affordances. Perceiving, acting, and knowing*. Hillsdale, NJ: Lawrence Erlbaum Associates.

Greenfield, A., & Shepard, M. (2007). *Architecture and situated technologies pamphlet 1*. The Architectural League of New York.

Grudin, J. (1990). The computer reaches out: The historical continuity of interface design. *Conference on Human Factors in Computing Systems CHI'90*, Seattle, USA, ACM.

Hillier, B., & Hanson, J. (1984). *The social logic of space*. Cambridge, UK: Cambridge University Press. doi:10.1017/CBO9780511597237

Jim, R., & Ken, S. (1996). Low vs. high-fidelity prototyping debate. *Interaction, 3*(1), 76–85. doi:10.1145/223500.223514

Jones, J. C. (1992). *Design methods*. New York, NY: Van Nostrand Reinhold.

Kaur, I. (2007). *Enhancing social awareness at the workplace. Unpublished Masters of Science in Media Arts and Sciences, School of Architecture and Planning*. Boston: MIT.

Kirsh, D. (2001). Changing the rules: Architecture and the new millennium. *Convergence: The International Journal of Research into New Media Technologies, 7*(2), 12. doi:10.1177/135485650100700210

Kirwan, B., & Ainsworth, L. K. (1992). *A guide to task analysis*. Taylor and Francis.

Kronenburg, R. (2007). *Flexible architecture that responds to change*. Laurence King.

LaGro, J. A. (2008). *Site analysis: A contextual approach to sustainable land planning and site design*. John Wiley & Sons, Inc.

Lang, J. (1975). *Designing for human behaviour: Architecture and the behavioural sciences*. John Wiley & Sons Inc.

Lawson, B. (1980). *How designers think: The design process demystified*. Architectural Press.

May, T. (2001). *Social research: Issues, methods and process*. Open University Press.

Mitchell, W. J. (2000). *E-topia*. MIT Press.

Moggridge, B. (2007). *Designing interactions*. MIT Press.

Moore, G. T. (1979). *Architecture and human behaviour: The place of environment-behaviour studies in architecture*. Winconsin Architect.

Negroponte, N. (1995). *Being digital. Hodder and Stoughton. Norman, D. A. (1988). The psychology of everyday things.* New York, NY: Basic Books.

O'Sullivan, D., & Igoe, T. (2004). *Physical computing.* Thomson Course Technology.

Sharp, H., & Rogers, Y. (2007). *Interaction design: Beyond human-computer interaction.* John Wiley & Sons.

Shove, E. (2003). *Changing human behaviour and lifestyle: A challenge for sustainable consumption?* P. S. Institute, ESRC Environment and Human Behaviour Programme.

Sparacino, F. (2002). *Narrative spaces: Bridging architecture and entertainment via interactive technology.* 6th International Conference on Generative Art, Politecnico de Milano University, Milan, Italy.

Sterk, T. E. (2003). *Using actuated tensegrity structures to produce a responsive architecture.* ACADIA, Annual Conference of the Association for Computer Aided Design In Architecture): Connecting, Crossroads of Digital Discourse, Indianapolis (Indiana).

Weiser, M. (1991). The computer for the 21st century. *Scientific American Special Issue on Communications, Computers, and Networks* (September).

KEY TERMS AND DEFINITIONS

Communication: The activity of conveying meaningful information as to engage with users.

Design Methods: A broad area of research which focuses on applying exploratory and rigorous methods to solve problems through design.

Interactive Architecture: A field of architecture in which objects and space have the ability to meet changing needs with respect to evolving individual, social, and environmental demands.

Retrofit Technologies: It refers to the addition of new technologies to older systems. It is particularly relevant to urban energy and carbon futures.

Smart Materials: Materials whoseich properties can be significantly changed in a controlled fashion via external stimuli.

Urban and Public Spaces: A social space that is open and accessible to all.

ENDNOTE

[1] Other terms used in the literature to refer to Interactive Architecture are: Intelligent Spaces; Smart Environments; Interactive Environments; Interactive Spatial Environments; Interactive Spatial Environments; Responsive environments

Chapter 17
Information Engagement through Interactive Sonification Design

Kirsty Beilharz
University of Technology-Sydney, Australia

ABSTRACT

Design for effective information engagement through interactive sonification and visualization can be divided into two parts: (1) interface and interaction - designing the method of manipulating, investigating and interrogating information representations; and (2) information design - designing the representation, interactivity and user-customizability of the data content. The user experience is affected by the responsiveness and intelligence (awareness, contextual knowledge, situated interactivity) of the representation design. The purpose of information visualization and sonification is to transform data into information, that is, to enable users to find meaningfulness in the data. Integral to the success of computational technologies in design is an understanding of designing around the human user, the user experience, ergonomics, aesthetics, usability, and attractive, engaging, "sticky" modes of interactivity.

INTRODUCTION

While data mining focuses on methods for interrogating datasets, it could be said that information visualization and sonification (auditory representation of data, or auditory graphing) attends to the aesthetics, interactivity, clarity and flexibility of data representation to enhance the experience of understanding, evaluating, and comparing information, usually by human users. Hence

human-centered customization of the interface, and interaction that allows multiple iterations or "views" of the data, aids human interaction with content (such as the ability to navigate, zoom and reorganize data) and these techniques can contribute to user control of auditory and graphical representations.

This chapter looks at information design, a subset of content in design, and at ways of leveraging the interface, e.g. with physical computing interaction and social interplay, in order to increase the satisfaction and engagement with the

DOI: 10.4018/978-1-61350-180-1.ch017

digital experience. Physical interaction and social interaction will be discussed in relation to data visualization and sonification but key concepts can be applied to other forms of representation and interaction design. Features such as the persuasiveness of the data become metrics of the performance of a representation. Increasingly, the goal of contemporary data representations often extends beyond informativeness to include social and non-expert engagement with the data representation through the media and popular forms of dissemination. Due to the efficiency of a graphical and auditory representation, information visualization is one of the most effective methods for conveying data in a penetrable, available form. User-centered interfaces allow lay people to interrogate, manipulate, compare and perform simple transformations of complex data sets that are otherwise only accessible to expert analysts when the data is in its raw form.

Visualization and sonification are becoming evermore important and ubiquitous in our understanding of complex data and for monitoring data events. Technologies such as web-cameras and sensors provide constant and potentially massive streams of information about the environment, information transactions, Internet activity, etc. and sensors and captors are increasingly widespread in urban, domestic, climatic and operational contexts. Less well explored are ways to effectively and ergonomically interact with live data utilizing the advantages of real-time, instantaneous responsiveness. While systems for computational analysis and software data interpretation are quite well established, more flexible and interactive systems for human access and understanding of information requires a different design approach. The way in which humans interact with digital information is also rapidly transforming as pervasive and physical, tangible, gestural interfaces for interaction are increasingly usual, offering the advantage that intuitive natural actions can be used to control computational processes in a myriad of physical locations. Therefore, interactive inter-

faces and designing the interaction experience is inseparable from the quality of the "experience" of negotiating information representations. This chapter examines these two major influences (the interaction experience and the information representation) in information engagement.

The chapter will draw on recent research in gestural, tangible, sensing, real-time interaction designs in the author's research lab[1], cases from pedagogical interaction design studios and work examining innovative real-time and interactive representation of information (i.e. information sonification and visualization).

BACKGROUND

The more established field of data visualization offers principles and insights that can be applied to data sonification representation and mapping processes. Edward Tufte (Tufte, 1983, 1992, 1997), Benjamin Fry (Fry, 2004), the *Gestalt* psychologists, and John Maeda's Laws of Simplicity for design and life (Maeda, 2006), have defined some prevailing principles of effective information communication, information design and representation design. These principles mostly construed for the visual domain are here interpreted for auditory representation and considered in conjunction with approaches informed by sound quality and musical attributes, such as subtlety and diversity of timbral expression, user-controlled features, interest and non-repetition. Listenable and interesting representations enhance the listening experience, facilitating engagement with the data. Sonification is the representation of data through non-speech sound. In recent years, visual representations have achieved a high level of aesthetic quality (Vande Moere, 2010). The strategies presented here provide approaches for bimodal, multimodal and auditory information representation because sound is an underexplored dimension in interaction design and information design.

Sonification exists for the purpose of conveying data to the listener, but is also commonly used for the creation of aesthetic works that are presented in the same context as purely musical works, or are used in an installation setting, e.g. interactive performative sonification (Weinberg & Thatcher, 2006). These works often do not aim to communicate a dataset, or at least do not use information transfer as a measure of their success. They also usually lack a connection between the user and the data being represented; the users are often uninterested in the data as it is of no relevance to them, or it is so complex as to be unintelligible. Their focus is rather on the aesthetic or musical content of the piece.

Another class of more traditional sonification exists purely for information transfer, and seems generally unconcerned with aesthetics. This precise problem has been identified by Fry in relation to visualization: "software-based information visualization adds building blocks for interacting with and representing various kinds of abstract data, but typically the aesthetic principles of visual design are treated as less important or even superficial, rather than embracing their strength as a necessary aid to effective communication" (Fry, 2004). Many sonifications of this type are produced through MIDI-based synthesis, and are stored as MIDI data, which leaves the specifics of timbral (tone color) quality to the particular combination of MIDI synthesizer and timbral program available at the time of playback, i.e. giving no quality assurance or precision to characteristics such as timbre, absolute loudness or dynamics, etc.

Paul Vickers posits that, "many sonifications have suffered from poor acoustic ecology which makes listening more difficult, thereby resulting in poorer data extraction and inference on the part of the listener" (Vickers, 2005; Vickers & Hogg, 2006). Vickers also points out that in recent contemporary (Classical) music of the past 60 years or so, composers have been employing algorithmic compositional techniques and since the computer-music age, algorithmic processes can be quickly enabled to proliferate material in a creative context. This seems to demarcate a common ground shared between sonification and music, in which strict algorithmic or (in the case of sonification) strict mapping relationships between values and sonic rendering cohabit with other parametric controls that govern sonic aesthetics. At the same time as some compositional processes have been computerized, composers have also explored sound at a more microcosmic or microscopic level (creating sonic materials, synthesizing musical materials) not only organizing at the level of the note object but creating the spectrum and characteristics of individual sounds, organising using metric and geometric methods as well as conventionally understood ones (Roads, 2001). This connects with one of Tufte's organizational principles: The reading of the micro and macro. We hear with Xenakis' use of the Serial Modulor approach (Beilharz, 2003; Xenakis, 1971) or the French Spectral School, a musical architecture that relates the structure of sonic grains and sub-note-sized organisms to grosser temporal durations and overall forms of pieces, spatial distribution and textural organization.

Tufte's (Tufte, 1992) theory for information design is about containing detailed information that can be zoomed in on, or mined at a deeper level, but it is also about (beyond comprehensiveness) organizational structures: "Detail cumulates into larger coherent structures" and "simplicity of reading derives from the context of detailed and complex information *properly organized*. A most unconventional design strategy is revealed: To clarify, add detail" (Tufte, 1992). In sonification, we can translate this idea as embedding zoom-able detail or nesting (unpack-able related hierarchies of information) in the detailed qualities of notes.

"Edgard Varèse defined music as organized sound, and sonifications organize sound to reflect mimetically the thing being sonified. What is apparent from listening to them is the wide variation in the [musical, aesthetic] quality" (Vickers & Hogg, 2006).

INTERACTIVE
SONIFICATION DESIGN

Information Design: Mapping, Representation, and Information Aesthetics

Principles from information visualization approaches can be applied to sonification, both to enhance information aesthetics and to facilitate bimodal representation based a shared understanding. Ben Fry's simplification of complex data visualization principles is manifest in his methodology (and tool) for *Computational Information Design* (Fry, 2004; Fry, 2008) that converges the fields of information visualization, data mining and graphic design normally employed in the complex task of representing data visually. One of the computational challenges presented beyond merely mapping data to representation is how to handle large volumes of data and how to glean a "big-picture" oversight or meaningful understanding. Fry's description of the process flow is not domain specific and applies equally well to sonification as visualization: "Acquire - parse - filter - mine - represent - refine - interact" (Fry, 2004). This process has reflexive and iterative rather than linear stages. This iteration is possible with the author's AeSon Toolkit[2].

Approaches that can rapidly, if qualitatively, convey the overview meaning and significant gist of the information representation are much more ergonomic that methods that require detailed analysis and short-term memorization, e.g. representing quantities with number values to be read rather than with size-scaled visual dots. The read test is also closer to the abstracted textual representation of the original dataset. This is akin to using speech in sound rather than non-speech audio that sonification employs to achieve an immediate, intuitive *"gestalt"* impression of meaning. That is, simplicity of rendering and reduced time for understanding the data are valuable qualities in representation. This view is underscored by John

Maeda's *The Laws of Simplicity* (Maeda, 2006). The goal is non-active information assimilation, i.e. pre-attentive display.

Examples of how quantity and relativity information can be represented visually include an object's number, shape, alignment (orientation) relative to the group, proximity, shape, size/scale, similarity versus dissimilarity of appearance. Also colour, motion and spatial position can impart pre-attentive signification.

Comparing these form modifiers with sonic representation, the broad division of similarity and dissimilarity within any representational parameter is important. For example like values can share similar timbre, pitch, duration, intensity (loudness/brightness) while outliers and dissimilar values can exhibit contrasting characteristics. This emphasizes the need for a subtle enough display that allows for variety or diversity within representational parameters and sufficient dimensions to convey the necessary dimensions of the dataset. Andrew Vande Moere and others (Vande Moere, 2010) have argued that the choice of representational form (akin to graphic design decisions) is a juncture in the design process where the mode of representation can be aligned with the aesthetics and semantics of the data, e.g. colours and icons in graphics or timbre and character in sound can equate with the tonality, gravity and message of the data. Information about fatalities in wars should be differently represented to the number of products sold for instance and this is a contextual design decision in which the data has a non-objective bearing on its representation.

Tufte (Tufte, 1983) advocates minimizing non-data ink, i.e. reducing superfluous and distracting elements in the representation that are not integral to clear understanding. Musically-speaking this is equivalent to minimizing irrelevant auditory information such as harmonization, beats and pulses that do not serve useful time-series purpose. On the other hand, helpful markers such as cues at peaks, critical thresholds and signifiers of patterns, cliques, accentuating repetitions or interesting features in the data would constitute the reason for non-graph intervention. Tufte attributes great importance to visual design for understanding data (Tufte, 1983, 1992), noting that "graphical excellence consists of complex ideas communicated with clarity, precision, and efficiency", its elegance arises from efficacy, functionality, the ability to create meaningful information. AeSon (Aesthetic Sonification Toolkit) adopts the approach that efficiency, simplicity, disqualification of irrelevant and clouding information, achieved by fastidious design, intuitive signification through pre-attentive formal representation and careful filtering in the mining phase can contribute to a less complicated rendering.

Card et al (Card, Mackinlay, & Shneiderman, 1999) espouse that the purpose of information visualization is "the use of computer-supported, interactive, visual representations of data to amplify cognition". That is, mere representation or graphing is not the culmination: Rather amplifying, enhancing, aiding cognitive understanding and analysis are the objectives. Sonification may often be more difficult for people initially than interpreting a visual graph however motivation lies in the potential for rich and concurrent multiple-meaning layers for ascribing information accessible intuitively or with minimal attentiveness. Sound is a good medium for layering information. Both information visualization and information sonification are concerned with making visible/audible and revealing information in abstract datasets. Interestingly, sound is often still described by many as an abstract medium due to its "invisible" quality and ephemeral time-dependent nature. However details of changing frequency and timbre can be measurably, easily, clearly and intuitively discerned and extremely fine distinctions in pitch can be discriminated by most people.

Visual quality, according to Fry (Fry, 2004), is often omitted from the discussion of information visualization due to its immeasurable, unqualifiable and subjective characteristic, yet this is precisely the crux impending on popular uptake,

acceptability and ergonomics of listening. Fry argues the importance of representational quality precisely because small aesthetic design decisions become dramatically amplified when applied to large and complex datasets. Tukey (Tukey, 1977) implies also that smallest inaccuracies and distortions in data can influence the quality of the graph, hence he places greatest importance on "procedures for analyzing data, techniques for interpreting the results of such procedures, ways of planning the gathering of data to make analysis easier, more precise or more accurate". Hence timbral control is an area of refinement, scaling and fine-tuning ascribed to the user in the AeSon toolkit, to allow for individual customization of the listening experience. It is useful to allow some user intervention and tailoring of the interface to suit their needs and tastes.

Clustering similar data and use of differentiating features are two methods identified by Fry (Fry, 2004) that can improve clarity and interaction. Teasing this out and applying it to a sonic context, color could be considered literally: Spectrum, timbral profile, tone colour or the general gist of illuminating relevance in a distinctive way, e.g. with a high-pass filter, amplifier, or modulator. Highlighting location is integral to an interface design that acknowledges the user interaction, navigating and locating or orienting the user.

In data representations intended for physical interaction (touchpad, drawing with a stylus on a graphic tablet, using a multi-touch surface such a large tangible display or Apple iPhone/iPad-style screen) orienting the user and the ability to locate sonic objects in two-dimensional space are critical features in the spatiality of the interface. With three-dimensional controllers such as a Nintendo Wii controller or six-degrees-of-freedom device, the user can manipulate sonic objects in the three spatial dimensions and use the rotation, tilt, yaw sensors for motion control, scaling, scrolling and panning the auditory representation of data. This gestural interaction and the relationship between intuitive spatial manipulation of information is further intended to give the user pre-attentive and intuitive control of the interaction relying on proprioception and natural spatial motion.

Low latency for interactive sonification environments and the ability to graph or map the same datasets in a variety of ways in order to interrogate it with a fresh "view/audit" are necessary. In the AeSon Toolkit, the user can scale the data at different granularities and refine the sonic dimensions applied to the axes and adjust tempo or pace of time-series sets, performing multi-dimensional scaling transformations. Contrast and differentiation are used to transform the aesthetic character of the representation, as well as to clarify meaning.

In Fry's information visualization (Fry, 2004), size, weight and placement are criteria used for interpretation. Musically, there are a number of ways to represent the idea of size (i.e. contextual scale and importance), such as density of a cluster of sounds - for example Edgar Varèse's "masses of sounds" or Iannis Xenakis' "clouds"- statistical clusters of values whose density, mass and distribution affect the perceived size and opacity of sound; dimension of the sound; intensity (loudness, spectrum); spatial proximity - perceived nearness appears larger, hence vary reverberation and virtual spatial audio characteristics to adjust sensations of nearness and farness and movement; agitation or excitement effectively attracting attention; articulation. Weight or importance and hierarchy demonstrate some overlap. Hence, if these are construed as different dimensions in the data, then orthogonal mapping approaches should be applied in the sonification to ensure a lack of cross-fertilization, e.g. sharpness or brightness could be used to distinguish hierarchy while loudness is equated with weight. In other words, the interplay of certain musical characteristics is context dependent. An interface that allows for various representations and re-examination of the data in different configurations can assist in detangling interoperating characteristics.

Spatial logic in relation to the user's own sense of space and nearness, farness in perception

determine the naturalness of gestural interactions. Sonic interaction that employs a spatial, physical interface, benefits from natural rules of drawing sonic objects closer, to the foreground, panning sounds to the left and right of the display-space and the Y-axis attributed to pitch can utilize spectrum shifts to produce the perception of height and depth in 3D. Proportion rules require strict scaling and multiplying functions. Scale and zoom in a time-series dataset effectively describes the time-stretching or distribution of the data over time and ability to examine a finer granularity, "magnifying" features of form. An important part of interaction is allowing the user to inspect the information at a useful scale and in different ways, to move from "overview" or global view to "microview" whereby the user can reveal greater detail. In AeSon a spatial sliding axis principle is used, similar to the "pinch" gesture on the iPhone interface that simply transforms how much of the sample dataset fills the inspection "window" (in auditory terms, what section of data is heard in the duration).

John Maeda's "Laws" or design principles are such universal paradigms that they can be applied to design, business, and life. These laws provide a basic understanding of characteristics of "good" design, some seeming especially relevant to information sonification, e.g. *achieving efficacy and clarity* (Maeda, 2006): Thoughtful reduction to achieve simplicity; organisation which makes a system of many appear fewer; avoiding time-wastage; contextualize and utilize peripheral information to contribute to the context of the central thread; subtract the obvious and elucidate the meaningful. From these principles we take the notion of constructive simplicity in the representation to avoid confounding and masking streams of data, while preserving the multivariate richness afforded by the underlying data. Mapping distinctive data dimensions to different sonic qualities can assist in the clarification and stratification of concurrent information.

In *Envisioning Information* (Tufte, 1992), Tufte talks about escaping "flatland", i.e. for graphic design and two-dimensional printing this means finding representational techniques that interleave layers of information, which can be loosely interpreted as multidimensionality in sonification. That is, within a succinct *gestalt* view or time-frame for assimilation, overlaying various concurrent meanings to create an information-rich display, to "sharpen the information resolution ... to increase (1) the number of dimensions that can be represented ... and (2) data density". In sonification, condensing the amount of information that can be accommodated within a space involves maximizing information reviewed in the time-scale. Multi-dimensionality also adds diversity and interest, hence it is both quantitatively and qualitatively enriching.

On layering and separation, Tufte states: "Confusion and clutter are failures of design - not attributes of information", hence organization can be achieved using (1) proper relationships among information layers, and (2) representation relevant in "proportion and harmony" (Tufte, 1992) which reiterates qualities found in music. Separation and delineation can be achieved by foregrounding and emphasizing important information, akin to differentiating the graph from its background in graphic design or eradicating competing patterns, pitches, interfering elements, confounding density of information. In musical and sonification contexts, we can use distinguishing pitch register, timbres and filtering to distinguish competing elements, as well as temporal off-set (rhythmic separation, asynchronicity).

Multimodal and Auditory Representation

Representations of data are tools for investigating and ultimately for understanding data resulting from measurements of a particular phenomenon.

Representations can be used to explore data, when the user is unsure of the meaning of a data collection, or they can be used to confirm a hypothesis, when a user seeks verification of something they already suspect to be true. Sometimes these two purposes are described as exploratory data analysis and confirmatory data analysis (Tukey, 1977). Graphs are often more useful for the exploratory phase, as they can highlight outliers, and describe multiple trends, and draw similarities between variables intuitively. After the character of the data is established, statistical tests can be used to confirm the significance of the effects seen in visual representations.

Representations are often used in various ways: Walker and Nees (Walker & Nees, 2005) describe the various possibilities using terms such as *trend analysis*, *point estimation*, *pattern detection*, and *point comparison*. They state that few auditory graphs can achieve these generic tasks, supporting the idea that audio in representation is sometime most useful as an indicative (cueing) feature or redundant and reinforcing element in conjunction with visual representation where exact quantitative measurements are required. However, for observing time-based transformation, peaks, troughs, trends and subtle differentiations in value, as well as to articulate outliers and anomalies, sound can be an extremely helpful communicator.

There are a number of distinct data elements that a representation may attempt to convey to a user. Measures of central tendency (e.g. various types of means, the median, or the mode) describe the general centre of the dataset, while measures of dispersion (e.g. standard deviation, variance) can describe its spread.

In an auditory and visual bimodal situation, strengths of sonification include immediacy, denoting significant points, time-based and representation. Clear parallels between tone color (timbre) and visual color; scale (size) of visual representation and magnitude of loudness (intensity); spatial panning (audio channels) and spatial distribution on screen or display; distribution over pitch range and height (y-axis) of a time-series visual graph, time distribution or periodicity (rhythm, tempo) and visual distance (x-axis) establish grounds for multimodal confluence and reinforcement.

Sonification places the representation in the time domain, and therefore it must grapple with the limitations of perception in the time domain (e.g. memory, comparison, masking effects that can occur between concurrent sounds). Visual perception and auditory perception are different.

The texture of the auditory representation is generally determined by the number and length of notes presented. Sonification uses a specified number of data-points represented as sound events (typically notes) presented at a constant rate or tempo, although there are many exceptions. This constant rate also often determines the length of notes – they are designed to sound only until the next note starts. This determines that none of the notes will sound simultaneously, and also makes sure there will be no silence. It is common in traditional sonification for notes to be presented at a consistent rate throughout the sonification. This has the effect of avoiding any dissonance between notes due to temporal overlap, meaning that an unintended effect of the choice of pitch mapping is avoided in all cases. An alternative method that provides more control over the textural complexity of the sonification is to choose a pitch mapping where all or most of the possible note combinations are consonant.

Contingency plays another important role in time domain representations. The intervallic leaps made to reach each note affects the perception of that note. Also, depending on the effect of rhythmic accents, musical notes usually have different meanings in different parts of the bar.

Temporal fusing is also a very important time domain effect. If two note onsets are simultaneous (e.g. occurring within approximately 30 milliseconds of one-another) it is likely that a chord will be perceived, rather than two separate notes, especially if the notes are harmonically consonant. A chord's components are difficult to separate, and the character of the chord is usually different to either component presented separately.

Repetition is a valued musical attribute. Very few musical compositions are completely devoid of repetition; it is one of the primary ways the musical form is defined. By contrast, there are few cases of sonification that incorporate repetition systematically, outside of the user replaying the entire audio sample. One solution to the control of repetition is interaction, which can provide a method for interrupting the flow of time, and replaying sections of interest in a dataset. This is commonplace in computer-based audio playback setups.

Pitch is the most commonly manipulated attribute of sound for data representation. It is also the most complicated attribute to control from the perspective of fusions, dissonance and their implied meanings. Shepard has described interrelations between pitched sounds using a geometrical spiral shape (Shepard, 1982). Other authors have described the geometry of chordal shapes (Tymockzo, 2006). The most obvious connection between notes at the octave, where fusion typically occurs as all the harmonics of the two notes. The musical connotations of coincidental pitches and progressions of sequential notes can be obfuscated by allowing harmonious modes in which "functional harmony" or voice-leading is implied (i.e. a mode with a weak sense of "tonic" or home-base), or by giving control of harmony and notes to the user with the expectation that the variety of iterations will diffuse semantic implications imposed by harmony rather than data characteristics. The latter approach is applied in AeSon Toolkit (Figure 1), in which the user selects a subset of notes, pitch distribution range and register for the sonification rendering. This can be altered for every rendition or even changed "on the fly" during playback. Musical scales such as the whole-tone scale or pentatonic scale have a more diffuse tonal centre than, say, the Western diatonic scale, therefore interfering less in the implicit structural characteristics of the sonified data.

Figure 1. 'AeSon' Aesthetic Sonification Toolkit interface allows the user to choose pitches, pitch distribution or range and register. The location of the node on the touch-screen moves the sound in auditory space.

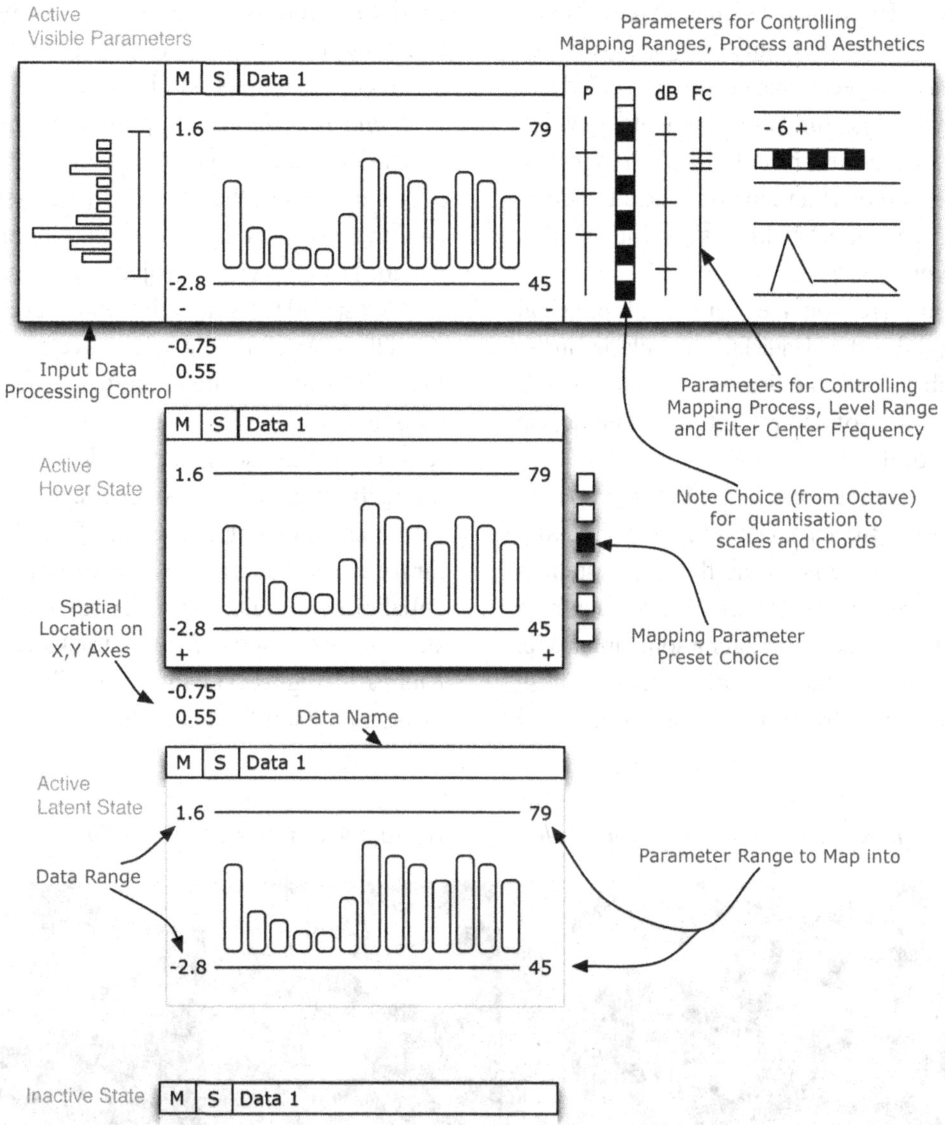

Interaction Design: Interface, Interactivity, Gesture

Building on the naturalness and intuitiveness of information design and representation, an interactive experience both enhances the user's engagement and, sharing the same uncomplicated ergonomics and intuitiveness, the method of interaction can assist seamless data investigation by a non-expert. An aim of physical computing and gestural interaction in the context of data representation is to encourage the user to manipulate, transform, compare and interrogate the dataset without requiring complex analytical tools and knowledge, and even to do so in a playful, natural environment without the constraints of a desktop computing paradigm. Some of the physical computing technologies that have been used by our

307

students and research projects aim to bridge the gap between the spatiality of sound, the physicality of the body and motion and visual spatial. Tactual objects that can be manipulated, touch-surfaces on which data "objects" can be moved, scaled and transformed and gestural environments in which movements trigger representational changes are some of the methods that can motivate interaction and contribute to the "stickiness" or engagement of the data enquiry process.

Following are some examples of physical computing and gestural interfaces developed in the research lab and pedagogical studios that exploit different features of natural, intuitive interaction with sound or data.

Camera-tracking color in *Sonic Kung Fu* gestural interface utilizes data captured by tracking the mid-point of a color zone that the system is calibrated to recognize (Figure 2). The data from the interaction is used to trigger a sonic interface, promoting spatial and gestural interaction, in this case activated by gloves. Such an interface requires no specialized knowledge to activate it and induces full-body gestural interaction and spatial awareness by the user. It can be applied in a playful or museum environment to achieve a universally understood interaction.

Sonic Tai Chi also employs camera-tracking of spatial gestures to control both the visual display, the rules of the Artificial Life system's behavior, as well as the spatial panning of the live sound. Thus the visual projection and responsive audio respond to the location and degree of activity of the user. Dynamic responsive environments like this, using gesture to modify generative systems and the auditory and visual display both respond to the user and provide a high level of interactivity and responsiveness, which can add to the engagement of the interface. Large gestural environments also establish the potential for collaborative multi-user interplay on the human side. Whereas *Sonic Tai Chi* tracks color, *Sonic Kung Fu* (Figure 3) captures outlines of bodies using an optical flow calculation.

Figure 2. Sonic Kung Fu camera tracking color of gloves to detect gestural interaction

Figure 3. Sonic Tai Chi by Joanne Jakovich and Kirsty Beilharz at BetaSpace, Sydney Powerhouse Museum

Hyper-Shaku: Border-Crossing is a musical application of sonification using breath noise spectrum and loudness data captured with a microphone live from the performer to activate various aspects of the real-time response. Motion of the player's face is tracked as well as loudness and noisiness of the acoustic instrumental output to modify the controlling parameters of a granular synthesis (e.g. grain length, grain distribution, size, etc.) and affect the thresholds in a Neural Oscillator Network modeled after a network of human brain synapses. In this model, impulses or messages are only sent when the input to a synapse node reaches a determined threshold; thus by altering the input and thresholds, variations in response from the system can be achieved. The Neural Oscillator Network serves to perpetuate a series of repercussions or networked consequences of an initial input signal. The breath-controlled interaction gives a level of moderation to the performer. It is called *Hyper-Shaku* because the computational system augments the traditional acoustic end-blown Japanese bamboo flute, *shakuhachi*. The *Border-Crossing* refers to cultural, as well as human-machine blending and cross-over.

Rubik's Studio sound controller was a project by students, Daniel Gallard and Piers Gilbertson. Using color-tracking and Reactivision fiducial marker-tracking of individual identifiers on each surface of the cube to control groups of sounds and individual timbres. Fiducial markers, individually unique identifiers that can be captured with a video camera and tracking identifying software, provide a low-latency motion and positional detection and tracking system. In this example (Figure 5), positioning the markers on a Rubik's cube immediately implies the paradigm for interaction to the user. The colors of the faces were also used to control the musical sound mixer. The cube had to be rolled or placed on a surface that housed the camera, illuminated and tracked from below the glass surface. The integration of tracking technology in a familiar interface makes the interaction available to an inexperienced user and adds a playful element to a normally predictable sound manipulation task. Thus the interface became a creative tool. The clear link between visual color and *timbre* (tone color) and matching or chaotic faces of the cube problem forged a strong semantic link between the physical interaction and auditory result, assisting with intuitive understanding of the interaction.

The *Wireless Gamelan*[3] project by Jeremiah Nugroho, Sam Ferguson and Kirsty Beilharz describes a musical outcome that has been activated in two different ways. The sounds range from hard metallic sounds to lower pitched resonant gong sounds. The first performance utilized the RFID tag technology (Radio Frequency Identification) capsules the size of a grain of rice, enclosed in glass, each with a unique identifying digital code that can be recognized by a scanner device (Figure 6). Musical tones were activated on a sequence of gamelan gong samples, the rhythm activated by passing the RFID tag in front of the suspended scanner and sequence used to modify the musical characteristics. Other controls manipulated the quadraphonic spatial placement and spectrum. The technology laid the foundation for the performative interpretation, exploring aspects of Cyborg culture (because these small ID chips can be implanted) and evaluating audience perceptions of embodiment of the trigger device. From the perspective that the actuator or trigger becomes inseparable from the body, not an extension or instrument but integrated with the performers own hand, performative issues of proprioception, latency, gesture control, accuracy and natural motion, the interactive technology has the ability to transform the interaction. Embodied controllers transform the role of the performer from that of instrumentalist to dancer or actor, in which the choreography of the body becomes the instrument of change, internalizing the interaction.

The second iteration of the Wireless Gamelan uses bio-data sonification to trigger the gamelan

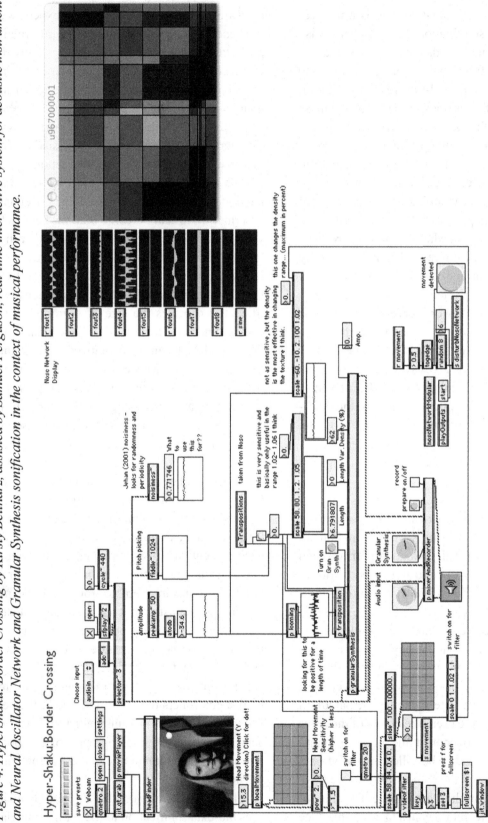

Figure 4. HyperShaku: Border Crossing by Kirsty Beilharz, assisted by Samuel Ferguson, real-time interactive system for acoustic instrument and Neural Oscillator Network and Granular Synthesis sonification in the context of musical performance.

Figure 5. Rubik's Studio using fiducial marker-tracking and color tracking for sound control and creative music mixing in real time

Figure 6. RFID activated Wireless Gamelan. Hand gestures used to trigger sounds by moving the rice-sized RFID tags within range of the suspended scanning device.

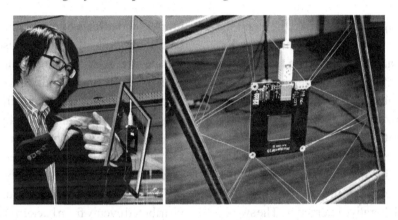

sounds. Using the BioWave EMG (facial muscle signals), EOG (eye messages) and EEG (brain signals) data from the headband contact sensors, connected to the Infusion Systems WiMicroDig[4], it transmits a live datastream by Bluetooth to the control patch in Max/MSP software. The BioFlex sensors on the arms and legs capture EMG (muscle signals) and the BioBeat sensor captures EKG (heartbeat signals) (Figure 7). An additional sensor, the BioEmo, is a galvanic skin sensor, which detects excitement or anxiety using the humidity and hence conductivity of the skin surface between a pair of contacts. To examine aesthetic rendering of bio-data, *Wireless Gamelan* mapped the heartbeat to a background pulsing effect in the music and used EMG to trigger an

array of gamelan (traditional Indonesian gong instrument) sounds. The brain and facial muscular signals were used to modulate pitch and filter the timbre of the gamelan, conveying relative stress and tension vs. relaxation and stasis. This is part of ongoing research concerning aesthetics and the user experience in the user-centered design of wearable technologies.

The multi-touch surface, used with data sonification as described above, provides a physical metaphor between the movements of the hands and graphical objects on the screen surface, connecting it with the movement of sonification elements in the auditory display. The primary purpose of our user evaluations was to explore bi-modality or benefits of multimodality for information

Figure 7. Bio-data sonification from facial muscle, heartbeat and brain-signal activity data used to influence virtual gamelan sounds

display, not to compare, for example, the graphing potential of visualization against sonification for the same representational task. The tangible interface gives a definitive "concreteness" to the otherwise rather abstract sonic entities that may be difficult visualize or conceptualize with spatial, contoured, coloration characteristics. A touch-table, due to its greater dimensions (compared with a multi-touch Smartphone, iPad or tablet PC), and multi-user capability, adds the potential for multi-user collaborative interaction. The swipe, drag, pinch, scroll, scale gestures of multi-touch interfaces are widely familiar due to the ubiquity of devices like the iPhone. Fixtures like the touch-table open up a different scope because it is room-based and, conjoint with a stereo or spatial speaker array, can lead to a more immersive and surround-sound experience for manipulating sound and using sonification to compare data.

In the formative stages of software interface and prototype design, we conducted small user studies to ascertain: The kinds of statistical and information enquiry operation users wanted to conduct with a multimodal touch-table configuration; visual and auditory representation qualities that appealed to users; response to data stimuli; conceptual associations with interaction stimuli; response to different kinds of visual and auditory

graphs; and affects of multimodal representation on understanding the data. We also conducted card sorting exercises to examine the ways in which users spatially and visually grouped information on a physical table surface using hand gestures. In a questionnaire answered by 9 participants, 78% preferred a touchable graphical audio and visual representation compared with 22% who preferred a visual-only touchable representation.

The 12 participants involved in the pilot study distributed evenly from backgrounds of economics (proficient in data analysis), sound/audio experts, students and others without special affiliation with data, sound or visual graphing, ranged in age from 18-45 years old. All were interested in new technologies. Presented with a number of topics for statistical representation, 45% expressed interest in the economy, 33% in environmental data, and 11% in each health and global statistics. Key areas that emerged with relatively high frequency in word association activities relating to *data* stimuli included: Information, statistics, processing, and memory. Key areas that emerged with relatively high frequency in word association activities relating to *information* stimuli included: Data, knowledge, technology, and education. The only key area that emerged with relatively high frequency in word association activities relating to *data analysis* was statistics. Key areas that emerged with relatively high frequency in word association activities relating to *interaction* stimuli included: People and communication. Key areas that emerged with relatively high frequency in word association activities relating to *statistics* stimuli were data and information. In response to visual graph stimuli, significant descriptors were: Change, variation, and information.

When presented with the same data using a) a visual graph (probably of familiar format), b) audio-only sonification and c) a multimodal audio and visual representation, in each case the graphical representation emerged as the easiest to understand, easiest for perceiving the relationship between time and data and easiest to perceive the trends and data conveyed. The multimodal representation emerged as the next most successful method, followed by the audio-only sonification in all three criteria. On the one hand, this feedback seems to undermine the advantages of multimodal display and expose the inadequacy of audio-only representation, however we assume that users are generally more familiar with graphical data representation. There are also situations of competing messages and low visibility when sonification can

enhance understanding. User feedback attributed importance to various interface design features that will be incorporated into the subsequent iteration of the physical multi-touch table design: The ability to form relationships between data, compare data, transform groupings and 'zoom in' on a subset of the data (examine more closely). Users also identified the usefulness of a 'track changes' feature; share information on social networks, and to be able to capture records of interaction with the data. Comparison, ranking and sharing findings featured highly as important criteria in both representation and long-term analysis.

The work, *Fluid Velocity* encapsulates pressure, motion and infrared sensors in the familiar interface of the bicycle to interact with visual projection and stereo sound installation, bridging the interaction between physical and virtual (on-screen) (Figure 8). This installation employed the IRCAM WiSeBox developed by Emmanuel Flety with Max/MSP software for WiFi transmission of data from captors located on the bicycle frame and handlebars to transform the 3D 'creature' on screen and alter the filtering and panning of the electronic music. Pressure on the handlebars, rotation, braking and pedalling velocity affected

Figure 8. Fluid Velocity installation at Tin Sheds Gallery, Sydney, uses a familiar physical interface with embedded sensors to interact with a virtual creature on screen and control musical characteristics. Developed by Kirsty Beilharz, Hong Jun Song, and Samuel Ferguson.

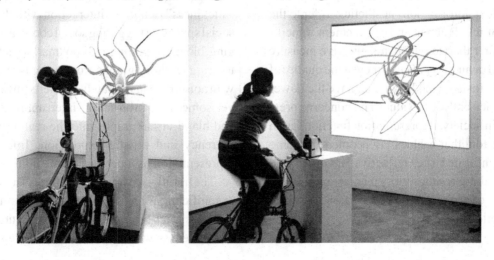

the angularity, splay, tentacle-thickness, number of limbs and waviness of the virtual multi-pod 3D creature in front of the rider. It uses binary, pressure, infrared proximity, accelerometer and gyroscopic sensors. Like a touch-table, embedding interaction in familiar devices, interfaces and situations takes advantage of assumed paradigms and can further enhance the playfulness and engagement of the interactive experience.

Persuasiveness and Engagement in Data Interaction

A relatively recent consideration in achieving persuasiveness of data comes from leveraging participation, opinion, user feedback, and social spin-offs generated by data availability. Interfaces that engage social networking, polling and permit user intervention and knowledge building in the data visualization process can add persuasiveness to the metrics of effective data representation and data interaction.

With the global awakening of open data[5] availability, through freely available datasets, e.g. statistical, demographic, climate and economic data, as well as ubiquitous sensors and captors in our daily lives collecting a continuous stream of live data, there is a growing need to transform this data into a comprehensible, usable informative form that can be interactive and meaningful for everyday people: The democratizing of data. In this context, information "aesthetics" refer to the degree of involvement and engagement it facilitates, rather than to denote a subjective measure for visual or auditory appeal or even the quality of the work. Insights hidden in data have the power to influence collective values and concerns present within society. Representation functions as an effective tool that enables lay people to become (better) informed (i.e. reflective, involved and thereby taking responsibility), in response to the problems of accountability, transparency, citizen participation and e-government.

Until very recently, traditional information graphing was chiefly the domain of scientists, journalists and economic experts. Statistical yet interesting data appeared as charts and streams of inharmonious auditory graphs, often giving higher priority to the phenomena present in the data than the meaning and principles behind it.

Persuasiveness of information can be enhanced by aesthetic data display, incorporating qualities influenced by graphic design, data art, music and intuitive interactivity. In the information society of today, arts, design, media and sciences have a common interest in utilising innovative forms of visualization to represent the knowledge, relevance and meaning hidden within information structures. Now, with the ability to create compelling data representations on the home computer, an increasing number of artists and designers have pushed the conceptual horizon of information visualization and data sonification towards a communication medium in its own right. Information representation has been embraced by media, educational, governmental and advocacy organisations for its ability to inform and engage its audience.

In the fields of data-art and data-driven music creation, we can observe that artists leverage the interestingness and usefulness of data as a creative source for beautiful, intriguing outcomes. Thus it is important to understand which aesthetic representational qualities imbue data with greatest "stickiness" (length of interaction with the data), social spin-offs (triggering social cooperation, tagging, blogging, polling and bookmarking sites) and to bring auditory graphs from a status compared with noise, earcons and auditory alerts (meaningful yet sometimes infuriating, interrupting signals) and bland visual graphs into the realm of social currency and artistic expression: Information representation as a persuasive medium.

The traditional way of evaluating visualization or sonification consists of measuring usability parameters, such as *effectiveness* (the accuracy and completeness with which users achieve specific tasks) and *efficiency* (the resources expended in relation to the effectiveness criterion, of specific user tasks). This focus on quantifying performance has driven the prevalent research focus on optimizing productivity of a representation application. As a result, the role of "user experience" has generally been limited to the self-reporting of perceived levels of "satisfaction" and "beauty". New approaches are required that accurately capture the qualities of a *design* approach in convergent visualization and sonification, and in particular for measuring its impact on users. With the advent of large-scale, collaborative data-representation websites targeting mass audiences, some researchers have recently proposed a groundbreaking shift: To evaluate such "popular" representations using more qualitative, ethnographic and experimental methods. Examples include the recent investigation of asynchronous collaboration in the context of information visualization (Heer, Viégas, & Wattenberg, 2009), or the analysis of conversational processes on a collaborative social visualization website (Viegas, Wattenberg, McKeon, Ham, & Kriss, 2008; Wattenberg, Jesse, & Matt, 2007). Projects like these have started to use *a case study approach* to evaluate the value of a public representation, and integrate visitor log analyses, user activity, user observation, interviews, surveys and the content analysis of online commenting, reviews and critiques on external websites.

This new approach necessarily includes subjective measures that are new for the visualization field, such as surveys, interviews, contextual enquiry and other ethno-methodological techniques. In sonification, this includes qualitative metrics for understanding dimensions that *add meaning*, sometimes merely reinforcing features, rather than assessing the performative graphing dimensions alone, e.g. asking users to give feedback on subjective yet influential parameters: Timbre (tone-colour); audio spatialization; harmony; or pulse (rhythm/beats). To accurately determine the engagement of users, this study will incorporate the two models of *affect* (i.e. information versus

interaction) and will take into account the users' awareness and subjective interpretation of emotional response to technology (Kuniavsky, 2003).

Measuring *persuasive* effectiveness includes a comparative analysis of the representation's functional roles: As a *tool* (e.g. showing information that motivates), as a *social actor* (e.g. providing a context for social support), or as a *medium* (e.g. allowing people to explore cause-and-effect relationships, providing people with vicarious experience that motivates) (Fogg, 2003), as well as surveying users before and after (immediately and after a predefined period) about themes that relate to the meaning of the data that was represented. The aim is to discover correlations between information awareness, behavioral or attitude changes, and the functional parameters of the representation that caused them.

FUTURE RESEARCH DIRECTIONS

Our future work includes the investigation of new representation paradigms that are able to augment the literacy of citizens about socially relevant themes, through the mediation of open data in the form of info-aesthetic visualization and sonification. We are continuing to develop software for aesthetic data sonification and inter-action tools for multi-touch devices and control surfaces to reinforce the relationship between spatial, gestural human interaction and spatial audio representation and the bimodal integration between sonification and visualization for analyzing data. Specifically, eco-data and bio-data are two focus areas of the Sense-Aware Lab for sonification research, as well as new applications of gestural interaction in music. In investigating hyper-instrument augmentation of traditional acoustic instrumental capabilities, live generative environments for ensemble performance pose an exciting new frontier.

Meanwhile, developing aesthetic and interactive sonification methodologies and evaluation to a level comparable with the more established domain of information visualization is necessary for a wider audience to develop an understanding and appreciation of auditory representation. As the pervasiveness and ubiquity of computing accelerates in everyday life, the design of integrative systems that understand new gestural and natural computing paradigms, shifting away from deskbound screen-based computing are essential to engagement and persuasiveness in interaction design.

CONCLUSION

This chapter has examined four areas essential to user-centered interaction design with special attention to designing interactivity including audio, both as a stand-alone information representation channel and as a modality reinforcing and collaborating in the representation of information in a multimodal context. In information design, many of the design and aesthetic principles applied in information visualization are relevant to the mapping and information interaction in sonification. Sonification can also adopt some aesthetic and semantic principles from music to achieve a more intuitive and natural understanding. Information design is discussed from the perspective of mapping to audio parameters, representation for audio and bimodal display and information aesthetics that can increase the efficiency, comprehensibility and elegance of representation.

Sound alone as a medium for data representation, sonification, is underutilized compared with visualization and also in bimodal contexts, either as a redundant reinforcing element or playing an independent role signaling important informational cues and revealing time-based trends that can be well discriminated using sound. This chapter elaborates on some of the most effective uses of sounds, whilst examining known constraints and strengths, presenting ways to optimize the performance of audio in multimodal representations.

Interactivity intended to be intuitive, natural and spatial is considered both from the perspective of giving a sense of physical connection with abstract concepts of auditory representation, metaphors of moving sonic representations of data in space and due to its potential for rapid, uncomplicated manipulations of data for comparison, time-based transformations and common processes in data analysis. Physical, tangible and gestural interaction can universalize the interface for non-expert users and facilitate an engaging "sticky" interactive experience. A step to democratizing ubiquitous and open data sources is to reveal the information in it in ways that are available to all people. This relies on designing the representation and the interaction around the user. The examples of gestural and physical interaction design discussed in this chapter are not isolated to information interactivity, but are equally pertinent for other kinds of interaction design, e.g. sonic interaction, musical performance and also multimodal installation, wearable technologies and tangible manipulations.

Engagement is vital for any interaction design but persuasiveness and influence on group opinions, the ability for data representation to inform and transform society is a relatively new and untapped capability facilitated by social networks and other online communities, for whom the aesthetics, interactivity and availability of data representation (visualization and sonification) can create information and participatory meaningfulness. This situation requires new representation design methodologies and evaluation methodologies able to measure social factors, persuasiveness and interactivity.

ACKNOWLEDGMENT

The Sense-Aware Research Lab in the Faculty of Design, Architecture & Building at the University of Technology, Sydney infrastructure was established with a UTS RIBG funding. The projects reported in this chapter were developed under the Australian Research Council Discovery Project DP0773107 'Gesture-Controlled Interaction with Aesthetic Sonification'. Thanks to Samuel Ferguson and Claudia Alessia Calo for their involvement in the user evaluation of the multi-touch table; and to co-designers on other projects - Joanne Jakovich, Jeremiah Nugroho, Samuel Ferguson and Hong Jun Song.

REFERENCES

Beilharz, K. (2003). Designing sounds and spaces: Interdisciplinary rules & proportions in generative stochastic music and architecture. In N. Cross & E. Edmonds (Eds.), *Expertise in design - Design thinking research* (vol. 6, pp. 3-21). UTS Sydney: Creativity and Cognition Studios Press.

Card, S. K., Mackinlay, J. D., & Shneiderman, B. (1999). *Readings in information visualization: Using vision to think*. San Francisco, CA: Morgan Kaufmann Publishers.

Fogg, B. J. (2003). *Persuasive technology - Using computers to change what we think and do*. San Francisco, CA: Morgan Kaufmann.

Fry, B. (2004). *Computational information design*. Massachusetts Institute of Technology.

Fry, B. (2008). *Visualizing data*. O'Reilly Media.

Heer, J., Viégas, F., & Wattenberg, M. (2009). Voyagers and voyeurs: Supporting asynchronous collaborative visualization. *Communications of the ACM, 52*(1), 87–97. doi:10.1145/1435417.1435439

Kuniavsky, M. (2003). *Observing the user experience: A practitioner's guide to user research*. San Francisco, CA: Morgan Kauffman.

Maeda, J. (2006). *Laws of simplicity*. The MIT Press.

Roads, C. (2001). *Microsound*. Cambridge, MA: The MIT Press.

Shepard, R. N. (1982). Geometrical approximations to the structure of musical pitch. *Psychological Review, 89*, 305–333. doi:10.1037/0033-295X.89.4.305

Tufte, E. R. (1983). *The visual display of quantitative information*. Cheshire, CT: Graphics Press.

Tufte, E. R. (1992). *Envisioning information*. Cheshire, CT: Graphics Press.

Tufte, E. R. (1997). *Visual explanations: Images and quantities, evidence and narrative*. Cheshire, CT: Graphics Press.

Tukey, J. W. (1977). *Exploratory data analysis*. Reading, MA: Addison-Wesley.

Tymockzo, D. (2006). The geometry of musical chords. *Science, 313*(5783), 72. doi:10.1126/science.1126287

Vande Moere, A. (2010). *Infosthetics: Where form follows data*. Retrieved January 20, 2010, from infosthetics.com

Vickers, P. (2005). *Ars Informatica - Ars Electronica: Improving sonification aesthetics*. Paper presented at the Understanding and Designing for Aesthetic Experience Workshop, 19th British HCI Group Annual Conference, Edinburgh, Scotland.

Vickers, P., & Hogg, B. (2006). *Sonification Abstraite/Sonification Concrète: An 'aesthetic perspective space' for classifying auditory displays in the Ars Musica domain*. Paper presented at the 12th International Conference on Auditory Display.

Viegas, F. B., Wattenberg, M., McKeon, M., Ham, F. v., & Kriss, J. (2008). *Harry Potter and the meat-filled freezer: A case study of spontaneous usage of visualization tools*. Paper presented at the International Conference on System Sciences.

Walker, B. N., & Nees, M. A. (2005). *An agenda for research and development of multimodal graphs*. Paper presented at the 11th International Conference on Auditory Display (ICAD2005).

Wattenberg, M., Jesse, K., & Matt, M. (2007). ManyEyes: A site for visualization at Internet scale. *IEEE Transactions on Visualization and Computer Graphics, 13*(6), 1121–1128. doi:10.1109/TVCG.2007.70577

Weinberg, G., & Thatcher, T. (2006). Interactive sonification: Aesthetics, functionality and performance. *Leonardo Music Journal, 16*, 9–12. doi:10.1162/lmj.2006.16.9

Xenakis, I. (1971). *Formalized music: Thought and mathematics in composition*. Bloomington, IN: Indiana University Press.

KEY TERMS AND DEFINITIONS

Aesthetics: In this context, information "aesthetics" refer to the degree of involvement and engagement it facilitates, rather than to denote a subjective measure for visual or auditory appeal or even the quality of the work.

Information Visualization: Visual representation of data, often a graphical form, intended to enable the user to derive information from the dataset.

Sonification: The non-speech auditory representation of data, often synonymous with auditory graphing.

ENDNOTES

[1] Sense-Aware Research Lab: University of Technology, Sydney - Faculty of Design, Architecture and Building.

[2] AeSon: Aesthetic Sonification Toolkit developed by Professor Kirsty Beilharz and Dr. Samuel Ferguson under Australian Research Council Discovery Project 'Gestural Interaction with Aesthetic Data Sonification' DP0773107 www.kirstybeilharz.com.au/aeson.html

[3] The *Gamelan* is a traditional instrumental ensemble of percussion instruments from Indonesia, comprised of struck metalophones and gong instruments, played by a group of people. Gongs have distinctive overtone spectra and often produce audible bi-tones and individual tunings. Samples and physically modeled virtual instruments can recreate these complex sounds, modifiable by pitch modulation, and spectral filtering.

[4] The BioWave sensors and MicroDig Bluetooth microprocessor are products of Infusion Systems.

[5] Open data is freely available, public domain data, e.g. the Australian Bureau of Statistics or U.S. established data.gov website. Availability does not equate to understanding the data in a usable, informative form.

Chapter 18
Supporting Design Thinking with Evocative Digital Diagrams

Christiane M. Herr
Xi'an Jiaotong-Liverpool University, China

ABSTRACT

This chapter presents a digitally supported approach to creative thinking through diagrammatic visuals. Diagrammatic visuals can support designing by evoking thoughts and by raising open questions in conversational exchanges with designers. It focuses on the educational context of the architectural design studio, and introduces a software tool, named Algogram, which allows designers to employ diagrams in challenging conventional assumptions and for generating new ideas. Results from testing the tool and the way of approaching conceptual designing encouraged by it within an undergraduate design studio suggest a potential for refocusing of attention in digital design support development towards diagrams. In addition to the conventional emphasis on the variety of tool features and the ability of the tool to assist representational modeling of form, this chapter shows how a diagram-based approach can acknowledge and harness the creative potential of designers' constructive seeing.

INTRODUCTION

Designerly thinking manifests itself in a variety of modes of approaching design tasks, among them reasoning, intuition, commonsense, art, science, drawing, problem-solving and experience. Designerly thinking tends to explore what works within a particular context and is less concerned with formal criteria as they apply to other fields of study. In this way, designers can handle, and even seek, paradox, ignorance, ambiguity and even

destruction just as they can handle and seek clarity, explicit knowledge, logic and formal rigour. This chapter aims to chart a new direction in what Shneiderman (2000) describes as "inspirationalist" approach to supporting creativity. This approach encourages creativity through strategies encouraging free association, play, divergence or lateral thinking in order to offer new ways of perceiving design tasks (DeBono 1973). Creativity support developed from this perspective often employs visual techniques which can assist in reimagining that which is presented. Goldschmidt (2003) has suggested that sketching aids designers in

DOI: 10.4018/978-1-61350-180-1.ch018

creative exploration by providing opportunities to "see again" that was initially expressed visually in drawings. Sketching thus allows designers to interpret drawings and "ascribe meaning" (Goldschmidt 2003, p. 83) to the unintended consequences of their drawings. Goldschmidt (1991) describes the experiences of drawing designers as dynamic exchanges between designers and their sketches and characterizes sketches as "interactive imagery". Sketching enables designers to transcend the realm of the representational by inviting or evoking new ways of seeing and thinking. While the links between creative thinking and sketching in the design-related professions have been examined in numerous studies over the past twenty years, in particular within the ongoing discourse in the journal *Design Studies* (see for example Schön 1988, Schön & Wiggins 1992, Suwa & Tversky 1997, Purcell & Gero 1998), research on diagrams has primarily been carried out in the fields of cognitive science, psychology and artificial intelligence. Studies originating from these fields have tended to focus on the role of diagrams in multi-modal reasoning and in visual forms of rational problem-solving through logical inference (see for example Glasgow, Narayanan & Chandrasekaran 1995). From this viewpoint, diagrams are defined as: "A diagram D is a set of labeled 2D objects all located clearly inside (i.e., no intersection or touching) a common region (or bounding box) B. The objects are of three types - points, curves, regions" (Chandrasekaran et al. 2005). This definition emphasizes the distinguishing and demarcating function of diagrams denoting clear formal relationships where diagrams serve a representational purpose, but refer to symbolically encoded contents. Even a more general definition of diagrams as given by Kamps (1999) emphasizes their role as devices to "visually represent factual knowledge". This view of diagrams is common in the context of digitally supported designing, since it allows the translation of diagrams into formats that can be handled digitally. In the context of architectural designing, however, diagrams may

also be understood and employed in yet different ways. When describing the role of diagrams in architectural design processes, in particular in communication between architects and clients, Szalapaj (2005) critically comments on the way diagrammatic reasoning is treated in artificial intelligence research. He argues that treating diagrams as mere inputs to computer systems based on an information-processing approach "completely misses the point of diagrammatic reasoning in architectural design" (ibid., p. 222). In the context of design processes, he emphasizes, diagrams may more productively be thought of as supporting creative thinking by influencing and expanding visual thinking processes. Both diagrams and sketches can function as abstract and ambiguous types of representations that encourage design exploration by enabling multiple interpretations (Goel 1995). This study approaches diagrams and diagramming similarly to sketches and sketching and focuses particularly on the use of evocative diagrams to support creative processes in the educational context of the design studio. In this role, diagrams do not merely function as symbolic representation or visualization tools, but as interactive imagery supporting creative thinking processes as described by Goldschmidt (1991). Szalapaj's (2005) critical comments on the information-processing viewpoint may be extended to the notion of "diagrammatic reasoning" itself, which seems to limit the scope of visual thinking processes to the realm of the rational. When designing, architects may not only reason rationally but for example seek productivity through maintaining ambiguity (Goel 1995) and by relying on emotion and intuition. Depending on their intentions, architects may thus create diagrams as tools enabling clear communication, or as media enabling creativity, or as anything in between. Accordingly, diagrams may conform to, (mis)appropriate or transform established visual codes that allow for symbolic forms of representation. Accordingly, Mark Garcia (2010), from an architectural viewpoint, characterizes diagrams as: "A diagram is the spatialisation of a selective abstraction and/or reduction of a concept or phenomenon. In other words, a diagram is the architecture of an idea or entity." (p. 18).

Both diagrams and sketches are visual devices that may be used to explain, visualize or to support creative processes, and a clear and conclusive distinction between them may not be possible. In tendency, sketches, in particular in architectural design, are understood to describe aspects of form or shape, whereas diagrams are typically understood to present more abstract or symbolic relationships or patterns. The ability of diagrams to mark out and delineate abstract relationships through relatively simple visual devices such as lines has led to their frequent use in the description of systems or systematic relationships in fields that embrace scientific approaches to research. Although systemic relationships tend to be seen as objective properties of the observed, judged from an objective or disembodied viewpoint, Rittel (1992) has argued that a system "reflects someone's understanding of something"(p. 59, translated from German by the author). In this chapter, I adopt a similar perspective towards diagrams and argue from the premise that whether a drawing is perceived as a sketch or a diagram depends mainly on the choice of the designer looking at it. This choice may however be influenced by perceived similarity to precedents or conventions: A drawing consisting of overlapping circles for example is likely to conjure up Venn or bubble diagram readings. A designer may choose to read any form as a diagram, which is common among architects emphasizing a conceptual approach to creating and contextualizing their work: A picture of concentric circles on a rippled water surface may for example be seen in terms of its particular form but also in terms of the more abstract associations of fluidity or resourcefulness it may evoke in the viewer - it may even be read as a bubble diagram. This simple example shows how the choice to regard a drawing as form-based sketch or as a relational abstract diagram may support a variety of directions in creative exploration.

In educational contexts, both form-oriented sketching and abstract/relational diagramming are primarily taught as tools for representational purposes rather than as tools to explore. Students tend to learn to sketch and diagram exploratively and tacitly, through experiencing (drawn) conversations with themselves or with their tutors. In digital design tool development, a similar focus on representation of form along with related visual codes and conventions, and on inception and refinement of geometry seems prevalent. Research on digital support for design processes during which concepts and ideas are cultivated alongside or independently of form-making is still comparatively rare (see the thorough review of design support tools in Parthenios 2005). To inspire and support design thinking with digital means, this project takes a designerly line of inquiry. The main question guiding this investigation is how diagram-based digital tools may be understood as evocative media in creative design conversations. This chapter presents the theoretical foundations of this approach and reports on the implementation of and a reflection on a digital design support tool named Algogram. Algogram was developed for an educational context, supporting architecture students' creative processes early on in a design studio. Examples of students' design outcomes are presented and discussed based on observations of students' creative processes. Keeping with insights gained from diagram-based architectural practice, the role of digital technology in designing is considered here in terms of the creative processes it enables. This chapter thus does not focus on the implementation of the tools themselves but considers technology as a valuable asset in dynamic and dialogical processes of creating new ideas in between designers and their diagrams.

Aims, Method, and Scope of the Study

In order to investigate digitally supported diagramming in the context of an architectural design studio, this study employed an action research approach as introduced by Schön's (1983) description of reflective practice and developed by, among many others, Kemmis and McTaggart (1990) and Freeman (1998) in the context of education. This allowed for the study of design processes not only from the perspective of the disengaged neutral observer but also from the viewpoint of the engaged designer and digital toolmaker (Fischer & Herr 2007). Grounded in the applied contexts of education and design, both action research and research in design recognize similar challenges that limit the applicability of the scientific research paradigm to such contexts: As Rittel and Webber (1972) argued, design problems (and processes) are not repeatable, resist generalization and predictability, and are highly contextual. Action research offers notions of rigour and validity that are tied to ways of accounting for the processes observed rather than to providing generalizable findings (see Herr and Anderson 2005). The implementation of Algogram, a diagram-based digital tool to assist students' creative processes in the architectural studio was set up to test the approach in an applied setting and to generate feedback to refine the theoretical approach as well as to inform ongoing tool development. For this purpose, a small group of nine students was studied in detail and primarily qualitative data was collected. Observational data included records of students' sketchbooks, interim and final design presentations, field notes as well as individual interviews with students after the final design presentation. To understand students' design processes when working with Algogram, the design outcomes were compared to those of other groups within the same studio not working with Algogram to clarify and confirm previous observations. The scope of the study is limited to detailed observation of a small group of nine

participating students by the author as an involved observer who acted as toolmaker and studio co-tutor. The aim of this study was to develop an understanding of diagram-based digital design support to feed back into and improve ongoing tool development as well as theory development.

BACKGROUND

For the development of Algogram, a digital diagram-based tool to support designing, this project drew mainly on four areas of previous research. First, a general review of the role of diagrams in architectural creativity. Second, models of creative design processes that provide a framework for directing design support development. Third, studies on the potential of tools to support creative thinking in such design processes. Fourth, previous studies employing diagrams within digitally supported design processes. In the following, the study presented in this chapter is contextualized within these four areas in successive separate paragraphs.

In contemporary (Western) architectural design practice and design education, architectural form is typically generated through and explained by abstract concepts and narratives. Questions of form and composition often receive less attention than conceptual narratives describing underlying principles, relationships, generative processes, patterns or rules. Ways of reading form and visual understanding have moved beyond mere representation of form, and relate increasingly to abstract and systemic notations. In conceptual design approaches as they are cultivated in leading design practices and design schools today, conceptual ideas are taking centre stage, as the work of UNStudio, MVRDV, BIG as well as Diller and Scofidio illustrates. In this context, diagrams have gained a key position in architectural thinking and designing over the past two decades, forming a core approach to dealing with design tasks and contexts that are not only increasingly difficult to grasp in their entirety, but also increasingly layered and intangible. Architects make use of many types of diagrams to address both technical and creative challenges in their design work. This chapter concentrates on diagrams as they are used to suggest, challenge and inspire creative ideas. Often deceptively simple in their visual presentation, yet potent in suggesting new ways of thinking, diagrams can be thought of as generative conceptual devices. Whereas architectural sketches conventionally focus on partial and formally representational aspects of physical form, such as mass, scale, space or light, diagrams exceed the representational. Diagrams are employed to express and make accessible systemic and holistic aspects of architectural thinking. As Spuybroek (2001) states, diagrams can be seen as part of a general contemporary shift from surfaces towards interfaces: In diagrams, visual images become surfaces that do not only record but require active seeing to be read. Diagrams provide opportunities for both analysis and synthesis. Analytical or explanatory diagrams are perhaps among the most conventional and best-known types of diagrams: Eisenman (Cassara 2006, p. 204) describes such analytical diagrams as means to animate buildings already designed. Diagrams can however also perform an operational and synthetic role during the design process (ibid.), where their purpose lies in generating new thoughts and ideas. It is this designerly understanding and use of diagrams as generative design tools that underlies the approach to design tool development taken in this study.

Diagrams can provoke and evoke creative seeing. In making use of the visual but stopping short of iconic representation of form, generative diagrams introduce gaps that are to be filled by creative imagination and thus provide designers with "templates for invention" (ibid.). In this way, generative diagrams provide a foothold for creative imagination but at the same time postpone representational questions of form so potential ideas can be developed further. Opening up the visual field of diagrams for experimentation involves

reducing representational expectations and allowing for the incomplete and continual processes of reworking (Benjamin 2000, p. 144). Designerly seeing acknowledges and embraces the seeking, self-positioning, perspective-choosing, experience dependent, attention-placing, interest-driven choice making that the process of vision entails (Herr & Fischer 2010). Discussing his educational work with digital and analogue diagrams, Spuybroek (2001) explains that diagrams support conception by postponing images and seeing.

Goldschmidt (1991) describes two modes of seeing: "Seeing that" and "seeing as". When "seeing that", a quick initial account is taken of things perceived visually. When "seeing as", seeing becomes interpretive and constructive and can transform conventional interpretations and expectations. In Spuybroek's (2001) description, seeing refers to what Goldschmidt (1991) describes as "seeing as". In Goldschmidt's account of designers' creative drawing processes, seeing as and seeing that form part of creative dialogues that stimulate new ways of seeing and thinking. Visual construction and reconstruction can be invited if what has to be constructed or reconstructed is yet unfinished and open-ended. Dogan and Nersessian (2002) similarly emphasize that abstraction in conceptual diagrams helps to avoid early commitment to a specific solution, thus enabling creative exploration. The power of conceptual diagrams lies in their capability to elicit interpretation. For these reasons, designers' conceptual drawings often employ deliberately rough, unfinished, ambiguous and spontaneous modes of drawing. When employing diagrams to generate new ideas, architects carefully maintain a state of suspension: Providing enough visual cues to inspire thinking, yet avoiding the overly representational. Diagrams create spaces where creative decisions can be suspended to support constructing and developing of new ideas.

Taking a designerly perspective on design support, this study adopts Schön's (1983) view of designing as reflective practice. Schön portrays designing as cycles of activity where doing, seeing and reflecting are intimately linked. In this model, creativity originates from recurring reconsideration and rethinking. Schön (ibid., p. 153) emphasizes the role of sketching in the creative thinking process, where sketching serves not only to externalize and pin down thoughts as representational drawings, but also to provide designers with materials that encourage constructive and creative seeing (Schön & Wiggins 1992). In this model, new ideas derive from the nature of the dialogical process: Creativity is neither only in the tool, nor in the mind of the designer, but arises from the in between the two. This central role of the conversational in-between in creative thinking is affirmed from the viewpoint of cybernetics. Glanville (2007) suggests that participants of conversations build meanings through the conversation itself rather than relying on the communication of predetermined meanings, whereby differences of understanding during conversation are the source of new thoughts. In this view, meaning and novelty are generated from and inextricably linked to the conversations between designers and their media of working and interaction. The conversational, novelty-generating processes designers initiate are directed, yet not linear. Gedenryd (1998, p. 112) stresses that no causal relationship can be drawn between cognition to action in the world. Activity and thinking are related within an integrated whole that should not be tied to any general organizational scheme. Gedenryd describes design processes as inquiries based on interaction, in which "transitions may come from anywhere and go anywhere, at any point" (ibid.). In the context of design processes, identifying singular process stages or linear, goal-driven progressions seems both arbitrary and futile. To support creative designing, digital tools should be able to support processes that are flexible, dynamic, opportunistic, in between participants of conversations and hardly predictable.

Contemporary architectural practice has become permeated with digital tools, which are applied in areas as diverse as drafting, modeling of form, fabrication and management. These processes are however only loosely related to creative thinking or inspiration. The application of digital tools tends to be associated with a loss of the holistic process of inquiry as Gedenryd (1998) describes. Instead, technology becomes the focus and object of concern. This can be gleaned from Mueller's (2006, p. 39) typical description of how designers augment their creative thinking with the aid of CAD systems. He claims that "the idea of computer systems only as tools of drawing production for construction documents is no longer adequate". As the major advance, he suggests that architects may now "gain value from computers not only in the secondary role of drawing production, but in their core problem-solving activity, which is the design of three-dimensional spaces". Mueller (ibid.) thus suggests that CAD's primary potential lies in capacity to support designers with the representational tasks of modeling in two or three dimensions. This tendency to see digital tools as instruments assisting linear, goal-directed and mostly form-focused workflows also seems to underly Shea's (2006, p. 55) description of digitally supported generative design processes. Shea suggests that computers, in addition to their existing roles as draughtspersons, visualisers, data-checkers and performance analysts, can also generate concepts and stimulate design solutions. But she adds that this process of generating concepts and stimulating design solutions should be based on "robust and rigorous models of design conditions, design languages and design performance" (ibid.). Shea's description of generative tools associates generative processes with production and analysis of a large number of geometrical variations. For her, the notion of design concepts seems to be associated with general layout of form. In both Shea's (2006) and Mueller's (2006) views, the potential of the in-between of conversational processes seems hardly considered when positioning digital tools within creative design processes. If new ideas and inspiration derive from ambiguity and misunderstanding within conversations (Goel 1995, Glanville 2007), how can designers integrate digital tools into their creative processes? Mueller (2006) notes that designers, in order to work with digital design tools, often press tools to go beyond preconceived applications. In a study on digitally supported creativity and tool use, Fischer & Herr (2007) illustrate this readiness to bend, twist and abuse design tools contrary to the expectations of tool developers for the purposes of designers' creative inquiries. Designers accept ideas and inspirations where they find them, and not necessarily where tool developers expect designers to find them. While tool developers may put much work in streamlining workflows and adding features to tools, designers tend to latch onto misunderstandings or spontaneous ideas only partly related to tool developers' intentions – in design contexts, limitations of software may even have enabling effects. To support designers' ways of working, this study reframes the role of digital tools in providing support for creative inquiries.

Although diagrammatic practice in architectural design, including digitally supported design, is common in contemporary practice, only few research studies have been directed toward this topic. The majority of drawing-related research in CAD tends to be focused on traditional representational sketching, such as sketch recognition, management and storage of sketches, and translation of sketches into 3D models. Diagram-based modes of reasoning have been investigated by Gross and Do (Gross 1996), who have presented a software prototype named "electronic cocktail napkin" to support conceptual sketching and diagramming. Gross and Do (ibid.) distinguish between form-focused sketches and diagrams, and define diagrams as a type of drawing that aims to capture as well as generate design concepts and guiding principles. Do & Gross (2001, p.136) provide a great description of how abstract and propositional diagrams work in architectural design processes: Diagrams serve to explore, explain, demonstrate,

or clarify relationships among parts of a whole. However, they stress that diagrams are made of symbols and carry pre-defined meanings. In the "electronic cocktail napkin" Do & Gross (1996) then turn their focus to how computers may become able to read, understand and interpret the drawings provided by designers. Reflecting on the current state of the field, Gross (2007) anticipates that future accomplishments will enable humans to communicate with computer software by using sketching, drawing, diagramming, and other forms of marking with a stylus. The challenges he envisions revolve mainly around the parsing, recognizing, interacting through, and understanding of visual languages. By defining diagrams as consisting of symbolic shapes constituting visual languages that can be decoded or otherwise read, diagrams are placed within the context of the information-processing centered viewpoint of artificial intelligence introduced earlier. In this understanding, diagrams are mostly stripped of their evocative, yet-undefined potential. Although paving the way for computer-aided diagram recognition in analogy to sketch or speech recognition, this understanding of diagrams has little in common with the way Spuybroek (2001) characterizes diagrams as interfaces or "open, porous surfaces that are no longer images but nonetheless make us of visualization". How do diagrams exceed the visual and the symbolical? Spuybroek asserts that "these images aren't 'seen', as in a passive recording technique, but precisely in an active way, where the seeing is permeated with acting." The potential of diagrams to inspire creative thinking, it seems, cannot be located in the marks on paper or on screens, but is generated in processes of active reading that transcends decoding of symbolic content. This creative seeing, is neither a trivial or deterministic activity, nor does it lend itself to automated recognition. In the following sections, a software prototype developed for an architectural design studio is introduced and discussed that builds upon this understanding of diagrams as visual interfaces provoking creative seeing in dialogue with architectural designers.

ALGOGRAM

Evocative Digital Diagrams

Algogram is a software prototype developed to support architectural students' creative thinking. It is based on the design-centred view of diagrams laid out in the previous sections of this chapter and implemented as a scripted utility in 3D Studio MAX. Algogram was the result of a series of four previous software prototypes of digital design support based on cellular automata. A detailed discussion of this development history can be found in Herr and Karakiewicz (2007). Earlier software prototypes focused mostly on issues of form and form generation based on an extended cellular automata model (see Herr 2008). Realizing the limits of a form-focused approach to design support, the main question driving the development of Algogram was how digital design support could be understood holistically as systems in which designers and digital tools can create new ideas from conversation and inspiration. This understanding acknowledges the ability of designers to respond creatively to questions and challenge and the capacity of digital design support to provoke inspiration through questions and challenge. Design support, in this context, aims at helping designers to ask designerly questions instead of producing and implementing geometry-related answers. Key to the digital design support project presented in this chapter is to allow for and harness ambiguity in productive ways as suggested by Gaver et al. (2003, p. 240), thus leaving space for ideas and decisions where conventional tools suggest and produce outcomes of a representational nature that tend to become too explicit too fast.

Although Algogram presents users with forms and allows for manipulation of forms, these forms are left unspecific: All elements in Algogram are created as generic spheres. The user interface of Algogram allows for three main activities: Creating, placing, coloring and naming of generic spheres (Figure 1), establishing of conditional relationships (named "rules") between individual spheres (Figure 1), and analysis functions (Figure 1). Due to the cellular automata-oriented background of Algogram's development, spheres can be linked to each other through simple rules. These rules take the form of simple conditional statements. At the time of Algogram's inception, these rule-based relationships were expected to provide the strongest potential for supporting designing. As diagrams typically emphasize less on aspects of form and shape and more on internal relationships, this link between cellular automata and diagrams provided a basis for implementing a cellular automata-based software to support designing. Cellular automata-based diagrams – or automated diagrams – were not intended to represent physical shape. Instead, they were intended to allow for multiple interpretations and mappings, suggesting issues and perspectives for consideration without imposing solutions. The automated, cellular automata-based component of such diagrams serves to give diagrams active capabilities to respond to configurational changes initiated by designers. Algogram thus presents an approach to digital design support where the computer is partly utilized as a tool to execute predetermined commands, and partly provides a playground for creative questioning and imagination.

In architectural terms, Algogram was intended to provide a generic way of representing architectural functions and their relationships through its spherical visual elements, which are related to both bubble diagrams - not so much in their functional, but in their generative capacity as described by Emmons (2006) - and Venn diagrams. These generic spheres represent architectural functions to avoid premature visualizing of diagrams as possible building forms. The spheres denote architectural functions but are not predefined: A sphere may thus be labeled freely

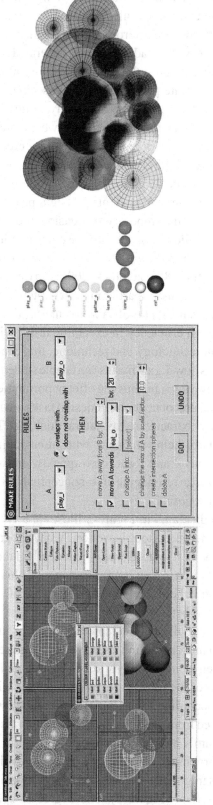

Figure 1. The Algogram interface: Utility interfaces for naming and placing of spheres, rules and analysis functions

depending on the design approach taken such as "tea drinking", "living" or "mountain". User-defined text labels and choosing from a set of predefined colors allow designers to express what spheres may present to them. Diagrammatic representations in Algogram can be manipulated either manually or by establishing automated relationships between elements by defining rules, which are used to numerically control relative positions of spheres and their intersections. In addition, Algogram provides analysis functions to visualize the overall composition of particular diagrams in a chart overview (Figure 1). Algogam's spherical composition of functions in three-dimensional space exceeds the modes of thinking supported by conventional bubble diagrams in several aspects. Most significantly, Algogram draws attention to not the function itself, but the potential for interaction, exchange and overlap in between different functions. For this purpose, the term "hybrid" was employed to suggest yet-undefined potentials to be interpreted and yet undefined architectural solutions to be invented. In Algogram, hybrids are generated as new mixed-colour spheres according to the two original overlapping spheres with the volume of and placed at the position of the original overlaps. User-defined rules serve to transform spheres in terms of volume and position according to their neighbors: "Tea-drinking" spheres may thus be moved away from "street" spheres and reoriented towards "mountain" spheres. Rules are defined based on an if/then logic through a simple visual interface (Figure 1), with several additional and more detailed parameters.

Algogram in the Design Studio: Supporting Creative Seeing

Algogram was developed for and tested in a second-year architectural studio project at The University of Hong Kong. The group of nine students working with Algogram formed part of a larger studio project in which all students of that year participated. Data on the studio work of students and their design processes was collected in form of field notes, student sketches made over the course of the semester, student interviews and design proposals from students taking part in the study as well as sample proposals by students working in parallel studio groups not working with Algogram. The architectural approach taken in the group of students working with Algogram aims to transcend the limits of prescriptive typologies developed from the modernist dictum of "form follows function". Instead of following prescriptive function-based examples and reinforcing students' preconceptions of building types, Algogram aimed to open up new ways of conceptual thinking based on architectural functions. Instead of producing definite architectural plans as quickly as possible, students were encouraged to critically reflect on the initial architectural brief, with the intention to lead students to re-frame the design task. The initial design brief given to students was general and called for the design of a school, where the type of school was open for students' individual choice. As described in the preceding section, students could express their initial thoughts on how they intended to approach the design of their schools only based on generic spheres composed in three-dimensional configurations. By inviting students to work with this deliberately unspecific visual format, designerly conceptual questioning was brought to the foreground. According to Rittel and Webber (1973), the choice of explanation when describing design problems already suggests the way these problems will be addressed to resolve them. Algogram provides diagrams of a particular, yet under-determined format that encourage particular ways of seeing. The lack of predetermined features may be seen not as limiting, but instead, as enabling for the purpose of supporting creative processes.

In the case of Algogram, design proposals are not explained but visualized as implicit questions. In diagrams produced with Algogram, both initial spheres with user-defined function labels as well

as hybrids generated from overlapping functions are sources of ambiguity intended to stimulate students' creative interpretations. As there is no correct way to read diagrams generated with Algogram, reading them architecturally always necessitates interpretation or creative seeing. With visual and architectural ambiguity maintained throughout the first three studio weeks during which students worked with Algogram, creative seeing was required to develop design concepts and to translate diagrams into architectural form at later stages in students' design processes (Figure 2) This temporary suspension of definite decisions allows for the processes of continual reworking and designerly inquiry described by Gedenryd (1998), Spuybroek (2001) and Benjamin (2000) as discussed earlier in this chapter. Where conventional CAD tools aim to support designing through efficiency in executing tasks, with a focus on technology and technique, this chapter discusses how digital means can enable students to see in new ways and thus can offer opportunities to 'reframe' preconceptions of design tasks – which is usually characterized as 'lateral thinking'. This particularly helps students, who often jump to conclusions – and form – too quickly, and who find it hard to re-imagine or re-conceptualize their design proposals.

The diagrams in Figure 2 illustrate a typical approach students took in working with Algogram. Students first placed very generically labeled elements in a rough configuration – in this example, a school designed for learning of, and encounter between, different generations. The student initially defined spheres labeled "building", "landscape", and "sea, water" (Figure 2). She then generated hybrids from overlapping sections of the spheres. As hybrids inherit mixed colors according to the initial spheres they were generated from, the student used both hybrids and Algogram's analysis function to reflect on and make proposals regarding to which roles these hybrids might play in the functional composition of the school (Figure 2). The degree of sphere

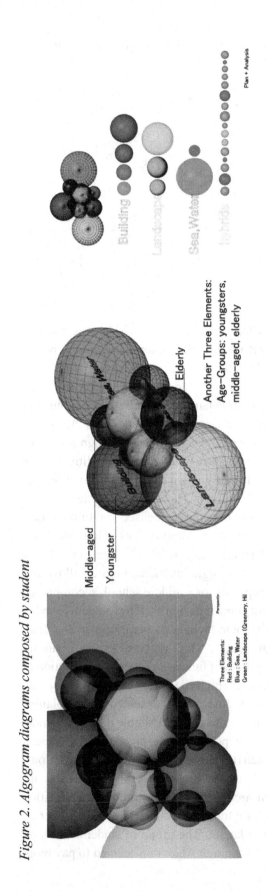

Figure 2. Algogram diagrams composed by student

surface opacity in the diagrams is a visual expression of the spheres' degree of intersection, and thus connection, to other spheres. In the example shown in Figure 2, this indicates that two centrally placed spheres labeled "landscape" are the most integral parts of the conceptual school design. Students were asked to work with Algogram during the first three weeks of their design projects. At this point, students started to translate Algogram-generated diagrams into more concrete architectural form through interpretation. Although students were initially hesitant to employ visual formats that did not denote form, they quickly grasped the potential inherent in this mode of thought development. Although visually simple, Algogram diagrams provided rich materials to inspire design discussions and to fuel students' creative imagination: Sphere sizes were for example presented as both indicative of form by indicating spatial volumes dedicated to a given architectural programme or alternatively, as designating the importance given to specific programme items through sphere size. In some cases, students described their use of both interpretations simultaneously in the same diagram. Several students continued to make use of the Algogram diagram format even after they stopped using Algogram. In a review of hand sketches of these students, the sphere format as placeholders to enable creative seeing tends to accompany the use of Algogram and also recurs after transitioning to conventional designing. In addition, the sphere-oriented format was often modified and integrated into the preferred drawing styles of individual students. Figure 3 illustrates manually drawn hand sketches that carry on the spherical function-based diagram format.

Students' work with Algogram-based diagrams during the first few weeks of the design process generated not only a productive and inventive conceptual design process centered on the rethinking of architectural functions, but it also resulted in a distinct visual language. Students quickly referred to "spheres", "hybrids" and "rules" when

Figure 3. Students' hand sketches following the Algogram-based diagram format after transitioning to hand-drawn plan development

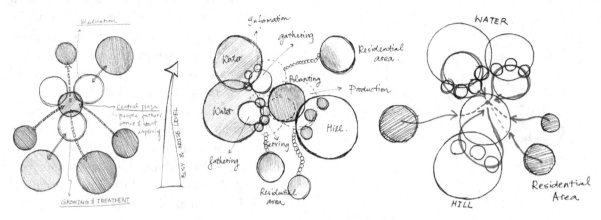

discussing their design proposals with teachers and among themselves. As illustrated in Figure 3, the diagram format was integrated into students' visual vocabulary, where it was used in individual variations to temporarily defer decisions related to architectural form-giving while students were thinking about internal relationships, flows of movement or functional coherence. Within the group of students and teachers working with Algogram, this was not clearly perceived until the design critiques at the end of the semester. At that point, invited guest critics were surprised and occasionally confused when interpreting students' conceptual reasoning, which most students illustrated by presenting early design stage diagrams generated in Algogram. A review of students' results in this studio project seems to indicate a broadened understanding of function-based architectural designing and a readiness to question and reinvent conventional architectural typologies. Where conventional function-based planning tends to suggest an additive and boundary-centered arrangement of spaces dedicated to single function use, students working with Algogram paid increased attention to designing the intersections and overlaps between functions. In the final design proposals, these efforts led to integrated and flowing spaces. Figure 4 illustrates a school for dancing, in which a student invented a variety of

spaces for situations in which dancing training and performing could interface with and be accessible to the public.

In groups of students working on the same design brief in parallel to the observed group, but without thinking through and with Algogram early on in the design process, design proposals seem to indicate a function-based additive design approach that emphasizes clear boundaries between functions. These students' design processes seem to have focused on finding new configurations or compositions of initially determined simple shapes, which were individually allocated to single functions. Figure 5 illustrates two proposals for a middle school, accompanied with conceptual design sketches students used to explain their layouts to reviewers in the final design critique. Both proposals show a similar arrangement of functions where the separation of functions is emphasized. The school shown to the right of Figure 5 was designed and explained based on a conventional bubble diagram, which, albeit conceptual in scope, preconditions a design approach of linking yet not integrating functions. Overall, students in other groups tended to approach architectural tasks through composition of overall form rather than rethinking internal function layout. The group of students working with and through Algogram seemed to pay more

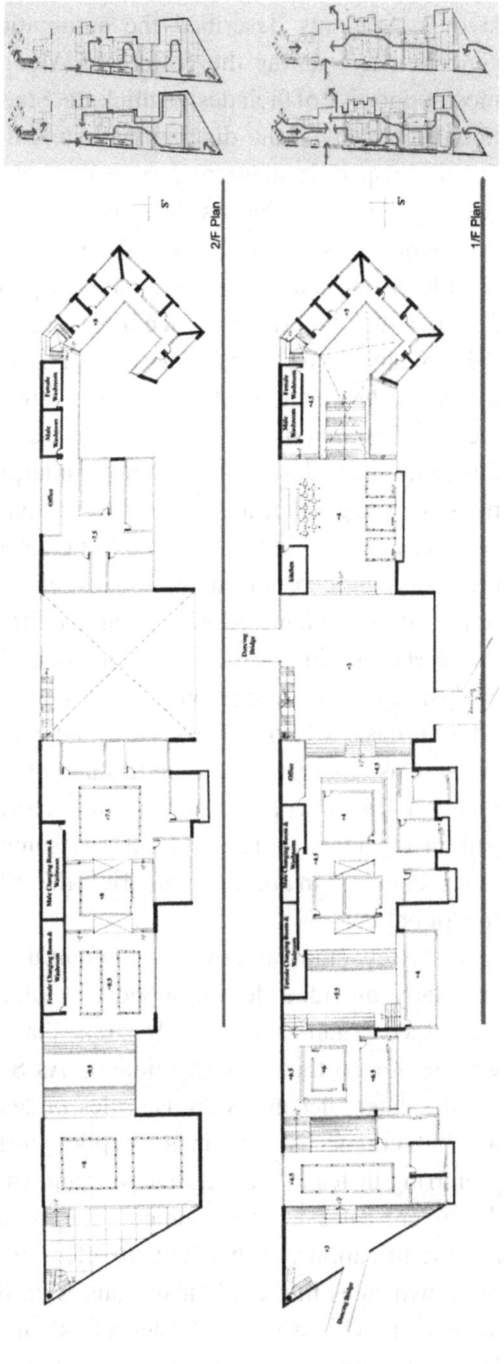

Figure 4. Plans of a school for dancing developed based on early conceptual work in Algogram

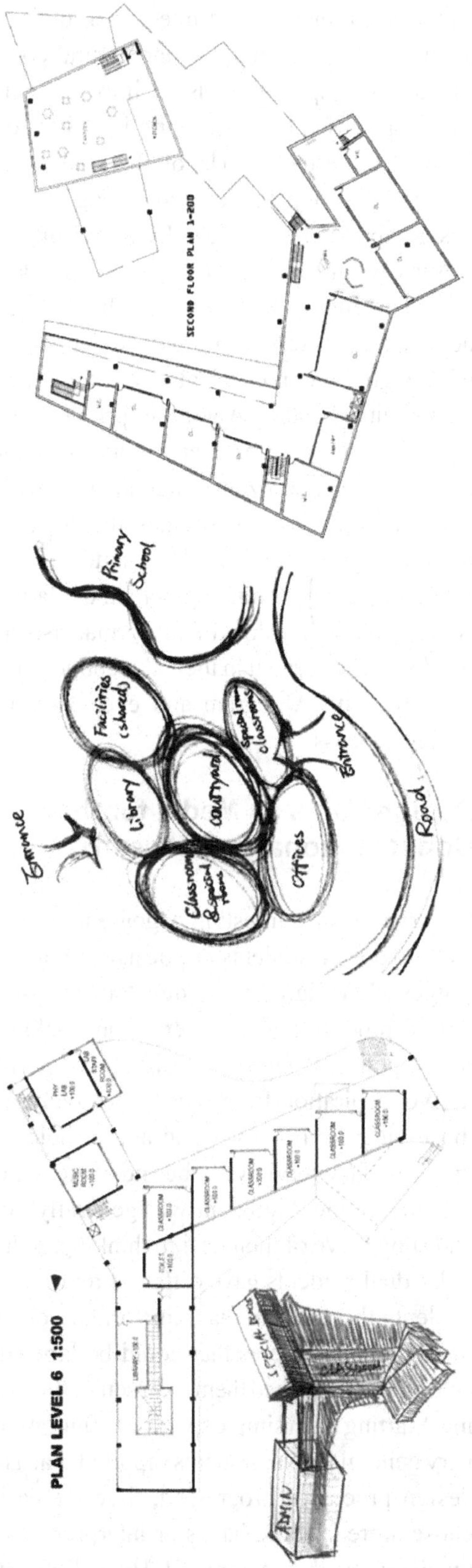

Figure 5. School proposal designed without Algogram

attention to questions of integrating their architectural proposals in urban and natural contexts, as shown in sphere labels such as "mountain", "sea" or "city". Reconsidering buildings on the basis of their functional layout led students of the Algogram group to develop strong individual design approaches that challenge existing architectural typologies, as the proposal for a dancing school in Figure 4 illustrates. The comparison between the observed group of students working with Algogram and students working in parallel teams without using Algogram primarily serves to clarify previous observations and does not aim to provide generalizable statements. The comparison however substantiates the observation that the diagram format itself seems to have played a role in students' thinking, which explains why students used variations of this format also in their hand sketches drawn in their sketchbooks during working with Algogram and even later in the design process.

Design Tools as Media for the Conversational In-Between

Observations from testing Algogram with architectural design students in a design studio setting suggest that digital tools developed to support design processes may benefit from making use of the potential inherent in designers' ability to derive inspiration from seeing creatively. When discussing the role of Algogram in their design processes in interviews at the end of the semester, students found Algogram was generally helpful and supportive of their design thinking, although individual students gave different reasons. Most students thought the diagram format consisting of unspecific spheres that could be labeled and colored freely helped them to structure their thinking. Starting from simple sphere configuration and very general labels, students reported that as their design processes progressed, they increasingly chose more specific labels or interpretations for the diagrams they composed. Hybrids generated

in between intersecting and overlapping spheres were perceived as reminders of design potential and interpreted as implicit questions provoking innovative solutions to architectural function layouts. Students described the automatically generated hybrids as the feature of Algogram most supportive of their design thinking. Students initially perceived the diagrammatic and deliberately unspecific diagram format presented in Algogram as confusing, as students expected the geometric precision and clarity of visuals they were used to from their previous digitally supported 3D modeling experience. Once they understood the evocative intentions underlying Algogram diagrams, however, students readily embraced the visual simplicity but implicit richness of the diagrams, and developed multiple interpretations for the geometrical properties of spheres. As interpretations were not fixed but created on the spot and according to personal preferences or priorities, students often maintained different interpretations in parallel. Students valued the analysis chart function provided by Algogram as a visual basis to provide overview and analysis as well as inspiration for understanding their functional layout composition in terms of a visual pattern rather than a numerical or textual summary as it is common in architectural briefs describing functional layouts.

Only few students however thought that the originally intended design support by offering rule-based organization of Algogram diagrams was helpful to their design thinking. As Schön (1988) stated, designers do use rules in designing but not necessarily in an explicit format, preferring instead flexible, diverse, contextually dependent rules that are subject to exceptions and modifications. In this context, attempting to pin down rules into explicit formats is unlikely to be of much assistance to designers engaged in developing ideas. Maintaining implicit and open-ended diagrammatic visual formats allowed students working with Algogram to focus on the interplay between visuals provided by Algogram and their personal interpretations of these visuals. This interplay allowed for multiple interpretations, misunderstandings, personal associations and deviation from conventional architectural typologies. By maintaining this creative dialogue in the digital realm and (temporarily) suspending translation of diagrams into form, Algogram provides a breeding ground for inspiration. Architectural design students working with Algogram readily developed new visual languages and personal interpretations, and were encouraged to reframe their initial conventional understanding of how a school may be designed. Diagrams generated with Algogram provided material for fruitful discussions in design tutorials, perhaps because they allowed students and teachers to maintain several options while negotiating a shared understanding of school design proposals. When compared with conventional bubble diagrams, diagrams generated with Algogram seemed to provide more opportunities for rethinking of conventional architectural typologies: Algogram diagrams created yet-undefined objects – the hybrids – that students had to reinterpret to make sense of the three-dimensional functional layout.

In terms of tool development, this approach to digital design support may provide an alternative way of thinking about supporting design processes through evoking ideas. It resonates with Glanville's (1992) characterization of the use of digital tools as media enabling creative processes of a conversational nature. Introducing limitations through the diagram format in the case of Algogram seems to have encouraged students to imagine creatively. This approach is different from tool development for manipulation of geometry, where the addition of features in the software is expected to greater capacity in modeling geometry, and thus, to better outcomes. Instead of automating human designers' actions, digitally supported design processes may be understood not only as holistic processes of inquiry involving both activity and thinking in parallel and in relation to each other as described by Gedenryd (1998): Algogram

suggests a form of digitally supported designing where designers are not only tool users but form part of systems that derive their strength as much from computation as from human inspiration.

FUTURE RESEARCH DIRECTIONS

The study reported in this chapter presents initial steps in the research area mapped out in the beginning of the chapter. It offers at least two main avenues for future research. The first potential research direction addresses the question of how digital tools can offer support for and evoke creative seeing. The second research direction addresses the diagrammatic notation formats that may support such creative seeing in contexts other than architectural function planning. These two directions are outlined briefly in the following, and may be particularly valuable to pursue within educational contexts, as the example of the architectural design studio presented in this chapter demonstrates.

To be able to evoke creative seeing through digital tools, tool developers may find it useful to consider designers' ability to step out of conventional or predetermined use patterns and transform their perception of their tools and environments. For tool developers, this means creating opportunities for unpredictability and misunderstanding, and for accommodating the accidental and spontaneous (see Glanville 1992). As described by Gaver et al. (2003), investigating ways of employing ambiguity may provide a fruitful direction for this purpose. Deterministic automating of design processes may not be the most appropriate approach to support creative designing. Instead, digital tools may be thought of as part of holistic dynamic processes of inquiry that allow for transformative and divergent thinking. In such processes, opportunities for design inspiration may be created in between human designers and digital design support. Where previous research is often focused on tools as answers or solutions to problems, tools may be considered part of a flexible and opportunistic processes of creative inquiry, where tools serve as media to support designers in imagining more and better problems and questions.

The second area of potential future research concerns the visual format of digitally supported and generated diagrams. In the case of Algogram, diagrammatic visuals were developed to support and challenge architectural function layout. Other diagram formats beyond those presented may provide similarly engaging but also similarly non-deterministic visual materials for designers to work with on other aspects of architectural design, such as structural layout design. In this study, Algogram-generated diagrams provided student designers with implicit questions. Other contexts may require different visuals to provide questions and inspire the "seeking, self-positioning, perspective-choosing, experience-dependent, attention-placing, interest-driven choice making" of designerly seeing (Herr & Fischer 2010).

CONCLUSION

This chapter presents a study of architectural design process support through evocative diagrammatic digital visuals. It discusses the theoretical foundations as well as a design studio test application of Algogram, a prototype software that provides designers with simple generic three-dimensional diagrams that serve to provide implicit questions rather than form-based outcomes. The approach to design support presented in this chapter embraces and harnesses designers' ability to see creatively and constructively. Based on the assumption that designing does not happen either in the tool or in the mind, but in between participants of conversations, Algogram deliberately employs a diagrammatic visual format that requires active creative seeing to make sense to designers working with it. Based on a series of previous prototypes of generative applications of cellular automata

in architectural design, Algogram reflects the understanding that in design processes initiated and driven by diagrams, designers are able to develop personal design approaches that are less limited by tool developers' intentions. Requiring designers working with Algogram to see creatively encourages claiming of ownership and authorship, an essential ingredient for successful design processes. Diagrams generated with Algogram were observed to stimulate ideas by provoking questions and challenging assumptions more than by providing form-based answers. In the case of Algogram, such questions and challenges are not defined explicitly but remain implicit in diagrams that evade conventional interpretations. This research project opens up new views on the potentials and future of digital design support, which may not only seek to assist designers merely in modeling and evaluating geometry, but also to integrate humans into design conversations in which where the role of computers is to present designers with evocative ambiguities rather than modeling precise geometry.

REFERENCES

Benjamin, A. (2000). *Architectural philosophy*. London, UK: Athlone Press.

Boden, M. A. (1991). *The creative mind: Myths and mechanisms*. New York, NY: Basic Books, Inc.

Cassara, S. (Ed.). (2006). *Peter Eisenman: Feints*. Milano, Italy: Skira.

Chandrasekaran, B., Kurup, U., & Banerjee, B. (2005). A diagrammatic reasoning architecture: Design, implementation and experiments. In *Proceedings of the AAAI Spring Symposium, Reasoning with Mental and External Diagrams: Computational Modeling and Spatial Assistance*, (pp. 108–113). Stanford University, CA.

DeBono, E. (1973). *Lateral thinking: Creativity step by step*. New York, NY: Harper Colophon.

Do, E. Y.-L., & Gross, M. D. (2001). Thinking with diagrams in architectural design. *Artificial Intelligence Review*, *15*(1-2), 135–149. doi:10.1023/A:1006661524497

Dogan, F., & Nersessian, N. (2002). Conceptual diagrams: representing ideas in design. In Hegarty, M., Meyer, B., & Narayanan, N. H. (Eds.), *Diagrammatic representation and inference* (pp. 353–355). Berlin, Germany: Springer. doi:10.1007/3-540-46037-3_37

Emmons, P. (2006). Embodying networks: Bubble diagrams and the image of modern organicism. *The Journal of Architecture*, *11*(4), 441–461. doi:10.1080/13602360601037867

Fischer, T., & Herr, C. M. (2007). The designer as toolbreaker? Probing tool use in applied generative design. In G. Yu, Q. Zhou & W. Dong (Eds.), *CAADRIA 2007: The Proceedings of The Twelfth International Conference on Computer-Aided Architectural Design Research in Asia* (pp. 381-389). Nanjing, China: School of Architecture, Southeast University and School of Architecture Nanjing University.

Freeman, D. (1998). *Doing teacher research: From inquiry to understanding*. Pacific Grove, CA: Heinle & Heinle.

Garcia, M. (2010). Introduction: Histories and theories of the diagrams of architecture. In Garcia, M. (Ed.), *The diagrams of architecture: AD reader* (pp. 18–45). Chichester, UK: Wiley.

Gaver, W. W., Beaver, J., & Benford, S. (2003). Ambiguity as a resource for design. *Proceedings of the Conference on Human Factors in Computing Systems*, 5-10 April 2003, Fort Lauderdale, FL, (pp. 233-240). New York: ACM Press.

Gedenryd, H. (1998). *How designers work: Making sense of authentic cognitive activity*. Unpublished doctoral dissertation, Lund University, Sweden.

Glanville, R. (1992). CAD abusing computing. In *CAAD Instruction: The New Teaching of an Architect? eCAADe 1992 Conference Proceedings*, Barcelona, (pp. 213-224).

Glanville, R. (2007). Grounding difference. In Müller, A., & Müller, K. H. (Eds.), *An unfinished revolution? Heinz von Foerster and the Biological Computer Laboratory – BCL 1958-1976*. Vienna, Austria: Edition Echoraum.

Glasgow, J., Narayanan, N. H., & Chandrasekaran, B. (1995). *Diagrammatic reasoning: Cognitive and computational perspectives*. Menlo Park, CA: AAAI Press.

Goel, V. (1995). *Sketches of thought*. Cambridge, MA: MIT Press.

Goldschmidt, G. (1991). The dialectics of sketching. *Creativity Research Journal*, *4*(2), 123–143. doi:10.1080/10400419109534381

Goldschmidt, G. (2003). The backtalk of self-generated sketches. *Design Issues*, *19*(1), 72–88. doi:10.1162/074793603762667728

Gross, M. D. (1996). The electronic cocktail napkin: a computational environment for working with design diagrams. *Design Studies*, *17*(1), 53–69. doi:10.1016/0142-694X(95)00006-D

Gross, M. D. (2009). Visual languages and visual thinking. In C. Grimm & J. J. L. Viola, Jr. (Eds.), *Sketch Based Interfaces and Modeling: Proceedings of the 6th Eurographics Symposium on Sketch-Based Interfaces and Modeling*, (pp. 7-11). New York, NY: ACM.

Herr, C. M. (2008). *From form generators to automated diagrams: using cellular automata to support architectural design*. Unpublished doctoral dissertation, The University of Hong Kong, Hong Kong.

Herr, C. M., & Fischer, T. (2010). Digital drifting: Minimally instructive education for tool-aided creativity in Asia. *Cybernetics & Human Knowing, 17*(1-2), 37–57.

Herr, C. M., & Karakiewicz, J. (2007). Algogram: Automated diagrams for an architectural design studio. In A. Dong, A. Vande Moere, & J. Gero (Eds.), *CAAD Futures 2007: The Proceedings of The Twelfth International Conference on CAAD Futures* (pp. 167-180). Dordrecht, The Netherlands: Springer.

Herr, K., & Anderson, G. L. (2005). *The action research dissertation: A guide for students and faculty*. Thousand Oaks, CA: Sage Publications.

Kamps, T. (1999). *Diagram design: A constructive theory*. Berlin, Germany: Springer.

Kemmis, S., & McTaggart, R. (Eds.). (1990). *The action research reader*. Victoria, Australia: Deakin University.

Mueller, V. (2006). Integrating digital and non-digital design work. In Chaznar, A. (Ed.), *Blurring the lines* (pp. 38–45). Chichester, UK: Wiley-Academy.

Parthenios, P. (2005). *Conceptual design tools for architects*. DDes Dissertation, Harvard Design School.

Purcell, A. T., & Gero, J. S. (1998). Drawings and the design process: A review of protocol studies in design and other disciplines and related research in cognitive psychology. *Design Studies, 19*(4), 389–430. doi:10.1016/S0142-694X(98)00015-5

Rittel, H. (1992). *Planen Entwerfen Design. Ausgewaehlte Schriften zu Theorie und Methodik*. Stuttgart, Germany: Kohlhammer.

Rittel, H., & Webber, M. (1973). Dilemmas in a general theory of planning. *Policy Sciences, 4*, 155–169. doi:10.1007/BF01405730

Schön, D. (1983). *The reflective practitioner: How professionals think in action*. New York, NY: Basic Books.

Schön, D. A. (1988). Designing: Rules, types and worlds. *Design Studies, 9*(3), 133–143. doi:10.1016/0142-694X(88)90047-6

Schön, D. A., & Wiggins, G. (1992). Kinds of seeing and their functions in designing. *Design Studies, 13*(2), 135–156. doi:10.1016/0142-694X(92)90268-F

Shea, K. (2006). Generative design. In Chaznar, A. (Ed.), *Blurring the lines* (pp. 54–61). Chichester, UK: Wiley-Academy.

Shneiderman, B. (2000). Creating creativity: User interfaces for supporting innovation. *ACM Transactions on Computer-Human Interaction, 7*(1), 114–138. doi:10.1145/344949.345077

Spuybroek, L. (2001). Machining architecture. In L. Spuybroek & Lang, B. (Eds.), *The weight of the image*. Rotterdam, The Netherlands: NAi Publishers.

Suwa, M., & Tversky, B. (1997). What do architects and students perceive in their design sketches? A protocol analysis. *Design Studies, 18*(4), 385–403. doi:10.1016/S0142-694X(97)00008-2

Szalapaj, P. (2005). *Contemporary architecture and the digital design process*. Oxford, UK: Architectural Press.

KEY TERMS AND DEFITIONS

Architectural Function: Designation of spaces for specific types of use such as 'eating', 'sleeping', 'street' or 'garden'.

Code: A system in which arbitrarily chosen words, letters, or symbols are assigned specific meanings.

Conversation: Informal exchange with others or the self in which novelty arises from repeated interpretation of what is exchanged. Designing is conversational in this sense.

Diagramming: To present visually, typically with a focus on relational and systemic aspects.

Hybrid: Stemming from heterogeneous sources or composed of incongruous character-istics, here referring to a feature of the Algogram software.

Sketching: To present visually, typically with a focus on shape and form.

Venn diagram: A type of diagram that utilizes circles to represent sets and their relationships.

Chapter 19
Architectural Design Education and Parametric Modeling:
An Architecturological Approach

Caroline Lecourtois
School of Architecture of Paris La Villette, France

François Guéna
School of Architecture of Paris La Villette, France

ABSTRACT

This chapter presents an original teaching method carried out at the School of Architecture of Paris La-Villette (ARIAM-LAREA) whose aim is to prepare future architects for parametric design. Unlike most of the parametric design studio, the authors of this chapter do not want to teach a specific design method. They believe that the students have to find out their own method from the knowledge of architectural usages of parametric design. Theoretical courses linked to a studio will better train them in the usage of parametric tools. During theoretical courses focused on parametric design activity, the authors ask the students to analyze computer activities of architects in order to identify their design methods. The students are trained under a method to analyze design activities based on "Applied Architecturology." During the studio, they ask the students to reuse the identified methods. The students apply the methods in their own project and adapt them in order to build their own parametric design method. The works produced by the students in the courses and in the studio bring up new questions for the ARIAM-LAREA research laboratory and constitute bases for the development of new software tools for parametric architectural design.

INTRODUCTION

Parametric modeling has been taught in several architectural design studios all over the world. But generally the parametric modeling is viewed as a component of a design method being taught to students. These design methods are most often focused on sustainable design or CAD/CAM technologies.

When the design method is focused on sustainable design, the teaching objective is to teach the possibilities of the parametric architectural design

DOI: 10.4018/978-1-61350-180-1.ch019

especially for adapting the shape to climate conditions or designing building shape inspired by forms and structures of the nature (fruits for example) (Matcha 2007). Generally, parametric modeling tools are used in conjunction with environmental performance evaluation tools (Holzer 2008).

When the design method is focused on CAD/CAM technologies, the teaching objective is to provide an in-depth understanding of the CAD/CAM technology and to convey how it can be applied in current architectural design practice (Bechthold 2007; Karzel and Matcha 2009).

The same teaching methods are commonly used. The students are first trained in using tools required by the design methods (parametric modelers, environmental performance evaluation tool or CNC manufacturing devices) and in how to communicate data between these tools. The teachers of the studio provide this training or, sometimes, appeal to expert competencies outside the studio. Often the training staff of the developer or vendor provides the training but consultants can be also found across other academic institutes. Sometimes, before this training, teachers of the studio provide preliminary course for introducing parametric modeling software, the use of parameters and their impact on the geometry.

When they have been trained to use the tools, several progressive exercises are proposed to students for learning the methods before designing their own project. The teachers propose appropriate methods by designing small objects (pieces of furniture for example) or small-scale architectural projects (Holzer 2008; Matcha 2007; Spaeth 2007).

This chapter presents an original teaching method carried out at the School of Architecture of Paris La-Villette (ARIAM-LAREA) whose aim is to prepare future architects for parametric design. Unlike most of the parametric design studio, we do not want to teach a specific design method. We believe that the students have to find their own method.

This teaching practice jointly uses two didactical methods: Teaching and training. Teaching is carried out in theoretical courses of the post-graduate program and training in a studio at the same level of studies. Architecturology is taught in the theoretical courses as basic knowledge on the architectural design and as an introspection and verbalisation method for analysing the architectural design activity. The students are led to investigate the functionalities of software tools using parametric modeling techniques in order to find out their potential to assist architectural design. In the studio the students use parametric modeling software tools (such as Grasshopper, Generative Component or Digital Project) for designing their architectural project. We train the students in using parametric tools in specific courses linked to the studio.

The aim of this teaching approach is to lead the students to discover the impact of those software tools on their production and to build new design methods. The works produced by the students in the courses and the studio bring up new questions for the ARIAM-LAREA research laboratory and constitute bases for the development of new software tools for parametric architectural design.

The first part of this chapter explains the specific approach of Architecturology taught in the theoretical courses. Architecturology is taught as an analysis tool that permits exploring design methods of architects. The aim of the theoretical courses is for the students to produce architecturological analysis of design methods in order to develop their own methods of parametric design. The second part presents how we approach, in the theoretical courses, the specific aspects of parametric modeling used by different teams of architects. It testifies our pedagogy and shows how our students explore cases to personalize their own approach to Computer-aided Design (CAD). The third part presents some student productions of parametric design from the studio. The last section or conclusion presents the impact of these experiments on our research and the specifications of a new parametric design tool we are currently developing.

BACKGROUND OF THE THEORETICAL COURSES: ARCHITECTUROLOGY

Architecturology is a French field of research whose scientific purpose is to examine the cognitive activity of architectural design (called conception) (Albertsen 1999). The focus of this field is the building of new means to examine conception in terms of measurement operations.

Architecturology was initiated by Ph. Boudon in the 70s and developed, from 2005, by the researchers of LAREA (Laboratory of Architecturology and Epistemological Researches on Architecture) (Boudon 1992). Nowadays, Architecturology is regarded as scientific knowledge on conception and conceived architecture. It provides a scientific language by which we can examine different objects dealing with conception, including the cognitive mechanisms of architecture produced with computer.

It is currently being developed in our laboratory at ARIAM-LAREA. The scientific structure of Architecturology is composed with two branches: The first one is the scientific language representing a general and systemic knowledge on conception (named Fundamental Architecturology). The second one (named Applied Architecturology) regroups methodologies of research that consist of "testing" the *a priori* concepts of Fundamental Architecturology on objects dealing with conception, in order to discover new knowledge on these objects.

The paradigm of Fundamental Architecturology is based on the distinction made by G. Canguilhem between *scientific objects* and *natural objects* (Canguilhem 1975). It also shares philosophies of E. Kant and J. Piaget (Kant 1781; Piaget 1968), positioning the experience on our prior knowledge and, in rejecting the idea that knowledge is derived from observation of reality.

Furthermore, three principles are at the origin of its paradigm. These principles incorporate the cogitations of B. Zevi, H. Focillon and E. Panof-

sky: 1) architecture deals with space (Zevi 1959; Focillon 1934), 2) architecture is thought before existence (Panofsky 1967), 3) space of architecture is measured (Focillon 1934).

Consequently, the *scientific object* of Architecturology (conception) concerns the following question: "How did designers give measurement to their artefact?" and knowledge explicating this question was constructed as a theoretical fiction (Boudon 2005). The method to construct this theoretical fiction was inspired by knowledge developed by F. Saussure, L. T. Hjemslev and R. Jakobson, on language (Boudon 1992).

Fundamental Architecturology is composed of different kinds of concepts. These concepts are related to the place in the systematic language and its designation. The first one is *space of conception* that represents the scientific object of Architecturology (Lecourtois 2006). The second one is *architecturological scale* that is plural and represents twenty-one classes of cognitive operations for giving measurement related to different fields of reference. The third one is *properties of scales* and *relationships between scales*. *Properties of scales* determine the manners that scales intervene in the process of design. *Relationships between scales* determine spatial or temporal relations between scales in relation to a project. All of these concepts help to describe the operating mechanisms of architectural conception in general detached from reality (Boudon et al. 2000).

Applied architecturology includes research methods that can be qualified as empirical or clinical and confronts cases from the theoretical point of view (Lecourtois 2004; 2005; 2006; 2011). The construction of these research methods is based on the distinction of E. Panofsky between the lower and the higher level of significance (Panofsky 1967: 138). Applied Architecturology aims to build at a higher level - or secondary layer– of meaning that helps to overcome the layer of sensible qualities and to build a "scientific" interpretation of the design work.

These methods of research can be used in order to question the usages of parametric modeling in architectural conception. With its focus on elemental cognitive operations, Applied Architecturology allows us to identify and distinguish the cognitive operations of design, the operations of modeling and the cognitive operations of design that modeling implies.

UNDERSTANDING PARAMETRIC DESIGN USING APPLIED ARCHITECTUROLOGY

This section explains how we use Applied Architecturology to understand the role of parametric modeling in architectural design. The aim of our research is to build a new pedagogical menu to help future architects to be more effective by using parametric modelling in their design. The new menu is already being tested in a new studio that we began in 2010.

Our hypothesis is that to better apply new methods of CAD, architects must know how they design and how to explain their approaches. Therefore, Architecturology is presented to them as a means to analyze and to understand their own practice and the practices of other architects who use parametric modeling.

Consequently, our educational system consists partly of analysing the use of software in architectural design. This allows us to understand the basic cognitive operations that assist and accompany such uses. The aim of this analysis is to identify the operational implications of these practices and to raise awareness in developing computer-aided architectural methods fitted to each student.

The cases that we study are coming from agencies that develop the uses of parametric modeling tools for design such as Foster & Partner, Gehry Partners, Zaha Hadid, S. Calatrava, SOM (Skidmore, Owings and Merrill), R&Sie, etc. The various implications of these tools within the design process in these agencies suggest the possible assistance of design operations.

From Architecturology, we analyze the cases to verbalize the cognitive activity of architectural design and computer support for design by distinguishing cognitive operations of design from modeling operations of architectural design.

Two particular projects (one by Foster & Partner and the other by SOM) are specifically analyzed to explain to the students the implications of computer in design and the relationships between cognitive operations of conception, modeling operations and assessment operations. The selected project of Foster & Partner is the City Hall of London. The selected project of SOM is the Infinity Tower.

Case I: The Design of the City Hall of London (Foster & Partner)

For this project, a team of parametric modeling specialists (Specialist Modelling Group) seems to have worked with designers from the first stages of architectural conception. Consequently, the cognitive operations of conception (or design operations) have been implemented by both the designers and modelers. A quick presentation of H. Withehead about the process of design introduces our architecturological point of view.

"Originally, the concept was to create a large "lens" looking out over the river, with a set of floor plates attached at the back in a serrated profile, which resulted in a "pine cone" glazing effect. At first sight, the inspiration for the form may seem somewhat arbitrary, which was, in fact, how it began; as the team started work on the project one of the partners was heard to say, "We are doing something by the river. I think it is a pebble." we took up the idea and attempted to create a "parametric pebble". The problem we faced was how to formulate a "pebble" in descriptive geometry. Our first thoughts were to start with a sphere, which has a minimal ratio of

surface area to volume, and then explore how it could be transformed." (Withehead H. in Kolarevic 2003: 85)

Six different *architecturological scales* help to investigate the relationships between design operations and modeling operations: Geographical scale, visibility scale, model scale, economical scale, geometrical scale and, representational scale (other *architecturological scales* could help to describe and articulate some relationships).

Geographical scale and visibility scale: The context of the project being nearby the river has inspired the designers to think that a building should provide views of the river: To build a "lens". The building was considered to provide surprising views of London through a ramp from the lower ground level to the top. The original form of the project was interpreted by the specialists of parametric modeling as a pebble.

Geographical scale and model scale: The idea to model a pebble proceeds from the context of the project and the form of the project with which the designers had considered the relationship with its environment. The question for the specialist modeling group was how to model a pebble that corresponds to the other intentions of the project. Is a pebble a deformed sphere? Or is it something else that must be able to adapt itself to the environment? Therefore the modeling of a pebble introduces the general concept of what is a pebble.

Model scale, economical scale and geometrical scale: From the beginnings of the project, the team has worked on a form that could integrate an energy assessment. The computer model has been considered in order to be able to test different forms in relation to energy performances and the sun-path. Therefore the geometric shape of the design had to be determined by a parametric model that is able to change according to the assessments.

Geometrical scale and representational scale: Consequently to the previous remarks, the construction of the computer model was a stage of architectural conception. The question for the team was to choose the best approach to geometrically defining a shape that could be transformed according to future assessments.

To determine the best model to represent the project in order to be able to articulate the concept is what we call, in Architecturology, to implement a representational scale. In this case, the team had to choose the parameters and their possible variations by anticipating future usage of assessment modeling.

Although architects and specialists of parametric modeling have different roles in this case, some cognitive operations of architectural design have been implemented by both parties. The approach to modeling includes rules for developing the project. The modeling operations consist of choosing the approach to representing a geometrical shape which depends on the conception of the project. Therefore the operations are necessary to be attached.

The question that we ask the students is to identify the modeling operations that could have helped the cognitive operations of design from this case.

Case II: The Design of Infinity Tower (SOM)

The second project presented in the theoretical courses is the design of Infinity Tower by SOM. This tower seems to have been developed according to a certain modeling operation named "twist" that combines a sweeping operation with rotation. The use of parametric modeling in this tower design exemplifies a quote of Victor Gane and John Haymaker: "*To design parametrically means to design a system that sets up a design space which can be explored through the variations of the parameters.*" (Gane & Haymaker 2007: 293).

Knowing the modeling operation (twist), the issue we concern is the cognitive operations that derive from the operation. In this case, the angle of rotation seems to have been a design parameter to choose according to two architecturological operations of conception: An "optical scale" and a "visibility scale". The "optical scale" deals with how the tower will be seen in its context. It is here combined with a "technical scale" in such a manner that the structural framework is specifically thought to be shown. The "visibility scale" deals with the eyesight that the future tower will offer to the ocean and the city skyline. These two (or three) architecturological scales become two (or three) types of assessment criteria. Designers have to choose between options calculated by the parametric model in order to satisfy these assessment aspects.

The name of the tower suggests the use of another architecturological scale: A "semantic scale". Infinity tower can be interpreted as a roofless tower, a non-limited tower at its top. This effect seems to have really been emphasized and implemented with the treatment of the structural framework which continues into the sky. Nevertheless, understanding the method that SOM adopts to implement the parametric model, we can say that the infinity of the tower is only within the computer model. The architectural project of the infinity is not possible in reality, but may exist in the parametric model to propose different "reality" for the project.

The parametric model of Infinity Tower defines a certain *space of conception* for the project by enabling different kinds of pre-determined *constraints*. Theses constraints can be dimensional or geometric (Gane & Haymaker 2007) and determine different design limits. Dimensional constraints establish relationships between a variable and its possible values. Geometric constraints establish relationships between two different variables.

In the architecturological language, to choose the constraints for parametric modeling, is to conceive this modeling process. Therefore it is to implement *operations of conception* in the context of a geometric scale. Consequently, complexity between two *spaces of conception* determines parametric modeling for architectural design. In order to explain each of them independently and to have means to explore their relationships, we propose to theoretically distinguish them with two different concepts. The concept of *space of conception* is kept to represent the cognitive operations of conception in order to conceptualize and determine the architectural project. To represent the cognitive operations in order to develop the parametric model for conceptualizing and determining the architectural project, we propose the new concept of *space of modeling* (Lecourtois 2010).

This complexity can be described in terms of *operation of induction*. A variable of the parametric modeling is necessary to become a variable of the design project and therefore, become a factor to conceptualize and to articulate its measurements. The opposite side of the question is to know how a variable of the architectural conception can be inducted to determine the choice of a variable for parametric modeling.

In Architecturology, variables of design can be either physical or abstract elements to consider in order to give them measurements. So for parametric modeling, it is more important to consider what each parameter determines. For example, in the case of Infinity Tower, variables of the design conception were: A distinction between a core and a footprint, the shape of the footprint, the edges of the shape of the footprint, and so on. All these variables have been considered in relation to the physical context of the project and certainly in relation to the possibility of parametric modeling. Nevertheless, variables of the design conception for the project must be determined by the development of the parametric model. The development of the parametric model at the conceptual design stage includes determining parametric variables and their constraints. It induces a "cutting" operation on geometric elements to construct the parametric model. In other words, the parametric model introduces and conceives the conception of "cutting" the space through many architectural elements such as core, corridor, columns, envelope, beams, and so on.

This case highlights the complexity of parametric architectural design and the constraints that the parametric modeling required for architectural design. If assessment operations are not directly implemented by the computer, in their own space of conception, designers will need to reason in front of the options produced by the computer.

The above interpretations about the selected cases and parametric design are explored in the theoretical courses whose aim is to understand the different ways "digital" architects apply parametric design in their practice and the possible principles behind the applications. By understanding these important theories and practices, in our studio, we aim for the students to develop their own method to parametric design by utilizing such software as Rhino and its plug-in Grasshopper, Generative components, Digital Project and so on, for architectural design.

STUDENT DESIGN OUTCOMES

Coupling the studio with the theoretical courses, we aim for the students to develop their own practices of parametric design from the knowledge of parametric design by other "digital" architects and Architecturology. This section presents some students projects that were designed under this pedagogical system.

The program of the project is to design an aquatic center in Paris that could host official Olympic swimming competitions. The site of the project is situated nearby a water channel and a disaffected railway.

The first case of student project presented in Figure 1, have been developed from the idea of Bubble.

To design this project, the student has applied different architecturological scales as neighboring scale, model scale, geographical scale, functional scale, and so on. The cognitive operations she has chosen to assist with the parametric model are optical scale, geometrical scale and economic scale.

The parametric model helps to determine the segmentation of the covering of the structure. This

Figure 1. Bubble aquatic center

segmentation is implemented from geometrical constraints of the covering pieces and the aspect of the building seen in its urban context. Parametric modeling is able to automatically calculate variations of the paneling. The evaluation of the aspect is done by the designer herself from her own esthetics criteria. So, optical scale and geometrical scale are directly assisted with the model. Moreover they are objects in the parametric model.

Economical scale is indirectly assisted by the parametric model. The parametric model has been considered to be coupled with a CAM that would help to optimize the construction of the paneling. The covering is thought as a mosaic of metal sheets that the parametric model could calculate (each differently) and the CAM would optimize the cutting of a large metal plate.

The second case of student project has been inspired from the project of the Waterloo Station of Grimshaw and the station of Liège in Belgium by S. Calatrava.

Like in the previous case, the student has applied different architecturological scales to design the project. Here, the shape in plan of the accordion has been determined with the shape of the project site (parcellar scale). The volume of the swimming pool has been considered with a regular structure that slices the plan.

The major cognitive operations that have been assisted by parametric modeling are related to the classes of operations named technical scale in Architecturology.

The student wanted to build his project with a single balloon frame repeated several times along the plan. The section of each balloon frame situated on the project has to be adapted to the shape of the plan. So, the student built a parametric model of the frame attached to the shape of the project site. The parametric model has been used to automatically calculate each frame of the project. The dimension of each frame depends on the scope of a span and the section of its constituted beams.

In other words, the parametric modeling process of this project assisted a technical scale, that is to say, helped to determine and to calculate the

structure of the project. The upper image in Figure 2 represents the technical simulation of the frame developed from parametric modeling.

The third case of student project was inspired by the notion of "random" - applying parametric modeling to cut elevation with a random algorithm. A reference of this project was the agencie of Périphériques (Louis Paillard, Anne-Françoise Jumeau, Emmanuelle Marin-Trottin, David Trottin).

Computer was used here to assist different cognitive operations. The parametric modeling helped to test different random segmentations of the elevations in order to choose the more suitable variation in relation to the architectural esthetics and the lighting inside. So, it assisted an optical scale (that answers the question: How the building is viewed?), a visibility scale (that answers the question: What views does the building provide, from inside to outside?) and a functional scale (that answers the question: How the building is functioned in relation to its brief?).

RDM6, a French freeware (http://iut.univ-lemans.fr/ydlogi/rdm_version_6.html), was used to calculate the structure of the building. So the combination of RDM6 and the parametric modeling tool has helped to design and evaluate different technical solutions to build the project (a technical scale).

Our pedagogical system permits the students to explore different assessment tools to design by testing them in an architectural project. With the theoretical language that we present to them, they are able to explain what they do or want to do with computer for design. They also understand through the practice what could be more suitable for their design. Their experiences help us to understand the potential of computer and to develop the specifications of a new parametric design system. We use our teaching, to develop this new software system combining parametric modeling and freehand sketching. The conclusion of this chapter explains how our teaching influences this research program.

Figure 2. The Accordion Olympic pool

CONCEPTION DIGITALE
UNE PISCINE OLYMPIQUE

LU LIN
10465

PERSPECTIVES INTERIEURES

PLAN MASSE 1:1000

Echelle: 1:2000

Figure 3. "Random" elevations for a swimming pool

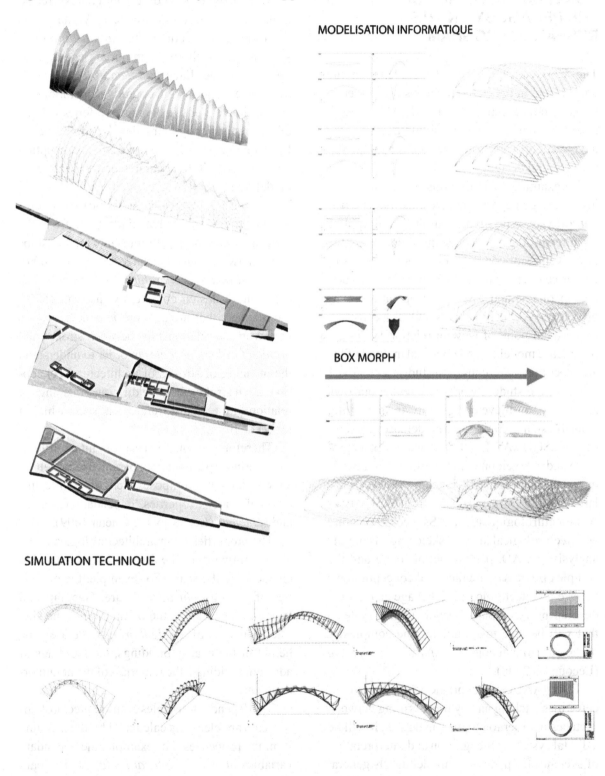

MODELISATION INFORMATIQUE

BOX MORPH

SIMULATION TECHNIQUE

CONCLUSION: IMPACT OF THE PEDAGOGY ON THE RESEARCH PROGRAM

The works produced by the students in the courses and in the studio (analysis and projects) bring up new questions for the ARIAM-LAREA research laboratory and constitute bases for the development of new software tools for parametric architectural design.

To examine CAD in terms of operations allows us to go beyond the investigation on existing software. With Architecturology and Applied Architecturology, students question about the effectiveness of computer on design in terms of cognitive operations: Design operations, modeling operations and assessment operations. The presentation of their works is built as a constructive critical point of view in relation to design, parametric modeling and doctrinal method of the architect they have chosen to study.

From the student works, we renew our own research work to develop new software that aims to embed design operations and modeling operations, named ESQUAAS. ESQUAAS is a computer program under development. It combines parametric modeling and freehand sketching (www.ariam-larea.archi.fr). Its name comes from "ESQUisses Architecturologiquement ASsistées" meaning architecturological aids for sketching). From the analysis of CAD, parametric modeling and the complex process of architectural conception, we believe architecturological language can help to develop new computer design support systems that will be able to "maintain" the complexity of the operational cognitive *space of conception* (Lecourtois 2008).

ESQUAAS can support the possibility to conceive by sketching and by transforming between sketches in order to progress in design. It will be a digital system of recognition and interpretation of sketches for parametric modeling. Its general aim is to permit building a parametric model with architecturological language. Therefore it will interpret sketches according to the context created by each architecturological concept. We have seen from the above sections that *architecturolgical scale* is one of the most important concepts of this knowledge. Each *architecturological scale* determines a group of cognitive operations of conception related to a domain of reference. Each of them is currently being developed in order to form an operational micro-system of conception that will constitute a parameter for parametric modeling in ESQUAAS.

So far ESQUAAS is already able to recognize graphic traces of twelve kinds built from the concept of *dromies* that represents relationships between two strokes (Guéna & Lecourtois 2009). For us, *dromies* and *architecturological scales* constitute a design complexity that can clarify the manners that architecture is conceived. We now work on relationships between strokes and *architecturological scales* in order to understand the meaning of strokes of architectural conception. Each stroke can have different meanings in relation to the architecturalogical scale which it proceeds from.

Therefore we construct each architecturological scale into a parameter for parametric modeling. Three elements compose each of architecturological scale: Properties, dependant variables and *scalemes* (Lecourtois & Guéna 2009).

The properties of an architecturological scale are determinants of the domain of reference that characterize the scale. For example, the properties of a *geographical scale* are: Geographical location, topography, the orientation of the site. The properties of a *neighboring scale* are: The height of the nearby buildings, the moldings of adjacent buildings, the materials of the neighborhood and so on.

The dependant variables of an architecturological scale are elements calculated by the machine from the properties. For example, the dependant variables of a *geographical scale* are: The path of the sun and the race of the prevailing winds. Those of a *neighboring scale* can be: The shadow of neighboring buildings and the template of the neighborhood and so on.

The scalemes of an architecturological scale are basic cognitive operations of conception. For example, the scalemes of a *geographical scale* are: Orientating, locating, cutting and giving measurement. Those of a *neighboring scale* can be: Locating in relation to the neighboring front, cutting, giving measurement and so on.

ESQUAAS will permit to link strokes to architecturological scales in order to drive design in a parametric model. Each scaleme will be an option to choose in order to articulate the values of the variables. Our students' experiences of applying parametric modelling in architecture help us to define and construct each architecturological scale as a parameter in ESQUAAS. Further experiments on objects conceived with parametric modeling are also conducted to understand the relationships between operations of conception and modeling operations.

REFERENCES

Albertsen, N., & Lundequist, J. (Eds.). (1999). Architecturology, Nordisk Arkitekturforskning. *Nordic Journal of Architectural Research, 1*, 99. Göteborg, Författarna och Nordisk Arkitekturforsking.

Bechthold, M. (2007). Teaching technology: CAD/CAM, parametric design and interactivity. In *Proceedings of eCAADe 25*.

Boudon, P. (1992). *Introduction à l'architecturologie*. Paris, France: Dunod.

Boudon, P. (2005). *Fiction théorique et "théorie fiction"*. *Les Cahiers Thématiques, Fiction théorique* (pp. 50–63). Jeanmichelplace.

Boudon, P., Deshayes, P., Pousin, F., & Schatz, F. (2000). *Enseigner la conception architecturale, cours d'architecturologie*. Paris, France: Editions de la Villette.

Boudon, P., & Pousin, F. (1988). *Figures de la conception architecturale*. Paris, France: Dunod.

Canguilhem, G. (1975). *Etudes d'histoire et de philosophie des sciences. Concernant les vivants et la vie*. Paris, France: Vrin.

Focillon, H. (1934). *La vie des formes*. Paris, France: PUF.

Gane, V., & Haymaker, J. (2007). Conceptual design of high-rises with parametric methods. In *Proceedings of eCAADe 25*.

Guéna, F., & Lecourtois, C. (2009). Aided architectural sketching with Markov models: Dromies and recognition. In *Proceedings of eCAADe 27*.

Holzer, D. (2008). Let's get physical, teaching sustainable design for performance-driven form finding. In *Proceedings of eCAADe 26*.

Kant, E. (2006). *Critique de la raison pure*. Flammarion. (Original work published 1781)

Karzel, R., & Matcha, H. (2009). Experimental design-build: Teaching parameter-based design. In *Proceedings of eCAADe 27*.

Kolarevic, B. (2003). *Architecture in the digital age, design and manufacturing*. Taylor and Francis.

Lecourtois, C. (2004). *De la communication sur l'espace: espace conçu et espace perçu de l'architecture et de l'urbanisme*. Unpublished doctoral dissertation, Université de Nanterre.

Lecourtois, C. (2005). *Architecturologie appliquée à une sémiotique de l'esquisse architecturale*. In Actes du Colloque SCAN05.

Lecourtois, C. (2006). Apprentissage d'un regard architecturologique pour un enseignement de la conception architecturale. In P. Boudon (Dir.), *Conceptions: Epistémologie et poïétique*. Paris, France: L'Harmattan.

Lecourtois, C. (2006). Conception de l'espace et espace de conception. *TIGR (Travaux de l'Institut de Géographie de Reims), Nouvelles approches de l'espace dans les sciences de l'homme et de la société.*

Lecourtois, C. (2008). Enseigner la conception architecturale assistée par ordinateur. In *Actes du colloque BASC 2008, Biskra Algérie.* Retrieved August 2011, from http://www.ariam-larea.archi. fr/ index.php?page=publications-noms

Lecourtois, C. (2010). *Meta-complexité architecturale et assistance informatique.* Paper presented at the Meeting of MCX, Lille, France.

Lecourtois, C. (2011), Studying collaborative design. Epistemology and research methodology. In G. Carrara, A. Fioravanti & A. Trento (Eds.), *Connecting brains shaping the world =>collaborative design spaces,* (pp. 25-37). Europia Productions.

Lecourtois, C. (in press). Genèse cognitive d'un musée: Le cas du Musée Guggenheim de Bilbao. *Architecture muséale, espace de l'art et lieu de l'œuvre.* Collection Figures de l'art. *Presse Universitaire de Toulouse.*

Lecourtois, C., & Guéna, F. (2009). Eco-conception et esquisse assistée. In Bignon, J.C., Halin, G., & Kubicki, S. (Eds.), *Conception architecturale numérique et approches environnementales* (pp. 63–75). Presses Universitaires de Nancy.

Lindsay, B. (2001). *Digital Gehry.* Basel, Switzerland: Birkhäuser.

Matcha, H. (2007). Parametric possibilities: Designing with parametric modelling. In *Proceedings of eCAADE 25.*

Panofsky, E. (1967). *Architecture gothique et pensée scolastique.* Paris, France: Editions de Minuit.

Piaget, J. (1968). *Le structuralisme.* PUF.

Spaeth, A. B., Schwägerl, K., & Stamm, I. (2007). Parameters in the design process. In *Proceedings of eCAADe 25.*

Zevi, B. (1959). *Apprendre à voir l'architecture.* Paris, France: Editions de Minuit.

KEY TERMS AND DEFINITIONS

Applied Architecturology: Methods of research that use the architecturological language or, the knowledge on the cognitive activity of conception, in order to develop new research and new knowledge on objects dealing with conception.

Architecturological Scale: Operational micro-system that regroups cognitive operations of measurement related to a domain of reference. Twenty-one architecturological scales compose the architecturological language as classes of manners to give measurement to space.

Architecturology: A field of research in which the scientific object is the cognitive activity of conception.

Dependant Variables of Architecturological Scale: Elements calculated by the machine from the properties of architecturological scales.

ESQUAAS: A new software we are currently developing to provide free-hand sketching in parametric modeling.

Properties of Architecturological Scale: Determinants of the domain of reference that characterize the scale.

Scaleme: Basic cognitive operations of conception.

Chapter 20
Design Education and Institutional Transformation

Dean Bruton
Southern Cross University, Australia

ABSTRACT

This chapter aims to develop awareness of the changing characterization of design and design education in response to the impact of global crisis and the ongoing introduction of innovative computational design methods and technologies. This chapter presents a strategic vision that includes a range of major concerns in relation to design education's learning and teaching needs in higher education. The purpose of the chapter is to reconsider the foundation and consequent assumptions required of a vital relevant design education in the 21ˢᵗ century. It reflects on a general academic reassessment of the nature of design education in the light of the impact of computational methods and technologies and asserts a need for the re-envisioning of design education pedagogies in terms of networked interaction and global issues. Specifically it maintains that computational methods and techniques and the institutional adoption of interaction as a key factor in education has transformed the conception and construction of content as well as the delivery of communications across the broad spectrum of both the arts and sciences. It acknowledges the theory of institutional transformation, explores the evidence for such a theory, and discusses design education's potential pedagogical strategies for reform of higher education.

INTRODUCTION

The general perspective of this chapter describes the change in characterization of design in response to global crisis and rapid digital technological developments. Design education is viewed as needing radical revision in light of the failure of the modernist and postmodernist agenda and the emergence of a heuristic understanding of the na-

ture of institutional transformation. Humanitarian concerns together with technological innovations initiate and drive changes to notions of design, methods and techniques for design pedagogy and goals of design practice. Furthermore documented analysis of institutional change suggests a need for improved educational understanding and utilization of design across the broader spectrum of all programs of study. While space constraints preclude systematic empirical assessments of this

DOI: 10.4018/978-1-61350-180-1.ch020

new framework, the penultimate section offers a brief illustrative application to the study of design education reform guided by lessons learnt from social revolutions, the most dramatic types of institutional change.

BACKGROUND

In the last decade the digital revolution has changed the characterization of design from a relatively narrow discipline-based study to a study of a range of design related interdisciplinary concerns. Julka Almquist and Julia Lupton state, "Design research has no single definition. It is an interdisciplinary form of inquiry categorized in multiple ways, including: Research with a focus on theory, practice, and/or production, as design epistemology, design praxiology, and design phenomenology, and humanities-based design studies" (Almquist and Lupton 2009). As Nigel Cross and others document how design theorists have been searching for ways to expand the understanding and incorporation of design into other programs of study (Cross 2001). In 2007, the OECD reported that 34% of Australians aged 25-64 years had a tertiary education, ranking it the seventh highest (equal with Norway) amongst the 30 OECD member countries, and six percentage points above the OECD average (28%) (Australian Bureau of Statistics, 2010). Canada, Japan, New Zealand and USA respectively outranked Australia. Is tertiary education today adequate for the design challenges of global crisis?

In 1996 a significant review of design education at a two day workshop called *Design@2006* recommended that the then design education of tomorrow should have a content focus on new thinking, research projects, and other activities that inform the education of new breed of designer and that a symposium on Design Education was to be held annually. Distance learning and interactive technology are key growth areas. Krippendorf in a 1997 report called 'Design in the Age of In-

formation' (Krippendorf 2008) noted four topics surfaced: Rising technological opportunities, new design principles, design education, and a list of key research issues. Both Cross and Krippendorf include Herbert Simon's definition of design: "The natural sciences are concerned with how things are...design on the other hand is concerned with how things ought to be" (Simon 1969). New design principles were boldly announced: "Design principles are propositions whose truth does not lie in the past but in their ability to guide actions towards desirable futures" (p27). Change fronts for design education at that time (1997) were in sum:

- Academia needs more collaboration
- Change in thinking of companies and institutions and grant programs
- Human-centered design – "that departs from our traditional objectivism" (Krippendorf 2008, p30)
- Collaborative environments (real and virtual)
- Interdisciplinary team work
- Reflective practice
- New boundaries exploration

The needs for action to occur were resources for equipment, digital links, and faculty student research. Optimistically, the call was put out in the final sentence of the report for a next step to be taken by visionary leaders within schools, government, design forums and companies (p37). In one larger working group that dealt specifically with design education a recognition of the changes required surfaced; "The participants of our discussion group agreed on the need for quite radical changes in current design curricula, pedagogies, and academic structures" (p57). The discussion in sum suggests the following actions:

- Addition of design drawing to the 'three Rs' (Reading, Writing and Arithmetic) in the guide of Planning, Creating and Visualising

- Better incorporation of emerging technologies
- Emphasis on team work and inter-disciplinarity
- Collaborative work across departments
- Change of understanding in 'other' departments to recognize nature and value of design
- Cross-disciplinarity – including government and industry
- Funding for PhD research in design
- Upgrading institutional learning environments
- Move toward online learning and information technology investment for universities (pp 58-60).

These outcomes sound familiar to those involved in higher education and digital media design. A decade later the development of design education appears even more urgent as global issues increasingly call for attention and rapidly applicable design solutions.

DESIGNING DESIGN EDUCATION

Institutional Transformation Theory

The 'macro' picture of world politics contributes additional support for institutional change in the 'micro' design environment. In 1998 the 'scientific' approaches of the past were seen as part of the problem and observers of institutional transformation such as Kurt Weyland support the idea that rationalist approaches to change are too simplistic and that design needs to take into account the contextual factors as heuristics of human and environmental contingency (Weyland 2008). Davis admits the theory as it stood in 1970 was woefully inadequate. According to Davis (1970) many economic historians focus their efforts on economically rational behavior as an explanation of past events, "institutions are taken as given and

the 'antiquarian' interests of the more traditional historians have been scorned" (Davis and North 1970).

Fortunately, Weyland developed theories of institutional transformation in association with cognitive psychological views of behavior. He refutes the view that rationalism alone can explain and predict institutional change. Using examples from the history of significant social change he observes that revolutionary decision making involves dissatisfaction of the status quo and periods of uncertainty that drive innovative solutions for new behavior. He contends that, "the heuristics of availability and representativeness drive the spread of violent contention" (Weyland 2008, p300). Weyland attempts to go beyond historical and rational choice institutionalism, by elaborating the core of a new theory that can account for the discontinuous, disproportionate, and frequently wavelike nature of institutional change in world politics.

Applying this to the world of higher education may be problematic as the diversity of government is far less pronounced. Perhaps Weyland gives a clue into the nature of change and why design education has not spread into the fundamental core of the educational system's 'Three Rs'. He asserts that cognitive-psychological findings on shifts in actors' propensity for assuming risk help explain periods of dramatic reform. Using this theory suggests moribund educational institutional behavior can be followed by revolutionary breakthroughs as educators respond to growing issues of concern that lead to efforts at bold transformation. He suggests solutions chosen in haste often emulate other countries' innovations because of the "boundedly rational learning" of moribund institutions.

Design Process

A redefined design process fuses the so-called 'aha' moment with the scientific method: "On the one hand are those accounts that emphasize the effect of sudden insights, and on the other hand are those that emphasize gradual and cumulative change. Unfortunately, these different perspectives have largely existed in mutual isolation or are presented in mutual opposition" (Crilly 2010). This chapter proposes the mutual respect for both approaches to the design process be integrated into a subject area called "Representation" – the fourth "R" and, that this subject be included in various forms across the education spectrum from pre-school through to higher education and beyond into adult education. As Lawson (Lawson 2005) suggests, "The designers of today can no longer be trained to follow a set of procedures" but "must learn to exploit and appreciate new technology as it develops" (p6). Design is considered in terms of agency instead of problem solving.

Traditional Notions of Design Process

Plato's pupil Aristotle (384–322 B.C.E.) agreed with his teacher that there is goal-directed activity in nature, but attributed this activity to the inherent tendencies of objects to fulfill their natural ends. The design process properly so-called moves beyond traditional notions of product design canons described as design thinking (Lawson 2005) and as a mechanical process (Ullman 2009) that may be seen from the UK Design Council articles online (Council 2010). For example, the Alessi design process is described as containing a rigorous monitoring and evaluation module to ensure design ideas are viable for production. A formal set of assessment criteria is applied to a new concept to decide if it should be developed for production. The formula measures the proposal along four dimensions:

"— *Function (F): The function of the design. Does it work? Is it practical, functional and labor saving?*

—*Sensoriality, Memory, Imagination (SMI): Does the design please the senses? Is it memorable? Does it engender emotion?*

— *Communication, Language (CL): Will the product give its owner status? Does it fit with current trends?*

— *Price (P): Can the product be made and sold at a sensible price, both relative to substitute products and to the customer's sense of its value? Items are given a score from 0 to 5 along each of these four dimensions, with five being the highest score, and three being neutral. A prospective design must have an overall score of more than 12 (equivalent to four neutral ratings) to be considered worth taking forward to the next stage"* (Council 2010).

This kind of rationalized value analysis is commonly favored in engineering education and uses quantification within creative problem solving strategies (Savransky 2000). Using a variation of this approach together with digital media tools may be a valuable "loose" quantitative system direction for future design education.

New Trends in Understanding of the Design Process

Due to the addition of code and programming considerations notions of contemporary design process are often variations that use digital media based on industry standard software. Many proprietary tools are developed by innovative major companies such as Pixar. Parametric design augmented with advanced programming knowledge suggests a new pioneering path for the next generation of creative design innovation as indicated by the rapid growth of the incorporation of Building Information Modeling (BIM) in higher education design programs. Programming plug-ins for movie industry production pipelines is a well known specialist sought after skill that adds a new dimension to existing notions of the visual designer and this process involves a set but flexible path that includes deeper understandings of the mathematical basis of design (Massive, 2010). Similarly in architecture and product design, generative design plug-ins such as Paracloud GEM simplifies complex design processes (Nir, 2010). Edward R. Tufte expands notions of design thinking by emphasizing the need for facts in design research, representation and presentation (Tufte, 2009). In similar mode, Neri Oxman takes up this challenge to develop design outcomes based on scientific data using a material-based design method she terms Variable Property Design (VPD). In response to Rivka Oxman's new digital understandings of the design (Oxman R., 2006), Neri Oxman offers alternative digital media approaches to design by reversing the traditional model of the design process (Oxman, 2010).

International Comparisons

Statistics give a somewhat belated glimpse into the international trends in the use of information technology. Korea had the highest proportion of households with Internet and broadband Internet access (94% each) in 2008. Turkey had the lowest, with 8% of households having Internet access, and 2% with broadband Internet access. Only 12% of Turkish households had access to a home computer. Australia, Canada and the United Kingdom had very similar levels of home computer access (78%), Internet access (about 72%) and broadband Internet access (about 62%). Japan had a higher proportion than Australia of households with access to a home computer (86% compared to 78% in Australia), but lower proportions of households with access to the Internet (64% and 72%), or with broadband access (59% and 62%) (Australian Bureau of Statistics, 2010).

FORM OF DESIGN EDUCATION: THE OLD VS THE NEW ECONOMY

Impending Change in the Form of Design Education

For over a decade some critics such as (Watson 1995) suggest today's higher education maintains a delivery structure based on the C17th church lectern. In response to the C20th digital revolution many suggest a need for change for higher education to survive the C21st. The current generation of students has been introduced to a ubiquitous computing environment since birth and any conceive of communications differently to their forbears. Alternative rituals for living and learning now challenge conventional approaches to higher education.

The need for networking and interdisciplinary considerations when designing educational experiences is increasingly apparent as each year classes are filled with new bloggers. Home computers have become cheaper and more affordable over time, and as a result are becoming increasingly common in Australian households. According to the ABS in 2008-09, nearly four out of every five (78%) households in Australia had access to a home computer, compared with just over two out of every five (44%) households in 1998. In 2008-09, households with children under 15 years of age had higher rates of computer access (91%) than those without children under 15 years (73%) (ABS 2009a) (Australian Bureau of Statistics, 2010). Fears of major players dominating the global education market have been assuaged by commentators such as Robin Mason "Because it is too difficult; there is too little money to be made, too many complex issues to handle and too great a need for people skills rather than technical skills" (Mason 1998). By contrast, Ray Kurzweil, one of the best-known and controversial advocates for the role of machines in the future of humanity envisions an event the 'singularity' in which technological change becomes so rapid and so profound that our bodies and brains will merge with our machines. In practical terms, this means that human aging and pollution will be reversed, world hunger will be solved, and our bodies and environment transformed by nanotechnology to overcome the limitations of biology, including death (Kurzweil 2005). According to this view we will be able to create virtually any physical product just from information, resulting in radical wealth creation.

Detractors such as Roger Penrose view the likelihood of the advent of a computer mind with deep suspicion (Penrose & Gardner, 2002). This kind of global consideration suggests impending change due to developing computer technologies will further impact on design education. In 2000 a report on Australian school students indicate a strong level of computer use that begins early and develops advanced skills often from home. "Some 56% of all students and 75% of current primary students began using computers before Year 4" (Australian Bureau of Statistics). Informed institutional planning is needed to develop a design education culture for the next generation's students to ensure their use of computers evolves from entertainment use to more sophisticated uses.

Institutional Design Planning

For Alexander, three models may assist in institutional design planning: 'Historical', 'Rational Choice' and 'Sociological' (Alexander 2005). Past planning seems to be a direct response to traditional conceptions of design as an adjunct to industrial production. This chapter proposes that design be reconsidered as part of a process of representation and visualization of design solutions. That planning for future educational institutions explicitly includes the fundamental building blocks of creative thinking strategies and digital media visualization systems. Design Education may be better served by approaches such as those of Canadian designer/educator Gustavo Machado who offers a socially and environmentally conscious open-source (ad-free) online initiative with

an almost utopian dream: Redesign the world inspired by Buckminster Fuller's famous quote: "The best way to predict the future is to design it." - Buckminster Fuller (1895-1983).

Using a wiki style of learning has fundamental flaws in aspects of credibility but the spirit of free and open access to information provides a wealth of new inspiration such as the idea of an expanding learning economy. "The knowledge economy and a growing consumer value on personal growth drive a diverse market for educational and learning experiences ranging from food, toys, and games to housing and travel" (Machado 2010). For Machado, "Public schools are, and will continue to be, a part of the learning economy. The challenge is to identify innovative ways to create relationships among the various players in the expanding learning economy. The emergence of community value networks that map the flow of tangible and intangible sources of value in the learning economy will improve relationships and reveal new sources of value and benefit from the public education system. Innovative communities, like the eLearning city in Espoo, Finland, will treat their educational resources as an urban learning commons—a shared, critical resource that requires collective management to avoid abuse and deterioration" (Machado 2010). The themes that emerge from this discourse are:

- Resilient School Communities
- Amplified Educators and Learners
- A Global Learning Economy
- Design as Philosophy
- Contested Authorities
- Diversifying Learning Geographies: Deserts and Oases

Current trends indicate that information technologies drive learning to become a key customer filter that shapes decisions in the market across income categories, expanding markets adjacent to public education. Leveraging networking tools, open knowledge repositories, and peer-to-peer production methods (rather than hierarchical production systems), learners and educators will increasingly experiment with sharing and exchanging learning resources across market boundaries growing a more integrated learning economy. According to Australian Bureau of Statistics there is currently very little data available for rates of participation of Australian adults in social networks. However, this is not the case for children. Of the two million Australian children aged 5-14 years using the Internet at home in 2009, 22% visited or used social networking sites. The proportion was higher for older children aged 12-14 years (48%) compared to 11% for children aged 9-11 years and 3% for children aged 5-8 years (Australian Bureau of Statistics, 2010).

Models for organizing learning experiences over time will diversify and extend beyond those found today in private, parochial, home schooling, and charter schools. Public schools become hubs in value networks. Lower network-coordination costs make it cost-effective to meet the needs and desires of "long-tail" niche markets in industries as diverse as music, health, and education. Numerous and diverse niche markets of learners become targets for all sorts of providers of learning experiences in the expanding learning economy (public, private, parochial, charter, home and other informal schools, and commercially based providers). Value network mapping becomes an important tool for tracking the exchange of tangible and intangible learning assets that flow between public schools and the rest of the learning economy. These exchanges create richer relationships between public schools and the community.

DISCUSSSION

Revision of University Communications

Some suggest the demise of the lecture theatre and the need for face to face communication for learning and teaching. As online technologies improve the delivery of video and interactive content delivery many argue that universities need to revise their infrastructure to become relevant to new tropes of information management. What evidence for this?

The growth of an incorporation of avatars into learning (Braswell & Childress, 2006), the development of new building measurement and BIM construction tools (Strong, 2008) and the adoption of mobile computing devices (Ryu & Parsons, 2009) are factors that contribute to these theories of educational change. The call for reconsideration of design is evident in the agendas of major design and education forums: "Stakeholders should use design as a strategic and creative force that can trigger innovation breakthroughs and transformations into the system. This must start with creating a new methodology for design thinking which facilitates the creation of future scenarios" (ICSID, 2009).

Design Education and Digital Media Learning

The media-rich pervasive learning environment is popular because it is visual and accessible. Immersive media enable anytime, anyplace learning, stimulating new educational practices and research. The need for visual literacy has never been greater to ensure a critical stance is enabled through an understanding of the power of representation tools. Interaction across multiple media is paramount in design education. The focus becomes one of context—our physical location, the information we can access, and the people to whom we can connect, physically and virtually.

The new learning in digitally enriched physical spaces revitalizes kinetic learning and the opportunities for learning through emotion and movement. Some key trends driving this new learning environment are:

- *Personal Digital Media:* These are collaborative, social, and interactive media such as web logs, wikis, and social bookmarking such as Facebook, Twitter, and MySpace. With approximately 47.3 million users, Myspace.com is a recent and controversial example of a virtual digital media forum. Already 87% of teens go online and 57% share text and personal creations online (Knowledge Works Foundation, 2010). According to Facebook, they have more than 750 million active users of which 50% log on to Facebook on any given day. The average user has 130 friends. People spend over 700 billion minutes per month on Facebook. The average user is connected to 80 community pages, groups and events and creates 90 pieces of content each month (http://www.facebook.com/press/info.php?statistics, accessed 19 August, 2011). The use of social networking for formal education is in its infancy but these figures indicate that the nature of educational communications is rapidly and irrevocably changing.
- *Urban Digital Media Environment:* The physical space for interaction in the virtual world is growing as urban digital media are added to the neighborhoods, malls, and public spaces often with wireless technology. The sense of place changes in relation to virtual tags that map the location and visual appearance of a mindset. The sense of interaction changes as places respond to environmental change as in smart housing environments where the smart house adjusts the blinds or the tinted windows to keep the interior temperature under control.
- *Serious Games:* The use of game engines in design education has significantly changed the traditional pedagogy used in architecture and design schools. Game engines are being used to develop models of architectural heritage, engineering simulations

and location-based cell phone games (The GoGame: Play like it is your job 2008). This mode of pedagogy can reach learners in context specific immersive settings using cell phones and PDAs to augmented-reality devices (like eyeglasses). Simulation style games such as World of Warcraft, a massively multiplayer online role playing game (MMORPG), is the most popular non-card game title, as measured by number of players. Nielsen figures about 1.2 million male players in the US along with 600,000 women played World of Warcraft in December, 2008 (Neilsen 2009).

CONTENT OF DESIGN EDUCATION

Computational Methods and Technologies

What is design knowledge and how do we teach it? Simply put, design theorists such as Margolin, Buchanan (Margolin & Buchanan, 1996), Fuller (Fuller, 1979), Thackara (Thackara, 2010), Norman (van Geel, 2011), and Gero (Gero, 1990) suggest there is a distinct kind of knowledge and activity to be learnt in design education. DiGiano believes learning centered technology synthesizes learning, instructional design and educational technology. The conditions for effective leaning "are the fundamental pursuit of the field known as 'the learning sciences', the amalgam of a range of a range of disciplines including education, computer science, cognitive science, developmental and social psychology, anthropology and linguistics"(DiGiano, 2008, p3). Hoadley and Cox propose seven categories of design knowledge (stages, values, roles, principles, patterns, techniques, and design psychology). They conclude that as design knowledge differs from other types of knowing, it requires novel forms of teaching (DiGiano, 2008, p12). Design knowledge has been represented as a visual language (Wilde

& Wilde, 1991) that can be taught with grammar (Leborg, 2006), and principles (Faimon & Weigand, 2004). Similarly new media described as a language by Manovich (Manovich, 2000) offers new interdisciplinary paths to understand designing. DiGiano states: "Technology alone is insufficient for meeting learning goals" (DiGiano, 2008, p13).

There is a need for authentic setting and challenges with the design education programs. Communicating across disciplines and cultures is an issue that needs addressing to overcome the standard divide and conquer approach students typically take on: Working in collaborative groups is problematic if all do not own the 'big picture' making a multiple-course sequence still an issue to resolve in standard university settings. The design of the campus for effective personal environment interaction requires consideration of these issues. For example, Strange and Banning suggest the principles to follow for interaction are encapsulated in four conditions for successful learning: "Inclusion, safety, involvement, community" (Strange, 2001). One of the key issues is: How can campus designs bring about and enhance a sense of community? Deciding on the physical features that lead to a feeling of community is a major online visual identity as well as a culturally responsive physical learning environment conundrum.

Learning Mode Reform

As personalization has become more cost effective in design education new roles, processes, and relationships in the learning economy spawn new career paths in education that may include content experts, learning coaches, network navigators, classroom managers, and cognitive specialists. Open content and curriculum and other publicly available resources contribute to new ecologies of teaching, learning, and assessment. Interactive and collaborative digital spaces, such as wikis, provide shared learning portfolios where students,

educators, parents, and other learning stakeholders can perform assessments and real-time interventions. Nearly three-quarters (72%) of Australian households had home Internet access in 2008-09, more than four times the proportion in 1998 (16%) (ABS, 2010). As William J Mitchell forecast the concept of permanent, large-scale infrastructure will likely give way to more temporary, localized, and ad hoc solutions: "Architects of the twenty-first century will shape, arrange, and connect spaces (both real and virtual) to satisfy human needs" (Mitchell, 1995, p105). The built environment aims to become instrumented and responsive via sensor-based technologies that track resources and manage logistics so that adaptive learning environments respond to the changing needs of administrators, students, and their families. Ideally facilities management becomes a strategic function, working collaboratively with those involved in curriculum development, technology integration, and pedagogical objectives.

CURRENT TRENDS IN DESIGN EDUCATION

In 2009 a selective study of European higher education institutions was undertaken to develop a glimpse of current trends of education that is concerned with design and digital media. Interviews were recorded with staff of *Gobelins – School of the Image*, Paris (Riewer, 2009); *National Film and Television* School in Beaconsfield, UK (John Rowe, 2009), *Escape Studios*, London (Danskin and Jenner 2009) and *FilmakAcademie*, Stuttgart (Hirtes, 2009). Confirmation of many of the issues raised above can be seen in the comments of CEOs and the current activities of these institutions. In sum, the study found that the impact of digital media in design education has altered the way designers understand the design process and design education. The design process is often understood as a mutable series of pipelines that transform in keeping with new media technologies.

Design in higher education appears to lag behind industry developments due to tight budgets and funding systems, institutional resource constraints and outdated program content. For example, developing an exemplary pedagogical approach for visual effects education in a university system relies on expensive state of the art stereo visualization equipment and facilities. Conceptually, the emulation of industry by academe is problematic because it assumes industry may always lead the academic research programs – a situation that undermines university research funding. Online technologies are increasingly a part of the fabric of design institutions as evidenced by the strong web presence of all institutions in the study.

The use of online marketing is a key feature of *Gobelins* who offer Summer Schools, *Escape Studios* who offer many hands on digital media design courses online in keeping with the example set by *Animation Mentor* (Larson 2010) who provide an 18 month animation design courses online with staff from *Pixar* and *ILM*. The transformation of universities is yet to arrive in the same way it has developed in the animation and visual effects feature production industry. Indications are that higher education will increasingly merge to form global education entities in much the same pattern seen with the merging of software companies such as *Avid* (Avid team 2010) who see the sense in combining forces to innovate.

How might interventions be realistically funded? These are questions for the social/political agenda largely outside the domain of design educators. Once Government funding and industry involvement reflect a public awareness of the need for a design education that embraces digital media many of the innate conflicts involved will be overcome. Perhaps some of these interventions may never be achieved because there are strong legal impediments (or professional registration blockages). Maybe this doesn't matter, if there is a commitment to a visionary approach for something that is partially or wholly achievable in the next few years.

Solutions and Recommendations

New computer technologies drive innovation using interdisciplinary collaboration. Higher education institutions are increasingly using industry contract staff and are developing online marketing and documentation resources. Teleconferencing is fundamental for international communication. Relating these interventions into the business and understanding of design education requires partici-

Table 1. Models of design education practice in 21st century contexts: Globalization and technological change

Comparative Characteristics	Design Education for Reform	Conventional Design Education
Desired Outcome	Creative innovation in response to globalization and eco crisis	Product oriented and narrow focus on economic outcomes
System Targeted for Change	Curriculum design and implementation	No concerted movement for change
Scope of Concern	Creativity and innovation through Design	Profit and progress
Education Roles for Change	Media Contacts Industry Associations Related Industry Partners Students/Student Associations International Committees University Academic Teaching and Research Staff University Enrolment/Executive Staff Education Minister/Government	Limited educational role due to inadequate funding and communication between industry, government agencies and education

pation from many in the construction/conveyance of knowledge and experience in education. The following chart attempts to outline a course of action for future institutional reform.

FUTURE RESEARCH DIRECTIONS

With the Deweyan goal of "social democracy" in mind, Striano sees two different trends in the development of educational systems: "One is the passage from national control to transnational control and guidance. The other trend is a progressive decentralization of the governance of educational systems, which is strictly connected with a tendency toward privatization of educational institutions and practices (see, for example, the growing phenomenon of home schooling) as well as the involvement of other agents in the educational process (Striano 2009, p381). Rethinking design education within the globalization framework is proposed as a future direction for institutional reform. Inclusivity is enabled through computing networks suggesting a new paradigm for education. The integration of all students within a school system and within a global network offers new synergies that challenge current face to face learning and the exclusive conventions of higher education structures (Acedo, Ferrer and Pamies 2009, p230). Finding ways to incorporate the international student community may change the traditional rhetoric of university ownership in relation to diversity of student population.

The content of design education changes in relation to the user. The development of nothing less than a customized learning environment for every student in every school is part of the US national education reform. Weiss reports on "a new model of education in which students do a substantial amount of work outside the school building – online, in the "outdoor classroom," and in peer-to-peer or small-group networks – and can be grouped according to their areas of interest, regardless of their age, grade level or geographic location, to pursue topics that cut across disciplines. It's also a model that reshapes and expands the role of the teacher – from being the sole source of information to being a guide, mentor and coach in the learning process" (Weiss 2006).

Incorporation of fundamental creative thinking strategies (Hurson, 2007) and reconsidering critical assessment tools, such as in the classic rethink of the MIT (Massachusetts Institute of Technology) approach to design which requires sophisticated computing (Gabriel, 1995) may feature as core content elements of a reformed design education. For example *The Future of Education* (The Future of Education, 2010) provides an online forum to interact with like-minded educators concerned about finding better ways to use computing technology. The traditional design education concerns for aesthetics will intersect with the future international issues that need dramatic and innovative responses as indicated by the observations of Brown et al: "As the twenty-first century continues to unfold so our relationships with the designed world become ever more crucial in determining how we shape and experience life. Alongside environmental change must be placed a second potential crisis—poverty of imagination. Now having the technologies to realize most anything we wish to do, the question is no longer 'how can this be made' but 'what do we want to do.' And this challenge requires the kinds of creative imagination so intrinsic to design" (Brown, Buchanan, Doordan, & Margolin, 2010).

REFERENCES

Acedo, C., & Ferrer, F., & Pa mies, J. (2009). Inclusive education: Open debates and the road ahead. *Prospects*, *39*, 227–238. doi:10.1007/s11125-009-9129-7

Alexander, E. R. (2005). Institutional transformation and planning: from institutionalization theory to institutional design. *Planning Theory, 4*(3), 209–223. doi:10.1177/1473095205058494

Almquist, J., & Lupton, J. (2009). Affording meaning. *Design Issues, 26*(1), 3–14. doi:10.1162/desi.2010.26.1.3

Australian Bureau of Statistics. (2000, 25-January). *Real time: Computers, change and schooling - A national sample study of the Information Technology skills of Australian school students*. Retrieved November 13, 2010, from http://www.abs.gov.au/ausstats/abs@.nsf/ Previousproducts/1301.0Feature%20Article182000?opendocument&tabname= Summary&prodno=1301.0&issue=2000&num=&view=

Australian Bureau of Statistics. (2010, 15-September). *1370.0 - Measures of Australia's Progress, 2010*. Retrieved November 13, 2010, from http://www.abs.gov.au/ausstats/ abs@.nsf/Lookup/by%20Subject/ 1370.0~2010~Chapter~Home%20computers%20%284.8.3%29

Avid Team. (2010, 5-April). *The future of digidesign: An open letter to customers*. Retrieved April 5, 2010, from http://duc.digidesign.com/showthread.php?t=270775

Braswell, R., & Childress, M. D. (2006). Using massively multiplayer online role-playing games for online learning. *Distance Education, 27*(2), 187–196. doi:10.1080/01587910600789522

Brown, B., Buchanan, R., Doordan, D., & Margolin, V. (2010, Winter). Introduction. *Design Issues, 26*(1), 1–2. doi:10.1162/desi.2010.26.1.1

Council, D. (2010). *Eleven lessons: Managing design in eleven global brands: A study of the design process*. Retrieved March 22, 2010, from http://www.designcouncil.org.uk/

Crilly, N. (2010). The structure of design revolutions. *Design Issues, 26*(1), 54–66. doi:10.1162/desi.2010.26.1.54

Cross, N. (2001). Designerly ways of knowing: Design discipline versus design science. *Design Issues, 17*(3), 49–55. doi:10.1162/074793601750357196

Danskin, L., & Jenner, J. (2009, 21-September). *Interview with Lee Danskin and Jason Jenner, Escape Studios, London* (D. Bruton, Interviewer)

Davis, L., & North, D. (1970). Institutional change and American economic growth: A first step towards a theory of institutional innovation. *The Journal of Economic History, 30*(1), 131–149.

DiGiano, C., Goldman, S., & Chorost, M. (2008). *Educating learning technology designers: Guiding and inspiring creators of innovative educational tools*. New York, NY: Routledge.

Faimon, P., & Weigand, J. (2004). *The nature of design*. Cincinnati, OH: How Design.

Forum for the Future. (2008, 1-Jan). *Case study 07-08 education for engineers*. Retrieved April 6, 2010, from http://www.forumforthefuture.org/projects/E21C-education-for-engineers

Fuller, R. B. (1979). *R. Buckminster Fuller on education*. New York, NY: University of Massachusetts Press.

Gabriel, R. (1995). *The rise of 'worse is better'*. Retrieved November 13, 2010, from http://www.jwz.org/doc/worse-is-better.html

Gero, J. (1990). Design prototypes: A knowledge representation schema for design. *AI Magazine, 11*(4).

Group, B. S. I. (2010). *BS 7000 series – Design management systems*. Retrieved April 5, 2010, from http://www.bsigroup.com/en/Standards-and-Publications/ Industry-Sectors/Manufacturing/ Design--product-specification/ BS-7000-Series--Design-Management-Systems/

Heller, S., & Dooley, M. (2008). *Teaching motion design*. New York, NY: Allworth Press.

Hirtes, S. (2009, 23-September). *Interview with Sabine Hirtes at Filmakademie, Germany* (D. Bruton, Interviewer)

Hurson, T. (2007). *Think better: An innovator's guide to productive thinking*. New York, NY: McGraw-Hill Professional.

ICSID. (2009). *ICSID World Design Congress, 23 - 25 November 2009, Singapore*. Retrieved November 13, 2010, from http://www.icsidcongress09.com/ phase2/permalink.asp?id=8

Knowledge Works Foundation. (2010). *Media-rich pervasive learning*. Retrieved Augustl 19, 2011, from http://resources.knowledgeworks.org/ MAP/map/23/Media-Rich-Pervasive-Learning. aspx

Krippendorf, K. (2008). *Design in the age of information: A report to the National Science Foundation (NSF). North Carolina State University, School of Design*. Raleigh, NC: University of Pennsylvannia.

Kurzweil, R. (2005). *The Singularity is near: When humans transcend biology*. New York, NY: Viking.

Larson, K. (2010). *Animation mentor*. Retrieved September 20, 2009, from http://www.animation-mentor.com/

Lawson, B. (2005). *Design thinking* (4th ed.). Oxford, UK: Architectural Press.

Leborg, C. (2006). *Visual grammar*. New York, NY: Princeton Architectural Press.

Leonardo. (2010). *About Leonardo*. Retrieved April 6, 2010, from http://www.leonardo.info/ leoinfo.html

Machado, G. (2010). *An expanding leaning economy*. Retrieved April 4, 2010, from 2006 http://www.designeducation.ca

Manovich, L. (2000). *The language of new media*. Cambridge, MA: MIT Press.

Margolin, V., & Buchanan, R. (1996). *The idea of design*. New York, NY: MIT Press.

Mason, R. (1998). *Globalising education*. New York, NY: Routledge.

Massive. (2010). *What is Massive?* Retrieved April 4, 2010, from http://www.massivesoftware. com/ whatismassive/

Mitchell, W. J. (1995). *City of bits: Space, place, and the Infobahn*. Cambrudge, MA: MIT Press.

Neilsen. (2009, April). *The state of the video gamer: PC game and video game console usage, fourth quarter 2008*. Retrieved April 5, 2010, from http://blog.nielsen.com/nielsenwire/ wp-content/ uploads/2009/04/ stateofvgamer_040609_fnl1. pdf

Nir, E. (2010). *Explore beyond your imagination*. Retrieved April 5, 2010, from http://www. paraclouding.com/GEM/

Oxman, N. (2010). *The new structuralism* (Oxman, R., & Oxman, R., Eds.). London, UK: John Wiley & Sons.

Oxman, R. (2006). Theory and design in the first digital age. *Design Studies*, *27*(3), 229–265. doi:10.1016/j.destud.2005.11.002

Pearce, P., & Pearce, S. (1980). *Experiments in form*. New York, NY: Van Nostrand Reinhold.

Penrose, R., & Gardner, M. (2002). *The Emperor's new mind: Concerning computers, minds, and the laws of physics*. London, UK: Oxford University Press.

Pink, D. (2005). *A whole new mind*. Crows Nest, Australia: Allen & Unwin.

Price, H. (2009, 11-September). *Interview with Hanna Price at Framestore, London* (D. Bruton, Interviewer).

Riewer, E. (2009, 10-September). *Interview with Eric Riewer at Gobelins, Paris* (D. Bruton, Interviewer).

Rowe, J. (2009, 19-September). *Interview with John Rowe at NFTS, UK* (D. Bruton, Interviewer).

Ryan, J. (2008, 16-December). *The next leap: A competitive Ireland in the digital era.* Retrieved April 5, 2010, from http://www.iiea.com/publications/ the-next-leap-a-competitive-ireland-in-the-digital-era

Ryu, H., & Parsons, D. (2009). *Innovative mobile learning: tecHniques and technologies.* Hershey, PA: IGI Global.

Savransky, S. D. (2000). *Introduction to TRIZ methodology of inventive problem solving.* Boca Raton, FL: CRC Press. doi:10.1201/9781420038958

Simon, H. (1969). *The sciences of the artificial.* Cambridge, MA: MIT Press.

Strange, C. C. (2001). *Educating by design.* San Francisco, CA: Jossey Bass.

Striano, M. (2009). Managing educational transformation in the globalized world: A Deweyan perspective. *Educational Theory, 59*(4), 381–393. doi:10.1111/j.1741-5446.2009.00326.x

Strong, N. (2008). Designing an integrated practice with building information modeling. In Solomon, N. (Ed.), *Architecture: Celebrating the past, designing the future* (p. 185). New York, NY: The American Institute of Architects.

Thackara, J. (2010). *What should design researchers research? Report from 2020.* Retrieved August 19, 2011, from http://observersroom. designobserver.com/ johnthackara/post/what-should-design-researchers- research-report-from-2020/23398/

The Future of Education. (2010). *The future of education - Charting the course of teaching and learning in a networked world.* Retrieved April 6, 2010, from http://www.futureofeducation.com/ ?xg_source=msg_mes_network

The GoGame: play like it is your job. (2008). Retrieved April 5, 2010, from http://www.thegogame. com/ team/index.asp

Tufte, E. (2009, 1-July). *Design thinking: How facts change everything (if you let them).* Retrieved November 13, 2010, from http://sloanreview.mit. edu/the-magazine/ articles/2009/summer/50409/ how-facts-change-everything-if-you-let-them/

Ullman, D. G. (2009). *The mechanical design process* (4th ed.). McGraw Hill.

van Geel, J. (2011, 1 11). *Strategy & leadership.* Retrieved August 19, 2011, from http:// johnnyholland.org/2011/01/11/ design-research-and-innovation-an- interview-with-don-norman/

Watson, B. (1995). Reliquishing the lecturn: Cooperative learning in teacher education. *Journal of Teacher Education, 46*(3), 209–215. doi:10.1177/0022487195046003007

Weiss, S. (2006). *Digital learning Spaces 2010: Technology in education.* Denver, CO: Education Commission of the States.

Weyland, K. (2008). Toward a new theory of institutional change. *World Politics, 60*(2), 281–314. doi:10.1353/wp.0.0013

Wilde, J., & Wilde, R. (1991). *Visual literacy.* New York, NY: Watson Guptill.

KEY TERMS AND DEFINITIONS

Design Education: The learning process that enables planning and form making.

Digital Media: Communications with computer technology.

Reform, Institutional Transformation: Change by a community of language users.

Visual Literacy: Ability to communicate with visual language.

Chapter 21
Teaching Spatial Thinking in Design Computation Contexts:
Challenges and Opportunities

Halil I. Erhan
Simon Fraser University Surrey, Canada

Belgacem Ben Youssef
Simon Fraser University Surrey, Canada

Barbara Berry
Simon Fraser University Surrey, Canada

ABSTRACT

A new generation of design computation systems affords opportunities for new design practices. This calls for potentially new teaching requirements in design education, in particular the development of the requisite spatial thinking skills. In this chapter, the authors review the pertinent literature, followed by two case examples that illustrate how spatial thinking was taught in two undergraduate design courses. The authors' experiences suggest that early exposure to spatial thinking concepts, coupled with practice using computational design tools in the context of a project, can significantly help students to improve the skills necessary to design in a digital environment. Through the use of team projects, the authors discovered the potential variances in design representations when students switched between digital and physical modeling. They propose further research to explore the spatial processes required in computational design systems and the implications for design education.

INTRODUCTION

Design computation involves the use of software systems when conceptualizing, representing, and realizing design. Today, the rich variety of design computation systems used in research and design practice reflects the diversity of design needs and tasks, different design contexts, as well as rapid advances in information technologies. This range of tools is used for supporting collaboration, algorithmic modeling, digital modeling, symbolic modeling, simulations, testing, fabrication, etc.

DOI: 10.4018/978-1-61350-180-1.ch021

The classical notion of Computer-Aided Design (CAD) is becoming obsolete as design systems are evolving to be more complex, intelligent and 'supportive' of creativity (Shneiderman, 2007). In response to these changes, the practice of design is reforming itself. For example, parametric modeling systems enable interaction with the 'design models' at multi-levels and multi-perspectives; and use representations at each level of sharing information (Aish & Woodbury, 2005). An algorithmic representation generating complex forms receives input from physical representation of the same form in 3D design space. 'Form creation' using these systems enabled designers to not only 'imagine' but also 'specify' for construction of complex free-form structures. New possibilities have been offered to designers that have never been available before. This new generation of design computation systems affords opportunities for new design practices.

These systems heighten the requirements for spatial skills, particularly for domains involving complex forms of spatial design such as engineering, architecture, urban planning, and product design, just to name a few. This is seen in current design practice where designers define spatial characteristics of a design in the virtual world that eventually will be built in the real world. In the virtual world, spatial thinking skills are required for (i) conceptualizing complex design forms, (ii) using computational systems as design-support and representation tools, and (iii) communicating solutions. The challenge of moving between these two contexts becomes more pronounced during the iterative process of design. Although both worlds employ the same design concepts, they have structurally different representations of spatial entities. Thus, there may be distinct spatial thinking skills required when creating these representations and moving between virtual and real worlds. We believe that design-focused courses may fall short in highlighting and developing these skills. Therefore, spatial thinking needs to be intentionally integrated into the learning process to prepare students for designing in virtual and physical worlds.

The following two examples illustrate different spatial requirements when performing design tasks in virtual and real worlds. The first shows differences in representations and operations performed on them. Imagine two Lego bricks of equal size relocated from parallel state to perpendicular state with four end-cells connected. Figure 1 shows the same task performed in digital and real worlds. The digital tool requires incremental, precise, and discrete operations planned and executed with the goal in mind. However, in the physical world (Figure 1, right) the task is intuitive and the requisite spatial operations of rotation, translation and alignment of two objects in relation to one another are continuous when compared to its digital version.

The second example demonstrates how strategies for decomposition and composition of objects in these two worlds can be different. Let us look at the construction of a simple cube with three holes centered on its faces (Figure 2). In the physical (real) world, an obvious solution is 'cut-

Figure 1. Task of snapping two Lego pieces in digital world and real world requires planning at different detail level and of spatial operations.

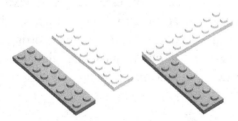

Figure 2. Construction of a cube with three holes in a parametric system

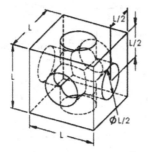 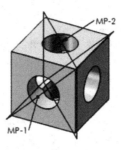

ting' the cube from a material, like wood or Styrofoam, and 'drilling' the holes individually. The spatial decomposition includes a cube with three holes; operations to compose this structure are cutting and drilling. Although the same strategy in the virtual world can also achieve the desired model, it defies the purpose of using digital tools for exploration; and limits the other opportunities presented by computational systems. An alternative to this strategy in virtual world can be based on spatial thinking on how parts of the model can be created. For instance, first the cube can be defined parametrically by creating an 'extruded' feature from a square profile, which its edges are linked to a parameter called 'length' (L). Second, a single hole is created by applying an 'extrude-cut' operation on a circle with a diameter of half of the parameter L. Instead of creating the holes individually, they can be 'mirrored' about the two diagonal mirror planes (MP-1 and MP-2), again created as reference geometry by the designer. A change on L, updates the model without any further effort. Operations like mirror, copy, cut etc. require different components for creating objects in the physical world. In the virtual world, there are other methods of creating the same cube, such as algorithmically, which from the structure and operations perspective, they present completely new challenges for designers including the development of spatial thinking. Obviously, the strategies for building the same object in virtual and real worlds are not necessarily identi-

cal. More importantly, they require the use of spatial thinking skills for developing such strategies with different representations and operations.

These examples, and the following two cases that we discuss below, suggest that there may be differences in learning these 'spatial thinking' skills in virtual and real worlds. Hence, how does one learn to perform these and other spatial operations in these two contexts, and what are the implications of these tools in design education? Our goal in this chapter is to describe, by using two case examples, how spatial thinking was integrated in design (computation) contexts. We offer a brief review of the literature on: (i) spatial thinking in design; and (ii) teaching contexts of spatial thinking. The two case studies describe our experiences teaching specific spatial skills within the context of two undergraduate courses, where students were taught 'spatial' thinking and design using digital and analog media. We analyze the challenges faced by students in switching between digital and physical spaces and identify implications for future research on specific issues that emerged in teaching spatial thinking skills in these two courses.

SPATIAL THINKING, REPRESENTATIONS, AND DESIGN

The literature describes spatial thinking as a cognitive process that shows unique characteristics

Figure 3. Components of spatial thinking

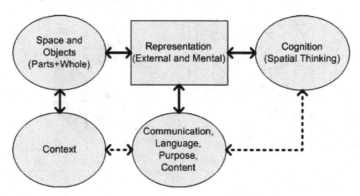

when compared to other forms of thinking such as verbal and logical. Its main difference is noticed in its' functions and the representations it uses. The National Research Council of the USA (NRC, 2006) emphasizes three main functions that make 'spatial thinking' significant: descriptive, analytical, and inferential functions. The descriptive function serves for identification of objects, their features and relations. The analytic function enables reasoning on the structure of objects and their composition; and finally, an inferential function that focuses on behavioral and functional properties of objects and their dependencies. These functions contribute to understanding what exists, such as in nature, and formulating what is needed, as in design and engineering (NCR, 2006). Examples of the first are the study of planetary systems and the molecular structure of a material. The latter involves designing environments and objects, entailing complex cognitive tasks for defining and shaping parts, part-whole relationships, topological structures, spatial interactions of the parts, and function-feature mapping. The complexity and scale to which spatial thinking applies varies widely. It also serves when we are dealing with abstract and non-spatial contexts (Gattis, 2003).

Representation is inseparable from thinking and communicating spatially and the main form of representation in spatial thinking is visual. This includes both mental and external representations.

The former plays an important role in creativity (Finke 1993; Sorby 2009); but is not sufficient enough to specify the spatial setting being conceived; hence externalization is essential (Figure 3). Arguably, the most natural form of externalizing mental representations is through sketching which is instrumental in creative discoveries (Verstijnen et al.1998; Mohler and Miller, 2008). More detailed representations, for example, the blue prints of a building or schematic diagrams of a natural phenomenon visually describe objects of interest incorporating spatial elements and their representations with more information coded than sketching. Physical prototypes are also a form of abstract representation of design showing the conceived object in 3D space. Computational representations involve applying complex operations on the representations of design models in the form of digital objects. These objects, like their counterparts as solid-body or deformable objects in the real world, can be formed using additive or subtractive operations; can be transformed using operations such as rotate and translate; and can be composed by or decomposed to its constituents. Deformable objects can be stretched, compressed, twisted, sheared, scaled, etc. in the computable representations. While all of these types of operations are central in design and all are performed using the similar type of spatial representations, how these operations are performed and detailed varies significantly between digital and physical contexts (refer to Figure 1 and Figure 2).

Spatial thinking and visuospatial representations play a primary role in the design process (Chandrasekaran, 2004; Bertel et al., 2006). Designers create, edit, communicate, and evaluate the designs by means of these representations (Visser, 2006). Using these representations, spatial thinking involves definition of a space (as a frame of reference to locate spatial entities) (Tversky, 2005); identification of objects and their relationship to each other (parts and whole, proximity, containment, location, etc.) (Casati & Varzi, 1999); manifestation of spatial-concepts in specific contexts (contextualization) (Rink, 2005); and identification of and discoursing about design and its spatial entities (Visser, 2006).

The reconstruction study of the Bah'ai House of Worship project conducted by Cichy (2006) is an example showing the role of representations in design computation (Figure 4). In this project, the Spline-Curves and –Surfaces guide the design of the main architectural features: The 'fin' structures arrayed every forty degrees about the center axis. The sketches, as abstract representations, capture the conceptual design with an overall spatial form defined with its salient parameters, such as Spline control points. They

not only pay attention to the architectural form but also describe how they can be constructed in a parametric design system. These sketches are the first stage in identifying parts, their features, and relationships to each other. The parametric definitions on the sketches are translated into the digital representations, which require complex reference geometries and control object created along with architectural forms. During the process, the spatial decomposition-composition strategies are developed, and the representations become the record of these strategies. A significant part of the architecture in this project is the space-frame supporting the fins. It is created algorithmically that the corresponding spatial elements are not visible to the designer until the form is generated. The model in the parametric design system requires further processing to assess if it can be built. This may demand several iteration of physical-model building by using the input generated from the digital model.

There are other types of representations that do not directly map on the spatial elements but spatial features of the objects being conceived. Non-visual representations of spatial objects also exist in the form of mathematical equations or computer programs. The spatial skills to work with these highly abstract while isomorphic rep-

Figure 4. A reconstruction study of Bah'ai House of Worship designed by Hariri Pontarini Architects. (Left to right) Conceptual sketches for planning, parameter identification of array structure of base components, and complex design form generated after the parametric modeling process, (Cichy, 2006)

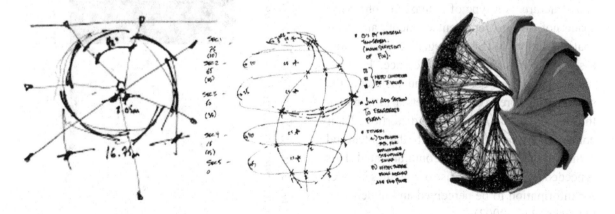

resentations with the actual design are also different. For example translation of an object in space can be performed using a 4x4 matrix or a computer function that takes an object, a coordinate system, and rotation parameters as input (Figure 5). Furthermore, prose representations of spatial structures are also possible, but they are generally less precise and subject to interpretation. A natural language conveys a richer set of relations while the spatial relations in graphics can express proximity and grouping relations on multiple dimensions, spatial and otherwise (Tversky, 2005).

Representations and Graphics in Spatial Thinking

External representations utilize elements and the spatial relations among them to convey meaning and ease of interpretation (Tversky 2005). Examples include maps, charts, and diagrams. In using similarities, figures of depictions, and schematic forms to represent elements in the world, diagrams maintain some spatial correspondences to the entities they represent. For instance, proximity in representations is used to convey proximity in spatial as well as other relations at several levels of abstraction.

The use of visual representations can be compared to speaking a form of "visual language" that can be used to communicate. Thus, the elements of graphics in these representations compare to words of a language while their spatial relations and structure as a type of syntax. Graphics use space not only to represent elements and their spatial relations but also to organize information, assist memory, and aid in inference. External representations are schematic and abstract in the sense that they preprocess the essential information through omission, addition, or distortion. Their content and format should describe the content and format of the concepts to be communicated. This is needed for the effective use of graphics in order for information to be perceived and understood (Tversky et al., 2002).

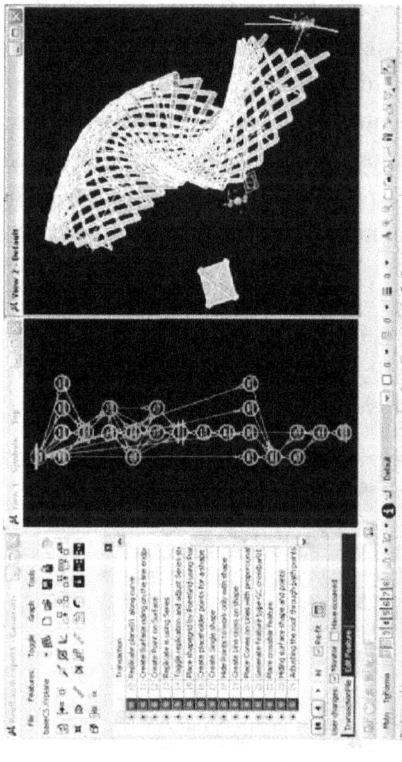

```
Function (int num, double radius,
double amp) {
Point pt = {};
double angle = 0;
double angleStart = 0;
for (int i = 0; i<num; ++i) {
pt[i] = {};
for (int j = 0; j<num; ++j) {
pt[i][j] = new Point();
angle = ((j/num)*(2*PI)) + angleStart;
pt[i][j].ByCartesianCoordinates(baseCS,
(Sin(Degrees(angle))*amp)+(i*(radius*2)),
Sin(Degrees(angle))*amp); }
angleStart = angleStart +
((2*PI)*((num+1)/num)); }
return pt; };
```

Figure 5. (Left) Symbolic and geometric representations of a parametric shell in Bentley's GenerativeComponents (www.bentley.com); (Right) implementation of a point-generating algorithm in GCScript in GenerativeComponents.

A growing body of research suggests that purely spatial explanations cannot sufficiently account for people's spatial reasoning about the physical world. Schwartz and Black (1996) showed that people can combine physical knowledge and analog imagery in the course of drawing an inference about a simple physical mechanism involving coordination. They showed that people use physical and contextual knowledge when applying spatial transformations. Later, Schwartz (1999) indicated in his studies that physical imagery is developed through physical action and not so much through visual perception. He further hypothesized that physical imagery may stem from doing and not from viewing. His model includes images representing physical information that is fundamental to the coordination of interactions between the imagined elements. Schwartz goes on to posit that understanding the physical properties helps people act and react in a "dynamic world filled with forces" (Schwartz, 1999).

Spatial Thinking and Synthesis

Visual representations are used to synthesize separate components into new configurations using various spatial operations. Visualization and synthesis employed in a wide variety of creative tasks range from the development of scientific models, to architectural design as well as many aspects of everyday problem solving. The successful performance on such a task is known to require a complex number of spatial operations to be carried out, including manipulations of position, size, and orientation (Anderson & Helstrup, 1990). Individuals with such spatial thinking skills have the ability to move parts around in an image and to arrange the parts in an efficient and accurate manner (Finke & Slayton, 1988).

Spatial procedural knowledge used in synthesis can be enhanced through "practice and feedback" (Lohman and Nichols, 1990). Their studies using rotation, reflection, and transposition as the main types of transformations emphasized the impor-

tance of practice with feedback and particularly its value for design-related activities. Practice with feedback helps developing a richer spatial knowledge base that could yield an enhancement in the speed and accuracy in performing these transformations. Their findings suggest that giving feedback had the most impact on the performance of low-ability and female subjects. They also advocated providing individuals with experiences that allow for the gradual enhancement of a "declarative knowledge base" in order to produce the largest changes in their spatial abilities (Lohman & Nichols, 1990).

TEACHING CONTEXTS OF SPATIAL THINKING

Spatial thinking has been a focus in research in the last four decades, evidenced by efforts to characterize the nature of spatial thinking by cognitive psychologists, scientists, engineers, and designers with different foci ranging from exploring its role in learning to problem solving, to its influences on behavioral patterns. Some of the research focuses on 'learning' and 'teaching' a particular set of spatial thinking skills in different contexts; for example, geographic information management, psychology, data mining, visualization, and design (NRC 2006; Golledge & Smitson, 1997; Newcombe & Huttenlocher, 2003; Casati & Varzi, 1999; Tversky, 2005). We agree with the National Academies that "…spatial thinking is at the heart of many great discoveries in science, that it underpins many of the activities of the modern workforce, and that it pervades the everyday activities of modern life." (NRC 2006, p.1).

Recent research and literature presents a significant amount of evidence showing the importance of spatial thinking. Sorby (1999) summarizes broad categories of spatial thinking that includes: Spatial perception, visualizations, mental rotations, spatial relations and spatial orientation. Their impact in the design curriculum has become more visible in different areas. In early university education, for example, academia has started to emphasize the importance of spatial concepts and particularly in problem discovery and problem solving (Sorby 2009). The most explicit course offerings related to spatial thinking are graphical communication courses offered by engineering, architecture, and art departments (Golledge & Stimson, 1997; Do, 2010; Sharp & Zachary, 2004; Dunwoody, 2010; & Sorby. 2009). Purdue University has been involved in engineering graphics design education and research since the late 1980's (Mohler & Miller, 2008). Michigan Technical University (MTU) has also been involved in the education and research associated with teaching 3D spatial abilities in general since the early 1990's (Sorby, 1999). The University of Southern California is one of the few universities offering dedicated courses in spatial thinking at the graduate level in a geographic information context (Golledge, 2010). The Georgia Institute of Technology is one of a few institutions that introduces 'visual reasoning' for first-year college students (Do, 2010).

The educational approach to teaching spatial thinking in higher education and specifically the techniques used to develop spatial skills in design education is our interest in this chapter. The conventional approach to teaching design has relied upon lectures, tutorials and practice labs as an overarching framework. The range of teaching techniques used to support students in developing their 2D and 3D spatial skills include: Lectures for teaching concepts and processes, sketching for applying projection techniques, and solid modeling (Sorby, 2009); mentored sketching to motivate students in lectures (Mohler & Miller, 2006); physical modeling (Erhan et al, 2009); hands-on problem solving, animations and computer games to focus on manipulating objects (Mohler & Miller, 2006). Sorby (2009) and her colleagues at MTU created and implemented a set of nine multimedia modules aimed at supporting first-year engineering students to enhance their spatial skills. The multimedia software package

of CAD exercises, including labs, proved to be an effective way for students to learn specific topics related to spatial thinking. Others have explored the use of problem-based approaches to learning spatial skills in measurement science with promising results. For instance, Shortis et al. (2002) have used simulations and animations to guide undergraduate students to develop context-specific spatial skills focused on spatial relations.

Although spatial thinking is at the core of design computation, we have yet to see a course that explicitly addresses spatial thinking applied in this context. Our approach is different from the other courses mentioned in the literature that we are aware. The first difference is on accepting how design computation, as discussed in the Introduction and the Bah´ai House of Worship example, uses representations that are not directly isomorphic to their physical world counterparts. The space, objects, and compositions can include features – such as reference geometries, mirroring, copying, and isolation from physics rules etc – suggest that the functions of spatial thinking within these contexts may require a different approach. Secondly, when these representations are used for the creation of real-world representations, the transition may require mapping from one spatial feature to the other. Our case courses differ on how to teach the translation occurring between the virtual and physical worlds in design, and the importance of spatial thinking in this process. We propose that by enhancing the ability of design students to think spatially and communicate visually in physical and virtual worlds in their own terms, they can be equipped with the problem solving and processing skills required in new and emerging design contexts. This chapter describes how undergraduate design students in two, unrelated courses, representing different disciplines, can be introduced to the foundational concepts and skills of spatial thinking, the fundamental skills of design computation, including digital representations and transitioning to physical modeling. The related teaching activities are described in the two case studies that follow.

TEACHING SPATIAL THINKING: TECH106 AND IAT337

Developing courses to integrate spatial thinking in design computation contexts is a significant undertaking. Although beyond the scope of the chapter, the process of developing these two courses provides context for the two cases that will be presented. An interdisciplinary team consisting of five faculty members, an instructional designer, and graduate students collaborated on the initial design, development, and delivery of the first case. This team worked closely together for over one year in what was a unique opportunity to incorporate their deep content knowledge while drawing upon their extensive experience in teaching engineering, product, and architectural design and integrating their research interests in computing, spatial cognition, and visual analytics (Erhan et al., 2008). Over three years, a smaller team has continued to instruct and evolve the design of this case. Moreover, the experience of designing the first course has informed the design and delivery of the second. Incidentally, an instructor and the instructional designer from the original team collaborated on the design of the second course.

These two courses offered as part of two different curricula. The first case study introduces the teaching approach taken in an introductory course titled "Spatial Thinking and Communicating" (TECH 106) offered as part of a six-course, cohort-based academic program at Simon Fraser University whose goal is to provide first-year university students with an interdisciplinary experience (TechOne Program, 2010). Students taking this course learn to apply 'spatial thinking' concepts and problem-solving skills in design through individual and group activities that allow them to switch between physical and digital representations in a linear and incremental process. The second case study describes an upper-division undergraduate course titled "Representation and Fabrication" (IAT 337) offered as part of the

School of Interactive Arts & Technology (SIAT) at Simon Fraser University. Third-year design students from SIAT are required to enroll in this course. Other students from the Informatics and Media-Arts streams may choose to do so. The students taking the first course – if they chose to continue in the SIAT Design stream – are required to take the second course. In the first offering, about 40% of the students taking Tech106 declared their majors as SIAT; and about 25% selected the Design stream.

In both cases, we describe the teaching and learning activities in relation to the spatial skills drawn from the literature. Table 1 shows how the two courses differ from and complement each other in terms of course goals, objectives, activities, and tools used. TECH 106 students choose this course before they choose their major. They are new to the university; and may or may not have design background or interests. The students taking IAT 337, take this course as part of their degree requirements. Before this course, they take prerequisite courses such as 'spatial design' that is concerned with making and understanding spaces used by people. The course goals in the first course focus around 'spatial thinking' that involves using different representation media, such as Lego Digital Designer, sketching, concept (mental) maps, and physical mock-ups. The students use these representations to iterate on space, objects, and object relations. As part of a design curriculum, IAT 337 focuses on use of design computation media for design representation, exploration, and realization. Both courses use individual and team assignments. The table below describes the structure of these courses in detail.

CASE 1. TECH 106: SPATIAL THINKING AND COMMUNICATING

The goal of TECH 106 is to provide students with the foundational knowledge and technical skills required to envision three-dimensional

Table 1. Course descriptions presented in the case studies

	TECH 106	SIAT 337
Context	Cohort-based, 1st year, interdisciplinary program	Required course in "Design" stream in SIAT's 3rd year
Students	New to university; may or may not have design background or interests	~25% of students have taken TECH 106
Delivery Method	Lecture: 1.5 hours/week Studio-lab: 3 hours/week	Lecture: 2 hours/week Studio-lab: 2 hours/week
Course Goals	Introduce spatial thinking, graphical representation and communication. Introduce concepts such as space, objects and operations; competencies and functions of spatial thinking. Provide the basic knowledge and technical skills for decomposing and composing 2D and 3D structures, visualization and thinking in 3D. Apply spatial thinking on solving problems using sketching, digital modeling, and physical modeling.	Use computer tools to represent designs for digitally enabled objects. Use computer-based representations as input to prototyping and fabrication systems. Study issues involved in preparing representations within a realistic design context. Understand concepts of coherence of design ideas across related artefacts, design rules and component and concept reuse. Apply the above concepts to the problem of designing a family of related artefacts.
Learning Objectives	Describe and use spatial thinking. Use graphical representations and communication in different problem domains such as engineering, arts, and business. Examine and interpret 3D representations. Visualize and define spatial problems and proposed solutions. Create and manipulate 2D and 3D representations and the solutions to given spatial problems. Select representation tools and techniques and make association among them when working on problems requiring spatial thinking. Use a computational design tools.	Represent spatial (geometry, location, orientation) properties of design solutions in design computation tools using parametric and constraint based methods. Reason and select representation techniques that match the nature of design solution. Use digital representations to build physical representation of designs. Move strategically between digital and physical representations of design for agility. Use representation tools in design and particularly in the design of a family of artifacts.
Developed Spatial Skills	Spatial visualization Spatial operations such as mental rotation Definition of object, space, and operations Use of representations Conceptualization of spatial components and their relations in different contexts	Composition and decomposition Translating digital to physical and physical to digital representations Inferencing from functional-behavioral properties of objects using both digital and physical representations
Digital Tools	Digital Lego Designer; SolidWorks	SolidWorks; CorelDraw; 3D Printer; Laser Cutter; (CNC outside the lab)
Assessments	Individual assignment and team work Mid-term focused on technical skills and fundamental concepts. Practice-based weekly assignments including lab activities focusing on development of SW skills and spatial skills. Course project intended to "integrate" spatial thinking, physical and digital representations, reasoning on space, objects, and operations. Comprehensive final exam.	Individual assignments. Course project to advance the students' knowledge and skills in digital and analog spatial representations while improving their skills in working in a collaborative setting.

structures, visualize and think in three dimensions and to analyze and solve specific spatial thinking problems using a range of analog and digital tools including: Sketching, physical models and computer-based modeling. This is not a traditional design studio course; rather it aims at engaging students in questioning how they 'think' as they design. This way they can develop a meta-design knowledge encapsulating spatial thinking as part of it (Williams, 1983; Voss & Wiley, 1995).

Course Overview and Learning Outcomes

The inaugural term for this 14-week long course was the Fall-2007 semester. Since then, there have been five offerings; the latest of which took place during Fall 2009. By the end of the course, students will be able to: Describe and use spatial thinking, use graphical representations and communication in different problem domains such as engineering, arts, and business, examine and interpret 3D representations, visualize and define spatial problems and proposed solutions, create and manipulate 2D and 3D representations of their solutions to given spatial problems, select representation tools and techniques and make association among them when working on problems requiring spatial thinking, and use a computational modeling tool (such as a Computer-Aided Design system).

Teaching Spatial Concepts and Skills

Students were introduced to the nature of spatial thinking through lectures, discussions of real-world examples, and presentations on tools used in spatial thinking. This was followed by an exploration of spatial thinking concepts including identification of spatial entities and objects, mental and on-representation translation and rotation, assemblies, associations between objects, and objects and space, representation tools, and reasoning. Students were exposed to sketching techniques, both freehand and using computer applications. These techniques are imperative to spatial thinking as they complete the representation used in communicating ideas not only to others, but also to themselves. As the course progressed, more advanced concepts in spatial thinking, such as proportions, shape and geometry, coordinates, properties of points, lines, circles and arcs were

introduced (Erhan et al., 2008). Following this introduction, a considerable part of the course was devoted to spatial visualization techniques through translating between 2D and 3D and using multi-view projections, cross-sections and axonometric projections (isometric, perspective). Details of the methods were presented in lecture sessions, along with a variety of in-lab and homework assignments and were a vital, integral component in supporting students in developing their spatial skills. We also covered the basics of dimensioning in order to allow students to include precision and accuracy in their representations and communicate related geometric properties, such as size information, of spatial entities.

Introducing Design Computation Tools

During the initial course design process, the team developed the requirements and specifications for the final project. This unpacking of the course project helped us realize the need for creating a simplified version of the major elements of the project in as far as they relate to design computation and physical modeling. During weeks one and two, students were introduced to Lego Digital Designer (Lego Digital Designer, 2010) and invited to "play" with the tool and to practice tasks using a pre-defined library of objects. Simple spatial skills such as selecting objects, rotating, attaching, detaching and copying were performed under guided instruction by TA's and instructors. Students built and animated a two-gimbal system within this environment. This "lite" experience set the stage for students to undertake more challenging spatial tasks within the more complex and industrial-strength computational environment of SolidWorks (Tickoo & Maini, 2007). Concepts of constraints, degrees of freedom, and modeling theory were introduced in lectures as well as in the context of this tool via examples, tutorials, and hands-on laboratory assignments. Tasks related to part modeling and assemblies

Figure 6. Sketch of a two-Gimbal System (right) and its corresponding concept map (left)

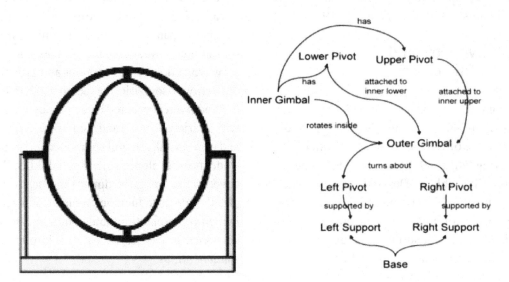

were done individually and then collaboratively to fulfill the requirements of the lab assignments and the team project. Our approach after the first offering of the course was to expose students early, starting from week 4 of the semester, and often to SolidWorks so that all of them can develop their modeling skills using this tool. We found that this early exposure was beneficial and helpful to them when it came time to deal with the requirements and added complexity of the project.

Modeling and Building a Gimbal System Using LEGO

This learning activity represented the first opportunity for students to practice some of the spatial thinking concepts and skills required for successful completion of the team project. This exemplified a first attempt at performing the spatial tasks required for digital and physical modeling: The development of a two-gimbal system. Students created a concept map for such a system, developed a corresponding digital model using Lego Digital Designer (LDD) and built a real two-gimbal mechanism using physical LEGO bricks. Our intent was to allow students to relate concepts learned during the first two weeks of

the term; such as space, context, representation, reasoning, and make references between them in a playful and familiar situation. Figure 6 displays the concept map of an example two-gimbal system.

Significant differences exist between digital and physical bricks and in how students develop models using digital vs. physical parts. Throughout the process of using real LEGO bricks to build a physical two-gimbal mechanism, students were encouraged to pay attention to their experiences while keeping in mind issues related to the approach employed in selecting Lego bricks regarding their shape, size, function, and location; the strategy they used in decomposing and composing parts including the order of assembly; and the challenges they faced while using physical LEGO parts compared to digital ones. Figure 7 shows a representative example of a digital and two physical models generated by students.

Designing an Animated Mechanical Toy

The primary goal of this major project was for the students to demonstrate spatial skills required in digital and physical modeling. It involved the design and building of an animated mechanical

Figure 7. A digital (left) and two physical (center and right) Lego models of a two-gimbal system.

toy (AMT) (Peppé, 2002) that incorporates two main components: A simple mechanical box and an original and creative figure integrated with it. The mechanical box contains mechanisms, such as gears and cams that are assembled together to generate different types of movement. When activated by a crank handle, the mechanism animates the attached figure. Two types of mo-tion were required: A translational motion and a rotational one.

The course project involved four distinct and yet iterative steps as shown in Figure 8. The first step dealt with brainstorming for AMT ideas, creating the concept map of the selected figure, and producing multi-view and isometric draw-ings as well as annotated sketches of students' designs (see Figure 9 for an example). Students

Figure 8. The steps involved in the design process of the AMT

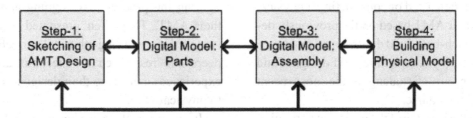

Figure 9. CheckMate AMT: Pictorial drawings of the figure (left), mechanical box (center), and multi-view drawing of figure (right)

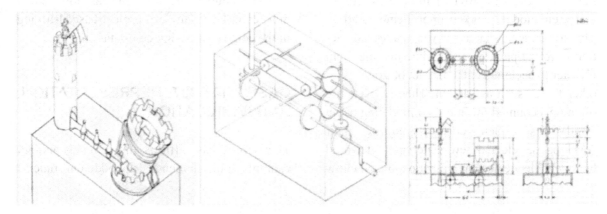

Figure 10. CheckMate AMT: Digital model (left) and physical model (right)

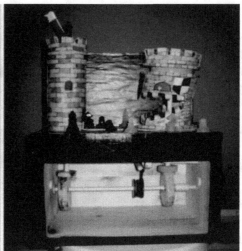

were asked to submit sketches that clearly depict how the mechanisms can be brought together as an assembly in the mechanical box so the figure actually moves as specified. In the second step, students were tasked with creating digital models of their AMT parts using SolidWorks (Dassault Systèmes, 2010). This was followed by assembling these parts into an animated digital model. Finally, the last step consisted of constructing a physical model of their AMT based on the previously developed sketch-based and digital representations. Figure 11 displays an example AMT designed and built by a group of students in the most recent offering of the course.

During the last step of the project in particular, teams practiced working with and refining materials that would enable their physical models to function. Teams improvised in order to ensure that their models worked upon demonstration. This often meant that teams were called into action to refine parts by hand while making them in order to account for the impact of gravity and other forces such as friction. These aspects are often unaccounted for in digital modeling using SolidWorks. Students creatively adjusted their AMT parts, selected new materials that would better enable the design to function, or somehow

modified their efforts to ensure that the model would work upon demonstration. Improvisation, defined by Gerber (2007) as a creative act without prior thought, may be used to support design as well as build perspectives and skills that are highly valuable for designers, including learning through error. The final requirement for the project was for teams to create a presentation highlighting the process of designing and building their AMT. They then presented and demonstrated their working physical models to their peers and responded to questions about their experiences in moving their designs from digital to physical worlds.

In summary, this case has provided a detailed description of the teaching and learning activities involved in digital and physical modeling in a first-year course. The following case illustrates a more complex example of project-based learning in the context of design computation.

CASE 2. IAT 337: REPRESENTATION AND FABRICATION

This second case affirms and provides another example of the challenges embedded in students

Figure 11. Student projects analyzing spatial properties of existing objects, modeling their properties, and exploring variations in SolidWorks and (spatial) configuration management

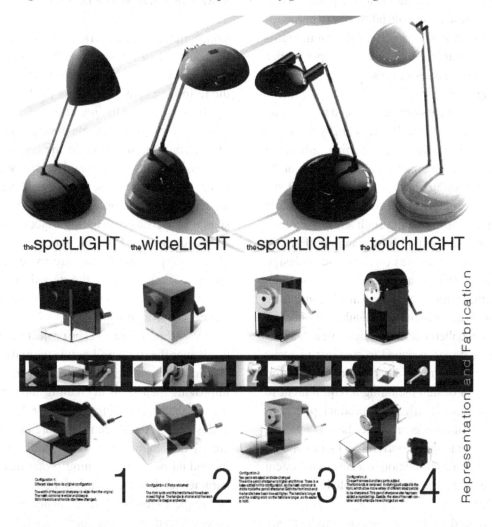

dealing with design in digital and physical environments. It describes a third year course that introduces students to the use of computational tools to represent designs for digitally enabled objects as input to prototyping and fabrication systems. It focuses on the student team project to illustrate the challenges faced by students in designing within a computational environment. In particular, the transition from digital to physical modeling is explored. Students in this course studied issues related to the preparation of representations within a realistic design context. A series of representation types were introduced

in order to understand concepts of coherence of design ideas across related artifacts, design rules and component and concept reuse. Students also applied these concepts to the problem of designing a family of related artifacts.

Course Goal and Learning Outcomes

This course prepares students to apply advanced software tools for representing designs and the techniques needed to use such tools for the generation of accurate and precise specification of parts and their assembly. It teaches how to use data from such representations as input to computer numerical control fabrication equipment and combine representation and fabrication techniques into an iterative design process. Designing a family of related artifacts provides an opportunity for reconciling issues of reuse, design rules and inter-design coherence.

Initially, students were introduced to concepts and advanced spatial skills including representations for designs, (digital) sketching, advanced solid modeling, parametric modeling, and methods of representing object behavior and analysis. Students were also introduced to fabrication tools used in physical modeling such as laser cutters, 3D printers and n-axis milling machines. Early in the course, the focus was on the reuse of design ideas across designs and design projects. Such reuse is often critical to a design firm's continuing success and can be realized through techniques of inter-design coherence and design rules. A team-based project was assigned to students to assist them in applying representation and fabrication techniques in design including a requirement to build a product family on a product platform. The heavy emphasis on a project-based approach affords students the opportunity to learn spatial skills in design computation in a lab environment where the instructor plays a key role in coaching the students.

By the end of the course, the students are expected to apply different representation types for describing spatial (form, geometry, size, composition) properties of design solutions in design computation tools using parametric and constraint-based methods. They learn how to select representation techniques that match the nature of their proposed design solution. Students use digital representations to build physical representations of these design solutions. They move strategically between these two types of design representations.

Spatial Feature Modeling and Team-Based Project

Conceptual and hands-on activities are taught over the course of 14 weeks. In addition to the content presented in the lectures, the students completed the following activities during the labs:

Assignments: The intention of the assignments is to prepare students through the practice of specific spatial skills, for the course project. The assignments are ordered in a way to allow students to acquire these skills over the course of the term: i) use computational software to model spatial properties of existing objects; ii) design an object derived from the modeled object; iii) utilize computational software to configure for spatial variations using the new design model; and iv) present designs and their variations (see Figure 11 for an illustration).

Team-Based Project: The project was planned to advance the students' knowledge and comptencies in digital and analog representations while improving their skills in creating and using them in a collaborative setting. The most relevant issues in design that the students explore in the project are: i) developing a product platform with its individual parts; ii) defining properties of parts parametrically to explore variation in dimensions and shape; iii) creating different designs using the parts defined in the platform; and iv) switching between digital and analog representations in the process. In the three offerings of this course, the course project involved the design and building of a kinetic sculpture with different themes. In the first year, the theme was 'interactive toys', the second year 'sustainability', and in the third year 'nature'. Kinetic sculptures are interesting as they present a rich context for experimenting with spatial object definitions that are relatively isolated from pragmatic design requirements, encourage both artistic and mechanical exploration, and allow for prototypes that can be quickly built, thus providing opportunities for students to

Figure 12. Example representations used in a student project called "Pirate Ship". The design explores parts-whole relationships, structural and functional features of parts, and (re)configuration in a product platform.

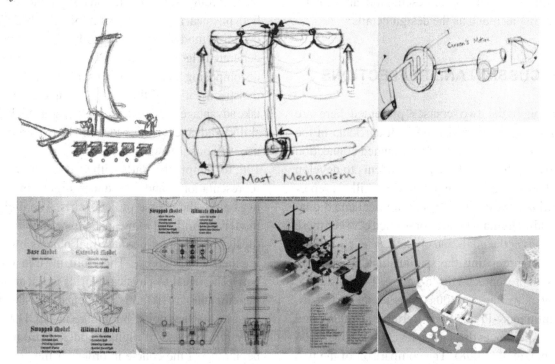

be highly creative with their designs. Figure 12 shows representations used by a group of students when exploring their design ideas of a pirate ship.

Designing a Product Platform

During the project, students analyzed existing kinetic sculptures to describe how the kinetic mechanisms work. The descriptions were pre-sented in different types of representations including technical drawings, functional prototypes, posters, animations etc. before the class. This effort requires the use and development of spatial thinking skills. When designing their projects, the students referred to their analyses, adapted and changed their designs, and described their reasoning again using both digital and analog representations (Figure 13 shows examples of such

Figure 13. Example prototypes of some kinetic sculptures designed by the students of IAT 337

analog representations). Although this resembles a 'design' process in a regular design course, the emphasis is on the representation and spatial thinking as much as the design details.

DISCUSSION AND REFLECTIONS

Although the two courses presented here are offered as part of two different curricula in the same institution, there is an assumed connection between them: Both require students to develop and use complex spatial thinking skills in representing their design ideas in physical and digital worlds. The main logical connection between these courses at the goals and objectives levels formed after appreciating the spatial thinking skills in design presented in the literature (Tversky, 2005; Novick & Bassok, 2005; and Sternberg, Lubart, Kaufman, & Pretz, 2005; Bertel et al. 2006); and our experiences during the developing TECH 106 (Erhan et al., 2008). The comparison of the two courses in relation to the design computation and spatial thinking aspects is shown in Table 2. IAT 337 is an advanced-level design course where the digital tools and digital fabrication techniques are used extensively for both representation and construction of design artifacts. Hence, issues such as compatibility, precision, constructability etc. are discussed in detail. While TECH 106 studies 'design' implicitly, the latter course explicitly introduces different structured design processes. Further, TECH 106 focuses on 'spatial thinking' as its main goal, and intentionally avoids explicit discussion of design processes. The students taking

IAT 337 design product platforms and families composed of modular replaceable parts. This takes place through several iterations of production of both physical and digital prototypes, in which the design is modeled parametrically and if needed generated algorithmically. This process involves decomposing and composing spatial objects and the specification of their relationships. Students take advantage of their 'developed' spatial thinking skills to advance in this process. The two courses use various (design) representations. TECH 106, for simplicity, starts with analog (on-paper) representations, and introduces digital modeling before the course project starts. The digital models are utilized as means to experiment with (design) ideas, and produce real objects by using them as a reference. Therefore, the transition between virtual to physical worlds is linear and incremental. In IAT 337, students use sketching as a starting point, but unlike in TECH 106, they are exposed to digital modeling from the beginning of the course in order for the created models to be used as the main means for design exploration. As often as possible, the students produce physical prototypes from these models using digital fabrication techniques. This process is hence iterative and continuous.

When measuring the students' progress in achieving the course objectives, we relied on the learning assessment tools, such as the course project, assignments, and tests mentioned in Table 1. We didn't, however, have a chance to conduct formal pre- and post-tests measuring the development of their spatial abilities. The second form of evaluation was the instructional team's obser-

Table 2. Overall differences and similarities in teaching design (computation) and spatial thinking between TECH 106 and IAT 337

Course/Context	Design Process	Spatial Thinking	Representations	Virtual/Physical Transition
TECH 106	Implicit	Explicit	Analog -> Digital -> Physical	Linear/Incremental
IAT 337	Explicit	Implicit	Digital <--> Physical	Iterative/Continuous

vations during the course development and delivery. They revealed that in both courses, the complexity of the design computation software, SolidWorks, interfered with the project related tasks: The students could easily get lost in using the software when they were completing their work. Their struggle when moving between the different stages in the design process and translating representations between virtual and physical worlds was another main concern.

The two courses have gone through some changes throughout their multiple offerings. These changes were based on the results of the team meetings regarding the students' progress and the new knowledge acquired in spatial thinking. For TECH 106, one of the main improvements was the integration of the pre-lab activities in the course to bridge the conceptual material presented in the lectures and practical applications in the lab. As a pilot project in the third academic year of offering TECH 106, the students were asked to reflect upon their progress during the completion of each step in the course project. They kept an individual journal that included sketches and text to describe their spatial thinking. At the end of the project, the teams compiled their collective thoughts from the journals to complete their final report. Although the journals were not graded, we noticed the team presentations were more organized and focused on spatial abilities in the context of the course project. From our experience, we propose formally integrating a journal component in the course. The major change in IAT 337 was in how the students learned to use the computational design tool. In the first offering, the software was introduced step-by-step following a very structured process. However, this was found less effective since not all the software features were relevant and more importantly the students were able to discover the needed features as they needed them. The studio-labs were a productive setting for this as they could ask their peers, teaching assistants, or instructors. The course, then, focused on equally emphasizing the students' design models and

what software features can help them in building them. The assignments were modified in order to focus on assessing how the students use the tool in modeling rather than what aspects of the tool the students can use.

In TECH 106, the students expressed their enjoyment and found the lab activities to be very engaging although undertaking the project was a major effort. Learning a feature-based parametric modeling system, such as SolidWorks, requires well-integrated tutorials that are focused on the specific spatial tasks required in the project. The industry training modules were too generic for the purpose of the learning requirements in TECH 106. Our choice to introduce the LEGO parts and LEGO Digital Designer as the initial learning activity was important for two reasons: These parts were familiar to most students and readily available, and we could afford to have sets of LEGO parts for literally 100s of students. The Lego component was a "fun" activity for applying the spatial concepts taught in the lectures. In IAT 337, the students always worked with physical and digital models simultaneously. This helped them to experiment with material types and their physical properties. Using the iterative design approach, students could benefit from prototypes of different resolutions in order to maintain the consistency between digital and physical modeling throughout the design process.

As a design team, we learned a tremendous amount about designing these courses that support spatial thinking in the context of design computation. These courses have reinforced the value of team projects for learning spatial thinking skills and in particular the importance of clearly specifying project requirements in order to assist students in focusing on the task(s) at hand. To mitigate some of the "distortions" and to help students move from digital to physical contexts, it may be beneficial to guide them in the development of prototypes of their projects. This would provide an opportunity for students to work with and test different materials early in the design process, thus enabling them to build a functioning and robust model that more closely corresponds to their digital models.

FUTURE RESEARCH DIRECTIONS

Based on our experiences with these two courses, we believe that there are fruitful areas for research in the future. This could involve exploring students' actual progress of developing spatial thinking skills in these contexts. This might entail conducting surveys, tests, and evaluations. In line with this, there is a need to assess whether the introduction of spatial thinking explicitly makes a difference in design and design computation. Although the learning assessments show a high-level achievement of the course objectives in both courses, these were set by the instructional design team, and therefore are not necessarily unbiased or may not be even appropriate for any reliable conclusion. Similar concerns apply when making conclusions on whether the introduction of the design process explicitly matters when teaching spatial thinking in the context of computational design. Additional research is required to identify and understand the spatial processes that take place during design computation and how these differ from those in the physical world.

There are numerous computational design approaches such agent-based systems, genetic algorithms, shape grammars that may require different spatial skills than parametric systems that we used in these case studies. These computational approaches present potentially interesting opportunities for additional investigation. For example, the compilation of shape grammar rules may need 'form analysis' skills, while applying them to generate new designs involves the selection of the rules to achieve a desired form. Similarly, studying the types of spatial skills required to work with genetic algorithms could be different from other computational approaches where the forms are generated by evolving through inheritance, mutation, selection, and crossover operations.

We suggest undertaking a longitudinal study to measure the impacts of being exposed to explicit spatial thinking concepts and tasks over the course of a four-year design program. The results of this work would inform the curricula of undergraduate design education. In fact, we believe that it would be valuable to explore the curricular-wide impacts of teaching spatial thinking skills.

ACKNOWLEDGMENT

We would like to thank our colleagues John Dill, Mike Sjoerdsma, and Janet McCracken who collaborated with us in developing and teaching Tech106, as well as the TechOne Program and the School of interactive Arts & Technology at Simon Fraser University and their staff for their support. We also wish to acknowledge the many students whom we learned with and from during our experience of teaching these two courses.

REFERENCES

Aish, R., & Woodbury, R. (2005). Multi-level interaction in parametric design. In *Smart Graphics*, 151-162. http://dx.doi.org/10.1007/11536482_13.

Akin, O. (2001). Variants in design cognition. In C. Eastman, W. Newstetter & M. McCracken (Eds.), *Design knowing and learning: Cognition in design education* (pp. 105-124). Elsevier Science.

Anderson, R. E., & Helstrup, T. (1993). Visual discovery in mind and on paper. *Memory & Cognition, 21*(3), 283–293. doi:10.3758/BF03208261

Bertel, S., Jupp, J., Barkowsky, T., & Bilda, Z. (2006). *Constructing and understanding visuo-spatial representations in design thinking*. Design Computing and Cognition Workshop, Eindhoven, The Netherlands.

Casati, A., & Varzi, A. C. (1999). *Parts and places: The structures of spatial representation*. Boston, MA: MIT Press.

Chandrasekaran, B., Kurup, U., Banerjee, B., Josephson, J. R., & Winkler, R. (2004). An architecture for problem solving in diagrams. In *Diagrammatic Representation and Inference: Third International Conference, Diagrams 2004*, (pp. 151-165).

Cichy, M. A. (2006). *Parametric design: An implementation of Bentley Systems generative components*. Unpublished M.Arch. thesis, University of Waterloo, Canada.

Dassault Systèmes. (2010, May 10). Retrieved from htpp://www.solidworks.com

Do, E. Y.-L. (2010, April 22). *GIS 172: Visual reasoning*. Retrieved from http://code.arc.cmu.edu/visual

Dunwoody, A. B. (2010, May 10). *APSC 151: Computer-aided engineering graphics*. Retrieved from http://courses.engineering.ubc.ca/apsc151

Erhan, H., Ben Youssef, B., Sjoerdsma, M., Dill, J., Berry, B., & McCracken, J. (2008, July 27-29). Spatial thinking and communicating: A course for first-year university students. In *Proceedings of the Fifth CDEN/RCCI International Design Engineering Conference*. Halifax, Nova Scotia (Canada).

Finke, R. (1993). Mental imagery and creative discovery. In Roskos-Ewoldsen, B., Intons-Petersen, M. J., & Anderson, R. (Eds.), *Imagery, creativity, and discovery* (pp. 255–285). New York, NY: North-Holland. doi:10.1016/S0166-4115(08)60145-4

Finke, R. A., & Slayton, K. (1988). Explorations of creative visual synthesis in mental imagery. *Memory & Cognition*, *16*(3), 252–257. doi:10.3758/BF03197758

Gattis, M. (2003). Space as bases for abstract thoughts. In Gattis, M. (Ed.), *Spatial schemas and abstract thought* (pp. 1–15). MIT Press.

Gerber, E. (2007, April 28-May 3). Improvisation principles and techniques for design. In *Proceedings of the 25th ACM Conference on Human Factors in Computing Systems* (CHI 2007) (pp. 1069-1072). San Jose, CA (USA).

Golledge, R. G. (1992, September 21-23). Do people understand spatial concepts: The case of first-order primitives. In *Proceedings of the International Conference GIS - From Space to Territory: Theories and Methods of Spatio-Temporal Reasoning in Geographic Space* (pp. 1-21).

Golledge, R. G. (2010, May 8). *GEOG 581: Concepts for spatial thinking and GEOG 583: Spatial analysis and modeling*. Retrieved from http://college.usc.edu/geography/ courses/graduate.html.

Golledge, R. G., & Stimson, R. J. (1997). *Spatial behaviour: A geographical perspective*. New York, NY: Guilford Press.

Lego Digital Designer. (2010, April 23). Retrieved from http://ldd.lego.com

Lohman, D. F., & Nichols, P. D. (1990). Training spatial abilities: Effects of practice on rotation and synthesis tasks. *Learning and Individual Differences*, *2*(1), 67–93. doi:10.1016/1041-6080(90)90017-B

Mohler, J. L., & Miller, C. L. (2008). Improving spatial ability with mentored sketching. *Engineering Design Graphics Journal*, *72*(1), 19–27.

Muller, W. (1989). Design discipline and the significance of visuo-spatial thinking. *Design Studies*, *10*(1), 12–23. doi:10.1016/0142-694X(89)90021-5

National Research Council (NCR). (2006). *Learning to think spatially*. Washington, DC: The National Academies Press.

Newcombe, N. S., & Huttenlocher, J. (2003). *Making space: The development of spatial representations and reasoning*. Cambridge, MA: MIT Press.

Novick, L. R., & Bassok, M. (2005). Problem solving. In Holyoak, K. J., & Morrison, R. G. (Eds.), *The Cambridge handbook of thinking and reasoning* (pp. 321–349). New York, NY: Cambridge University Press.

Peppé, R. (2002). *Automata and mechanical toys*. Crowood Press.

Rink, M. (2005). Spatial situation models. In Shah, P., & Miyake, A. (Eds.), *Handbook of higher-level visuospatial thinking* (pp. 334–382). Cambridge, UK: Cambridge University Press.

Schwartz, D. L. (1999, May). Physical imagery: Kinematic versus dynamic models. *Cognitive Psychology*, *38*(3), 433–464. doi:10.1006/cogp.1998.0702

Schwartz, D. L., & Black, J. B. (1996, April). Analog imagery in mental model reasoning: Depictive models. *Cognitive Psychology*, *30*(2), 154–219. doi:10.1006/cogp.1996.0006

Seepersad, C. C., Green, M. G., & Schmidt, K. J. (2006). Learning journals as a cornerstone for effective experiential learning in undergraduate engineering design courses. In *Proceedings of the 2006 ASEE Annual Conference*. Chicago, Illinois.

Sharp, J., & Zachary, L. W. (2004). Using the van Hiele K-12 geometry learning theory to modify engineering mechanics instruction. *Journal of STEM Education Innovations and Research*, *5*(1&2), 35–41.

Shneiderman, B. (2007). Creativity support tools: Accelerating discovery and innovation. *Communications of the ACM*, *50*(12), 20–32. doi:10.1145/1323688.1323689

Shortis, M., Leahy, F., Ogleby, C., Kealy, A., & Ellis, F. (2002). *Learning spatial design and analysis concept*. Retrieved from http://www.geomsoft.com/markss/ papers/Shortis_etal_spatDA.pdf

Sorby, S. A. (1999). Developing 3-D spatial visualization skills. *Engineering Design Graphics Journal*, *63*(2), 21–32.

Sorby, S. A. (2009). Educational research in developing 3-D spatial skills for engineering students. *International Journal of Science Education*, *31*(3), 459–480. doi:10.1080/09500690802595839

Sternberg, R. J., Lubart, T. I., Kaufman, J. C., & Pretz, J. E. (2005). Creativity. In Holyoak, K. J., & Morrison, R. G. (Eds.), *The Cambridge handbook of thinking and reasoning* (pp. 351–369). New York, NY: Cambridge University Press.

TechOne Program. (2010, April 26). Retrieved from http://students.surrey.sfu.ca/techone

Tickoo, S., & Maini, D. (2007). *SolidWorks 2007 for designers*. CADCIM Technologies.

Tversky, B. (2005). Functional significance of visuospatial representations. In Shah, P., & Miyake, A. (Eds.), *The Cambridge handbook of visuospatial thinking* (pp. 1–34). Cambridge, UK: Cambridge University Press.

Tversky, B. (2005). Visuospatial reasoning. In Holyoak, K. J., & Morrison, R. G. (Eds.), *The Cambridge handbook of thinking and reasoning* (pp. 209–240). New York, NY: Cambridge University Press.

Tversky, B., Morrison, J. B., & Betrancourt, M. (2002, October). Animation: Can it facilitate? *International Journal of Human-Computer Studies*, *57*(4), 247–262. doi:10.1006/ijhc.2002.1017

Verstijnen, I. M., van Leeuwen, C., Goldschmidt, G., Hamel, R., & Hennessey, J. M. (1998, October). Sketching and creative discovery. *Design Studies*, *19*(4), 519–546. doi:10.1016/S0142-694X(98)00017-9

Visser, W. (2006). *The cognitive artifacts of designing*. Mahwah, NJ: Lawrence Erlbaum Associates.

Voss, J. F., & Wiley, J. (1995). Acquiring intellectual skills. *Annual Review of Psychology, 46*, 155–181. doi:10.1146/annurev.ps.46.020195.001103

Williams, L. V. (1983). *Teaching for the two-sided mind*. Prentice Hall, Inc.

ADDITIONAL READING

Akin, O. (2004). *A Cartesian Approach to Design Rationality*. Ankara: METU Faculty of Architecture Press.

Bates-Brkljac, N. (2007). Investigating perceptual responses and shared understanding of architectural design ideas when communicated through different forms of visual representations. In *Proceedings of 11th International Conference Information Visualization*, pp. 348-353.

Eastman, C., Newstetter, W., & McCracken, M. (2001). *Design Knowing and Learning: Cognition in Design Education* (1st ed.). Elsevier Science.

Ferguson, E. S. (1992). *Engineering and the Minds' Eye*. Cambridge, MA: The MIT Press.

Frank, M., Lavy, I., & Elata, D. (2003). Implementing the project-based learning approach in an academic engineering course. *International Journal of Technology and Design Education, 13*, 273–288. doi:10.1023/A:1026192113732

Gibson, I. S. (2003). From solo-run to mainstream thinking: Project-based learning in engineering design. *European Journal of Engineering Education, 28*(3), 331–337. doi:10.1080/0304379031000108768

Goel, V. (1995). *Sketches of Thoughts*. The MIT Press.

Gregor, S., & Jones, D. (2007). The Anatomy of a Design Theory. *Journal of the Association for Information Systems, 8*(5), 313–335.

Grinter, L. E. (1955). Report of the committee on evaluation of engineering education. *Journal of Engineering Education, 46*, 25–60.

Hegarty, M., & Waller, D. A. (2005). Individual Differences in Spatial Abilities. In Shah, P., & Miyake, A. (Eds.), *The Cambridge Handbook of Visuospatial Thinking* (pp. 121–169). Cambridge: Cambridge University Press.

Hensel, M. (2004). Are We Ready To Compute. In Leach, N., Turnbull, D., & Williams, C. (Eds.), *Digital Techtonics* (pp. 120–126). Chichester: Wiley-Academy.

Hespanha, S. R., Goodchild, F., & Janelle, D. G. (2009). Spatial thinking and technologies in the undergraduate social science classroom. *Journal of Geography in Higher Education, 33*(1), S17–S29. doi:10.1080/03098260903033998

Johnson, G., Gross, M. D., Hong, J., & Do, E. Y. L. (2009). Computational Support for Sketching in Design: A Review. *Foundations and Trends in HCI, 2*(1), 1–93.

Kastens, K. A., & Ishikawa, T. (2006). Spatial thinking in the geosciences and cognitive sciences: A cross-disciplinary look at the intersection of the two fields. In Manduca, C. A., & Mogk, D. W. (Eds.), *Earth and mind: How geologists think and learn about the earth* (pp. 53–76). Boulder, CO: The Geological Society of America. doi:10.1130/2006.2413(05)

Kolmos, A. (1996). Reflections on project work and problem-based learning. *European Journal of Engineering Education, 21*(2), 141–148. doi:10.1080/03043799608923397

Levine, M., Marchon, I., & Hanley, G. (1984, March). The Placement and Misplacement of You-Are-Here Maps. *Environment and Behavior*, *16*(2), 139–157. doi:10.1177/0013916584162001

Mark, E., Gross, M. D., & Goldschmidt, G. (2008). A Perspective on Computer Aided Design after Four Decades, Earl Mark, Gross, M.D., Goldschmidt, G. In *26th international conference on Education in Computer-Aided Architectural Design in Europe* (eCAADe), Antwerp, Sept 17-20, 2008. pp. 169-178.

McKim, R. H. (1980). *Experiences in Visual Thinking*. Boston, MA: PWS Publishers.

Meredith, M. (2008). Never enough (transform, repeat ad nausea). In Sakamoto, T., & Ferre, A. (Eds.), *From Control To Design, Actar-D* (pp. 6–9). New York, Barcelona.

Merriwether, A. M., & Liben, L. S. (1997, April). Adults' Failures on Euclidean and Projective Spatial Tasks: Implications for Characterizing Spatial Cognition. *Journal of Adult Development*, *4*(2), 57–69. doi:10.1007/BF02510081

Olkun, S. (2003, April). Making connections: Improving spatial abilities with engineering drawing abilities. *International Journal of Mathematics Teaching and Learning*, Center for Innovation in Mathematics Teaching, University of Plymouth, UK.

Oxman, R. (2008). Towards a Performance based Generation and Formation Model in Architectural Design. *International Journal of Architectural Computing*, *6*(1), 1–17. doi:10.1260/147807708784640090

Piaget, J. (1983). Piaget's Theory. In Kessen, W. (Ed.), *History, Theory, and Methods* (4th ed., *Vol. I*, pp. 103–128). Handbook of Child Psychology New York: Wiley.

Piaget, J., & Inhelder, B. (1956). *The Child's Conception of Space* (Langdon, F. J., & Lunzer, J. L., Trans.). New York: Norton. (Original work published 1948)

Prusinkiewicz, P. (2004). Art and science for life: Designing and growing virtual plants with L-systems. *in* C. Davidson and T. Fernandez (eds.), *Nursery Crops: Development, Evaluation, Production and Use*: Proceedings of the XXVI International Horticultural Congress. *Acta Horticulturae* 630, pp. 15-28.

Schnier, T., & Gero, J. S. (1998). From Frank Lloyd Wright to Mondrian: Transforming evolving representations. In Parmee, I. (Ed.), *Adaptive Computing in Design and Manufacture* (pp. 207–219). London: Springer. doi:10.1007/978-1-4471-1589-2_16

Sims, V. K., & Mayer, R. E. (2002, January). Domain Specificity of Spatial Expertise: The Case of Video Game Players. *Applied Cognitive Psychology*, *16*(1), 97–115. doi:10.1002/acp.759

Sorby, S. A. (2005). Assessment of a "new and improved" course for the development of 3-D spatial skills. *Engineering Design Graphics Journal*, *69*(3), 6–13.

Wickens, C. D., Vincow, M., & Yeh, M. (2005). Design Applications of Visual Spatial Thinking: The Importance of Frame of Reference. In Shah, P., & Miyake, A. (Eds.), *The Cambridge Handbook of Visuospatial Thinking* (pp. 383–425). Cambridge: Cambridge University Press. doi:10.1017/CBO9780511610448.011

KEY TERMS AND DEFINITIONS

Animated Mechanical Toy: It refers to a toy object comprised of a mechanical box and a figure integrated with it. The mechanical box contains mechanisms, such as gears, cams, cranks, etc. that are assembled together to generate different types of movement. When actuated by a handle, the mechanism animates the attached figure.

Design Computation: Is the use of computation-driven methods, such as constraint-based modeling, shaper grammar, frame-based modeling, object-oriented modeling, and generative algorithms as an aid in creating design solutions and their representations.

External Representation: (in the present context) Is an abstract description of existing or conceived objects through a form of media that is shareable with self and others and created for a specific purpose.

Kinetic Sculpture: An expressive art form composed of mechanical and interactive parts as figures that are spatially interconnected.

Mental Representation: (in the present context) Is an abstract imagery of existing or conceived objects in visuospatial memory with its spatial and semantic properties.

Project-Based Learning: Employs instruction and learning activities centered upon creating a product in order to learn specific concepts and skills.

Spatial Thinking: Is a collection of declarative and perceptual spatial concepts and thought processes including the ability to operate, transform, or combine these concepts and processes. The main components of spatial thinking are concepts of space, tools of representation, and processes of reasoning.

Spatial Visualization: (in the present context) Description of objects and their spatial properties using visual imagery that enables mental or external spatial transformations.

Chapter 22
Inserting Computational Technologies in Architectural Curricula

José P. Duarte
Techical University of Lisbon, Portugal

Gabriela Celani
University of Campinas (Unicamp), Brazil

Regiane Pupo
University of Campinas (Unicamp), Brazil

ABSTRACT

This chapter describes two case studies concerning the introduction of computational design methods and technologies in new undergraduate architectural curricula, one in Portugal and the other in Brazil. In both cases, the immediate goal was to introduce state-of-the-art technologies in the curriculum to promote creative design thinking. The ultimate goals were to fulfill the criteria of intellectual satisfaction, acquisition of specialized professional skills, and contribution for the economic development of society that should underlie university education. The chapter describes the theoretical framework, the various courses and labs that were devised and implemented, as well as the strategies used to implement them. Then it presents the final results and concludes with a discussion of the pros and cons of each strategy. The main lesson drawn from both efforts was that cultural and organizational aspects are at least as important as technical aspects for the successful integration of computer media in architectural education.

INTRODUCTION

The insertion of "new technologies" in architectural teaching and practice has been everything but smooth. The meaning of the term itself is ambiguous and tends to be reduced in a very simplistic manner to the use of the computer or, even more simplistically, to the use of CAD software. Not surprisingly, the issue divides educators and professionals alike and prompts them to take extreme positions. On one side, one finds those who tend to assign a central role to the computer; on the other, one encounters those who refuse

DOI: 10.4018/978-1-61350-180-1.ch022

to admit that it can have any role at all. Reality, nevertheless, demonstrates that the role of the computer can facilitate the resolution of certain design problems but may jeopardize the solution of others. Time and experience permit to categorize problems and so the contact of architectural students with new technologies in the early stages of their learning and training process is important. This chapter describes two cases concerned with the integration of computational design methods and technologies in undergraduate curricula in new programs in architecture, one at the Technical University of Lisbon School of Engineering (Instituto Superior Técnico – IST, TU Lisbon) in Portugal, and another at the School of Civil Engineering, Architecture and Urban Design of the University of Campinas (Faculdade de Engenharia Civil, Arquitetura e Urbanismo da Universidade Estadual de Campinas – FEC, Unicamp) in Brazil.

In their paper "The Ideal Computer Curriculum" Mark, Martens & Oxman (2005) discussed how devising an architectural curriculum in the digital age is a matter of finding a balance between the need for integrating state of art technology and the demand of keeping traditional subjects to meet the requirements of professional accreditation. They identified a list of computer courses that could be included in the architectural curriculum organized into three levels: Basic, intermediate and advanced. Then they identified two different strategies to integrate computer courses in the architectural curriculum, one that was set within the framework of the typical curriculum structure and another that displaced a great number of traditional courses. Finally they gave examples of possible curricula for each of the two cases. In the first curriculum, most of the digital design topics were integrated in existing courses, except for two mandatory courses in geometric modeling and structural analysis. By contrast, in the second curriculum, most of the computer topics were offered in seven separate mandatory courses. In both curricula, students could take additional, elective courses on computer-related subjects.

They concluded that the first strategy was better because the latter "would not likely prepare students well for a career in architecture as the profession is likely to demand."

The IST case described in this chapter is closer to the first curricula described by Mark, Martens & Oxman (2005) in the sense that it includes fewer computer courses and the CAD content is better intertwined with architectural content, although not by including computer topics in traditional courses but the reverse. The IST curriculum includes only three mandatory courses, two in the first years and one in the last year, and no elective courses on computer topics. Although the title of the first two subjects make reference to CAD, computer topics are taught by addressing architectural problems, such as how to model and describe a building (CAD I) or how to write a program to generate a certain type of architectural forms (CAD II). And in the last subject, (CAAD) the goal is the development of architectural design projects with the use of computer technologies. This means that all the courses have a creative component.

At UNICAMP the curriculum includes four mandatory and five elective CAD courses, but although their objective is to allow students to incorporate computer technologies in their design process, their focus is still mainly instrumental. In fact, in none of these subjects the development of a design project with the use of different technologies in an integrated way is carried on, like in the IST case. Each CAD subject at UNICAMP concentrates on a specific computer topic (e.g. rapid prototyping, animation, generative systems, etc.) and small projects are carried on in each subject more with the objective of fixing specific concepts than with the objective of showing the use of technologies in an integrated way. In other words, students are left with the responsibility of putting the parts together. Thus, this curriculum is closer to the second case described by Mark, Martens & Oxman (2005), because it includes more CAD courses but CAD topics are less intertwined into design content as a whole.

However, the most remarkable feature of both cases is that the computer is not seen as a mere representational device, but as a potentially conceptual tool and so all the effort in setting up both curricula was placed on enabling such use of the computer, first by gradually building students' skills and then approaching design problems using different media, including computers.

Another difference between the two cases lies on the strategies used to integrate the computer courses. The process of integrating the courses was dynamic and, in fact, one may distinguish three different moments in the process of integration: (1) before the interventions described in this chapter; (2) after such interventions, when the delineated strategies were put in place, and (3) a few years on. When the IST program was created in 1998, there were two computer courses and the strategy initiated in 2000 was to change their contents and add a studio course. The peak of this strategy was reached in 2004 when students in the revised curriculum reached the fifth year and took the studio. Then the process backlashed under the pressure of traditionally oriented instructors who did not accept that the computer could be more than a representational tool, and the studio was taken out of the curricula. In the IST case, computer courses were first introduced in the undergraduate program and only later were they introduced in graduate programs, mainly because this was the order in which these were created at the school. When the Unicamp program was created in 1999, there were already five mandatory computer courses. The strategy was the opposite from IST, as changes in the curricula were first implemented at the graduate level by setting up classes in which the computer was used as conceptual tool, a process initiated in 2002. By linking the work in such classes to ongoing research, namely theses, it was possible to demonstrate the potential of the computer to go beyond representation capabilities. Then such changes were introduced at the undergraduate

level in a gradual manner, driven by demand of students and then instructors. Currently, there are five computer oriented mandatory courses and five electives courses at the undergraduate level but computer topics have permeated other courses as well.

Such differentiated strategies were crucial to the difference in outcomes. The IST curriculum led to noticeable results faster (publications, design and scientific awards, etc.) but was rejected by traditional teaching staff who pushed the beginning courses to intermediate years and cancelled the advanced course, whereas in the Unicamp case the opposite is true. The argument laid in this chapter is that the success of the integration of computers in architectural education depends not so much on the number of courses, but on how computers are used and how they are introduced into the curricula following a process in which cultural and organizational aspects are, at least, as important as technical ones.

THEORETICAL FRAMEWORK

In setting up the new curricula, five theoretical references were taken into account. Almost two decades ago, Akin (1989) identified two different viewpoints regarding the role of computers in architecture. One, supported by early computer enthusiasts and pioneers, argued that the computer would eventually replace the architect. The other viewpoint, hold by more conservative designers, defended that it could merely add to existing design capabilities. Akin, however, was in favor of a third view, which considered that new technology "continues to change the way we design, rather than to merely augment or replace human designers" (p.301). The belief in this view was the starting point for the design of the new curricula described in this chapter. The work of early pioneers who used the computer in the design of buildings with success made evident that turning the back to the new technologies was not the solution. As a result, some schools introduced CAD courses in their programs, but usually only in the last years of their curricula. The computer was then used as a drafting tool in the last stages of the design process to produce accurate or presentation drawings. Only when the goal shifted into giving students the opportunity to use the computer as a conception tool, rather than a mere representation device, was it considered desirable to include CAD education in the early years of formation.

The second reference was Schon's theory of the reflective practitioner. (Schon 1987; Schon & Wigging, 1992) In his texts, Schon puts forth an approach for educating competent professionals so that they are able to tackle complex and unforeseen problems in their practice. He describes designing as a conversation with the materials of a design situation. Working in some visual medium - drawing, in the experiments reported in the texts - the designer sees what is 'there' in some representation of a site, draws in relation to it, and sees what has been drawn, thereby informing further designing. In this see-move-see cycle, the designer not only visually registers information but also constructs its meaning, that is, identifies patterns and assigns meanings to them. Schon elaborates on the conditions that enable this cycle to work effectively, and thus draws some recommendations for design education and for the development of computer environments. In Schon's approach, to be able to construct visual representations of a design context is a key element of an effective designing process. Accordingly, hand drawing is an essential skill in traditional design education. The goal in setting up the CAD curricula was to promote the kind of process described by Schon, but with computer-based media.

The third references was Mitchell and Mc-Cullough's (1994) diagram showing the integrated use of digital media for surveying, representing and fabricating buildings, (Figure 1, top) which showed the emerging relationships between the building, and its drawings, physical model and

digital model, and illustrated the possible translations among the various representations. The fourth reference was Mitchell's (1975) categories of models for representing design problems: Analogue, iconic, and symbolic, which we reinterpreted in a diagrammatic form similar to the first diagram. (Figure 1) The proposed extended combination of the two models is shown in Figure 2 with the computer-related courses included in the two curricula addressed in this chapter. The iconic digital model or just digital model may include geometry, textures, and lights. The symbolic digital model or computational model refers to the codification of architectural forms into a computer program. The analogue digital model or virtual model refers to the simulation of buildings in the real world as well as in imaginary worlds. A virtual model can have different degrees of simulation and its basic version may be obtained from the digital model by adding the fourth dimension (time, movement). The two curricula presented in this chapter were set up to ensure that students had the opportunity to learn and experiment with all the translations among the different representations. This meant that they had to be given access to both the capabilities found in traditional design studios and those offered by digitally-mediated design. The specific courses in which students had the first contact with the translation mechanisms involving digital media at each school are identified in the diagram.

Finally, the fifth reference was the work of Wojtowicz, Chen, Mitchell and others (Wojtowicz et al., 1992, 1993; Chen et al., 1994) on the virtual design studio. These authors describe the theoretical and the practical aspects, as well as the methods and the infrastructure required for setting up and undertaking design studios using new information and communication technologies. Over the years, other authors have approached this topic using the latest technology, but the principles and set up have remained more or less constant. For a detailed reference on their work

Figure 1. Precedent theoretical models for integrating traditional and digital media: at the top, a diagram adapted from Mitchell and McCullough (1994); and at the bottom, a diagram reinterpreting Mitchell's design problems representation models (1975).

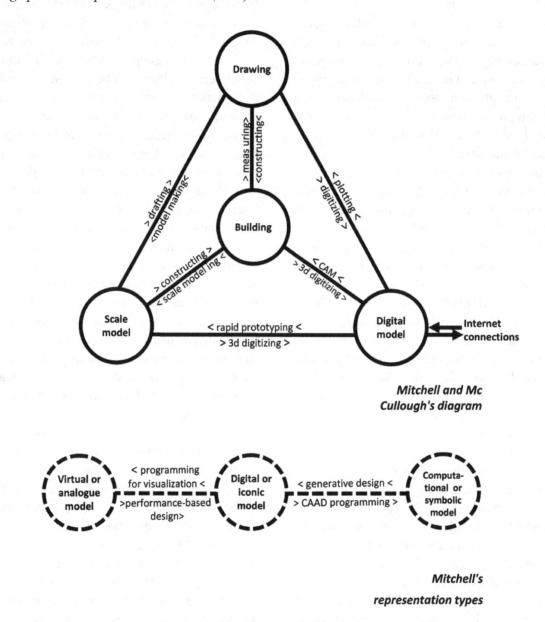

Mitchell and Mc Cullough's diagram

Mitchell's representation types

see the Cummincad archive of research papers. (http://cumincad.scix.net)

To complete the set up required for the digital and virtual design studio, the courses mentioned above needed to be complemented with a sophisticated infrastructure.

At IST, part of the infrastructure was common to the entire school, including wide network access and online course information. In fact, the school is connected to the e-U, an European-wide wireless network that links all the universities and permits anyone to login from any campus, regardless of

Figure 2. Proposed theoretical model for integrating traditional and digital media: diagrams combining and extending the diagrams in Figure 1 that show the various models and processes of conversion among them used in the design process. The diagrams also identify the courses in which such processes are addressed or utilized at IST (top) and at UNICAMP (bottom).

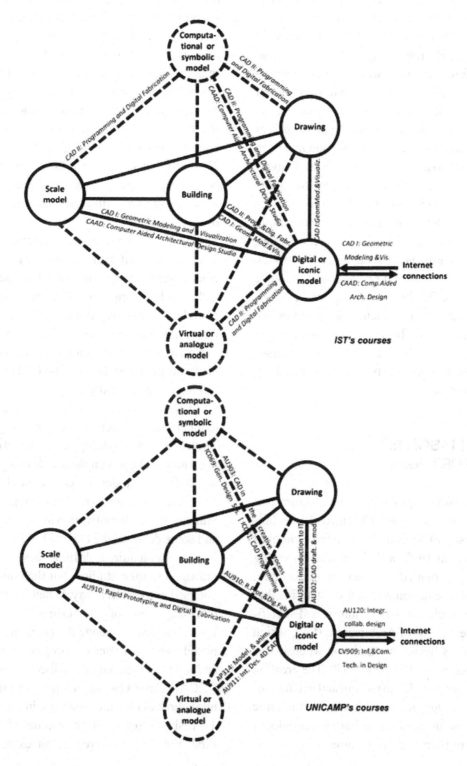

the institution of origin. In addition, the school has implemented and turned mandatory to place the contents of all courses online using a system developed locally called Phoenix. The remaining infrastructure was specific to the Program in Architecture and included advanced geometric modeling, rapid prototyping, virtual reality and video-conferencing laboratories. Their installation began in 2005, although somewhat similar facilities from other departments were used before.

At Unicamp an online teaching environment called Teleduc was created in 2001 and had been used by most courses since then, so the University had already assimilated the culture of remote collaborative environments when the changes reported in this text took place. In regards to rapid prototyping and digital fabrication technologies, a laboratory started being set up in 2007, through investments that targeted research and graduate education specifically; not undergraduate teaching. This is due to a characteristic of the public funding policies in Brazil, where research in technology is considered a priority. The courses and the labs at each of the two schools are briefly described below.

THE TU LISBON IST CASE, PORTUGAL

The undergraduate program in architecture was created at Instituto Superior Técnico, the Technical University of Lisbon (TU Lisbon) School of Engineering, in 1998, with the aim of providing a technology-oriented education in architecture. This sort of orientation was non-existent in other architectural schools in the country, and specifically at the School of Architecture (FA), which maintained its beaux arts tradition when it was incorporated in TU Lisbon in 1979. The creation of the new program led to the unusual situation of having two programs in architecture at the same university but the goal was to have a technology-oriented program and an art-oriented one. The

new program was initially set up as a five-year professional degree to guarantee accreditation by the architectural association. Courses were organized into five categories: Basic sciences, design support systems, building technology, history and theory, and architectural design. When the program was set up, it included only two computer-related courses: Computer Programming and CAD. The first was a required course in all the degrees offered by the school, and it consisted of a C language programming class. The second course consisted mainly of an AutoCAD-based 2D drafting course. In addition, there was a GIS course and computer-based surveying techniques were taught in a traditional course called *Survey of Buildings*.

It did not take long for problems to emerge. The contents and exercises of the programming course were the same across all the degrees and had no architectural content. Architecture students complained that they did not perceive how programming skills could be applied in designing and they saw no point in taking the class. As a result, many dropped and failed. The CAD course was offered in the second year.

In this course, AutoCAD was taught in the manner used to teach civil engineering students. The teaching methodology consisted of enumerating AutoCAD commands and showing how they worked. Then students were given 2D drawings and were asked to copy them using AutoCAD. Students saw little motivation in copying drawings and some dropped the class. Those who finished it used the acquired skills to develop accurate drawings in their studios, but the computer was not used in a creative way. When it became clear that things were not going in the desired direction, it was decided to change the curricula. This happened two years after the program was initiated and led to the strategy described herein.

CAD classes had been introduced in architectural curricula for the first time in the country at TU Lisbon's School of Architecture (FA) in 1986. First, they were offered as an extra-curricular course to senior undergraduate students and then as a mandatory class in the last two years. As time went by, these courses tended to be offered in earlier years. So, following the idea of introducing computers early in architectural formation, drawn from the theoretical references listed above, it was decided to maintain the courses in early years but to reformulate them, first by swapping their contents, so that students learnt first how to draw with the computer and then how to program. The idea was to use a scripting language of an existing CAD package in the programming course so that exercises could have architectural content. Finally, a computer-based studio was created in the last year to take full advantage of the computer and architectural skills that students had learnt in previous years. The resulting courses, CAD I, CAD II, and CAAD are described below, followed by a description of the labs that were created to support them.

The IST program accepted 50 students each year, divided into two cohorts of approximately equal number. This means that CAD I and II had between 25 and 30 students, including those who failed these courses in previous years. The CAAD Studio was offered as an alternative to a traditional design studio, which permitted that the number of students taking the course could vary between 8 and 24 students each year, depending on the specific content of the course and students' interest. For instance, when the course was offered as a remote collaborative design studio, the maximum number of accepted students was just 12.

CAD I: Geometric Modeling and Visualization, 1st Semester, (4h x 14 Weeks)

This course is the first in the series of three devised for the new undergraduate Program in Architecture at IST with the intention of proving students with state of art designing and representation skills. It introduces the fundamentals of geometric modeling and visualization techniques while presenting

students with the most common hardware and software solutions. In the proposed approach, the computer is not understood as a mere electronic version of traditional drafting media, but as a tool that creates new opportunities to architectural and urban design. Students are asked to select a building, to construct its virtual model and then to manipulate it creatively for analyzing and describing its architectural qualities. The goal is to teach students about architectural qualities and in doing so get them to learn how to model with the computer.

Students can work in teams of two and work proceeds through a series of 5 small exercises that build up to a final project: 2D and 3D modeling, image processing, realistic rendering and web design. In previous years, students selected buildings from World famous architects or local city landmarks. In the latter case, the work in the class is articulated with a research project that is being developed in collaboration with a firm, which aims at developing a 3D model of the city for research and practice purposes.

CAD II: Programming and Digital Fabrication, 2nd Semester (4h x 14 Weeks)

This course introduces the theoretical and practical fundamentals for the exploration of computational aspects of architectural form and knowledge. The basic concepts of computer programming are addressed using Autolisp, AutoCAD's scripting language. Students are expected to acquire the basic skills required for developing their own design tools. As such, students are introduced to various paradigms for encoding and computing with architectural forms – parametric design, shape grammars, genetic algorithms, and cellular automata – as well as different techniques for producing them through rapid prototyping – cutting, additive, and subtractive processes. Students are asked to select a class of forms and encode them into a computer program.

Like in CAD I, students can work in teams of two and work proceeds through a series of 5 small exercises that build up to a final project: Batch, parametric and rule-based programs, web design, and rapid prototyping. In previous years, students work addressed both historical themes, for instance a program for generating Romanesque churches (Figure 3), and contemporary themes, for instance, a program for generating twisted towers and decomposing them into discrete parts for fabrication.

CAAD: Computer Aided Architectural Design Studio, 9th and 10th Semesters (2 x 4h x 14 Weeks)

This course integrates the skills acquired in the previous two courses while introducing new tools, such as advanced geometric modeling, rapid prototyping, virtual reality, remote collaboration and structural analysis. It aims at exploring the use of advanced computer-aided design and production techniques to address complex problems and de-velop innovative solutions in collaboration with the industry. It may have the format of a remote collaborative design studio open to senior students in Architecture and Engineering of at least two universities, and the specific topic varies each year. For instance in one academic year, the problem was to design a technology-oriented cultural centre that included non-regular double-curved surfaces made of ceramic elements. In another year, it aimed at conceiving innovative ceramic roof coverings. For detailed accounts of these studios see Duarte, Caldas & Rocha (2004) and Caldas & Duarte (2005), respectively.

More recently, the studio addressed the customization of mass housing. This studio built on previous research aimed at devising a methodology for designing housing systems. (Duarte 2005; Benrós & Duarte 2009) This methodology encompasses a design system, a building system, and a computer system. The design system encodes the rules for generating solutions tailored to specific design contexts. It determines the formal structure and the functional organization of the house. The building

Figure 3. CAD II: Programming and fabrication. Program for generating Romanesque churches (Ricardo Mesquita, 2003/04): from the digital model to the 3d physical model produced by FDM.

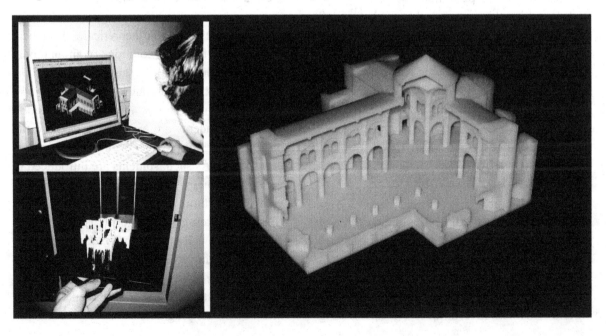

system specifies how to construct such solutions in accordance with a particular technology that is suitable for the context. Finally, the computer system enables the easy exploration of solutions and the automatic generation of information for fabricating and building the houses. It was the first time that this methodology was used in its full extent. In the CAD II class, students had already developed programs for exploring solutions for housing design systems conceived by other students in a more traditional way. However, in the CAAD Studio the conceptual and temporal separation between conceiving the design system and developing the program were blurred, and students conceived the design system by developing a computer program (Figure 4). This was exactly the sort of approach that was sought when these classes were devised. Computer-based media has become a way of stimulating creative design thinking and engaging students in a reflective practice as proposed by Schon.

Regardless the specific themes, the key ideas in the studio are to use advanced media both for designing and exploring solutions at the conceptual design stage and for producing the information needed to build them at the construction

Figure 4. CAAD: Computer Aided Architectural Design. Design system for customized housing conceived by programming it in Autolisp. (Luís Rasteiro, Joana Pimenta, and Pedro Barroso 2005/06). Explanation of how rules are applied in the generation a solution, partial universe of design solutions, view of a street generated using the program, and FDM models of solutions.

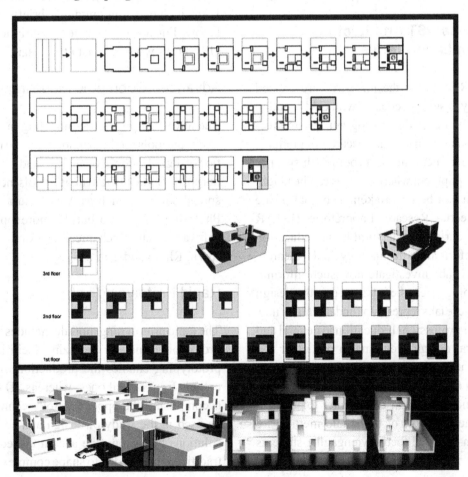

Figure 5. ISTAR, IST Architecture Research Laboratories: Views of the advanced geometric modeling, rapid prototyping, remote collaboration, and virtual reality facilities included in the computational architecture laboratory

detailing stage. In addition, students are asked to develop the protocols required for geographically distributed, multidisciplinary design teams to operate effectively. In short, students are expected to operate within the context of a virtual design studio. Students are arranged in groups of up to 3 and the number and content of the exercises depend on the specific topic of the studio.

ISTAR Labs: IST Architecture Research Laboratories

The ISTAR Labs are the infrastructure created specifically to support courses with CAD content in the IST undergraduate Program in Architecture, as well as courses and research in graduate programs. Lab here means a room with specific technical equipment where courses can be taught or research can be undertaken. The goal of the IST Architecture Research Laboratories (ISTAR Labs) is to enrich architectural higher education through information technology and research. The ISTAR labs investigate how such information technologies can be integrated in the design process. These labs represent a fundamentally new strategy for professional education in general and architectural design programs in particular – a strategy that employs educational technology to build upon the established strength of the studio method, and the design community experience with it. The strengths of the studio method are its problem-oriented focus by engaging students in complex ill-defined problems that require cre-

ativity and cross-disciplinary work. The proposed strategy is to create a robust research environment and a rich online environment that complement the physical studio environment. The ISTAR Labs encompasses two main labs: The Bioclimatic Architecture Lab (LAB, after the Portuguese acronym) and the Computational Architecture Lab (LAC) (Figure 5), addressed in this chapter. LAC includes four modules briefly described below. For a more detailed description see the URL http://www.civil.ist.utl.pt/istar/.

Advanced Geometric Modeling Lab

The advanced geometric modeling module possesses the tools for the development and manipulation of digital models for analysis and visualization purposes. Some of the available tools include wide spread software such as Architectural Desktop, Photoshop, 3D Studio, but also more sophisticated software such Mechanical Desktop, Autodesk Revit, Rhino and Catia.

Rapid Prototyping Lab

The rapid prototyping module includes both rapid prototyping and 3D digitizing facilities. Rapid prototyping enables the production of physical models from digital ones, whereas 3D digitizing accomplishes the opposite. Both techniques can be used in the study of design and construction solutions that cannot be accomplished with the traditional means due to shape complexity. These solutions include new building forms for aesthetic innovation and pleasure, but also for better technical performance. The solutions rapid prototyping and 3D digitizing solutions available are those considered appropriate for a teaching environment for being cleaner, for not demanding special security measures, for possessing easy maintenance. Such solutions include: A laser cutter, a milling machine, and a vinyl cutter, all falling into the category of subtractive process, and an FDM 3D printing machine, which is an additive process. The available solutions can be complemented by more sophisticated solutions that exist in other IST laboratories.

Virtual Reality Lab

The virtual reality module enables the creation of virtual models from digital ones, with different degrees of immersion and interaction. Virtual models can be used for conveying solutions to clients, for studying the impact of large-scale architectural and urban interventions, for testing and experiment with innovative constructions techniques in a degree not allowed by physical and digital models. The big advantage of virtual reality is that the user can experience the built environment in a way that is closer to reality without actually having to build it. The lab includes a desktop solution, and a room unit. The desktop solution can be used by a single user, and it allows only a small degree of immersion and user interaction with the environment, whereas the room unit can be used by several users at once and allows a higher degree of immersion.

Remote Collaboration Lab

The remote collaboration module provides the means for enabling distance teaching, learning, and working. An important part of the work involved in the design of a building is done in collaboration. Traditionally, such a collaboration required participants to be co-located. Later, technological

evolution would then introduce synchronous and asynchronous means of communication, such as fax machines, telex, and phone. More recently, other forms of communication emerged such as e-mail, video-conferencing, and Web-based applications. The goal of this lab is to study how such new forms of communication affect and should be used for effective design collaboration. It includes several wide spread desktop solutions for videoconference through IP, and one mobile larger unit that enables both IP and ISDN communication.

THE UNICAMP CASE, BRAZIL

The Architecture and Urban Design course at the University of Campinas (Unicamp), Brazil, was created in 1999, with a curriculum that emphasized the relationship between building technology and design. In its very beginning it accomplished the need for making students proficient in the use of the computers by means of five different IT subjects throughout the six years of the program. This was considered an innovation, since most architecture courses in Brazil have only one or two CAD subjects, usually for 2D and 3D computer drafting training. However, even in this avant-garde environment, in the original curriculum CAD was seen merely as a representation tool, as in most schools in Brazil. As a result, in 2003 the course was criticized by the State Education Council, who suggested that a young, innovative pedagogical project should not give CAD a secondary role. In response to this criticism, in the past five years the CAD curriculum at Unicamp has progressively evolved, introducing new CAD-related issues, such as BIM, digital fabrication, and the use of computers in the creative process.

The Unicamp program accepts exactly 30 students each year, organized into one single cohort. Mandatory courses typically have 30 students and elective courses may vary between 10 and 20 students. Classes are held at a computer laboratory equipped with 40 desktops and/or at the rapid prototyping laboratory, LAPAC, which is described below. The present CAD curriculum at Unicamp includes four mandatory subjects, plus 5 elective courses:

AU301: Introduction to IT and Computer Graphics, 1st Semester (2h x 15 Weeks)

The objective of this subject is to level freshmen students in terms of their ability to communicate ideas properly, using digital media for visual, textual, numerical and hypertext explanations. The subject includes the introduction to graphic design and raster and vector graphic representation concepts. Students are asked to develop graphic projects about a central theme (an architectural work) with the use of image processors, desktop publishing, mind map and web design software. At the end of this class students are ready to communicate their ideas using digital media.

AU302: CAD Drafting and Modeling, 2nd Semester (4h x 15 Weeks)

In this course students are introduced to CAD systems, BIM concepts, digital geometric modeling, parametric modeling, and definition of classes of objects. They are encouraged to develop architectural models in 3D, from which they can automatically generate 2D representations. At the end of this subject students are supposed to be ready to develop their design projects tri-dimensionally. However, this subject must also prepare them for the production of traditional bi-dimensional architectural representations, such as construction documents and detailing.

AU303: CAD in the Creative Process, 3rd Semester (2h x 15 Weeks)

The objective of this subject is to introduce computational design concepts. After an introduction about the history and definitions of computer-aided design, generative strategies, such as symmetry, parameterization, randomness, substitution, hierarchical systems, recursive application of rules, performance-based and constraint-based design, and evolutionary computation are introduced. Students develop short design exercises in the computer using CAD scripts, CAD plug ins and on-line applications that implement shape grammars, fractals, parametric design, cellular automata and genetic algorithms. Programming is simply presented as a tool that allows the implementation of generative strategies, but it is not taught in this course.

AP314: Modeling and Animation, 5th Semester (4h x 15 Weeks)

This course develops students' ability to use CAD software for representation purposes. It includes 3D modeling, rendering and animation.

AU120: Integrated Collaborative Design (BIM), 10th Semester (6h x 15 Weeks)

This course is a studio in which course collaborative design instruments and environments are introduced and used to develop a design exercise. The course includes methods and organizational strategies for integrated collaborative design and design coordination. Case studies of projects developed by multidisciplinary teams, with a high level of control of activities and budget are presented. Students develop a design project in a collaborative way, using BIM software and a virtual collaborative design environment.

Elective Courses

In addition to the mandatory courses above, the school also offers five elective courses, namely *Information and Communication Technologies in Design (CV909), Rapid Prototyping and Digital*

Fabrication (AU910), *Integrated Design in 4D CAD (AU911)*, *Design Automation and CAD Programming (IC061)*, and *Generative Design Systems (IC069)*. The two last subjects are graduate subjects that can be taken by senior undergraduate students. The goal of these courses is to complement the skills acquired in the mandatory courses and enable the students to explore in a deeper way the use of new media in architecture and urban design. The programming course was once offered as an undergraduate elective, but half of the students dropped it, even though programming was introduced within an architectural context, through CAD scripting. As a graduate elective, only a few undergraduate students show interest in the subject. Some of the possible reasons for this have been discussed by Celani (2008).

Besides, digital technologies have been introduced in other subjects that are not necessarily part of the CAD curriculum. Such is the case, for example, of a subject called *Topography and Geographic Information Systems for Architecture*. This is a traditional topography course into which digital media was introduced. Besides the usual content, concepts of remote sensing, Global Positioning Systems and Geographic Information Systems are presented. The same happened in a subject called *Architectural scale models*. In 2009 rapid prototyping and digital fabrication technologies were first introduced in this course. Students developed scale models with the use of 3d-printing and laser-cutting. As a final project, they produced a collaborative sculpture made of CNC-cut parts (Figure 6).

Unfortunately, the school's limited number of faculty members in the field of computation makes it impossible to offer the electives with the desirable frequency. In order to overcome this limita-

Figure 6. Students assembling the collaborative sculpture (left) and the sculpture displayed at the School of Civil Engineering, Architecture and Urban Design

tion, extra-curricular activities related to the field, such as invited lectures and workshops, have been offered as a way to encourage students to further develop their computational design skills. Another strategy used has been the development of individual undergraduate research projects that are carried on at the digital fabrication lab. Some of these projects are described below.

LAPAC: Automation and Prototyping for Architecture and Construction Laboratory

In 2007-2008 a rapid prototyping and digital fabrication laboratory was created in the school. The goal of this lab is to provide the technological means for supporting the courses listed above. The lab includes a laser cutter, a CNC milling machine, and a 3D printing machine (Figure 7),

in addition to several modeling and simulation software. For a more detailed description of the lab see Pupo & Celani (2008), and http://www.fec.unicamp.br/~lapac/.

The use of the new machines was first introduced to senior-year students, as a new resource for producing scale models (Figure 8). The enthusiasm of the students with the new available techniques made them increase the number of physical models produced during the design process, thus contributing to the quality of the outcome. After this experience, rapid prototyping was introduced in the Architectural Models subject (4th semester), which now includes both traditional and automated fabrication techniques. Students now can use the laboratory for producing models for any architectural design studio they are taking.

Figure 7. LAPAC's rapid prototyping machines

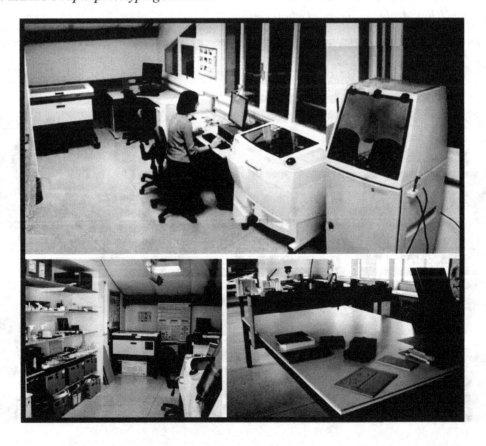

Figure 8. Scale models produced by senior-year students

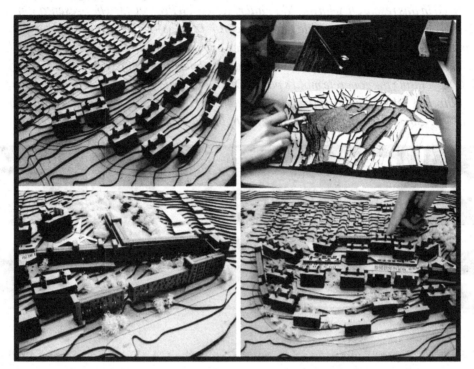

A strategy that has been used is the offering of one-year undergraduate research scholarships. This type of research consists of individual or small team projects about anything students are particularly interested in, under the advice of a professor. The only requirement to develop a research project in the digital prototyping and fabrication lab is that the student must overlap his or her personal interest with the use of the available technologies. For example, a student interested in accessibility developed tactile maps using rapid prototyping techniques; another student interested in origami conducted a research about how to make origami using the laser cutter; a student interested in historical architecture produced scale models of her favorite buildings, and so on. As a result, these students deepen their knowledge about technology and its applications in architecture (Celani, 2008).

The results are presented to other students during an annual interdisciplinary seminar at the University. On top of a cash stipend, students are given credits in their academic records as an extra incentive. Some of the research projects conducted by undergraduate students at LAPAC are shown in Figure 9.

RESULTS

When the new curriculum was devised at IST, the goal was to provide students with state of art computer technology and prompt the use of such a technology in a natural way in the design process. When the courses and labs were created the expected results were: (1) to support architectural teaching and research; (2) to investigate how computers and information technology can be integrated in the design process; (3) to create a research environment that supports creative and innovative design teaching and practice; (4) to develop new expertise oriented towards new architectural and building solutions; (5) to provide technology-oriented consulting services

Figure 9: Research Project #1: The hand-made model being 3d-scanned; Research Project #2: One of the models produced in this research, with the 3d-printer; Research Project #3: The presentation model of the campus; Research Project #4: The tactile map; Research Project #5: The wind-tunnel experiment, with the laser-cut model; Research Project #6: The dry ice experiment with the 3d-printed model; Research Project #7: The laser-cut scale model of the wind reactor-generated shape (Eduardo Corradi); Research Project #8: CNC-cutting the concrete mold's parts (Danilo Higa da Rocha); Research Project #9: A scale model of a sculpture, 3d-printed from the 3d-scanned file (Laura Cancherini); Research Project #10: A screenshot of Photomodeler software showing the digitations of a capital (Luciana Iódice).

to the AEC industry. These results were achieved to a certain extent. The technology was successfully integrated in the architecture program and use of the skills that students acquired in the described courses extended to other courses. The courses and the labs have served as the basis for developing several master and doctorate theses. The work of students has led to innovative and creative approaches with recognized results. For instance, one student won the FEIDAD Award in 2005 and another got the Best Paper Award at the 2007 CAAD Futures conference. In addition, several patents were obtained, some of which have yielded new products for the construction industry that are now being commercialized. This, in turn, has prompted the industry to take the initiative to commission new projects. Finally, the courses and the labs contributed for increasing the students' employability, particularly by firms known for their technology-oriented approaches. Interestingly enough, students' good results in the technology-oriented realm did not collide with their design skills, as they also obtained significant results at this level. In fact, both the students who

took the CAAD studio and those who took the alternative traditional studio got awards in design competitions over the years.

However, despite the good results, the strategy followed at IST back-lashed. The preeminence of the computer-based classes, particularly among students, led instructors who were in favor of a traditional approach to fight against computer-oriented classes. The argument was that before students learnt how to use the computer before, they should learn how to draw, and that free-hand drawing skills were essential to architectural design thinking. Our argument was that students should learn free-hand and computer drawing in parallel so that they could become proficient in both techniques and use them naturally in the design process. We believed that computer-based means of representation could support design thinking in a way similar to that of hand drawing. Traditionally oriented instructors outnumbered technology-oriented ones and the result was they voted to move computer classes to later years of the program in architecture. At the end of this power struggle, the computer-based classes were reduced to only two, with the first being offered only in the 5th semester (third year). The CAAD studio first became an elective course and then it was cancelled. The GIS course also was cancelled.

This outcome is not so surprising if we consider that, according to literature in management, (Beamish, 2008) to successfully introduce any new technology into an existing organization, one must conquer the support of the organization's members. No technology can be successfully introduced without such a support. Cultural and organizational aspects play a role in the process that is as important as those of technological aspects. Despite the fact that the new program in architecture was created inside an engineering school with the goal of enabling a technology-oriented formation, the prevalent culture of the community of architecture instructors had a different orientation. Obviously, the sheer struggle for power also influenced the course of events. Instructors with no background in technology and specifically in computers saw the raise of computer technology as a threat to their position and their interests and so acted accordingly.

One possible way of avoiding this negative reaction that has been followed in recent years is to team up technology-oriented instructors with traditionally oriented ones. When both become responsible for the success of a class, particularly a studio, they have no option than putting their differences aside and work together. In addition, while one concentrates on the successful teaching and use of the technology, the other can make sure that design aspects are not overlooked and neglected. Obviously, this strategy depends on the willingness of the two instructors to work together in first place, but this is something that head of the program is in good position to overcome.

At the time these events were taking place, a graduate student from Unicamp was spending a period of study at TU Lisbon as part of her Ph.D. studies on prototyping and fabrication technologies. She was interested in how such technologies could be introduced in the curriculum at Unicamp,

who was in the process of implementing its own laboratory to strengthen the role of technology. As a result, digital fabrication technology was implemented into mandatory and elective subjects at Unicamp. There the strategy was first to make digital fabrication technologies available to students outside the formal curricula and then led students to transport these technologies into the formal courses and use this as drive to change the existing courses and create new ones.

At Unicamp the curriculum changes were based on the assumption that the introduction of computational design theories and techniques would naturally result in the use of new technologies in the design process and in the increase of design creativity. With the introduction of rapid prototyping techniques students started to give more importance to physical models in the creative process, which was a great contribution to their design outcomes. The number and quality of scale models was increased, along with the quality of the designs. However, the use of IT still remained restricted to representation issues for most students, even in students who had taken CAD programming and generative design elective subjects.

One possible reason for this is the fact that all the new subjects have been introduced as complements to the course's main core, which is still formed by traditional architectural design studios, as in most schools. In these studios instructors usually teach design in the same way they are used to work in their professional practices, which does not include the use of state-of-the-art design computing techniques. This has shown us that changing the school's design culture is as important as creating laboratories and introducing new subjects.

A strategy that has been adopted to overcome this limitation is offering workshops to the faculty and creating discussion forums about the use of the new techniques in the creative process. Another possibility would be to introduce CAD programming and generative design techniques earlier in the curriculum, as mandatory subjects linked to a design studio as done at IST.

DISCUSSION AND CONCLUSION

In her paper "Theory and design in the first digital age" Rivka Oxman (2006) proposed a theory of digital design that tried to map the different levels of interaction of the user with digital media and integration of the computer into design. Oxman identified four components of digital design - representation, generation, evaluation, and performance - and four types of interaction with increasing levels of integration - interaction with non-digital representations, interaction with digital constructs (e.g. a CAD model), interaction with a digital representation generated by a mechanism (e.g. a rule-based generated CAD model), interaction with a digital environment (e.g. interaction with the coded rules that generate the CAD model). Then she identified eight main models of design, being the first, the paper model, in which the user interacts only with non-digital representations. In the second model, called CAD descriptive model, s/he interacts with a CAD model, an explicit representation of a particular form. In the third, the generation evaluation model, the designer also makes use of analytical simulation techniques that are predictive models of design. In the fourth, called formation model, s/he interacts with dynamic representations for form generation such as in parametric design and scripting, rather than with its explicit representation. In the fifth, the generative model, s/he interacts with more complex mechanisms of form generation like shape grammars. The difference between formation and generative models are basically in the level of knowledge embedded in the process used to generate architectural form. The sixth and seventh are performance models, in which the formation and generative mechanisms are coupled with performance-driven techniques, so that the form is the result of the manipulation of these mechanisms to obtain a form with a specified performance. The eighth is a compound model that combines all the other models.

According to this theory, the TU Lisbon IST and Unicamp cases represent two different approaches for integrating digital technologies in architectural curricula. They both aimed at achieving the compound model identified by Oxman but they followed two radically different strategies.

In the IST case, the strategy was to introduce digital technologies early in the formation process at the undergraduate level, starting with the CAD descriptive model (CAD I), then the generation evaluation and the formation models (CAD II), and finally the generative and performance-based models (CAAD). In the latter case, not all the models were explored at once in the same course every year because it was not feasible in just one course, but the idea was to explore some of these models every year so as to form students with varied skills over time. The implementation process was top down, with the few mandatory courses being forced into the curriculum. It permitted to achieve noticeable results faster (awards, etc.) but it caused a negative reaction on the behalf of traditional teaching staff. At the end the computer-related classes were pushed back to latter years of the curricula.

In the Unicamp case, the original curriculum, created in 1999, was similar to Martens & Oxman's second curriculum, because there were many computer courses, but they were not integrated in the design curriculum. When the digital fabrication laboratory was created, the strategy was to introduce digital technologies at the graduate level and then to permeate gradually the undergraduate design curricula. This was accomplished by offering workshops to undergraduate students outside the curricula who then transported these techniques to the design studio. Eventually there was also a demand for the creation of separate courses on these topics, mainly because the design teaching staff did not possess the required skills. The implementation process was bottom-up, with several mandatory courses being added gradually to the curriculum. It avoided a negative reaction but took longer to achieve visible results. At the end more courses on computer topics are offered at Unicamp then at the beginning at IST.

The Unicamp case shows that Martens & Oxman's ideal introduction of computer technologies within the design curriculum is not always possible, because it requires design instructors who are ready for this type of approach. In certain cases the introduction of digital fabrication facilities along with research projects, workshops and elective courses may be more efficient because it allows the students themselves to carrying the new contents to the design studio.

Both the experiences at UTL and Unicamp have shown that it is important to introduce CAD subjects as early as possible in the architectural curriculum. This includes not only representation skills, but also fabrication and generative knowledge. Adding computational design subjects in the curriculum and creating rapid prototyping and digital fabrication laboratories is important. However, the greatest challenge to the real revolution in CAD curriculum is changing the design culture in the school. This has been true for the two programs described herein, despite of all their differences.

In the seminal paper "The theoretical foundations of Computer-aided Architectural Design", Mitchell (1975) proposed different levels for the "division of tasks between human designer and machine". According to him, the "least ambitious level of use of the machine is to allocate to it only tasks of representation", which is followed by "the task of evaluating solutions produced for consideration by the human designer". Unfortunately, in most of the architectural curricula these are the only functions given to the computer.

The automated generation of design alternatives by means of computer programming (not just by the use of black-box software!), even if just for small, well-defined, design problems, represents a far more ambitious pedagogical use

of the machine, and thus should also be included in the architectural curriculum. To be able to develop this type of application, students must learn alternative ways of representing design problems – not just the graphic ones – since computers operate with symbolic representations. It is important to introduce these skills early in the curriculum, so students can get used to them and start developing their own algorithms. In the beginning of their education they may use these skills just to automate repetitive procedures, and as they become more experienced in design they can start using them for design exploration. In theory, the capacity to automatically generate a great number of alternatives may contribute to the discovery of novelty and the increase of creativity.

This proposal may look contradictory to Schon's theories about the importance of visualizing and manipulating shapes for reflecting on design problems. However, graphic diagrams play a fundamental role in the definition of symbolic representations, allowing one to establish parametric relationships. Besides, nowadays graphic representations can be used even for developing computer programs. "Visual programming" environments, such as Grasshopper, bring symbolic representations closer to the architect's way of thinking.

Still according to Mitchell (1975), "The most ambitious potential level of use of the machine is to attempt to develop systems capable of dealing intelligently and flexibly with ill-defined problems; that is of displaying the capabilities characteristic of a good human designer." (p. 149) In order to develop this kind of skill in architecture students, it would be interesting to encourage interdisciplinary work with computer sciences and engineering students.

In summary, we have described two approaches to introducing new technologies in architectural curricula, each with its own pros and cons. It is hard to say which is better as the success of the approach depends on the specific culture of the institution and its social and technical environment, as well as on the ability of the "technology promoter"—the person or people in charge of leading the process and teaching the computer-oriented classes—to undertake extensive, sometimes painful, negotiations. If one has the social skills and the willingness to undertake such negotiations, one might be able to avoid the type of backlash described in the IST case and, therefore, one might be better off following a similar approach as it leads to visible results faster. Otherwise, it might be wiser to follow the approach described in the Unicamp case and let students and time get there.

In conclusion, the introduction of technologies in an integrated way in any architectural curriculum has to take into account the school's traditions and the faculty's beliefs. Different paths, sometimes not so direct, may be necessary in each case. The whole enterprise needs to have the participation of the entire community, so that new technologies can be really integrated in the architectural education and not seen as an interference, a threat, or a luxury, whether in specific CAD subjects or within the design studio.

More information on the courses and the labs can be found at http://www.civil.ist.utl.pt/~dac/ and www.fec.unicamp.br/~lapac.

ACKNOWLEDGMENT

The authors thank the students, the teaching assistants, and the colleagues who participated in the classes and labs described in this chapter for their enthusiasm, commitment, and hard work. The work described in this paper, and particularly the collaboration between the two labs was supported by FAPESP and CAPES in Brazil, and FCT in Portugal.

REFERENCES

Akin, O. (1990). Computational design instruction: Towards a pedagogy. In Mitchell, W. J., & Purcell, P. (Eds.), *The electronic design studio* (pp. 302–316). Cambridge, MA: MIT Press.

Beamish, A. (2008). *Learning from work: Designing organizations for learning and communication. Stanford, CA*. Stanford: Business Books.

Benrós, D., & Duarte, J. P. (2009). An integrated system for providing mass customized housing. *Automation in Construction, 18*, 310–320. doi:10.1016/j.autcon.2008.09.006

Breen, J. (2004). Changing roles for (multi)media tools in design - Assessing developments and applications of (multi)media techniques in design education, practice and research. In B. Rudiger, B. Tournay, & H. Orbaek (Eds.), *Architecture in the Network Society, 22nd eCAADe Conference Proceedings* (pp. 530-539). Copenhagen, Denmark: Royal Danish Academy of Fine Arts.

Caldas, L. G., & Duarte, J. P. (2005). Fabricating innovative ceramic covers: re-thinking roof tiles in a contemporary context. In J. Duarte (Ed.), *23rd eCAADe Conference Proceedings* (pp. 269-276). Lisbon, Portugal: IST Press.

Celani, G. (2007). A importância da pesquisa na formação de docentes: O caso da informática. *Cadernos de Pós-graduação em Arquitetura e Urbanismo, 7*(1), 1–10.

Celani, G. (2008). Teaching CAD programming to architecture students. *Revista Gestão & Tecnologia de Projetos, 3*(2), 1–23.

Chen, N., Kvan, T., Wojtowicz, J., Van Bakergem, D., Casaus, T., Davidson, J., et al. (1994). Place, time, and the virtual design studio. In A.C.Harfmann & M.Fraser (Eds.), *Reconnecting, 14th ACADIA Conference Proceedings* (pp. 115-132). St. Louis, MO: Washington University.

Duarte, J. P. (2005). Towards the mass customization of housing: The grammar of Siza's houses at Malagueira. *Environment and Planning. B, Planning & Design, 32*(3), 347–380. doi:10.1068/b31124

Duarte, J. P., Caldas, L. G., & Rocha, J. (2004). Freeform ceramics: Design and production of complex forms with ceramic elements. In B. Rudiger, B. Tournay, & H. Orbaek (Eds.), *Architecture in the Network Society, 22nd eCAADe Conference Proceedings* (pp. 174-183). Copenhagen, Denmark: Royal Danish Academy of Fine Arts.

Mark, E., Martens, B., & Oxman, R. (2001). The ideal computer curriculum. In H. Penttila (Ed.), *Architectural Information Management, 19th eCAADe Conference Proceedings* (pp. 168-175). Helsinki, Finland: Helsinki University of Technology.

Mitchell, W. J. (1975). The theoretical foundation of computer-aided architectural design. *Environment and Planning B, 2*, 127–150. doi:10.1068/b020127

Mitchell, W. J., & McCullough, M. (1994). *Digital design media*. New York, NY: Van Nostrand Reinhold.

Oxman, R. (2006). Theory and design in the first digital age. *Design Studies, 27*, 229–265. doi:10.1016/j.destud.2005.11.002

Pupo, R. T., & Celani, G. (2008). Prototipagem Rápida e Fabricação Digital para Arquitetura e Construção: Definições e Estado da Arte no Brasil. *Cadernos de Pós Graduação em Arquitetura e Urbanismo, 8*(1), 31–41.

Schon, D. (1987). *Educating the reflective practitioner*. San Francisco, CA: Josey-Bass Publishers.

Schon, D. A., & Wigging, G. (1992). Kinds of seeing and their functions in designing. *Design Studies, 13*(2), 135–156. doi:10.1016/0142-694X(92)90268-F

Wojtowicz, J., Davidson, J. N., & Mitchell, W. J. (1992). Design as digital correspondence. In K. Kensek & D. Noble (Eds.), *Computer Supported Design in Architecture: Mission, Method, Madness, 12th ACADIA Conference Proceedings* (pp. 89-101). Charleston, SC: Clemson University.

Wojtowicz, J., Papazian, P., Fargas, J., Davidson, J. N., & Cheng, N. (1993). Asynchronous architecture. In F. Morgan & R. Pohlman (Eds.), *Education and Practice: The Critical Interface, 13th ACADIA Conference Proceedings* (pp. 107-117). College Station, TX: Texas A & M University.

KEY TERMS AND DEFINITIONS

Analogue Model: A dynamic model that simulates how design objects behave in reality from a certain viewpoint.

Architectural Curriculum: The set of ordered courses that form an undergraduate program in architecture.

Computational Model: A model that encodes the instructions for generating a certain kind of design objects.

Digital Model: An iconic model built and stored in the computer.

Iconic Model: A static model that depicts the look and feel of design objects without giving any information regarding how to generate them and how they behave.

Model: A representation of reality in a simplified, schematic, abstract way, showing just the elements that are strictly necessary to understand specific aspects of the phenomenon being studied.

Symbolic Model: A computational model encoded with a language of symbols.

Virtual Model: An interactive dynamic model that simulates how design objects behave and appear to users.

Chapter 23
Computational Methods and Technologies:
Reflections on Their Impact on Design and Education

Ning Gu
The University of Newcastle, Australia

Michael J. Ostwald
The University of Newcastle, Australia

ABSTRACT

Computational Design Methods and Technologies: Applications in CAD, CAM and CAE Education surveys five major categories of contemporary computational technologies and explores their applications in, and interactions with, design and design education. The five categories of technologies are: Generative and parametric design systems; BIM; collaborative virtual environments; virtual and augmented reality systems; and interactive and intelligent environments. This final chapter reflects on the impact of these computational design methods and technologies, using Ostwald's System-enabler Model as an underlying conceptual structure. The chapter explores changing relations between the representational, proportional, indexical, and operational systems in the design process, as well as emerging opportunities and challenges that arise from these methods and technologies. The impact of these new technologies and approaches is also discussed in the context of design education. The chapter draws together this significant body of work in order to provide a point of reference for the interpretation and critique of the new design knowledge and phenomenon encompassed in the five categories.

INTRODUCTION

By the time a person has finished reading *Computational Design Methods and Technologies: Applications in CAD, CAM and CAE Education*, they will have been immersed in the domain of computational design, observing and exploring the latest developments, methods and technologies. The 22 chapters they will have completed survey a range of technologies and explore their application in, and interactions with, design and design education. For ease of understanding, these

DOI: 10.4018/978-1-61350-180-1.ch023

contemporary computational technologies can be generally classified into five categories including generative and parametric design systems, BIM, collaborative virtual environments, virtual and augmented reality systems, and interactive and intelligent environments. However, many of these categories combine common ideas and have similar goals meaning that these five groupings may be a useful way of thinking about a complex field, but they are not necessarily definitive. Another way of considering this point is to realize that, to understand all five categories in isolation is important, but to fully appreciate their impact on design and education a broader perspective must be taken. This is, in part, the purpose of the present chapter which provides a critical reflection on the collective impact of these recent computational methods and technologies on design practice and education. Such reflection is essential for assisting readers to contextualize the knowledge presented throughout this work and to discuss the overall impact of these methods and technologies in such a way as to highlight the future challenges for the design field and their potential for transforming design practice and education.

In order to reflect on the overall impact of computational methods and technologies on design and education, the chapters revisits a variation of Ostwald's System-enabler Model (presented in Chapter 1). The System-enabler model is a conceptual way of thinking about the architectural design process from the point of view of the frameworks that support and define the design process. Importantly the model is not discipline specific; it is applicable to a wide range of fields including architectural design, engineering design, industrial design and interior design. The System-enabler Model identifies and combines four primary meta-systems that define the context of design. These four include the Representational, Proportional, Indexical and Operational Systems all of which are necessary for a design to be developed, promulgated and realized. However, in order for this to occur, the process, and each of the four systems, require various forms of practical, technical and conceptual support. By exploring the changing relations between these systems and their enablers, the model provides a consistent structure for describing and evaluating the impact of contemporary computational methods and technologies on the design process. This structure is used in the present chapter to support a process of critical reflection on the five main categories of computational design technologies presented throughout this book. However, in addition to these four original ways of viewing the design process suggested by Ostwald's System-enabler model, an additional lens is added in this chapter. This fifth way of viewing the design process is concerned with education; a necessary part of the broader design process.

THE SYSTEM-ENABLER MODEL

Traditional design models typically focus on simulating or replicating the different stages of the design process. These stages, such as conceptual design, developed design, documentation, review and reflection, have been well documented in the literature (Schön, 1983; Cross, 1997; Lawson 2005). Although these traditional models provide a sound foundation for designers and researchers to understand and reflect on the design process, they provide very limited insights into those methods, techniques and technologies that enable and support the design process. Ostwald's System-enabler Model takes a different approach that

"... is focused on the relationship between the meta-conditions of design (representation, proportion, information, operation) and the tools, devices and technologies that enable these conditions to be met. Thus, this is a framework recording the relationship between conceptual systems and practical enablers and therefore could be described as a system-enabler model of the design process."

The System-enabler model is predicated on the existence of four primary meta-systems each of which corresponds to one of the anticipated, but rarely defined, dimensions of the design process. These four systems, the Representational, Proportional, Indexical and Operational, have the following features.

- In the design process, the Representational System is the most visible manifestation of the desired outcome; that is, the architect's or engineer's sketches, drawings and models that are used to describe the building being proposed.
- The Proportional System relates the dimensional information contained in the design representation (the drawings and models) to the real world in a consistent way.
- The Indexical System assists in converting the unbuilt proposition into constructed reality by defining specific structural, tec-

tonic or material components and performance criteria.
- The final system the Operational, emerged in the mid to late 19th Century due to the increased complexity and demands of the construction process. Because of growing time and cost based risks, the operational part of the design process is now often collaboratively undertaken with construction and project managers.

In the System-enabler Model, a specific design process is considered in terms of the relations and interactions between these four systems. By characterizing and conceptually modeling typical variations of the design process throughout history, it is possible to explain how this process has evolved in the past, and predict how the development of new methods and technologies will enable future transformation. For example, the typical design process in the late 20th Century has been illustrated by Ostwald (Figure 1), showing

Figure 1. The design process in the late 20th Century interpreted using Ostwald's System-Enabler Model

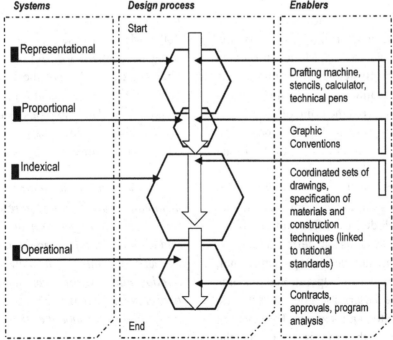

the emergence of CAD as an enabling factor. One impact of the rise of CAD has been that the traditional separation between the Representational and Proportional Systems has been gradually reduced, closing a gap that has existed since antiquity. It is also worth reiterating, when considering this stage of the System-enabler Model that, its terms, frameworks and concepts are all applicable to the majority of the design disciplines including engineering design, industrial design and interior design because it is constructed around meta-issues (Miller 1995; Dorst 1997; Cross 2000). Readers can refer to Chapter 1 for further information and a complete demonstration of the model.

THE IMPACT OF COMPUTATIONAL DESIGN METHODS AND TECHNOLOGIES

This section is divided into two parts both of which explore the changing relations and interactions between the Representational, Proportional, Indexical and Operational Systems in the design process. The first considers the emerging design opportunities and challenges that result from such changes and are enabled by these computational methods and technologies. The second section expands this analysis to examine the impact of these methods and technologies on design education.

Evolving Definitions and Boundaries

With the emergence and adoption of different enabling technologies, the traditional relationship between the critical systems or frameworks which define the design process has irrevocably changed. Four changes are identified in this section as representing the potential of various technical and methodological developments to support new design agendas and innovative practices.

A different role for the Representational System: The traditional role of the Representational System, along with its historic separation from the other meta-systems, has been challenged by computational design paradigms including shape grammars (Chapter 3) and parametric design (Chapter 4). Generative and parametric design technologies possess the capacity to represent a design, but their primary purpose is to support an algorithmic approach to encoding knowledge into the design process. This knowledge typically comprises sets of interrelated and dependent rules which support the interpretation, generation and analysis of design. Collectively these rules capture not only the end-state of the design itself (the product), but also the ways the end-state has been achieved (the process), together with other design alternatives that have been tested and rejected (the potentials). On one hand, these contemporary design mechanisms enable the dual roles of the Representational System to support both design generation and design representation. Conversely, they also enable, through rule design, the early consideration of factors that are normally considered much later as part of Indexical or Operational systems. Many design practitioners and researchers see great opportunities in this change, which suggests a heightened potential for designers to make more informed decisions. At the same time, this new power also poses clear challenges for designers, requiring them to re-examine their traditional understanding of design and the design process if they are to benefit from the use of generative and parametric design skills. Moreover, one of the greatest challenges is to use these new approaches for more than just form generation, but for considering the complete range of design values; firmness, commodity and delight.

The disappearance of the Proportional System: As suggest previously (Figure 1), the use of CAD systems in the building lifecycle has completely altered the traditional separation of the Representational, Proportional and Indexical Systems in design. In particular, it has significantly reduced the function of the Proportional System and even questioned its necessity in the design process. Although scale is still an important factor for consideration during design, CAD systems enable virtual models to be freely scalable as required. This level of freedom is further enhanced with recent developments in virtual and augmented reality systems (Chapter 12, Chapter 13 and Chapter 14), which not only significantly improve the quality of digital design representation, but also aim to seamlessly integrate the digital representation within the actual design context (in the case of augmented reality). Moreover, the disappearance of the Proportional System opens up new possibilities to connect the Representational and Indexical Systems. For augmented reality in particular, this connection infers the seamless integration between the virtual world and the physical world. However, while virtual and augmented reality systems have shown promising potential for design purposes, this has been largely limited to development and testing within laboratories and academic environments. A closer collaboration between designers and industry partners will provide a much needed platform to verify the viability of these technologies and to assist them to mature to such an extent that industry is able to use them to their full potential. Such a change will also provide a wider variety of case scenarios for better utilizing the technologies in design.

The integration of the Indexical and Operational Systems: Design is often understood as a reflective practice; a learning and exploration process where cyclic iteration is a critical component of the creative process (Schon, 1983). While designers can independently achieve the required degree of reflection to maintain a creative practice, the growing complexity of design projects and the influence of the global economy and the exigencies of international practice have, arguably, made such cases of reflection increasingly rare. Today, designers work collaboratively with people from within their own discipline along with experts from across other fields. This change has placed issues of teamwork, negotiation and shared ownership of knowledge at the forefront of the design process. As a result, collaborative design

has increasingly become a specialized research subject which is especially important for the design and building sector, as multi-disciplinary collaboration is the norm in current architecture, engineering, and construction (AEC) practice. Collaborative technologies can support design in several ways and this book introduces two important types including:

- Collaborative virtual environments (Chapter 9, Chapter 10 and Chapter 11) for supporting remote design collaboration where design activities can occur at the same time with the participants remotely located.
- BIM (Chapter 6, Chapter 7 and Chapter 8) - an advanced approach to object-oriented CAD, which extends the capability of traditional CAD systems by attributing additional building information to and defining intelligent relationships between the elements in the digital 3D model.

The communication between design and construction can also be further enhanced through digital fabrication (Chapter 5) directly from the CAD model to reduce errors and material wastage and to assist transparency and accountability. Although the full benefits and challenges of these technologies are still to be realized, collaborative virtual environments and BIM have the potential to support a better integrated building project life-cycle by connecting and even embedding the Representational System within, or alongside, Indexical and Operational Systems. In particular, if correctly used, BIM can play an important role in supporting innovation, as highlighted by Shelden (Chapter 6) and supported with selected successful industry examples:

"... (BIM) is a key technical component of this evolution in practice, encompassing newly available modeling, fabrication and communications technologies. BIM represents a key enabler of other

innovations, by creating value and incentives for rethinking aspects of conventional practice, from contractual roles and responsibilities to the format and content of project information."

Computational technologies as new design elements for built environments: Contemporary living is inseparable from computation. In his trilogy – *City of Bits* (1995), *e-topia* (1999) and *Me++* (2003) – William J. Mitchell examined the roles and impact of computational technologies on everyday life. One of Mitchell's observations is that technology is constantly transforming both human life and the environment. The emergence of such transformative technologies is arguably the most important catalyst for innovation in all domains, including design. While Mitchell has provided the vision, designers and researchers are now implementing it with respect to our traditional notions of the built environment. Rather than seeing the future of the constructed world as a more confusing array of computers and cables, we can utilize computational technologies as new design elements through which built environments will be transformed into interactive and intelligent environments (Chapter 15, Chapter 16 and Chapter 17), where the physical and the digital are blurred. In this context, the challenge for interactive and intelligent environments is how they can be used to support the design of adaptive places that can usefully respond to changing patterns of usage, new cultural values and social agendas.

The Challenges of Teaching Computational Design

This book presents many examples of state-of-the-art teaching practices using computational design, ranging from shape grammars (Chapter 3), parametric design (Chapter 4) to BIM (Chapter 7 and Chapter 8), collaborative virtual environments (Chapter 9 and Chapter 10) and virtual and augmented reality systems (Chapter 12 and Chapter 14). Each of these examples combines

insights into design, computation and pedagogy to document courses that meet the needs of the future building and construction industry. The people responsible for these examples have shared their experiences of teaching such courses and the lessons they have learnt from their students and colleagues. As emphasized in these cases, teaching computational design is much more than just teaching the students to use the tools. Besides technical tutorials, a successful computational design course requires the careful development and application of supplementary or new design theories that can best direct and utilize the particular design technologies they are focused on. Various conceptual frameworks, principles and guidelines developed by the contributing authors provide an important step towards building such a theoretical foundation for computational design and for teaching computational design. For example, the DDNET semantic system developed by Oxman (Chapter 2) provides a methodological and pedagogical basis for contemporary computational design. This overall framework is then developed in accordance with other specific principles and guidelines for different computational design topics including "slow computing" (Chapter 3), BIM curricular integration strategies (Chapter 7), constructivist learning theory (Chapter 9), game modding (Chapter 12), interactive architecture design methodology (Chapter 16), information engagement methods through interactive sonification and visualization (Chapter 17), diagram-based approach (Chapter 18), Architecturological approach (Chapter 19) and many others.

When applying new computational design methods and technologies in design curricula, it is important for academics to not only maximize the advantages of these technologies and methods to enhance the students' design and learning, but to also carefully address the new challenges that emerge from the application of these methods and technologies. These issues can range from the need for relatively high level institutional transformation (Chapter 20), to specific skill set learning (Chapter 21) and curricular implementation (Chapter 22). Among these computational design courses, some have been founded on well-understood theories and have been verified and revised over decades with different student cohorts and in different design disciplines. Others are relatively new, and have been developed and modified "on the fly", in parallel with rapid changes in technology and with theoretical developments. Nevertheless, such examples have enhanced and transformed the traditional design curricula at different levels and in their own unique ways. Ultimately, academics and institutions can refer to the experiences and reflections, as well as principles and guidelines reported in this book, to make more informed decisions in initiating and/or adopting computational design curricula that suit their own needs.

Finally, from the point of view of the System-enabler model, the pedagogical framework is one of several secondary systems, including the professional and the social, which could be incorporated into the model. Each of these additional systems is complicit in shaping the meta-processes of design development and realization. For example, the Professional System could be said to govern rights of participation; that is, the ability of a designer to be accepted into an association of peers that confers on them the right to engage in design in an authorized (or legal) way. The Pedagogical System has some similarities to the professional system in that it too plays a gatekeeper role, ensuring minimum standards and transferrable skills. But at a finer level, beyond the issues of participation and standards, the Pedagogical System has also changed over time.

In the historic familial or apprentice models of education (Chapter 1), the young designer typically learnt under the tutelage of a practicing professional. The advantage of this relationship was that practical knowledge was directly transferred and applied by successive generations of students and teachers. However this model also famously produced homogeneity of design and

effectively enshrined the same approaches to construction and materiality in the building industry for hundreds of years. Rapid developments in design thinking and practice only began to occur after the professionalization of design educators and the associated rise of research as an intrinsic part of a discipline's development. This last shift in the System-enabler model, which effectively moves the Pedagogical System from the top or start of the model, into a role which parallels the rest of the stages, is important for understanding many of the chapters about education presented in this book. In the modern world change is occurring so swiftly and comprehensively that the Pedagogical System cannot simply precede practice and it cannot be separated from research and development. The chapters on education in this volume affirm the importance of the cyclic renewal of design practice through immersion in research and appropriate teaching strategies. It is only through such approaches, and informed debate and development, that new technologies and new ideas are normalized into design thinking. It is only then, when demonstrable evidence is available for the efficacy of these ideas and devices, that the foundations are built for the next stage of development – with the rise of new enablers and the shifting role of primary and secondary systems – that support the design process.

CONCLUSION

While in one sense, this chapter represent the conclusion of *Computational Design Methods and Technologies: Applications in CAD, CAM and CAE Education*, it is also, for the new reader at least, the start of a larger journey into the world of computational design. The purpose of this chapter is not to provide a hermetic or perfect conclusion, but to create a foundation for further work and to act as a point of reference for the development and critique of new design knowledge. As exemplified in the 22 chapters in this volume, the rapid development of computational design technologies and methods has significantly impacted on design and design education beyond the simple replacement of traditional design tools with CAD, CAM and CAE systems. With the emergence and adoption of these technologies and methods, the systems that govern the design process – the Representational, Proportional, Indexical, and Operational along with the Pedagogical, Professional and Social – have been forced to change, creating opportunities for innovation, efficiency and productivity. However, such systems and enablers, are neither necessarily positive nor negative, they do not, in and of themselves, imply an astounding or ground-breaking future. Instead, the potential for these systems and enablers is in the hands of designers, educators and their clients. The real challenge is for designers to adopt these enablers, in an intelligent and considered way, and to use them for the betterment of the wider built environment and the society which inhabits it.

REFERENCES

Cross, N. (1997). Descriptive models of creative design: Application to an example. *Design Studies*, *18*(4), 427–440. doi:10.1016/S0142-694X(97)00010-0

Cross, N. (2000). *Engineering design methods: Strategies for product design*. New York, NY: Wiley.

Dorst, K. (1997). *Describing design - A comparison of paradigms*. Delft, The Netherlands: Technische Universiteit Delft.

Lawson, B. (2005). *How designers think: The design process demystified*. Burlington, MA: Elsevier.

Miller, S. F. (1995). *Design process: A primer for architectural and interior design*. New York, NY: Van Nostrand Reinhold.

Mitchell, W. S. (1995). *City of bits*. Cambridge, MA: The MIT Press.

Mitchell, W. S. (1999). *e-topia*, Cambridge, MA: The MIT Press.

Mitchell, W. S. (2003). *Me*. Cambridge, MA: The MIT Press.

Schön, D. A. (1983). *The reflective practitioner: How professional think in action*. New York, NY: Basic Books.

KEY TERM AND DEFINITION

System-Enabler Model: Developed by Prof. Michael Ostwald (in Chapter 1), the System-enabler Model offers a way of considering the design process in any discipline from the point of view of its overarching frameworks and the tools that support these frameworks. The System-enabler Model identifies four primary meta-systems in design including the Representational, Proportional, Indexical and Operational Systems. Additional systems, including the pedagogical can also be usefully incorporated into the model as the present chapter demonstrates. The four main systems are integrated and supported by a range of enabling technologies. In this chapter, the model is used to structure reflections on the impact of contemporary computational methods and technologies on design and education.

Compilation of References

(1985). Exploring Vygotskian perspectives in education. InForman, E. A., & Cazden, C. B. (Eds.), *Culture, communication, and cognition: Vygotskian perspectives*. Cambridge, UK: Cambridge University Press.

(2004). *Digital Project™*. Los Angeles, California: Gehry Technologies.

Castle, H. (Ed.). (2002). *Reflexive architecture*. London, UK: Wiley-Academy.

Fear, B. (Ed.). (2001). *Architecture and animation*. London, UK: Wiley-Academy.

3DWorld Editors. (2007). Imagina20. *3dWorld, 1*. Achten, H., & Turksma, A. (1999, 8-10 April). *Virtual reality in early design: The design studio experiences*. Paper presented at the AVOCAAD Second International Conference, Brussels (Belgium).

Abbott, J., & Ryan, T. (1999). *Constructing knowledge, reconstruction schooling*.

Abowd, G. D., & Mynatt, E. D. (2000). Charring past, present, and future research in ubiquitous computing. *ACM Transactions on Computer-Human Interaction, 7*(1), 29–58. doi:10.1145/344949.344988

Acedo, C., & Ferrer, F., & Pa mies, J. (2009). Inclusive education: Open debates and the road ahead. *Prospects, 39*, 227–238. doi:10.1007/s11125-009-9129-7

Addington, M., & Schodek, D. (2005). *Smart materials and technologies for the architecture and design professions*. Architectural Press.

AIA. (2007). *Integrated project delivery: A guide, version 1*. AIA National / AIA California Counsel.

AIA. (2008). Contract document [Building information modeling protocol exhibit.]. *E (Norwalk, Conn.)*, 202.

Aipperspach, R., & Hooker, B. (2009). The heterogeneous home. *Interaction, 16*(1). doi:10.1145/1456202.1456211

Aish, R., & Woodbury, R. (2005). Multi-level interaction in parametric design. In *Smart Graphics*, 151-162. http://dx.doi.org/10.1007/11536482_13.

Akin, O. (2001). Variants in design cognition. In C. Eastman, W. Newstetter & M. McCracken (Eds.), *Design knowing and learning: Cognition in design education* (pp. 105-124). Elsevier Science.

Akin, O. (1990). Computational design instruction: Towards a pedagogy. In Mitchell, W. J., & Purcell, P. (Eds.), *The electronic design studio* (pp. 302–316). Cambridge, MA: MIT Press.

Alberti, L. (1986). *The ten books of architecture*. New York, NY: Dover Publications.

Albertsen, N., & Lundequist, J. (Eds.). (1999). Architecturology, Nordisk Arkitekturforskning. *Nordic Journal of Architectural Research, 1*, 99. Göteborg, Författarna och Nordisk Arkitekturforsking.

Alexander, E. R. (2005). Institutional transformation and planning: from institutionalization theory to institutional design. *Planning Theory, 4*(3), 209–223. doi:10.1177/1473095205058494

Almquist, J., & Lupton, J. (2009). Affording meaning. *Design Issues, 26*(1), 3–14. doi:10.1162/desi.2010.26.1.3

Ambrose, M. A. (2006). *Plan is dead: To BIM, or not to BIM, that is the question*. Computing in Architecture / Re-Thinking the Discourse (pp. 182–189). Sharjah, United Arab Emirates: ASCAAD.

Ambrose, M. A. (2009). BIM and comprehensive design studio education. In *Proceedings of the 14th International Conference on Computer Aided Architectural Design Research in Asia* (pp. 757-760). Yunlin, Taiwan: CAADRIA.

Amonashvili, S. A. (1984). Development of the cognitive initiative of students in the first grades of elementary education. [in Russian]. *Voprosy Psihologii, 5*, 36–41.

Anderson, J. (1976). *Language, memory and thought*. Hillsdale, NJ: Erlbaum Associates.

Anderson, J. (1983). *The architecture of cognition*. Cambridge, MA: Harvard University Press.

Anderson, R. E., & Helstrup, T. (1993). Visual discovery in mind and on paper. *Memory & Cognition, 21*(3), 283–293. doi:10.3758/BF03208261

Anders, P. (2007). *Designing mixed reality: Perception, projects and practice* (pp. 276–283). Association for Computer Aided Design in Architecture.

Anders, P., & Lonsing, W. (2005). *AmbiViewer: A tool for creating architectural mixed reality* (pp. 104–113). Association for Computer Aided Design in Architecture.

ArchiForm3d. (2010). *3D rendering gallery*. Retrieved 28 March, 2010, from http://www.archiform3d.com/3d-gallery/index.php

Argyris, C., & Schon, D. A. (1978). *Organisational learning: A theory of action perspective*. Reading, MA: Addison-Wesley.

Armpriest, D., & Gulling, D. (2010). Teaching architecture technology: Shifts in subject matter and pedagogical practices from 2006 to 2009. In B. Goodwin & J. Kinnard (Eds.), *RE.building, 98th ACSA Annual Meeting* (pp. 762 - 768). Washington, DC: ACSA Press.

Australian Bureau of Statistics. (2000, 25-January). *Real time: Computers, change and schooling - A national sample study of the Information Technology skills of Australian school students*. Retrieved November 13, 2010, from http://www.abs.gov.au/ausstats/abs@.nsf/ Previousproducts/1301.0Feature%20Article182000?opendocument&tabname= Summary&prodno=1301.0&issue=2000&num=&view=

Australian Bureau of Statistics. (2010, 15-September). *1370.0 - Measures of Australia's Progress, 2010*. Retrieved November 13, 2010, from http://www.abs.gov.au/ausstats/ abs@.nsf/Lookup/by%20Subject/1370.0~2010~Chapter~Home% 20computers%20 %284.8.3%29

Autodesk. (2007). *Revit building information modeling: BIM goes to school*. Retrieved November 16, 2007, from http://students2.autodesk.com/ama/ orig/BIM_Goes_To_School.pdf

Autodesk. (2007b). *Frequently asked questions*. Retrieved October 16, 2007, from http://usa.autodesk.com/adsk/servlet/index?siteID=123112&id= 8497694#section2

Avid Team. (2010, 5-April). *The future of digidesign: An open letter to customers*. Retrieved April 5, 2010, from http://duc.digidesign.com/ showthread.php?t=270775

Azuma, R. (1997). A survey of augmented reality. *Presence (Cambridge, Mass.)*, (August): 335–385.

Baird, F., Moore, C. J., & Jagodzinski, A. P. (2000). An ethnographic study of engineering design teams at Rolls-Royce Aerospace. *Design Studies, 21*(4), 333. doi:10.1016/S0142-694X(00)00006-5

Balakrishnan, B. (2004). *Digital media & virtual reality: A multi-modal approach for architectural design representation*. MA Thesis, The Pennsylvania State University, University Park, PA, May.

Baptiste, N. (1995). Adults need to play, too. *Early Childhood Education Journal, 23*(1), 2. doi:10.1007/BF02353377

Bardram, J. E. (1997). Plans as situated action: An activity theory approach to workflow systems. In *Proceedings of ECSCW 1997*, September 7-11, Lancaster, UK, (pp. 17-24). Kluwer Academic Publishers.

Bardram, J. E. (1998). *Collaboration, coordination, and computer support: An activity theoretical approach to the design of computer supported cooperative work*. Doctoral Dissertation (PB-533), DAIMI, University of Aarhus.

Barrows, H. S. (1986). A taxonomy of problem-based learning methods. *Medical Education, 20*, 481–486. doi:10.1111/j.1365-2923.1986.tb01386.x

Bauerlein, M. (2008). Online literacy is a lesser kind. *The Chronicle Review, 55* (4), B10. Retrieved May 13, 2010, from http://proquest.umi.com.lib-proxy.mit.edu/ pqdlink?index=31&did=1564036981&SrchMode =3&sid=2&Fmt=3&VInst=PROD &VType= PQD&RQT=309&VName=PQD&TS= 1277424696&clientId=5482&aid=1

Beamish, A. (2008). *Learning from work: Designing organizations for learning and communication. Stanford, CA.* Stanford: Business Books.

Becerik-Gerber, B., & Kensek, K. (2010). Building information modeling in architecture, engineering and construction: emerging research directions and trends. *Journal of Professional Issues in Engineering Education and Practice*, 136(3), 139 – 147. American Society of Civil Engineers, 2010-7.

Bechthold, M. (2007). Teaching technology: CAD/CAM, parametric design and interactivity. In *Proceedings of eCAADe 25.*

Bedny, G., & Meister, D. (1997). *The Russian theory of activity current applications to design.* London, UK: Lawrence Erlbaum Assoc.

Beilharz, K. (2003). Designing sounds and spaces: Interdisciplinary rules & proportions in generative stochastic music and architecture. In N. Cross & E. Edmonds (Eds.), *Expertise in design - Design thinking research* (vol. 6, pp. 3-21). UTS Sydney: Creativity and Cognition Studios Press.

Belcher, D., & Johnson, B. (2008). *MxR: A physical model-based mixed reality interface for design collaboration, simulation, visualization and form generation* (pp. 464–471). Association for Computer Aided Design in Architecture.

Bellamy, T. R., Williams, A. P., Sher, W. D., Sherratt, S. M., & Gameson, R. (2005). Design communication: Issues confronting both co-located and virtual teams. *Proceedings of the Association of Researchers in Construction Management 21st Annual Conference*, London.

Benjamin, A. (2000). *Architectural philosophy.* London, UK: Athlone Press.

Benjamin, D., & Yang, S.-I. (2006). *Life size.* New York, NY: Graduate School of Architecture, Planning and Preservation of Columbia University.

Bennetts, R. (2008). Reasserting the architect's position in pursuit of sustainability. In S. Roaf & A. Bairstow (Eds.), *The Oxford Conference: A re-evaluation of education in architecture* (pp. 11-16). Southampton, UK: WIT Press.

Benros, D., & Duarte, J. (2009). An integrated system for providing mass customized housing. *Automation in Construction, 18,* 310–320. doi:10.1016/j.autcon.2008.09.006

Bergdoll, B., & Christensen, P. (2008). *Home delivery: Fabricating the modern dwelling.* New York, NY: Museum of Modern Art.

Bernstein, P., & Deamer, P. (2010). *Building (in) the future: Recasting labor in architecture.* Princeton Architectural Press.

Bertel, S., Jupp, J., Barkowsky, T., & Bilda, Z. (2006). *Constructing and understanding visuo-spatial representations in design thinking.* Design Computing and Cognition Workshop, Eindhoven, The Netherlands.

Biloria, N., Oosterhuis, K., & Aalbers, C. (2005). Design informatics. In *Smart Architecture: Integration of Digital and Building Technologies* (pp. 226–235). Savannah, GA: ACADIA.

Blender. (2010). *Blender: Features.* Retrieved 1 May, 2010, from http://www.blender.org/ features-gallery/ features/

Bobrow, E. (2009, April 23). ArchiCAD's new virtual building explorer. *AECbytes Tips and Tricks Issue, 41.* Retrieved 7 August, 2010, from http://www.aecbytes.com/ tipsandtricks/ 2009/issue41-archicad.html

Boden, M. A. (1991). *The creative mind: Myths and mechanisms.* New York, NY: Basic Books, Inc.

Bonewetsch, T., Kobel, D., Gramazio, F., & Kohler, M. (2006). *The informed wall: Applying additive digital fabrication techniques on architecture.* Synthetic Landscapes (pp. 489–495). Louisville, KY: ACADIA.

Boudon, P. (1992). *Introduction à l'architecturologie.* Paris, France: Dunod.

Boudon, P. (2005). *Fiction théorique et "théorie fiction".* Les Cahiers Thématiques, Fiction théorique (pp. 50–63). Jeanmichelplace.

Boudon, P., Deshayes, P., Pousin, F., & Schatz, F. (2000). *Enseigner la conception architecturale, cours d'architecturologie.* Paris, France: Editions de la Villette.

Boudon, P., & Pousin, F. (1988). *Figures de la conception architecturale.* Paris, France: Dunod.

Bourdieu, P., & Wacquant, L. J. D. (1992). *An invitation to reflexive sociology.* Chicago, IL: University of Chicago Press.

Bowen-James, A. (1997). Paradoxes and parables of intelligent environments. In P. Droege (Ed.), *Intelligent environments: Spatial aspects of the information revolution* (pp. 354–383). Amsterdam, The Netherlands: Elsevier.

Bransford, J., Brown, A., & Cocking, R. (Eds.). (2000). *How people learn: Brain, mind, experience and school.* Washington, DC: National Research Council.

Braswell, R., & Childress, M. D. (2006). Using massively multiplayer online role-playing games for online learning. *Distance Education, 27*(2), 187–196. doi:10.1080/01587910600789522

Breen, J. (2004). Changing roles for (multi) media tools in design - Assessing developments and applications of (multi)media techniques in design education, practice and research. In B. Rudiger, B. Tournay, & H. Orbaek (Eds.), *Architecture in the Network Society, 22nd eCAADe Conference Proceedings* (pp. 530-539). Copenhagen, Denmark: Royal Danish Academy of Fine Arts.

Brennan, S. E., & Lockridge, C. B. (2006). Computer-mediated communication: A cognitive science approach. In Brown, K. (Ed.), *ELL2, Encyclopedia of language and linguistics* (2nd ed., pp. 775–780). Oxford, UK: Elsevier Ltd.

Broadbent, G. (1969). *Design methods in architecture.* London, UK: Lund Humpries for the Architectural Association.

Brown, B., Buchanan, R., Doordan, D., & Margolin, V. (2010, Winter). Introduction. *Design Issues, 26*(1), 1–2. doi:10.1162/desi.2010.26.1.1

Brownell, B. (2006). *Transmaterial: A catalog of materials that redefine our physical environment.* New York, NY: Princeton Architectural Press.

Bruner, J. (1966). *The process of education: Towards a theory of instruction.* Cambridge, MA: Harvard University Press.

Bruner, J. (1973). *Going beyond the information given.* New York, NY: Norton.

Bruner, J. (1986). *Actual minds, possible worlds.* Cambridge, MA: Harvard University Press.

Building Design and Construction Magazine Website. (2007). *BIM adoption accelerating, owners study finds.* Retrieved November 20, 2007, from http://www.bdcnetwork.com/ bim-adoption-accelerating- owners-study-finds

Burke, A., & Tierney, T. (2007). *Network practices: New strategies in architecture and design.* New York, NY: Princeton Architectural Press.

Burrow, A., & More, G. (2005). *Architectural designers and the interactive audience.* Paper presented at the Second Australasian Conference on Interactive Entertainment.

Burry, M. (2001). *Cyberspace: The world of digital architecture.* Melbourne, Australia: Images.

Burry, M. (2003). Between intuition and process: Parametric design and rapid prototyping Architecture. In B. Kolarevic (Ed.), *Digital age: Design and manufacturing* (pp. 147–162). New York, NY: Spon Press.

Burry, M. (2010). Models, prototypes and archetypes. In M. Ostwald, P. Downton, & A. Fairley (Eds.), *Homo Faber volume 3: Modelling, identity and the post digital* (pp. 187 – 196). Melbourne, Australia: Melbourne Museum.

Burry, M. (1999). Paramorph: Anti-accident methodologies. In Perella, S. (Ed.), *Architectural design: Hypersurface architecture II* (pp. 78–83). Chichester, UK: Wiley.

Buxton, B. (2007). *Sketching user experiences.* Morgan Kaufmann.

Caldas, L. G., & Duarte, J. P. (2005). Fabricating innovative ceramic covers: re-thinking roof tiles in a contemporary context. In J. Duarte (Ed.), *23rd eCAADe Conference Proceedings* (pp. 269-276). Lisbon, Portugal: IST Press.

Calderon, C. (2009). *Interactive architecture design.* Harvard Graduate School of Design, Design and Technology series 2009-2.

Campbell, D., & Wells, M. (1994). *A critique of virtual reality in the architectural design process.* Technical Report: R-94-3. Retrieved 28 March, 2010, from http://www.hitl.washington.edu/ publications/r-94-3/

Canguilhem, G. (1975). *Etudes d'histoire et de philosophie des sciences. Concernant les vivants et la vie.* Paris, France: Vrin.

Card, S. K., Mackinlay, J. D., & Shneiderman, B. (1999). *Readings in information visualization: Using vision to think.* San Francisco, CA: Morgan Kaufmann Publishers.

Cartwright, D., & Zander, A. (1968). *Group dynamics: Research and theory.* New York, NY: Harper Collins College Div.

Casati, A., & Varzi, A. C. (1999). *Parts and places: The structures of spatial representation.* Boston, MA: MIT Press.

Cassara, S. (Ed.). (2006). *Peter Eisenman: Feints.* Milano, Italy: Skira.

Caudell, T., & Barfield, W. (2001). *Fundamentals of wearable computers and augmented reality.* New Jersey: Lawrence Erlbaum Associates.

Celani, G. (2007). A importância da pesquisa na formação de docentes: O caso da informática. *Cadernos de Pós-graduação em Arquitetura e Urbanismo, 7*(1), 1–10.

Celani, G. (2008). Teaching CAD programming to architecture students. *Revista Gestão & Tecnologia de Projetos, 3*(2), 1–23.

Celani, M. G. C. (2008). Teaching programming to architecture students. *Revista Gestão & Tecnologia de Projetos, 3*(2), 1–23.

Chandrasekaran, B., Kurup, U., & Banerjee, B. (2005). A diagrammatic reasoning architecture: Design, implementation and experiments. In *Proceedings of the AAAI Spring Symposium, Reasoning with Mental and External Diagrams: Computational Modeling and Spatial Assistance,* (pp. 108–113). Stanford University, CA.

Chandrasekaran, B., Kurup, U., Banerjee, B., Josephson, J. R., & Winkler, R. (2004). An architecture for problem solving in diagrams. In *Diagrammatic Representation and Inference: Third International Conference, Diagrams 2004,* (pp. 151-165).

Chen, I. R., & Schnabel, M. A. (2009). Retrieving lost space with tangible augmented reality. International Conference on the Association for Computer-Aided Architectural Design Research in Asia (pp. 135-142).

Chen, N., Kvan, T., Wojtowicz, J., Van Bakergem, D., Casaus, T., Davidson, J., et al. (1994). Place, time, and the virtual design studio. In A.C.Harfmann & M.Fraser (Eds.), *Reconnecting, 14th ACADIA Conference Proceedings* (pp. 115-132). St. Louis, MO: Washington University.

Chen, Y. L., & Hung, P. C. (2009). Intuitive augmented reality navigation system design- implementation by Next-Gene20 Project, *International Conference on the Association for Computer-Aided Architectural Design Research in Asia* (pp. 351-360).

Chen, Y., Fram, I., & Maver, T. W. (1998). A virtual studio environment for design integration. *Advances in Engineering Software, 29*(10), 787–800.

Chen, C.-T., & Chang, T.-W. (2006). *1:1 spatially augmented reality design environment* (pp. 487–499). The International Conferences on Design & Decision Support Systems in Architecture and Urban Planning.

Chen, Q., Grundy, J., & Hosking, J. (2003). *An E-whiteboard application to support early design-stage sketching of UML diagrams. Prodeecings of HCC.* IEEE.

Chidambaram, L., & Jones, B. (1993). Impact of communication medium and computer support on group perceptions and performance: a comparison of face-to-face and dispersed meetings. *Management Information Systems Quarterly, 17*(4), 465–491. doi:10.2307/249588

Chiu, M.-L. (2002). An organizational view of design communication in design collaboration. *Design Studies, 23*(2), 187–210. doi:10.1016/S0142-694X(01)00019-9

Choi, J. W. (2006). A technological review to develop an AR-based design supporting system. In X. Wang & M. A. Schnabel (Eds.), *Mixed reality in architecture, design and construction* (pp. 53–57). Sydney, Australia: Springer.

Choo, S. Y., Heo, K. S., Seo, J. H., & Kang, M. S. (2009). Augmented reality- effective assistance for interior design: Focus on tangible AR study. *The 27th Conference on Education in Computer Aided Architectural Design in Europe: Communicating Space(s)* (pp. 649-656). Istanbul.

Chung, D. H. J., Zhiying, S. Z., Karlekar, J., Schneider, M., & Lu, W. (2009). *Outdoor mobile augmented reality for past and future on-site architectural visualizations* (pp. 557–571). Computer Aided Architectural Design Futures.

Cichy, M. A. (2006). *Parametric design: An implementation of Bentley Systems generative components*. Unpublished M.Arch. thesis, University of Waterloo, Canada.

Clancey, W. J. (2001). Field science ethnography: Methods for systematic observation on an expedition. *Field Methods, 13*(3), 223–243. doi:10.1177/1525822X0101300301

Clark, S., & Maher, M. L. (2005). *Learning and designing in a virtual place: Investigating the role of place in a virtual design studio. Proceedings of eCAADe, 2005*. Technical University of Lisbon.

Clear, T., & Kassabova, D. (2005). Motivational patterns in virtual team collaboration. In A. Young, & D. Tolhurst (Eds.), *Proceedings of Australasian Computing Education Conference 2005, Conferences in Research and Practice in Information Technology,* Newcastle, Australia, vol. 42.

Cleland, D., & Ireland, L. (2002). *Project management: Strategic design and implementation* (4th ed.). New York, NY: McGraw-Hill.

Cole, M. (1990). Cultural psychology: A once and future discipline? In J. J. Berman (Ed.), *Cross-cultural Perspectives, Nebraska Symposium on Motivation* (vol. 37, pp279-335). Lincoln, NE: University f Nebraska Press.

Coller, B. D., & Scott, M. J. (2009). Effectiveness of using a video game to teach a course in mechanical engineering. *Computers & Education, 53*(3), 900–912. doi:10.1016/j.compedu.2009.05.012

Collins, A. (1991). Cognitive apprenticeship and instructional technology. In Idol, L., & Jones, B. F. (Eds.), *Educational values and cognitive instruction: Implications for reform* (pp. 121–138). Hillsdale, NJ: Lawrence Erlbaum.

Constructech. (2007). BIM builds its case. *Constructech Magazine, 10*(9), 25-28.

Cooke, A., & Friedman, A. (2001). Ahead of their time: The Sears Catalogue prefabricated houses. *Journal of Design History, 14*(1), 53–70. doi:10.1093/jdh/14.1.53

Council, D. (2010). *Eleven lessons: Managing design in eleven global brands: A study of the design process.* Retrieved March 22, 2010, from http://www.design-council.org.uk/

Cowdroy, R. M., & Williams, A. P. (2002). Assessing design activity: Issues and actions. *Proceedings of the 7th International Design Conference, DESIGN 2002,* Croatia.

Cox, R., & Brna, P. (1995). Supporting the use of external representations in expert problem-solving: the need for flexible learning environments. *Journal of Artificial Intelligence in Education, 6*(2).

Crilly, N. (2010). The structure of design revolutions. *Design Issues, 26*(1), 54–66. doi:10.1162/desi.2010.26.1.54

Cromarty, J. (2008a). *Draft2 text*. Retrieved 1 May, 2010, from http://julescromarty.blogspot.com/ 2008/10/draft2-text.html? zx=c8500b3429f482e7

Cromarty, J. (Producer). (2008b). *Draft2_Cromarty. mov: Machinima*. Retrieved from www.russelllowe.com/publications/ cdmt/Draft2_Cromarty.rar

Cross, N. (1997). Descriptive models of creative design: Application to an example. *Design Studies, 18*(4), 427–440.

Cross, N. (2000). *Engineering design methods: Strategies for product design*. New York, NY: Wiley.

Cross, N., Christiaans, H., & Dorst, K. (1996). Introduction: The Delft Protocols Workshop. In N. Cross, H. Christiaans, & K. Dorst (Eds.), *Analysing design activity* (pp. 1-14). John Wiley & Sons.

Cross, N. (1982). Designerly ways of knowing. *Design Studies, 3*(4), 221–227. doi:10.1016/0142-694X(82)90040-0

Cross, N. (1997). Descriptive models of creative design: Application to an example. *Design Studies, 18*(4), 427–440. doi:10.1016/S0142-694X(97)00010-0

Cross, N. (2000). *Engineering design methods: Strategies for product design*. New York, NY: Wiley.

Cross, N. (2001). Designerly ways of knowing: Design discipline versus design science. *Design Issues*, *17*(3), 49–55. doi:10.1162/074793601750357196

Cross, N., Christians, H., & Dorst, K. (Eds.). (1996). *Analysing design activity*. Chichester, UK: Wiley.

Crysuki. (2008). *Enodo new info* (formerly IMAGTP). Retrieved August 8, 2010, from http://www.incrysis.com/forums/ viewtopic.php?pid=467288

Crytek. (2010). *Crytek, MyCryENGINE*. Retrieved 8 August, 2010, from http://mycryengine.com/

CSIRO. (2008). *Wireless tracking for challenging applications*. Retrieved May 31, 2010, from http://www.csiro.au/science/ Position-Location-System.html

Cuff, D. (1991). *Architecture: The story of practice*. Cambridge, MA: MIT Press.

Cunningham, D. (1991). Assessing construction and constructing assessments: A dialogue. *Educational Technology*, *31*(5), 13–17.

Danskin, L., & Jenner, J. (2009, 21-September). *Interview with Lee Danskin and Jason Jenner, Escape Studios, London* (D. Bruton, Interviewer)

Dassault Systèmes. (2010, May 10). Retrieved from htpp://www.solidworks.com

Dave, B. D., & Danahy, J. (1998). Virtual study abroad and exchange studio. Digital design studios: Do computers make a difference? *ACADIA Conference Proceedings*, (pp. 100-115). Québec, Canada: ACADIA.

Dave, B., & Moloney, J. (2009). Augmenting time and space in design inquiries. *International Conference on the Association for Computer-Aided Architectural Design Research in Asia* (pp. 523-532).

Davey, C. (2008). *Design against crime*. Retrieved April 2010 from http://www.designagainstcrime.org/

Davidson, P. (2006). *The regular complex*. Paper presented at the NSK Wolfram Science Conference, Washington, DC. Retrieved May 10, 2010, from http://www.wolframscience.com/conference/ 2006/presentations/davidson.html

Davies, C. (2005). *The prefabricated home*. London, UK: Reaktion Books.

Davis, L., & North, D. (1970). Institutional change and American economic growth: A first step towards a theory of institutional innovation. *The Journal of Economic History*, *30*(1), 131–149.

Davydov, V. V. (1988). Problems of developmental teaching: The experience of theoretical and empirical psychological research. In *Soviet Education*, Part I: *30*(8), 15-97; *Part II: 30*, 3-38; *Part III: 30*(10), 3-77.

Davydov, V. V. (1990). *Types of generalisation in instruction: Logical and psychological problems in the structuring of school curricula*. Reston, VA: National Council of Teachers of Mathematics.

DeBono, E. (1973). *Lateral thinking: Creativity step by step*. New York, NY: Harper Colophon.

Dede, C., Salzman, M., & Loftin, R. B. (1996). The development of virtual world for learning Newtonian mechnics. In P. Brusilovsky, P. Kommers & N. Streitz (Eds.), *Multimedia, hypermedia and virtual reality* (87-106). Berlin, Germany: Springer.

Dede, C. (1995). The evolution of community support for constructionist learning: Immersion in distributed virtual worlds. *Educational Technology*, *35*(5), 46–52.

DeLuca, D., & Valacich, J. S. (2006). Virtual teams in and out of synchronicity. *Information Technology & People*, *19*(4), 323–344. doi:10.1108/09593840610718027

Dennis, A. R., & Valacich, J. S. (1999). Rethinking media richness: towards a theory of media synchronicity. *Proceedings of the 32nd Hawaii International Conference of System Sciences*.

Design, C. A. S. E. Inc. (2010). *Conceptual design modeling in Autodesk Revit Architecture*, 2010. White Paper, Autodesk.

Dewey, J. (1957). *Experience and education*. New York, NY: MacMillan.

Dewey, J. (1966). *Democracy and education*. New York, NY: Free Press.

Dias, J. M. S., Lopes, A. C., & Marcos, J. S. (2005). *Seamless indoor and outdoor location, guidance and visualization in mobile computing*. International Conference on Construction Applications of Virtual Reality.

Dickey, M. D. (2005). Three-dimensional virtual worlds and distance learning: Two case studies of active worlds as a medium for distance education. *British Journal of Educational Technology, 36*(3), 439–451. doi:10.1111/j.1467-8535.2005.00477.x

Dickey, M. D. (2007). Teaching in 3D: Pedagogical affordances and constraints of 3D virtual worlds for synchronous distance education. *Distance Education, 24*(1), 105–121. doi:10.1080/01587910303047

Dick, W., & Carey, L. (1985). *The systematic design if instruction.* Glenview, IL: Scott Foresman.

DiGiano, C., Goldman, S., & Chorost, M. (2008). *Educating learning technology designers: Guiding and inspiring creators of innovative educational tools.* New York, NY: Routledge.

Dix, A., Finlay, J., Abowd, G., & Beale, R. (1993). *Human-computer interaction Europa.* Printice Hall.

Do, E. Y.-L. (2010, April 22). *GIS 172: Visual reasoning.* Retrieved from http://code.arc.cmu.edu/visual

Do, E. Y.-L., & Gross, M. D. (2001). Thinking with diagrams in architectural design. *Artificial Intelligence Review, 15*(1-2), 135–149. doi:10.1023/A:1006661524497

Dogan, F., & Nersessian, N. (2002). Conceptual diagrams: representing ideas in design. In Hegarty, M., Meyer, B., & Narayanan, N. H. (Eds.), *Diagrammatic representation and inference* (pp. 353–355). Berlin, Germany: Springer. doi:10.1007/3-540-46037-3_37

Dokonal, W., & Hirschberg, U. (Eds.). (2003). *Digital design.* Graz, Austria: eCAADe and Graz University of Technology.

Dong, K. (2008). *BIM in education: Collaborative design studios integrating architecture, engineering, & construction.* 2008 buildingSMART alliance™ National Conference, December 8-13, 2008, presentation.

Dorst, K. (1997). *Describing design - A comparison of paradigms.* Delft, The Netherlands: Technische Universiteit Delft.

Dourish, P. (2001). *Where the actions is: The foundations of embodied interaction.* The MIT Press.

Dourish, P., & Bell, G. (2007). The infrastructure of experience and the experience of infrastructure: meaning and structure in everyday encounters with space. *Environment and Planning. B, Planning & Design, 34,* 16. doi:10.1068/b32035t

Dowhal, D. (1997). A seven – dimensional approach to graphics. *ACM Asterisk Journal of Computer Documentation, 21*(4), 26–37. doi:10.1145/270871.270875

Driver, R., Aasoko, H., Leach, J., Mortimer, E., & Scott, P. (1994). Constructing scientific knowledge in the classroom. *Educational Researcher, 23*(7), 5–12.

Drury, C. G. (1992). Methods for direct observation of performance. In Wilson, J. R., & Corlett, E. N. (Eds.), *Evaluation of human work.* London, UK: Taylor and Francis.

Duarte, J. P., Caldas, L. G., & Rocha, J. (2004). Freeform ceramics: Design and production of complex forms with ceramic elements. In B. Rudiger, B. Tournay, & H. Orbaek (Eds.), *Architecture in the Network Society, 22nd eCAADe Conference Proceedings* (pp. 174-183). Copenhagen, Denmark: Royal Danish Academy of Fine Arts.

Duarte, J. (2005). Towards the mass customization of housing: The grammar of Siza's houses at Malagueira. *Environment and Planning B, 32*(3), 347–380. doi:10.1068/b31124

Duarte, J. P. (2004). MIT-Miyagi 2002: An experiment in using grammars for remote collaboration. In Bento, J., Duarte, J. P., Heitor, M., & Mitchell, W. J. (Eds.), *Collaborative design and learning* (pp. 79–115). Westport, CT: Praeger Publishers.

Duarte, J. P. (2005). Towards the mass customization of housing: The grammar of Siza's houses at Malagueira. *Environment and Planning. B, Planning & Design, 32*(3), 347–380. doi:10.1068/b31124

Duarte, J. P. (2008). *Mass customization of housing: Models and algorithms. Unpublished Habilitation Exam, Course Report and Synthesis Lesson.* School of Architecture, Technical University of Lisbon.

Dubberly, H., Pangaro, P., et al. (2009). What is interaction? Are there different types? *ACM Interactions,* January.

Dunwoody, A. B. (2010, May 10). *APSC 151: Computer-aided engineering graphics*. Retrieved from http://courses.engineering.ubc.ca/apsc151

Durand, J. (1802–1805). *Leçons d'Architecture Partie Graphique des Cours d'Architecture*. Paris, France: Chez l'Auteur.

Durand, J. N. L. (1809). *Précis des leçons d'architecture données à l'École royale polytechnique.* Chez l'auteur.

Durkheim, E. (1973). *Emile Durkheim on morality and society*. Chicago, IL: University of Chicago Press.

Eastman, C. (2008). *BIM handbook: A guide to building information modeling for owners, managers, designers, engineers, and contractors*. Hoboken, NJ: Wiley.

Eastman, C., Teicholz, P., Sacks, R., & Liston, K. (2008). *BIM handbook: A guide to building information modeling for owners, managers, designers, engineers, and contractors* (pp. 27, 208). Hoboken, NJ: Wiley Publishing.

Eastman, C. (2004). New methods of architecture and building. In *Fabrication: Examining the Digital Practice of Architecture* (pp. 20–27). Cambridge, Canada: ACADIA & AIA Technology in Architectural Practice Knowledge Community.

Eastman, C. M. (1970). On the analysis of intuitive design processes. In Moore, G. T. (Ed.), *Emerging methods in environmental design and planning* (pp. 21–37). Cambridge, MA: The MIT Press.

Eastman, C., Teicholz, P., Sachs, R., & Liston, K. (2008). *BIM handbook: A guide to building information modeling for owners, managers, designers, engineers, and contractors*. New York, NY: John Wiley & Sons.

Emmons, P. (2006). Embodying networks: Bubble diagrams and the image of modern organicism. *The Journal of Architecture*, *11*(4), 441–461. doi:10.1080/13602360601037867

Engstrom, Y. (1987). *Learning by expanding: An activity-theoretical approach to developmental research*. Helsinki, Finland: Orienta-Konsultit.

Engstrom, Y., Miettinen, R., & Punamaki, R.-L. (1999). *Perspectives on activity theory*. Cambridge, UK: Cambridge University Press.

Enright, J. (2009). Applications in cross-curriculum teaching the synthesis of the design studio and building technology seminar. *ARCC Journal 09. Affecting Change in Architectural Education*, *6*(1), 14–22.

Epic Games Inc. (2004). *Unreal Tournament 2004, Bonus Disc: Atari.*

Epic Games Inc. (2010). *Unreal Technology: Editor*. Retrieved 29 April, 2010, from http://www.unrealtechnology.com/ features.php?ref=editor

Erhan, H., Ben Youssef, B., Sjoerdsma, M., Dill, J., Berry, B., & McCracken, J. (2008, July 27-29). Spatial thinking and communicating: A course for first-year university students. In *Proceedings of the Fifth CDEN/RCCI International Design Engineering Conference* [CD-ROM]. Halifax, Nova Scotia (Canada).

Ericsson, K. A., & Simon, H. A. (1993). *Protocol analysis: Verbal reports as data*. Cambridge, MA: The MIT Press.

Evans, G. (1996). Environmental psychology as a field within psychology. *IAAP Newsletter*, Fall.

Faimon, P., & Weigand, J. (2004). *The nature of design*. Cincinnati, OH: How Design.

Finke, R. (1993). Mental imagery and creative discovery. In Roskos-Ewoldsen, B., Intons-Petersen, M. J., & Anderson, R. (Eds.), *Imagery, creativity, and discovery* (pp. 255–285). New York, NY: North-Holland. doi:10.1016/S0166-4115(08)60145-4

Finke, R. A., & Slayton, K. (1988). Explorations of creative visual synthesis in mental imagery. *Memory & Cognition*, *16*(3), 252–257. doi:10.3758/BF03197758

Fischer, M., Stone, M., Liston, K., Kunz, J., & Singhal, V. (2002). Multi-stakeholder collaboration: The CIFE iRoom. *Proceedings of the CIB W78 Conference 2002: Distributing Knowledge in Building*, *6*(13).

Fischer, T., & Herr, C. M. (2007). The designer as tool-breaker? Probing tool use in applied generative design. In G. Yu, Q. Zhou & W. Dong (Eds.), *CAADRIA 2007: The Proceedings of The Twelfth International Conference on Computer-Aided Architectural Design Research in Asia* (pp. 381-389). Nanjing, China: School of Architecture, Southeast University and School of Architecture Nanjing University.

Fisher, D. (2008). *Dynamic architecture*. Retrieved 14 July, 2008, from http://www.dynamicarchitecture.net/home.html

Fisher, R. A. (1922). On the interpretation of χ2 from contingency tables, and the calculation of P. *Journal of the Royal Statistical Society*, *85*(1), 87–94. doi:10.2307/2340521

Fleming, M. L., & Levie, W. H. (1993). *Instructional message design: Principles from the cognitive and behavioral science*. Hillsdale, NJ: Educational Technology Publications.

Flemming, U., Coyne, S., Pithavadian, R., & Gindroz, R. (1986). *A pattern book for Shadyside: Technical report*. Department of Architecture, Carnegie-Mellon University, Pittsburgh, PA.

Flemming, U. (1987). More than the sum of parts: The grammar of Queen Anne houses. *Environment and Planning B*, *14*(3), 323–350. doi:10.1068/b140323

Flemming, U. (1990). Syntactic structures in architecture. In McCullough, M., Mitchell, W. J., & Purcell, P. (Eds.), *The electronic design studio* (pp. 31–47). Cambridge, MA: The MIT Press.

Focillon, H. (1934). *La vie des formes*. Paris, France: PUF.

Fogg, B. J. (2003). *Persuasive technology - Using computers to change what we think and do*. San Francisco, CA: Morgan Kaufmann.

Forrest, R., La Grange, A., & Yip, N.-m. (2002). Neighborhood in a high rise, high density city: Some observations on contemporary Hong Kong. *The Sociological Review*, *50*(2), 215–240. doi:10.1111/1467-954X.00364

Forum for the Future. (2008, 1-Jan). *Case study 07-08 education for engineers*. Retrieved April 6, 2010, from http://www.forumforthefuture.org/ projects/E21C-education-for-engineers

Fosnot, C. (1996). Constructivism: A psychological theory of learning. In Fosnot, C. (Ed.), *Constructivism: Theory, perspectives, and practice* (pp. 8–33). New York, NY: Teachers College Press.

Fox, M., & Kepm, M. (2009). *Interactive architecture*. Princeton Architectural Press.

Frazer, J. H. (1995). *An evolutionary architecture*. London, UK: The Architectural Association Publications.

Freeman, D. (1998). *Doing teacher research: From inquiry to understanding*. Pacific Grove, CA: Heinle & Heinle.

Fruchter, R. (2006). The FISHBOWL: Degrees of engagement in global teamwork. *Proceedings of EG-ICE*, *2006*, 241–257.

Fry, B. (2004). *Computational information design*. Massachusetts Institute of Technology.

Fry, B. (2008). *Visualizing data*. O'Reilly Media.

Fukuda, T., Kawaguchi, M., Yeo, W., & Kaga, A. (2006). Development of the environmental design tool "Tablet MR" on-site by mobile mixed reality technology. The *24th Conference on Education in Computer Aided Architectural Design in Europe: Communicating Space(s)* (pp. 84-87). Volos, Greece.

Fuller, R. B. (1979). *R. Buckminster Fuller on education*. New York, NY: University of Massachusetts Press.

Gabriel, G., & Maher, M. L. (1999). *Coding and modelling communication in architectural collaborative design*. ACADIA' 99.

Gabriel, R. (1995). *The rise of 'worse is better'*. Retrieved November 13, 2010, from http://www.jwz.org/doc/worse-is-better.html

Gabriel, G. C., & Maher, M. L. (2002). Coding and modelling communication in architectural collaborative design. *Automation in Construction*, *11*(2), 199–211. doi:10.1016/S0926-5805(00)00098-4

Gagne, R. M., Briggs, L. J., & Wager, W. W. (1988). *Principles of instructional design*. New York, NY: Holt Rinehart and Winston.

Gagnon, G., & Collay, M. (1996). *Teacher's perspectives on a constructivist learning design*. Retrieved from http://www.prainbow.com/ cld/cldp.html.

Gane, V., & Haymaker, J. (2007). Conceptual design of high-rises with parametric methods. In *Proceedings of eCAADe 25*.

Gao, S., & Kvan, T. (2004). An analysis of problem framing in multiple settings. In Gero, J. (Ed.), *Design computing and cognition* (pp. 117–134). Dordrecht, The Netherlands: Kluwer Academic Publishers.

Garcia, M. (2010). Introduction: Histories and theories of the diagrams of architecture. In Garcia, M. (Ed.), *The diagrams of architecture: AD reader* (pp. 18–45). Chichester, UK: Wiley.

GarrysMod. (2010a). *GarrysMod: About*. Retrieved 1 May, 2010, from http://www.garrysmod.com/about/

GarrysMod. (2010b). *Wiremod*. Retrieved 1 May, 2010, from http://wiki.garrysmod.com/?title=Wire_Addon

Gasper, P. (1999). Definitions of constructivism. In Audi, R. (Ed.), *Cambridge dictionary of philosophy* (2nd ed., p. 855). Cambridge, UK: Cambridge University Press.

Gattis, M. (2003). Space as bases for abstract thoughts. In Gattis, M. (Ed.), *Spatial schemas and abstract thought* (pp. 1–15). MIT Press.

Gaver, W. (1991). *Technology affordances*. Conference on Human Factors in Computer Systems CHI'91, New Orleans, ACM.

Gaver, W. W., Beaver, J., & Benford, S. (2003). Ambiguity as a resource for design. *Proceedings of the Conference on Human Factors in Computing Systems*, 5-10 April 2003, Fort Lauderdale, FL, (pp. 233-240). New York: ACM Press.

Gedenryd, H. (1998). *How designers work: Making sense of authentic cognitive activity*. Unpublished doctoral dissertation, Lund University, Sweden.

Gee, J. (2003). *What video games have to teach us about learning and literacy*. New York, NY: Palgrave MacMillan.

Gerber, E. (2007, April 28-May 3). Improvisation principles and techniques for design. In *Proceedings of the 25th ACM Conference on Human Factors in Computing Systems* (CHI 2007) (pp. 1069-1072). San Jose, CA (USA).

Germen, M., Artut, S., Ayiter, E., Balcısoy, S., & Sharir, Y. (2006). The representation and navigation of complex data. The *24th Conference on Education in Computer Aided Architectural Design in Europe: Communicating Space(s)* (pp. 406-410). Volos, Greece.

Gero, J. (1990). Design prototypes: A knowledge representation schema for design. *AI Magazine, 11*(4).

Gero, J. S. (1990). Design prototypes: A knowledge representation schema for design. *AI Magazine, 11*(4), 26–36.

Gero, J. S., & McNeill, T. (1998). An approach to the analysis of design protocols. *Design Studies, 19*, 21–61. doi:10.1016/S0142-694X(97)00015-X

Gibson, J. J. (1977). *The theory of affordances. Perceiving, acting, and knowing*. Hillsdale, NJ: Lawrence Erlbaum Associates.

Gifford, B. R., & Enyedy, N. D. (1999). Activity centered design: Towards a theoretical framework for CSCL. In *Proceedings of Computer Supported Collaborative Learning 1999*, December 12-15, Palo Alto, CA, USA, (pp. 189-196). Lawrence Erlbaum Associates.

Gindroz, R., & Robinson, R. (2004). *Urban design associates: The architectural pattern book*. New York, NY: W.W. Norton & Company.

Gips, J. (1999). *Computer implementation of shape grammars*. Paper presented at the NSF/MIT Workshop on Shape Computation, Cambridge, MA.

Gips, J. (1975). *Shape grammars and their uses: Artificial perception, shape generation and computer aesthetics*. Basel, Switzerland: Birkhaüser Verlag.

Glanville, R. (1992). CAD abusing computing. In *CAAD Instruction: The New Teaching of an Architect? eCAADe 1992 Conference Proceedings*, Barcelona, (pp. 213-224).

Glanville, R. (2007). Grounding difference. In Müller, A., & Müller, K. H. (Eds.), *An unfinished revolution? Heinz von Foerster and the Biological Computer Laboratory – BCL 1958-1976*. Vienna, Austria: Edition Echoraum.

Glasersfeld, E. v. (1983). Learning as constructive activity. *Proceedings of the 5th Annual Meeting of the North American Group of PME*. Montréal, Canada: PME-NA.

Glasersfeld, E. v. (1995). A constructivist approach to teaching. In Steffe, L., & Gale, J. (Eds.), *Constructivism in education* (pp. 3–16). Lawrence Erlbaum Associates, Inc.

Glasersfeld, E. v. (Ed.). (1987). *Learning as a constructive activity: Problems of representation in the teaching and learning of mathematics*. Hillslade, NJ: Lawrence Erlbaum.

Glasgow, J., Narayanan, N. H., & Chandrasekaran, B. (1995). *Diagrammatic reasoning: Cognitive and computational perspectives*. Menlo Park, CA: AAAI Press.

Goel, V. (1995). *Sketches of thought*. Cambridge, MA: MIT Press.

Goh, Y., McMahon, C., & Booker, J. (2005). Development and characterization of error functions in design. *Research in Engineering Design, 18*, 129–148. doi:10.1007/s00163-007-0034-x

Goldschmidt, G. (1991). The dialectics of sketching. *Creativity Research Journal, 4*(2), 123–143. doi:10.1080/10400419109534381

Goldschmidt, G. (1994). On visual design thinking: The vis kids of architecture. *Design Studies, 15*(2), 158–174. doi:10.1016/0142-694X(94)90022-1

Goldschmidt, G. (1995). The designer as a team of one. *Design Studies, 16*(2), 189–209. doi:10.1016/0142-694X(94)00009-3

Goldschmidt, G. (2003). The backtalk of self-generated sketches. *Design Issues, 19*(1), 72–88. doi:10.1162/074793603762667728

Golledge, R. G. (1992, September 21-23). Do people understand spatial concepts: The case of first-order primitives. In *Proceedings of the International Conference GIS - From Space to Territory: Theories and Methods of Spatio-Temporal Reasoning in Geographic Space* (pp. 1-21).

Golledge, R. G. (2010, May 8). *GEOG 581: Concepts for spatial thinking and GEOG 583: Spatial analysis and modeling*. Retrieved from http://college.usc.edu/ geography/ courses/graduate.html.

Golledge, R. G., & Stimson, R. J. (1997). *Spatial behaviour: A geographical perspective*. New York, NY: Guilford Press.

Goodwin, R., McGillick, P., Helsel, S., Tawa, M., Benjamin, A., & Wilson, G. (2006). *Richard Goodwin: Performance to porosity*. Victoria, Australia: Craftsman House, an imprint of Thames and Hudson.

Gramazio, F., & Kohler, M. (2008). *Digital materiality in architecture*. Lars Müller Publishers.

Graphisoft. (2010). *Graphisoft virtual building explorer for ArchiCAD*. Retrieved 1 May, 2010, from http://www. graphisoft.com/ products/virtual-building-explorer/

Greenfield, A., & Shepard, M. (2007). *Architecture and situated technologies pamphlet 1*. The Architectural League of New York.

Gropius, W. (1956). *The new architecture and the Bauhaus*. Boston, MA: Charles T. Branford Company.

Gross, M. D. (2009). Visual languages and visual thinking. In C. Grimm & J. J. L. Viola, Jr. (Eds.), *Sketch Based Interfaces and Modeling: Proceedings of the 6th Eurographics Symposium on Sketch-Based Interfaces and Modeling*, (pp. 7-11). New York, NY: ACM.

Gross, M. D. (1996). The electronic cocktail napkin: a computational environment for working with design diagrams. *Design Studies, 17*(1), 53–69. doi:10.1016/0142-694X(95)00006-D

Group, B. S. I. (2010). *BS 7000 series – Design management systems*. Retrieved April 5, 2010, from http://www. bsigroup.com/en/Standards-and-Publications/ Industry-Sectors/Manufacturing/ Design--product-specification/ BS-7000-Series--Design-Management-Systems/

Gruber, L., Gauglitz, S., Ventura, J., Zollmann, S., Huber, M., Schlegel, M., et al. (2010). The city of sights: Design, construction, and measurement of an augmented reality stage set. *International Symposium in Mixed and Augmented Reality* (pp. 157-163). Seoul, Korea.

Grudin, J. (1990). The computer reaches out: The historical continuity of interface design. *Conference on Human Factors in Computing Systems CHI'90*, Seattle, USA, ACM.

Gu, N., & Maher, M. L. (2005). Dynamic designs of 3D virtual worlds using generative design agents. *Proceedings of CAAD Futures 2005*, Dordrecht, The Netherlands: Springer.

Guba, E. (1981). Criteria for assessing the trustworthiness of naturalistic inquiries. *Education Communication and Technology Journal, 29*(2).

Guba, E., & Lincoln, Y. (1998). Competing paradigms in qualitative research. In Denzin, N., & Lincoln, Y. (Eds.), *The landscape of qualitative research*. California: Sage Publications.

Guéna, F., & Lecourtois, C. (2009). Aided architectural sketching with Markov models: Dromies and recognition. In *Proceedings of eCAADe 27*.

Gül, L. F. (2007). *Understanding collaborative design in different environments: Comparing face-to-face sketching to remote sketching and 3D virtual worlds*. Key Centre for Design Cognition and Computing. Sydney, University of Sydney. PhD.

Gül, L. F., & Maher, M. L. (2006). The impact of virtual environments on design collaboration. *24th eCAADe Conference Proceedings*, Volos, Greece. ISBN 0-9541183-5-9

Gül, L. F., Gu, N., & Maher, M. L. (2007). *Designing virtual worlds: A case study of design education in and of 3D virtual worlds*. CONNECTED 07, International Conference on Design Education, Sydney.

Gul, L., Wang, X., Tanyel, B., Bülbül, T., Çağdaş, G., & Tong, H. (2008). Global Teamwork: 2008, a study of design learning in collaborative virtual environments. In *CD Proceedings of 2008 Design Research Society Biennial Conference*.

Gül, L. F., Gu, N., & Williams, A. (2008). Virtual worlds as a constructivist learning platform: Evaluations of 3D virtual worlds on design teaching and learning. *ITCon. Special Issue Virtual and Augmented Reality in Design and Construction, 13*, 578–593.

Gül, L. F., & Maher, M. L. (2009). Co-creating external design representations: Comparing face-to-face sketching to designing in virtual environments. *CoDesign, 5*(2), 117–138. doi:10.1080/15710880902921422

Hallnäs, L., & Redström, J. (2001). Slow technology – Designing for reflection. *Personal and Ubiquitous Computing, 5*, 201–212. doi:10.1007/PL00000019

Hanson, J., & Sinclair, K. (2008). Social constructivist teaching methods in Australian universities - Reported uptake and perceived learning effects: A survey of lecturers. *Higher Education Research & Development, 27*(3), 168–186. doi:10.1080/07294360802183754

Hao Hsiu Hsu, V. (Producer). (2008). *ARCH1101 experiment 3: Animation*. Retrieved from www.russelllowe.com/publications/ cdmt/VincentHaoHsiuHsu.rar

Harel, I., & Papert, S. (1991). *Constructionism*. Norwood, NY: Ablex Publishing Corporation.

Havok. (2010). *Havok physics*. Retrieved 1 May, 2010, from http://www.havok.com/ index.php?page=havok-physics

Heath, C., & Luff, P. (1996). Convergent activities: Line control and passenger information on the London underground. In Engestrom, Y., & Middleton, D. (Eds.), *Cognition and communication at work* (pp. 96–129). Cambridge University Press.

Hedegaard, M. (1986). Instruction of evolution as a school project and the development of pupils' theoretical thinking. In M. Hildebrand-Nilshon & G. Ruckreim (Eds.), *Workshop contributions to selected aspects of applied research. Proceedings of the 1st International Congress on Activity Theory* (Vol. 3), Berlin, Germany: System Druck.

Hedegaard, M. (1987). Methodology in evaluative research on teaching and learning. In van Zuuren, F. J., Wertz, F. J., & Mook, B. (Eds.), *Advances in qualitative psychology: Themes and variations* (pp. 53–78). Lisse: Swets & Zeitlinger.

Hedegaard, M. (1990). The zone of proximal development as basis for instruction. In Moll, L. (Ed.), *Vygotsky and education: Instructional implications and applications of sociohistorical psychology* (pp. 349–371). Cambridge, UK: Cambridge University Press.

Heer, J., Viégas, F., & Wattenberg, M. (2009). Voyagers and voyeurs: Supporting asynchronous collaborative visualization. *Communications of the ACM, 52*(1), 87–97. doi:10.1145/1435417.1435439

Hein, G. E. (1991). *Constructivist learning theory*. Retrieved from http://www.exploratorium.edu/IFI/ resources/constructivistlearning.html

Heller, S., & Dooley, M. (2008). *Teaching motion design*. New York, NY: Allworth Press.

Hennessy, S., & Murphy, P. (1999). The potential for collaborative problem solving in design and technology. *International Journal of Technology and Design Education, 9*(1), 1–36. doi:10.1023/A:1008855526312

Henning, W. (2004). Everday cognition and situated learning. In Jonassen, D. (Ed.), *Handbook of research on educational communications and technology* (pp. 143–168). Mahwah, NJ: Erlbaum.

Hensel, M., & Menges, A. (Eds.). (2008). *Versatility and vicissitude: Performance in morpho-ecological design.* London, UK: Wiley-Academy.

Hensel, M., Menges, A., & Weinstock, M. (Eds.). (2004). *Emergence: Morphogenetic design strategies.* London, UK: Wiley-Academy.

Hensel, M., Menges, A., & Weinstock, M. (Eds.). (2004). *Architectural design, emergence: Morphogenic design strategies.* London, UK: Wiley.

Herbig, P., & O'Hara, B. (1994). The future of original equipment manufacturing: A matter of partnership. *Journal of Business and Industrial Marketing, 9*(3), 38–43. doi:10.1108/08858629410066854

Herr, C. M. (2008). *From form generators to automated diagrams: using cellular automata to support architectural design.* Unpublished doctoral dissertation, The University of Hong Kong, Hong Kong.

Herr, C. M., & Karakiewicz, J. (2007). Algogram: Automated diagrams for an architectural design studio. In A. Dong, A. Vande Moere, & J. Gero (Eds.), *CAAD Futures 2007: The Proceedings of The Twelfth International Conference on CAAD Futures* (pp. 167-180). Dordrecht, The Netherlands: Springer.

Herr, K., & Anderson, G. L. (2005). *The action research dissertation: A guide for students and faculty.* Thousand Oaks, CA: Sage Publications.

Herr, C. M., & Fischer, T. (2010). Digital drifting: Minimally instructive education for tool-aided creativity in Asia. *Cybernetics & Human Knowing, 17*(1-2), 37–57.

Heylighen, F. (1993). Epistemology, introduction. *Principia Cybernetica.* Retrieved from http://pespmlcl.vub.ac.be/EPISTMI.html

Hiipakka, J., Ilmonen, T., Lokki, T., Grohn, M., & Savioja, L. (2001). Implementation issues of 3D audio in a virtual room. *Proceedings of SPIE,* vol. 4297.

Hillier, B., & Hanson, J. (1984). *The social logic of space.* Cambridge, UK: Cambridge University Press. doi:10.1017/CBO9780511597237

Hill, J., Song, L., & West, R. (2009). Social learning theory and web-based learning environments: A review of research and discussion on implications. *American Journal of Distance Education, 23,* 88–103. doi:10.1080/08923640902857713

Hinwood, J. (2010a, 11 August). *Crysis image capture and concept.* http://jarrodhinwood.blogspot.com

Hinwood, J. (Producer). (2010b). *Keller and Merkel_s elevators.flv.* Retrieved from www.russelllowe.com/publications/ cdmt/Hinwood.rar

Hirtes, S. (2009, 23-September). *Interview with Sabine Hirtes at Filmakademie, Germany* (D. Bruton, Interviewer)

HKS. (2007). *HKS licenses Unreal Engine 3 for groundbreaking architectural applications.* Retrieved November, 2009, from http://www.hksinc.com/news/2007_10_HKS_Licenses_Unreal.htm

Holzer, D. (2008). Let's get physical, teaching sustainable design for performance-driven form finding. In *Proceedings of eCAADe 26.*

Hookway, B., & Perry, C. (2006). Responsive systems, appliance architectures. *Architectural Design, 76*(5), 74–79.

Hoon, M., & Kehoe, M. (2003, 24-27 October). *Enhancing architectural communication with gaming engines.* Paper presented at the ACADIA22, Connecting Crossroads of Digital Discourse, Indianapolis (Indiana).

Hornby, A. S., & Wehmeier, S. (Eds.). (2007). *Oxford advanced learner's dictionary.* New York, NY: Oxford University Press.

Hoyt, B. (2000). Techniques to manage participation and contribution of team members in virtual teams. *WebNet Journal, 2*(4), 16–20.

Huang, Y., & Ho, K.-S. (2008). *An integrated environment of representing digital antiques.* International Conference on Construction Applications of Virtual Reality.

Huitt, W. (2003). *Constructivism: Educational psychology interactive.* Valdosta, GA: Valdosta State University.

Hunter, M. (Producer). (2009). *BENV2423: Experiment 1.* Retrieved from www.russelllowe.com/publications/cdmt/MathewHunterEXP1.rar

Hurson, T. (2007). *Think better: An innovator's guide to productive thinking*. New York, NY: McGraw-Hill Professional.

Hye Bin, S. (2006). *Hye Bin Sung: DESN104 experiment 3 website*. Retrieved 1 May, 2010, from http://www.russell-lowe.com/desn104_2006t2/website_misc/student_work/hye_bin_sung_exp3_website/index.html

Ibrahim, M. M. (2007). Teaching BIM, what is missing? The challenge of integrating BIM based CAD in today's architectural curricula. *Embodying Virtual Architecture: The Third International Conference of the Arab Society for Computer Aided Architectural Design*, ASCAAD 2007, (pp. 651–660), 28-30 November 2007, Alexandria, Egypt.

ICSID. (2009). *ICSID World Design Congress, 23 - 25 November 2009, Singapore*. Retrieved November 13, 2010, from http://www.icsidcongress09.com/ phase2/permalink.asp?id=8

Intille, S. S. (2006). The goal: Smart people, not smart homes. *Proceedings of the International Conference on Smart Homes and Health Telematics*.

Iwamoto, L. (2008). *Digitally fabrications, architectural and material techniques*. New York, NY: Princeton Architectural Press.

Jansen, D. (2006). *The electronic design automation handbook*. Kluwer Academic Publishers.

Jarvenpaa, S., & Leidner, D. (1998). Communication and trust in global virtual teams. *Journal of Computer-Mediated Communication*, 3.

Jaworski, B. (1993). *Constructivism and teaching - The socio-cultural context*, v. 1.0. Retrieved from http://www.grout.demon.co.uk/ Barbara/chreods.htm

Jeng, T. 92009). Toward a ubiquitous smart space design framework, *Journal of Information Science and Engineering (JISE), 25*(3).

Jeng, T. C., Chen, J., Wang, C., Wu, P., Chung, S., & Cheng, J. ... Yang, J. (2008). House of the future relies on multimedia and wireless sensors. *SPIE Newsroom*. Retrieved from http://spie.org/x19165.xml?ArticleID=x19165

Jim, R., & Ken, S. (1996). Low vs. high-fidelity prototyping debate. *Interaction, 3*(1), 76–85. doi:10.1145/223500.223514

Johns, R., & Lowe, R. (2005). *Unreal Editor as a virtual design instrument in landscape architecture studio*. Paper presented at the Trends in Real-Time Landscape Visualization and Participation, Anhalt University of Applied Sciences.

Johnson, B. (2001). Unfocused interaction in distributed workgroups: Establishing group presence in a Web-based environment. In B. de Vries, J. van Leeuwen, & H. Achten (Eds.), *Proceedings of the International CAAD Futures Conference*, 8-11 July 2001, Eindhoven, The Netherlands, (pp. 401-414).

Johns, R., & Shaw, J. (2006). Real-time immersive design collaboration: Conceptualising, prototyping and experiencing design ideas. *Journal of Desert Research, 5*(2), 15.

Jonassen, D. H. (1999). Designing constructivist learning environments. In Reigeluth, C. M. (Ed.), *Instructional design theories and models* (pp. 215–239). Mahwah, NJ: Erlbaum Associates.

Jones, M. W. (2006). Ancient architecture and mathematics: Methodology and the Doric temple. In S. Duvernoy & O. Pedemonte (Eds.), *Nexus VI: Architecture and mathematics* (pp. 149–170). Torino, Italy: Kim Williams Books.

Jones, J. C. (1992). *Design methods*. New York, NY: Van Nostrand Reinhold.

Jordan, N., & Henderson, L. (2010). *Teaching for collaboration: Bringing our practice to our teaching. JBIM, Journal of Building Information Modeling, Spring 2010* (pp. 31–33). Houston, TX: Matrix Group Publishing, Inc.

Julesz, B. (1971). *Foundations of Cyclopean perception*. Chicago, IL: The University of Chicago Press.

Kahneman, D., & Tversky, A. (1996). On the reality of cognitive illusions. *Psychological Review, 103*(3), 582. doi:10.1037/0033-295X.103.3.582

Kalay, Y. E., & Marx, J. (2001). Architecture and the Internet: Designing places in cyberspace, reinventing the discourse. *Proceedings of the 21 Annual Conference of the ACAADA, How Digital Tools Help Bridge and Transform Research, Education and Practice in Architecture* (pp. 230-241). Buffalo, New York.

Kamps, T. (1999). *Diagram design: A constructive theory*. Berlin, Germany: Springer.

Kant, E. (2006). *Critique de la raison pure*. Flammarion. (Original work published 1781)

Kan, W. T. (2008). *Quantitative methods for studying design protocols*. Sydney: The University of Sydney.

Karakiewicz, J. (2004). City as a megastructure. In Jenks, M., & Dempsey, N. (Eds.), *Future forms for sustainable cities* (pp. 137–151). Oxford, UK: Architectural Press.

Karzel, R., & Matcha, H. (2009). Experimental design-build: Teaching parameter-based design. In *Proceedings of eCAADe 27*.

Kaur, I. (2007). *Enhancing social awareness at the workplace. Unpublished Masters of Science in Media Arts and Sciences, School of Architecture and Planning*. Boston: MIT.

Kavakli, M., & Gero, J. S. (2003). Difference between expert and novice designers: An experimental study. In Lindemann, U. (Ed.), *Human behaviour in design: Individual, teams, tools* (pp. 42–51). Berlin, Germany: Springer.

Kelly, H. (2005). *Pre-summit paper harnessing the power of games for learning*. Paper presented at the Summit on Educational Games. Retrieved from www.FAS.org

Kemmis, S., & McTaggart, R. (Eds.). (1990). *The action research reader*. Victoria, Australia: Deakin University.

Kensek, K. (2009). Sustainable parametric objects. In *AUGI | AEC Edge, Fall 2009* (pp. 31 – 35). Extension Media LLC. Retrieved July 27, 2010, from http://digitaleditiononline.com/ publication/?i=25028

Kenzari, B. (2008). Digital design and fabrication. *Proceedings of the 13th International Conference on Computer Aided Architectural Design Research in Asia* (pp. 61-67). Chiang Mai, Thailand: CAADRIA.

Kiernan, S., & Timberlake, J. (2005). *Refabricating architecture: How manufacturing methodologies are poised to transform building construction*. New York, NY: McGraw-Hill.

Kim, J. S. (2005). *Tangible user interface for CAVE based on augmented reality technique*. MS Thesis, Virginia Polytechnic Institute, Blacksburg, VA.

Kim, M. J., & Maher, M. L. (2008). The impact of tangible user interfaces on spatial cognition during collaborative design. *Design Studies*, *29*(3), 222–253. doi:10.1016/j.destud.2007.12.006

Kinayoglu, G. (2009). Using audio-augmented reality to assess the role of Soundscape in environmental perception: An experimental case study at UC Berkeley campus. The *27th Conference on Education in Computer Aided Architectural Design in Europe: Communicating Space(s)* (pp. 639-648).

Kirsh, D. (2001). Changing the rules: Architecture and the new millennium. *Convergence: The International Journal of Research into New Media Technologies*, *7*(2), 12. doi:10.1177/135485650100700210

Kirwan, B., & Ainsworth, L. K. (1992). *A guide to task analysis*. Taylor and Francis.

Knerr, D. (2004). *Suburban steel: The magnificent failure of the Lustron Corporation, 1945–1951*. Columbus, OH: The Ohio State University Press.

Knight, T. (1999). Shape grammars in education and practice: History and prospects. *International Journal of Design Computing, 2*. Retrieved from http://wwwfaculty.arch.usyd.edu.au/ kcdc/ijdc/vol02/papers/ knightFrameset.htm

Knight, T. W. (1989). Color grammars: Designing with lines and colors. *Environment and Planning. B, Planning & Design*, *16*, 417–449. doi:10.1068/b160417

Knight, T. W. (1994). Shape grammars and color grammars in design. *Environment and Planning. B, Planning & Design*, *21*, 705–735. doi:10.1068/b210705

Knight, T. W. (2003). Either/or → and. *Environment and Planning. B, Planning & Design*, *30*, 327–333. doi:10.1068/b12927

Knight, T., & Stiny, G. (2001). Classical and non-classical computation. *Architectural Research Quarterly*, *5*(4), 355–372.

Knowledge Works Foundation. (2010). *Media-rich pervasive learning*. Retrieved Augustl 19, 2011, from http://resources.knowledgeworks.org/ MAP/map/23/Media-Rich-Pervasive-Learning.aspx

Kolarevic, B. (2003). *Architecture in the digital age: Design and manufacturing*. New York, NY: Spon Press.

Kolarevic, B. (Ed.). (2003). *Architecture in the digital age*. New York, NY: Spon Press.

Kolarevic, B., & Malkaawi, A. (Eds.). (2005). *Performative architecture: Beyond instrumentality* (pp. 85–96). New York, NY: Spon Press.

Kolarevic, B., Schmitt, G. N., Hirschberg, U., Kurmann, D., & Johnson, B. (2000). An experiment in design collaboration. *Automation in Construction, 9*(1), 73–81. doi:10.1016/S0926-5805(99)00050-3

Koshnevis, B. (2004). Automated construction by contour crafting-related robotics and information technologies. *Construction and Automation, 13*(1), 1–19.

Kostof, S. (1977). The practice of architecture in the ancient world: Egypt and Greece. In S. Kostof (Ed.), *The architect: Chapters in the history of the profession* (pp. 3–27). New York, NY: Oxford University Press.

Krippendorf, K. (2008). *Design in the age of information: A report to the National Science Foundation (NSF). North Carolina State University, School of Design*. Raleigh, NC: University of Pennsylvannia.

Kronenburg, R. (2007). *Flexible architecture that responds to change*. Laurence King.

Krygiel, E. (2008). *Green BIM: Successful sustainable design with building information modeling*. Hoboken, NJ: John Wiley & Sons.

Krygiel, E., & Nies, B. (2008). *Green BIM: Successful sustainable design with building information modeling* (p. 209). Indianapolis, IN: Wiley Publishing.

Kuhn, T. S. (1996). *The structure of scientific revolutions*. Chicago, IL: University of Chicago Press.

Kuniavsky, M. (2003). *Observing the user experience: A practitioner's guide to user research*. San Francisco, CA: Morgan Kauffman.

Kurzweil, R. (2005). *The Singularity is near: When humans transcend biology*. New York, NY: Viking.

Kuutti, K. (1994). *Information Systems, cooperative work and active subjects: The activity-theoretical perspective*. Ph.D. Thesis, Research Papers Series A 23, Department of Information Processing Science, University of Oulu, Finland.

Kvan, T. (2001). The problem in studio teaching - Revisiting the pedagogy of studio teaching. *Proceedings of the 1st ACAE Conference on Architecture Education*, National University of Singapore.

Kvan, T., Mark, E., Oxman, R., & Martens, B. (2004). Ditching the dinosaur: Redefining the role of digital media in education. *International Journal of Design Computing, 7*.

Kvan, T., West, R., & Vera, A. (1997). *Tools and channels of communication: Dealing with the effects of computer mediation on design communication*. 1st International Conference on Creative Collaboration in Virtual Communities, University of Sydney.

Kvan, T. (2004A). Collaborative design: What is it? *Automation in Construction, 9*(4), 409–415. doi:10.1016/S0926-5805(99)00025-4

Kvan, T. (2004B). Reasons to stop teaching CAAD. In Chiu, M.-L. (Ed.), *Digital design education* (pp. 66–81). Taipei, Taiwan: Garden City Publishing.

Kvan, T., Schmitt, G. N., Maher, M. L., & Cheng, N. Y.-W. (2000). Teaching architectural design in virtual studios. In Fruchter, R., Pena-Mona, F., & Roddis, W. M. K. (Eds.), *Computing in civil and building engineering* (pp. 162–169). Stanford. doi:10.1061/40513(279)21

Kymmell, W. (2006). *Outline for a BIM curriculum*. Retrieved September 25, 2007, from http://www7.nationalacademies.org/ FFC/willem_kymmell_csu.pdf

LaGro, J. A. (2008). *Site analysis: A contextual approach to sustainable land planning and site design*. John Wiley & Sons, Inc.

Lahti, H., Seitamaa-Hakkarainen, P., & Hakkarainen, K. (2004). Collaboration patterns in computer supported collaborative designing. *Design Studies, 25*(4), 351–371. doi:10.1016/j.destud.2003.12.001

Laiserin, J., & Barron, C. (2003). Graphisoft on BIM. *The Laiserin Letter, 19*.

Lakos, M. (2010a, 11 August). *Bridge development.* Retrieved from http://www.millielakos.blogspot.com

Lakos, M. (Producer). (2010b). *Running through bridge. mp4, Elevator1.mp4.* Retrieved from www.russelllowe. com/publications/ cdmt/Lakos.rar

Landa, L. (1983). The algo-heuristic theory of instruction. In Reigeluth, C. M. (Ed.), *Instructional design theories and models.* Hillsdale, NJ: Lawrence Erlbaum Associates.

Lang, J. (1975). *Designing for human behaviour: Architecture and the behavioural sciences.* John Wiley & Sons Inc.

Larson, K. (2010). *Animation mentor.* Retrieved September 20, 2009, from http://www.animationmentor.com/

Latour, B. (1987). *Science in action: How to follow scientists and engineers through society.* Cambridge, MA: Harvard University Press.

Latour, B. (1994). *We have never been modern.* Hertfordshire, UK: Harvest Wheatsheaf.

Lave, J., & Wenger, E. (1991). *Situated learning: Legitimate peripheral participation.* Cambridge, UK: Cambridge University Press.

Lawson, B. (2005). *How designers think: The design process demystified.* Burlington, MA: Elsevier.

Lawson, B. (2004). *What designers know.* Elsevier Architectural Press.

Lawson, B. (2005). *Design thinking* (4th ed.). Oxford, UK: Architectural Press.

Lawson, B. (2005). *How designers think.* London, UK: Architectural Press.

Leborg, C. (2006). *Visual grammar.* New York, NY: Princeton Architectural Press.

Lecourtois, C. (2004). *De la communication sur l'espace: espace conçu et espace perçu de l'architecture et de l'urbanisme.* Unpublished doctoral dissertation, Université de Nanterre.

Lecourtois, C. (2005). *Architecturologie appliquée à une sémiotique de l'esquisse architecturale.* In Actes du Colloque SCAN05.

Lecourtois, C. (2006). Apprentissage d'un regard architecturologique pour un enseignement de la conception architecturale. In P. Boudon (Dir.), *Conceptions: Epistémologie et poïétique.* Paris, France: L'Harmattan.

Lecourtois, C. (2006). Conception de l'espace et espace de conception. *TIGR (Travaux de l'Institut de Géographie de Reims), Nouvelles approches de l'espace dans les sciences de l'homme et de la société.*

Lecourtois, C. (2008). Enseigner la conception architecturale assistée par ordinateur. In *Actes du colloque BASC 2008, Biskra Algérie.* Retrieved August 2011, from http:// www.ariam-larea.archi.fr/ index.php?page=publications-noms

Lecourtois, C. (2010). *Meta-complexité architecturale et assistance informatique.* Paper presented at the Meeting of MCX, Lille, France.

Lecourtois, C. (2011), Studying collaborative design. Epistemology and research methodology. In G. Carrara, A. Fioravanti & A. Trento (Eds.), *Connecting brains shaping the world =>collaborative design spaces,* (pp. 25-37). Europia Productions.

Lecourtois, C. (in press). Genèse cognitive d'un musée: Le cas du Musée Guggenheim de Bilbao. *Architecture muséale, espace de l'art et lieu de l'œuvre.* Collection Figures de l'art. *Presse Universitaire de Toulouse.*

Lecourtois, C., & Guéna, F. (2009). Eco-conception et esquisse assistée. In Bignon, J. C., Halin, G., & Kubicki, S. (Eds.), *Conception architecturale numérique et approches environnementales* (pp. 63–75). Presses Universitaires de Nancy.

Lee, L. A., & Reekie, R. F. (1949). *Descriptive geometry for architecs and builders.* London, UK: Arnold.

Legaspi, H. (Producer). (2009). *Arch7201_Legaspi.flv.* Retrieved from www.russelllowe.com/publications/ cdmt/ Arch7201_Legaspi.rar

Lego Digital Designer. (2010, April 23). Retrieved from http://ldd.lego.com

Lehtinen, S. (2002, 18-20 September). *Visualization and teaching with state-of-the-art 3D game technologies.* Paper presented at the Connecting the Real and the Virtual - Design E-ducation, 20th eCAADe Conference, Warsaw (Poland).

Leicht, R. M. (2009). *A framework for planning effective collaboration using interactive workspaces.* Ph.D. Thesis, Department of Architectural Engineering, The Pennsylvania State University, University Park, PA, USA.

Leidner, D., & Jarvenpaa, S. (1995). The use of Information Technology to enhance management school education: A theoretical view. *MIS Quarterly*, September.

Lektorsky, V. A. (1984). *Subject, object, cognition.* Moscow, Russia: Progress.

Leonardo. (2010). *About Leonardo.* Retrieved April 6, 2010, from http://www.leonardo.info/leoinfo.html

Leont'ev, A. N. (1978). *Activity, consciousness, and personality.* Englewood Cliffs, NJ: Prentice-Progress.

Leont'ev, A. N. (1981). *Problems of the development of the mind.* Moscow, Russia: Progress.

Lertlakkhanakul, J., Lee, I., & Kim, M. (2005). Using the mobile augmented reality techniques for construction management. *International Conference on the Association for Computer-Aided Architectural Design Research in Asia* (pp. 396-403).

Li, S. (Producer). (2007). *shawn_li_workshop.wmv.* Retrieved from http://www.russelllowe.com/cdmt/shawn_li_workshop.rar

Liang, R.-H., & Huang, Y.-M. (2009). Visualizing bits as urban semiotics. *International Conference on the Association for Computer-Aided Architectural Design Research in Asia* (pp. 33-42).

Lieberman, H., Liu, H., Singh, P., & Barry, B. (2004). Beating common sense into interactive applications. *AI Magazine, 25*(4), 63–76.

Lin, H. C., Shen, Y. T., & Jeng, T. (2005). IP++: Computer- augmented information portal in place. *International Conference on the Association for Computer-Aided Architectural Design Research in Asia* (pp. 185-192).

Lin, J. (2010). Design for quantitative and qualitative performance: a pedagogical approach for integrating environmental analysis into the early stages of the design process. In B. Goodwin & J. Kinnard (Eds.), *RE-Building, 98th ACSA Annual Meeting* (pp. 189 - 196). Washington, DC: ACSA Press.

Lindsay, B. (2001). *Digital Gehry.* Basel, Switzerland: Birkhäuser.

Liu, Y. T. (2005). *5th FEIDAD Award: Demonstrating digital architecture.* Bern, Switzerland: Birkhäuser.

Liu, Y., Wang, Y., Li, Y., Lei, J., & Lin, L. (2006). Key issues for AR-based digital reconstruction of Yuanmingyuan garden. *Presence: Teleoperator and Virtual Environments, 15*(3), 336–340. doi:10.1162/pres.15.3.336

Lloyd, P., Lawson, B., & Scott, P. (1996). Can concurrent verbalisation reveal design cognition? In Cross, N., Christians, H., & Dorst, K. (Eds.), *Analysing design activity* (pp. 437–463).

Lohman, D. F., & Nichols, P. D. (1990). Training spatial abilities: Effects of practice on rotation and synthesis tasks. *Learning and Individual Differences, 2*(1), 67–93. doi:10.1016/1041-6080(90)90017-B

Lonsing, W., & Anders, P. (2011). Three-dimensional computational structures and the real world. *International Conference on the Association for Computer-Aided Architectural Design Research in Asia* (pp. 209-218). Hong Kong.

Lowe, R. (2007a). *ARCH1102: Course outline.* Retrieved 29 April, 2010, from http://www.russelllowe.com/arch1102/ course_info/course_outline.html

Lowe, R. (2007b). *ARCH1501: Course outline.* Retrieved 1 may, 2010, from http://www.russelllowe.com/ arch1501/course_outline.html

Lowe, R. (2007c). *HL2 tutorial: Model with complex collision.* Retrieved 1 May, 2010, from http://www.russelllowe.com/desn285_2006t2/ tutorials/model_with_complex_collision.html

Lowe, R. (2008a). *BENV2423: Course outline.* Retrieved 1 May, 2010, from http://www.russelllowe.com/ benv2423/index.htm

Lowe, R. (2008b, 9-12 April). *Beyond the boundary object: Sketches, computer games and blogs facilitating design development.* Paper presented at the CAADRIA, Chiang Mai (Thailand).

Lowe, R. (2009a, 21 June 2009). *ARCH1101: Architecture design studio 1, discussion forum.* Retrieved 29 April, 2010, from http://groups.google.com/group/arch1101

Lowe, R. (2009b). *BENV2423: Course outline*. Retrieved 1 May, 2010, from http://www.russelllowe.com/benv2423_2009/index.htm

Lowe, R. (2009c). *Computer game modding for architecture*. Paper presented at the 14th International Conference on Computer Aided Architectural Design Research in Asia. Retrieved from http://cumincad.scix.net/cgi-bin/works/Show?caadria2009_176

Lowe, R. (2010a). *ARCH1101-2010 blog*. Retrieved 1 May, 2010, from http://www.arch1101-2010.blogspot.com/

Lowe, R. (2010b). *ARCH1101: Architecture design studio 1, discussion forum*. Retrieved 1 May, 2010, from http://groups.google.com/group/ arch1101-2010/topics

Lowe, R. (2010c). *SketchUpToCrysis_mpeg4.avi*. Sydney, Australia: Lowe, R.

Lowe, R., & Goodwin, R. (2009, 5-6 November). *Computer gaming technology and porosity*. Paper presented at the 9th International Conference on Construction Applications of Virtual Reality, Sydney, Australia.

Lum, E. (n.d.). *On design intent*. Retrieved from http://www.aia.org/practicing/ groups/kc/AIAB081947

Lynn, G. (1993). Architectural curvilinearity: The folded, the pliant and the supple. In Lynn, G. (Ed.), *AD architectural design: Folding in architecture* (pp. 8–15). London, UK: Wiley.

Lynn, G. (1999). *Animate form*. New York, NY: Princeton Architectural Press.

Machado, G. (2010). *An expanding leaning economy*. Retrieved April 4, 2010, from 2006 http://www.design-education.ca

Maeda, J. (2006). *Laws of simplicity*. The MIT Press.

Maher, M. L. (1999). *Variations on a virtual design studio*. The 4th international Workshop on CSCW in Design, Universite de Technologie de Compiegne.

Maher, M. L., & Merrick, K. (2005). Agent models for dynamic 3D virtual worlds. *Proceedings of 2005 International Conference on Cyberworlds*, Singapore, (pp. 27-34).

Maher, M. L., & Simoff, S. (2000). Collaboratively designing within the design. *Proceedings of Co-Designing 2000*.

Maher, M.-L. (1995). Using the Internet to teach in a virtual design studio. In *Proceedings of DECA 95: Information Technology and its Influence on Design Education*, RMIT, Melbourne, 1995.

Maher, M. L., Bilda, Z., & Gül, L. F. (2006). *Impact of collaborative virtual environments on design behaviour. Design Computing and Cognition '06*. the Netherlands: Springer.

Maher, M. L., Bilda, Z., & Gul, L. F. (2006a). Impact of collaborative virtual environments on design behaviour. In Gero, J. (Ed.), *Design Computing and Cognition '06* (pp. 305–321). Dordrecht, The Netherlands: Springer. doi:10.1007/978-1-4020-5131-9_16

Maher, M. L., Rosenman, M., Merrick, K., & Macindoe, O. (2006b). DesignWorld: An augmented 3D virtual world for multidisciplinary, collaborative design. [Osaka, Japan.]. *CAADRIA, 2006*, 133–142.

Mahoney, J. (2004). What is constructivism and why is it growing? *Contemporary Psychology, 49*, 360–363.

Maitland, B. S. (1985). A problem-based course in architecture. In Boud, D. (Ed.), *Problem-based learning in education for the professions*. Sydney: HERDSA.

Mallasi, Z. (2004, 7-9 December). *Identification and visualisation of construction activities' workspace conflicts utilising 4D CAD/VR tools*. Paper presented at the eDesign in Architecture: ASCAAD's First International Conference on Computer Aided Architectural Design, KFUPM, Saudi Arabia.

Manovich, L. (2000). *The language of new media*. Cambridge, MA: MIT Press.

Margolin, V., & Buchanan, R. (1996). *The idea of design*. New York, NY: MIT Press.

Mark, E., Martens, B., & Oxman, R. (2001). The ideal computer curriculum. In H. Penttila (Ed.), *Architectural Information Management, 19th eCAADe Conference Proceedings* (pp. 168-175). Helsinki, Finland: Helsinki University of Technology.

Marks, M., Mathieu, J., & Zaccaro, S. (2001). A temporally based framework and taxonomy of team processes. *Academy of Management Review, 26*, 356–376.

Marx, K., & Engels, F. (1968). *The German ideology.* Moscow, Russia: Progress.

Mason, R. (1998). *Globalising education.* New York, NY: Routledge.

Massive. (2010). *What is Massive?* Retrieved April 4, 2010, from http://www.massivesoftware.com/ whatis-massive/

Matcha, H. (2007). Parametric possibilities: Designing with parametric modelling. In *Proceedings of eCAADE 25.*

Maver, T. W. (1995). CAAD's seven deadly sins. In M. Tan & R. The (Eds.), *The Global Design Studio, Proceedings CAAD Futures* (pp. 21-22). Singapore: Centre for Advanced Studies in Architecture, National University of Singapore.

May, T. (2001). *Social research: Issues, methods and process.* Open University Press.

McCullough, M. (2005). *Digital ground: Architecture, pervasive computing, and environmental knowing.* The MIT Press. Norman, D. A. (2010). *Living with complexity.* The MIT Press.

Mead, G. H. (1938). *The philosophy of act.* Chicago, IL: University of Chicago Press.

Meredith, M. (2008). *From control to design: Parametric/ algorithmic architecture.* Barcelona, Spain: Actar.

Merriam-Webster Online Dictionary. (2007). *Visualization.* Retrieved from http://www.merriam-webster.com/ dictionary/visualization

Messner, J. I., & Horman, M. J. (2003). Using advanced visualization tools to improve construction education. *Proceedings of CONVR 2003, Conference on Construction Applications of Virtual Reality*, Blacksburg, VA, (pp. 145-155).

Microsoft. (2004). *Computer gaming to enhance CS curriculum* (p. 11). Retrieved from http://research.microsoft.com/ en-us/collaboration/papers/ computergamingtoenhancecscurriculum.doc

Milgram, P., & Kishino, F. (1994). A taxonomy of mixed reality visual displays. *IEICE Transactions on Information Systems. E (Norwalk, Conn.)*, 77-D(12).

Miller, S. F. (1995). *Design process: A primer for architectural and interior design.* New York, NY: Van Nostrand Reinhold.

Minsky, M. (2000). Commonsense-based interfaces. *Communications of the ACM, 43*(8). doi:10.1145/345124.345145

Mitchell, W. J., & McCullough, M. (1995). *Digital design media.* New York, NY: Van Nostrand Reinhold.

Mitchell, W. J., Yee, S., Naka, R., Morozumi, M., & Yamaguchi, S. (1998). The Kumamoto-Kyoto-MIT Collaborative Project: A case study of the design studio of the future. In N. A. Streitz, S. Konomi, & H.-J. Burkhardt (Eds.), *Cooperative Buildings, Integrating Information, Organisation, and Architecture. Proceedings of the First International Workshop, CoBuild'98*, Darmstadt, Germany, February 1998, (pp. 80-93).

Mitchell, W. S. (1999). *e-topia*, Cambridge, MA: The MIT Press.

Mitchell, W. J. (1975). The theoretical foundation of computer-aided architectural design. *Environment and Planning B, 2*, 127–150. doi:10.1068/b020127

Mitchell, W. J. (1995). *City of bits: Space, place, and the Infobahn.* Cambrudge, MA: MIT Press.

Mitchell, W. J. (2000). *E-topia.* MIT Press.

Mitchell, W. J., & McCullough, M. (1994). *Digital design media.* New York, NY: Van Nostrand Reinhold.

Mitchell, W. S. (1995). *City of bits.* Cambridge, MA: The MIT Press.

Mitchell, W. S. (2003). *Me.* Cambridge, MA: The MIT Press.

Moggridge, B. (2007). *Designing interactions.* MIT Press.

Mohler, J. L., & Miller, C. L. (2008). Improving spatial ability with mentored sketching. *Engineering Design Graphics Journal, 72*(1), 19–27.

Moloney, J. (2001, 9-12 December). *3D game software and architectural education.* Paper presented at the Meeting at the Crossroads. Short Paper Proceedings of the 18th Annual Conference of the Australian Society for Computers in Learning in Tertiary Education., Melbourne, Australia.

Moloney, J. (2002, 18-20 September). *String CVE collaborative virtual environment software developed from a game engine*. Paper presented at the 20th eCAADe Conference Proceedings, Warsaw (Poland).

Moloney, J. (2007). Screen based augmented reality for architecture. *International Conference on the Association for Computer-Aided Architectural Design Research in Asia* (pp.577-584).

Moloney, J., & Dave, B. (2011). From abstraction to being there: Mixed reality at the early stages of design. *International Journal of Architectural Computing*, *9*(1), 1–16. doi:10.1260/1478-0771.9.1.1

Monedero, J. (2000). Parametric design: A review and some experiences. *Automation in Construction*, *9*(4), 369–377. doi:10.1016/S0926-5805(99)00020-5

Moore, G. T. (1979). *Architecture and human behaviour: The place of environment-behaviour studies in architecture*. Winconsin Architect.

More, G., & Burrow, A. (2007). *Observing the learning curve of videogames in architectural design*. Paper presented at the The Fourth Australasian Conference on Interactive Entertainment: IE2007, RMIT University, Melbourne Australia.

Morrison, T., & Ostwald, M. J. (2007). Shifting dimensions: The architectural model in history. In P. Downton, M. Ostwald, A. Mina, & A. Fairley (Eds.), *Homo Faber: Modelling architecture* (pp. 142–156). Melbourne, Australia: Melbourne Museum.

Mueller, V. (2006). Integrating digital and non-digital design work. In Chaznar, A. (Ed.), *Blurring the lines* (pp. 38–45). Chichester, UK: Wiley-Academy.

Muller, W. (1989). Design discipline and the significance of visuo-spatial thinking. *Design Studies*, *10*(1), 12–23. doi:10.1016/0142-694X(89)90021-5

Murphy, E. (1997). *Constructivism: From theory to practice*. Retrieved from http://www.stemnet.nf.ca/~elmurphy/emurphy/cle.html

MyCryEngine. (2010). *Five reasons to license CryENGINE3*. Retrieved 1 May, 2010, from http://mycryengine.com/?conid=43

National Research Council (NCR). (2006). *Learning to think spatially*. Washington, DC: The National Academies Press.

Negroponte, N. (1995). *Being digital. Hodder and Stoughton. Norman, D. A. (1988). The psychology of everyday things*. New York, NY: Basic Books.

Neilsen. (2009, April). *The state of the video gamer: PC game and video game console usage, fourth quarter 2008*. Retrieved April 5, 2010, from http://blog.nielsen.com/nielsenwire/ wp-content/uploads/2009/04/stateofvgamer_040609_fnl1.pdf

Newcombe, N. S., & Huttenlocher, J. (2003). *Making space: The development of spatial representations and reasoning*. Cambridge, MA: MIT Press.

Ng, H. (Producer). (2009). *HayleyNGEXP1.flv*. Retrieved from www.russelllowe.com/publications/ cdmt/HaleyNGEXP1.rar

NIBS- National Institute of Building Sciences. (2009). *Annual Report to the President of the United States*. Retrieved from www.nibs.org

Nir, E. (2010). *Explore beyond your imagination*. Retrieved April 5, 2010, from http://www.paraclouding.com/GEM/

Noguchi, M. (2003). The effect of the quality-oriented production approach on the delivery of prefabricated homes in Japan. *Journal of Housing and the Built Environment*, *18*(4), 353–364. doi:10.1023/B:JOHO.0000005759.07212.00

Novak, M. (1997). Cognitive cities: Intelligence, environment and space. In P. Droege (Ed.), *Intelligent environments: Spatial aspects of the information revolution* (pp. 386–419). Amsterdam, The Netherlands: Elsevier.

Novick, L. R., & Bassok, M. (2005). Problem solving. In Holyoak, K. J., & Morrison, R. G. (Eds.), *The Cambridge handbook of thinking and reasoning* (pp. 321–349). New York, NY: Cambridge University Press.

Oaariki, O. (2006). *Oren Oaariki: DESN104, experiment 3 website*. Retrieved 1 May, 2010, from http://www.russelllowe.com/desn104_2006t2/ website_misc/student_work/oren_oaariki_exp3_website/index.html

Oblinger, D. G., & Oblinger, J. L. (Eds.). (2005). *Educating the Net generation*. Washington, DC: Educause.

O'Brien, M. (Producer). (2010). *Exp3Part1.mp4, Exp3Part2.mp4, Exp3Part3.mp4*. Retrieved from www. russelllowe.com/ publications/cdmt/OBrien.rar

O'Coill, C., & Doughty, M. (2004, 15-18 December). *Computer game technology as a tool for participatory design*. Paper presented at the Architecture in the Network Society, 22nd eCAADe Conference, Copenhagen (Denmark).

Ondrejka, C. R. (2004). *Aviators, moguls, fashionistas and barons: Economics and ownership in Second Life*. SSRN eLibrary.

Online Schools. (2010). *Video game statistics*. Retrieved 21 March, 2010, from http://www.onlineschools.org/blog/video-game-statistics/

Oosterhuis, K. (2002). *Architecture goes wild*. Rotterdam, The Netherlands: 010 Publishers.

Ostwald, M. J. (2004). Freedom of form: Ethics and Aesthetics in digital architecture. *The Philosophical Forum*, *35*(2), 201–220.

Ostwald, M. J. (2006). Ethics and geometry: Computational transformations and the curved surface in architecture. In S. Duvernoy & O. Pedemonte (Eds.), *Nexus VI: Architecture and mathematics* (pp. 77–92). Torino, Italy: Kim Williams Books.

Ostwald, M. J. (2010a). Ethics and the auto-generative design process. *BRI: Building Research and Information*, *38*(4), 390–400.

Ostwald, M. J. (2010b). On the value of labour: Rethinking the physical model and questioning the CAD/CAM model. In M. Ostwald, P. Downton, & A. Fairley (Eds.)m *Homo Faber volume 3: Modelling, identity and the post digital* (pp. 175 – 186). Melbourne, Australia: Melbourne Museum.

O'Sullivan, D., & Igoe, T. (2004). *Physical computing*. Thomson Course Technology.

Otto, G., Messner, J., & Kalisperis, L. (2005). Expanding the boundaries of virtual reality for building design and construction. *Proceedings of the ASCE Computing in Civil Engineering Conference*, Cancun, Mexico.

Oxman, N. (2010). *Material-based computation*. PhD Thesis Dissertation, Dept. of Architecture, MIT, Cambridge, 2010

Oxman, R., & Oxman, R. (Eds.). (2010). Special issue: The new structuralism: Design, engineering and architectural technologies/ *Architectural Design, 80*(4).

Oxman, N. (2007). Get real towards performance-driven computational geometry. *IJAC: International Journal of Architectural Computing*, *4*, 663–684. doi:10.1260/147807707783600771

Oxman, N. (2010). *The new structuralism* (Oxman, R., & Oxman, R., Eds.). London, UK: John Wiley & Sons.

Oxman, R. (1994). Precedents in design: a computational model for the organization of precedent knowledge. *Design Studies*, *15*(2), 141–157. doi:10.1016/0142-694X(94)90021-3

Oxman, R. (2003). Think-maps: Teaching design thinking in design education. *Design Studies*, *25*(1), 63–91. doi:10.1016/S0142-694X(03)00033-4

Oxman, R. (2006). Theory and design in the first digital age. *Design Studies*, *27*(3), 229–265. doi:10.1016/j.destud.2005.11.002

Oxman, R. (2008). Performance based design: Current practices and research issue. *IJAC International Journal of Architectural Computing*, *6*(1), 1–17. doi:10.1260/147807708784640090

Oxman, R. (2009). Performative design - A performance-model of digital architectural design. *Environment and Planning B*, *36*, 1026–1037. doi:10.1068/b34149

Oxman, R., & Oxman, R. (2010). The new structuralism - Design engineering and architectural technologies. In *Architectural design: New structuralism* (pp. 79–85). London, UK: Wiley. doi:10.1002/ad.1101

Oxman, R., & Streich, B. (2001). Digital media and design didactics in visual cognition. In Hannu, P. (Ed.), *Architectural Information Management, Proceedings of eCAADe19* (p. 357). Helsinki, Finland.

Palladio, A. (1965). *The four books of architecture*. New York, NY: Dover Publications.

Pan, C. (2010, 11 August). *Client spaces*. Retrieved from http://www.arch1101-2010kb.blogspot.com/

Pan, C., & Jeng, T. (2008). *Exploring sensing-based kinetic design for responsive architecture*. Proceedings of CAADRIA2008. Thailand: Chiang Mai.

Panofsky, E. (1967). *Architecture gothique et pensée scolastique*. Paris, France: Editions de Minuit.

Papagiannakis, G., & Magnenat-Thalmann, N. (2007). Mobile augmented heritage: Enabling human life in Ancient Pompeii. *International Journal of Architectural Computing, 5*(2), 396–415. doi:10.1260/1478-0771.5.2.396

Parthenios, P. (2005). *Conceptual design tools for architects*. DDes Dissertation, Harvard Design School.

Pearce, P., & Pearce, S. (1980). *Experiments in form*. New York, NY: Van Nostrand Reinhold.

Pelosi, A. (2010a). List of game engines used. In R. Lowe (Ed.) (email to author ed., pp. 1).

Pelosi, A. (2010b, 7-10 April). *Obstacles of utilising real-time 3D visualisation in architectural representations and documentation*. Paper presented at the CAADRIA 2010, New Frontiers, Hong Kong.

Penrose, R., & Gardner, M. (2002). *The Emperor's new mind: Concerning computers, minds, and the laws of physics*. London, UK: Oxford University Press.

Peppé, R. (2002). *Automata and mechanical toys*. Crowood Press.

Perkins, D. (1991). Technology meets constructivism: Do they make a marriage? *Educational Technology, 31*(5), 18–23.

Petzold, F., Bimber, O., & Tonn, O. (2007). CAVE without CAVE: On-site visualization and design support in and within existing building. The *25th Conference on Education in Computer Aided Architectural Design in Europe: Communicating Space(s)* (pp. 161-168).

Phan, V. T., & Chool, S. Y. (2010). Augmented reality-based education and fire protection for traditional Korean buildings. *International Journal of Architectural Computing, 8*(1), 75–91. doi:10.1260/1478-0771.8.1.75

Phye, G. (1997). Learning and remembering: the basis for personal knowledge construction. In Phye, G. (Ed.), *Handbook of academic learning: Construction of knowledge* (pp. 47–64). San Diego, CA: Academic Press. doi:10.1016/B978-012554255-5/50003-X

Piaget, J. (1968). *Le structuralisme*. PUF.

Pickersgill, S. (2007, 11–13 July). *Unreal Studio: Game engine software in the architectural design studio*. Paper presented at the Computer Aided Architectural Design Futures, Sydney (Australia).

Picon, A. (1997). Les annales de la recherche urbaine. *Le Temps du Cyborg dans la Ville Territoire, 77*, 72-77.

Picon, A. (2010). *Digital culture in architecture: An introduction for the design profession*. Bern, Switzerland: Birkhäuser.

Pink, D. (2005). *A whole new mind*. Crows Nest, Australia: Allen & Unwin.

PlayUpTools. (2010). *PlayUp homepage*. Retrieved 1 May, 2010, from http://www.playuptools.com/

Pottmann, H. (2010). Architectural geometry as design knowledge. In Oxman, R., & Oxman, R. (Eds.), *Architectural design: New structuralism: Design engineering and architectural technologies* (pp. 72–76). London, UK: Wiley.

Powers, M. (2001). *Applying a constructivist pedagogy to design studio education*. ARCC Spring Research Conference, Virginia Technique.

Prasolova-Førland, E., & Wyeld, T. G. (2006). Online 3D cave performance of T. S. Elliot's Cocktail Party: An example of virtual stage. In *Proceedings of Web-Based Education 2006*, Puerto Vallarta, Mexico, January 23-25.

Prasolova-Førland, E., & Wyeld, T. (2008). The place metaphor in 3D CVEs: A pedagogical case study of the virtual stage. *International Journal of Emerging Technologies in Learning, 3*(1), 54–60.

Price, C. (2006). A crisis in physics education: Games to the rescue! *ITALICS, Innovation in Teaching And Learning in Information and Computer Sciences, 5*(3).

Price, H. (2009, 11-September). *Interview with Hanna Price at Framestore, London* (D. Bruton, Interviewer).

Pupo, R. T., & Celani, G. (2008). Prototipagem Rápida e Fabricação Digital para Arquitetura e Construção: Definições e Estado da Arte no Brasil. *Cadernos de Pós Graduação em Arquitetura e Urbanismo, 8*(1), 31–41.

Purcell, A. T., & Gero, J. S. (1998). Drawings and the design process: A review of protocol studies in design and other disciplines and related research in cognitive psychology. *Design Studies, 19*(4), 389–430. doi:10.1016/S0142-694X(98)00015-5

Purdue University. (2007). *CGT 460: Building information modeling for commercial construction. Course syllabus.* Retrieved October 16, 2007 from http://www2.tech.purdue.edu/ cgt/courses/cg460

Rankin, J., Issa, M., & Christian, A. J. (2006). Exploring the principles of interactive collaborative workspaces. *1st International Construction Specialty Conference*, Calgary, Alberta, Canada, May 23-26.

Rashid, H., & Couture, L. A. (2002). *Asymptote: Flux.* New York, NY: Phaidon.

Reigeluth, C. M. (1983). *Instructional design: What is it and why is it?* Hillsdale, NJ: Lawrence Erlbaum Associates.

Reiser, J., & Umemoto, N. (2006). *Atlas of novel tectonics.* New York, NY: Princeton Architectural Press.

Resnick, L. B. (1986). Introduction. In Resnick, L. B. (Ed.), *Knowing, learning and instruction: Essays in honor of Robert Glaser* (pp. 1–24). Hillsdale, NJ: Lawrence Erlbaum Associates.

Resnick, L., Levine, J. M., & Teasley, S. D. (1991). *Perspectives on socially shared cognition.* Washington, DC: American Psychological Association. doi:10.1037/10096-000

Rheingold, H. (1991). *Virtual reality.* New York, NY: Summit Books.

Riese, M., & Simmons, M. (2004). The glass office - SCL office and showroom in Brisbane, Australia. In *Fabrication: Examining the digital practice of architecture* (pp. 28–33). Cambridge, Canada: ACADIA & AIA Technology in Architectural Practice Knowledge Community.

Riewer, E. (2009, 10-September). *Interview with Eric Riewer at Gobelins, Paris* (D. Bruton, Interviewer).

Rink, M. (2005). Spatial situation models. In Shah, P., & Miyake, A. (Eds.), *Handbook of higher-level visuospatial thinking* (pp. 334–382). Cambridge, UK: Cambridge University Press.

Rittel, H. (1992). *Planen Entwerfen Design. Ausgewaehlte Schriften zu Theorie und Methodik.* Stuttgart, Germany: Kohlhammer.

Rittel, H., & Webber, M. (1973). Dilemmas in a general theory of planning. *Policy Sciences, 4*, 155–169. doi:10.1007/BF01405730

Roads, C. (2001). *Microsound.* Cambridge, MA: The MIT Press.

Rocker, I. M. (2006). When code matters. *AD Architectural Design, 76*(4), 16–25.

Rosenman, M. A., Smith, G., Ding, L., Marchant, D., & Maher, M. L. (2005). Multidisciplinary design in virtual worlds. *Proceedings of CAAD Futures 2005.* Dordrecht, The Netherlands: Springer.

Rosser, J., Lynch, P., Cuddihy, L., Gentile, D., Klonsky, D., & Merrell, R. (2007). The impact of video games on training surgeons in the 21st century. *Archives of Surgery, 142*(2), 5. Retrieved from http://archsurg.highwire.org/ cgi/content/full/142/2/181doi:10.1001/archsurg.142.2.181

Rowe, J. (2009, 19-September). *Interview with John Rowe at NFTS, UK* (D. Bruton, Interviewer).

Rubens, P. (2003, December 15). Fax - The technology that refuses to die. *BBC News World Edition.* Retrieved from http://news.bbc.co.uk/1/hi/ magazine/3320515.stm

Russell, P., & Elger, D. (2008). The meaning of BIM. *Architecture in Computro, Conference Proceedings* (pp. 531-536) Antwerpen, Belgium: eCAADe.

Ryan, J. (2008, 16-December). *The next leap: A competitive Ireland in the digital era.* Retrieved April 5, 2010, from http://www.iiea.com/publications/ the-next-leap-a-competitive-ireland-in-the-digital-era

Ryu, H., & Parsons, D. (2009). *Innovative mobile learning: tecHniques and technologies.* Hershey, PA: IGI Global.

Sacks, R., & Barak, R. (2010). Teaching building information modeling as an integral part of freshman year civil engineering education. *Journal of Professional Issues in Engineering Education and Practice, 36*(1), 30–37. doi:10.1061/(ASCE)EI.1943-5541.0000003

Santos, P., Gierlinger, T., Stork, A., & McIntyre, D. (2007). Display and rendering technologies for virtual and mixed reality design review, *International Conference on Construction Applications of Virtual Reality* (pp. 165-175).

Santos, P., Stork, A., Gierlinger, T., Pagani, A., Araujo, B., & Jota, R. ... McIntyre, D. (2007). IMPROVE: Collaborative design review in mobile mixed reality. *Proceedings of Human Computer Interaction International*, (pp. 543–53).

Sasaki, M. (2007). *Morphogenesis of flux structures.* London, UK: AA Publications.

Sass, L. (2005). A wood frame grammar: A generative system for digital fabrication. *International Journal of Architectural Computing, 1*(4), 51–67.

Sass, L. (2006). Synthesis of design production with integrated digital fabrication. *Automation in Construction, 16*(3), 298–310. doi:10.1016/j.autcon.2006.06.002

Sass, L., & Oxman, R. (2006). Materializing design, the implications of rapid prototyping in digital design. *Design Studies, 26*, 325–355. doi:10.1016/j.destud.2005.11.009

Sass, L., & Oxman, R. (2006). Materializing design. *International Journal of Design Studies, 27*(3), 325–355. doi:10.1016/j.destud.2005.11.009

Savransky, S. D. (2000). *Introduction to TRIZ methodology of inventive problem solving.* Boca Raton, FL: CRC Press. doi:10.1201/9781420038958

Schlueter, A., & Thesseling, F. (2008). Balancing design and performance in building retrofitting, a case study based on parametric modeling. In A. Kudless, N Oxman, M. Swackhamer (Eds.), *Silicon + Skin > Biological Processes and Computation, ACADIA 08 Conference Proceedings* (pp. 214- 221). Association of Computer Aided Design in Architecture.

Schnabel, A. M., Wang, X., Seichter, H., & Kvan, T. (2007). From virtuality to reality and back. *Conference on International Association of Societies of Design Research* (IASDR) (pp. 1-15).

Schnabel, M. (2008). *Mixed reality in architecture, design and construction.* Dordecht, The Netherlands: Springer.

Schnabel, M. A., Kvan, T., Kruijff, E., & Donath, D. (2001). The first virtual environment design studio, architectural information management. *19th eCAADe Conference Proceedings*, Helsinki, Finland.

Schnabel, M. A., Kvan, T., Kuan, S. K. S. & Li, W. (2004). 3D crossover: Exploring - Objets digitalise. *International Journal of Architectural Computing – IJAC, 2*(4), 475-490.

Schnabel, M., Wang, X., & Seichter, H. (2008). Touching the untouchables: Virtual-, augmented-, and reality. *International Conference on the Association for Computer-Aided Architectural Design Research in Asia* (pp. 293-299).

Schnabel, M. A., & Bowller, N. (Eds.). (2007). *Disparallel spaces.* Sydney, Australia: The University of Sydney.

Schn, D. A., & Wiggins, G. (1992). Kinds of seeing and their functions in designing. *Design Studies, 13*(2), 135–156. doi:10.1016/0142-694X(92)90268-F

Schodek, D., & Bechthold, M. Griggs, K., Kao, K., & Steinberg, M. (2007). *Digital design and manufacturing: CAD/CAM applications in architecture and design.* New York, NY: John Wiley & Sons.

Schodek, D., Bechthold, M., Griggs, K., Kao, K. M., & Steinberg, M. (2005). *Digital design and manufacturing, CAD/CAM applications in architecture and design.* New York, NY: Wiley Academy Press.

Schön, D. A. (1983). *The reflective practitioner.* New York, NY: Basic Books.

Schön, D. (1983). *The reflective practitioner: How professionals think in action.* New York, NY: Basic Books.

Schon, D. (1987). *Educating the reflective practitioner.* San Francisco, CA: Josey-Bass Publishers.

Schön, D. A. (1983). *Educating the reflective practitioner.* New York, NY: Basic Books.

Schon, D. A. (1983). *The reflective practitioner.* London, UK: Temple, Smith.

Schön, D. A. (1983). *The reflective practitioner: How professional think in action.* New York, NY: Basic Books.

Schön, D. A. (1988). Designing: Rules, types and worlds. *Design Studies*, *9*(3), 133–143. doi:10.1016/0142-694X(88)90047-6

Schon, D. A., & Wigging, G. (1992). Kinds of seeing and their functions in designing. *Design Studies*, *13*(2), 135–156. doi:10.1016/0142-694X(92)90268-F

Schoon, I. (1992). *Creative achievement in architecture: A psychological study*. Leiden, The Netherlands: DSWO Press - Leiden University.

Schutz, W. (1958). *Firo: A three-dimensional theory of interpersonal behaviour*. New York, NY: Holt, Rinehart, and Winston.

Schwartz, D. L. (1999, May). Physical imagery: Kinematic versus dynamic models. *Cognitive Psychology*, *38*(3), 433–464. doi:10.1006/cogp.1998.0702

Schwartz, D. L., & Black, J. B. (1996, April). Analog imagery in mental model reasoning: Depictive models. *Cognitive Psychology*, *30*(2), 154–219. doi:10.1006/cogp.1996.0006

Sears & Roebuck. (1990). *Home builders catalogue, The complete illustrated 1910 edition*. New York, NY: Dover Publications.

Seepersad, C. C., Green, M. G., & Schmidt, K. J. (2006). Learning journals as a cornerstone for effective experiential learning in undergraduate engineering design courses. In *Proceedings of the 2006 ASEE Annual Conference*. Chicago, Illinois.

Segal, L. (1995). Designing team workstations: the choreography of teamwork. In Hancock, P., Flach, J., Caird, J., & Vicente, K. (Eds.), *Local applications of the ecological approach to human-machine systems* (pp. 392–415). Hillsdale, NJ: Lawrence Erlbaum.

Seichter, H. (2007). *Augmented reality and tangible interfaces in collaborative urban design* (pp. 3–16). Computer Aided Architectural Design Futures.

Seifert, T. (2004). Understanding student motivation. *Educational Research*, *46*, 137–149. doi:10.1080/0013188042000222421

Serlio, S. (1996). *Sebastiano Serlio on architecture: Books I–V of Tutte l'Opere d'Architettura et Prospetiva*. New Haven, CT: Yale University Press.

Sharp, H., & Rogers, Y. (2007). *Interaction design: Beyond human-computer interaction*. John Wiley & Sons.

Sharp, J., & Zachary, L. W. (2004). Using the van Hiele K-12 geometry learning theory to modify engineering mechanics instruction. *Journal of STEM Education Innovations and Research*, *5*(1&2), 35–41.

Shea, K. (2006). Generative design. In Chaznar, A. (Ed.), *Blurring the lines* (pp. 54–61). Chichester, UK: Wiley-Academy.

Shepard, R. N. (1982). Geometrical approximations to the structure of musical pitch. *Psychological Review*, *89*, 305–333. doi:10.1037/0033-295X.89.4.305

Sheppard, S. (2008). *We're on to something with Project Newport*. Retrieved 7 August, 2010, from http://labs.blogs.com/its_alive_in_the_lab/ 2008/12/were-on-to-something-with-project-newport.html

Sherif, M. (2008). Building information modeling and architectural practice: On the verge of a new culture. *International Conference on Critical Digital Matters*, (pp. 85-90) Cambridge, MA: Harvard University Graduate School of Design.

Shiratuddin, M. F., & Fletcher, D. (2007, 22-23 October). *Utilizing 3D games development tool for architectural design in a virtual environment*. Paper presented at the Conference on Construction Applications of Virtual Reality 2007, Penn State University.

Shneiderman, B. (2000). Creating creativity: User interfaces for supporting innovation. *ACM Transactions on Computer-Human Interaction*, *7*(1), 114–138. doi:10.1145/344949.345077

Shneiderman, B. (2007). Creativity support tools: Accelerating discovery and innovation. *Communications of the ACM*, *50*(12), 20–32. doi:10.1145/1323688.1323689

Shortis, M., Leahy, F., Ogleby, C., Kealy, A., & Ellis, F. (2002). *Learning spatial design and analysis concept*. Retrieved from http://www.geomsoft.com/markss/papers/Shortis_etal_spatDA.pdf

Shove, E. (2003). *Changing human behaviour and lifestyle: A challenge for sustainable consumption?* P. S. Institute, ESRC Environment and Human Behaviour Programme.

Simon, H. (1969). *The sciences of the artificial*. Cambridge, MA: MIT Press.

Singhal, S., & Zyda, M. (1999). *Networked virtual environments: Design and implementation*. New York, NY: ACM Press.

Smith, D. K., & Tardif, M. (2009). *Building information modeling: A strategic implementation guide for architects, engineers, constructors, and real estate asset managers*. Hoboken, NJ: John Wiley & Sons.

Smith, G., Maher, M. L., & Gero, J. S. (2003). Designing 3D virtual worlds as a society of agents. *Proceedings of CAAD Futures 2003*, the Netherlands, Kluwer Academic Publishers.

Smith, M. K. (2002). Jerome S. Bruner and the process of education. In *The encyclopedia of informal education*.

Sorby, S. A. (1999). Developing 3-D spatial visualization skills. *Engineering Design Graphics Journal, 63*(2), 21–32.

Sorby, S. A. (2009). Educational research in developing 3-D spatial skills for engineering students. *International Journal of Science Education, 31*(3), 459–480. doi:10.1080/09500690802595839

Sowa, J. (1991). *Principles of semantic networks*. San Francisco, CA: Morgan Kaufman.

Spady, W. G. (2001). *Beyond counterfeit reforms: Forging an authentic future for all our learners*. Lanham, MD: The Scarecrow Press.

Spaeth, A. B., Schwägerl, K., & Stamm, I. (2007). Parameters in the design process. In *Proceedings of eCAADe 25*.

Sparacino, F. (2002). *Narrative spaces: Bridging architecture and entertainment via interactive technology*. 6th International Conference on Generative Art, Politecnico de Milano University, Milan, Italy.

Spuybroek, L. (2001). Machining architecture. In L. Spuybroek & Lang, B. (Eds.), *The weight of the image*. Rotterdam, The Netherlands: NAi Publishers.

Spuybroek, L. (1998). Motor geometry. *Architectural Design, 68*(5/6), 7.

Spuybroek, L. (2004). *NOX: Machining architecture*. New York, NY: Thames and Hudson.

Stauber, R., & Bollrath, L. (2007). *Plastics in automotive engineering: Exterior applications*. Munich, Germany: Hanser.

Steiner, I. D. (1972). *Group process and productivity*. New York, NY: Academic Press, Inc.

Sterk, T. E. (2003). *Using actuated tensegrity structures to produce a responsive architecture*. ACADIA, Annual Conference of the Association for Computer Aided Design In Architecture): Connecting, Crossroads of Digital Discourse, Indianapolis (Indiana).

Sterk, T. (2005). Building upon Negroponte: A hybridized model of control suitable for responsible architecture. *Automation in Construction, 14*(2), 225–232. doi:10.1016/j.autcon.2004.07.003

Sternberg, R. J., Lubart, T. I., Kaufman, J. C., & Pretz, J. E. (2005). Creativity. In Holyoak, K. J., & Morrison, R. G. (Eds.), *The Cambridge handbook of thinking and reasoning* (pp. 351–369). New York, NY: Cambridge University Press.

Stiny, G. (1975). *Pictorial and formal aspects of shapes and shape grammars*. Basel, Switzerland: Birkhaüser Verlag.

Stiny, G. (1977). Ice-ray: A note on Chinese lattice designs. *Environment and Planning. B, Planning & Design, 4*, 89–98. doi:10.1068/b040089

Stiny, G. (1980). Introduction to shape grammars. *Environment and Planning B, 7*(3), 343–35. doi:10.1068/b070343

Stiny, G. (1980). Kindergarten grammars: Designing with Froebel's building gifts. *Environment and Planning. B, Planning & Design, 7*, 409–462. doi:10.1068/b070409

Stiny, G., & Mitchell, W. J. (1978). The Palladian grammar. *Environment and Planning B, 5*(1), 5–18. doi:10.1068/b050005

Stockburger, A. (2007). Playing the third place: Spatial modalities in contemporary game environments. *International Journal of Performance Arts and digital Media, 3*(2 & 3), 13.

Stockwell, S., & Muir, A. (2003). The military-entertainment complex: A new facet of information warfare. *FibreCulture, 1*, 1. Retrieved from http://journal.fibreculture.org/ issue1/issue1_stockwellmuir.html

Strange, C. C. (2001). *Educating by design*. San Francisco, CA: Jossey Bass.

Strauss, C., & Fuad-Luke, A. (2008). The slow design principles: A new interrogative and reflexive tool for design research and practice. In C. Cipolla & P. P. Peruccio (Eds.), *Changing the change* (pp. 1440-1454). Allemande Conference Press.

Striano, M. (2009). Managing educational transformation in the globalized world: A Deweyan perspective. *Educational Theory*, *59*(4), 381–393. doi:10.1111/j.1741-5446.2009.00326.x

Strong, N. (2008). Designing an integrated practice with building information modeling. In Solomon, N. (Ed.), *Architecture: Celebrating the past, designing the future* (p. 185). New York, NY: The American Institute of Architects.

Suchman, L. A. (1987). *Plans and situated actions: The problem of human-machine communication*. Cambridge, UK: Cambridge University Press.

Sullivan, C. (2007). Integrated BIM and design review for safer, better buildings: How project teams using collaborative design reduce risk, creating better health and safety in projects. *McGraw Hill Construction Continuing Education*. Retrieved November 16, 2007, from http://construction.com/CE/ articles/0706navis-3.asp

Suwa, M., Purcell, T., & Gero, J. S. (1998). Macroscopic analysis of design processes based on a scheme for coding designers' cognitive actions. *Design Studies*, *19*(4), 455–483. doi:10.1016/S0142-694X(98)00016-7

Suwa, M., & Tversky, B. (1997). What do architects and students perceive in their design sketches? A protocol analysis. *Design Studies*, *18*(4), 385–403. doi:10.1016/S0142-694X(97)00008-2

Suwa, M., & Tversky, B. (2002). How do designers shift their focus of attention in their own sketches? In Anderson, M., Meyer, B., & Olivier, P. (Eds.), *Diagrammatic representation and reasoning*. Springer. doi:10.1007/978-1-4471-0109-3_14

Szalapaj, P. (2005). *Contemporary architecture and the digital design process*. Oxford, UK: Architectural Press.

Taiebat, M., & Ku, H. (2010). Industry's expectations of construction school graduates' BIM skills. *46th Annual Associated Schools of Construction International Conference Proceedings, in conjunction with the Annual Meeting of the International Council for Research and Innovation in Building and Construction (CIB) Working Group 89*, Wentworth Institute of Technology, (p. 35). Retrieved from ascpro.ascweb.org/chair/paper/ CEUE217002010.pdf

Techel, F., & Nassar, K. (2007). Teaching building information modeling (BIM) from a sustainability design perspective. *Em 'body' ing Virtual Architecture: The Third International Conference of the Arab Society for Computer Aided Architectural Design* (ASCAAD 2007), November 28-30, 2007, Alexandria, Egypt, (pp. 635-650).

TechOne Program. (2010, April 26). Retrieved from http://students.surrey.sfu.ca/techone

Terzidis, K. (2006). *Algorithmic architecture*. Oxford, UK: Elsevier.

Thabet, W., Shiratuddin, M. F., & Bowman, D. (2002). Virtual reality in construction: A review. In *Engineering computational technology* (pp. 25–52). Civil-Comp Press. doi:10.4203/csets.8.2

Thackara, J. (2010). *What should design researchers research? Report from 2020*. Retrieved August 19, 2011, from http://observersroom.designobserver.com/ johnthackara/post/what-should-design-researchers-research-report-from-2020/23398/

The Future of Education. (2010). *The future of education - Charting the course of teaching and learning in a networked world*. Retrieved April 6, 2010, from http://www.futureofeducation.com/ ?xg_source=msg_mes_network

The GoGame: play like it is your job. (2008). Retrieved April 5, 2010, from http://www.thegogame.com/ team/index.asp

Tickoo, S., & Maini, D. (2007). *SolidWorks 2007 for designers*. CADCIM Technologies.

Tolsby, H., Sorensen, E. K., & Dirckinck-Holmfeld, L. (2000). *Designing virtual portfolios for communities of practice*. In the Seventh World Conference on Computers in Education, WCCE 2001, Copenhagen, Denmark, 2000.

Tonn, C., Donath, D., & Petzold, F. (2007). Simulating the atmosphere of spaces– The AR-based support of 1:1 colour sampling in and within existing buildings. *The 25th Conference on Education in Computer Aided Architectural Design in Europe: Communicating Space(s)* (pp. 169-176).

Tonn, C., Petzold, F., & Donath, D. (2008). Put on your glasses and press right mouse button: AR-based user interaction using laser pointer tracking. *The 26th Conference on Education in Computer Aided Architectural Design in Europe: Communicating Space(s)* (pp. 201-208).

Tonn, C., Petzold, F., Bimber, O., Grundhöfer, A., & Donath, D. (2009). Spatial augmented reality for architecture – Designing and planning with and within existing buildings. *International Journal of Architectural Computing*, *6*(1), 41–58. doi:10.1260/147807708784640126

Tran, B. (Producer). (2009). *BillyTranEXP1.flv*. Retrieved from www.russelllowe.com/publications/ cdmt/ BillyTranEXP1.rar

Tsai, J. J.-H., Wang, X., & Huang, Y. (2008). Studying different scales of collaborative designs in real and virtual environments. [Newcastle, Australia.]. *ANZAScA*, *08*, 277–284.

Tufte, E. (2009, 1-July). *Design thinking: How facts change everything (if you let them)*. Retrieved November 13, 2010, from http://sloanreview.mit.edu/the-magazine/ articles/2009/summer/50409/ how-facts-change-every-thing-if-you-let-them/

Tufte, E. R. (1983). *The visual display of quantitative information*. Cheshire, CT: Graphics Press.

Tufte, E. R. (1992). *Envisioning information*. Cheshire, CT: Graphics Press.

Tufte, E. R. (1997). *Visual explanations: Images and quantities, evidence and narrative*. Cheshire, CT: Graphics Press.

Tukey, J. W. (1977). *Exploratory data analysis*. Reading, MA: Addison-Wesley.

Tversky, B. (2005). Functional significance of visuospatial representations. In Shah, P., & Miyake, A. (Eds.), *The Cambridge handbook of visuospatial thinking* (pp. 1–34). Cambridge, UK: Cambridge University Press.

Tversky, B. (2005). Visuospatial reasoning. In Holyoak, K. J., & Morrison, R. G. (Eds.), *The Cambridge handbook of thinking and reasoning* (pp. 209–240). New York, NY: Cambridge University Press.

Tversky, B., Morrison, J. B., & Betrancourt, M. (2002, October). Animation: Can it facilitate? *International Journal of Human-Computer Studies*, *57*(4), 247–262. doi:10.1006/ijhc.2002.1017

Tymockzo, D. (2006). The geometry of musical chords. *Science*, *313*(5783), 72. doi:10.1126/science.1126287

Ullman, D. G. (2009). *The mechanical design process* (4th ed.). McGraw Hill.

Van Berkel, B., & Bos, C. (1999). *UN Studio: Move*. Amsterdam, The Netherlands: Architectura & Natura.

van Geel, J. (2011, 1 11). *Strategy & leadership*. Retrieved August 19, 2011, from http://johnnyholland. org/2011/01/11/ design-research-and-innovation-an-interview-with-don-norman/

Vande Moere, A. (2010). *Infosthetics: Where form follows data*. Retrieved January 20, 2010, from infosthetics.com

Verlinden, J., & Horvth, I. (2009). Analyzing opportunities for using interactive augmented prototyping in design practice. *Artificial Intelligence for Engineering Design, Analysis and Manufacturing*, *23*(3), 289–303. doi:10.1017/S0890060409000250

Verstijnen, I. M., van Leeuwen, C., Goldschmidt, G., Hamel, R., & Hennessey, J. M. (1998, October). Sketching and creative discovery. *Design Studies*, *19*(4), 519–546. doi:10.1016/S0142-694X(98)00017-9

Vickers, P. (2005). *Ars Informatica - Ars Electronica: Improving sonification aesthetics*. Paper presented at the Understanding and Designing for Aesthetic Experience Workshop, 19th British HCI Group Annual Conference, Edinburgh, Scotland.

Vickers, P., & Hogg, B. (2006). *Sonification Abstraite/ Sonification Concrète: An 'aesthetic perspective space' for classifying auditory displays in the Ars Musica domain*. Paper presented at the 12th International Conference on Auditory Display.

Vidler, A. (1977). The third typology. In Cuthbert, A. (Ed.), *Designing cities* (pp. 317–339). UK: Blackwell Publishing.

Viegas, F. B., Wattenberg, M., McKeon, M., Ham, F. v., & Kriss, J. (2008). *Harry Potter and the meat-filled freezer: A case study of spontaneous usage of visualization tools*. Paper presented at the International Conference on System Sciences.

Viet, T. P., Yeon, C. S., Hak, W. S., & Ahrina, C. (2009). AR: An application for interior design. *International Conference on the Association for Computer-Aided Architectural Design Research in Asia* (pp.115-124).

Visser, W. (2006). *The cognitive artifacts of designing*. Mahwah, NJ: Lawrence Erlbaum Associates.

Vitruvius, M. (1914). *The ten books on architecture*. New York, NY: Dover Publications. [written circa 20BC]

Voss, J. F., & Wiley, J. (1995). Acquiring intellectual skills. *Annual Review of Psychology, 46*, 155–181. doi:10.1146/annurev.ps.46.020195.001103

Vygosky, L. S. (1978). *Mind in society*. Cambridge, MA: Harvard University Press.

Vygosky, L. S. (1981). The genesis of higher mental functions. In Wertsch, J. V. (Ed.), *The concept of activity in Soviet psychology* (pp. 144–188). Armonk: M.E. Sharpe.

Wachsmann, K. (1961). *The turning point of building*. Wurzburg, Germany: Reinhold Publishing Corporation.

Walker, B. N., & Nees, M. A. (2005). *An agenda for research and development of multimodal graphs*. Paper presented at the 11th International Conference on Auditory Display (ICAD2005).

Wang, R., & Wang, X. (2009). Experimental investigation of co-presence factors in a mixed reality-mediated collaborative design system. The 6th International Conference on Cooperative Design, Visualization, and Engineering (pp. 333-340). Luxembourg: Springer-Verlag.

Wang, X. (2007). *Mutually augmented virtual environments for architectural design and collaboration* (pp. 17–29). Computer Aided Architectural Design Futures.

Wang, X., & Chen, R. (2009). An experimental study on collaborative effectiveness of augmented reality potentials in urban design. *CoDesign, 5*(4), 229–244. doi:10.1080/15710880903320020

Wang, X., & Dunston, P. S. (2005). Real time polygonal data integration of CAD/augmented reality. In *Architectural Design Visualization, Computing in Civil Engineering* (pp. 1–8). American Society of Civil Engineers, ASCE. doi:10.1061/40794(179)10

Wang, X., & Dunston, P. S. (2006). Compatibility issues in augmented reality systems for AEC: An experimental prototype study. *Automation in Construction, 15*(3), 314–326. doi:10.1016/j.autcon.2005.06.002

Wang, X., & Dunston, P. S. (2006). Potential of augmented reality as an assistant viewer for computer-aided drawing. *Journal of Computing in Civil Engineering, 20*(6), 437–441. doi:10.1061/(ASCE)0887-3801(2006)20:6(437)

Wang, X., & Dunston, P. S. (2008). User perspectives on mixed reality tabletop visualization for face-to-face collaborative design review. *Automation in Construction, 17*(4), 399–412. doi:10.1016/j.autcon.2007.07.002

Watanabe, M. S. (2002). *Induction design: A method for evolutionary design*. Basel, Switzerland: Birkhäuser.

Watson, B. (1995). Reliquishing the lecturn: Cooperative learning in teacher education. *Journal of Teacher Education, 46*(3), 209–215. doi:10.1177/0022487195046003007

Wattenberg, M., Jesse, K., & Matt, M. (2007). ManyEyes: A site for visualization at Internet scale. *IEEE Transactions on Visualization and Computer Graphics, 13*(6), 1121–1128. doi:10.1109/TVCG.2007.70577

Weinberg, G., & Thatcher, T. (2006). Interactive sonification: Aesthetics, functionality and performance. *Leonardo Music Journal, 16*, 9–12. doi:10.1162/lmj.2006.16.9

Weiser, M. (1991). The computer for the 21st century. *Scientific American Special Issue on Communications, Computers, and Networks* (September).

Weiss, S. (2006). *Digital learning Spaces 2010: Technology in education*. Denver, CO: Education Commission of the States.

Wenger, E. (1999). *Communities of practice: Learning, meaning and identity*. Cambridge: MA Cambridge University Press.

Wertsch, J. V. (1990). *Voices of the mind*. Cambridge, MA: Harvard University Press.

Westrik, J., De Graaff, E., Chen, S. E., Cowdroy, R. M., Kingsland, A., & Ostwald, M. J. (1994). Development and management of the new PBL-based curriculum in architecture. In *Reflections on problem based learning* (pp. 189–200). Sydney, Australia: Australian Problem Based Learning Network.

Weyland, K. (2008). Toward a new theory of institutional change. *World Politics*, *60*(2), 281–314. doi:10.1353/wp.0.0013

Whisker, V. E., Baratta, A. J., Yerrapathruni, S., Messner, J. I., Shaw, T. S., & Warren, M. E. … Johnson, F. T. (2003). *Using immersive virtual environments to develop and visualize construction schedules for advanced nuclear power plants*. 2003 International Congress on Advances in Nuclear Power Plants (ICAPP), Córdoba, Spain.

White, M., Petridis, P., Liarokapis, F., & Plecinckx, D. (2007). Multimodal mixed reality interfaces for visualizing digital heritage. *International Journal of Architectural Computing*, *5*(2), 322–337. doi:10.1260/1478-0771.5.2.322

Whyte, J. (2002). *Virtual reality and the built environment*. Oxford, UK: Architectural Press.

Wikipedia. (2010a). *List of level editors*. Retrieved 14 August, 2010, from http://en.wikipedia.org/ wiki/List_of_level_editors

Wikipedia. (2010b). *Steam (content delivery)*. Retrieved 1 May, 2010, from http://en.wikipedia.org/ wiki/Steam_(content_delivery)

Wilde, J., & Wilde, R. (1991). *Visual literacy*. New York, NY: Watson Guptill.

Wilhem, J., Baker, T., & Dube, J. (2001). *Strategic reading: Guiding students to lifelong literacy*. New Hampshire, USA, Heinemann, Reed Elsevier Inc.

Williams, L. V. (1983). *Teaching for the two-sided mind*. Prentice Hall, Inc.

Wilson, B., & Lowry, M. (2000). Constructivist learning on the Web learning technologies. In Burge, L. (Ed.), *Reflective and strategic thinking*. San Francisco, CA: Jossey-Bass, New Directions for Adult and Continuing Education.

Winn, W. (1993). *A conceptual basis for educational applications of virtual reality. Human interface technology laboratory*. Washington Technology Center, University of Washington.

Wittgenstein, L. (1953). *Philosophical investigations*. London, UK: Basil Blackwell.

Wojtowicz, J., Davidson, J. N., & Mitchell, W. J. (1992). Design as digital correspondence. In K. Kensek & D. Noble (Eds.), *Computer Supported Design in Architecture: Mission, Method, Madness, 12th ACADIA Conference Proceedings* (pp. 89-101). Charleston, SC: Clemson University.

Wojtowicz, J., Papazian, P., Fargas, J., Davidson, J. N., & Cheng, N. (1993). Asynchronous architecture. In F. Morgan & R. Pohlman (Eds.), *Education and Practice: The Critical Interface, 13th ACADIA Conference Proceedings* (pp. 107-117). College Station, TX: Texas A & M University.

Wojtowicz, J. (1994). *Virtual design studio*. Hong Kong: HKU Press.

Woods, D. (1985). Problem-based learning and problem-solving. In Boud, D. (Ed.), *Problem-based learning in education for the professions* (pp. 19–42). Sydney, Australia: Higher Education Research and Development Society of Australasia.

Wooldridge, M. (2000). *Reasoning about rational agents*. Cambridge, MA: MIT Press.

Wyeld, T. G., Prasolova-Førland, E., & Chang, T.-W. (2006). The 3D CVE as a cross-cultural classroom. In *Proceedings of Game/Set/Match 2006*, Delft, Berlageweg, Holland, March 29-April 01.

Wyeld, T. G., Prasolova-Forland, E., & Teng-Wen, C. (2006). *Virtually collaborating across cultures: A case study of an online theatrical performance in a 3DCVE spanning three continents*. Sixth International Conference on Advanced Learning Technologies.

Wyeld, T. G., Prasolova-Førland, E., & Viller, S. (2007). Theatrical place in a 3D CVE: An online performance of Plato's allegory of the cave in a distributed 3D CVE. In [Guadeloupe, French Caribbean.]. *Proceedings of The Second International Multi-Conference on Computing in the Global Information Technology, ICCGI, 2007*(March), 4–9.

Wyeld, T., & Prasolova-Førland, E. (2008). Using activity theory to assess the effectiveness of a learning community: A case study in remote collaboration using a 3D virtual environment. In Akoumianakis, D. (Ed.), *Virtual communities of practice and social interactive technologies: Lifecycle and workflow analysis*. Hershey, PA: IGI Global.

Xenakis, I. (1971). *Formalized music: Thought and mathematics in composition*. Bloomington, IN: Indiana University Press.

Zaero-Polo, A., & Moussavi, F. (2003). *Morphogenesis: FOA's ark*. Barcelona, Spain: Actar.

Zevi, B. (1959). *Apprendre à voir l'architecture*. Paris, France: Editions de Minuit.

Zhang, Y., Sotudeh, R., & Fernando, T. (2005). The use of visual and auditory feedback for assembly task performance in a virtual environment. *Proceedings of the Twenty-First Spring Conference on Computer Graphics (SCCG'05)*, (pp. 59–66).

About the Contributors

Ning Gu is a Senior Lecturer in the School of Architecture and Built Environment at the University of Newcastle, Australia. He researches in the broad areas of design computing. He is particularly interested in collaborative design, generative design, and virtual worlds. Ning is a pioneer of applying leading-edge Information Technologies in design and learning, and has established an international collaborative design studio using *Second Life*. He has also designed and implemented a wide variety of collaborative virtual environments and applied them in his teaching and research in numerous Australian and international tertiary design institutions including the University of Newcastle, the University of Sydney, MIT, and Columbia University. He has published extensively in the fields of design computing and design education.

Xiangyu Wang is Professor in the School of Built Environment at Curtin University. Dr. Wang is an internationally recognized leading researcher in the field of Virtual (VR) and Augmented Reality (AR) in Architecture, Engineering, and Construction (AEC), Education, and Training. He was awarded US National Science Foundation grant to investigate the skill development and transfer from virtual training systems. His current focus is on Building Information Modelling (BIM), AR, and VR integration for AEC and Education/Training. He is the Chair of Australian National Committee of International Society in Computing in Civil and Building Engineering (ISCCBE). He has been invited to give several keynote speeches in BIM research and industrial conferences in Asian area. His work has been published into over 170 refereed books, book chapters, technical journals, and conference papers.

* * *

Kirsty Beilharz is Professor of Music, Sonification, and Interaction Design, conjointly in the Faculty of Arts & Social Sciences and the Faculty of Design, Architecture, & Building at the University of Technology, Sydney, and course director of the Bachelor of Sound and Music Design degree. Formerly, Beilharz directed graduate Digital Media at the University of Sydney Design Lab. Beilharz's research integrates music and generative (algorithmic and Artificial Life) processes applied to sound, real time audio-visual interaction, and data sonification. Her design research includes gestural interaction using multimodality, multi-touch interaction, physical computing, wearable technologies, hyper-instruments, and aesthetics and interactivity in sonification, with a special interest in the representation of bio-data and eco-data. Beilharz is also an internationally recognized composer whose music has been performed by ensembles including Sydney Symphony Orchestra, Nouvel Ensemble Moderne Canada, and Ensemble Recherche Freiburg, and she is a practitioner of the Japanese shakuhachi.

Barbara Berry received her MA in Adult, Administrative, and Higher Education from the University of British Columbia, Vancouver Canada. She is currently an Education Consultant in the Teaching and Learning Centre at Simon Fraser University (SFU), Surrey, British Columbia. She provided consulting support services to the TechOne Program instructional teams between 2007 and 2010. She currently consults with the School of Interactive Arts and Technology (SIAT) and the Faculty of Health Sciences (FHS) at SFU. Her research interests include student learning, learning design in STEM-based and health sciences curricula, as well as teaching and learning requirements in spatial thinking and design. Barbara has professional experience in training and development in the software industry as well as health sector. She is a member of the Society for Teaching and Learning in Higher Education (STLHE).

Dean Bruton is an Australian artist/designer, author, and visual arts program coordinator who developed the Master's in Digital Media Program at the School of Architecture, Landscape Architecture and Urban Design at The University of Adelaide from 2003-2011, and earlier, the New Media courses at the SA School of Art, University of South Australia. His specialist research interests include art, architecture, and design practice and its relation to digital media, particularly pedagogy, heritage, and aspects of interdisciplinary visual arts theory/production. Currently his book, "Digital Design: A critical introduction" is in production and will be launched by Bloomsbury Press, UK in April 2012. As Associate Dean International (Architecture) he gave public lecture presentations at Penn State University, USA and a number of Chinese universities including South China University of Technology, Guangzhou, China. He is currently leader of the Digital Arts program at Southern Cross University, Lismore, Australia.

Carlos Calderón is an academic at the School of Architecture, Planning, and Landscape at Newcastle University. Calderon is a qualified Civil Engineer and has a PhD in Applied Computing. He has taught widely in Architecture Schools and currently leads a MSc programme and postgraduate modules at Newcastle's part 2 Architecture Programme. His research interests lie at the intersection of the built environment and computation around three main areas: Energy and carbon futures in cities; smart materials and environments; and intelligent systems and digital design. His work has been recognised in multiple publications and funded projects. He has been a visiting fellow to the Virtual System Laboratory, Gifu University, and Harvard University Graduate School of Design, USA.

Gabriela Celani holds a B.A. (1989) and an M.Sc. in Architecture and Urban Design (1997) from the University of São Paulo, and a Ph.D. in Design and Computation (2002) from the Massachusetts Institute of Technology, where she was advised by professors Terry Knight and William Mitchell. She has also developed post-doctoral research at the Technical University of Lisbon, with Prof. José Duarte. She is presently a Professor at the University of Campinas, where she founded LAPAC, the Laboratory for Automation and Prototyping in Architecture and Construction, in 2007. She is the author of *CAD Criativo*, an introduction to VBA programming for implementing generative design tools, and has translated Mitchell´s *The Logic of Architecture* and Moore, Mitchell, and Turnbull's *The Poetics of Gardens* into Portuguese. Gabriela is also co-founder and co-editor of PARC, an online journal of research in architecture, and acts as a reviewer for many CAAD conferences and journals.

Clark Cory is an Associate Professor in the Department of Computer Graphics Technology at Purdue University. Clark's primary professional responsibility is undergraduate instruction in architectural and construction graphic communication, and visualization utilizing Building Information Modeling. These include integrating courses for Computer Graphics majors and several service courses for engineering and liberal art students. He has been the major champion for developing a Construction Graphics Communication specialty area within the Computer Graphics Department at Purdue. He is also active as a member and academic advisor for student organizations at Purdue- National Home Builders Association and The Design Build student organization. Most recently, Clark has helped in the Design/Build component offering two graduate level courses for the Solar Decathlon House, an international competition sponsored by DOE. Clark has had over 40 years' experience in the AEC industry with positions ranging from general laborer to project manager of 25 residential structures per year.

José Pinto Duarte is currently Full Professor at the Technical University of Lisbon Faculty of Architecture, researcher at the Instituto Superior Técnico, and a Visiting Scientist at MIT. He holds a B.Arch. (1987) in Architecture from the Technical University of Lisbon and an S.M.Arch.S. (1993), and a Ph.D. (2001) in Design and Computation from MIT. He was the founder of the ISTAR Labs - IST Architecture Research Laboratories (http://www.civil.ist.utl.pt/istar), co-author of "Collaborative Design and Learning" (with J. Bento, M. Heitor and W. J. Mitchell, Praeger 2004), and author of "Personalizar a Habitação em Série: Uma Gramática Discursiva para as Casas da Malagueira" (Fundação Calouste Gulbenkian, 2007). He was awarded the Santander/TU Lisbon Prize for Outstanding Research in Architecture by the Technical University of Lisbon in 2008. His main research interests are mass customization with a special focus on housing, and the application of new technologies to architecture and urban design in general.

Halil I. Erhan received his BArch degree from Middle East Technical University in Turkey. During his Master's study at Clemson University, he investigated 3D model integration in representing building design and construction information. As a result of this study, he became interested in design computation. He pursued this interest in his PhD study at Carnegie Mellon University. He is currently a Professor of Design and Informatics at the School of Interactive Arts and Technology, Simon Fraser University. His research interests span from design of complex systems and design cognition to software design strategies and education. Particularly, he concentrates on generative aspects of complex systems developed for supporting wide spectrum of design activities and visual analytics of decision dependencies in design information space. He is a member of CAADRIA, ACADIA, and ACM [Sigchi and Sigsoft].

François Guéna is Professor at the National School of Architecture of Paris-la-Villette where he leads a Digital Design Program and manages the ARIAM-LAREA laboratory. After graduating from the Special School of Architecture (ESA) in 1980, he joined the Center of Informatics and Methodology in Architecture (CIMA) where he participated in the development of Computer Aided Architectural Design (CAAD) systems. He graduated from the University Paris VI with a Master and a PhD degree in Computer Sciences. He holds the French post-doctoral degree, allowing him to supervise PhD students (HDR). In 1998, he co-founded the ARIAM research team and became the director after merging with the LAREA laboratory in 2005. The main topic of his research is to integrate artificial intelligence into CAAD systems in order to improve human computer interactions and collaborative design.

Leman Figen Gül is an Associate Professor at the Architecture Program at the TOBB Economy and Technology University, Turkey. Dr. Gül's work is featured with design studies and design education. Her research interests include investigating design cognition in virtual worlds, digital design and fabrication, design teaching, human-computer interactions, and computer-supported cooperative work. She received her BArch (1993) and her MUCon (1996) in the Urban Conservation Program at the Mimar Sinan University in Istanbul and MDes (2003) in Digital Media and PhD (2007) in Architecture at the University of Sydney. She was a Lecturer and Tutor at the University of Sydney, a Research Fellow at the University of Newcastle (Australia), and an Associate Professor at the International University of Sarajevo before joining TOBB University of Economics and Technology in 2011.

Christiane M. Herr is an Architect, Researcher, and Teacher focusing on the areas of digitally supported design, conceptual design, structural design, design studio teaching, and traditional Chinese approaches to creative thinking. Christiane is a German National and has worked and studied in Australia, Hong Kong, China and Taiwan for more than 10 years. In her PhD work at The University of Hong Kong, Christiane explored cellular automata as a means to establish architectural design support, which led to her strong interest in diagrams and designerly ways of seeing. Christiane's approach to education for creativity relies strongly on second-order cybernetics and radical constructivism. In her research work, Christiane focuses on the integration of designerly and scientific modes of inquiry through empirical, grounded, and action research approaches. Christiane is a member of conference organizing and review committees for the ASC and CAADRIA and member of review committees of various journals and conferences.

Yinghsiu Huang is currently an Assistant Professor and The director of Interactive, Cognition, and Product Design Laboratory (ICP Lab) at the Department of Industrial Design, Tung-Hai University, Taiwan. He obtained his Ph.D. degree in Graduate Institute of Architecture at National Chiao Tung University, Taiwan. Dr. Huang's research interests are ranging from human cognitive studies in design media to design computing, including imagination of design process, interactive interface, physical computing, collaborative design in virtual reality and augmented reality environment, and digital archive technology. He has published papers into a wide range of highly recognized international journals and conferences (*Design Studies*, CAADRIA, eCAADe.) He has organised several conferences and workshops in Taiwan. He also has a digital archive project funded by National Science Council of Taiwan, ROC, to study the digitalization processes of sculptures and simulate these sculptures in VR and AR environments.

Taysheng Jeng received the B.S. degree in Architecture from National Cheng Kung University, Tainan, Taiwan, in 1986, the M.A. degree in Architecture from University of California at Los Angles, in 1993, and the Ph.D. degree in Architecture from Georgia Institute of Technology, Atlanta, Georgia in 1999. He is an Associate Professor and Chairman of the Department of Architecture of National Cheng Kung University in Taiwan. His research interests include interactive architecture, smart space, digital design, and computer-aided design.

Jeff WT Kan is the Deputy Dean of the School of Architecture, Building, and Design, Taylor's University, Malaysia. He completed his PhD in Design Computing and Cognition at the University of Sydney. During his study, he was awarded an International Postgraduate Research Award by the Australian Department of Education to undertake his PhD. His study focused on developing and using quantitative methods to study the cognitive behaviour of designers. He formerly taught Design Studio and Computer-Aided Design at the Department of Architecture, Chinese University of Hong Kong. He has published papers on architectural visual Information System, online interactive teaching materials, architectural visual impact studies, protocol analysis of designers, and methods to study design activities.

Shih-Chung (Jessy) Kang, PhD graduate of Stanford University, currently works in Department of Civil Engineering at National Taiwan University as an Associate Professor. He focuses on the automation of crane for years, publishing more than 50 academic papers in the field. He obtained multiple grants from National Science Council of Taiwan, leading the research on developing cranes and robots for automatic construction. In the year of 2008 and 2009, he obtained the excellent teaching award and excellent service award respectively from National Taiwan University. In 2011, he published "Robot Development Using Microsoft Robotics Developer Studio," a textbook for hands-on robotics courses.

Karen M. Kensek earned her SB from the Massachusetts Institute of Technology and her Master's of Architecture from the University of California, Berkeley. Her teaching and research areas at USC focus heavily on Building Information Modeling (BIM), performance-based architecture, and sustainable design tools. She is a Past President of ACADIA (the Association of Computer Aided Design in Architecture), was the leader for the 2008 Revit BIM Experience Award from Autodesk and the AIA TAP 2010 BIM Award (honorable mention for coursework and curriculum development), and was host for five symposia at USC on BIM with a co-emphasis on sustainable design, construction, analytics, customization, and parametrics.

Mi Jeong Kim is an Assistant Professor of Housing and Interior Design at Kyung Hee University. She received her Ph.D (2007) in the Key Centre of Design Computing and Cognition at the University of Sydney. She worked as a postdoc fellow in the Department of Engineering Research Support Organization in UC Berkeley before joining Kyung Hee University. Her current research interest includes design and evaluation of new interaction techniques for 3D design, empirical studies and new technologies for computer-supported collaborative design, designing in and for virtual worlds, cognitive design studies, future housing studies such as smart home, and Information Technology in construction.

Terry Knight is a Professor of Design and Computation in the Department of Architecture, School of Architecture and Planning, at the Massachusetts Institute of Technology. She conducts research and teaches in the area of computational design, with an emphasis on the theory and application of shape grammars. Her book, *Transformations in Design*, is a well-known introduction to the field of shape grammars. Her recent research includes work on visual-physical grammars: rule-based, customizable building assembly systems that support cultural sustainability through the incorporation of vernacular patterns and local resources. She is also exploring the incorporation of sensory aspects of design, apart from the visual, into grammars. She holds a BFA from the Nova Scotia College of Art and Design, and an MA and PhD in Architecture from the University of California, Los Angeles.

Caroline Lecourtois is a DPLG architect and holds PhD in Urbanism and Space Management from the University of Nanterre (Paris X). She is a Professor of Architectural Design at the National School of Architecture of Paris-la-Villette. She is also a researcher at the laboratory of ARIAM-LAREA. Her field of research is Architecturology, and her scientific object is the cognitive activity in architectural design made with computers. With François Guéna, she deals with different research on collaborative design, digital architectural style, and parametric modeling in design. She also works with agencies of architecture to apply her results of research in design activities. She has written epistemological and scientific articles on architectural conception, architectural qualities, applied Architecturology, design education, and collaborative design (www.ariam-larea.archi.fr).

Robert Leicht is an Assistant Professor of Architectural Engineering at Penn State University. He is the leader of the Lean and Green Research Initiative and Director of the Partnership for Achieving Construction Excellence. His research interests focus on high performance collaboration, notably interdisciplinary collaborative efforts, within Architecture, Engineering, and Construction. Within collaboration, his interests revolve around how processes, technologies, and competencies evolve through different environments, organizations, and teams to develop high performance facility outcomes. In addition to his research efforts he has several years of construction industry experience, most notably with DPR Construction where he was hired to setup and lead the East Coast's virtual building effort. In this capacity, he focused his efforts to integrate the design and construction teams on projects, using building information models and related virtual tools as enablers to more integrated efforts and lean processes.

Russell Lowe lectures in Architecture at the University of New South Wales. He coordinates the first year architectural design studio and teaches in the Master's of Architecture graduation studio. Russell is a member of CAADRIA (Computer Aided Architectural Design Research in Asia) and has published on the use of computer gaming technology to engage with uses and concepts outside of the entertainment industry. Lowe has developed unique insights into opportunities for collaborative thinking that take advantage of the multiple perspectives that new media and computer game environments afford. His prize winning research on architectural space spans from clinical simulation to fine art films, which have been exhibited worldwide in film festivals as well as private and public art galleries and museums.

John Messner is the Director of the Computer Integrated Construction (CIC) Research Program at Penn State and an Associate Professor of Architectural Engineering. He specializes in virtual prototyping and BIM, along with globalization issues in construction. The CIC Research Group is currently performing the BIM Execution Planning project for the buildingSMART alliance. He has also received NSF grants for investigating the application of advanced visualization in construction engineering education and the AEC Industry. As a part of these grants, he led the development of the Immersive Construction Lab, an affordable, 3 screen immersive display system for design and construction visualization. Dr. Messner is also a principle investigator on two globalization projects for the Construction Industry Institute. He previously worked as a project manager on various construction projects for a large general contractor. He has taught courses in virtual prototyping, BIM, strategic management in construction, international construction, and project management at Penn State.

Michael J. Ostwald is Dean of Architecture at the University of Newcastle (Australia), a Visiting Professor at RMIT University (Melbourne), and past President of the Association of Architecture Schools of Australasia. He presently holds an Australian Research Council "Future Fellowship" and is Director of CIBER (Centre for Interdisciplinary Built Environment Research). He has a PhD in Architectural History and Theory and a higher Doctorate (DSc) in Design Computing and Mathematics. He has lectured in Asia, Europe, and North America and has written and published extensively on the relationship between architecture, philosophy, and geometry. Michael Ostwald is a member of the editorial boards of the *Nexus Network Journal* (Architecture and Mathematics), *Architectural Theory Review,* and *Architectural Science Review* and former foundation Editor of *Architectural Design Research.*

Rivka Oxman holds B.Sc., M.Sc., and D.Sc. degrees from the Technion Israel Institute of Technology where she is an Associate Professor in the Faculty of Architecture and Town Planning. She has been the Vice Dean of the Faculty of Architecture and Town Planning. Prof. Oxman is an Associate Editor of the international journal, *Design Studies*, and a member of editorial boards of other leading international scientific journals and conferences on design research, design theory, and digital design. In 2006 she was appointed as a Fellow of the Design Research Society (FDRS) for her contributions and established record of achievement in design research. Recently she has co-authored with Robert Oxman a book called "The New Structuralism: Design, Engineering and Architectural Technologies" (Architectural Design, 2010) published by Wiley. She has been a Visiting Professor at Stanford University; Delft University of Technology, and held research appointments at MIT, Berkeley, and Harvard University. She has been invited to deliver keynote lectures in leading conferences around the world: ACADIA 2000; CAAD Futures 1997, 2011; SIGRADI 2004; 2009; CAADRIA 2011.

Ekaterina Prasolova-Førland is an Associate Professor and project coordinator at the Program for learning with ICT, Norwegian University of Science and Technology (NTNU). She holds a M.Sc. in Technical Cybernetics and a PhD in Computer Science from the same university. Her research interests include educational and social aspects of 3D Collaborative Virtual Environments and augmented environments as well as virtual universities, mobile learning, and educational games. She is author and co-author of more than 50 publications on the topic. She is currently involved in two EU-financed projects focusing on creativity and serious games in 3D virtual worlds. Recently, she started working for the Norwegian Armed Forces, developing educational simulations for training cultural awareness in military operations.

Regiane Pupo holds a Diploma of Architecture and Urban Design from Pontifícia Universidade Católica in Campinas (PUCCAMP), a Master's Degree from the Federal University of Santa Catarina (UFSC), and a PhD from the State University of Campinas (UNICAMP), all in Brazil. In 2007 she lived in Lisbon, Portugal and established the ISTAR Labs at Instituto Superior Técnico (IST). She has run the Laboratory for Automation and Prototyping for Architecture and Construction (LAPAC) at UNICAMP as a post-doc researcher and a Professor in the fields of Computational Design, Rapid Prototyping, and Digital Fabrication for Architecture from 2009 to 2011. Currently, she is a Professor at the Federal University of Santa Catarina, where she teaches at the Industrial Design course.

Lawrence (Larry) Sass is an architectural researcher exploring an emerging field known as digital design and fabrication. He believes that all buildings will be printed with machines run by computers and that the age of hand crafted, hand operated construction will be a thing of the past. This includes prefabricated construction, which is a century old tradition of handcrafted construction indoors. He believes that people will be replaced by machines and that components for each building will be fabricated worldwide immediately after the building is designed. Cost savings will come from assembly only construction sites; both manual and robotic. The challenge for architectures schools will be researching and teaching creative digital design and fabrication across scales from furniture and skyscrapers. This transformation also includes teaching computational methods that support design production, from artificial intelligence to high level computer programming, and last, new methods of production with computer controlled machines, assembly and finishing robots, and material invention. Larry is an

Associate Professor in the Department of Architecture at MIT teaching courses specifically in digital fabrication and design computing since 2002 after earning a PhD '00 and SMArchS '94 also at MIT. He has a BArch from Pratt Institute in NYC, has published and has exhibited his work at the Modern of Museum Art in New York City.

Shanna Schmelter - Morrett is a graduate from Purdue University where she received her Master's degree in Computer Graphics Technology in May 2008. While at Purdue, she studied Construction Graphics and focused her research on creating a Building Information Modeling (BIM) curriculum for future students. Currently she works for a general contractor, Holder Construction Co. in Atlanta, GA, where her current efforts are focused on BIM management, modeling, coordination, and customer service for multiple projects. Also, she plays a lead role in development and delivery of the company's BIM Training program, is a frequent presenter at customer and partner training events, and continues to support BIM curriculum development with university partners.

Marc Aurel Schnabel is an Architect and Professor at the School of Architecture, The Chinese University of Hong Kong. He is leading research and education in the field of Computational Architecture and Design. As Immediate Past-President of CAADRIA, the international Association for Computer Aided Architectural Design Research in Asia, he is affiliated with various professional and scientific committees. He established the Digital Architecture Research Alliance, DARA, which brings together researchers who push the boundaries of current digital spatial design. He taught and worked in Germany Australia, and Hong Kong for over fifteen years, and since then, has become highly recognized for his work in the areas of virtual environments and parametric design learning. He publishes extensively in international journals about novel perspectives in computational architecture and the communication of three-dimensional space using innovative design methods. He recently curated two Digital Architectural exhibitions, *Disparallel Spaces* at the Tin Sheds Gallery and *8448 cubed* at Gaffa Gallery and hosted an international conference on computational architecture.

Dennis R. Shelden is Associate Professor of the Practice of Design and Computation in the Department of Architecture, School of Architecture and Planning, at the Massachusetts Institute of Technology, and Chief Technology Officer of Gehry Technologies, a building industry technology company formed in 2002 by the research and development team of Frank Gehry Partners. He joined Gehry Partners in 1997 and was Director of Research and Director of Computing before co-founding Gehry Technologies. Prior to joining Gehry Partners, he performed structural engineering, energy systems, and technology development work at firms including Arup, Consultants' Computation Bureau and Cyra Systems. Professor Shelden lectures and conducts research in building industry process advancement and in design computation and cognition. He holds a BS in Architectural Design, an MS in Civil and Environmental Engineering, and a PhD in Computation and Architectural Design from MIT.

Jerry Jen-Hung Tsai is a researcher in design computing. He was awarded his PhD in Design Computing and Cognition at the University of Sydney. His research focuses on representation, energy integrations and interactions in buildings, collaborative design, interactions between human, machine, and environment, ambient intelligence, and smart environment. He is an author or editor of two books and a number of papers, international journals, and book chapters. He is also an architect, interior designer, and industrial designer. Formerly he was an honorary Lecturer at Architecture, Design, and Planning, University of Sydney and an Assistant Professor in Department of Art Creativity & Development at Yuan Ze University in Taiwan. He has been a visiting scholar in universities in Italy, Malaysia, and Taiwan. He is now based in Sydney and working collaboratively on research projects and book publication with researchers in Australia, Malaysia, and Taiwan.

Anthony Williams is currently the Head of School of Architecture and Built Environment at the University of Newcastle, Australia. He researches across of broad range of areas relating to Design Cognition and Education with considerable work in the area of collaborative design, both face to face and virtual domains, his specific interest is in studying the collaborative activity in a real world context. He is currently working on projects relating to spatial abilities and their implication on novice designers as well as a project on design creativity and strategies to assess them. He is widely published in the area of design education.

Theodor Wyeld is the Director of Studies, Digital Media Studies in the Department of Screen and Media, School of Humanities, at Flinders University, Adelaide, Australia. He researches in the field of 3D Information Visualisation and teaches Interaction Design and 3D Design. He has published widely in these fields and chairs the annual European Information Visualisation Society Conference. He recently established a spinout company, thereitis.com, based on his invention for a large 3D information array. He holds degrees in Architecture, and Master's in Planning and in Design, and is currently completing his PhD in Cognitive Psychology at the Swinburne University of Technology, Melbourne, Australia.

Belgacem Ben Youssef received his PhD from the Cullen College of Engineering at the University of Houston (Houston, Texas, USA). He is currently an Associate Professor of Computer Engineering in the College of Computer & Information Sciences at King Saud University in Riyadh, Saudi Arabia. Prior to that, he was an Assistant Professor in both the TechOne Program and the School of Interactive Arts & Technology at Simon Fraser University (Vancouver, British Columbia, Canada). His research interests include parallel computing, computational tissue engineering, visualization, digital signal processing, and spatial thinking in learning and design. Dr. Ben Youssef has also two years of industrial experience in software development and technical project management in the telecommunications and business sectors. He is a member of both the IEEE Computer Society and the ACM.

Xingquan Zhu received his PhD degree in Computer Science from Fudan University, Shanghai China, in 2001. He is a recipient of the Australia ARC Future Fellowship and a Professor of the Centre for Quantum Computation & Intelligent Systems, Faculty of Engineering and Information Technology, University of Technology, Sydney (UTS), Australia. Dr. Zhu's research mainly focuses on data mining, machine learning, and multimedia systems. Since 2000, he has published more than 110 referred journal and conference proceedings papers in these areas. Dr. Zhu is an Associate Editor of the *IEEE Transactions on Knowledge and Data Engineering* (2009-), and a Program Committee Co-Chair for the 23rd IEEE International Conference on Tools with Artificial Intelligence (ICTAI 2011) and the 9th International Conference on Machine Learning and Applications (ICMLA 2010).

Index